W9-BGI-996

A New History of Southeast Asia

LONG BEACH PUBLIC LIBRARY
101 PACIFIC AVENUE
LONG BEACH, CA 90822

A New History of Southeast Asia

FEB - - 2011

M. C. Ricklefs
Bruce Lockhart
Albert Lau
Portia Reyes
Maitrii Aung-Thwin

Edited by M. C. Ricklefs

959 N532

A new history of Southeast
    Asia

33090012551000   BREW

© M. C. Ricklefs, Bruce Lockhart, Albert Lau, Portia Reyes, Maitrii Aung-Thwin 2010

All rights reserved. No reproduction, copy or transmission of this publication may be made without written permission.

No portion of this publication may be reproduced, copied or transmitted save with written permission or in accordance with the provisions of the Copyright, Designs and Patents Act 1988, or under the terms of any licence permitting limited copying issued by the Copyright Licensing Agency, Saffron House, 6–10 Kirby Street, London EC1N 8TS.

Any person who does any unauthorized act in relation to this publication may be liable to criminal prosecution and civil claims for damages.

The authors have asserted their rights to be identified as the authors of this work in accordance with the Copyright, Designs and Patents Act 1988.

First published 2010 by
PALGRAVE MACMILLAN

Palgrave Macmillan in the UK is an imprint of Macmillan Publishers Limited, registered in England, company number 785998, of Houndmills, Basingstoke, Hampshire RG21 6XS.

Palgrave Macmillan in the US is a division of St Martin's Press LLC, 175 Fifth Avenue, New York, NY 10010.

Palgrave Macmillan is the global academic imprint of the above companies and has companies and representatives throughout the world.

Palgrave® and Macmillan® are registered trademarks in the United States, the United Kingdom, Europe and other countries

ISBN 978–0–230–21213–8 hardback
ISBN 978–0–230–21214–5 paperback

This book is printed on paper suitable for recycling and made from fully managed and sustained forest sources. Logging, pulping and manufacturing processes are expected to conform to the environmental regulations of the country of origin.

A catalogue record for this book is available from the British Library.

A catalog record for this book is available from the Library of Congress.

10   9   8   7   6   5   4   3   2   1
19   18   17   16   15   14   13   12   11   10

Printed in China

3 3090 01255 1000

Contents

Illustrations

Maps and Tables

Maps

Tables

Preface

Hall's *History*

This *New History of Southeast Asia* aims to succeed to the role played for over half a century by one of the enduring works of scholarship in this field – *A History of South-East Asia* by Professor D.G. E. Hall (1891–1979). Hall's book was the first genuinely scholarly history of Southeast Asia, from the earliest times to what was then the present. The first edition – of 807 pages – was published in 1955. A second edition followed in 1964, a third in 1968, and a fourth (posthumously) in 1981, by which time the book had grown to be 1070 pages long.

Hall's connection with Southeast Asia began when he was appointed as Professor of History at the new Rangoon University – arriving there in 1921 while a nationalist strike against the university was still going on. His job was to teach Western history and political ideas, including British constitutional history, so his deepening interest in Burmese history sometimes had to take a back seat. When the nationalist students returned to the university, they included many who would become the first-generation political elite of independent Burma. On a visit to Burma in the early 1950s, Hall was picked up at his government guest house for dinner by a group of former students who were now, in fact, the cabinet of Burma; they presented him with what they called their homework: a copy of the new nation's constitution. Hall returned to Britain before World War II and became head of an English private school, but maintained his scholarly interest in and commitment to the history of Burma, and expanded that interest to other parts of the region.

In 1949 Hall was appointed as the first holder of the Chair in South East Asian History at the School of Oriental and African Studies (SOAS) of the University of London. He realized that a book was needed to bring together the scattered scholarship on Southeast Asian history, so he set about writing it. Thus came about his *History of South-East Asia*. Hall insisted on hyphenating 'South-East', although his chair was not hyphenated and his American friends spelled it as one word. 'American writers have standardized the form "Southeast" …', he wrote, 'but there seems to be no valid reason for coining a new form in preference to either "South-East" or "South East".' Invoking a powerful authority for an Englishman of his generation, Hall added that 'The Royal Navy uses the hyphen.'[1] So 'South-East Asia' it became in Hall's title.

---

[1]   D. G. E. Hall, *A History of South-East Asia* (4th edn, Basingstoke: Macmillan, 1981), 3.

Nevertheless, the one-word version – Southeast – has long since become standard. So while the authors of this book follow Hall's vision in many ways, we do not follow his spelling.

I came to know Hall first when I was a PhD student at Cornell University, where he was invited to give a semester-long seminar, and subsequently far better when I lived in England. He was a colleague of mine during my years of teaching at SOAS (1969–79), for he was still invited to make a contribution there on occasion, although already in his eighties. When my family and I moved to the town of Hitchin, where Hall had been born, raised, and still lived, we were frequently in contact.

In his later years, Hall's eyesight began to fail and by the time he was compiling the fourth and last edition of his *History* he had gone blind. His mind remained active and he worked by dictating to a secretary. He wanted, however, to include some of the latest scholarship on the history of Java in the eighteenth and nineteenth centuries that he had been unable to read. Since I was at work in this field, he asked me whether I would author a chapter for his last edition and I happily agreed. Unexpectedly, I subsequently found that I had thereby agreed to a sort of academic version of apostolic succession.

A few years after Hall's death, his publishers – Macmillan, now Palgrave Macmillan – asked me whether I would do a new edition of Hall's book. I said no for several reasons. The subject was, I felt, already too big for any one historian to be able to command the literature. I had many other responsibilities. And I had other priorities for work in my own field of Indonesian history. Macmillan repeated the request from time to time for 25 years or so, and each time my answer was the same. Occasionally I contemplated taking this project on with some colleague, but anyone who was qualified for the task seemed to have even more reasons to refuse than I. In the meantime, the fourth edition of Hall's *History* continued to sell, being still the best single-volume history of Southeast Asia despite becoming more and more out-of-date.

Then, in 2006, nearing the end of a career of professional peregrinations, I found myself invited to become Professor in the Department of History of the National University of Singapore. Here was a large group of Southeast Asian historians, whose expertise extended from the earliest times to the present and covered all nations of Southeast Asia, with command of both the indigenous and non-indigenous languages and the scholarly disciplines necessary to master the field. At last, a 'new Hall' could be written. I found that – despite the expected clash of priorities that arise when such a proposal is put – four of my new colleagues agreed that this task was of such importance that other work could be postponed in order to do it. Palgrave Macmillan also reacted with enthusiasm – perhaps unsurprisingly, after a quarter-century of trying to get a positive answer to their requests.

Nevertheless, for all of our admiration for Hall's work – and in my case for all of my personal affection for and fond memories of a kind, old-fashioned gentleman scholar – this book is very different from his.

We are a team of specialists, with our expertise focused on particular areas and periods of Southeast Asian history. We thus bring together a level of expertise that neither Hall nor any other single author could muster. By working as a team, we have endeavored to create a book that is consistent in its coverage and style while reflecting the latest work available in secondary sources and the fruits of our own work in primary sources.

We have also sought to go beyond narrative. Inevitably a book like this, if it is to be of use to students in their studies and to general readers as a reference, must provide a general, factual narrative. The exigencies of presentation push much of that narrative into country-defined segments. But we aim to go beyond this when we can to indicate the broad issues and themes that spread across the region as well as those that dominate in particular historiographies. Furthermore, since Southeast Asia is a region that has been an international crossroads throughout its history – open always to multiple outside influences and inspirations which Southeast Asians turned to their own purposes – we have sought to situate the indigenous history of the region in its international contexts where appropriate. And, of course, there is a half-century of history discussed here beyond the chronological limits of Hall's book.

The study of Southeast Asian history

The field is very different today from Hall's time. Before about the mid-twentieth century, there were three general groups of scholars at work on Southeast Asia's past. The first were Orientalists and epigraphers who studied the stone and metal inscriptions of ancient kingdoms and often combined them with external sources – those in classical Chinese in particular – to reconstruct the political chronology of the past. The second were philologists working on indigenous literatures, whose main objective was often to attempt to reconstruct a (hypothetical) '*ur*-text'. The third were trained historians who concentrated on the sorts of sources that historians of the day commonly concentrated on: archival records, letters, memoirs, and such-like – which in the case of Southeast Asia usually meant colonial records in European languages. So a trained historian, employing historical source criticism and employing both indigenous and external sources, was a rare thing. Hall himself sought to work in this way, but his own use of Burmese-language sources was limited.

The number of university departments in this field was also limited but grew rapidly in the 20 years after World War II. In 1950, the only university with a Professor of History working on Southeast Asia was SOAS, with Hall in the Chair. There was fine work going on in Leiden and Paris, but little of it would fit our present-day idea of what historians do. At Cornell University, however, a new program was growing that would soon become a major center for the discipline. Others followed in the United States and, particularly, in Australia, where Monash University and the Australian National University became centers for Southeast Asian historical studies. As the new nations of Southeast Asia came into being, the study of their own history naturally developed in their universities, although it must be said that at times this study was obliged to conform to political agendas in a way unpalatable to professional historians.

There have long been scholars of Southeast Asia who were Southeast Asians themselves – before the expansion of the 1960s these already included Hoesein Djajadiningrat, Pe Maung Tin, Poerbatjaraka, Daw Mya Sein, Lé Thanh Khôi,

Le Van Dinh, Soedjatmoko, Song Ong Siang, Phya Anuman Rajadhon, Horatio de la Costa, T. M. Kalaw, C. A. Majul, Carlos Quirino, Gregorio F. Zaide, Maung Maung, and the Thai princes Chula Chakrabongse, Damrong, and Dhani Nivat, among others – and as the field grew it became even more thoroughly international in its personnel and approaches.

The qualifications expected of a Southeast Asian historian have become more exacting. A book or doctoral thesis done only on the basis of Western-language sources is now a great rarity. Command of both indigenous languages and those in which relevant foreign sources are written is now expected of any serious scholar. And the field has moved far beyond the early efforts just to establish a basic political chronology. Other disciplines – particularly anthropology – inform our work. Now we ask our sources questions about social structures, economic relations, beliefs and values, as well as about events, their causation, and their consequences. We try to understand what it might have meant to be a Southeast Asian in a particular place and time.

This book aims to help its readers to approach such questions themselves and to guide them to the further readings that will take them deeper into our subject.

M. C. Ricklefs

Acknowledgements

The authors and publishers wish to thank the following for permission to use copyright material:

Timothy P. Barnard for photographs of Labuanbajo Port on p. 17; A Cham Temple at My Son, Vietnam on p. 28; Wat Phra Si Sanphet, Ayuthia on p. 74; Theravada Monks on p. 75; and Living on the Perfume river on p. 430.

Corbis for photographs of Manuel Quezon on p. 286, © Bettmann/Corbis; Norodom Sihanouk on p. 357, © Pierre Perrin/Sygma/Corbis; President Soeharto on p. 382, © Kapoor Baldev/Sygma/Corbis; and Lee Kuan Yew on p. 445, © How Hwee Young/epa/Corbis.

Getty Images for photographs of Ho Chi Minh on p. 352, Three Lions/Hulton Archive/Getty Images; and President Sukarno on p. 381, Beryl Bernay/Hulton Archive/Getty Images.

PA Photos Ltd for photographs of Ngo Dinh Diem on p. 353, Horst Fass/AP/Press Association Images; Ne Win on p. 370, AP/Press Association Images; Sarit Thanarat on p. 374, AP/Press Association Images; Corazon Aquino and Diosdado Macapagal on p. 392, AP/Press Association Images; Mahathir Mohamad on p. 429, Andy Wong/ AP/Press Association Images; Prince Ranariddh and Hun Sen on p. 438, David Longstreath/AP/Press Association Images; and Aung San Suu Kyi on p. 465, Khin Maung Win/AP/Press Association Images.

Every effort has been made to trace the copyright holders but, if any have been inadvertently overlooked, the authors and publishers will be pleased to make the necessary arrangements at the first opportunity.

Orthography

There have been different – sometimes competing – transcription systems used for most of the languages of Southeast Asia. In this book we have sought to make the transcriptions as simple, as 'minimalist', as possible in the interest of accessibility. Fully diacritical versions of local words and names will be found in the Index.

In general, sounds are pronounced as they are in English (with *g* as a hard consonant), but the following should be noted.

In Sanskrit words, *ś* is pronounced like English *sh*.

In Arabic, the *'ayn* is indicated by ' (and is one of the most difficult Arabic sounds for non-native speakers to pronounce: a sort of *a* sound made in the pharynx), while the *hamza* glottal stop is indicated with '.

Pinyin spellings are used for Chinese, but the first time a name or term appears the older Wade-Giles transcription is also given.

In Burmese, *ky* is pronounced like English *ch* and *gy* is pronounced like English *j*. An *h* before a consonant indicates that it is aspirated.

In Thai, an *h* after a consonant indicates that it is aspirated.

Vietnamese has a highly developed system of diacritical marks: all are omitted in the text of the book but may be found in the Index.

In Javanese, *c* is pronounced like English *ch*; *th* and *dh* are retroflexes.

Modern Indonesian and Malay share an agreed-upon spelling system, with some peculiarities for English speakers. *C* is pronounced like English *ch* and *sy* is pronounced like English *sh*. In Indonesian, colonial-era spellings are sometimes used for personal names; in such cases, *dj* is pronounced like English *j*, *tj* is pronounced like English *ch*, *j* is pronounced like English *y*, and *oe* is pronounced like English *u*.

Given the loss of indigenous scripts of the Philippines, Tagalog (the basis of the Filipino or Pilipino national language) has long been written in the Western alphabet and poses no transcription problems today.

Southeast Asian languages have various ways of distinguishing singular from plural nouns. Here we have simply added the English form *s* or *es* to the indigenous word where it is to be understood as a plural.

Abbreviations and Acronyms

AFPFL	Anti-Fascist People's Freedom League (Burma)
AFTA	ASEAN Free Trade Area
AH	*Anno Hijrae,* the Islamic era
AJ	*Anno Javanico,* the Javanese era
APEC	Asia-Pacific Economic Cooperation
ARVN	Army of the Republic of [South] Vietnam
ASEAN	Association of Southeast Asian Nations
BCE	before the Common Era
BDA	Burma Defence Army
BIA	Burma Independence Army
BSPP	Burma Socialist Program Party
BU	Budi Utomo
c.	*circa*
CCP	Chinese Communist Party
CE	Common Era
CIA	Central Intelligence Agency (USA)
CPP	Communist Party of the Philippines *or* Cambodian People's Party
CPT	Communist Party of Thailand
d.	died
DRV	Democratic Republic of Vietnam
EDSA	Epifanio de los Santos Avenue, Manila
EEIC	English East India Company
FMS	Federated Malay States
g.	governed
GAM	*Gerakan Aceh Merdeka* (Independent Aceh Movement)
GATT	General Agreement on Tariffs and Trade
GCBA	General Council of Burmese Associations
GCSS	General Council of Sangha Sammeggi
GDP	Gross Domestic Product
ha	hectares
ICP	Indochinese Communist Party
IMF	International Monetary Fund
ISA	Internal Security Act (Malaysia and Singapore)
JI	Jemaah Islamiyah (Islamic Community, an Indonesian terrorist group)
km	kilometer, kilometers
KMM	Kesatuan Melayu Muda (Young Malay Union)
LP	Liberal Party (formerly *Partido Liberal,* the Philippines)

MIC	Malayan Indian Congress
MCA	Malayan Chinese Association
MCP	Malayan Communist Party
MD	Malayan dollars
MDU	Malayan Democratic Union
MILF	Moro Islamic Liberation Front
MNLF	Moro National Liberation Front
MNP	Malay Nationalist Party
MPAJA	Malayan People's Anti-Japanese Army
NGO	Non-Governmental Organization
NLD	National League for Democracy (Burma)
NLF	National Liberation Front (Vietnam)
NP	Nationalist Party (formerly *Partido Nacionalista*, the Philippines)
NPA	New People's Army (the Philippines)
NU	Nahdlatul Ulama
OSVIA	Opleidingschool voor Inlandsche Ambtenaren, Training School for Native Officials (Indonesia)
PAP	People's Action Party (Singapore)
PAS	Parti Islam SeMalaysia (All-Malaysia Islamic Party)
PAVN	People's Army of Vietnam
PDI	Partai Demokrasi Indonesia (Indonesian Democracy Party)
PHP	Philippine Peso
PKI	Partai Komunis Indonesia (Indonesian Communist Party)
PNI	Partai Nasional Indonesia (Indonesian Nationalist Party)
PRC	People's Republic of China
r.	reigned
SI	Sarekat Islam (Islamic Union)
SLORC	State Law and Order Restoration Council (Burma)
SP	Spanish Peso
STOVIA	School tot Opleiding van Inlandsche Artsen, School for Training Native Doctors (Indonesia)
UK	United Kingdom of Great Britain and Northern Ireland
UMNO	United Malays National Organization (Malaya/Malaysia)
UMS	Unfederated Malay States
UN	United Nations
USD	United States dollars
USAFFE	United States Army Forces in the Far East
USSR	Union of Soviet Socialist Republics
VNQDD	Viet Nam Quoc Dan Dang (Vietnamese Nationalist Party)
VOC	Vereenigde Oost-Indische Compagnie, (Dutch) United East India Company
YMBA	Young Men's Buddhist Association

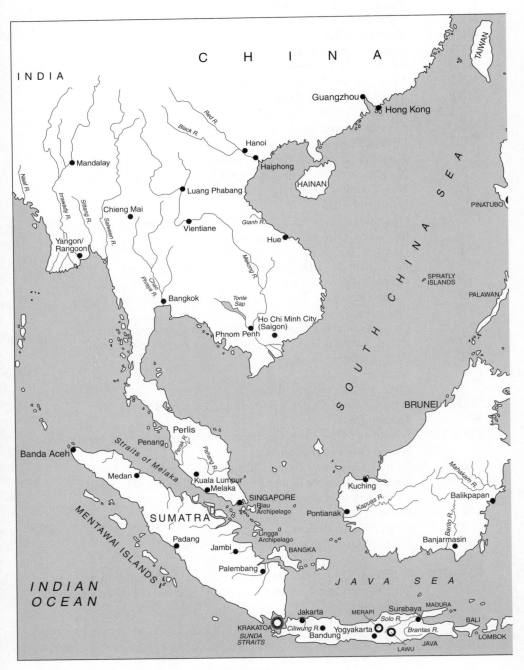

Map 1 Major physical features of Southeast Asia

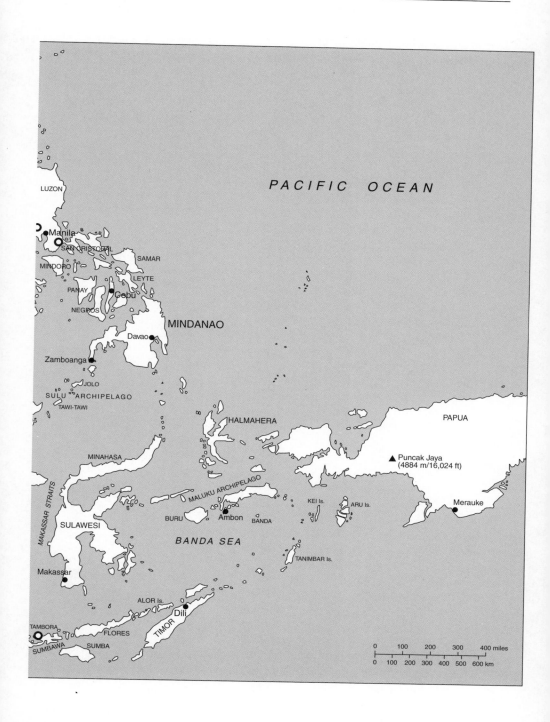

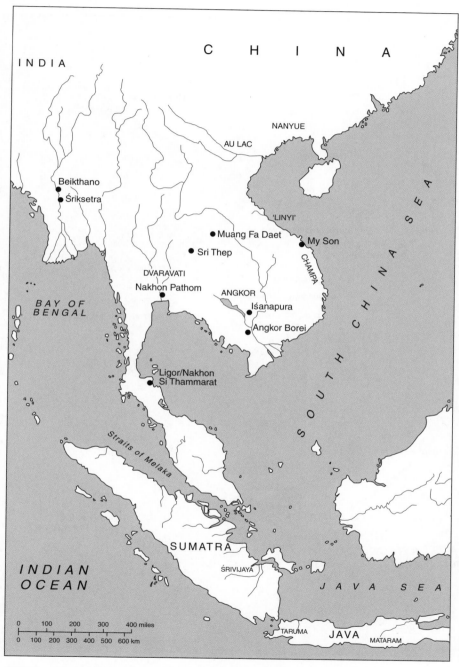

Map 2 Principal early polities of Southeast Asia to c.800

Map 3 Locations of 'Classical' kingdoms c.800–1400

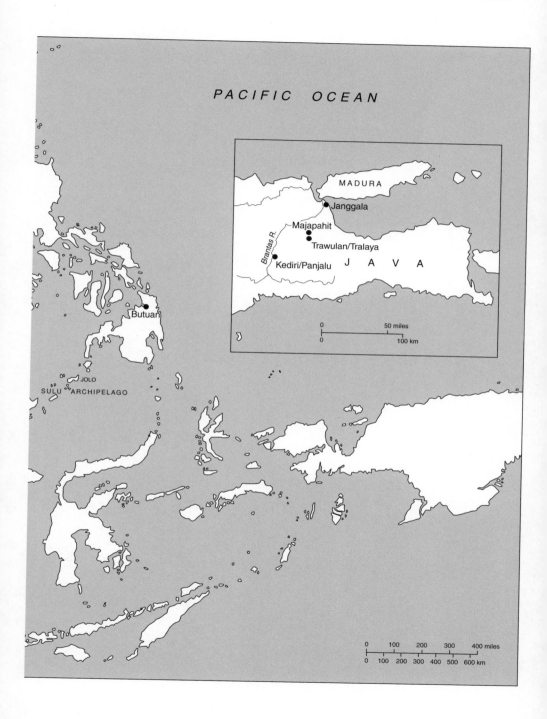

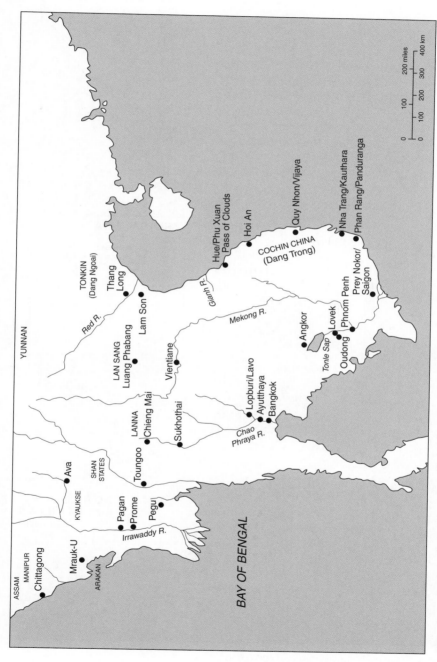

Map 4 Mainland Southeast Asia c.1400–1800

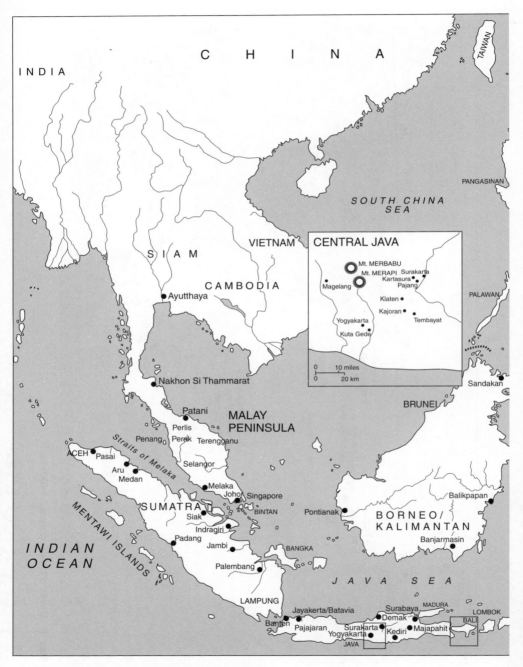

Map 5 Maritime Southeast Asia c.1400–1850

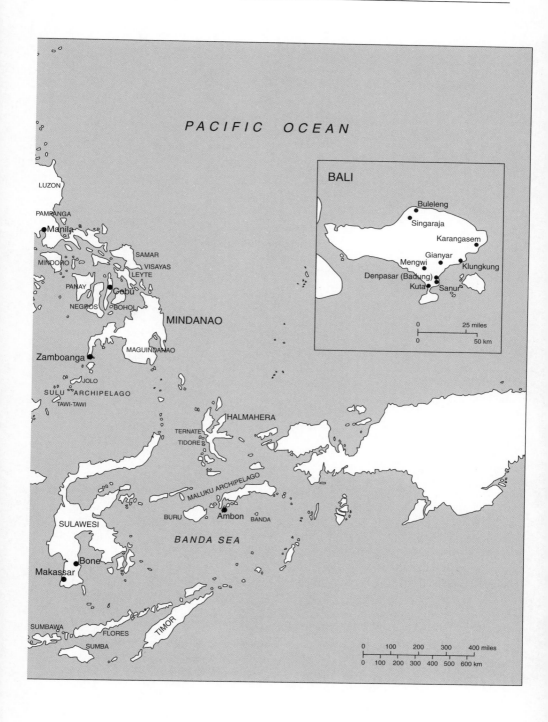

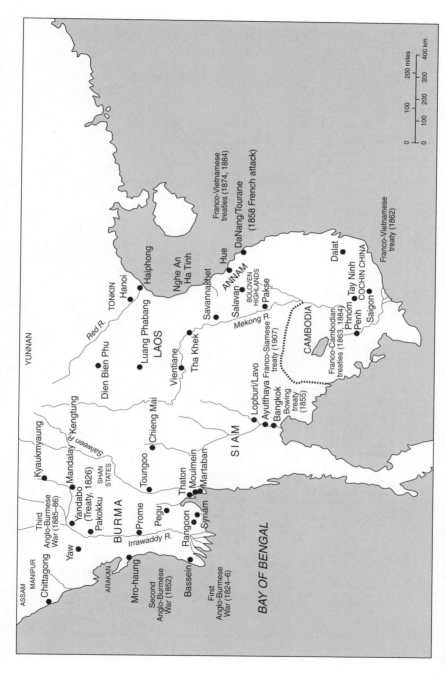

Map 6 Colonial Mainland Southeast Asia, with dates of major wars, conquests or treaties of colonization

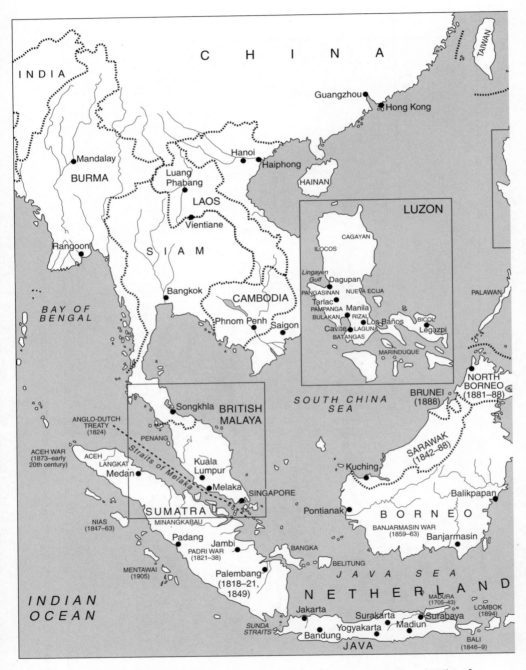

Map 7 Colonial Maritime Southeast Asia, with dates of major wars, conquests or treaties of colonization

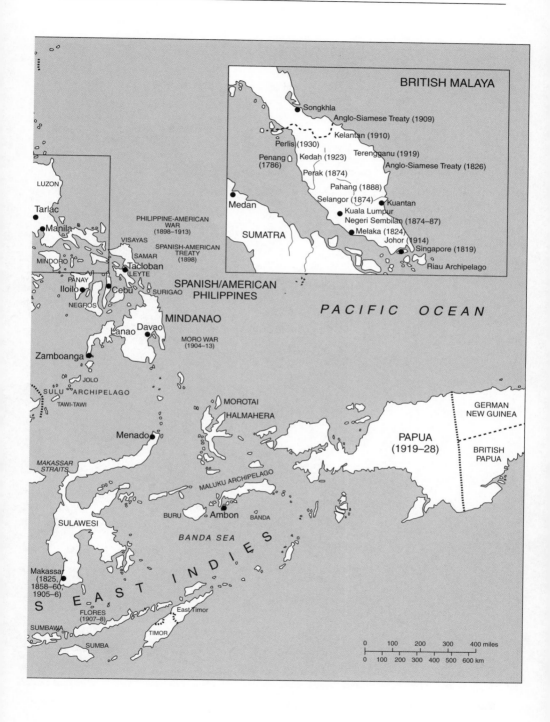

Map 8 Recent and contemporary Southeast Asia

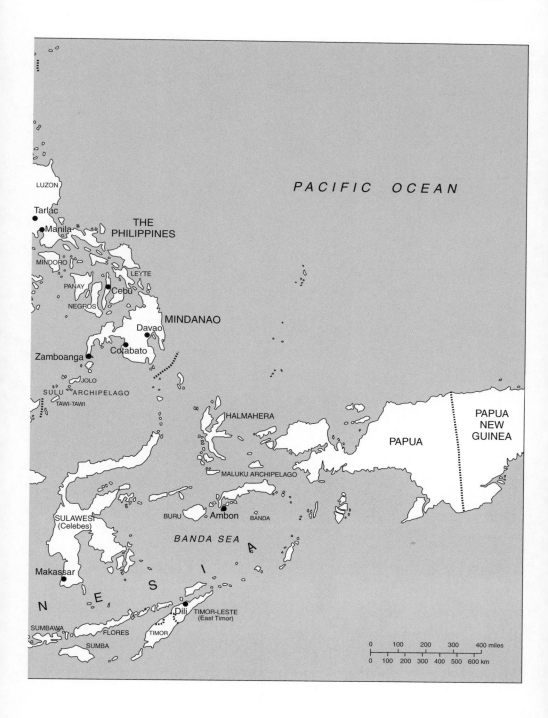

1
Ethnic Groups, Early Cultures and Social Structures

Introduction

The ethnic, cultural and linguistic diversity of Southeast Asia is by no means a recent phenomenon; archeological evidence suggests that this diversity extends back thousands of years into the distant past. Much of the prehistoric era, of course, remains difficult to reconstruct. Carbon dating and other techniques allow us to sketch out a rough chronology for the prehistoric period, along with some general inferences about agriculture, social ranking, and primordial spiritual beliefs. Linking these traces of long-vanished peoples to present-day inhabitants is another matter, however. A skull can be measured and identified in terms of some human group, but it cannot tell us what language the person spoke. Common patterns in burial practices or pottery motifs in different areas suggest communication links and cultural ties, but we cannot be certain whether these different peoples were related to each other or simply in regular contact. Moreover, scholarly theories about migration into and within Southeast Asia have changed drastically over the past half-century, thus reshaping our understanding of the broader pre-historic picture.

Ethnohistory

It is often helpful to approach the ethnic mosaic of Southeast Asia through an overview of the main linguistic families. Language and ethnicity do not always overlap, because over time individuals and groups can change their speech as well as their ethnic identity. However, focusing on language does allow us to make some general observations about different groups of peoples and also to suggest long-term patterns in the movement of these peoples. After a brief introduction of the major families, we will attempt to place each of them within the larger history of Southeast Asia.

With a few exceptions found in the easternmost islands of Indonesia, all indigenous Southeast Asian languages can be assigned to one of five families: Austroasiatic, Austronesian, Tai, Tibeto-Burman, and Hmong-Mien. The term 'indigenous' is used here to exclude the languages spoken by more recent immi-grants from China and India. The *Austroasiatic* languages – often referred to as Mon-Khmer – include Vietnamese and Cambodian (Khmer), as well as Mon (spoken in parts of Myanmar and Thailand) and the languages of several dozen ethnic groups scattered through the uplands of Vietnam, Laos, Cambodia, and Thailand. Mon-Khmer languages are also spoken by a few groups found in southern Thailand and Malaysia. By contrast, the *Austronesian* (Malayo-Polynesian) languages are found mainly in insular Southeast Asia – with the exception of Malay, which is also spoken in southern Thailand, peninsular Malaysia and Singapore, and a few of those in the highlands of central and southern Vietnam and north-eastern Cambodia. Virtually all of the languages of Indonesia and the Philippines belong to this group.

The *Tai* – sometimes called Tai-Kadai – family spans a wide belt of territory stretching from both sides of the China-Vietnam border to Assam in northeast-ern India. It includes the national languages of Thailand and Laos, as well as the tongues spoken by some upland groups found in those countries, Vietnam, and Myanmar. The *Tibeto-Burman* family includes Burmese, the national language of Myanmar, as well as a band of languages spoken in the uplands of northern Southeast Asia. Finally, the *Hmong-Mien* (previously called Miao-Yao) languages are spoken by the descendants of a wave of migrants from China, who settled in the uplands of Vietnam, Laos, and Thailand over the last century or so.

The earliest inhabitants of Southeast Asia were hunter-gatherers, meaning that they had no agriculture as such, but lived on what they could hunt, forage or gather from the forest, rivers, and sea. A crucial development came with the arrival of rice agriculture, which is believed to have spread from southern China over the course of the third millennium BCE. At this point it is important to stress the fact that the 'border' between 'China' and 'Southeast Asia' was once much further north than it is now. The Han people – those that we now think of as 'ethnic Chinese' – only expanded southward at a much later point in time, and in many respects present-day southern China below the Yangzi river had much closer ethnic, linguistic, and cultural ties to Southeast Asia. The spread of cultivated rice was a long, slow process measured in centuries, and there is no evidence that hunter-gatherers eagerly abandoned foraging to become farmers. Archeological evidence from different sites across the region suggests that the two means of livelihood coexisted in close proximity to each other and, in some cases, within the same communities.

Current scholarship agrees that nearly all the languages presently spoken in Southeast Asia can be traced back to distant roots somewhere in southern China, and many – though not all – Southeast Asians are descended from peoples who migrated from different parts of that region. It seems probable that the knowledge and practice of rice agriculture spread outward from the Yangzi river area along with the ancestors of the various Southeast Asian languages as their speakers moved south. The two major linguistic families – Austronesian and Austroasiatic – can both be linked to migration. The Austronesian-speaking peoples are now believed to have originated on the south-eastern coast of China, from where they moved to Taiwan. The indigenous or 'aboriginal' peoples of that island still speak languages from this family. Probably some 4000–5000 years ago, Austronesians took to the sea and launched one of the largest migrations in history, spreading through most of the Pacific islands, the southern part of Southeast Asia, and as far west as the island of Madagascar. Many of the existing inhabitants of the islands were culturally and linguistically assimilated into the migrant populations, though in a few places – notably the island of Papua or New Guinea – they remained separate.

On the mainland it was the Austroasiatic speakers who became the dominant group, completely absorbing the existing inhabitants and their languages. As was the case for the island world, it seems that these new arrivals were agriculturalists who gradually assimilated the hunter-gatherer populations. Although small groups of hunter-gatherers survive even today, they have adopted Austroasiatic languages. The two great linguistic families overlap on the Malay peninsula, where many of the groups known in Malaysia as '*orang asli*' ('original people') are Austroasiatic – rather than Malay-speaking. The chronology of Austroasiatic migration into Southeast Asia remains fuzzy. It is probable that they were directly responsible for the spread of rice cultivation into the region beginning around 3000 BCE, although some scholars believe that they may have come even earlier and subsequently acquired this knowledge from other groups in southern China.

By the end of the prehistoric period, then, most inhabitants of Southeast Asia would have been speaking languages from one of these two families, and those whose ancestors had pre-dated the arrival of the Austroasiatics and Austronesians were largely absorbed into the population descended from the latter two. By the beginning of the Common Era, there were speakers of Tibeto-Burman languages in Southeast Asia as well, concentrated in the territory of present-day Myanmar. The most important group, the Pyu, flourished during the early centuries of the first millennium CE, but they were subsequently assimilated by the ethnic Burmese, a later group of migrants speaking a related language. The last large-scale migration came in the late first and early second millennia, when Tai speakers began to move southward and westward from a homeland probably located in the present-day China-Vietnam border region. The Tai spread as far west as Assam and as far south as the Malay peninsula. While they seem to have adopted certain cultural features – notably Buddhism – from the Mon-Khmer-speakers among whom they settled, they achieved political dominance almost everywhere and, in some cases, completely assimilated the original inhabitants.

By the thirteenth century the distribution of ethnic groups and language families across Southeast Asia had taken roughly its present pattern, with a few important exceptions. First of all, the Vietnamese, whose civilization began in the Red river delta area, gradually expanded southward through a centuries-long process of migration, colonization, and assimilation. This expansion took place at the expense of the Cham along the coast and the Khmer (ethnic Cambodians) in the Mekong delta. Second, the last few centuries have seen a steady trickle of upland peoples moving southward from China. Many of these recent arrivals are Hmong or Yao, while others speak Tibeto-Burman languages. Finally, the advent of colonial rule brought large-scale migration of

Indians and Chinese into various parts of the region, and they constitute significant minorities in several countries today. Significant numbers of Chinese also resettled in Vietnam before colonial rule and in Siam outside the framework of colonization.

Culture

The lowland cultures of Southeast Asia have been profoundly shaped by influences from outside the region, a subject which will be discussed in the next chapter. However, the impact of imported cultural elements has by no means erased the beliefs and practices which pre-dated them, many of which have survived and even blended with those which arrived later. It is always risky to extrapolate backwards from present-day cultural traits. Nevertheless, certain phenomena are both sufficiently widespread and deeply enough rooted in many parts of the region for us to suggest that they provide at least glimpses of the primordial cultures that existed before the arrival of belief systems from India, China, and elsewhere.

Early Southeast Asia was above all a world of spirits – and, indeed, remains so today. Belief in spirits, usually known as animism, has existed at some point in time in virtually every society in history. In certain parts of the world the strength of monotheistic religions – Christianity, Islam, and Judaism – has weakened or eradicated the earlier worship of spirits. Elsewhere, however, animism remains a powerful force, and few Southeast Asians have been so deeply influenced by a Western materialist worldview that they have abandoned their beliefs in spirits. Not a few Muslims and Christians in the region interact with the spirit world above and beyond their regular worship of God, and even those more conservative believers who renounce all animistic practices in their own lives often do not deny the existence of the spirits.

Spirits come in many categories. One of the most common varieties consists of those believed to reside in specific locations such as mountains, caves, rivers, trees, or stones. Many such natural objects and sites are believed to be home to powerful spirits, and the observant traveler will frequently encounter incense sticks or colorful cloths near or actually on top of a rock or tree. Spirits associated with mountains and rivers may be venerated in specific shrines, often without an actual physical image, or honored in well-known legends. In some cases the stories attempt to provide a 'biography' that links the spirit to a specific period in history, but more often their roots go deep back into an unrecorded past. These spirits occasionally appear in the historical record; in eleventh-century Vietnam, for example, a newly crowned ruler was reportedly warned by the spirit of a local mountain that his brothers were plotting to seize the throne.

A second category is the ancestral spirit. Respect for one's (live) elders and (deceased) ancestors is nearly universal in Southeast Asian cultures, and in many cases there is some form or other of actual ancestor worship. Two important exceptions are the Thai and Lao, whose worldview attributes little or no significance to ancestral spirits. These spirits may be represented by physical images, as among the Toraja of Sulawesi in Indonesia; by engraved tablets and – more recently – photographs, as in Vietnam; or simply by decorated altars such as those used to propitiate the *neak ta* of the Khmer. Even a Muslim or Christian home may have pictures of deceased ancestors prominently displayed, although no sacrifices are performed.

The exact degree of ancestral involvement in the daily affairs of their descendants varies from culture to culture. Vietnamese will make daily offerings and prayers and may take the initiative to report household developments on the assumption that their deceased ancestors are still interested in family affairs. Among the Batak and Minahasans of Indonesia, many of whom are now Muslims and Christians, it has traditionally been believed that such spirits actively fight against their more malevolent counterparts to protect their own descendants. Some groups of Chin highlanders in Burma believe that the acts of the living impact the rank of their dead kin, and thus they are in a position to solicit the latter's blessing by performing rituals on their behalf. Similarly, the Batak would carry out ceremonies to enhance the status of their ancestors in the afterlife, thus making them more effective protectors.

A third category is the guardian spirit, who is responsible for the protection of a defined social unit, whether it be a household, village, town, or city, or even an entire country. In some cultures ancestral spirits may fulfill this role, particularly for the family. Often, however, there are separate household spirits who are connected to the physical space itself rather than to the family or lineage of those who live there. Many Tai-speaking peoples have a small shrine located somewhere on the family property. In present-day Thai cities this structure will be large and ornate where government buildings, banks, and other large businesses are concerned. Traditional Vietnamese villages each had their own guardian spirit – in some cases the recognized founder of the village, in others a powerful legendary or historical figure.

Generally speaking, monotheism in the strict sense of the term only came to Southeast Asia with Islam and Christianity. A number of cultures in the region, however, do contain a primordial belief in a overarching deity or supreme creator. One example is the Lahu, found in China's Yunnan province and now in northern Thailand and Burma, whose creator spirit was assimilated to the Christian God when missionaries began evangelism work among them. Early Spanish accounts of some Filipino peoples also mention supreme deities, notably among the Tagalogs. Nevertheless, polytheism was much more widespread. Some cultures, such as the Minahasans, worshipped a pair of deities in the form of a sun god and earth goddess. Many ethnic groups had a whole pantheon of deities or spirits, one of whom might be worshipped as a creator but was not supreme. In a few cultures, such as the Balinese and the Cham, these deities were later given Indic names with exposure to Indian culture.

The two most fundamental concerns of primordial Southeast Asian cultures were fertility – both agricultural and human – and protection from harm. Several peoples, such as the Balinese and Thai, believe in a rice goddess who is linked to bountiful crops. Shrines for guaranteeing a woman's ability to bear children were created around phallic-shaped stones, which later became associated with the Hindu deity Śiva, or other sites whose resident spirits – often female – were believed to be receptive to the petitions of barren and pregnant women alike. Meanwhile, every culture had its own varieties of malevolent spirits intent on causing harm to living beings. In some cases these spirits would be explicitly identified and directly propitiated to ensure that they left people alone. In other cases recognizably benevolent powers such as the ancestors mentioned above would be the recipients of offerings and prayers asking for their protection from evil spirits, known and unknown.

The system of animistic beliefs is structured around two main components: taboos and offerings. Taboos are steps taken to prevent offending the spirit in question; they range from avoiding any mention of the spirit's name to the omission of a particular bird or animal from one's diet, to abstaining from sex or other activities in the proximity of an altar or other sacred site. Offerings, generally accompanied by some form of prayer or petition, are made with varying frequency depending on the particular spirit involved; a household spirit might be propitiated on a daily basis, whereas a village guardian could be the focus of an annual festival. Normally a village will have one or more kinds of 'specialists' to perform rituals and/or communicate with the spirits when necessary. These mediums, shamans, 'spirit doctors' – to name the three most common categories – have survived in most Southeast Asian societies. Even among those groups which have converted to Christianity or Islam, both of which are notably hostile to animistic practices, it is still possible to find such practitioners, though their roles may be more restricted than was the case in traditional society.

One of the distinctive features of Southeast Asian cultures – though not one unique to the region – is the importance of female ritual specialists and mediums. It seems to have long been the case that women frequently enjoy close links to the spirit world, and in various parts of the region many of the most renowned spirit mediums are female. Moreover, many male mediums are homosexual or even transsexual, thus explicitly linking themselves to the female gender. In many cases the spirits themselves are female, such as the rice goddesses just mentioned or the Holy Mothers (*Thanh Mau*) of the Vietnamese, and the most important deity of the Cham people is the goddess Po Nagar. With the subsequent introduction of religions like Theravada Buddhism, Islam, and Christianity, which tend to assign women a subordinate role in the spiritual hierarchy, tensions have arisen because of the traditional association of spiritual powers with women. In some cases the original female-dominated beliefs and practices survive and coexist with the later arrivals from outside the region.

Kinship and the extended family are important in virtually all Southeast Asian societies. Westerners used to simply referring to 'brothers', 'sisters', 'uncles', 'aunts', and the like will be struck by the variety of terms used to denote members of one's family. It is nearly universal to distinguish clearly between older and younger siblings, and generally between paternal and maternal relatives of various generations. Most languages in the region make extensive use of kinship terms as forms of address and, in some cases, as pronouns; in Vietnamese, for example, there is no polite word for 'you' which does not also mean 'elder brother', 'aunt', 'grandfather', and so on. Modern Thai, Lao, and Indonesian, by contrast, do have polite words for 'I' and 'you' which are not derived from terms for family members, but in many situations the speaker will switch to using kinship terms as pronouns instead. The use of these terms to designate the speaker and the listener reflects the awareness of finely gradated distinctions of age and status found in many of the region's cultures.

Kinship is important for determining inheritance rights, the pool of possible spouses, and social obligations, as well as one's fundamental place in a particular sub-group of one's society. Anthropologists identify several different kinds of kinship, and all of them can be found within Southeast Asia. Patrilineality is common; such groups emphasize the father's lineage and generally identify an individual as the son of a particular man, whether through a family name or a patronymic, whereby one's father's name is linked to one's own. In matrilineal societies, such as the Minangkabau of Sumatra and the E-de (Rhadé) of Vietnam's Central Highlands, family lineages are structured around the woman's line rather than the man's. Some societies practice bilateral kinship, whereby both the paternal and maternal lineages are important. Among royal families this could prove complicated when it came to determining the legitimate successor to a ruler; this is believed to have been a problem in Angkorean Cambodia, for example.

Social and political structures

Like elsewhere in the world, the family and clan or lineage have traditionally been at the foundation of most Southeast Asian societies, though their significance and function vary widely from one culture to another. We have just referred to the extensive systems of kinship terminology, which is a clear illustration of the importance attributed to the family in general and to the need to distinguish among different members in particular. The family/household almost universally remains the fundamental unit, whether it is reinforced by the collective worship of a particular group of ancestors or by the shared activity involved in earning a living.

Families in many societies are organized into clans and/or lineages. One's membership in one of these units may be indicated by one's name, the particular taboos one follows, the ancestors one makes offerings to, or simply by one's own sense of identity. It should be noted that in many of the region's cultures, family names are quite recent inventions. Exceptions are the Vietnamese, who have had them since the period of Chinese rule during the first millennium, and the Christian Filipinos, some of whom began to acquire them in the sixteenth century. The Thai began to use family names in the early twentieth century, and the Lao somewhat later. Khmer and Burmese names are more complicated; in some cases the full names of children may incorporate an element of their father's name in order to show the family connection, but not always, and family names as such are almost non-existent. Malays use patronymics, while Javanese have a variety of naming patterns that may or may not show a common affiliation. Among the upland peoples the Hmong are known for their particularly strong clan structure; the number of clan names is fixed, and two Hmong who share the same clan name will usually feel some sense of kinship even if their respective roots are geographically very far apart.

Clans and lineages are often the main form of social organization below the village level. They will usually have their own chiefs or elders, who have considerable influence among the members of their kinship unit. In some cultures this unit may be connected to a specific place or structure, whether it be a lineage hall as found in Vietnam, a longhouse as was (and is) common among highland groups in certain areas, or an entire village. In the latter case the leadership of the clan or lineage may overlap with the leadership of the village. At the very least the clan or lineage elders would normally play an important role in village affairs.

Not all Southeast Asians traditionally lived in a village, but it was by far the most common socio-political unit. Even most upland groups, who were frequently characterized by foreign observers as 'tribes', tended to have some kind of settlement which could be considered as a village. 'Tribe' is no longer a politically correct term, having come to be viewed as pejorative. For a long time, however, it served to denote groups of people living under a particular leader but without a formal structure of government. The main exception would be hunter-gatherers, whose lack of involvement with agriculture meant that they were more likely to move around through the forests in a series of temporary settlements. Ethnic groups practicing slash-and-burn agriculture, by contrast, normally have villages within the general proximity of the fields where they grow their crops.

The nature, structure, and size of the Southeast Asian village vary widely. Villages may be quite loosely organized and less clearly defined in terms of their geographical space, or they may be tightly structured with clear boundaries. Villagers may worship a common ancestor or guardian spirit. There may be a single headman, usually from the most powerful family or clan in the community. Alternatively, the leadership may be composed of elders whose position is recognized by virtue of their age and/or status within the community, of officials appointed or elected either by the villagers themselves or – in later times – by the government, or perhaps of a combination of the two groups of people.

During the pre-modern period, a number of Southeast Asian peoples had no structure above the village level. Villages were often self-contained units whose leadership effectively represented the highest level of authority within that particular ethnic group. The clan and/or lineage leaders, along with a priest or someone else with spiritual powers, constituted the 'ruling elite'. Well into the twentieth century many upland groups such as the Chin of Burma, the E-de (Rhadé) of Vietnam, and a number of the peoples of Borneo (in present-day Eastern Malaysia, Brunei, and Kalimantan, Indonesia) had no supra-village power structure. While villages could and often did form alliances for various purposes, notably for fighting against common enemies, they were autonomous and did not submit to the authority of an outside ruler.

Over time, some ethnic groups developed more formal and structured patterns of leadership under rulers such as chiefs and kings. The qualitative distinction between these two categories of ruler is admittedly rather subjective. In the Southeast Asian context we generally speak of kings and kingship for those peoples who were exposed to cultural influence from outside the region, initially Indic and Chinese and later Theravada Buddhist and Islamic. Southeast Asian kingship will be considered in detail in the next two chapters, while the discussion in this section will focus on chiefs. The title is sometimes used for the leader of a village, but it is less confusing to refer to that individual as a head-man and reserve the term 'chief' for someone with supra-village authority.

Scholars generally refer to societies ruled by chiefs as either chiefdoms or chieftaincies. The main characteristic of such societies is that a group of villages are bound together by some form of ties which are more permanent than a temporary war alliance. The chief's authority may be based on personal prestige, martial accomplishments which have earned the submission of neighboring groups, kinship ties, or a combination of these. There is little or no 'government' in the modern sense; the chief's main concern is to be able to acquire financial resources in the form of taxes, tribute, or gifts, and to mobilize manpower in the event of a conflict. These requirements necessitate the assertion of his (or, occasionally, her) authority at certain times but do not involve day-to-day governance. Village autonomy remains important, and a chief who attempts to intervene or interfere in village affairs beyond the rights which are attributed to him will encounter serious problems unless he has sufficient personal prowess to enforce his will.

Chiefdoms and chieftaincies are usually perceived as rather fragile structures, held together mainly by the force of the ruler's personality and by the shared interests of the various villages involved. The chief's authority is exercised by consensus, by recognition on the part of those willing to accept it. In exchange for the loyalty and material things which he receives from his subjects, he must be able to provide protection and allow them to benefit from his prestige, spiritually if not materially. In many cultures rulers are believed to bring about prosperity through their own personal attributes. If at some point his personal prestige begins to wane and the advantages of submitting to his authority become less evident, the territory under his control is likely to shrink or to fragment into pieces as rival leaders go their way and assert their independence from their former overlord.

Leadership and authority in Southeast Asian societies, then, have always been highly personal in nature. They may be backed up by physical coercion (or the threat of it) reinforced by rituals and ceremonies, or validated by the prestige attached to an individual or his lineage. Such authority can be very transitory, however, and it was only with the arrival of religious beliefs and concepts of kingship from outside the region that chiefly power became royal power and chiefdoms were transformed into relatively more permanent kingdoms. As will be shown in Chapter 2, this transformation was a long, slow process, and the early kingdoms of Southeast Asia demonstrated many of the same weaknesses and problems as their predecessors. While most lowland chiefs were becoming 'kings', their upland counterparts continued to articulate and exercise their authority in older ways. For several centuries, the qualitative differences between the power of a lowland king and an upland chief were not significant, even though their respective domains may have varied in size.

Lowland and upland, fields and forests, land and sea

Every country in Southeast Asia except for urbanized Singapore is characterized by at least one of three important demographic distinctions. The first is between inhabitants of the lowlands and those who live in the hills and mountains, usually referred to as 'uplanders' or 'highlanders'. The second distinction is between those who live in fixed settlements and practice either wet- or dry-rice (swidden) agriculture and those who engage in hunting and gathering for subsistence, usually in the forests. Finally, several countries have small populations whose lives center around the sea and who live on boats, as opposed to fishing communities who depend on the ocean for their livelihood but are nevertheless part of the land-based population.

These distinctions are not just geographical, economic, or demographic; they are also ethnic. Peoples living in the highlands, in the forests, or on boats along the coasts are always ethnic minorities in their respective countries. In many, but not all, cases they have come to be designated as 'indigenous peoples', as opposed to the ethnic majorities or other minority groups who migrated at a later point in time. This classification is not without its difficulties, especially when the majority group has been present for centuries and considers itself as equally 'indigenous'. Nevertheless, the category of 'indigenous peoples' remains in active use among anthropologists and activists involved with advocating for the rights of these often marginalized minorities.

Early patterns and sequences of migration into Southeast Asia are often difficult to determine because of the lack of a written record and the fact that many groups have only faint memories in their oral traditions of earlier movement from somewhere else. Linguistic and ethnological analysis allows for a general historical picture, but it remains quite hazy and is further complicated by the fact that in some areas there has been intermixing between groups of people inhabiting different geographical space. Nevertheless, we can attempt to trace a broad overview of the ways in which different ethnic groups have come to be linked to separate geographical areas.

In most of mainland Southeast Asia, the Austroasiatic (Mon-Khmer) speakers constitute the 'oldest inhabitants'. As noted above, these languages originated outside the region but were introduced with early waves of migration, and there is no remnant of any languages spoken before that time. The pre-Austroasiatic period was the Stone Age, and the populations living in the mainland area at that time were absorbed by the migrants. In those areas which were not disturbed by further migration, the Austroasiatic speakers became the dominant lowland groups: Mon, Khmer (Cambodians), and Vietnamese. The exact roots of the Vietnamese as an ethnic group are still unclear; they seem to have moved down from the midland regions of northern Vietnam and may have incorporated groups speaking languages from other families.

Burma

The ethnohistory of the various groups in Burma is full of speculation, but it seems likely that the country's territory has been almost completely populated by migration. The ancestors of the ethnic Burman majority came from Tibet, as did their predecessors the Pyu, who provided the ethnic and cultural foundations for the future Burmese kingdom and were gradually but completely assimilated by the Burmans. Both the Pyu and the Burmans were lowland peoples, and the cities and kingdoms which dominate the Burmese historical record belonged to them.

The uplands are inhabited by a variety of ethnic groups speaking Tibeto-Burman or Mon-Khmer languages and by the Shan, who are Tai-speakers and Theravada Buddhists. If we assume that the Mon-Khmer speakers have been in the mainland region the longest, that would suggest that the oldest inhabitants of present-day Burmese territory are the Wa and Palaung, who belong to the Austroasiatic family and are found in the northeastern region along the border with China's Yunnan province. Historically they were not part of the Burmese kingdoms but were included within the borders of colonial Burma after the advent of British rule.

Several of Burma's most important minorities speak Tibeto-Burman languages: the Chin and Kachin are the best-known. It should be pointed out that these names came into use in English as collective designations for several different ethnic groups speaking related languages; there is not a single, homogeneous 'Chin' or 'Kachin' group. The original homeland of these peoples lies further north in what is now Tibet; as they migrated down into present-day Burma, there was probably little or no competition for the upland areas where they settled. Traditionally these groups were animists, as were the Wa and Palaung, but missionary work under British rule resulted in significant numbers of Chin and Kachin becoming Christians.

A major upland group is the Shan, who live intermingled with many of the peoples just mentioned. They represent the westernmost edge of the Tai-speaking zone; the Ahom of northeastern India originally spoke a Tai language as well but eventually adopted the local Assamese tongue. As adherents of Theravada – although in a form somewhat distinct from that of the Burmans – they have generally resisted conversion to Christianity. The Shan have the most highly developed socio-political structure among the highland peoples of Burma; until the end of British rule they were divided into a multitude of small states known as *mong*, each with its own ruler. While this structural strength has not usually translated into domination over their neighbors, they have been influential in the highland areas, and the British anthropologist Edmund Leach described in a famous study how some groups of Kachin alternated between their own indigenous and relatively egalitarian structure and a more hierarchical one modeled after the Shan.

The other significant group found in Burma's highlands is the Karen, whose language is most probably Tibeto-Burman, although its exact affiliation remains uncertain. As with the Chin and Kachin, 'Karen' is a collective term for several different groups, and its comprehensiveness in this respect is debated among scholars, even though they generally use it with certain qualifications. The ancestors of the Karen are believed to have migrated from Tibet at some point, but once again the timeframe for this movement is unclear. Many Karen live in the highlands, but some communities also live in the lowlands and practice wet-rice agriculture. The village has traditionally been the significant socio-political unit among the various groups of Karen, with no chief or ruler holding authority above that level.

Cambodia

Cambodia presents a diametrically opposite case, since lowlanders and high-landers come from the same Mon-Khmer stock. Over the centuries some groups separated themselves from the lowland Khmer and settled at higher altitudes. As elsewhere, these groups – known collectively as *Khmer Loeu* ('upland Khmer') – have usually been differentiated on the basis of agriculture and religious practices. In Cambodia these highland minorities are concentrated in the northeastern region; several of them (such as the Brao and Stieng) are found on both sides of the border with Vietnam. One of the largest minorities, the Kuy, straddles the Thai border; they have adopted wet-rice farming and, in some cases, Buddhism. The northeastern highlands are home to small populations of Jarai and Rhadé, Austronesian speakers who are found in greater numbers in central Vietnam. In the lowland areas of Cambodia there are also numerous pockets of Muslim Cham and, along the northern border, ethnic Lao.

The Tai world

The great migration of the Tai-speaking peoples, already mentioned earlier in this chapter, considerably disrupted the ethnic patterns of the mainland region. Tai speakers came to dominate politically and culturally the lowland areas of Thailand and Laos. The Mon were assimilated over much of the territory of what is now Thailand, though later a sizable population shifted to what is now southern Burma. Most of the rest of the original inhabitants moved to higher altitudes, where they practiced dry-rice agriculture and remained unexposed to Buddhism, two key factors which would come to differentiate them from lowlanders.

The two areas of mainland Southeast Asia where the most significant displacement took place were present-day northern Thailand and Laos. The former region is believed to have been inhabited by Mon and Lawa, the latter also a Mon-Khmer-speaking group. Like the Mon further south, those in the north were absorbed by the Tai migrants. This was probably the case for some of the Lawa as well, but they have survived as a separate group, practicing either wet- or dry-rice agriculture depending on their location. Their oral traditions contain memories of chiefs and kings, but supra-village structures disappeared even before the arrival of the Tai, apparently with the expansion of Mon power. Certain Northern Thai chronicles and rituals make allusion to the Lawa, and the spirits of a Lawa couple have long been venerated as the guardians of Chiang Mai.

Laos has a diverse population of Mon-Khmer speakers scattered through the country's highland regions. The largest of these groups is the Kmhmu, found in several northern provinces. Central and southern Laos are home to a number of upland minorities, many of whom have kin on the Vietnamese side of the border as well. These Mon-Khmer-speaking groups are the descendants of the original inhabitants of present-day Laos; their ancestors left or were driven to higher altitudes when the Tai-speaking Lao migrated in during the first millennium. Several groups have oral traditions of conflict with the new arrivals, including anecdotes about having been tricked by the more clever Lao into giving up their native lands. These groups have traditionally been known to Tai speakers as *Kha*, meaning slaves, which indicates their inferior social and cultural status *vis-à-vis* the lowlanders, as well as – in some cases – their vulnerability to slave-raiding activities.

Vietnam

The upland areas of northwestern Vietnam are essentially part of the Tai world, the two main groups being the Black and White Thai, who practice wet-rice agriculture in upland valleys; they have retained traditional Tai animistic beliefs and have not converted to Buddhism in either its Vietnamese or Theravada form. By contrast, the Tay and Nung of northern Vietnam have had much closer political and cultural ties to the ethnic Vietnamese and have been more deeply influenced by their beliefs. The connections between these upland and lowland groups extend deep into the past, and it is widely believed that while the Vietnamese people's language is Mon-Khmer, their pre-Sinicized cultural roots may lie with the Tay and Nung.

Mon-Khmer-speaking groups are scattered around different parts of upland Vietnam. In the northwestern region they are a relatively small presence and were traditionally subordinated to the more powerful Black and White Thai, whose local rulers dominated much of the region. Their numbers are much stronger in the upland areas of central Vietnam, both the western parts of the coastal provinces and the region known as the Central Highlands (Tay Nguyen) which borders on Lao and Cambodia. These groups range in size from the more numerous Muong and Ba-na (Bahnar) down to small populations numbering only a few hundred. The Muong deserve special mention here because they are the closest kin to the ethnic Vietnamese, and it is probable that the two were originally one people, later divided when some chose to migrate to the lowlands.

The Central Highlands are also home to several large groups of Austronesian speakers whose ancestors came over the sea and then migrated inward and upward from the coast. The best-known of these are the E-de (Rhadé) and Gia-rai (Jarai). These peoples have retained close links to the lowland Cham, who once occupied the entire central coast but are now confined to a smaller area of that coast and a second area along the Cambodian border. Also Austronesian speakers, the Cham were more heavily exposed first to Indian culture and then to Islam. They will reappear in later chapters, as they were important neighbors – and frequent enemies – of the Vietnamese.

Finally, mention should be made of the Khmer (ethnic Cambodian) minority in the Mekong delta. This southernmost region of Vietnam was first colonized by the Vietnamese in the seventeenth century, and despite coexistence and some intermarriage, the Khmer population has never been assimilated. They have retained their own language and their Theravada Buddhism, as opposed to the Mahayana practiced by ethnic Vietnamese. Their presence is one of the factors which make the Mekong delta a culturally eclectic region, different in many ways from either the lowland or upland areas further north.

The 'newest' highlanders

The settlement patterns just described have been in place for roughly the past thousand years, and much longer in the case of groups other than the Tai. Over the past century or so, one final round of migration has brought new arrivals who are now scattered across northern mainland Southeast Asia. The five main groups are the Hmong, Yao (Mien), Lahu, Lisu, and Akha. Originating from different parts of southern and southwestern China, these highlanders have been moving across borders for over a hundred years. As the most recent migrants, they have been forced to settle in the highest inhabitable altitudes, above the areas occupied by Mon-Khmer speakers or upland Tai. Their predominant form of agriculture has been slash-and-burn cultivation of dry rice and other crops and, in more recent times, the opium poppy. Although few of them have adopted the Buddhism of their lowland neighbors, they have to varying degrees been responsive to the efforts of Western missionaries, and Christian communities can be found among all five groups, most notably the Hmong.

The island world

As mentioned above, Malay and virtually all the other indigenous languages of Indonesia and the Philippines belong to the Austronesian family. The immigration of Austronesian speakers several thousand years ago led to the virtually complete disappearance of other tongues, and even those ethnic groups whose ancestors may have already been around when this migration took place have since adopted the languages of the later arrivals. Moreover, there has been considerable intermarriage and assimilation over the centuries, so that attempting to differentiate clearly between 'original' inhabitants and 'later' migrants is almost impossible. Having said this, it is certainly the case that there remains a tremendous degree of ethnic diversity within the island world, as well as clear distinctions among the various groups in terms of their respective cultures and ecological niches. The term 'Malay' (*Melayu*) itself is very fluid and has been used at different times to refer to different groups speaking related languages. It now most commonly refers to the majority group in Malaysia and Brunei and to the largest minority in Singapore. In the past, however, it has been used more broadly to designate other lowland peoples such as the Javanese and even many of those in the Philippines – which is part of the 'Malay world' in its larger sense.

In Malaysia a number of non-Malay ethnic groups are referred to collectively as *orang asli* ('original people'). These groups are scattered around Peninsular Malaysia and parts of Southern Thailand. The small northern group known as 'Semang' are usually classified as 'Negritos', a classification distinguishing them from the 'Mongoloids' represented by the Malays, Javanese, and many other inhabitants of the island world. They are foragers and speak languages belonging to the Austroasiatic family. Another set of Austroasiatic speakers are usually referred to collectively as 'Senoi'. Like 'Semang', this is a group label which can be broken into various sub-groups. They are more numerous and are scattered over a larger swath of the Malay peninsula; they mainly practice dry-rice agri-culture. There is debate among scholars as to whether the ancestors of these groups were in fact the 'original' inhabitants of the territory, their designation in Malay notwithstanding.

The island of Borneo, which includes Eastern Malaysia (Sabah and Sarawak), Brunei, and Indonesian Kalimantan, is divided among three governments dominated by lowlanders but with substantial upland and forest-dwelling popu-lations. The ethnic classification of these populations is very complicated, and considerable disagreement remains as to the suitability of certain terms such as 'Dayaks' (referring to various peoples in Kalimantan) or 'Ibans' (in Sarawak). Ethnic identity on the island has clearly undergone significant shifts at different points in time, particularly with conversion to Islam and, more recently, Christianity. Many of these groups continue to practice swidden agriculture or foraging, depending on their location.

Like Borneo, most of the islands of eastern Indonesia are home to more than one ethnic group, and the distinction between lowland and upland dwellers remains important in some places, notably the large island of Sulawesi. The lowland regions of Sulawesi have long been dominated by the political rivalry between various Bugis and Makassarese kingdoms, while groups like the Minahasans and Toraja remained in the uplands. As one moves eastward through the archipelago, the inhabitants become less Mongoloid and more Melanesian – on Flores and Timor, for example – and the island of New Guinea (Papua) represents the 'frontier' between Southeast Asia and the Pacific island world to the east.

In the Philippines we can distinguish two different groups of uplanders. Several groups of Negritos are found in different parts of the archipelago, while the mountainous Cordillera of Luzon is home to a number of groups for whom the collective term 'Igorots' is frequently used. Many of these groups practice wet- or dry-rice agriculture, the Ifugao being particularly famous for their terraced fields (Figure 1). Several other groups called Lumads are found in the southern region of Mindanao. While the Negritos may well be the descendants of a population which predated the Austronesian speakers who arrived long ago, many scholars now believe that the rest of the population comes from the same stock and that the distinctions between uplanders and lowlanders are largely cultural and linguistic. In particular, uplanders were largely removed from the process of conversion to Islam and Christianity which took place in the lowlands.

Finally, we will briefly consider the scattered groups of sea- and shore-dwelling peoples, sometimes referred to as 'sea nomads' or, in many parts of the region, as *'orang laut'* ('sea people' in Malay). These groups can be found along the western coast of the Malay peninsula as far north as the Thai-Burmese border (where they are called Moken); in the Riau-Lingga area where Singaporean, Malaysian, and Indonesian territorial waters meet; in a stretch of water extending from Malaysian Sabah on northern Borneo to the Tawi-tawi archipelago in southern Philippines; and in various parts of eastern Indonesia. In the latter two regions two of the most common names for these *orang laut* are 'Sama'/ 'Samal' and 'Bajau', though neither these designations or the

Figure 1 Ifugao terraces

groups they refer to can be neatly defined. Generally speaking, the 'sea nomads' are less nomadic than they once were, and some have settled permanently on land, though they still have close links to their boat-dwelling kin (Figure 2).

Attempting to place these sea-dwelling groups in the broader narrative of Southeast Asian history is a difficult and complex task. In some places they were seen as pirates and were involved in raiding activities of various kinds, including slave-trading. In others their primary occupation was to gather various marine products for trade, notably the sea cucumber or *trepang*, which despite its name is actually a living creature valued as both food and medicine, particularly among the Chinese. Historians are increasingly coming to recognize the importance of *orang laut* as 'clients' of coastal rulers who relied on them for manpower and – to some extent, at least – incorporated them into their social and commercial networks. While today these groups are drastically reduced in numbers and, in some cases, marginalized and even exploited by the societies they belong to, it is clear that in the past they filled an important niche in pre-colonial maritime polities.

As this chapter has made clear, the history of Southeast Asia cannot be told merely in terms of lowland peoples living in cities, towns, and villages. While the multi-ethnic nation-states created by Western colonialism and its legacy of borders do not correspond to the kingdoms of earlier centuries, neither would it be accurate to argue that colonial rule dragged upland or forest-dwelling peoples out of isolation and into contact with the 'outside world'. There are a few isolated examples where this observation would be valid, but not many.

Figure 2   Labuanbajo port scene, Flores, Indonesia

Most groups living outside the lowland areas, though they generally enjoyed considerable autonomy and even total independence *vis-à-vis* the political centers found in those areas, did have social and trading contacts with lowlanders. In many cases these contacts were mutually beneficial, as when each side could trade what it had for something it needed. In some cases they were exploitative, when slave-raiding took place or when a lowland state was strong enough to collect taxes instead of engaging in two-way trade. The attempt to reconstruct a multi-ethnic history which takes into consideration the roles and the significance of groups occupying different ecological niches is one of the most challenging tasks facing the historian of Southeast Asia today.

2
Early State Formation

Introduction: approaches to early Southeast Asian history

We distinguish between prehistory, which is the domain of the archeologist, and proto-history, which designates the period when a particular region has yet to produce its own written record but does at least appear in foreign sources. For Southeast Asia, the transition between these two stages takes place during the early centuries of the Common Era. Fairly precise information on the region can be found in Chinese sources from the third and fourth centuries. Epigraphy (inscriptions) in Sanskrit, and subsequently in local languages, begin to appear shortly thereafter. These two sets of materials comprise our main sources for the study of early Southeast Asian history, but each presents its own problems. Chinese scholars wrote detailed accounts of distant countries for which they had acquired scattered bits of information, which they filtered through their own cultural prejudices and general worldview. Inscriptions, on the other hand, present us with even more scattered morsels of knowledge about rulers, their claims to power and glory, and their deeds – mainly donations to and foundations of temples, along with the occasional military victory.

Western historians writing during the first half of the twentieth century relied heavily on the Chinese texts to reconstruct a narrative of the Southeast Asian past, attempting to squeeze information from the epigraphy into the chronological framework provided by the Chinese sources. While Indian and Arab writers did mention Southeast Asia as well, they provided little substantive information that could contribute to a historical narrative. Scholars generally accepted the Chinese view of a region filled with 'kingdoms' and 'empires' of various sizes, ruled by successive 'dynasties' and 'bureaucracies' and presumably patterned after the model of the Middle Kingdom. Most textbook maps of Southeast Asia during the first millennium have depicted a handful of large polities with contiguous borders, more or less analogous to the modern assortment of nation-states. The 'foundation', 'rise', and 'fall' of these various 'kingdoms' and 'empires' constituted the core of early Southeast Asian history as it was generally understood.

Over more recent decades, however, scholars have begun to raise serious questions about the ways in which the Southeast Asian past has been mapped out, literally and figuratively. To what extent did Chinese writers distort the realities of their neighbors to the South by assuming that these countries were structured like their own empire? To what degree did colonial-era histories impose the assumptions and views of Western imperialism when studying the past? A new generation of historians has sought to address these questions by rethinking Southeast Asian history (particularly during the first millennium) and retelling the story based as much as possible on local evidence rather than foreign accounts. At the same time, there has been a greater effort to understand the region's history in cultural terms – that is, to study it not just as a sequence of events but also as the interplay of concepts, ideas, and beliefs originating both inside and outside Southeast Asia, an approach that has generally shaped the whole of this book.

It has long been recognized, of course, that early Southeast Asia was heavily influenced by the cultures of China (in the case of Vietnam) and India (almost everywhere else in the region). The twin phenomena of Indianization and Sinicization were fundamental to the evolution of many – though not all – of the cultures in the region. Our understanding of the impact of these external forces and their interaction with indigenous cultural elements has, however, changed dramatically, which in turn has reshaped our view of the centuries when this interaction was taking place. Colonial-era scholars tended to look at early Southeast Asian history and culture through 'Indian' and 'Chinese' lenses. These 'lenses' had several components. First, the foreign cultural elements were viewed as dominant over – and generally superior to – the cultures that they came to influence. Second, the influx of these foreign elements was seen as the defining force and catalyst for the 'beginning' of Southeast Asian history. Finally, the polities of Southeast Asia were long viewed as more or less imperfect copies of Chinese and Indian originals.

The influential history by French scholar George Coedès, entitled *The Indianized States of Southeast Asia*, is the quintessential example of this approach. For Coedès, the narrative of Southeast Asian history effectively begins with the arrival of Indian culture, which serves as the catalyst for the forces of political, cultural, and economic change that shaped the region for the next millennium. One could go even further and infer from his discussion that it was Indian culture which essentially created and defined Southeast Asia as a region, a supposition that is heightened by his omission of Vietnam and the Philippines from his study. Pre-Indianized Southeast Asia is relegated to a few introductory pages on prehistory, geography, and ethnology. Coedès's approach was largely followed by D. G. E. Hall in his own work, and subsequent histories by other authors made little attempt to delve into the region's past before Indianization, leaving this topic to the archeologists.

Such an approach to early Southeast Asia is no longer acceptable. Not only has our understanding of the region's pre- and proto-history been greatly enriched by further archeological research, but now the findings of this research have been incorporated directly into the historical narrative. There are at least two important consequences of this change. First, rather than viewing Southeast Asian history as having started rather abruptly with the impact of Indian culture – or Chinese, in the case of Vietnam – scholars now emphasize a gradual process of cultural change which moves from prehistory to proto-history. Second, there is much more attention to the economic activities which linked the region to the Indian Ocean and elsewhere for several centuries before actual cultural Indianization began. Recognition of the dynamic trade patterns which were already in effect in the final centuries BCE has replaced the assumption that such economic dynamism only began later on. At the same time, this allows us to explore more deeply the linkages between trade and cultural exchange, which tended to take place in tandem and following the same routes.

Historians are also looking more closely at the polities that appeared in the early centuries CE with the onset of Indianization. Not only is there a more concerted attempt to differentiate between these early polities and the later kingdoms of the 'classical' era, but scholars are also raising more questions about the nature and structure of these polities. There is a general consensus that Southeast Asia in the proto-historical period was made up predominantly of chiefdoms or chieftaincies. As described in the previous chapter, these polities were structured around the personal authority, prestige, and charisma of a particular leader and were fundamentally fragile in many respects. When Indian culture began to penetrate the region, chiefs became *rajas* and *maharajas* with courts which were centers of this culture, and they began to articulate their power and authority in new ways. We cannot assume, however, that these developments made them inherently stronger or their 'kingdoms' more stable or tightly structured. This point will be developed further below.

Indianization

Indian cultural influence spanned a wide area of Southeast Asia, and even today Indian elements can be identified in the languages and cultures of much of the region. This historical phenomenon has been called by different names. Some scholars prefer 'Sanskritization', because one of the earliest concrete signs was the appearance of inscriptions in that language in different parts of Southeast Asia. Others have favored 'Hinduization' because of the importation of Hindu deities such as Śiva, Visnu, and Brahma. This term ignores the significance of Buddhism, however, and for that reason is now seldom used. 'Indianization' is the broadest and most general term and will be used here.

Indianization as we understand it in the Southeast Asian context parallels a process which occurred in the Indian sub-continent itself with the southward spread of the Hindu-related cultural elements from their roots in the Aryan north. Local chiefs adopted Sanskrit titles and Hindu conceptions of kingship along with new religious beliefs. Sanskrit became the language of ritual and literature while the vernacular (local) tongues remained in common use. Local spirits and deities were not eliminated, but rather were incorporated into the broader pantheon of Hinduism. Thus 'Indianization' in India was a process of interaction and syncretism between local beliefs and concepts and those coming from outside a particular region.

We understand the Indianization of Southeast Asia as largely the same process. Beginning roughly at the start of the Common Era, elements of Indian culture began to spread eastward. Much of this process is still unclear, but it seems certain that there were numerous points of contact between areas in India and Southeast Asia, as evidenced by the diversity of artistic and linguistic

Figure 3 Hindu priest, contemporary Bali

influences found in early artifacts from the region. There is no precise time-frame, but the first Sanskrit inscription (from Vo Canh in southern Vietnam) dates from the third century CE. Trying to establish an endpoint for Indianization is even more difficult, but we can suggest that by the end of the first millennium direct Hindu and Buddhist influence from India had tapered off significantly. Henceforth the most important new cultural forces moving from India to Southeast Asia would be largely Islamic, while Buddhism would now come mainly from Sri Lanka. Java, however, was an exceptional case, as there is evidence to suggest that new Hindu texts and ideas were still being imported in the second half of the fifteenth century – at the same time as Islam was spreading. Bali, of course, has remained predominantly Hindu until today (Figure 3).

The geographer and historian Paul Wheatley made the often-quoted observation that 'the Sanskrit tongue was chilled to silence at 500 meters'. Indian culture was effectively a lowland phenomenon, though some aspects of it did penetrate upland cultures over the long run. The Black Thai of northwestern Vietnam and eastern Laos, for example, use a writing system ultimately derived from an Indian script even though they never adopted Buddhism or other aspects of Indian culture. Even this development, moreover, was a reflection of their links to other Tai-speaking groups rather than of any direct exposure to Indianization. A second example is the Batak of Sumatra, whose original culture (before subsequent conversion to Christianity or Islam) included Hindu deities and divination which incorporated elements of Indian astronomy. These examples are somewhat exceptional, however, and generally speaking the impact of Indianization or the lack of it is one feature which distinguishes lowland from upland cultures.

Virtually all of mainland Southeast Asia – including the peninsular region which is now ethnically and culturally linked more to the island world – was

Indianized to some degree. The main exception is the area which is now northern Vietnam. It is known that Indian and Central Asian priests and monks did occasionally appear among the Vietnamese during the early centuries of Chinese rule, but substantive traces of Indian culture are few and far between.

Indianization in maritime Southeast Asia was more selective. Java and Bali were the most heavily exposed to Indian culture, and even today Bali remains arguably the most thoroughly Indianized place in the region. Evidence of Indian culture can be found in other parts of the Indonesian archipelago as well. When we reach the Philippines, however, the evidence becomes much scantier. Those ethnic groups which were in direct contact with other parts of the Malay world further west may have acquired some elements of Indian culture. The sixteenth-century Spanish missionaries, for instance, recorded that the Visayans called their deities *diwata* – a term which is clearly of Sanskrit origin (borrowed via Malay), though the actual spirits were indigenous and had no connection with Hinduism. Similarly, there are vocabulary items in Tagalog that are ultimately of Sanskrit origin. Thus the Philippines found themselves on the easternmost periphery of Indianized Southeast Asia, and in many ways outside it.

Much ink has been spilled over the question of how Southeast Asia was Indianized. Some colonial-era scholars believed that the region must have once been actually colonized by Indians, but today the idea of a 'Greater India' built on Indian settlements is accepted only by Hindu nationalists. Other theories have centered on warriors (*ksatriya*) and traders (*vaisya*) who would have traveled around the region, spreading their culture as they went. Some scholars, however, have argued that such men could not have been effective 'missionaries' and that such a role could only have been played by Brahmin priests and other holy men. These hypotheses tend to assume that it was Indians coming to Southeast Asia who brought their beliefs to a receptive local audience. More recently, though, it has been pointed out that many Southeast Asians themselves were veteran sea travelers – notably those from the Malay world – and could certainly have been active in taking Indian culture back to their home areas. This argument is part of a broader trend to assign more agency or initiative to Southeast Asians rather than seeing them as more or less passive – although welcoming – recipients of Indian culture. Thus, while there could have been Brahmins traveling to the region, it is equally plausible that Southeast Asians were ordained in India and then returned home to disseminate their newly acquired beliefs.

Indianization is a broad and complex phenomenon which touches many aspects of the Southeast Asian worldview. At its core is the adoption of Indian religious practices, whether it be the worship of Hindu deities or of the Buddha. Southeast Asian Buddhism was originally Mahayana of Indian origin, with Sanskrit as its sacred tongue; the subsequent large-scale conversion to the Theravada school was influenced by Sri Lanka. The religious artifacts of Southeast Asia from the first millennium CE are almost completely Hindu and Buddhist, as is much of its most famous architecture.

What we will never be able to ascertain for certain is just how deeply these beliefs penetrated into Southeast Asian cultures at the time, or the extent to which these religious practices were identified as something new, different, or distinctively 'Indian'. Again, scholars have long been divided on this issue. Those colonial-era writers who talked of 'Further India' or 'Greater India' believed that Indian culture (including the caste system) was disseminated in the region lock, stock, and barrel, transforming Southeast Asian societies into smaller replicas of India. A few dissenting voices minimized the impact of Indianization outside a small group of elite. Most famously, the Dutch scholar J. C. van Leur regarded the Indian elements as no more than a thin and flaking glaze on top of local culture. The general preference at present is to think in terms of interaction between Indian and Southeast Asian cultures, whether as the 'localization' of the former by the latter or as a syncretic mixture of the two. This approach to Indianization has been reinforced by the comparisons with cultural change in India mentioned above.

The introduction of Indian religions was accompanied by many other cultural elements as well. Sanskrit, as the sacred language of both Hinduism and Mahayana Buddhism, had a major impact on the 'original' lowland languages of Southeast Asia: Javanese, Malay, Mon, Khmer, and Cham. Thai and Lao, by contrast, were more heavily influenced by Pali, used in Theravada Buddhism (as was the case for Burmese), and much of their linguistic Indianization occurred through the mediation of Khmer. These cultures were pre-literate when they acquired the use of Sanskrit, and it was thus in that language that their earliest inscriptions were written. Later they wrote in their own languages using scripts derived from various writing systems in India.

Southeast Asian elites also became familiar with themes and styles of Indian art and architecture. The diversity of such influences in early Southeast Asia reflects the local and chronological variations in India itself, indicating that the cultural connections between the two regions were complex and varied. Indian conceptions of law were introduced into Southeast Asian cultures, as were the classic works of literature such as the *Ramayana*, which appears in various distinctive forms throughout the Indianized region. Characters and themes from both the *Ramayana* and the *Mahabharata* also found their way into the art of shadow puppetry, most commonly known by its Javanese name of *wayang kulit*. Most Southeast Asian cultures adopted some variation of an Indian calendar as well as elements of Indian astronomy.

An Indian traveler to Southeast Asia would have found many familiar elements, but few of them would have had exactly the appearance and shape that they did back in India. What was most important, however, was that Indianization not only linked Southeast Asian countries to India culturally and psychologically, but also created a common ecumene within the region to which these cultures belonged. Each people and each polity was distinctive, yet when it came to articulating political authority or developing an elaborate court culture, the various Southeast Asian elites all drew on similar sources.

From proto-history to early history

The writing of early Southeast Asian history was long predicated on the assumption that when the first polities appeared in the first centuries CE, they were essentially smaller versions of the larger kingdoms and empires which dominated the region by the second millennium. This point has already been made earlier in the chapter, and we return to it here in more detail, because this is one of the ways in which our picture of early Southeast Asia has changed most significantly. Because most information on these polities comes from Chinese accounts and local inscriptions, it is now widely felt that the history written by earlier scholars was distorted by these sources in two significant ways. First, Chinese sources tended to assume that their neighbors in Southeast Asia, which they usually classified as vassals of China, were essentially small replicas of China itself: kingdoms – since there could only be one empire – with fixed borders and centralized governments. Second, inscriptions by Southeast Asian rulers boasted of their military prowess and territorial conquests, often giving what was probably an exaggerated impression of the actual extent of their realm.

As a result of these sources – and because colonial scholars themselves thought mainly in terms of large kingdoms and empires – the landscape of Southeast Asia during the first millennium was believed to be occupied by a few large and powerful polities: Funan (later replaced by Chenla), Champa, Śrivijaya, Dvaravati, Java, and (by the end of the millennium) Pagan. Until very recently, history texts showed maps of Indianized Southeast Asia which were completely covered by these large countries, whose respective territories were mapped out by approximate borders which presumably remained more or less constant for much of their existence. The historical narratives themselves concentrated on dividing the centuries into successive royal dynasties, with valiant attempts at determining precise reign dates and titles for each ruler. The main focus was what is often termed 'kings and battles', on the assumption that these were the most important aspects which should provide the backbone of these narratives. There was little discussion of the nature of these rulers' power or the ways in which it was exercised. Dynasties rose and fell, monarchs ruled until they died or their thrones were usurped, and the borders of the kingdoms and empires expanded or contracted through military campaigns, annexations, and territorial losses.

Our present understanding of these polities – how they were structured, how they were ruled, and how and why they 'rose' and 'fell' – is dramatically different in several important ways. First of all, it is no longer assumed that a ruler's adoption of Indian titles or his self-identification with Śiva, Visnu, or the Buddha necessarily made him a significantly more powerful or fearsome monarch than his predecessors who were simply chiefs. Second, the personal and fragile nature of royal authority is understood and emphasized much more than before. Third, the significance of acquiring or controlling territory is now seen as generally less important than that of maintaining control over people (manpower). Finally, the polities themselves are seen as more complex and even fragile entities.

All four of these points come together in the concept of a *mandala* which was popularized by Oliver Wolters as a model for understanding early Southeast Asia. This term is derived from the Sanskrit word for 'circle' and is used to describe polities where power radiated outwards from a single center or capital. Rather than being spread more or less evenly within fixed borders and remaining fairly consistent through successive reigns, the center's authority and control waxed and waned according to the power and charisma of a particular ruler. There was relatively little government as we would understand it in the modern sense or even in the form found, say, in much of Southeast Asia by *c.*1500. Rather, the ruler relied on networks of personal ties to mobilize people and collect revenue on the one hand, and to distribute largesse and rewards in order to maintain loyalty on the other. This would have been one of the main continuities with earlier chiefdoms or chieftaincies. The fact that authority was now 'royal' and articulated in new ways did not mean that a ruler had to work any less hard to acquire and maintain it.

Nor could he be certain that his successor would hold on to the full extent of his kingdom. As late as the thirteenth century in new kingdoms like Lanna and Sukhothai, it was very possible for a fairly extensive realm to fall to pieces within a year of the death of a powerful ruler whose son, brother, or nephew inherited his throne but lost much of his territory. Belonging to a particular dynastic line and enjoying the status of designated heir to the throne meant much less once the more powerful king was no longer around to enforce his choice. Moreover, the principle of primogeniture, which – most of the time – governed succession in many European monarchies as well as in countries like China and Vietnam, failed to take root in much of Southeast Asia. Societies with bilateral kinship were particularly vulnerable in this respect, as there could be numerous claimants to a single throne on the basis of their paternal and/or maternal ties.

For this reason, the shape and structure of these early Southeast Asian polities has sometimes been compared to a concertina. Under a strong ruler able to impose his will firmly on his existing territory and probably to expand it through a combination of charisma, intimidation, conquest, and marriage alliances, the kingdom would expand. Under a weak ruler who lacked this ability, the 'concertina' would contract as local leaders at the peripheries of the *mandala* went their own way and either openly declared their independence from the center or simply ignored their obligations. It is thus much more difficult than was once imagined to map out early Southeast Asia in terms of large entities with relatively fixed borders. Instead, we should think in terms of polities scattered around the region whose size and scope were in constant and sometimes violent flux. We will now look briefly at a few of these early peoples.

Pyu

The people known to us as the Pyu were among the earliest known inhabitants of what is now Burma or Myanmar. The most important – but by no means the only – sites associated with them are Beikthano, Halin, and Thayekittaya (often referred to by its Sanskrit name Śrikṣetra). Carbon dating of artifacts from these sites suggests that Beikthano was occupied as early as the second century BCE, while the latter two locations were important as late as the ninth century CE. Thus the Pyu culture would have predated the first exposure to Indian culture and flourished through the beginnings of the later Pagan kingdom. Pagan was dominated by the Burmans, who were separate from the Pyu but had close ethnic and cultural ties to them. They eventually assimilated the Pyu, but there is strong evidence that the foundations of Pagan culture were in fact Pyu.

The few surviving inscriptions in the Pyu language have been only partially deciphered, and our knowledge of the Pyu period is thus quite spotty. A few names of kings can be identified for Halin and Śrikṣetra, but no more than that. The archeological evidence is more substantial, and each of the three major sites has been extensively excavated, along with Mongmao (Maingmaw). All four sites were walled settlements and presumably represented the main Pyu power centers, but whether they were autonomous or linked under a single ruler is not clear.

It is evident that the Pyu were one of the earliest Southeast Asian peoples to adopt elements of Indian culture. The name 'Beikthano' itself means 'city of Visnu', and statuary of both Hindu deities and the Buddha has been unearthed at various Pyu sites. Indian influences are also evident in the architecture, the coinage, and the various scripts used in the early epigraphy. Pyu artifacts also demonstrate links to other Indianized cultures in Southeast Asia and to Nanzhao in Yunnan (southern China), and Pyu coins have been unearthed as far away as the Mekong delta – an important reminder of the fact that culture and trade followed the same routes.

Dvaravati

The Sanskrit name Dvaravati is associated with a group of sites scattered throughout Central Thailand (in a large semi-circle around Bangkok) and parts of the Northeast. Dvaravati was long known only through old Chinese texts, but in the 1960s coins were unearthed which actually bore the name in Sanskrit. Although earlier scholars believed that Dvaravati was a single large kingdom spanning much of present-day Thailand, it is now generally accepted that we can assume almost nothing about political structures, and it seems more likely that there were multiple centers under different rulers. Dvaravati would thus constitute a cultural area rather than a kingdom.

Dvaravati is associated with the Mon, who were the original inhabitants of large areas of modern Thailand before the migration of the various groups of Tai speakers, by whom they were almost completely assimilated in subsequent centuries. This particular Mon civilization flourished from the seventh century until the end of the first millennium, after which it was gradually absorbed into the new Tai polities or, in some cases, the expanding Khmer empire centered at Angkor. The archeological heritage of Dvaravati is very rich, and many sites have revealed structures and artifacts extending back further in time than the period just mentioned. There is also evidence of contacts and connections with other cultural complexes in the region.

The major Dvaravati sites (among them Nakhon Pathom, Uthong, and Ku Bua in the Central region and Sri Thep and Muang Fa Daet in the Northeast) are characterized by moats, some of which are still visible today in aerial photographs. These towns were centers of a rich Indianized culture – predominantly various forms of Buddhism, though with some worship of Śiva and Visnu. A number of inscriptions in various languages have been found, but they do not allow us to attempt any kind of reconstruction of historical events. Dvaravati's legacy is above all artistic, with a wide variety of statuary and other religious objects. Particularly important are the *Dharmachakra* ('*Dharma* wheels', referring to the teachings of Buddhism) votive tablets for personal devotion to the Buddha, and (in the Northeast) the *sema* stones which marked off the boundaries of the sacred space in temples.

Aside from its art, Dvaravati's most important legacy was probably its cultural impact. Along with the neighboring Pyu, the Mon were apparently among the earliest Southeast Asians to adopt Buddhism, and thus that faith was well established on the mainland when the Tai-speaking migrants arrived. It was almost certainly the latter's contact with the Mon, whom they conquered, that exposed them to Buddhism in particular and Indianized culture in general. Dvaravati's centralized location meant that the Mon would have had trade and cultural contacts with other parts of the region as well.

Cham

As mentioned in Chapter 1, the Cham were once the southern neighbors of today's Vietnamese. Their territory stretched from the northern-central coast down to the edge of the Mekong delta. Although they are Austronesian speakers and originally migrated from what is now Indonesia, their presence on the mainland dates from before the Common Era. A pre-Indianized civilization known as the Sa Huynh culture, characterized by the burial of the dead in earthen jars, is linked to the coastal region of Vietnam and is believed by many scholars to represent the precursor to the later Cham kingdoms.

In the early third century CE, Chinese sources record the existence of a kingdom known to them as Linyi which was apparently located in the central coastal region, south of the Vietnamese territory then under Chinese rule. Linyi is generally acknowledged as an early Cham kingdom, although its size and the length of its existence as a separate entity are unknown. The Chinese were notoriously reluctant to change the names by which foreign countries were known to them, and they continued to use 'Linyi' until the mid-eighth century, when they abruptly switched to 'Huanwang'. The name Champa appeared in local Sanskrit inscriptions in the late sixth century, and it was that name which came to designate the various Cham polities in Western sources.

The territory formerly inhabited by the Cham is home to many ancient architectural structures and has yielded a tremendous quantity of inscriptions and artifacts. For more than a century, scholars have pored over the inscriptions in an attempt to reconstruct the history of the Cham. We have the names of dozens of kings ruling from several different capitals scattered up and down the coast. Until recently, most scholars believed that there was a single 'kingdom of Champa' ruled by a succession of dynasties, with occasional changes of capital depending on which family was in power. Now, however, it is more commonly accepted that there were multiple Cham polities coexisting through much of their history. This topic will be discussed in more detail in the following chapter.

Figure 4   Cham temple at My Son

Until the mid-eighth century – when 'Linyi' became 'Huanwang' in the Chinese records – Cham political and cultural activity was centered predominantly in what is now Quang Nam province, near the central city of Da Nang. The most famous site in this area is My Son (Figure 4), a complex of temples dedicated to Śiva which still survives today, though in a much dilapidated form. Worship of Śiva and Vishnu was widespread among the Cham during this period, although Mahayana Buddhism would predominate for roughly a century afterward, and both Hinduism and Buddhism coexisted with indigenous Cham religion. Indianization made the Cham culturally different in many ways from the Sinicized Vietnamese to the north, although the two peoples could find some common ground through Mahayana. In later centuries, the Vietnamese began to conquer and assimilate the Cham, as will be described in subsequent chapters. The absorption of Cham religious elements would produce various regional sub-cultures within Vietnam.

Khmer

Narratives of Cambodian history before the establishment of the kingdom of Angkor in the very early ninth century have long been dominated by the names of Funan and Chenla (Zhenla), the two main 'players' mentioned in the Chinese sources. Funan was allegedly a large and powerful state centered in the

Mekong delta which was overthrown by its vassal Chenla around the early seventh century; Chenla in turn was supposed to have split into two separate countries, 'Land Chenla' and 'Water Chenla'. Although 'Funan' and 'Chenla' do not correspond to any names appearing in the wealth of Cambodian inscriptions, this story of competing large polities made sense to both Chinese and Western scholars and became the standard version of Cambodian history before Angkor.

In conformance with the revisionist wariness regarding both the distortions of Chinese sources and the existence of large, powerful kingdoms in early Southeast Asia, 'Funan' has now been trimmed down to size and 'Chenla' more or less discarded as a single entity. The role of the Mekong delta in the early centuries of the first millennium is undeniable. The important site of Oc Eo has produced coins and other artifacts from as far away as the Roman Empire, clear evidence of the flourishing trade which encouraged the emergence and growth of these early polities. Further inland is Angkor Borei (in Takeo on the other side of the Vietnamese-Cambodian border), whose period of significance seems to have paralleled that of Oc Eo (second through sixth centuries), and the two sites were apparently linked by a series of canals.

Angkor Borei and Oc Eo may well have been part of a single early Khmer kingdom, but the picture for the seventh and eighth centuries makes the tale of one or even two 'Chenlas' less plausible. Certain important political centers have been identified from inscriptions, notably Iśanapura, which had at least two different locations, both in present-day Kompong Thom province. It is not, however, certain that these were capitals for unified kingdoms. The patterns of inscriptions and the knowledge we have of the various rulers who wrote them suggest that the period between the political decline of the Mekong delta region – apparently because of shifting regional trade patterns – and the rise of Angkor was characterized by rivalry among multiple centers in different parts of present-day Cambodia. The founding of Angkor in 802 was thus the culmination of a process of consolidation rather than the reunification of an earlier Chenla polity which had been fragmented.

The pre-Angkorean period of Cambodian history has a geographical span extending from southern Vietnam through northeastern Thailand and southern Laos. The temple complex of Vat Phou in the Lao province of Champassak is linked to early Khmer rulers, and the earliest Khmer temples in Thailand date from this period as well. As elsewhere, the predominant religious influences were Indian, particularly Śivaite and Vishnuite. Sanskrit was widely used in inscriptions, either by itself or in tandem with Khmer. While the architectural and archeological legacy of these early centuries is not as rich as that of Angkor, the political and cultural developments helped to lay the foundations for the glories of the Angkorean period.

Śrivijaya

The Malay peninsula (now southern Thailand and peninsular Malaysia) and the Indonesian island of Sumatra were part of a thriving sub-regional trade network that preceded the arrival of Indian culture by several centuries. The peninsula was dotted with coastal city-states which were linked to other areas further east and west and which are believed to have played a key role both in stimulating trade and prosperity and in transmitting culture from outside the region. One of the most important fruits of the centuries of economic and cultural activity was the polity of Śrivijaya, which appeared in the historical record in the late seventh century. It was certainly not the first kingdom to take shape on the island, for the Chinese had been receiving envoys from rulers there for two centuries. After Śrivijaya's emergence on the scene, however, it seems to have enjoyed an extended period of dominance, and there were no more diplomatic missions from neighboring kingdoms. Like Champa, Śrivijaya's history spans both this chapter and the next. Here we will concentrate on the 'window' in the seventh century, for which we have the earliest substantial information.

The rise of Śrivijaya appears to be linked directly to changing trade patterns which favored the Straits of Melaka region, notably at the expense of the Mekong delta coast where 'Funan' had earlier flourished. Śrivijaya seems to have been able to extend its influence over the Malay peninsula, as indicated by a late eighth-century inscription from Ligor (now Nakhon Si Thammarat in southern Thailand). Whether this influence was a long-term reality or a short-term phenomenon is unclear, however, and during the early centuries of Śrivijaya's history, at least, we should be careful about postulating the existence of any kind of 'maritime empire'. Nevertheless, the importance of maritime trade cannot be denied, and various sources confirm that Śrivijaya was above all a trading polity.

Unlike most of its Southeast Asian neighbors, Śrivijaya left behind no architectural legacy, only a few scattered inscriptions and a handful of artifacts. This paucity of material culture has made it difficult for scholars to reconstruct its civilization – or even, for that matter, to determine the exact location of its capital. After decades of debate, however, there is a general consensus that Śrivijaya's center was at Palembang(in Sumatra). We do know that it was deeply influenced by Buddhism. The seventh-century Chinese monk Yijing visited Śrivijaya and wrote admiringly of the kingdom's devotion to the faith and of the large international community of monks engaged in translating the Buddhist scriptures into various languages. As was the case elsewhere, no one religion enjoyed a total monopoly, and Vishnu statues have been unearthed in both Sumatra and the Malay peninsula, but Buddhism seems to have predominated.

Java

As with Sumatra, the historical and archeological account of Java during the first centuries of the first millennium CE is fairly skimpy and there is very little substantial evidence before the eighth century. In the mid-fifth century a ruler with the title Purnavarman who governed a polity named Taruma left a series of Sanskrit inscriptions in various places in western Java. Purnavarman was a lone Indianized voice in the wilderness, however, and there is a prolonged gap in the record until inscriptions and temples begin to appear in the seventh and

Figure 5   Arjuna complex, Dieng Plateau, eighth century

eighth centuries – this time in the central part of the island, which apparently remained the political and cultural center of gravity through the end of the ninth century. The development of Javanese polities will be covered in the next chapter; here we will briefly look at the civilization of Central Java before the important power shift eastward after 900.

The period between 700 and 900 saw the construction of several important temples which remain part of the Central Javanese landscape over a millennium later. The most famous are Borobudur and Prambanan. The latter, completed around 850, is Hindu, while the former, probably erected a half-century earlier, is Buddhist. Another site in the central part of Java, the Dieng Plateau, is home to a complex of temples dedicated to Śiva (Figure 5). The construction of such large and extravagant temples belonging to both Hinduism and Buddhism in the same time period and in fairly close proximity to each other provides one of the best examples of coexistence of the two faiths in early Southeast Asia. While Borobudur (Figure 6) and Prambanan are associated with two different ruling families, one of which (the Hindu Sanjaya dynasty) seems to eventually have come under the domination of its Buddhist neighbors, there is little evidence that political rivalry meant rivalry or tensions between the two religions.

Earlier generations of Dutch scholars frequently referred to Javanese culture as 'Hindu-Buddhist', and the term is certainly accurate in its emphasis on the equal importance of the two religious traditions. Most other parts of Southeast Asia tended to emphasize one or the other, although neither of the two faiths ever possessed a 'monopoly' for more than a very short period of time. As we will see in Chapter 3, both Buddhism and Hinduism remained important cultural forces in Java well into the second millennium. Even long after the island had become at least nominally Muslim in its totality, Hindu-Buddhist culture remained influential.

Figure 6   Borobudur Buddha image, ninth century

Sinicization in Vietnam under Chinese rule

Sinicization took place only in the area that is now northern Vietnam, beginning in the early second century BCE when the region was incorporated into a kingdom known as Nanyue ('Nam Viet' in Vietnamese), ruled by a self-styled emperor who rose to power with the fall of the powerful but short-lived Qin dynasty in China. This emperor and his descendants held the throne for nearly seventy years until the foundation of the Han, one of the strongest dynasties in Chinese history. The new Han rulers consolidated their power on both sides of the present-day Sino-Vietnamese border, conquering a stretch of territory extending down to what is now the Vietnamese province of Ha Tinh. This area would remain under Chinese rule for more than a thousand years, leaving a deep impact on the people who lived there.

Compared to the rest of Southeast Asia, we have a somewhat more detailed picture of the civilization that existed in Vietnam before the advent of outside cultural influence, though much of this picture is shrouded in myth. The most tangible evidence comes from the abundant artifacts of the rich Dong Son culture, which spread across much of the Red river delta and the surrounding areas from roughly the ninth century BCE through the early centuries of Chinese rule. The bronze drums which are the most impressive products of this civilization have become virtually iconic in Vietnamese minds as the most ancient symbol of their culture. Dong Son was the last Vietnamese culture before Chinese colonization, and it was to this foundation that the first elements of Sinitic culture were added.

Modern Vietnamese historians have linked the Dong Son civilization to the quasi-mythical Hung kings, who are said to have ruled the kingdom of Van Lang for centuries before the Chinese conquest. It is in fact very difficult to find evidence of 'kings' or 'kingdoms' in the pre-Chinese period, and it seems more likely that the ancestors of the Vietnamese were structured by clans or tribes and governed by chiefs like their neighbors elsewhere in the region. Whatever the case, the historical record becomes somewhat less opaque in the third century BCE with the appearance of a ruler known to the Vietnamese as King An Duong. Apparently from a neighboring region, he is said to have invaded and conquered the territory of the Hung kings and established a new kingdom of Au Lac. According to legend, the local spirits rose up to resist his attack, under the leadership of a giant white chicken, but he defeated them with the aid of a magic crossbow made from a turtle claw. (Chickens – even giant ones – have never had much chance against crossbows.)The ancient site of Co Loa, just outside present-day Hanoi, is believed to have been An Duong's capital.

Au Lac was short-lived, however, and within three decades was defeated by Emperor Zhao Tuo (Trieu Da in Vietnamese) of the Nanyue around 180 BCE. His capital was at Guangzhou (Canton), an area which at the time would have very much straddled the 'Chinese' and 'Southeast Asian' worlds. The emperor himself does not seem to have been a culturally or ethnically alien figure to the people of Au Lac, and he was long venerated by the Vietnamese as their first emperor. It was only relatively recently that he began to be perceived by some Vietnamese scholars as a 'Chinese enemy' and the millennium of Chinese rule began to be dated from his conquest rather than the defeat of one of his descendants by Han dynasty forces in 111 BCE. In any case, it was the events of the second century BCE which brought the ancestors of the Vietnamese into China's sphere of influence, where they would remain for 2000 years, first as part of the Middle Kingdom itself and then as an independent but tributary empire.

Chinese rule lasted until the early tenth century, when the fall of the powerful Tang dynasty provided the Vietnamese an opportunity to assert and maintain their independence. This was not the first such opportunity; the centuries-long period known in Vietnam as *thoi Bac thuoc* ('the time of Northern domination/subordination') was punctuated by periodic episodes of revolt. Times of dynastic instability or change in China frequently led to a loosening of the imperial hold over its peripheral regions. Many of the most famous names in the Vietnamese pantheon of heroes and heroines come from this period: the Trung Sisters (first century CE), Lady Trieu (third century), Ly Bi and Trieu Viet Vuong (sixth century), Mai Hac De and Phung Hung (eighth century). Some of these individuals came from the local elite, others from the common people. A few established short-lived kingdoms with imperial titles patterned after those of the Chinese overlords they were attempting to drive out. It was, however, only the prolonged chaos of the late Tang and subsequent

'Five Dynasties and Ten Kingdoms' period of the tenth century which led to a long enough interlude for the Vietnamese to establish a permanent polity of their own. The history of independent Vietnam will be discussed in the following chapter; what concerns us here is the cultural impact of the *Bac thuoc* period.

The most important aspect of Sinicization among the Vietnamese is what can be called their worldview – their system of values and beliefs. The core of Chinese culture is formed by three sets of beliefs known collectively as the 'Three Teachings' (*Sanjiao*): Confucianism, Buddhism, and Daoism. Confucianism, based on the teachings of the sixth-century BCE scholar Kongfuzi (Confucius), focuses primarily on creating and maintaining proper relationships between people, particularly those of different status, within the social or familial hierarchy. While Confucius paid little attention to the supernatural, his emphasis on filial piety towards one's parents shaped the ancestral worship which became fundamental to Chinese culture. Originally imported from India, Buddhism took root in China and the other countries in its sphere of influence. Buddhism contains moral teachings, but much of its emphasis is other-worldly, offering the way to reincarnation in a subsequent life, rebirth in a kind of Paradise, or the attainment of enlightenment (Nirvana). Finally, Daoism is a complex system of beliefs and practices focusing variously on achieving a life in harmony with unseen cosmic forces, gaining immortality, or obtaining blessings from various deities.

Most of the elements of these belief systems passed into Vietnamese culture during the millennium of Chinese rule. Although we know much less than we would like to know about Vietnamese cultural history during this period, it is clear that Buddhism and Daoism in particular were well-established by the time of independence in the early tenth century. Confucianism was considerably weaker at that time, but its influence strengthened in subsequent centuries, as will be explained in later chapters. Both Buddhist and Daoist beliefs easily coexisted and blended with Vietnamese beliefs. Local spirits, for example, are sometimes believed to guard Buddhist temples, which may incorporate altars to them. An excellent example of Sino-Vietnamese syncretism is the goddess Lieu Hanh, believed to be a daughter of the (Chinese) Daoist supreme deity, the Jade Emperor, who was exiled from her father's realm and was then incarnated in Vietnam. Her cult is much more widespread among Vietnamese than that of her father, yet the 'Chinese connection' in her biography remains.

Chinese culture left its mark on the Vietnamese in many other ways. Almost all family names and many personal names in Vietnam are derived from Chinese. Classical Chinese remained the main written language of Vietnam until the early twentieth century. When the Vietnamese devised a separate script to write their own tongue as it was spoken, this writing system (*chu Nom*) was also based on Chinese characters. The Vietnamese language itself, although related to Cambodian rather than Chinese, has been deeply influenced by the latter in terms of vocabulary and grammar, just as English bears the imprint of French dating from the Norman conquest of England in the eleventh century – and, through French, from Latin and Greek. Vietnamese artistic and literary styles often reflect Chinese influences as well.

One of the great ironies of Vietnamese history is that the process of Sinicization long outlasted the actual period of Chinese rule. The Vietnamese emerged from the *Bac thuoc* period with political independence but with a mentality – at least at the elite level – which remained firmly rooted within the Chinese world. For the next nine centuries or more, until a whole generation had grown up under French colonial rule, the standards of 'culture' and 'civilization' were defined largely in Chinese terms. Like the Japanese and Koreans, the Vietnamese were eager to prove themselves 'civilized' by Chinese standards. Diplomatic exchanges and purchases of books and art from the Middle Kingdom permitted the elite to maintain a heavily Sinicized lifestyle well into the twentieth century. Even at the village level, the various components of the *Sanjiao* belief system remained deeply rooted through the institutions of local schools and temples. These beliefs continue to form the base of Vietnamese culture even today.

3

'Classical' States at Their Height

Introduction

This chapter will focus on the half-millennium between roughly 800 and 1300 (but into the fourteenth century in Java), which is sometimes considered to represent the 'classical' period of Southeast Asian history. Some scholars have challenged the appropriateness of the term 'classical' as being Eurocentric, but it does have a certain value in the Southeast Asian context even if the historical era it refers to was quite different from the 'classical' period of Western civilization. Moreover, in much of the region the kingdoms examined in this chapter are in fact perceived by present-day Southeast Asians as a kind of 'golden age' in their respective histories, just as was formerly the case for Roman and Greek culture within a European context. The important thing is for us to understand 'classical' Southeast Asia on its own terms without artificially applying characteristics of 'classical' Europe.

This chapter in many ways represents a continuation of the previous one. Not only do some of the kingdoms described here straddle the two chapters chronologically, but also there is a high degree of continuity between the two periods. The political, cultural, and economic developments of the early centuries of the first millennium laid the foundations for the later classical period, and the smaller and more fragile polities described in Chapter 2 evolved into the larger and somewhat longer-lived kingdoms to be studied below. The 'Hindu-Buddhist' cultural framework remained dominant in Angkor (Figures 7–10), Champa, and Java; in Śrivijaya Buddhism dominated with little or no Hindu influence; while Burmese Pagan and the new kingdoms founded by Tai-speakers gradually adopted Theravada Buddhism. Vietnam, meanwhile, emerged from Chinese rule with a strong Mahayana Buddhist orientation combined with elements of Confucianism.

One significant difference between the 'classical' states and those of the earlier period is that the polities studied in this chapter were generally larger, lasted longer, and had a more stable political center than those which preceded them. The political, cultural, and geographical core of these kingdoms endured over a period of centuries, even while the size and borders (such as there were) fluctuated. As we saw in the previous chapter, the states that existed during the

Figure 7   Banteay Srei, Angkor, tenth century

earlier part of the first millennium were less stable and, in some cases, less clearly defined as kingdoms. The polities described here can generally be more easily mapped out and more clearly defined both politically and geographically than their often amorphous predecessors.

A second difference between the kingdoms of the classical period and their earlier counterparts is that we simply know more about them, and this through their own eyes rather than foreign sources, though the latter (notably Chinese and Arab) do have something to contribute at certain points in time. In addition to the architectural legacy found throughout the region, we have numerous inscriptions and even chronicles, though these tend to be written later and are often valuable more for what they tell us about how later writers saw their past than about the factual details of that past. While there are still gaps in our information, we can sketch out historical narratives for these kingdoms with greater certainty and usually greater detail than is possible for the earlier period.

The specific time-frame of the classical period varies from country to country, as is shown by the different sections of this chapter. For Cambodia it extends from the 'foundation' of the Angkorean polity in the first years of the ninth century until the shift of the Cambodian power center away from Angkor in the mid-1300s. We can roughly apply this time-frame to Cham history as well. The Burmese kingdom of Pagan was founded in the mid-ninth century, but most of what we know about its history only begins in the eleventh century and extends through the end of the 1200s. The 'classical' Tai world is associated with the kingdoms of Sukhothai and Lanna, both founded in the thirteenth century, and with the early history of Ayutthaya, which appeared in the mid-1300s; the first two polities will be discussed in this chapter and Ayutthaya in Chapter 5. In the case of Vietnam, it took nearly a century after the end of Chinese rule (in the early 900s) to establish more enduring kingdoms with regular dynastic succession, but there were only two ruling dynasties between 1010 and 1400.

For the maritime world, attempting to mark out chronological boundaries for the classical period is somewhat more challenging. In the case of the Sumatra-based polity known as Śrivijaya, its history spans the earlier centuries covered in Chapter 2 as well as much of the period discussed in this one. Most of what we know about Śrivijaya begins in the eleventh century and ends around the thirteenth, and by the 1200s our information is already becoming spotty. As for Java, its history can be fairly neatly divided into Central and Eastern periods, based on a shift in power center from one region of the island to the other around 900. The Central period was the focus of the previous chapter, and here we will concentrate on those kingdoms which dominated East Java.

The structure of classical kingdoms

The previous chapter's discussion raised questions about the structure of early Southeast Asian kingdoms and suggested that there was a higher degree of instability and fragility than was originally perceived by many historians. The concept of a *mandala* popularized by O. W. Wolters suggests the ways in which a ruler's power flowed outward from the center of his kingdom towards an often-distant periphery. And it was almost always 'his' kingdom, for female rulers were almost unknown during this period, although a woman could wield considerable authority over her royal husband. His authority was much more personal than institutional – or, in many cases, dynastic – and relied on networks of relationships more than fixed governmental or administrative structures. Consequently, this authority had to be re-established by each subsequent ruler upon his accession to the throne, and not all new kings were up to the task. Thus the size of a kingdom's territory could fluctuate considerably from one ruler to the next, as previously loyal vassals and subordinates chose to go their own way and govern autonomously until a ruler appeared in the center who was powerful enough to reimpose his authority.

To a large extent this pattern is believed to have continued through the classical period. In certain cases, notably Angkor and Java, it seems clear that the networks of relationships were gradually consolidated into something closer to what we would understand as an administration, but even here the personal element was still present. In other kingdoms there is strong evidence of continued fragility and instability which allows us to suggest that the *mandala* model remains applicable throughout this period. When Tai-speakers began to establish kingdoms in the thirteenth century, these polities also appear to have conformed to this model. As we will see below, both Sukhothai and Lanna underwent extended periods of instability and fragmentation after the deaths of powerful rulers. Although inscriptions and chronicles may present a picture of more centralized and stable rule, this picture does not always bear up under the close scrutiny of modern scholars.

For the polities of Śrivijaya and Champa, scholars have begun to think in terms of a model applied specifically to coastal regions. Originally conceived of by the archeologist Bennet Bronson to look at political and economic ties between 'upstream' and 'downstream' areas, this 'coastal state model' seeks to explain the ways in which rulers whose territory lay primarily in coastal regions could extend their authority inland, usually along the course of rivers which penetrated the hinterland away from the sea. Like the *mandala* concept, Bronson's model emphasizes the personal nature of a ruler's authority and the need for him to provide economic benefits for chiefs or other subordinate rulers in the inland forests and hills. In many cases, the people living in the hinterland regions belonged to different ethnic groups from those living along the coast, but it was possible for them to be loosely incorporated into the coastal ruler's sphere of authority as long as it profited them to recognize this authority. The most valuable product from the coast was usually salt, which would be traded for various commodities found in the forests and hills.

Whether a ruler's power is understood as extending in circles from a particular center (in the *mandala* model) or in a kind of semi-circle (in the coastal state model), it had to be constantly reinforced to be maintained, and it remained much more personal than institutional. It was not, however, just a matter of ensuring material benefits for followers and their chiefs. The authority of Southeast Asian rulers had a strong religious and ritual character. One of the most important points to be made is that the modern distinction between religious or spiritual power and secular power would have had little or no meaning for pre-modern rulers. Laws on 'secular' matters might invoke the authority of spirits or deities along with that of the king, while an inscription might record the ruler's sanction for donations to a temple. A Southeast Asian court would almost certainly have had priests to perform certain ceremonies, but the ruler would have participated in many of these ceremonies. Some rituals, notably the coronation, were specifically centered on the ruler. In other circumstances the royal family as lay-men and lay-women would be the most visible participants in religious activities to demonstrate their own piety to their subjects.

In some states, the king was actually presented as the incarnation of a god or of several gods at once. The Javanese monarch Hayam Wuruk was extravagantly depicted in the following terms in the Old Javanese epic poem *Deśawarnana* of 1365 CE:

> He is present in invisible form at the focus of
>   meditation, he is Śiva and Buddha,
>   embodied in both the material and
>   the immaterial;
> As King of the Mountain, Protector of the Protectorless,
>   he is lord of the lords of the world,

And as the deity of deities that one sets one's
heart upon, the inconceivable of the
inconceivable, being and non-being
are his expressions in the world.[1]

Cambodia

The name of Angkor is familiar to many people outside Cambodia, but the famous multi-towered structure which its name conjures up is only part of a much larger complex. The temple, Angkor Wat (Figure 8), was built in the twelfth century as one of many temples – and, presumably, palaces, though the latter have not survived – scattered around northwestern Cambodia. For more than half a millennium, from 800 until the fifteenth century, this area was the political and cultural center of gravity of what grew to be the largest Southeast Asian kingdom of its time. Technically speaking, 'Angkor' refers specifically to the area around the capital, but it is commonly used to refer to the entire kingdom of Cambodia during this period as well. If any polity in the classical period of the region's history deserves to be called an empire, it was almost certainly Angkor. In terms of its size and its durability, it was unmatched by any of its peers and by very few of its successors.

Although 'pre-Angkorean' and 'Angkorean' Cambodia are normally treated as two distinct periods of history, there is in fact a degree of continuity between them. In 802 a ruler known to us as Jayavarman II (r. 802– c.835) performed

Figure 8 Angkor Wat, twelfth century

---

1 *Deśawarnana* Canto I: 1–2, in Mpu Prapañca, *Deśawārṇana* (*Nāgarakrtāgama*) (trans. Stuart Robson; *VKI* vol. 169; Leiden: KITLV Press, 1995).

Figure 9 Thommanon, Angkor, twelfth century

a ceremony on a hill called Phnom Kulen proclaiming himself as king. This event is usually taken as the foundation of the kingdom of Angkor, but it represented the culmination of a series of earlier events as much as it did the start of a new phase in Cambodian history. The seventh and eighth centuries saw a gradual process of political consolidation by successive rulers combined with the progressive shift of power centers away from the Mekong delta and towards the great lake known as the Tonle Sap. It was apparently this process which was interpreted by the Chinese sources as a split in 'Chenla'. Jayavarman II's coronation did not immediately bring either lasting peace or stability in Khmer territory, and he had to spend much of his reign building military and marriage alliances to consolidate his control. His decades in power did, however, lay a foundation for his successors to build on and established that region as the main power center for the next few centuries.

'Angkor' was never a single site. There were several shifts of capital within the region, and these sites collectively constitute Angkor in its broadest sense. The specific city which came to serve as the capital was founded by a ruler named Yaśovarman (r. *c.*889–*c.*910) and bore his name (Yaśodharapura). Many Cambodian rulers were builders, each contributing one or more structures to Angkor's architectural legacy. Many of these structures were temples (Figure 9), dedicated to Śiva, Vishnu, or the Buddha depending on which was most venerated by a particular ruler and his family. Many temples included images of royal parents and other ancestors; although scholars are still trying to puzzle out the exact significance of these images, it seems clear that there was some kind of royal ancestor cult. Conversely, although it was long believed that Cambodian rulers were 'god-kings' (based on the appearance of the Sanskrit term *devaraja* in certain inscriptions), this assumption is now doubtful. Rulers were in many ways sacred and might claim special connections to a deity, but this does not mean that they were worshipped as 'gods'. They thus differed from the Javanese Hayam Wuruk mentioned above, who was 'Śiva-Buddha' and 'the deity of deities'.

Although Angkorean Cambodia was a long-lived polity, it was not always a stable one. The extensive epigraphy left behind by its rulers over the centuries contains clear evidence of frequent power struggles. It has been suggested that one reason for this was the principle of bilateral kinship: a ruler might cite ancestors from both the paternal and maternal branches of his family in order to bolster his legitimacy. The risk of this system was that it multiplied the potential claimants to the throne compared to a more straightforward pattern of succession from father to son. It is difficult to map out Angkorean history in terms of dynasties as such – unlike, say, Vietnam – and royal succession appears to have moved in various directions at different times, with occasional cases of usurpation by someone completely outside the ruling family. Some of the royal genealogies found in inscriptions seem to be at least partially fabricated, since a ruler whose legitimacy was uncertain might try to bolster it by claiming blood ties to an earlier king.

Internal unrest can also be explained in terms of the *mandala* model. It is clear from the historical evidence that, like all other Southeast Asian kingdoms, Angkor experienced alternations between strong and weak rulers. A handful of strong kings stand out: Jayavarman II, Yaśovarman, Suryavarman I (r. 1002–49), Suryavarman II (r. ?– c.1150), and Jayavarman VII (r. 1181– c.1220). In several cases the new ruler appeared out of a time of chaos to restore stability, reunify fragmented territory, and even expand the size of the kingdom. At least by the eleventh century if not earlier, there were powerful families governing various regions away from the capital. Their interests had to be accommodated, otherwise they might cease to acknowledge the ruler's authority or even attempt to place a new king on the throne. The long-term predominance of a political center (Angkor) did not ensure that every ruler who reigned there could count on support from all parts of his territory.

Although the ruler's power was to some extent personal (i.e., based on kinship and other ties) and to a large extent spiritual (based on links to the power of a deity), Angkor over time did develop a sizable bureaucracy. It is not easy to unravel the functions linked to the various titles which appear in the epigraphy, as the titles often have religious connotations. It is clear, however, that positions such as royal ministers were established, and the inscriptions testify to the presence of various categories of official at lower levels of the hierarchy as well. These officials are often mentioned in conjunction with land transactions – one of the most important subjects of the inscriptions. Historian Michael Vickery has observed that, whereas during the first two centuries of Angkor's history such inscriptions normally invoked the specific authority of the king, from the reign of Suryavarman I onward the sanction for transactions was frequently given by officials rather than the ruler. This testifies to the growing importance of the bureaucracy and is also linked to the rise of powerful families, from whom some of these officials would have come.

In recent years scholars have also begun to look more closely at Cambodian temples not just in terms of their religious function, but as social and economic networks which helped to provide structure for the kingdom as a whole above and beyond the role of government as such. As will be discussed below, this argument has also been put forth for Java, another important 'temple state'. Temples were the recipients of considerable grants of resources, including land and manpower ('temple slaves'). Specific temples might be linked to specific families or rulers, while connections among the various temples may have helped to forge networks of patronage and support within the elite. Once again we are reminded that the 'secular' and 'religious' spheres are not easily distinguished in these 'classical' Southeast Asian societies.

It is important to realize that, for most of its history, the territorial scope of the Angkorean kingdom extended beyond the present-day boundaries of Cambodia into southern Laos and northeastern Thailand. During the pre-Angkorean period some Khmer kings already exercised influence over parts of these regions, and subsequently several Angkor rulers were able to considerably expand the size of their territory. It should be remembered that during the early centuries of Angkor's existence the ancestors of the Thai and Lao had yet to arrive on the scene, and the areas of central and northeastern Thailand which came under Angkorean control were predominantly Mon. The current city of Lopburi north of Bangkok, for example, was originally a Mon power center, then a provincial outpost of the Angkorean polity, and finally a Thai *muang* (a political unit that will be discussed below).

Angkorean Cambodia reached its zenith under Jayavarman VII, who is generally considered to be the greatest king in the country's history. His inscriptions have been found as far away as what is now the Lao capital of Vientiane, although whether his authority actually reached that far and, if so, for how long is a matter of dispute. Certainly the Angkorean *mandala* at this time included a large chunk of modern Thailand, as well as the Mekong delta. Jayavarman VII was a prolific builder of both temples (Figure 10) – he was a devout Mahayana Buddhist – and public works such as roads, rest stations, and hospitals. Ironically, he is also the last Angkorean ruler about whose reign we have substantial information, for the historical record tapers off significantly after his death.

It may be an overstatement to argue that the decline of Angkor as a kingdom began with Jayavarman VII's passing, but it is certainly the case that it began to shrink. By the early thirteenth century Tai-speaking peoples had settled into northern Thailand and were expanding southward. It is not clear whether their expansion was directly responsible for the contraction of Cambodia's borders through the 1200s or, conversely, whether Angkor was weakening primarily for internal reasons and thus leaving its periphery vulnerable to the increasingly powerful Tai speakers. Whatever the case, the thirteenth century saw the establishment of Tai *muang* of various sizes, first outside the limits of the Angkorean *mandala* and then within its periphery – the important new kingdom of Sukhothai will be discussed below. The appearance and expansion of Ayutthaya in the Chao Phraya valley in the mid-fourteenth century effectively signaled the end of Angkor as a strong power in the region.

Some scholars have sought to explain the rise, flourishing, and eventual decline of Angkor in terms of a state-controlled hydraulic system, represented

Figure 10   Bayon, Angkor Thom, Jayavarman VII period

by the large reservoirs (*baray*) scattered around the kingdom's core territory. It has been argued that these reservoirs were the key to Angkor's prosperity and that when they eventually silted up, broke down, or simply became inadequate for the kingdom's needs, its end was inevitable. It is certainly the case that after Cambodia's political center of gravity shifted to the southeast in the fifteenth century, it remained there ever after and never returned to the northwest, suggesting that the strength of that region was based on the massive irrigation works. While geographers' calculations of land and water usage now suggest that the *baray* were not in and of themselves the mainstay of Angkorean agriculture, ongoing scholarly research is working to understand the relationship between the kingdom's demise and ecological damage linked to water resources.

From the late fourteenth century onward, Angkor was subject to increasing military pressure from Ayutthaya to the west, including at least one major invasion. By the mid-1400s the capital had shifted much closer to the location of present-day Phnom Penh, further away from the Thai and closer to coastal trade routes. In the nineteenth century, French explorers believed that they had 'rediscovered' Angkor Wat and that the ruined temples constructed by centuries of Angkorean rulers were unknown to Cambodians at the time, or at least not recognized as being the work of their ancestors. This assumption may have been flattering to the Frenchmen's egos, but it was far from the truth. Memories of Angkor had remained powerful in the Cambodian memory, as indeed they do today: virtually every single national flag, no matter what the ideology of the regime it served, has borne the image of Angkor Wat. Moreover, contrary to French assertions, Angkor remained an important pilgrimage site.

The transition to Theravada

The kingdoms just described continued to operate largely within the 'Hindu-Buddhist' framework, wherein the Buddhist component was predominantly Mahayana. One of the important developments of the classical period, however, was the arrival of Theravada Buddhism from Sri Lanka. Theravada will be discussed in more detail in Chapter 4, but it needs to be introduced here as a historical and cultural force. The historical roots of Theravada are very old and extend back to the earliest centuries of Buddhism and the splits which took place within the religion before it spread outward from India. Buddhism was present in early Southeast Asia in multiple forms, reflecting geographical and doctrinal variations in India. There is early evidence of Theravada among the Pyu in Burma as well as the Mon in the Dvaravati culture, and in this instance it would have been transmitted directly from India. The particular form of Theravada which was implanted in Southeast Asia over the long term, however, came from Sri Lanka, which became the spiritual center for this school of Buddhism. For this reason, Theravada is sometimes referred to as 'Sinhalese Buddhism' after the majority ethnic group in Sri Lanka. While conversion to Theravada did not represent a complete rupture with all of the beliefs and practices of the 'Hindu-Buddhist' period, Sinhalese Buddhism became the predominant form of religion, displacing both Mahayana and Hinduism. The centuries of coexistence and interaction of the two different faiths thus largely came to an end.

Most of the details about the arrival and spread of Sinhalese Theravada are shrouded in mystery, myth, and legend. The process left no document trail, and we are only able to make inferences from accounts written much later which are short on specifics as to the pace or agency of conversion. By the beginning of the second millennium, parts of mainland Southeast Asia were in regular contact with Sri Lanka, and the strength of Indianized Buddhism on the mainland would have made the region fertile ground for Theravada. It seems likely that monks from both Sri Lanka and Southeast Asia traveled back and forth with some regularity, and they would have been the most likely channels for transmission of new religious ideas and practices. Compared to Mahayana, Theravada is more centered on the monkhood (*Sangha*) as an institution and particularly as a means of achieving spiritual benefits, and the decision to ordain or re-ordain monks with practices imported from Sri Lanka was often the catalyst for religious change on the mainland. (This topic will be discussed in more detail in the following chapter.) It must also be pointed out that, by the end of the first millennium, Buddhism in India had significantly weakened in competition with both Hinduism and Islam, so that Sri Lanka became the most dynamic Buddhist center in the Indian Ocean region.

There is no clear time-frame for the large-scale shift to Theravada, but the process of religious change was under way by the early eleventh century at the latest and seems to have been more or less complete by the end of the fourteenth century. Angkorean Cambodia was a Theravada kingdom by the late 1200s, while Burmese Pagan's conversion seems to have occurred in the eleventh century. (As will be explained below, the Burmese polity inherited Buddhism from the Pyu but subsequently adopted a more specifically Sinhalese form.) The new form of Buddhism spread through the lowland Tai-speaking peoples during the thirteenth and fourteenth centuries – and perhaps earlier than that in some cases – so that by 1400 mainland Southeast Asia was predominantly Theravada, with the exceptions of Champa and Vietnam.

The spread of Theravada is frequently linked to the Mon people, and in the case of Burma the chronicles specifically attribute the conversion of Pagan to its conquest of a Mon kingdom. The accuracy of this version of events is now being debated, as will be discussed below. The role of the Mon is more clear-cut in the case of the area now known to us as Thailand. In the Northern, Central, and Southern regions Tai-speakers established kingdoms on territory inhabited predominantly by Mon. These new polities were Theravada, suggesting that the conquerors adopted the religion of those they conquered (and eventually assimilated), as there is no evidence that the Tai were Buddhists before migrating into the region. There are a lot of gaps in our knowledge of the religious history of the Mon, but there is clear evidence of Theravada (from India, not Sri Lanka) in the Dvaravati period; the earliest Theravada inscriptions date from the sixth century. At a later point in time it seems plausible that one or both of the important political and cultural centers of Lavo (Lopburi) and Haripunjaya (Lamphun) had either already converted or were in the process of converting to Sinhalese Theravada when they became part of the Tai world. This may have been the case as well for the southern area of Ligor, now Nakhon Si Thammarat.

Buddhist chronicles contain an interesting account of the history of Buddhism in Northern Thailand which clearly illustrates the various layers of beliefs found in the region. As is often the case with such accounts, the Buddha is reported to have flown into the region and made a prediction about a city to be founded centuries later, in this case Haripunjaya. Toward the end of the first millennium CE, two hermits founded a city at that site and wanted to find a virtuous ruler. Having heard that there was a powerful king at Lavo (Lopburi) with a daughter Camadevi who was a faithful Buddhist, they went there to ask her to come and reign. Her father sent her off to Haripunjaya with a large group of monks and various craftsmen, instructing her to be a good Buddhist ruler. Lavo/Lopburi was originally part of the Dvaravati cultural region and was later incorporated into the Angkor empire, hence this story could symbolize the spread of early Buddhist culture from south to north and may possibly suggest the rise of a specifically Mon kingdom.

The final act of the story came in the eleventh century, with a Mon ruler at

Haripunjaya named Adittaraja, whose existence had also been predicted by the Buddha. Unknown to the king, the Buddha had left a personal relic which had remained buried throughout the centuries. Through a complicated process, the existence of the relic was now revealed to him. It was unearthed, then disappeared, and then reappeared after the king cleaned the whole city, and he built a reliquary to house it. Relics are particularly closely associated with Theravada, and it has been suggested that this incident symbolizes the conversion of Haripunjaya from an earlier form of Buddhism to Theravada. It would henceforth remain as a strong 'outpost' of Buddhism in the region and was flourishing when Tai migrants arrived on the scene. In the late thirteenth century Haripunjaya was conquered by a Tai ruler, Mangrai, and its incorporation into his kingdom seems to have introduced – or at least consolidated – Buddhism among his people.

Pagan

It seems quite clear that in certain important respects at least, the kingdom and culture of Pagan were built on the foundations of Pyu civilization. By the mid-ninth century, the last remaining Pyu polity had been sacked by invaders from the kingdom of Nanzhao (in what is now the southern Chinese province of Yunnan), and a new kingdom was founded by the Burmans on what had formerly been Pyu territory. The Burmans appear to have descended from a later wave of migrants from Tibet than the Pyu, but they had prolonged contact with the latter and absorbed much of their culture. The kingdom of Pagan became a strong power with a flourishing Buddhist civilization which rivaled – and indeed challenged – Angkor for dominance in the mainland region.

We have relatively little concrete information about Pagan before the early eleventh century, at which point the actions of the rulers and the historical narrative in general become somewhat less obscure. The history of the eleventh century is dominated by two powerful rulers: Aniruddha (or Anawrahta) (r. 1044–77) and Kyanzittha (r. 1084–1111). These two kings oversaw the expansion of Pagan from its core in what is usually known as Upper Burma to include a large swath of territory to the south, extending down the peninsula. They also laid the foundations for the governance of Pagan through the thirteenth century.

The conversion of Pagan to Sinhalese Theravada and its subsequent consolidation as the kingdom's primary religion are also linked to these two reigns. Although the chronology of this change is still accepted, serious questions have been raised about the way in which it took place. For a long time it was believed that Pagan was bordered in the south by a Mon kingdom with its capital at Thaton and that Aniruddha conquered it after his conversion to Theravada by a visiting Mon monk. The chronicles on which this story is based acknowledge that Buddhism was already present in Pagan prior to this event but portray it as being in a corrupt state which was rectified by the adoption of the purer Theravada found among the Mon. The conquest of the Mon kingdom was said to have led not only to the rapid and full-scale conversion of the Burmans to Sinhalese Buddhism, but also to the adoption of Mon culture by the Pagan elite.

Pagan scholar Michael Aung-Thwin has challenged what he calls the 'Mon paradigm', pointing out that there is in fact virtually no substantial evidence of a Mon kingdom in Lower Burma at this point in time. He believes that the main religious elements in Pagan's culture were inherited from the Pyu, including Theravada, and that there was no conquest of a Mon kingdom or any large-scale adoption of Mon culture. This argument has generated considerable debate among scholars, several of whom feel that this so-called 'Pyu millennium' theory throws the baby out with the bathwater by undervaluing the Mon role. While there is a general consensus that the story of the invasion of Thaton is fictional, there is nevertheless evidence of a Mon presence in Lower Burma during the Pagan period, even if it was not necessarily the thriving Mon kingdom claimed by later accounts. The impact of the Mon on Pagan culture cannot be completely discounted, then, but the emphasis on the significance of the Pyu contribution does provide a greater degree of balance while reminding us that the cultures of most early Southeast Asian kingdoms were the result of multiple intersecting influences from various sources.

The predominant form of Theravada in Pagan after the eleventh century was Sinhalese rather than Indian, but it could have reached the Burmans through direct cultural contacts with Sri Lanka – which are known to have taken place – rather than originating with the Mon. Pagan's conversion to Theravada was neither as rapid nor as complete as later sources suggest, for other varieties of Buddhist belief as well as elements of Hinduism survived in the kingdom's culture. Even Kyanzittha, who is credited with consolidating Theravada among his people, was sufficiently eclectic to declare himself a reincarnation of Vishnu. This reinforces the image of conversion to Theravada as a gradual process which was slow to displace existing beliefs, some of which indeed were never completely supplanted.

Over the long run, however, Theravada became the foundation of Pagan's culture and society. Pagan inscriptions demonstrate the importance of temples not only as religious but also as economic institutions which accumulated large amounts of land and manpower through donations. Human beings could be attached to temples as bondservants. In turn, temples stimulated economic activity through the hiring of craftsmen, farmers, and others who provided needed services to monks who did not engage in worldly activities. This aspect of temples' economic roles was obviously a positive one which benefited the kingdom's economy. Michael Aung-Thwin has argued, however, that over the long run the regular donations to Buddhist temples – a crucial part of a layman's devotional life as a form of making merit – harmed the royal state by removing excessive quantities of land and manpower from its control. Theravada rulers could and did have the authority to enact a 'purification' of the *Sangha* on the grounds that it had become morally corrupt. This occurred on several occasions in Pagan's history, and Aung-Thwin suggests that above and beyond the religious motives for such purification, the rulers involved were also attempting to shift the balance of resources back in favor of the state. This argument has been contested by other scholars, and it is noteworthy that there is no evidence for such a phenomenon occurring in other Theravada polities in Southeast Asia. It is certainly true, however, that a large-scale transfer of resources and manpower out of state control could, over the long term, contribute to the weakening of that state.

Manpower was a particularly crucial asset for Pagan – probably more so than land, which was in plentiful supply compared to the population. The kingdom was structured around the control of manpower more than it was around territorial-based units, though these did exist as well, and the inscriptions show a wide variety of terms allowing for a complex and precise designation of different categories of people. Aung-Thwin has described Pagan's social structure as 'cellular' in that much of the population was grouped according to occupation and, it seems, ethnicity as well in some cases. These 'cells' at the grassroots, each headed by a local leader, were in turn under the authority of high-ranking individuals who 'ate' them – meaning that these individuals collected revenue from them, keeping a share for themselves and passing the rest on to the court. This pattern was not unique to Pagan, of course; it was found in other kingdoms as well, and even the same reference to 'eating' occurs in the Tai world. Pagan possessed a parallel system specifically for the control of its standing military, although it also could mobilize civilian manpower through its 'eaters' when needed.

Pagan as a polity clearly fit the model characterized as a *mandala*. The core of the kingdom was made up of several *kharuin*, a term which Aung-Thwin glosses as referring to spokes radiating outward from a center, just as power and authority spread outward from the center of a *mandala*. Different terms were used to designate less-settled areas which were relatively central but outside these core regions: 'stockade' or fortified areas to the north, where lay the main threats to Pagan's security; and 'conquered territories' along the kingdom's periphery. The latter were incorporated into Pagan through military expansion over the course of its history, and the exact nature of their relationship with the Burmese court probably varied from place to place.

The question arises whether over the long term Pagan suffered from the same structural fragility as other *mandala*s in the region. There is some evidence that it did not, and the territory under the control of successive rulers does not seem to have undergone the cycles of contraction and expansion that we see elsewhere. Pagan did experience periods of conflict, but they were due largely to succession battles and other rivalries at the center. It may be that the comparatively sophisticated system of manpower control just described ultimately proved to be a more effective kind of 'glue' than its counterparts in other Southeast Asian kingdoms.

It is certainly the case that Pagan enjoyed an extended period of prosperity, relative stability, and expansion, reaching its zenith in the late twelfth and early thirteenth centuries under Kings Narapatisithu (r. 1173–1210) and Nadaungmya (r. 1210–34). The kingdom's territory covered much of the lowland area of present-day Myanmar, and the devotion and wealth of the ruling class were reflected in a host of new temples (Figure 11). As the thirteenth century went on, however, it seems that Pagan's kings attempted to maintain the affluence and elegance of their predecessors without in fact having the same degree of prosperity.

Such a threat appeared in the 1270s with the emergence of the Mongol Yuan dynasty in China as a major contender for influence in Southeast Asia. The

Figure 11 Dhammayazika pagoda, Pagan, twelfth century

expansion of Yuan control into Yunnan brought the Mongols to Pagan's borders, and years of warfare ensued. Although Burmese diplomacy in the mid-1280s achieved a lessening of tensions, it was only temporary, and a major Mongol invasion was mounted in 1288. Neither the capital nor the kingdom itself appears to have actually fallen to the Mongol forces, who returned to China the following year. Nevertheless, the attack caused serious structural damage to the polity, which had already been weakened by conflicts within the elite, as well as by rebellion among the Mon in Lower Burma. A member of the Pagan dynasty ruled until the final years of the thirteenth century, when he was overthrown by a group of men known to history as the 'Three Shan Brothers', though their exact ethnicity is uncertain.

The turn of the century marks the end of Pagan as a kingdom, but it remained important as a symbol and as a memory of a powerful and prosperous past. The 1300s would see the rise of a separate Mon kingdom at Pegu, as well as a new Burman polity with its capital at Ava. The Ava kingdom represented reunification after decades of division, when the 'Three Brothers' and their successors had been ruling from various capitals, and Ava would become a major polity, albeit one which was short-lived compared to its predecessor. Like Angkor after its abandonment as a capital, Pagan continued to dominate the mental and cultural world of the Burmese, and for centuries afterward ambitious rulers attempted to strengthen their authority by establishing genealogical links to the Pagan dynasty.

The Tai world

Arguably the most significant change in the ethnic and geopolitical landscape of mainland Southeast Asia – and, indeed, perhaps the whole region – during the classical period was the arrival of the Tai-speaking peoples. (As was explained in Chapter 2, the term 'Tai' refers to a number of different ethnic groups speaking related languages.) It was once fashionable to believe that the origins of the Tai lay as far north as the Altai mountain range of Central Asia and that they experienced subsequent waves of large-scale migration progressively southward, eventually establishing a 'first Tai kingdom', known as Nanzhao (Nanchao), in China's Yunnan province. They were then believed to have made one final migration into Southeast Asia proper, driven out by pressure from the Mongols in the thirteenth century. This theory is no longer taken seriously, however, and there is a general agreement that the various Tai groups originated in the area spanning southeastern China and northwestern Vietnam, where sizable Tai-speaking populations remain today.

The idea of a large wave or flood of Tai speakers pouring into northern Southeast Asia has also largely given way to a picture of a slow but steady trickle of migrants moving southward along river valleys. In most Tai cultures the fundamental socio-political unit above the village level is the *muang*, which can mean 'city', 'town', or 'country', depending on the context; it essentially refers to all of the territory and population under the control of a single ruler. Tai oral and written traditions contain numerous stories about the ruler of one *muang* sending out one or more sons to establish another one subordinate to his own, and thus networks of such *muang* were established as the new arrivals prospered, grew more numerous, and extended their influence over their neighbors.

The chronology of this migration cannot be mapped out with any precision, as the chronicle accounts were produced much later and often contain many fanciful elements. Possibly as early as the tenth century, more probably in the eleventh, and certainly by the twelfth, what the Thai historian Khachon Sukphanit famously called 'beach-head states' (*muang*) were being established in various parts of what is now southern China, northern Thailand, and Burma. One of the earliest arose in Yunnan, where Nanzhao – which was in fact not ruled by Tai speakers, though they were present among its population – gave way to a successor kingdom called Dali, which by the twelfth century at the latest was being overshadowed by a new Tai *muang* at Chieng Hung (modern Jinghong). Roughly contemporary were Chieng Saen (now in the far north of Thailand) and possibly the first Shan states in northern Burma. The period between roughly 1000 and 1200 thus witnessed the establishment and expansion of Tai migrants all across the northern mainland region.

It is only in the thirteenth century that the historical record begins to take clearer shape, when groups of *muang* began to coalesce into larger if structurally fragile kingdoms which bore a close resemblance to other *mandalas* in the region. As was mentioned earlier, the appearance of these kingdoms (Sukhothai and Lanna) coincided with Angkor's contraction after its period of maximum expansion, but the degree of cause and effect linking the two important developments cannot be determined. Lanna was in present-day northern Thailand, outside Angkor's sphere of influence, but Sukhothai's core territory lay further south, at least partly in territory which would have been at the periphery of the Angkorean *mandala*. The earliest Sukhothai inscriptions present a picture of a rebellious territory which broke away from Khmer overlordship and established itself as a Thai kingdom.

In studying this early period of the history of 'Thailand', we need to be mindful of the fact that neither the northern nor central regions would have been purely 'Tai' in their ethnicity. Although there is no indication of the numbers of Tai speakers who gradually made their way down the various rivers that flow through these regions, it is certain that they would have been a minority among the speakers of Mon, Cambodian, and other Mon-Khmer languages who already occupied the territory. It was the Tai who emerged as the new rulers, however, as the Mon territories were conquered or otherwise subordinated while Angkor's authority receded to the southeast. The Mon populations were almost completely assimilated, the Khmer only partially. Even today minority groups speaking Khmer or closely related languages can be found in several provinces of northeastern Thailand.

Sukhothai was by no means the first Tai kingdom, but it was probably the largest and most important at that time, and it would remain so until it was overshadowed by Ayutthaya in the latter half of the fourteenth century. The most detailed glimpse of Sukhothai comes from the famous 1292 inscription attributed to King Ramkhamheng (r. 1279–98), which paints a picture of a peaceful and prosperous country where 'there are fish in the water and rice in the fields' and where the ruler demonstrated his devotion by inviting monks to sit on his throne and preach their sermons. According to the inscription, Ramkhamheng's father had been part of an alliance forged against Angkor a half-century earlier which succeeded in rolling back Cambodian influence in the region, although given the state of the Angkorean kingdom after the death of Jayavarman VII, the Thai 'victory' may not have been particularly hard-fought.

The scholar of Thai history David Wyatt argued that Ramkhamheng's inscription was in a sense an advertisement for his Sukhothai kingdom, implicitly publicizing the advantages of his peaceful and benevolent rule as opposed to the more oppressive overlordship of the Khmer. Ramkhamheng himself has come to symbolize a model of paternalistic Thai kingship. His title *Pho Khun* can be translated as something like 'Father Lord'. We should perhaps take his description of his rule with a grain of salt, but it is certainly plausible that Thai overlordship did represent a favorable and even welcome change from Khmer rule. More importantly, it seems clear that by this time Thai rule meant Theravada rule, whereas Angkor at the time of its overlordship in the region had yet to adopt Sinhalese Buddhism. Jayavarman VII, it will be remembered, was Buddhist, but Mahayana rather than Theravada.

A more problematic issue is the size and extent of Sukhothai. The inscription includes a long list of place-names allegedly under Ramkhamheng's control, stretching from Luang Phabang in present-day Laos to far down the Malay peninsula. Thai and foreign scholars alike have traditionally taken this list at face value, and Sukhothai appears on many maps as a large although irregularly shaped entity stretching hundreds of miles from north to south. In fact, however, it is highly unlikely that a ruler based in Sukhothai would have had the capacity for conquest or 'empire-building' needed to accumulate a stretch of territory this size, and there is no evidence that even the Chao Phraya river valley itself (immediately to the south of Sukhothai) was under the latter's authority. At the most, Wyatt suggested, he could conceivably have built a chain of marriage and military alliances, but even that seems unlikely on such a scale. Ramkhamhaeng would not have been the first ruler – or the last – to blithely give a fictitious list of places as his dependencies.

Sukhothai's century or so of independent history demonstrates the characteristics of a typical Southeast Asian *mandala*. Built up under Ramkhamhaeng and his predecessors, it fell apart after his death, although his successors – of whom the most prominent were Leu Thai (r. 1298–1346) and Li Thai (r. 1347–c.1370) – continued to rule over a smaller kingdom. These rulers left a magnificent architectural heritage of temples which have now been restored and organized into a national historical park. Sukhothai never achieved 'major power' status, however, and by the mid-fourteenth century its potential to expand southward into the Chao Phraya valley was blocked by the emergence of Ayutthaya, which eventually absorbed it. It remained an important political and cultural center distinct from those further south, however, and its time of power and prosperity marked an important stage in the historical development of the Tai world.

The second important kingdom to emerge during the thirteenth century was Lanna (sometimes written Lan Na), whose name means 'a million rice fields'. The language spoken there (and still spoken in northern Thailand today) was distinct from the Thai spoken further south in Sukhothai, and the northern Thai are acknowledged as a separate group from the Siamese of the central region. The founder of Lanna, Mangrai (r. 1292–1317 as king of Lanna), came from the ruling family of Chieng Saen, one of the oldest Tai *muang*, and his mother was from Chieng Hung. He succeeded to his father's throne in Chieng Saen in 1259 but spent the next few decades expanding his kingdom through conquest, marriage alliances, and out-and-out trickery. The latter strategy particularly targeted the Mon kingdom of Haripunjaya, his most significant rival for supremacy in the region: Mangrai sent a false defector to infiltrate the capital and gradually erode its defenses.

Mangrai took the throne of Haripunjaya in 1281 but continued to expand his territory and search for a new location for his capital. It is interesting that his explicitly Buddhist activities seem to have begun after the conquest of Haripunjaya, suggesting that this may have been the source of the Buddhism which spread among his people. In 1292 he settled on the site which became Chiang Mai, but its founding is usually dated from 1296, when he actually began to build the city. By Mangrai's death in the early 1300s, he had acquired a considerable expanse of territory, but guaranteeing its unity after his death was quite another matter. Like his friend and contemporary Ramkhamhaeng, he was unable to ensure a smooth succession, and Lanna fell into civil war for more than a decade. It was pulled together again by one of his descendants and endured as a separate political entity – though not always an independent one – into the nineteenth century, when it was gradually absorbed into Siam. Chiang Mai would remain the political and cultural center of the Northern Thai people (also called Yuan or Khon Muang) throughout the vicissitudes of Lanna's fortunes over the next few centuries and even after the kingdom's demise.

These thirteenth-century kingdoms represented what one might call the first 'super-*muang*', linked together through a combination of military conquest, diplomacy, marriage alliances, and even deception (if the account of Mangrai's actions is to be believed). They were larger and geopolitically more influential than their predecessors, yet they retained an essential structural fragility. Nor were either Sukhothai or Lanna able to expand significantly in terms of territory after the accomplishments of their respective founders. The next important development in the Tai world only took place in the fourteenth century with the appearance of Ayutthaya, which was stronger and more durable as well as expansionist.

Vietnam

The history of independent Vietnam between the end of Chinese rule in the tenth century and French colonization in the nineteenth century is broken into two parts by the twenty-year Ming occupation in the early 1400s. In this chapter we will look at the first part of this history, ending with the Ming invasion. This first period of independence can be divided into three sections: the tenth century, when Vietnam was ruled by a succession of rulers from different families and regions; the Ly dynasty (1009–1225), the country's first stable and durable imperial dynasty; and the Tran dynasty (1225–1400), whose fall led to the Ming occupation. While this five-century period saw relatively little territorial expansion, it brought considerable political and cultural consolidation and established the Vietnamese kingdom as a permanent and important player in the region.

As was noted in Chapter 2, the millennium of Chinese rule over northern Vietnam saw periodic episodes of resistance and revolt by the Vietnamese, who were able to profit from the times when political unrest in the Middle Kingdom translated into a weakening of its control over its periphery. These episodes of Vietnamese independence were short-lived until the early tenth century, when the decline and fall of the powerful Tang dynasty and the prolonged division of the subsequent 'Five Dynasties and Ten Kingdoms' gave the Vietnamese sufficient breathing room to establish and defend a country of their own. While in its early stage this country was far from unified – and, as we shall see, was perhaps not even a single entity – it was able to fight off two Chinese attempts to re-establish their authority, thus ensuring that the embryonic polity had a chance to grow.

During the final decades of Tang rule over what had come to be called the 'Protectorate of Annam', China's control over its Vietnamese periphery was nominal, and members of the local elite began to take matters into their own hands. Between roughly 905 and 930, three successive leaders from a single family named Khuc held the position of 'governor' under the theoretical authority of the absent Tang. The newly established Southern Han dynasty invaded in 930 to regain control, but its forces were soon driven out. The next few decades saw a succession of military leaders coming to power in different parts of the Red river delta. The most prominent among them were Ngo Quyen, who had himself crowned king in 939 after a famous naval victory over the Chinese at Bach Dang, and Dinh Bo Linh, who assumed the title of 'Emperor of Dai Co Viet' in 968. When he was murdered a few years later, one of his generals, Le Hoan, took the throne. He ruled for a quarter-century, and his death was followed by a power struggle between his sons; the victor ruled for four years and then died. A court official named Ly Cong Uan was crowned emperor, and his successors remained on the throne for more than two centuries.

The chaotic events of the tenth century are represented in traditional Vietnamese sources as a succession of short-lived 'dynasties' which eventually gave way to the Ly. In reality, however, these rulers look much more like Southeast Asian 'men of prowess' than Chinese emperors. They seem to have come to power through the support of networks of followers, ties to powerful families, and local or regional power bases, and they ruled from at least two different capitals. Nor did any of them succeed in ensuring that his son was accepted as ruler after him. The process of building and consolidating a stable dynasty was a slow one, and, all in all, Vietnamese history in the tenth century follows a familiar Southeast Asian pattern.

To some extent, however, this Southeast Asian-style polity was operating within a Chinese cultural framework. While Confucianism does not seem to have been strong as an ideology even among the ruling class – and, indeed, would not be so for some time to come – Buddhism and Daoism were clearly influential. In the absence of an extensive educational system or regular Chinese-style examinations, to a large extent Buddhist monks – and, to a lesser extent, Daoist priests – constituted the intellectual elite. The chronicles show such individuals acting as advisors and officials within the royal courts and welcoming diplomatic missions from China. A famous (though probably apocryphal) anecdote tells of a Vietnamese monk who was sent disguised as a boatman to receive an envoy from the Chinese Song dynasty; he astounded the visitor with his ability to recite classical poetry, thus demonstrating that the Vietnamese were a cultured people.

Mahayana Buddhism remained the predominant cultural force throughout the Ly and Tran dynasties. Confucianism as an intellectual influence was on the rise but only achieved its full status in the 1400s after the Ming occupation. Members of the Ly and Tran royal families and other members of the Vietnamese elite gave strong patronage to their religion, providing moral support for the monkhood and sponsoring the copying of Buddhist scriptures and the casting of bells for temples. Several emperors wrote philosophical treatises on Buddhism and occasionally a ruler abdicated to spend the rest of his life as a monk.

Vietnamese Buddhism was not, however, monolithic. The Ly and Tran elite favored the school known in China as *Chan* and in Vietnam as *Thien*. This school, known in the West by its Japanese name of Zen, emphasized devotion through meditation and sometimes arcane philosophical texts. *Thien* monks are recorded as having practiced various forms of asceticism, challenged their disciples with contradictory or incomprehensible questions, and even performed miracles and magical acts through their superior spiritual prowess. At the grassroots, however, Vietnamese are assumed to have followed more mundane forms of Buddhism based on making merit, reciting prayers, and repeating the Buddha's name. It was these Buddhist practices, closely akin to the Pure Land School originating in China, which endured in Vietnamese culture over the long run; the elite fascination with *Thien* seems to have been specific to this period.

The Ly and Tran dynasties are often linked together in Vietnamese minds, not only because of their shared Buddhist culture, but also because there is considerable continuity between them in terms of the evolution of Vietnam as a polity. During the centuries before the Ming occupation, Dai Viet – as the kingdom was known for most of this period – was gradually building an institutional framework and an administrative structure based on the Chinese model. This was a slow process, however, and government under the two dynasties was less complex, less bureaucratic, and in some ways perhaps more personal than it became from the fifteenth century onward.

There were at least two reasons why this was the case. First, both dynasties began with roughly a century of generally good and strong rulers before beginning a process of decline. Thus, members of the royal family played important roles in governing the country. Under the Tran in particular, princes held many important civil and military positions which were entrusted to mandarins under later dynasties. Princes and princesses possessed large tracts of land (especially under the Tran) and thus had considerable manpower under their direct control. This somewhat feudal structure is particularly characteristic of this period of Vietnamese history. Second, although there were prominent scholar-officials from the twelfth century onward – as monks were gradually relegated to more traditional religious roles – these 'literati' as a group did not enjoy the influence that they came to have under a larger and more Confucianist-oriented bureaucracy starting in the late fifteenth century. Examinations were not held as regularly, and the mandarinate as an institution did not reach the critical mass needed to give it real weight in government affairs, particularly at times when there was a healthy supply of powerful and competent princes.

It seems clear that the Vietnamese village was already the predominant social structure – along with the family – during this period, but we know relatively little about life inside it. The main source of information is the chronicles, which are written from the perspective of the court and have little to say about the countryside except when there was trouble. We can assume that most people grew rice, practiced some form of craft or artisanry, or perhaps did some of both. There is evidence of both privately and communally owned land – a dual system that would prevail through the French colonial period – but we lack the specific data to know how the balance between the two played out at the village level. Periodic peasant revolts suggest that there was tension and probably exploitation in the countryside, problems that were aggravated in times of drought, flooding, or epidemics, any one of which factors could trigger unrest. A wise government would reduce or even waive taxes when times were bad, but rulers were not always wise, and local officials had plenty of opportunities to squeeze more revenue out of the people under their authority.

The geographical core of Dai Viet for much of this period remained the area which had earlier been under Chinese control, corresponding to the northern and north-central regions of present-day Vietnam. The kingdom itself consisted mainly of the lowland and midland areas inhabited by ethnic Vietnamese. Chiefs of neighboring highland groups – probably speakers of Tai languages and Muong for the most part – occasionally appear in the chronicles either to offer tribute to the court in Thang Long (as Hanoi was then known) or else to rise up in revolt and be suppressed. In a few instances under the Ly, princesses were offered to these chiefs to establish marriage alliances. Generally, however, it is unlikely that they and their territories were administratively incorporated into the kingdom, and a weak ruler was probably unable even to collect tribute from the ethnically alien periphery.

Dai Viet was never at peace for more than a few decades at a time. Successive Chinese dynasties from the Southern Han in the early tenth century to the Song in the eleventh century and the Mongols in the thirteenth mounted invasions of their southern neighbor. Each of these campaigns was defeated, and great military leaders such as Ly Thuong Kiet (eleventh century) and Prince Tran Hung Dao (thirteenth century) are part of the Vietnamese pantheon of heroes. There were also long peaceful intervals in the Sino-Vietnamese relationship, however, with periodic tribute missions and official Chinese recognition of each new ruler in Thang Long. Vietnamese monarchs were 'emperors' within their own domain but only vassal 'kings' in their relations with China.

From the time of independence, Vietnamese relations with the Cham to the south were fraught and conflict-ridden. For most of this period the two peoples were roughly equal in strength. The Vietnamese seem to have had contacts with more than one Cham kingdom, although it is not easy to sort this out from the chronicles. There were periodic episodes of warfare, and Dai Viet annexed Cham territory in the eleventh and thirteenth centuries – once through warfare and once through an arranged marriage between a Tran princess and a Cham ruler – but it is not certain that this territory was firmly under Thang Long's control. In the 1360s and 1370s the Cham were strong enough to mount several invasions that penetrated as far as the Vietnamese capital. The balance of power would shift in Vietnamese favor in the fifteenth century, however, and the Cham never regained their former strength.

These first centuries of independence, then, constituted the formative period of the Vietnamese polity. The foundations for a Chinese-style imperial government were laid and then expanded over the course of time. Dai Viet had diplomatic relations and occasional military conflicts with several of its neighbors, but it also had trade contacts, particularly through the important northern port of Van Don. The cultural framework which had evolved during the millennium of Chinese rule remained largely intact and, indeed, was reinforced by periodic injections of new ideas and religious practices into Vietnamese society. Dai Viet was by no means a carbon copy of its northern suzerain, but it was clearly within the Sinicized cultural sphere, which set it apart in many respects from its Indianized neighbors elsewhere in the region.

Champa

As was emphasized in the previous chapter, it is now almost universally accepted that 'Champa' was not a single kingdom, but rather a series of kingdoms extending along the Vietnamese coast. The evidence for multiple polities becomes particularly clear during the period covered here, beginning from roughly the eighth century. These kingdoms would have shared a common Indianized Cham culture, though probably with local variations. Each is known to us by a Sanskrit name which is linked to a specific region. At times two or more of them were apparently in conflict with each other as one ruler attempted to extend his own influence at the expense of the others. It appears, however, that for most of the 'classical' period no one kingdom was able to achieve extended domination over the others.

It is not possible to construct a single, coherent narrative for Cham history during the period between 800 and 1400. What we have is a series of 'windows' provided by clusters of inscriptions and bursts of architectural activity in specific places at specific times. Information from outside sources (Chinese, Vietnamese, Cambodian) can fill in some of the gaps, but sometimes these sources serve to confound rather than clarify, especially because they tend to refer simply to 'Champa' without distinguishing which particular polity is involved. Since past scholars tended to assume that there was in fact only one Champa, it was necessary to posit periodic and drastic changes of capital and ruling family in order to knit all of the evidence into a single 'national' history. The recognition that there were multiple centers complicates the historian's task, yet it also frees us from the need to jam all of the diverse sources into one story.

As previously mentioned, the original 'core' of Cham civilization appears to have been located in the middle of the Vietnamese coast, near the present-day city of Da Nang, with the twin ancient sites of Tra Kieu (Indrapura) and My Son. Until the mid-ninth century and after the late tenth century, the ruling family or families located in this region (called Amaravati) seem to have worshipped Śiva above other deities. During the interval between these two periods (from 875 until almost 1000), however, there was a sudden shift in emphasis to Mahayana Buddhism with the appearance of the culture centered at Dong Duong in the same region. In reality the shift may have been less dramatic than it appears, since Buddhism and Hinduism coexisted in so many places. It is likely that the century-long flourishing of Buddhist art indicates the domination of a particular family who favored the Buddha over Śiva, just as successive Angkorean rulers favored Śiva, Vishnu, or the Buddha.

The mid- to late eighth century also saw the appearance on the historical record of two kingdoms further south: Kauthara (centered around what is now the city of Nha Trang) and Panduranga, the southernmost kingdom, which corresponds to present-day Phan Rang. These two regions remained both strong and separate from the various kingdoms in Amaravati. They would also outlast their northern counterparts once the Vietnamese began to expand. Panduranga would in fact be the final remnant of 'Champa', conquered by the Vietnamese but surviving as a distinct entity until the nineteenth century. Nha Trang is home to the important temple dedicated to Po Nagar, a Cham deity who was sometimes represented as Uma, the consort of Śiva, but nevertheless retained her separate identity.

Sandwiched between Amaravati and Kauthara was Vijaya, which flourished from around 1000 through the late fifteenth century, when it was conquered by Dai Viet. The remains of several walled citadels from this kingdom can still be found. The capital was located at what is now the town of Quy Nhon in the province of Binh Dinh. Temples and statuary from the Vijaya region show that its culture remained Indianized throughout this period. Thus by the second millennium there were apparently at least four different Cham polities coexisting with each other, although for the sake of convenience we may collectively refer to them as 'Champa'.

Two key themes to understanding the history of the Cham are trade and warfare. The long stretch of coastal territory occupied by the various Cham polities was in many places much more suited for maritime trade than for agriculture, as the soil was often poor and the lowland areas often narrow, squeezed in between the easternmost edge of the Central Highlands and the sea. Champa was, of course, well-placed to benefit from the active trade between the South China Sea and the Indian Ocean which provided much of the economic dynamic of Southeast Asian history. The Vietnamese coast for most of its length is characterized by numerous rivers and ports, and many of these were long under the control of Cham kingdoms. The 'coastal state model' described above would seem to be a perfect fit for these kingdoms, and the highland areas along the western edge of Cham territory were full of various exotic products which were in demand for the Chinese market and thus suitable for trade with the lowland regions. Ceramics – both locally produced and imported for re-export elsewhere – were another important trade item.

It should be pointed out as well that the Cham, with their ethnic and linguistic ties to the various peoples of the island world, could easily fit into the trade network linking Sumatra, Java, and the Malay peninsula to India and other parts of the Islamic world. During the earlier centuries covered in Chapter 2, direct trade connections with China seem to have been more important and concentrated mainly in the northernmost Champa kingdom. The appearance of Kauthara and Panduranga, however, coincided with a temporary disruption of trade with China followed by the growth of ports within Chinese-ruled Vietnam itself. Over the long term, multiple Cham ports flourished up and down the coast, but different regions seem to have been more closely linked to different trading networks depending on their location.

As far as warfare is concerned, the two greatest security threats to the Cham kingdoms came from the north (the Vietnamese) and the southwest (the Cambodians). The frequent conflicts between the Vietnamese and Cham have already been mentioned in the previous section. Linyi and its successors appear as a threat in Chinese and Vietnamese sources for much of the period of Chinese rule. The territory of the northernmost Cham kingdoms appears to have extended through what are now the provinces of Quang Binh and Quang Tri, thus abutting directly onto the southern edge of China's Vietnamese provinces (present-day Ha Tinh). After Vietnamese independence in the tenth century, this border area between the two kingdoms became a frequent point of conflict. Although Vietnamese histories claim that much of this northern stretch of Cham territory was annexed by Dai Viet in the eleventh century, it is not at all certain that the Vietnamese were in fact able to bring the ethnically alien Cham populations under their control. The same may be said of the provinces around modern Hue which were allegedly given to the Vietnamese as a bride-price for the Tran princess in the early 1300s.

Attempting to understand the dynamic of Cham-Vietnamese relations over the centuries is a difficult task, especially if we assume that Dai Viet may have had dealings and even wars with more than one Champa. The Vietnamese chronicles tend to portray the Cham in a subordinate role, referring to their 'tribute missions' comparable to those Dai Viet itself sent to China. In reality, however, there seems little likelihood that the Cham would have needed or wanted to play the role of a Vietnamese 'vassal'. As was mentioned above, there seems to have been a relative geopolitical balance of power until the late 1300s. In the very first years of the fifteenth century, however, the Cham felt sufficiently threatened to cede territory south of the Pass of the Clouds (between present-day Hue and Da Nang). By this time what had been the territory known as Amaravati was clearly lost to Dai Viet. The Vietnamese now had a presence south of what had been an important barrier to land-based military expansion, paving the way for a major military campaign against Vijaya later in the century. The year 1400, then, marks an important watershed in the strategic relationship between Vietnam and Champa.

The relationship between the Cham and Khmer evolved within a common Indianized cultural framework but was no less fraught than ties with the more culturally alien Vietnamese. Relations between the two peoples date back to the pre-Angkorean period, and in fact the name 'Champa' first appears in inscriptions in Cham and Khmer territory at the same time in the seventh century. Particularly as the southern Cham kingdoms developed, their proximity to Cambodia (ruled from Angkor from roughly 800 onward) heightened the potential for confrontations over trade routes and perhaps territory as well. The most violent conflicts appear to have occurred in the twelfth century, probably because of expansionist tendencies on the part of Angkorean rulers. It has long been believed that there was a major Cham naval raid on Angkor in 1177, although Michael Vickery has questioned whether this actually took place. In any case, subsequently Cambodia and its Cham neighbors appear to have resolved their differences, and the southern Cham polities did not face a major external threat until the Vietnamese campaigns of the late fifteenth century.

The 'border' between the Sinicized world of Vietnam and the Indianized civilization of Champa was significant well into the second millennium. Cultural and trade ties to Cambodia and the Malay world meant that the Cham were in many ways better connected with the rest of Southeast Asia than their neighbors to the north. As multiple Champas emerged and flourished, the Cham role in regional trade was strengthened and diversified. Had they been able to hold their own militarily against Dai Viet, their period of strength could probably have gone on much longer. There is too little information about internal developments in the Cham kingdoms after the great military campaigns against Vietnam in the 1370s to explain why the balance of power shifted so dramatically in so short a time. The death (following those battles) of the powerful Cham ruler known to the Vietnamese as Che Bong Nga was surely one factor, but there must have been structural issues as well. It is interesting to speculate whether a single, unified Champa would in fact have been able to withstand further Vietnamese pressure rather than suffering the territorial concessions and military defeats of the fifteenth century. In any case, by 1400 the glories of Cham civilization were beginning to fade, though many architectural works survived as reminders of Champa's classical past.

Śrivijaya

Śrivijaya has already made its appearance in the previous chapter, and it occupies center stage in maritime Southeast Asia for most of the period covered in the present chapter. Its importance in terms of geopolitical and commercial influence, however, is not matched by the amount of knowledge we possess regarding its history. In fact, we arguably know less about specific developments in the polity of Śrivijaya than about almost any other part of classical Southeast Asia. It is not possible to piece together a narrative of Śrivijaya's history based on the scattered descriptions and references in various foreign sources. At best we can make anecdotal and impressionistic observations about what it was and how it evolved.

Chapter 2 described the seventh-century 'window' when Śrivijaya made its appearance on the historical scene. A polity based at Palembang in southeastern Sumatra appears to have gained ascendancy over rivals located elsewhere on the island, and from the late 600s onward only 'Śrivijaya' was sending tribute missions to the Chinese court. It is generally believed that Palembang remained the center of power until the late eleventh century, when it shifted northward to Jambi. For various reasons to be discussed below, Śrivijaya's power seems to have been on the wane from that point onward, but it survived into the fourteenth century with its center at Jambi and later in the lands inhabited by the Minangkabau. By the early 1400s, however, the center of the Malay world had clearly shifted to Melaka.

At the time of Śrivijaya's 'discovery' in the early twentieth century by colonial-era scholars who pieced together information from various sources, it was viewed as a maritime 'empire' which at its height extended over Java and Sumatra and well up the Malay peninsula. Like its neighbors, though, it has been cut down to size by more recent scholarship, and our understanding of its structure has been significantly altered. Most scholars now conceive of Śrivijaya as a core – located at Palembang or Jambi – surrounded by networks of ties to vassal rulers and other outlying areas. While inscriptions and other sources suggest that Śrivijayan rulers were at certain points in time able to project their power to Java, the peninsula, or even further afield, we cannot assume that these more distant locations were incorporated into an 'empire' for long periods of time.

Bronson's model of upstream-downstream ties is particularly applicable to Śrivijaya as we now understand it. Trade in local and foreign commodities was in many respects Śrivijaya's *raison d'être* and provided the glue that held the polity together. A strong ruler would be able to build and maintain links to lesser rulers scattered around the island world, including the *orang laut* ('sea peoples') who constituted an essential source of manpower. These links would have included not only transactions of mutual economic benefit, but also ritualized expressions of loyalty and frequent communications between the overlord and his vassals. This system survived as long as trade prospered. When southeastern Sumatra as a region began to lose its attractiveness as a trade center and suffered a decline in its general prosperity, Śrivijaya was directly affected.

Scholars have sometimes described Śrivijaya as a 'thalassocracy' which dominated the maritime region through its powerful navy, but again the assumption that its dominant economic role was attributable to military strength must be reconsidered. The Malay peninsula and western Indonesian archipelago were dotted with ports, some of which predated Śrivijaya itself. Although relatively little is known about many of these entities beyond their names (frequently found in Chinese sources), they fitted into a complex trading network of which Śrivijaya may have been the center but was not necessarily the master. At best the rulers of Śrivijaya would have exercised overlordship or hegemony, but not necessarily direct control.

Nor did Śrivijaya's domination of the trade routes go unchallenged. There were episodes of conflict with Javanese rulers in the tenth century, although the details of Śrivijaya's relationship with Java during this period are unclear. The best-known and most serious challenge came from the South Indian Chola dynasty in the early eleventh century, when commercial rivalry between the two trade powers led to a crippling invasion of Sumatra in 1025. While this invasion did not culminate in a long-term Indian occupation, it seems to have significantly altered the regional balance of power. There is no evidence after that point of Śrivijayan authority on the peninsula, which became a major area of contention among various other rival powers.

As mentioned above, the 'capital' of Śrivijaya shifted from Palembang to Jambi a half-century after the Chola invasion, and some scholars see this change as marking the beginning of the polity's decline. Its dominant position clearly began to wane, and rival kingdoms in northern Sumatra (Samudra-Pasai), the Malay peninsula (Tambralinga, centered at present-day Nakhon Si Thammarat in southern Thailand), and East Java prospered at its expense. Samudra-Pasai's economic clout was linked to the pepper trade, while successive East Javanese polities were better situated than Sumatra to profit from the growing spice trade. Nevertheless, Chinese sources suggest that Śrivijaya's role in regional trade remained significant though at least the thirteenth century, even if it no longer had the dominance it had once enjoyed.

If Śrivijaya was not necessarily the hegemonic empire that earlier generations of scholars believed it to be, its power and wealth during its heyday are not in dispute. Chinese and Arab sources tell of the fabled riches of the kingdom and its rulers. Moreover, like its contemporaries elsewhere in 'classical' Southeast Asia, it exercised ongoing influence over the Malay world. Later chronicles explicitly linked the foundation and rise of Melaka to Palembang – where Śrivijaya once flourished – and the new kingdom established on the peninsula in the early 1400s was in many ways heir to the glory and prestige of its predecessor.

Java

Chapter 2 gave a brief overview of Javanese history through the end of the ninth century, when the island's political and cultural dynamism was concentrated in central Java. The early tenth century saw a major shift in the center of power to east Java. There it remained for several centuries, even if the central Javanese sacred sites built before 900 (particularly Prambanan and Borobudur) remained important. The reasons for this eastward shift are unclear. There is speculation about a threat from Śrivijaya, or perhaps a volcanic eruption which destroyed agricultural land and settlements, and was seen as a bad omen. Whatever the case, the eastern part of the island, particularly the Brantas river valley, now became the focus of Javanese political power and the rivalries and conflicts that went with it.

Java's history during the classical period is characterized by alternating periods of division and relative unity, with frequent changes of power centers when a ruler chose to shift his court (*kraton*). True unity appears to have been an elusive goal, however, and while the ideal of a single kingdom remained strong, it was generally a treasured memory rather than an achievable reality. This period of Javanese history can be roughly divided into four phases. (1) In 929 a new dynasty was established in the Brantas valley by Pu Sindok (r. 929–47), whose descendants ruled a relatively united kingdom through the reign of Airlangga (r. 1010–42). After a long and powerful reign, Airlangga abdicated to become a Hindu ascetic and divided his kingdom between his two sons. (2) For more than a century, east Java was divided into two rival kingdoms, Janggala and Panjalu (Kediri). (3) In 1222 a ruler named Ken Angrok (r. 1222–27) founded a new dynasty at Singhasari, which gradually eclipsed the previous ruling families and sought to re-establish a single kingdom. Neither he nor his successors was able to achieve this objective fully – not even the powerful ruler Kertanagara (r. 1268–92). Kertanagara was killed when a revolt broke out, followed by a Mongol invasion in 1293. (4) His son-in-law Vijaya allied with the Mongols against Singhasari's enemies and established a new capital at Majapahit. He ruled as Kertarajasa (r. 1293–1309), and Majapahit would survive as the last pre-Islamic Javanese kingdom into the sixteenth century.

The shift in power center from central to east Java had several important consequences. First, it enabled agricultural development because the Brantas valley was less populated than the central region, with more land which was not under the control of any chief or ruler. Second, it facilitated the exchange of goods between the coastal areas and hinterland, thus increasing the ruler's potential to control trade and acquire revenue. This is not to say that trade was unimportant in central Java, but coastal centers in particular became more significant in the east. Thirdly, increasing wealth enabled rulers to build more temples – even if no longer on the scale of Borobudur or Prambanan – to express their devotion and provide patronage, while also attracting more support. Consequently, the monarchy as an institution became generally more powerful, especially from Airlangga's reign.

Javanese society under the Eastern kingdoms became increasingly complex. The two key units in the traditional Javanese polity were the village and the court. The Javanese village resembled its Vietnamese counterpart in that it had both privately and communally owned land and a fairly sophisticated social structure including a stratum of local leadership. It was linked to other villages through a market system and through connections to local temples. Between the village and the *kraton* were the *watek*, which were ruled by individuals known as *rakrayan*. Many *watek* seem to have been originally independent chiefdoms or other polities which were subsequently absorbed into larger kingdoms yet retained a separate but clearly subordinate identity within those kingdoms. Over the period of time covered by this chapter, the *watek* increased in number and complexity, so that many villages were separated from the *kraton* by more than one layer of authority. *Rakrayan* were involved with the taxation of the villages under their authority and could make demands on their labor as well as being involved with the management of irrigation, but they did not exert control over the village land.

Most historians believe that the successive kingdoms mentioned above were not particularly centralized. There is evidence that *watek* and village alike were relatively self-sufficient in financial terms, meaning that while they had to collect revenue and send it to the *kraton*, they received very little of that revenue back in terms of subsidies or services. Kings ruled and invested considerable time and effort in projecting their authority in spiritual and ritual terms (to be discussed more below), but the actual structure of what we might consider 'government' was minimal for much of this period. The various Javanese kingdoms do not seem to have been held together by coercion or the threat of physical force.

In other sections of this chapter we have seen the importance of horizontal and vertical relationships as the 'glue' that held various Southeast Asian kingdoms together – at once more personal and more fragile than the structures of modern government. Such relationships were based on patronage and largesse, which (ideally) ensured that subordinates remained loyal to their superiors and fulfilled their obligations within the system. In the case of Java it is much more difficult to discern these kinds of ties, and many historians in fact tend to understand Javanese rulers as having to some extent bypassed the *rakrayan* and other regional leaders by creating direct ties to local temples which were loyal to the royal court. The main instrument for doing so was the *sima*, a kind of granting of tax-exempt status to a religious institution in a particular locality. Not only did the *sima* deprive the local authorities of any revenue from the land belonging to the temple, the latter might be under the direct patronage of a member of the royal family and, in some cases, even be dedicated to the worship of a deceased king or other royal family member.

The mention of worshipping deceased kings brings us to the issue of religious beliefs in classical Java, which is a topic of greater complexity than perhaps anywhere else in Southeast Asia. Java was one of the 'strongholds' of Indianized culture in the region and remained so after its mainland neighbors had converted to Theravada. Although the gradual conversion to Islam diluted the influence of Indic religion on Javanese culture, it by no means erased it, as is evident from the diverse varieties of Islamic and non-Islamic practices still found on the island today. The purest Indianized culture remains that of Bali (Figure

Figure 12   Gunung Kawi rock-cut temples, Bali, eleventh century

12), which was at times subordinate to Javanese rulers but never followed its larger neighbor in adopting Islam. Java is also unique among Southeast Asian cultures in having preserved a self-conscious memory of having imported culture from India: the story of Aji Saka, who is said to have brought the calendar and other trappings of Indic civilization to the island in the distant past.

During the classical era Javanese religious practices included four broad spheres: Śivaism and Vishnuism, Buddhism, and local deities such as the Goddess of the Southern Ocean. Of the first three, different elements were emphasized by particular rulers or courts at different times, while the indigenous Javanese deities were consistently important. A *kraton* might have living quarters reserved for religious leaders, and kings would visit different parts of their realm to perform ceremonies linked to specific spirits and deities. In the Indic worldview the court was the center of the *mandala* and ultimately a microcosm of the universe, but it was also linked to a network of uniquely Javanese sacred sites which were no less important.

Like their counterparts elsewhere, Javanese rulers drew on beliefs and traditions of kingship which went far beyond the mere performance of rituals. The importance of ancestors was considerable, and from early in the classical period Javanese kings were divinized after their death. Airlangga, for example, was worshipped as Vishnu, but only posthumously. Kediri rulers also placed particular emphasis on Vishnu, although they were not deified during their lifetime – and, interestingly enough, one of the factors in the eventual fall of that particular dynasty is said to have been an attempt by its last king to represent himself falsely as Śiva. Kertanegara, the last Singhasari ruler, was posthumously linked to both Śiva and the Buddha, and we find the same tendencies for Majapahit kings as well. There is also some evidence that the divinization of rulers while they were alive began in Singhasari and continued at Majapahit. These increasingly potent spiritual claims would have been directly linked to assertions of royal legitimacy and attempts to consolidate power over larger stretches of territory.

A line can be drawn between the earlier kingdoms of East Java and Majapahit, which in many respects was the ultimate Javanese state, with a powerful center ruling over a fairly large span of territory. The fourteenth century, following its foundation by Kertarajasa, marked the transition to a kingdom with a more powerful center which could collect revenue and products directly from outlying and subordinate areas rather than just receiving them as tribute or ritual offerings. At the same time, there was a general expansion of state revenue attributable to the overall state of peace and security during the 1300s, along with the expansion of roads and marketing networks, as well as an increase in the foreign demand for spices. The rise of the spice trade, it will be remembered, was probably a key factor in the shift of economic power from Śrivijaya on Sumatra to Javanese-based polities.

Majapahit rulers by no means enjoyed absolute power, however, and they faced potential competition from the traditional landed elite. The rulers were not strong or brave enough to try to break the power of this elite, so where possible they worked to bypass them, encouraging the growth of trade and artisanry and forging direct connections with these groups. The glories of Majapahit in the fourteenth century were recorded in two important chronicles, the *Deśawarnana* (formerly usually called the *Nagarakertagama*) and the *Pararaton*, which paint a picture of an unprecedentedly large and powerful kingdom. The most famous king from this period was Hayam Wuruk (r. 1350–89), who ruled with his powerful and competent minister Gajah Mada. A few decades later, however, the kingdom went into decline, as the commercial elite in the coastal trade centers began to break away from the authority of the *kraton*, and Majapahit's history began to look more like that of its predecessors.

The Philippines

A discussion of Southeast Asia during this period cannot omit the Philippines. Even though the archipelago was largely outside the Indianized sphere and for that reason evolved rather differently from the rest of the region, it appears on our historical radar screen during the classical period because of its participation in regional trade networks, particularly with China. Our knowledge of Philippine history before the Spanish colonization in the sixteenth century has many gaps. Even though several Philippine languages had scripts which were in active use when the Spanish arrived, there is no corpus of inscriptions or documents which would allow us to piece together any kind of historical narrative. Reconstructing the pre-colonial history of the Philippines is largely the task of archeologists, with some help from historians who have sifted through Chinese sources in search of references to polities scattered around the archipelago.

The precise impact of Indianization in terms of state formation in Southeast Asia has been widely debated. Although most scholars would no longer accept the arrival of Indian culture as the sole catalyst for the transition of early Southeast Asian polities from prehistoric chiefdoms into kingdoms, there is no denying that Indian concepts of kingship and the religious beliefs and rituals closely linked to them did play a formative role in the process whereby chiefs transformed into *rajas* and *maharajas*. In this respect it is significant that the Philippines, where there are few traces of Indic cultural influence, does not seem to have progressed beyond the chiefdom or chieftaincy stage until the arrival of Islam.

Throughout the period when 'classical' kingdoms were evolving elsewhere in the region, Philippine polities were characterized by what archeologist Laura Junker has characterized as 'political cycling', a model whereby these polities 'recurrently oscillate between political expansion and political fragmentation, fluctuating between "complex" forms with two-level administrative hierarchies and "simple" forms with one-level decision-making hierarchies'.[2] These chiefdoms – whether simple or complex – would have shared certain fundamental characteristics with their larger and more powerful neighbors to the west, notably their reliance on networks based on profits from trade. They were, however, in some ways more fragile and less durable than their counterparts, and thus they are considerably more difficult to identify and describe.

The first Philippine polities appear in the Chinese records during the Song dynasty (tenth–thirteenth centuries), a time when trade contacts between China and Southeast Asia expanded significantly. Reference is made in the tenth century to '*Mayi*', believed to be Mindoro (southwest of Luzon), and in 1001 the Song recorded the arrival of a tribute mission from Butuan ('*Puduan*'), located on northern Mindanao. A few smaller polities in the same archipelago are also mentioned, but their actual location is unclear, and the Chinese writers clearly had only the vaguest (and sometimes completely erroneous) notions of Philippine geography. 'Mayi' never followed Butuan's example in sending tribute but was evidently an important trading partner. Subsequently, under the Mongol Yuan dynasty (thirteenth–fourteenth centuries), the Chinese had contacts with 'new' polities located in the Sulu archipelago and on Luzon, probably at Manila. These polities were both geographically distant and politically distinct from each other, and it is impossible to map out their history in any greater detail. During the classical period we are still several centuries away from the arrival of Islam, which would contribute to the rise of several important Philippine sultanates. Yet this eastern periphery of the 'Malay world' was by no means isolated or stagnant, and the various polities just mentioned had their role to play in the growth of regional trade.

Conclusions

During the centuries covered in this chapter, Southeast Asia was transformed from congeries of small and sometimes obscure (to us, at least) kingdoms into

---

2 Laura Lee Junker, *Raiding, Trading, and Feasting: The political economy of Philippine chiefdoms* (Honolulu: University of Hawai'i Press, 1999), 85.

a lesser number of larger polities. In some respects these classical kingdoms shared significant continuities with their predecessors: structural fragility, an Indianized civilization (with the notable exceptions of Vietnam and the Philippines), and a reliance on networks of personal ties for governance more than a bureaucratic hierarchy. Imperial Vietnam was somewhat exceptional in this last sense as well, but only partly so. While the classical polities expanded in size and grew more cosmopolitan in population and outlook, at their core they were larger versions of the first Indianized kingdoms discussed in Chapter 2. Moreover, polities like Angkor, Pagan, and Śrivijaya effectively straddled the pre-classical and classical periods.

At the same time, these classical kingdoms in turn laid the foundations for the states of the early modern period, which were those encountered by the Western powers upon their arrival in the region. Ayutthaya (to be discussed in Chapter 5) is the only example of a classical state which endured well into the early modern era, but some of its neighbors (notably Dai Viet and Majapahit) provided structures, traditions, and ideas of governance which would outlast them in the years after 1500. At the psychological level, it is the polities examined here that came to constitute a 'golden age' for later generations, not only because of their perceived size and power, but also because of the strength and durability of their culture.

The strength of the continuities with early modern Southeast Asia varied, of course. The conversion to Islam and the consequent establishment of self-consciously Muslim polities weakened – though it did not destroy – the Indianized foundations of the kingdoms in the Malay world. This was less so in Islamized Java and much less the case with the mainland polities which adopted Theravada, where there was considerably less cultural and psychological 'disconnect' with the Hindu-Buddhist period. The Cham, of course, arguably remained Indianized as long as they maintained a separate polity, for the rump kingdom that survived into the early 1800s was more Indic than it was Muslim, despite the penetration of Islam. In Vietnam, the northern kingdom of Dang Ngoai (Tonkin) would adhere more closely to the model of fifteenth-century Dai Viet, while Dang Trong (Cochin China) to the south was less tightly based on that model, either politically or culturally.

4

New Global Religions and Ideas from the Thirteenth Century

Introduction

Significant new religions and associated practices appeared in Southeast Asia from about the thirteenth century. It is, however, easy to fall into the dual traps of religio-cultural stereotyping and theological anachronism when studying them. We should ensure that the phenomena we are picturing actually existed in some time and place, rather than being theoretical constructs imposed on that time and place by other and/or later observers.

The idea of 'orthodoxy' complicates the historical study of religion. In the world's largest religions – Hinduism, Buddhism, Islam, and Christianity, all of them represented in Southeast Asian history – since the sixteenth century, and particularly since the eighteenth, there have been major reform and revival movements seeking greater 'orthodoxy'. Such movements have intensified even more across all faiths since the 1960s and 1970s. Typically these reforms seek to return to a more pristine, 'original' version of the faith. This is a global phenomenon worthy of study in its own right, but it can complicate our understandings of the past. Seeing religions as they are defined by more recent reformers can lead us away from understanding how they were actually practiced in the historical societies that interest us.

In Buddhism, for example, what we know of the Buddha's original teachings may lead us to see Buddhism as an austere, philosophically rigorous, intellectually demanding set of doctrines that denies the existence of both the soul and a god, and demands non-violence from Buddhists. Yet as it developed in both its Theravada and Mahayana forms, Buddhism absorbed all sorts of other ideas and became a religion full of spiritual idiosyncrasies. It created hierarchies of enlightened beings and justified the idea of world-conquering kings whose hands were as bloody as those of the monarchs of other religions.

Or consider Christianity. Its evolution from the teachings of Jesus to the doctrines of the Catholic Church in Europe was remarkable. But even knowing that history might not lead us to expect that early Filipino Catholics would manage to preserve both a form of ancestor worship and divorce while professing to be devout Catholics. The Protestant Reformation in Europe gave birth to the severe austerities of Dutch Calvinism, which morphed into some quite inconsistent displays of ostentatious wealth when Calvinist Dutchmen became wealthy in the service of the VOC – while both praising their Calvinist divinity and often defrauding the Company of its revenues. Islam also offers such examples. The revelation recorded in the *Qur'an* may seem a long way from Islam as it existed on the ground in pre-reformist ages. But that is what Islam was at such times in such places.

An unfortunate characteristic of this period, however, inhibits our ability to understand these new religions as they actually existed in Southeast Asian societies. That is the fact that much of religious life between the thirteenth and nineteenth centuries is poorly documented. So we are often obliged to speculate on the basis of limited material. We have no other choice given the documentary realities of the age, but we must take care to base our conjectures on such evidence as survives, not on our – or others' – theoretical formulations of what a certain religion is supposed to have been like.

Theravada Buddhism

The roots of Theravada as a separate school of Buddhism from the Mahayana which is practiced in China, Vietnam, and elsewhere go back to the centuries following the Buddha's death, when a series of councils met to hash out issues of doctrine and practice, almost invariably resulting in further splits within the religion. Most of these early debates involved differing interpretations of the *Vinaya*, the detailed code of rules which governed the behavior of the monks, known by the collective term *Sangha*. Although the various schools would over the long term differ significantly in their understanding of the Buddha himself and what it meant to follow his teachings even at the level of the lay-person, the overarching importance of the *Sangha* as an institution meant that most of the crucial problems to be solved in the early history of Buddhism related to monks rather than lay believers.

By roughly the end of the third century BCE the sects of Mahayana and Theravada were going their separate ways. 'Theravada', derived from the Sanskrit word for 'elders', is the preferred name for the latter school. It is sometimes referred to as 'Hinayana', meaning 'Lesser Vehicle', as opposed to the 'Great Vehicle' (Mahayana); this name is considered derogatory, however, and 'Theravada' is preferred. Although Theravada survived for some time in India, Sri Lanka became its main center, and it was there that the Theravada scriptures – known as the *Tripitaka* or Three Baskets – were compiled. The *Tripitaka*, written in the Pali language, is different in content from the Sanskrit scriptures used by Mahayana and other schools. The use of Pali became one of the distinctive characteristics of Theravada, and its appearance in local inscriptions in a particular part of Southeast Asia is one of the few concrete tools we have for dating the spread of Sinhalese Buddhism through the region.

As mentioned in Chapter 2, it seems that both the Pyu and the Mon of the Dvaravati culture acquired Theravada directly from India several centuries before the Sinhalese variant arrived from Sri Lanka. By roughly the year 1000,

Sri Lanka had replaced India as the main source of Buddhist influences coming into Southeast Asia, because of the strength of Buddhism on the island as well as its decline in India at the expense of both Islam and Hinduism. Parts of the Hindu-Buddhist world began to adopt Sinhalese Theravada in the early eleventh century, and the process of conversion appears to have been complete by about 1400. Theravada never gained a foothold in the island world, and on the Malay peninsula it spread as far as the region to the south of present-day Nakhon Si Thammarat, but stopped at the territory now inhabited by the Malays. Once the latter began to convert to Islam, there developed a 'cultural frontier' between the two religions which would remain a geopolitical border as well – between Malay and Thai polities – until the early twentieth century.

Mahayana vs. Theravada: an overview

Although the split between Mahayana and Theravada originally concerned mainly the specific disciplines to be followed by monks, the core doctrines of the two branches evolved along very different lines, as did the practices which reflected these teachings. Mahayana, for example, venerates a number of different Buddhas and Bodhisattvas. 'Buddhahood' is in fact a state of existence which can be attained by more than one individual, and Mahayana has developed a pantheon of multiple Buddhas and Bodhisattvas with different roles. Theravada, by contrast, generally focuses on a single Buddha; although there is a widespread belief in a 'future Buddha' called Maitreya who will appear at some unspecified time, he is much less important than, say, the Amitabha Buddha who presides over the Western Paradise in Mahayana teachings.

The fundamental spiritual path to be followed by the believer also differs significantly. Mahayana and Theravada do, of course, share a core belief in reincarnation, the idea that after death one is reborn into another life. Both schools accept the Buddha's teaching that human existence is characterized by suffering stemming from attachment, that it is this attachment and suffering which drive the continued cycles of death and rebirth, and that only by achieving enlightenment can one be liberated from those cycles and reach the state known as Nirvana. Many Mahayana followers practice meditation and other spiritual disciplines in order to attain enlightenment, though many others will instead focus on reciting prayers and invocations of the Buddha's name in order to be reborn in the Western Paradise as an alternative to Nirvana. Theravada as it has come to be practiced, by contrast, tends to downplay enlightenment as a spiritual goal and to emphasize instead the making of merit to improve one's chances of a better life the next time around. Merit is accumulated by doing specific acts such as offering food to a monk, listening to a sermon, or being ordained as a monk oneself; *karma*, the balance of one's merit, will determine the conditions of one's rebirth in the next life. This is not to say that merit is of no significance for Mahayana, but in the latter it does not play the central role that it holds in the Theravada worldview.

A third difference between the two schools relates to Bodhisattvas, beings who are able to attain Buddhahood but choose not to in order to help others along their spiritual path. The most prominent Bodhisattva in East and

Southeast Asia is Guanyin, who represents a fusion of the male figure Avalokiteśvara in Indian Buddhism and a local female deity in Chinese culture. Although Guanyin has gained popularity among Theravada Buddhists in Thailand, with its large concentrations of ethnic Chinese, generally speaking she and other Bodhisattvas do not have an important place in the Theravada pantheon.

One of Theravada's most distinctive characteristics is the preponderant role of the *Sangha*. Monks and nuns are important figures in Mahayana as teachers and spiritual leaders, but many of the lay-person's acts of devotion – meditation, recitation of prayers, and so on – are performed either privately or in groups, without the need for the presence of an ordained individual. In Theravada, by contrast, many of the most important acts of merit-making directly involve monks and/or temples. For this reason monks in Theravada are sometimes referred to as 'fields of merit' because they are the main channel through which it is obtained. A brief period of ordination is a rite of passage for almost every male in the Theravada world, which is not the case for Mahayana.

A second, related characteristic of Theravada is the virtually complete absence of nuns. This was not always the case: women were ordained in the Buddha's time and continue to be so in most other schools of Buddhism. Most Theravada countries appear to have had female ordination at some point in their history, but the practice died out at different times in the various societies. There are women – often elderly – dressed in white who practice a higher degree of asceticism than most lay people, and they have sometimes been erroneously identified as 'nuns'. They are still lay-women, however, and do not enjoy the respect given to monks in their own culture or to nuns in Mahayana societies. Over the past few years, under the influence of feminism among Buddhist women, the practice of female ordination has been re-established, most notably in Sri Lanka. A few women from Southeast Asia have been ordained in this way, but this trend has met with considerable resistance from the male clergy, and so far their scope for ministry has been quite limited.

Theravada in Southeast Asian culture

The process of conversion to Theravada, whether earlier in its Indian form or later in its Sinhalese version, is largely unknown to us in terms of either its speed or its impact. This is partly because the change was not recorded in any contemporary sources and partly because so little is known about Southeast Asians' worldview during the Hindu-Buddhist period which preceded it. Did, for example, most people specifically identify themselves as 'Hindu' or 'Buddhist'? One of the few places where a clear alternation can be seen is among Angkorean rulers; in most other cases the two religions seem to have coexisted, as discussed in previous chapters. Even in the case of Cambodia it is difficult to imagine that the ruling class as a whole would have shifted their religious focus according to the faith of a particular king, though it is certainly possible that one or the other enjoyed greater prominence in specific reigns. For the 'average Southeast Asian' it is almost impossible to determine what he or she believed or understood in terms of religious doctrine.

Of the Theravada found among the Pyu and the Mon before the arrival of the Sinhalese version there is very little knowledge, and so our discussion will concentrate on the 'second wave', which became the predominant form of Buddhism in the mainland, replacing the Indian-derived variant where it was present. The group to be affected first would almost certainly have been the monkhood, for Theravada clearly set itself apart from other forms of Buddhism by its ordination. The legitimacy of the monkhood is derived from the correctness of its ordination procedures, and normally any religious reform is triggered by a change in ordination procedures. This has occurred several times in the history of Southeast Asian Buddhism, usually when monks from the mainland were exposed to new practices in Sri Lanka – generally a reformed method of ordination – and then brought these back to their native land. Once the ruler as the patron of the *Sangha* accepted and supported the new Sinhalese reform, there would be a massive round of reordinations. Not all monks accepted them, and in some cases the *Sangha* was split between new and old factions. In most cases, however, there was considerable pressure to conform to the royally supported reordination.

In the case of the initial arrival of Sinhalese Theravada early in the second millennium, it is likely that the rulers of various kingdoms found it appealing and supported the ordination and establishment of a new monkhood. Once a Theravada *Sangha* was in place, it would not have been difficult to propagate the new doctrines among a people already exposed to the teachings of Buddhism. Nor is it entirely certain that the change to Theravada was a 'top-down' process initiated by the elite; there may well have been initial conversions among the people. Royal sanction, though, would have accelerated and ultimately legitimized the process. However long the switch to Theravada may have taken, by the time it was completed, the Southeast Asian societies involved were affected from top to bottom.

It seems certain that conversion to Theravada did establish a clear 'Buddhist' identity for the Southeast Asians involved. The veneration of Hindu deities was not completely abandoned, but from now on the dominant religion was Theravada, and over time to be 'Burman', 'Thai', 'Lao', or 'Khmer' came to be equated with being Buddhist. Members of Theravada societies had the sense of being part of a wider Buddhist world, with cultural and psychological connections to Sri Lanka and ultimately to India. Most chronicles from the region begin with the history of Buddhism in India and connect that history seamlessly to their own past, often through prophecies uttered by the Buddha about future kingdoms to be established; such prophecies are often linked to stories of the Buddha flying to various parts of Southeast Asia. Thus the Burman, Thai, Lao, or Khmer past becomes embedded in a broader Buddhist framework.

While Theravada came to dominate the worldview of these peoples, it did not monopolize it. There were at least two important areas in which Buddhism continued to coexist with other belief systems. The first was court rituals, where in at least two cases – Cambodia and the Thai kingdom of Ayutthaya (Figure 13) and its successors – Brahmin priests continued to play a role. Court Brahminism was restricted to certain rituals – the consecration of a new ruler being the most important example – but in those particular ceremonies the role

Figure 13 Wat Phra Si Sanphet, Ayutthaya, fifteenth century

of the Brahmins was indispensable, and they could not be replaced by Buddhist monks. Brahmins were also involved with the use of the astrological system borrowed from India.

A second and more fundamental area in which Buddhism never crowded out existing beliefs was spirit worship. Any observer of local culture in Theravada societies will immediately be aware of the persistent strength of animist beliefs at all levels of society. Buddhism has generally been tolerant of spirit beliefs; while the occasional zealous ruler in Southeast Asian history has attempted to 'purify' his kingdom by suppressing animistic practices, no one has ever succeeded. It is generally argued that while Buddhism addresses the believer's concerns about the next life, it does not fully protect one against the risks present in this one. There are some intersection points between the two; Buddhist amulets and tattoos, for example, offer protection against misfortune and malevolent spirits. Monks (Figure 14), however, are generally not supposed to be directly involved with spirits, and the lay-person will have recourse to propitiatory ceremonies or the services of a spirit doctor or medium instead.

At the top stratum of society, Theravada brought both an ideology of Buddhist kingship and a specific model for interaction between the monarchy and the monkhood, which constituted the two most important institutions in a Theravada kingdom. The Sinhalese view of kingship did not differ dramatically from the earlier Indic models already in place in Southeast Asia, but it did become institutionalized in Theravada countries over the long term. The primary ideal was the *dhammaraja* or *dharma* king. *Dharma* (Sanskrit) or *dhamma* (Pali) refers to the teachings of Buddhism. A Theravada ruler was

Figure 14   Theravada monks, Cambodia

expected to demonstrate his adherence to these teachings and his patronage and protection for the religion within his kingdom. There was a specific list of qualities which he was supposed to embody, and a ruler who consistently failed to live up to these standards might raise serious questions about his legitimacy. As we have seen in previous chapters, for much of Southeast Asian history, ancestry and dynastic ties were never sufficient to guarantee a ruler's right to sit on the throne. Legitimacy was also defined in terms of one's *karma*, and either personal misfortune, immoral actions, natural disasters, or a combination thereof could undermine a ruler's claim to be the legitimate king.

This is not to say, of course, that all Theravada rulers led holy or saintly lives, any more than was the case for the 'Christian' crowned heads of Europe. They must, however, at least profess and demonstrate devotion to Buddhism, and their contacts with the *Sangha* were arguably the most important opportunity for them to do so. The relationship between the monarch and the monkhood is often viewed as a symbiotic one. On the one hand, the ruler needed to protect the *Sangha* and, more broadly, the Buddhist religion from harm and offer material support through his own merit-making and other forms of patronage. On the other hand, the monkhood played a part in buttressing the ruler's legitimacy through their acceptance of his offerings and their visible presence in his court. The most junior monk still outranked a king in spiritual terms, and even the most powerful ruler had to show proper deference to the

Sangha. Failure in this respect would not only be demeritorious, meaning that it would have a negative effect on one's *karma*, but it would also seriously jeopardize the king's standing as a proper Buddhist ruler.

At the village level, the monkhood was considerably more visible and ultimately more important than the monarchy. Unless a ruler happened to go into battle or embark on a royal tour, most of his subjects in rural areas were unlikely ever to lay eyes on him. They knew that he existed, of course, and the unseen monarch occupied the pinnacle of the kingdom's socio-political structure. In their day-to-day existence, however, the local monks loomed much larger in terms of both their importance and their influence. The temple would have been not only the locus of religious activity but also the social and cultural center as well – roles which have not been entirely displaced even today when local government is considerably more elaborate than was the case in earlier centuries. The monks themselves constituted an important part of the local elite, all the more since there was no group of local scholars such as those found in Vietnamese villages. The only schooling available in a Theravada village was offered by the temple.

It is important to understand the extent to which the culture of Theravada countries was permeated by Buddhism. Many of the written texts were copies of the Buddhist scriptures or other religious texts – such as the history of a particular statue or relic – and the historical chronicles as well were written within an explicitly Buddhist framework, as mentioned above. Outside of the royal palaces, there were no libraries except those found within temples. The most common works of art were the paintings on Buddhist themes found in temples and palaces and, of course, the statues of the Buddha himself, which combined artistic skill with their religious function. One of the most important sources of inspiration came from the *Jatakas*, a collection of stories about the Buddha's previous lives before his last incarnation, during which he attained enlightenment. These tales were expounded upon in sermons, repeated at festivals, and incorporated into paintings. What we might consider as 'secular' literature only appeared at a relatively recent date, although oral traditions certainly contained stories that were not explicitly religious.

Another important aspect of Theravada kingdoms which was constructed in Buddhist terms was law. The various Theravada societies of Southeast Asia produced a wide variety of laws and legal texts governing many different cases and situations. While these texts do incorporate values and punishments from the specific societies to which they belong, they are cast within a broader Buddhist framework. There are often references to the *Tripitaka* or the *Jatakas*, and the cosmology of rebirth based on *karma* and punishments in future lives is a core element. Some texts hearken back to the writings of Manu, depicted as a counselor to the first king, who is said to have written down the first legal code after finding it written in large letters at the edge of the universe. Like many other elements of Buddhism, the story of Manu is shared with Hinduism, but in the Theravada context the king he served was an ancestor of the Buddha himself, and in some texts the king and Manu become one and the same. Many legal texts were written by monks, while the authorship of others was credited to specific kings, since the ideal Buddhist ruler would have a strong sense of justice which entitled him to both adjudicate and legislate.

Both an individual's life-cycle and the yearly calendar have traditionally been structured around Buddhist holidays and other religious events. Arguably the most important event in a man's life, or that of his family, would be his ordination; this is also a chance for his female relatives to make merit by making his robes. At the village level, the year is structured around the agricultural cycle but also around the Buddhist calendar. The annual rainy season, for example, was traditionally a common time for men to be ordained, and the beginning and end of that season are both occasions for Buddhist festivals. The coronation of a new ruler in the capital might be celebrated, of course, but 'national' holidays with no religious significance only appeared in the twentieth century.

It is clear, then, that the arrival of Sinhalese Theravada was one of the most significant events in the history of Southeast Asia. A region extending from Yunnan in China through the Tai world and Cambodia to Burma now shared what Buddhist scholar Andrew Huxley has called a 'Pali cultural package'. This is not to say that the various Theravada cultures became identical, of course, but the core elements just discussed can be found throughout the region. At the same time, however, the transformation which helped to draw parts of Southeast Asia closer together also brought divisions. The Hindu-Buddhist world was sundered, as the Cham to the east and the Malay world to the south remained outside the boundaries of the Theravada sphere. Vietnam remained alien in many respects as well, and over the long term the differences between its Sinicized culture and the Theravada worldview of its western neighbors colored their relations. As the Malay world became progressively Islamized, it evolved in different directions as well, and the common cultural core once shared by much of Southeast Asia shrank considerably, though it did not disappear completely.

Islam

Islam rests upon seventh-century revelations in Arabic to the Prophet Muhammad, recorded in the *Qur'an*. The other canonical sources of religious knowledge are the Traditions (*hadith*) concerning the Prophet and his companions. Islam's most characteristic doctrine is its absolute monotheism, the doctrine of the unity of God (*tauhid*). The Confession of Faith proclaims that 'There is no God but God and Muhammad is the messenger of God'. The most heinous sin in Islam is *shirk*, ascribing partners to God, or polytheism. In Islam, God is transcendent. He created the world but did not enter into his creation. While humans have souls, they are not part of a divine soul: to suggest so would be *shirk*. Along with humankind, God also created angels. There will be a Day of Judgment when the dead will rise and the pious will enter Paradise, while the damned will go to Hell.

Islam sees itself as being the culmination of divine revelations to a long series of prophets of the Middle East, all of them true but incomplete until the final revelations to Muhammad. The recipients of these earlier revelations are the Jews and Christians – known as the 'people of the book'. The most developed area of Islamic culture is law. For Muslims, the *Qur'an* and *hadith* represent a full and final revelation. They must therefore convey all that is needed to regulate every aspect of individual and community life. Neither, however, is a clear set of laws. So rules for individuals and societies had to be deduced by Muslim scholars.

All humans are equal before God, so there are no priests with occult doctrines or powers in Islam. But there is a class of scholars (*ulama*) who are qualified to interpret Islam for its followers. Their considerations eventually produced four Orthodox (Sunni) – or Traditionalist – Schools of Law. As in all other religions, Muslim thinkers frequently disagreed among themselves. Islamic history is as full of conflict and violence over religious issues as that of any other faith. Its spread within Arabia and thence throughout the Middle East and into North Africa and India was often accompanied by violence – unlike in Southeast Asia, as will be seen below.

Muslims should implement the 'Five Pillars' of the faith: (1) the Confession of Faith; (2) five daily prayers in the direction of Mecca; (3) payment of alms; (4) fasting during the month of Ramadan; and (5) the pilgrimage to Mecca for those who can afford it. Islam soon developed further complexities, like all religions. From the early centuries, mysticism began to develop. Mystics (Sufis) were inspired more by the love of God than by the fear of God's judgments, which plays a major role in the *Qur'an*. Many legalistic *ulama* regarded Sufis as heretics, but by the twelfth century it was generally accepted that it was possible to be both a Sufi and an orthodox believer. A schism between Sunni and Shiite Islam, which arose in the early years of Islam, was never healed, but Shiism plays next to no role in Southeast Asian history.

Islamization and indigenization

We may be sure that Muslims were in contact with Southeast Asia from shortly after the time of the Prophet himself. Emissaries were sent to the court of China by the third of the Prophet's successors, the Caliph 'Uthman (644–56), and they must have reached there by sea through Southeast Asia. A community of Muslim traders several thousand strong was living in Canton in the ninth century and, again, must have got there through Southeast Asian waters.

Despite the reasonable presumption that Islam was represented in Southeast Asia by traders from an early time, so far no reliable evidence has been found of the conversion of Southeast Asians to Islam or of the foundation of Islamic states in the region until several centuries later. There is an eleventh-century Islamic gravestone for someone who was a daughter of a man named Maimun found in East Java, but this stone seems in fact to have been a gravestone from somewhere else that was reused as a ship's anchor, so it is irrelevant to the history of local Islamization. This time lapse before local conversions obviously calls for explanation.

Since Islamic ideas evidently traveled to Southeast Asia along the trade routes, it may seem natural to assume that traders were the main agents of conversion, but the delay in the founding of local Islamic communities raises analytical problems. If traders were the main bringers of Islam, why was it that locals evidently began converting to Islam only several centuries after traders had been traveling through Southeast Asia and – so we assume – necessarily pausing there for rest, to wait for favorable winds, or to trade locally? Why didn't this happen much sooner? Professor A. H. Johns proposed that the answer lay in the emergence of Sufism as a dominant form of Islam throughout the Muslim world from the thirteenth century, particularly after the fall of Baghdad to the Mongols in 1258. Since Southeast Asian religion before the coming of Islam was characterized by the mystical doctrines of Hinduism and Buddhism, it is easier to understand how locals might have been attracted to the new faith of Islam if it, too, was presented in a mystical form. This argument rests on only little direct evidence, but the chronology and logic are persuasive.

The earliest evidence so far known of a local Islamic community being founded comes from the northern part of Sumatra, the gravestone of one Sultan Sulaiman bin Abdullah bin al-Basir, who died in Lamreh in 1211. Then there is a gap until more gravestones mark the deaths of north Sumatran Islamic rulers from the late thirteenth century onwards. The first of these is the grave of Sultan Malik al-Salih of Samudra, who died in 1297. When the Venetian traveler Marco Polo visited north Sumatra in 1292, he noted the presence of Muslims in some places. The Moroccan visitor Ibn Battuta visited Samudra in 1345–46 and reported that the ruler followed the Shafi'i school of Islamic law, which remains the dominant school throughout Southeast Asia today.

We should note that in these early stages of Islamization, two processes probably took place, although they are reasonably well documented only in the case of Java. On the one hand, foreign Muslims settled down in Southeast Asia so that they and their descendants became locals; this was Islamization by settlement. On the other hand, local people embraced the new religion and became Muslims; this was Islamization by conversion. It is important to note that there is no evidence of any armed force from outside Southeast Asia imposing the new faith in the region, so here Islam did not spread as the result of external conquest, as happened in many parts of the Middle East, Africa, and Central and South Asia.

Based on archeological evidence, it is believed that an Islamic state was founded in Terengganu, on the eastern side of the Malay peninsula, in the fourteenth century. The evidence is a stone edict introducing elements of Islamic law into the local society, but because the date given at the end of the stone seems to be incomplete, the precise date is uncertain. The possible range is between 1302 and 1387. In Brunei in northern Borneo the gravestone of a ruler has been found who used both Arabic (*Sultan*) and Sanskrit (*Maharaja*) titles, reflecting the hybrid heritage of the area.

In East Java are preserved some particularly intriguing gravestones. These are found in the graveyards of Trawulan and Tralaya, near the site of the pre-Islamic kingdom of Majapahit. While these are undoubtedly the graves of Muslims, they are dated in the Hindu *Śaka* era and use Old Javanese rather than Arabic numerals for the years (Figure 15). So here again is seen the hybridity of culture in the early stages of Islamization. The series of these stones begins with one dated 1368–69 and extends into the fifteenth century. Perhaps the most remarkable thing about these stones, as analyzed by the great French scholar Louis-Charles Damais, is that their decorations suggest strongly that these were the graves of members of the Javanese elite, perhaps even members of the

Figure 15 Fragment of a Trawulan gravestone, with the date in Old Javanese numerals
Śaka 1338 (CE 1416–17)

Majapahit royal family. So the first evidence of conversions among the Javanese – the largest ethnic group among Southeast Asia's Muslims – suggests conversions starting at the very top of society. This is relevant to speculations about the reasons for local conversions, for it is easier to picture mystically inclined Hindu-Buddhist Javanese aristocrats being converted by magic-wielding Sufis than by down-to-earth traders.

Further Islamic states were founded in the region in the course of the fifteenth and early sixteenth centuries, as evidenced by surviving gravestones. At the very tip of north Sumatra, Aceh was established as an Islamic kingdom in the early sixteenth century; it would become one of the most important players in Indonesian history down to the present day. Aceh's first major Sultan died in 1530.

There was once an Islamic gravestone, now lost, of a local ruler from near Jolo, in the Philippines' Sulu archipelago; it was dated 1310, so we may presume that Islamic conversions or the settlement and indigenization of foreign Muslims was happening across much of the Malay-Indonesian area, even though we have no evidence of that for most of the region. The legends of the southern Philippines tell of Islam being brought there by Arabs and by Malay people from the western archipelago. How reliable these legends are is hard to judge, but it is reasonable to accept that local people who converted to

Islam would sometimes feel motivated to take their new faith to other parts of Southeast Asia.

The picture we have of this early stage of Islamization is of course fragmentary, dependant upon gravestones that happened to survive and occasionally on a traveler's report. From the early sixteenth century, however, we have an invaluable survey of the whole Malay-Indonesian area by an astute Portuguese visitor named Tomé Pires. He was in Melaka in 1512–15, just after its 1511 conquest by the Portuguese (to be discussed below). He visited Java and Sumatra himself and collected reports from others about the rest of the region.

According to Pires, most rulers in Sumatra were by then Muslims, but the southern tip and western coast of Sumatra were not. West Java was still Hindu, but central and east Java's north coast was Islamized; the states there were often at war with the still-Hindu king in the interior, where a rump of Majapahit still existed in Kediri (east Java). On Java's north coast Pires saw the two processes described here: both Islamization of local people and Javanization of foreign Muslims who settled there. Thus were the roots laid of a culture that was both Javanese and Islamic. In Kalimantan (Borneo), Brunei alone was Islamized; other states were still pre-Islamic, as were the islands along the chain from Bali to the east. But in Maluku – the 'spice islands' that so attracted the interest of Europeans – Islam was spreading from the rulers downwards.

The impact of Islam seems to have varied from place to place in the Malay-Indonesian area. In Java, where a Hindu-Buddhist 'high culture' is well documented for centuries before the coming of Islam, there was a process of cultural hybridization at work, such that Islamic Javanese culture retained strong pre-Islamic features. In most Malay-speaking areas of Sumatra, the Malay peninsula, and coastal regions throughout the archipelago, however, Islam seems to have made a greater impact in these early years. This difference is reflected in the use of scripts, for example: most Javanese documents down to the mid-twentieth century – except for some specifically religious works – were written in Javanese script, which derived from prior Indian-derived scripts and is similar to those used in Thai or Burmese. Malay, by contrast, was written in Arabic script. In the case of Bali, which shared the Old Javanese Hindu-Buddhist culture of Java, cultural barriers were such that the Balinese refused Islamization and have retained their Hindu culture down to today. We must recognize that Islamization was a process, not an event, and it continues still, as Islam seeks deeper roots and greater influence in Muslim societies – in which respect it is of course like other religions. For the earlier centuries, this process of Islamization is best documented in the case of Javanese society.

Sixteenth-century manuscripts survive showing that orthodox mystical (Sufi) Islam was being spread in Java at that time. One such manuscript, however, denounces Islamic heresies at length and leads to the suspicion that the proselytizers of Islam in Java saw plenty around them that seemed heretical. Another text of uncertain date, but certainly from some time and place where Islam was just spreading in a previously Hindu society – possibly even as late as the late eighteenth century in East Java – draws firm boundaries between Islam and pre-Islamic practices and between Muslims and non-Muslims. Tomé Pires reported that Javanese Muslims honored Hindu-Buddhist ascetics, of whom there were still many in Java in the early sixteenth century. These two sources are not necessarily contradictory: Pires may have seen and reported a common hybrid phenomenon, which the author of the Javanese text also saw, but roundly condemned.

Sultan Agung (r. 1613–46) – whose state-building on behalf of the Mataram dynasty will be discussed in Chapter 7 – is seen as the greatest reconciler of Javanese and Islamic identities. Until his time, the court (*kraton*) in Java retained many pre-Islamic practices. Its calendar, for example, remained the Indian *Śaka* calendar. In the early years of his reign, Agung does not seem to have altered such traditions. But in the 1630s he faced a rebellion evidently led by religious figures and centered on Tembayat, the holy grave-site of the reputed Islamizer of south-central Java, Sunan Bayat. Agung brutally crushed the rebels but then, in 1633, made a pilgrimage to Tembayat, building there a memorial gateway that still stands (Figure 19). He is said to have communed with the spirit of Sunan Bayat. Around the time of his pilgrimage, he also introduced a hybrid calendrical system that was based on the Islamic lunar calendar and introduced some major works of Islamically inspired literature to courtly culture (discussed further below).

Over subsequent years, Javanese sources confirm that the dominant form of religious life in Java was what has been called a 'mystic synthesis'. Within a generally Sufi style of Islam, the 'mystic synthesis' had three characteristic features: (1) a strong sense of Islamic identity – to be Javanese was, for most Javanese, to be a Muslim; (2) carrying out of the ritual 'Five Pillars' of Islam; and (3) nevertheless, an acceptance of the reality of local spirits. Thus, even devout people are recorded as accepting the reality of the Goddess of the Southern Ocean, the spirit of Mount Lawu, local village spirits, and so on.

Religious life in other areas of Muslim Southeast Asia is less well recorded – or in some cases less well researched – in the period before the nineteenth century and modern reform movements. But similar sorts of compromises and syntheses must have been widely found.

Islamic period literatures

Muslim Southeast Asia inherited literary traditions from at least three sources: indigenous traditions, Indian-derived Hindu-Buddhist traditions, and Islamic traditions. Out of this mix came a literary culture of great complexity, variety, and vitality.

One quite essential technological advance came with Islam: the bound book of paper pages. Prior to this time, indigenous works were mainly written on palm-leaves or inscribed on some harder material such as bone or stone. The former does not usually last very long in the tropical climate and its technology is rather laborious. Preparation of the palm-leaves into writing material takes time and effort. Writing is inscribed on the leaf, ink is rubbed over the leaf so that it fills the inscribed writing, and the ink is then wiped off leaving the dark ink only in the depressions made by the inscribed text. Stone and bone are harder to inscribe, but may last a great deal longer. Stone inscriptions can last for centuries in favorable circumstances, but it is hard to imagine writing a major work of literature on stone. And you certainly couldn't carry such a work from place to place. With Islam came the book, with all of its portability, ease of writing, capacity for containing voluminous works of literature, and relative durability – depending on the quality of the paper and binding, of course. So the book was among the things that facilitated the flowering of a rich literary culture in Islamized Southeast Asia.

The other innovation that seems probably to have come with Islamic culture is the writing of works of history. Historical studies were well developed in Arabic culture but are almost entirely unknown from pre-Islamic maritime Southeast Asia. While it is not certain that history-writing was little developed before Islam, certainly the chronicles that we now know of are from the Islamic period. We may generally divide the literary traditions of Islamized Southeast Asia into two large classes based on language: Malay and Javanese.

Literature in Malay was dominant in the western part of the Indonesian-Malay area and throughout the coastal regions of the rest of the archipelago, except for Java. Malay literature was typically written in Arabic script and in prose, although there was also some Malay writing in verse. Malay literature produced new versions of pre-Islamic classics such as the *Ramayana* to produce the Malay-language *Hikayat Seri Rama* or the *Mahabharata* to produce the Malay *Hikayat Pandawa Jaya*. But much of Malay literature was directly inspired by Islamic legends and teachings. Persian inspiration is seen in the work 'The Crown of Kings' (*Mahkota segala Raja-raja*, also known as *Taj as-Salatin*). The stories about 'the two-horned' (Alexander the Great) from the *Qur'an* inspired the Malay *Hikayat Iskandar Dhulkarnain*, while *Hikayat Amir Hamza* was a romantic story derived from Persian legends about the Prophet's uncle. From sixteenth- and seventeenth-century Aceh came very major works of Sufi teachings associated with a group of mystics whose disagreements became bitter and bloody: three indigenous Sumatrans – Hamzah Pansuri, Syamsuddin of Pasai, and Abdurrauf of Singkil – and the most prolific of the four, the Gujarati Nuruddin ar-Raniri.

Malay authors also wrote major historical chronicles about the kingdoms and rulers of the region. *Sejarah Melayu* not only told the story of the kingdom of Melaka, but also depicted standards of courtly Malay Muslim culture that were taken as authoritative throughout the Malay-dominated parts of the archipelago. The *Hikayat Aceh* tells of Aceh in the time of Sultan Iskandar Muda (r. 1607–36) and seems to have been inspired by the Persian *Akbarnama* in praise of the Mogul emperor Akbar (r. 1555–1606).

Javanese literature, while also much inspired by Islamic ideas, nevertheless is significantly different from Malay. Whereas there is very little known about pre-Islamic Malay literature, there is a major body of Old Javanese literature, mainly inspired by Indian classics such as the *Mahabharata* and *Ramayana*. This Old Javanese tradition had an abiding influence on Islamic-period Javanese (or 'Modern Javanese') literature. Indeed, Old Javanese literature seems to have been studied and written in the courts of Java at least into the eighteenth century, and is still preserved in Bali. We see continuing Old Javanese influence in such Modern Javanese translations of these pre-Islamic works as *Serat Rama* (from *Ramayana*), *Serat Bratayuda* (from *Bharatayuddha*), and *Serat*

Mintaraga (from *Arjunawiwaha*). Most Modern Javanese literature continued to be written in Javanese (rather than Arabic) script and employed verse rather than prose.

There were, however, also many new departures in Modern Javanese literature. Notably, chronicles (*babad*) began to be compiled. There are many of these about various kingdoms, historical periods or episodes. Some are very voluminous. The great *Babad Tanah Jawi* (History of the Land of Java) written in the court of Surakarta in 1836 is 18 volumes in its original manuscript.

Religious works from other parts of the Islamic world were also produced in Javanese versions and many works of mysticism were locally inspired. Sometimes such works were written in Arabic script. Some of the Malay-language works of the Acehnese mystics referred to above were turned into Javanese versions. Legendary heroes of Islam such as Joseph and Amir Hamza also were told of in lengthy Javanese verse romances. Javanese literature sometimes carried spiritual power. It seems clear that the major works of Islamically inspired literature that Sultan Agung caused to be introduced to courtly culture in the 1630s – notably *Carita Sultan Iskandar, Serat Yusuf,* and *Kitab Usulbiyah* – were believed to be magically powerful a century later. So also was a late eighteenth-century work *Kangjeng Kyai Surya Raja*, composed in 1774 by the crown prince who would later become Sultan Hamengkubuwana II of Yogyakarta (r. 1792–1810, 1811–12, 1826–28).

Other Islamized ethnic groups of the Malay-Indonesian area also had their own literatures. The literatures of the Bugis and Makasarese of South Sulawesi were notable for extensive and detailed chronicles and for diaries kept by monarchs and other members of the elite – a form of literature not known until very recent times elsewhere in the region.

Catholicism

Jesus of Nazareth is believed by Catholics to be the son of God and universal savior of humankind. The Catholic Church regards itself as the universal Church, upholding doctrines that apply across all times and cultures. In the mid-eleventh century, the Great Schism split Catholicism between the Western (Latin) and Eastern (Orthodox) branches, but it is only the former that was of significance in Southeast Asia. This is most commonly known as the Roman Catholic Church, referring to the head of the church hierarchy, the Pope (or Pontiff), who reigns in the Vatican City State in Rome. Catholicism is the only major world religion which has such a hierarchical structure. The Pontiff serves as the head of a hierarchy of bishops, whom he appoints. They administer dioceses, a divisional unit comprised of parishes in each of which is a church led by a priest.

Catholic priests do not marry and remain celibate. Parish priests are called 'secular' clergy. There are also religious orders of men – known as 'regular' clergy or 'friars' – and women (nuns). They are fairly independent, receiving minimal assistance from the Church for subsistence. Renowned for their missionary zeal and scholasticism, they run missions, hospitals, schools, and colleges.

According to the Catholic doctrine of apostolic succession, the Pontiff, the bishops, and the clergy are heirs to the spiritual authority that Jesus dispensed to his disciples, led by the apostle Peter. The scripture and traditions of the 'Church fathers', handed down and interpreted by bishops with the Pope's blessing, are the primary sources of faith.

In Catholicism, God is omnipotent, omniscient, and omnipresent. He has created the world but also ceaselessly takes an interest in believers. Everyone has an immortal soul, which, following death, is destined for Heaven or Hell on the basis of her or his actions in life. Catholics believe in the Trinity of God, Jesus, and the Holy Spirit, and in the resurrection of the dead. They venerate the Virgin Mary and other saints and remember the dead in Purgatory, which is a sort of intermediate location from which souls may eventually proceed to Heaven. Throughout their lives they atone for their sins by going to confession and doing penance, and may be granted absolution by a priest. During the Lenten Season, Catholics worship God by sacrificing their material needs through fasting and/or abstinence.

Catholic evangelization and indigenization

Chapter 6 below discusses the events that led the Portuguese and Spanish to Southeast Asia. By the early sixteenth century, the Spanish were making their first attempts to establish themselves in the Philippines, while the Portuguese were in the process of conquering the great Malay trading port of Melaka. Both had their eyes on the 'spice islands' of eastern Indonesia and each thought the other to be an interloper.

Not surprisingly, they turned to the Pope to answer the question of who had what rights and where in the newly discovered parts of the world. Neither the Pope, the Spanish, nor the Portuguese, of course, actually knew very much about where those 'spice islands' were on the other side of the globe, since knowledge of longitude was very poor in this age.

A 1493 ruling by Pope Alexander VI and the treaties of Tordesillas (1494) and Saragossa (1529) added a religious dimension to this competition by dividing the world into two spiritual jurisdictions. Portugal was to take charge of converting 'heathens' and building churches and monasteries in one half of the world (reached by sailing east from Europe) and Spain assumed responsibilities in the other half (reached by sailing west). The two monarchs were to have extensive authority over the Church in their respective hemispheres: this created the so-called *padroado/patronato real* (royal patronage). Whereas the *patronato* gave the Iberian crowns jurisdiction over the Church, in 1522 another Pope, Adrian VI, allowed the religious orders to disregard monarchical restrictions and to move freely in the new territories.

In accordance with the *patronato*, priests accompanied every Portuguese or Spanish expedition. After conquering Melaka (1511), the Portuguese started exploring eastern Indonesia. In 1534, as Portuguese trader Gonzalo Veloso settled in northern Halmahera, his compatriot the priest Simon Vaz – destined to become Indonesia's first Catholic martyr – won the first conversions in eastern Indonesia. His example was followed by zealous members of different religious orders. In this respect the Jesuits, renowned for their martial missionary discipline, were notable. One of their founders, Francis Xavier, purportedly worked miracles throughout the region, teaching thousands the rudiments of the Catholic faith. Another order, the Dominicans, thoroughly transformed Larantuka on Flores and Dili on Timor into centers of Catholic life. By the late sixteenth century, one-fifth of their 150,000 residents had been baptized. To what extent they identified themselves as Catholics or whether they would have been recognized as Catholics in contemporary Europe is open to question.

Over the following two and a half centuries the spread of Catholicism in eastern Indonesia slowed dramatically, as other powers challenged the Portuguese in the region. In 1575 the Sultan of Ternate ransacked their fortress and mission base there. In 1605 the VOC took Ambon from the Portuguese. In areas under its control, the Company banned Catholicism and promoted the Calvinist form of Protestantism (see below) instead. Nonetheless, some missions persevered. In Flores and Timor, Portuguese priests continued to work until 1772, their success limited by their small numbers, the lack of local clergy, and linguistic barriers between the friars and local people. Local religious rituals and ideas were absorbed into Catholic practices and doctrines.

Evangelization was markedly more successful in the Philippines. Under the Spanish *patronato*, the Magellan expedition (see Chapter 6) took the first steps. As recalled by the chronicler Antonio Pigafetta, the Spanish fleet was welcomed in northeast Mindanao by the tatoo-covered chief of Butuan and Caraga, Rajah Kolambu. Magellan convinced the *rajah* of the peaceful nature of his expedition and impressed local inhabitants with the pageantry of Spanish Catholicism. On Easter Sunday his chaplain celebrated the mass to the deafening sound of Spanish artillery. The Spaniards planted and did obeisance to a wooden cross on the highest spot on the island, proclaiming that the islanders now enjoyed the protection of Catholic Spain. Future Spanish ships would hence not harm the islanders or their property. The Spaniards added that the cross even secured inhabitants from thunder, lightning, and destructive storms.

This strategy of instilling awe and fear was repeated in a larger settlement of Cebu. Rajah Humabon received the foreigners, sealing his friendship with their leader through a blood compact. To ease diplomatic relations Humabon displayed an interest in the Spanish religion. Overjoyed by the possibility of conversion, Magellan enlightened him about basic Catholic precepts. Catholicism, he claimed, enjoyed the protection of Spanish arms and those who accepted it would be treated like Europeans. He promised that after baptism, Cebuanos would be given suits of armour and would no longer be haunted by demons.

Humabon was baptized as 'Don Carlos', after the Spanish Emperor Charles V; his subjects followed suit. Humabon's wife was presented with a statue of the *Santo Niño* (Holy Infant). In three months 1200 baptisms were conducted. Magellan urged them to burn their idols, for worship should be directed at the wooden cross on the island. A misunderstanding about accepting Catholicism soon emerged. Pigafetta wrote that locals celebrated baptisms by holding religious sacrifices led by priestesses (*babaylanes*), with ceremonial dance, drink, exhaltation of the sun and slaughter of a hog. This apparent indigenization of Catholicism hardly bothered the *conquistadores*.

To extend Spanish influence in the Visayas, Magellan demanded that the chiefs of nearby settlements recognize the primacy of Humabon/Don Carlos. Two obeyed; two did not. The Spaniards burned the latter's villages, forcing one chief to surrender. The second, Datu Lapu-lapu, remained undeterred; he and 2000 fighters met Magellan and his coterie on the shore. The low tide kept the Spanish fleet distant, rendering their cannon, musketeers, and crossbowmen ineffectual. Magellan and seven others were killed while another 26, including Pigafetta, were wounded. Two ships escaped but only one, the *Victoria*, in the end managed to return to Spain in 1522.

Despite this defeat, Spain persisted in the region. The possibilities of securing spices and precious metals encouraged the Crown to send more expeditions: those led by Juan Jofre de Loaisa (1525), Alvaro de Saavedra (1527), Ruy Lopez de Villalobos (1542) – who named the islands 'Las Filipinas', after Prince Phillip II – and Miguel Lopez de Legazpi (1564). The last successfully established an ongoing Spanish presence and laid the foundations for Catholicism in the archipelago. In 1565 it landed in Samar, eastern Visayas, to be greeted by a hostile populace.

Near Bohol, de Legazpi overpowered a Muslim trading junk. The captives provided a wealth of information. They reported that other junks, owned by Manila Muslims, regularly traded gold, wax, slaves, and silk in the region. The Spaniards were also informed that they could find abundant supplies in Cebu, whose inhabitants continually refused Islam. Finally, the captives reported that from Ternate the Portuguese had been launching destructive raids against the central Visayas. Evidently the locals there – not surprisingly – construed the newly arrived Spaniards as Portuguese, hence their deep resentment. Armed with this information, Legazpi invited the local chiefs, Datu Sikatuna and Datu Sigala, aboard his flagship *San Pedro*. Painstakingly he persuaded the leaders of the honest intentions of Spain in the Philippines. Their blood compact would later be used to signify an enduring connection between the Spanish and Filipino nations.

Cebu was more difficult for the Spaniards. Hundreds of warriors, inspired by Lapu-Lapu's resistance, met them there; Rajah Tupas defied offers of friendship. Incensed, the Spaniards bombarded the shores with gunfire, set local bamboo-and-nipa (palm thatch) settlements on fire, and forced inhabitants to flee to the hills. On 8 May 1565 Legazpi claimed the island in the name of Spain. Among other religious relics his crew found the statue of the *Santo Niño* given to Humabon's wife. The Catholic *conquistadores* took this discovery as divine encouragement.

Hungry and embattled, the *conquistadores* nevertheless had to flee Cebu in 1569 and sail northeast, towards Panay. Here they finally found momentary refuge, providing Legazpi with the opportunity to send significant missions to the north. In 1570 Captain Martin de Goiti and a crew of 120 men and 15 boats of Visayan allies attacked Manila. The Tagalog chief Rajah Soliman and his fighters defended their territory, but the Spaniards proved to be too strong. The seizure of the city and a sizable booty of gold prompted Legazpi to move from Panay to Manila. He was greeted with offers of peace by other chiefs who feared Soliman's fate. Legazpi then launched a relentless military campaign that ultimately conquered settlements along the coasts of Luzon and forced Muslims to retreat southwards to Palawan, Mindanao, and Sulu.

While the military paved the way, Catholicism completed its conquest of all but the southernmost islands of the archipelago. The missionary zeal of regular orders was crucial, trumping problems like local defiance, language gaps between the missionaries and communities, and lack of missionary manpower that plagued early evangelization efforts. Legazpi's pilot and chaplain, Fray Andres de Urdaneta, led the charge, along with five other Augustinian fathers. Drawing from missionary experiences in the Americas, the Augustinians delayed baptisms until the candidates demonstrated at least some evidence of Christian knowledge.

In 1569, after reinforcements from Mexico arrived, the Augustinians took Cebu under their wing and, remembering the image of the *Santo Niño* recovered there, called the new Spanish settlement *Santísimo Nombre de Jésus* (the Most Holy Name of Jesus). The friars then followed Legazpi to Panay. Displaying commitment and dedication, an Augustinian, Fray Juan de Alba, subsequently learned the Hiligaynon language to aid in converting the populace. Meanwhile the seizure of Manila prompted the friars also to proselytize in Luzon. Their eventual success heartened the Church to send more missionaries to the islands. Four orders joined the Augustinians: the Franciscans (1577), Jesuits (1581), Dominicans (1587), and Recollects (1606). They divided the archipelago into spiritual jurisdictions – the Augustinians and Dominicans took northern and central Luzon; the Franciscans, southern Luzon; the Jesuits, southern Visayas and Mindanao; and the Recollects, northeast Luzon, its northernmost islands, northern Visayas, Palawan, and Mindanao.

Missionization followed a regular pattern. Friars converted the local chief and his entourage, convinced that they would be followed by their constituencies. Friars then set up their mission, including a convent, church, and school. They provided children with pre-baptismal instruction, to ensure that future members of the community were Catholics and sympathetic towards the Spanish. To earn the trust of potential converts, friars eschewed Spanish and conducted catechism in the local languages. Of course translation was not always feasible: Latin and Spanish words for concepts such as God, the Holy Spirit, and grace were retained where they had no equivalents in the vernacular tongues. Visual aids complemented the teaching: depictions of a fiery hell instilled fear among converts, convincing them to remain faithful.

Steadily the number of baptisms rose. In the late sixteenth century half the population were baptized; in the late nineteenth, some 6.7 million or around 90 percent of the populace were considered by the Spanish to be Catholics. Instead of resting on their laurels, missionaries continually persevered to keep their flocks. Catechism was continued. Missionaries encouraged the chanting of prayers and sponsored elaborate annual processions in honor of a town's patron saint. The mystery and pageantry associated with such events attracted the populace to town centers where they were further indoctrinated. Violators of the dogma were shunned, corporally punished, or even put to death.

Nonetheless, Catholicism did not remain free of local influences. The persistence of local priestesses (*babaylanes*), the inadequate number of missionaries, and the lack of local priests led to insufficient learning (and so, improvization) of the faith among Catholics. For many Filipinos, conversion only meant placing the Catholic God alongside the traditional religious idols. Believers equated saints with spirits (*anitos* or *diwatas*), who were placated and cajoled for blessings and intercession. Inevitably syncreticism characterized religious practice. Sacraments were associated with curative and empowering rituals, while amulets and charms (*anting-anting*) that were customarily used to attract or ward off spirits were endowed with Christian trappings and so acquired a Catholic façade.

Catholic era literature

Unlike the literature in much of Southeast Asia, Catholic-era literature in the Philippines means printed literature, above all the material associated with the propagation of Catholicism. Printing was introduced in Manila in 1593. Through the xylographic (wood-block) method the Dominicans produced the *Doctrina cristiana* (Christian doctrine) in Tagalog, Spanish, Chinese, and Visayan along with the *Tratado de la Doctrina de la Santa Iglesia y de Ciencias naturales* (Treatise on the doctrine of the Holy Church and the natural sciences). *Doctrina*s outlined Christianity in the form of questions and answers and were used in conjunction with *confesionarios* (confessional pamplets) which were instrumental in keeping converts loyal to the Church. Cautiously altered across time, *doctrinas* and *confessionarios* signified the development of religious learning in the archipelago.

The so-called *arte* (grammar) and *vocabulario* (dictionary) also featured in this early literature. Volumes like San Buenaventura's dictionary of Tagalog (1613), Francisco Coronel's grammar of Pampango (1617), San Agustin's study of Tagalog (1703), and Francisco Encina's grammar of Cebuano (1758) prepared missionaries for work in their apostolates while also mapping the linguistic and cultural terrain in the Philippines.

Chronicles and histories like Pedro Chirino's *Relacion de las Islas Filipinas* (1610) and Juan de Plasencia's *Crónica de San Gregorio Magno de religiosos descalzos n.s. San Francisco en las Islas Filipinas* (1676) drew an ethnographic map of the islands. They witnessed the ways of local peoples and thus became indispensable to the writing of the country's history.

Protestantism

The Protestant Reformation began in early sixteenth-century Europe as an attempt to reform the Catholic Church, which critics saw as having corrupted the true teachings of Jesus. The first, symbolic step occurred when the German monk Martin Luther nailed his '95 theses' to the door of the church at Wittenberg in 1517, challenging basic ideas of the Catholic Church. Other critics joined his protests and soon the unity of the Christian Church in Western Europe collapsed in schisms. Protestants denied the authority of the Pope, rejected the idea that one could gain spiritual benefit through the purchase of indulgences, and condemned corruption in the Church hierarchy. For Protestants, the only true source of knowledge about Christian truths was the Bible, without the mediating authority of the Pope or of lesser priests whose rituals were claimed to create miracles, such as the conversion of wine and bread into the blood and body of Christ. For Luther and those who followed him, salvation was only possible through faith and all believers were equal before God.

For Southeast Asia, the most relevant form of Protestantism was not Lutheranism, but that founded by the French theologian John Calvin – most of whose life was spent in the Swiss city of Geneva – which became the foremost exemplar of what was called Reformed Christianity, or, more simply, Calvinism. His doctrines became dominant in, among other places, the northern part of the Netherlands, whereas Catholicism remained dominant in the southern provinces which broke away in 1830 to form the state of Belgium.

Calvin insisted upon the absolute sovereignty of God but this was of course within the defining Christian doctrine of the Trinity of God, Christ and Holy Spirit, so this absolute sovereignty differed from the uncompromising monotheism of Islam. Consistent with the idea of the omnipotence and omniscience of God, Calvinists adopted the idea of predestination. That is, God must know in advance who will be saved and who not, and the lives of the saved will carry signs in this world of their impending salvation: notably piety, sobriety, modesty, and hard work.

Calvinism suited the emerging bourgeois society of the Netherlands very well. Not surprisingly, those who became wealthy in this life saw it as a sign of divine favor and an indication of their impending salvation. When Dutch merchants founded the VOC in 1602, they saw it as an act of faith as well as an act of commerce. But whereas Dutch merchants at home lived that life of public modesty and sobriety that marked the elect, in Southeast Asia Dutch Protestants adapted quickly to opportunities for other lifestyles. The Governor-General of the VOC, Jan Pietersz Coen, famously observed that 'Our nation must drink or die'. Drunkenness was indeed very common among VOC servants in the tropics. As were corruption, violence, and early death from disease. VOC Europeans, many of whom were not Dutch by origin, often lived with indigenous women and some adopted hybrid or even fully local lifestyles. A few are known to have converted to Islam and thereby become indigenized. John Calvin would not have approved.

Protestant conversion

If the Dutch founders of the VOC thought they were doing God's work – which was also expected to bring them profits – in Southeast Asia they refrained from attempting to spread their faith. The VOC restricted the activities of Dutch ministers and allowed no proselytization among Muslims. The Company hired Calvinist ministers solely to look after the religions needs of the European Protestants whom it employed. No free-lance missionizing was tolerated.

The only significant conversion activity undertaken by the VOC concerned local people in East Indonesia who had already been converted to Catholicism by the Portuguese. In 1605 the VOC took Ambon from the Portuguese. There the Jesuit Francis Xavier had laid the foundations for Catholic mission activity and by the beginning of the seventeenth century there were probably around 60,000 indigenous Catholics there. But for the VOC, with its Dutch roots reaching back to the Protestant Reformation and the wars of religion still going on in Europe, Roman Catholicism was a greater enemy than Islam. So while the VOC had no interest in converting Muslims, it was determined that these Indonesian Catholics should become Calvinists. Portuguese priests were expelled from Ambon and the locals were converted to Protestantism. Down to today Ambonese society remains partly Protestant and partly Muslim.

The VOC's aversion to allowing Protestants to spread their faith remained throughout the Company's history. In the nineteenth century, however, after the VOC had gone bankrupt, its interests had been taken over by the Netherlands government and Christian parties became influential in that government, Dutch policy would change. First Protestant and then, late in that century, even Roman Catholic missionaries would be allowed to operate in Indonesia. Even in the nineteenth and early twentieth centuries, however, the Dutch colonial government often viewed these missionaries with concern and dislike, fearing that they would precipitate antagonism among Muslims that could endanger the stability of the colonial regime.

5

The Rise of New States from the Fourteenth Century

Introduction

Just as the religions discussed in the preceding chapter changed the long-term religious landscape of Southeast Asia, so also new states set the scene for the centuries ahead. Sometimes consolidating empires brought together disparate states under a new hegemony. Elsewhere, kingdoms that had previously loomed large declined and collapsed, often in the face of rising new competitor states.

As has been repeatedly emphasized above, in these centuries – before the communications revolution that began in the nineteenth century – it was typically quite difficult for a central monarch to control the outlying areas of the realm. Only in the case of Vietnam was there anything like a centralized, hierarchical bureaucratic structure to govern the state. Elsewhere, loyalties were often grounded in cultural allegiances, in the belief that the monarch was somehow superhuman and that lesser lords under the ruler reflected that superhumanity in lesser ways. Much of what we would now call 'governing' was done through networks and hierarchies of relationships rather than through an 'administration'.

Kingdoms were also governed by threat and fear. Behind the cultural and religious pretensions of Southeast Asian monarchs in this period, there lay 'hard' power. If there should be an outlying lord who paid obeisance to the spiritual superiority of the king, but who might, for example, neglect to pay a portion of the taxes he raised to the center, it was important that the king could send an armed force to compel more genuine subservience.

The geopolitical realties of the region influenced the ability to mobilize power. For much of the year, it was possible to move large forces up and down the wide river valleys of Southeast Asia: those of the Irrawaddy, Chao Phraya, Mekong, and Red rivers on the mainland, and the Brantas and Solo in Java. Here population was relatively dense and communications relatively easy. Where armed forces could move, so could trade. So these valleys could support substantial populations, considerable wealth, and powerful kingdoms. Similarly, across the shallow waters of the Straits of Melaka and the Java Sea it was relatively easy to move military forces by sea for much of the year. So kingdoms located in Sumatra, Malaya, south Kalimantan, and the north coast of Java often sought to extend their sway across those bodies of water, more than they sought to control the difficult hinterlands behind them.

Elsewhere topography and hence state-building was more challenging. The Salween river is long but flows mostly through deep gorges rather than a wide valley. The rivers of the Malay peninsula are short and difficult to navigate, as are most of the coastal rivers elsewhere in the archipelago. So communications and political control up and down such river valleys was more difficult than in places served by the navigable waterways.

Everywhere in Southeast Asia, however favorable topography might be, putting and keeping a state together was a formidable challenge. Countervailing forces were everywhere and the population was often mobile. If there was too much hardship and oppression, eventually ordinary people could abandon even a 'god-king' and walk or sail elsewhere, undermining the very foundations of the kingdom. No people meant no taxes and no army, and that meant no state.

Burma, c.1300–1752

Fragmentation and unification, c.1300–1550

Pagan's decline in the late thirteenth and early fourteenth centuries resulted in the fragmentation of this 'classical' community and the emergence of four smaller realms. The first of these occupied the hills northeast of the former capital inhabited by the newly arrived Shan, an ethnic group which was among the Tai communities that had been migrating into the mainland from their homeland in the present Sino-Vietnamese border area for the past few centuries. Closely coinciding with the arrival of the Shan was the founding of Ava, the second of these smaller realms, in 1364–65 as the new capital of the region we now call Upper Burma, continuing many of the traditions of Pagan through the lineage of three royal brothers. The relationship between this loosely connected polity and its Shan neighbors was as much contentious as cooperative. Frequent fighting between the two contributed to political fragmentation in Upper Burma. At the same time, Burmese literary traditions, patterns of donation to the religious sector, and trade networks provided links between the hill regions and the lowlands, suggesting that Ava's presence was a significant stabilizing factor in the Upper Burma region. A third, relatively autonomous realm emerged in the western zone of Arakan. No longer able to sustain control over this area, Ava recognized Mrauk-U, the political center of Arakan, as an independent polity rather than as a vassal of the Upper Burma court. Finally, Lower Burma began to assert its influence as the Mon kingdom of Ramanna was able to take advantage of Upper Burma's weakened power. Ramanna was insulated from Shan incursions and benefited from proximity to the growing maritime trade.

Of the four realms, Arakan's political and economic trajectory was aligned most closely with the commercial dynamics of the Bay of Bengal and the growing Islamic trade networks, even though the Arakanese shared linguistic and cultural traditions with Upper Burma. With its long coastline and protective mountain ranges on its eastern flank, Arakan adopted Buddhist and later Islamic models to suit its needs. Arakanese kings both patronized Buddhist temples and incorporated Islamic styles of authority, which was no doubt necessary as Mrauk-U increased its regional influence between 1430 and the 1450s. Despite its somewhat peripheral position, Mrauk-U was aggressive towards rival polities, first conquering Prome to the east and then Chittagong, the chief port of eastern Bengal, to the west in the first half of the 1500s. Geographic location, then, did not isolate Arakan completely from the patterns and processes characterizing the greater Irrawaddy river zone; it maintained diplomatic relations with emerging courts and adopted familiar cultural and political models of both Upper and Lower Burma, while at the same time being attuned to the rhythms of Islamic India.

While in a political sense local-level polities along the Irrawaddy and surrounding regions were exerting greater autonomy, these same communities were experiencing a growing cultural connectedness through the spread of Burman values, language, and literature. Perhaps due to southward migrations of Burmese speakers drawn to the maritime opportunities in places such as Prome and Toungoo, Burmese literature in the form of chronicles and Buddhist texts spread in areas normally occupied by Mon-speakers. By the late fifteenth and early sixteenth centuries, chronicles began to be circulated by traveling monks seeking patronage from local rulers who wanted to purify the standard of the monks in their domains, thereby themselves becoming *dhammarajas* (kings of the Buddhist law, a concept associating leadership with notions of Buddhist legitimacy).

The emergence of the Shan as new players had significant economic ramifications for those interior economies that were closer to the coasts in Lower Burma. Shan raids into the lowlands of Upper Burma disrupted existing trade networks, forcing southward migrations that benefited *parvenu* polities to the south that were still hungry for cultivators and traders. With their influx into Lower Burma, cultivation of new lands increased from around 300,000 acres (some 120,000 ha) in the 1350s to nearly 1,000,000 acres (approx. 400,000 ha) by the early 1500s. Along with the increased rice cultivation, cotton became attractive as an alternative crop in dry soils, providing communities in Lower Burma with a commodity that would eventually travel northward to China through Yunnan. Cotton, spices, gems, and salt would be traded up the Irrawaddy for goods such as iron, copper vessels, weapons, tea, silk, and silver that would be transported on the return leg from China. Lower Burma thus emerged as an inter-regional trade hub serving markets in China, India, and insular Southeast Asia.

If the period from the mid-fourteenth through the mid-fifteenth centuries was a time of fragmentation for the communities situated along the Irrawaddy river valley, the late fifteenth and early sixteenth centuries brought unification and intensive integration as the political center of gravity shifted southward towards Toungoo. Toungoo was particularly well suited to inherit the legacy of unification left by Pagan. It was predominantly Burman in ethnicity, having welcomed those who had migrated southwards, getting away from the instabilities caused by Shan raids in Upper Burma and seeking economic opportunities in Lower Burma. Charismatic leadership seemed also to characterize Toungoo. It had already begun to expand its territory in the 1350s with an attack on Kyaukse, the breadbasket of Upper Burma, which was nominally subject to the much weaker Ava court in the north. By the late fifteenth century, under Mingyinyo (r. 1486–1531), Toungoo launched an aggressive campaign of expansion that continued into the sixteenth century. Like the earlier Pagan kings, Mingyinyo devoted state resources to the reclamation of new lands and the refurbishment of irrigation works. In direct competition with Upper Burma's Ava, the king founded new 'exemplary centers' in 1491 and again in 1510, suggesting that the political, cultural, and economic balance had indeed tipped towards Toungoo.

The policy of expansion that had been established by Mingyinyo was continued by his son and successor Tabinshweihti (r. 1531–50) who concentrated on solidifying Toungoo's base of power in Lower Burma. He was perhaps already aware of the commercial potential of the coast. Tabinshweihti finally captured the crucial Mon port-city of Pegu in 1539 with the aid of Muslim mercenaries and formally established it as the capital of the new Toungoo dynasty.

Tabinshweihti's successor, Bayinnaung (r. 1551–81), extended Toungoo's territorial campaigns beyond any previous measure, unifying Upper Burma with Lower Burma for the first time since Pagan. In proclaiming himself a Buddhist *cakkavartin* (universal conqueror), he resurrected the model inaugurated by India's King Aśoka and emulated by the Pagan rulers Anawratha and Kyanzittha. His expansion northward made Upper Burma (still ruled from Ava), parts of Manipur, and the entire Shan realm tributaries of the new Pegu court. This reinforced cultural norms, language, and Buddhist orthodoxies that were becoming tied to notions of a collective Burmese identity. With Pegu's access to maritime revenue (through taxation, monopolies, and tolls), the relative weakness of the Ava and Shan polities, and the incorporation of new manpower into the military, Bayinnaung was able to conquer Ayutthaya, the capital of Siam, in 1569 and to extend his influence over Lanna and Lan Sang as well. The adoption of European-style firearms and the utilization of well-trained mercenaries may have been the deciding factor in the king's campaigns. He outfitted a fifth to a third of his forces with Portuguese firearms, which were superior to the available Chinese- and Muslim-style guns. With the Siamese now effectively his clients – although only until they were strong enough to reassert their independence – Bayinnaung was king of one of the largest stretches of territory in the history of Southeast Asia, stretching from Arakan to the borders of Cambodia and from Lower Burma north to the edge of Yunnan.

The growth of trade from the mid-1300s to the early 1500s facilitated regular village markets which provided the interior with a growing international exposure to foreign goods, ideas, and eventually new military technology. With growing commercial revenues, local leaders were able to hire mercenaries to buttress their military while providing cash to use as patronage of religious institutions which had previously enjoyed tax-free land grants. This new pattern of support, a product of a growing maritime trade and the influx of Chinese silver, allowed local elites with imperial ambitions to continue to express notions of authority and legitimacy through their support of Buddhist monasteries, pagodas and annual festivals. But now donations were made in cash, thereby preserving land-based tax revenues for the state and protecting the new center at Toungoo from the structural weaknesses that had faced the classical state of Pagan.

The collapse of Pegu and the return to Upper Burma (1550s–1620s)

Impressive territorial expansion did not come without challenges for the first Toungoo kings. Administering newly conquered polities often meant replacing existing rulers with new ones, creating tributary relationships that could hardly be monitored from Pegu. Imperial links were weaker the further communities were from the directly controlled Lower Irrawaddy basin. With infrequent visits from royal representatives, local priorities and concerns would continue to play an important role in how communities saw themselves and the world around them. Toungoo kings had to make do with loose and sometimes insecure relationships with their new Tai vassals, with whom they lacked enduring cultural bonds. Rebellion in the Tai periphery was frequent and due mainly to the over-extension of Burma's resources and the inability to overcome linguistic, patronage, and economic loyalties to competing Tai centers of prestige and status.

In some respects, the Pegu court faced similar structural challenges closer to home in the Lower Irrawaddy basin as well. To be sure, such provinces were more closely supervised through appointment of *bayins* (senior royal relatives), but the trappings of that position could inspire more autonomous behavior if royal authority weakened. *Bayins* could maintain their own armies, draw upon a local tax base, and even enjoy the privileges and ritual status associated with the Toungoo 'High King', such as the notion of *dhammaraja*. In some cases, these provincial appointments became hereditary, reinforcing the tendency for *bayins* to distance themselves from the center when the Pegu king died or there was a succession dispute. Other lowland positions of governance, such as those held by junior princes (*myo-zas*), were even more prone to resistance in the event of political instability, as they were linked only by tribute, infrequent troop demands, and nominal acts of loyalty.

Internal structural weaknesses were not the only pressures facing the Pegu court. By the end of the sixteenth and the beginning of the seventeenth centuries, maritime dynamism declined in what has been identified as a pan-regional economic crisis precipitated by declining availability of New World silver, a general rise in prices, a reduction in agricultural output, and the cooling of coastal trade due to an increase in overland Chinese commerce and a growing Dutch maritime presence that threatened the prominence of Southeast Asian trading networks. This combination of factors weakened the strategic position of Pegu and limited profit margins that the port had enjoyed earlier. In addition, comparative climatic studies suggest that an El Niño phenomenon produced weak monsoons, droughts, crop failures, famines, and in 1601 one of the coldest summers in 600 years – changes that the Pegu state, like states in India and elsewhere in the 1590s, could hardly withstand.

To make matters worse, the death of Bayinnaung in 1581 spurred a contest for the throne that allowed outlying tributaries to break away from Burma and realign their allegiances to alternative overlords. Protracted efforts at re-conquering Tai polities drained the Burmese kingdom of both resources and manpower, increasing the burden on Irrawaddy basin communities, who there-fore fled to other courts and monasteries for refuge and tax relief. With state resources weakened, formerly loyal regional *bayins* saw their opportunity and directed their armies from Toungoo and Arakan to attack the capital. Ayutthaya, too, joined in the campaign against Pegu, which these armies burned in 1599. While the more immediate causes of the decline might be attributed to these defections, Pegu was in part weakened by its successes. Over-extension, along with longstanding patterns of local autonomy, climatic change, and shifts in maritime trade all contributed to the disintegration of Lower Burma's massive territorial empire.

The court of Ava

Following a brief period of warfare in the Irrawaddy river basin, a new polity emerged with the restoration of Ava as a center of power in the 1630s–50s. Ava had appeared earlier in the fourteenth century as a successor to the Pagan state and now it provided refuge to a branch of the defunct Toungoo dynasty, which there reasserted its influence and developed pre-existing institutional and cultural patterns. Upper Burma was a strategic location and would provide sites for new capitals in both pre-colonial and post-colonial contexts. This was due to its agricultural and demographic superiority but also to cultural reasons: the most significant temples, religious centers, literary and handicraft traditions, and economic centers were located in the 'dry-zone', the heartland of Burmese communities. There were economic opportunities for commerce with Yunnan and relative stability with the pacification and incorporation of Shan polities into the Burman, Tai, and Chinese orbits. In Ava much of the vitality and inno-vation of cosmopolitan Pegu was restored and combined with the more endur-ing agrarian traditions of Upper Burma.

Ava leaders were more realistic in conceptualizing a unified kingdom along the Irrawaddy river, rather than over-reaching into areas they could not hope to administer. The Shan were also considerably weaker after being conquered by Bayinnaung, while pressure from China also contributed to their more marginal status. This allowed overland trade to flourish and also meant more stability for the rice-rich region of Kyaukse, a major producer of rice for the kingdom. In addition, Upper Burma enjoyed superior human resources, with its large and relatively stable population. The religious sector, which had previously drained the state of resources, continued to be maintained through cash donations rather than through tax-exempt lands while new (secular) administrative bodies were created to manage and control religious wealth, effectively curbing the economic power of the Buddhist *Sangha*. These transformations changed the relations between the state and *Sangha* by limiting the ability of the principal monasteries to accumulate landed estates. New or revitalized initiatives designed to privatize religious lands, limit the numbers of monks, and diminish the status of religious bondsmen (*hpaya-kyun*) resulted in a decrease in tax-exempt personnel and an increase in available manpower – the crucial resource for the pre-colonial state.

The resurgence of Upper Burma was marked by an effort to manage state resources more effectively, fine-tuning the experiences of the earlier Pagan and Pegu courts. More garrisons and forts (*taiks*) were established to link strategic points of the kingdom. Some new provincial centers were thereby founded that facilitated closer patronage relationships while curbing the ever-present problem of hereditary succession. Insubordination and rebellion were managed by recalling local *bayin* and *myo-zas* to the court, replacing them with junior princes or commoners who had little claim to the throne and relatively limited local client groups. These *myo-wuns* were not allowed to display royal insignia and were dependent on the king's patronage, thereby weakening the capacity of these provincial elites to become claimants to the throne. These new appointees effectively curbed the power of the *bayins* in the provinces while implementing a greater degree of supervision at the sub-provincial level.

Royal administration also grew more complex in legal and fiscal matters. In 1635, King Thalun (r. 1628–48) instituted a census that recorded the rights of landed elites, population figures, and tax and service obligations for lowland districts throughout the kingdom. New tax and patronage agreements at the village level were negotiated with the capital, linking more closely the administrative sinews of the kingdom. By 1650, Ava was able to administer over 40 percent of the population within a 120 mile/200 km radius as royal servicemen (*ahmu-dan*), an increase of nearly 20 percent over the mid-sixteenth century. Irrigation and cultivation programs were extended with the incorporation of this new manpower. Administrative support grew as well, as the capital increased numbers of officials and support staff, secretaries, and ministers that were assigned to manage new kingdom-wide procedures, laws, and routines. Even as the state in Burma returned to a more agrarian and familiar economic orientation, however, maritime revenues continued through the patronage of merchants, the increasing supervision of custom duties, and greater oversight of port authorities. All of these measures enhanced control of manpower and economic production in the kingdom while responding to opportunities on the coast.

Local autonomy and the decline of Ava (1650s–1752)

Ironically, Ava's administrative evolution and a wider trend of economic growth in the eighteenth century may have contributed to its fall. Growing trade seems to have amplified dynastic rivalries within the central court, as courtiers who did not have access to revenue from maritime commerce attempted to compensate by heavily exploiting the royal servicemen, undermining the attraction of the court as a patron. With the weakening of the central state, the throne was unable to keep provincial leaders under its authority and influence. Furthermore, ministerial authority increased at the expense of royal authority as officials close to the court sought to divert funds and resources to their own patronage networks, so as to secure their own power while competing with the court for influence. These trends compounded the inability to manage succession, a problem that affected the Burmese state for most of its history. Factional differences in the court in the late 1600s and early 1700s resulted in an inability to regulate royal servicemen, with many seeking alternative patronage from private patrons, rival princes, or the *Sangha*, or else migrating to other territories. Defecting *ahmu-dans* bolstered the military capacity of provincial princes, which forced King Mahadamayazadipati (r. 1733–52) to make concessions to local demands. The weakened Ava state faced invasions from Manipur, the revolt of Shan principal-ities, and the threat of attack from an increasingly rebellious leadership in the old Mon kingdom of Pegu. In 1752 with a large contingent of troops from Lower Burma, Pegu's King Banyadala drove Ava's remaining defenders back into the citadel walls and provided the final blow that effectively ended the Toungoo dynasty.

The Tai world

The fourteenth century saw a significant shift in power within the Tai world, with the appearance of the new kingdoms of Ayutthaya (or Ayudhya) in the Chao Phraya river valley south of Sukhothai and Lan Sang in what is now Laos. Neither kingdom sprang out of nowhere; both polities were the result of a consolidation process knitting together existing *muang*. Chapter 3 showed this development taking place in the thirteenth century with the kingdoms of Sukhothai and Lanna. The kingdoms that appeared in the mid-1300s would become the two dominant powers in the sub-region lying between Vietnamese and Burmese territory. Lan Sang would flourish for more than three centuries until its fragmentation around 1700, while Ayutthaya would evolve into the large, powerful, and prosperous polity known to the world as Siam.

Ayutthaya

Different sources offer widely varying accounts of the establishment of Ayutthaya under a ruler named Uthong who took the title Ramathibodi (r. 1351–69). Although the chronicles give a very specific date (1351) for the foundation of the kingdom, it is not at all certain that a new polity was in fact established at that point in time. It seems clear that like so many other Southeast Asian kingdoms, Ayutthaya represented the culmination of a process of alliance-building and territorial consolidation, although in this particular case there is no evidence of warfare. By the mid-fourteenth century the migration of Tai-speakers and the receding of Angkor's authority had led to a proliferation of new *muang* in the Chao Phraya valley, outside the sphere of influence of Sukhothai to the north. Lopburi (Lavo) had been an important Mon center, then a provincial power center under Angkor, and was now a Thai *muang*. To its south there was another small *muang* named Ayutthaya, which clearly already existed before 1351, and to its west a third *muang* called Suphanburi. These three *muang* collectively formed the core of the new, larger *mandala* which retained the name of Ayutthaya.

Ayutthaya existed as a kingdom for over four centuries; we can break down its history into several sub-periods or phases. The period stretching from its establishment through the end of the fifteenth century was one of consolida-tion and expansion, culminating in the reign of King Trailok (r. 1448–88), who is credited with having given long-term structure to both government and society through the codification of the *sakdina* system, an elaborate hierarchy of quantified rank which theoretically covered every individual in the kingdom. The second period, lasting through the mid-sixteenth century, was characterized by increased trade – including, after 1500, trade with Western commercial interests – as well as frequent warfare with Ayutthaya's neighbors. The Burmese kingdom emerged as the primary threat to Ayutthaya's security, as was made all too clear by the fall of the capital to the Burmese king Bayinnaung's invasion in 1569. A third phase extended from the re-establishment of the kingdom under a new dynasty through a time of vigorous foreign trade, culminating in the reign of King Narai (r. 1656–88). Finally, a coup against Narai's family at the time of his death brought in a new ruling family which held the throne until a second Burmese attack on Ayutthaya in 1767 brought an end to this phase of Thai history.

Thai historians have long given a rather stereotypical picture of Ayutthaya as an 'absolute monarchy' whose ideas of kingship and institutions were borrowed from Angkor and which thus represented a very different style of government from Sukhothai, with its 'paternalistic' and supposedly more 'authentically Thai' rulers. This picture is, however, probably oversimplified. It is certainly true that Ayutthaya was exposed to Khmer and Mon influences, located as it was along the former periphery of the Angkorean empire, and these two languages were both used within the kingdom for at least the first century or so of its existence. Also undeniable are the greater degree of bureaucratization and more ceremonially elaborate kingship compared to either Sukhothai or Lanna.

It must be pointed out, however, that in significant ways the Ayutthayan monarchy was not particularly 'absolute'; indeed, many scholars would argue that a genuine absolute monarchy did not come into existence until Chulalongkorn's reign in the late nineteenth century. Ayutthaya remained a Southeast Asian *mandala* in certain respects or – as Stanley Tambiah has characterized it – a 'galactic polity' whose various components had greatly differing relationships to the center. In the late 1300s there is already evidence of conflict between two of the *muang* which were linked together to form the new polity, and as Ayutthaya expanded its territory over the next few centuries, each new *muang* or region was a potential point of contestation. Sukhothai was a prime example; although nominally incorporated into Ayutthaya in the 1430s after decades of conflict, it seems to have retained a strong regional identity, and the kingdom's rulers could not always count on its loyalty. Mahathammaracha (r. 1569–90), who collaborated with the Burmese invasion and took the throne as Ayutthaya's new ruler, was linked to the old Sukhothai ruling class.

Ayutthaya was in some ways a more structured kingdom than many of its neighbors, and it developed a reasonably complex hierarchy of officials at various levels, although bureaucratic titles were often linked as much or more to control of manpower in particular areas than to specific functions. Structure did not guarantee stability or unity, however, and Ayutthaya demonstrated the fundamental challenge of most Southeast Asian polities: how to ensure that a network of relationships between central, regional, and local rulers would be solid and durable enough to allow the kingdom to weather the storm of a difficult succession or an outside invasion. Siamese rulers faced the perennial question of how best to control their nobility. Some preferred to have nobles scattered around the kingdom's territory, others to have them concentrated in the capital where their activities could be monitored. Each solution had its advantages and disadvantages; the line between nobility and royalty was often a fine one, and there were several occasions in Ayutthaya's history – twice in the seventeenth century – when a noble overthrew a king and established a new dynasty. The willingness of provincial nobles to mobilize manpower was a key factor in the defense of the kingdom's core region, and the lack of noble support was a major cause of the two Siamese defeats in 1569 and 1767.

Although the vast majority of Ayutthaya's population engaged in agriculture, its strength and prosperity cannot be understood without some discussion of trade. Chinese traders were present from at least the fourteenth century and probably earlier, and some versions of Uthong's origins suggest that he had links to this community. Trade patterns shifted at different times – one important variable being the changing policy of successive Chinese dynasties towards maritime commerce – but Siam remained an important regional player throughout. When the Europeans appeared on the scene – initially the Portuguese, followed by the Dutch, English, French, and other Westerners – they were easily integrated into the system, and they became an important presence within the kingdom. Even after the coup at Narai's death in 1688, which was partially due to a reaction against the growing influence of European interests in Siam, there was no attempt to reverse course by adopting a 'closed-door' policy. Ayutthaya's role as a major trading center was simply too well established and too lucrative for the ruling class to consider changing it.

Another long-term characteristic of Ayutthaya was its multi-ethnic and cosmopolitan character, particularly in the capital. It was never an exclusively 'Siamese' kingdom. The population included various other ethnic groups, particularly as military campaigns and conquest expanded the kingdom's territory, notably to the south. Immigrants from elsewhere –such as Japanese, Vietnamese, Cham, and Makassarese from eastern Indonesia – established their own communities; many of them were traders, and some were mercenaries in the court's service. Relations with these communities were sometimes tense, as was the case with the *Farang* (Westerners) as well, but it was inconceivable that any Ayutthayan ruler might try to close the door to a particular group, no matter how troublesome or even threatening they might be. The foreign communities included numerous Christians and Muslims, reflecting the relatively high degree of religious tolerance within Siamese society.

Ayutthaya's foreign relations were characterized by a mixture of warfare and diplomacy. There were periodic wars with Lanna and Lan Sang, but there were also periods of peace and exchanges of missions and even marriages between the royal families. Ayutthaya sought to extend its influence both eastward (Cambodia) and southward (down the peninsula into the Malay world). At the very least it was frequently able to demand tribute missions from these weaker neighbors, and at its strongest it was in a position to intervene in their affairs, particularly in terms of choosing compliant rulers. Relations with the *Farang* were more complex, since they often had considerable firepower backing up their demands. During the Ayutthaya period, however, Europeans were more interested in trading with Siam than attacking or colonizing it. Moreover, the Siamese court – particularly under Narai – was able to come to terms with Western diplomacy to an extent unknown elsewhere in the region, and diplomatic missions were exchanged with the Dutch and French. Ultimately Ayutthaya's troubles would arise from a combination of internal weaknesses and the Burmese threat, not from Western imperialism.

Lanna

The history of the Northern Thai kingdom during this period is a tumultuous and frequently unhappy one. Lanna's location made it vulnerable to attacks from aggressive neighbors, notably Ayutthaya, Burma, and Lan Sang. It also suffered from the kinds of internal structural weaknesses which plagued most kingdoms of the Tai world at their inception but which never seem to have been resolved in Lanna's case. Mangrai's successors in the fourteenth century were able to restore a fragile unity, but it was not durable, and the ruler in Chiang Mai frequently faced challenges from rebellious *muang* in different parts of his territory. The ambitions of powerful Burmese kingdoms first at Ava and then at Toungoo proved the most serious. Burma invaded in the late 1550s, removing the last of Mangrai's descendents from the throne. Lanna remained under the Burmese thumb for more than 200 years.

Lanna's real significance arguably lay in the strength of its Buddhist culture. With a separate language and a separate script from the Siamese, it retained a powerful identity over the centuries and influenced neighboring cultures as well. The Lanna *Sangha* had direct contact with their counterparts in Sri Lanka, and Sinhalese monastic reforms were introduced into the kingdom in both the fourteenth and fifteenth centuries. There is also increasing scholarly interest in the cultural connections with Lan Sang, which seems to have been significantly influenced by its neighbor.

Lan Sang

The early centuries of Lao history are quite obscure. At some point in time the ancestors of the Lao and other Tai-speaking peoples in present-day Laos migrated from their homeland, eventually settling on both sides of the Mekong river. (It is important to remember that until the nineteenth century, much of northeastern 'Thailand' was part of the Lao world.) It is assumed that they found the territory occupied by Austroasiatic speakers of various groups, and some of these peoples have retained memories in their oral traditions of conflicts with the new arrivals; in some cases the Lao are said to have tricked the original inhabitants into giving up their land. Although some may have remained in the lowlands and been absorbed into the Lao population, many retreated to the hills and mountains, where significant highland minorities remain even today.

At some point, perhaps concurrently with the establishment of new Tai *muang* further west, the Lao founded a kingdom at Xieng Dong Xieng Thong, now the city of Luang Phabang. This seems once to have been a power center for one or more Austroasiatic groups, but it became the principal political and cultural center for the Lao. The Lao historical narrative only begins in the mid-fourteenth century, however, when Fa Ngum (r. 1353–73), a prince from this kingdom, is said to have been exiled and to have made his way to Angkor, where he married a Cambodian princess. Eventually he returned to his ancestral home, working his way northward and forging alliances with various Lao *muang* until he conquered Luang Phabang from his own uncle and established a new kingdom called Lan Sang ('million elephants') in 1353. Lan Sang would exist as a unified kingdom for more than 300 years.

Lan Sang at its peak included all of present-day Laos, much of northeastern Thailand, and parts of Yunnan and northwestern Vietnam. Just how much authority the ruler in Luang Phabang – or, after a shift of capital in 1560, Vientiane – had over all this territory is open to question. The general impression given by chronicles and other sources is that Lan Sang as a kingdom was rather less structured than Ayutthaya despite their comparable size, although a hierarchy of officials did exist, many with similar titles to those found in other Tai kingdoms. Local *muang* seem to have retained considerable authority under the overlordship of the Lan Sang ruler; and if the kingdom as a whole faced fewer serious threats to its existence than its neighbors to the west, this may be due to a more secure location rather than to any real military or institutional strength. It did have occasional conflicts with Lanna, Ayutthaya, Burma, Angkor, and Dai Viet, but it was never as badly affected as the first two kingdoms were by their own wars with the Burmese. It was only in the eighteenth century, after Lan Sang had fragmented into several smaller parts, that the Lao polities became more vulnerable to outside intervention.

Like all kingdoms in Southeast Asia, Lan Sang did experience occasional political turbulence, but it also enjoyed extended periods of relative peace and prosperity under strong rulers. The most famous of these were Sam Saen Thai (r. 1373–1416), Phothisalat (r. 1520–47), Setthathilat (r. 1547–71), and Soulignavongsa (r. *c.*1637–94). The last of these in particular is credited with a 'golden age', both because of the length of his reign and because it was after his death that the kingdom fell apart. The change of capital from Luang Phabang to Vientiane, which occurred partly for strategic reasons, also seems to have connected Lan Sang more closely to the growing trade opportunities in the region. The Dutch VOC was sufficiently interested in Lan Sang's potential to send one of its merchants, Gerrit van Wuysthoff, to visit the kingdom in 1641–42.

One issue which is still a matter of puzzlement for historians is the expansion of Buddhism among the Lao. According to the story found in some chronicles, Theravada was imported in Fa Ngum's time because his Cambodian wife, despairing at the state of religion in her husband's kingdom, requested that monks and Pali scriptures be sent from Angkor. There are, however, no inscriptions or statues clearly indicating the presence of Theravada as early as the fourteenth century, and it may only have become firmly implanted in the fifteenth century, or even later in some regions. That does not, however, mean that Buddhism was absent before that point. There is evidence of Mon Buddhism in the region of Vientiane as early as the first millennium, though it is not clear whether this was due to an actual Mon presence east of the Mekong or simply to cultural influences from elsewhere. Over the long run, Lao culture came to be characterized by the same mixture of Theravada and spirit beliefs that is found throughout mainland Southeast Asia, with a particularly significant influence from Northern Thai Buddhism due to Lan Sang's close proximity to, and frequent contact with, the Lanna kingdom.

Vietnam

The 20-year Ming occupation of Dai Viet between 1407 and 1427 marks an important watershed in Vietnamese history in several respects. First, it was the only successful Chinese invasion following the gaining of independence in the tenth century. Second, it serves as a break between the earlier Ly and Tran dynasties, which were less tightly structured and more Buddhist in their orientation, and the Le dynasty (1428–1788), which became gradually more centralized and more Confucian in its ideology. Finally, the period after the Ming occupation was the time when the Vietnamese people began to expand southward on a large scale through conquest and migration.

One of the factors which directly provoked the Ming invasion was the fall of the Tran in 1400. An official named Ho Quy Ly had married into the royal family and gradually built himself a power base, eventually manipulating the succession to put his son (by a Tran mother) on the throne of a new Ho dynasty. Although he is given credit by modern historians for having worked to centralize the court's power after decades of fragmentation and decentralization under successive Tran rulers, at the time he and his son were seen as usurpers, and resistance led by Tran princes sprang up even as the kingdom faced a Chinese invasion. Father and son were captured by the Ming and carted off to China, bringing their short-lived dynasty to an end.

The instability caused by Ho Quy Ly's actions provided a window of opportunity for Ming Emperor Yongle (r. 1402–24). China had never completely resigned itself to the loss of its former Vietnamese provinces, and Yongle was also driven by a 'civilizing mission' to spread Chinese culture to his neighbors. The two decades of Chinese rule in Vietnam provided an excellent opportunity to do so, and the 'shot in the arm' given to Confucianism there had a lasting effect. Buddhism remained strong as an instrument of personal devotion, but from the fifteenth century onward, the ideology of government was more purely Confucian, and emperors would now pen musings on Confucian ideals rather than Buddhist philosophy.

Although the Ming had no trouble finding collaborators for their occupation regime, neither was there a lack of resistance, and by 1418 a rebellion had broken out based at Lam Son in Thanh Hoa province. Its leader, Le Loi, mounted a decade-long campaign of guerrilla warfare, building up a following in different parts of the occupied territory. By late 1427 he had succeeded in defeating the Ming forces, and they returned to China, leaving him free to establish a new dynasty with the help of his strategist and intellectual 'right-hand man', Nguyen Trai. The Le dynasty founded in early 1428 would prove to be Vietnam's longest-lived dynasty, though hardly its most stable.

The fifteenth century after the defeat of the Ming is often viewed as a period of strength and prosperity, particularly the reign of Emperor Le Thanh Tong (r. 1460–97). Le Loi (usually known by his reign title of Thai To, r. 1428–33) was able to draw on the base of support he had built up during the resistance against the Chinese in order to put a new government in place, and there was no major challenge to his authority. The new emperor only lived for five years, however, and after his death there was increasing factionalism within the court. The decades between Le Loi's death and Thanh Tong's accession in 1460 saw the prolongation of these quarrels, and it was only during the latter's reign that the relative peace and stability which prevailed outside the capital could be found inside the Court as well.

Thanh Tong represented the ideal Confucian ruler who was both scholarly and competent in government affairs. He is generally credited with the promulgation of the famous Hong Duc legal code, named for his reign title – although it now seems likely that at least parts of it had already been written under his predecessors. His reign saw both the consolidation of internal government and a policy of territorial expansion through conquest. He embarked on several major military campaigns, notably against the Lao and the Cham. An apparently punitive expedition against the Lao seems to have had mixed results, but the 1471 attack on the Cham kingdom centered at Vijaya added several southern provinces to Dai Viet's territory.

This golden age ended with Thanh Tong's death, however, and within three decades of his passing, the Le were temporarily overthrown and the kingdom plunged into civil war. The early sixteenth century saw a succession of bad rulers – two of whom were known by the epithets 'devil king' and 'pig king' respectively – and increasing rural unrest under the combined burdens of taxes, land rents, and demands for labor service. A major rebellion in 1516 culminated in an attack on the capital of Thang Long which forced the court to flee and seek refuge in a distant province. The rebels were defeated by royal troops under the leadership of a military officer named Mac Dang Dung who proved to have his own ambitions. He spent the next decade consolidating his power base and finally usurped the throne in 1527.

The Mac usurpation opened a period of civil strife which lasted until nearly the end of the century and came to involve four powerful families: the Mac, Le, Nguyen, and Trinh. Although the Mac would largely fade from the scene by 1600, the other three families ruled Vietnam (actually two Vietnams) until the late eighteenth century. The Mac initially benefited from antipathy to the Le and enjoyed a 'honeymoon' during their early decades in power. Although their policies in many respects followed those of the Le, culturally they are perceived as having moved away from the near-total emphasis on Confucian ideology in favor of more eclectic patronage for Buddhism and the veneration of local spirits. They also actively supported artisanry and other economic activities, thus laying the foundations for the growth in foreign trade of the seventeenth century.

Le supporters fled to Lao territory and re-established the dynasty there within a few years of the Mac seizure of power. Six decades of civil war ensued, with leadership of the anti-Mac struggle in the hands of the Trinh and Nguyen

Figure 16   Thien Mu pagoda, Perfume river, Hue, seventeenth century

families. The Trinh became increasingly powerful, and the Nguyen – under the leadership of Nguyen Hoang – decided to move to the southern periphery of Vietnamese territory and put distance between themselves and their rivals. Poor government by the Mac led to their defeat in 1592, and a Le emperor once more ruled in Thang Long, but now with a Trinh lord as his chief minister and virtual viceroy. Nguyen Hoang remained in the South in the region of Hue (Figure 16), where he and his successors would rule for the next 350 years.

From around 1600 until the 1770s there were effectively two Vietnams. The northern kingdom, ruled nominally by the Le but with power in the hands of the Trinh, was known to foreigners as 'Tonkin' and to the Vietnamese as 'Dang Ngoai'. The southern kingdom, ruled by the Nguyen, was known as 'Dang Trong' or 'Cochin China'. There was sporadic warfare between the two during the first half of the seventeenth century, but neither was able to defeat the other, and in 1672 a truce was signed, with a *de facto* border established at the Gianh river – ironically almost the exact location of the Demilitarized Zone between North and South Vietnam in the mid-twentieth century.

By the seventeenth century the nucleus of a European community existed in both Vietnams. Catholic missionaries were apparently resident in Tonkin by the late 1500s but appeared in Cochin China only after 1600. The first missionaries were Portuguese, but Frenchmen and Spaniards came to dominate the scene later on. Catholicism took root among the Vietnamese despite periodic bans from both royal courts – although the bans were not always strictly enforced, and in any case the long, open coastline made it easy for expelled missionaries to return. Vietnamese rulers shared their Chinese counterparts' contempt for Christianity as a 'heterodox teaching'; the foreign religion was not seriously linked to the threat of outside intervention until the nineteenth century.

Generally more welcome – though not always – were the Portuguese, Dutch, and English traders who set up shop in the two kingdoms. The Le/Trinh government was more suspicious and restrictive, limiting the foreigners' activities to the Red river trading port of Pho Hien and to the capital of Thang Long. Tonkin developed closer ties with the Dutch, while the Nguyen favored the Portuguese. Overall the southern kingdom was somewhat more open both intellectually and culturally, and its incorporation of the numerous Cham ports along the coast – the most important of which was at Hoi An (Figure 17), known to the Europeans as Faifo – provided it with a better 'infrastructure' for foreign trade.

The two Vietnamese kingdoms developed along quite different trajectories. Tonkin had no room for territorial expansion, and the prolonged tensions between its two ruling families meant that its internal stability was often problematic. It remained fairly ethnically homogeneous, with the exception of a small Chinese community. Cochin China was more multi-ethnic, particularly as it expanded through Cham and later Khmer territory. Ethnic diversity translated into cultural diversity as well: not only was the Nguyen kingdom in some ways less Confucian and more explicitly Mahayana, it also came to include a significant Theravada minority as well as the various religious systems found among the Cham, which by the seventeenth century included Islam.

Figure 17   Cantonese temple and assembly hall, Hoi An

Champa

As was mentioned in Chapter 3, for the Cham the transition from the four-teenth to the fifteenth century marked the permanent shift from a position of strength to one of weakness and defeat at the hands of the Vietnamese. The brief reign of the Ho dynasty saw the expansion of Dai Viet's authority south of the Pass of the Clouds. Vietnamese ambitions were of course halted by the Ming occupation, and it is not clear how firmly the early Le rulers controlled the southernmost edge of their kingdom. It seems, however, that the Cham power centers to the north faded away, and that Vijaya (present-day Quy Nhon) was the strongest remaining kingdom. By the mid-1400s, Dai Viet was in a position to take the offensive; the major campaign of 1471 destroyed Vijaya and conquered the territory under its control. A number of Cham fled south to the neighboring kingdoms of Kauthara and Panduranga.

The border between Cham and Vietnamese territory now lay at a point roughly halfway between Quy Nhon and Nha Trang, although once again it is not certain that Dai Viet fully controlled the territory down to this point. During the sixteenth century the prolonged Vietnamese civil war appears to have allowed the Cham some breathing room and perhaps even the opportu-nity to reclaim some of the territory lost in 1471. By the early 1600s, however, the Nguyen family ruling from the area around Hue were effectively independ-ent from the restored Le in the north and were in a position to consolidate their southern border. Over the course of the seventeenth century they gradually pushed further and further south, and by 1700 all of the former Cham territory was integrated into the Nguyen kingdom, though Panduranga survived as a kind of vassal until the 1830s.

When the Vietnamese occupied Cham territory, they acquired considerably more than land. Cham ports had long played an important role in regional trade and were probably at least as important a factor as – if not more impor-tant than – agriculture in the long-term survival of the Cham kingdoms. One of the interesting phenomena now being studied by art historians and archeol-ogists is the sudden appearance in the fifteenth century of several kinds of ceramics produced in the Vijaya region. This burst of local production has been attributed to the Ming dynasty's crackdown on maritime trade early in that century, which apparently stimulated the Cham to fabricate and export their own ceramics to replace what could no longer be imported. Cham ceramics production does not seem to have survived the Vietnamese invasion of 1471, but the thriving trade ports certainly did, and they contributed significantly to the growth and prosperity of the Nguyen kingdom. Meanwhile, the invasion provoked a Cham exodus westward to Cambodia and southward to various kingdoms in the Malay world which served to reinforce the ties between that world and the surviving Cham polities.

Cambodia

The entire period of Cambodian history between about 1300 and 1500 is almost impossible to reconstruct with any accuracy. The Cambodian chronicles recounting events of this period have been found to contain a good deal of fiction, as well as individuals and events from later periods which were 'transplanted' to an earlier point in the narrative. For this reason we can only paint a general picture of the period with broad brush strokes.

From the fifteenth century onward – and indeed even earlier – the history of Cambodia is closely intertwined with that of the Thai. For the first century or so after Ayutthaya's appearance, there were periodic episodes of warfare with Angkor, which was the new kingdom's main rival outside the Tai world. By the early 1400s, Ayutthaya seems to have been in control of at least part of the remaining territory still ruled by Angkor and to have put its own king on the throne. By mid-century the Cambodians threw off the Siamese yoke, and a ruler named Yat took the throne, but with his capital established further to the southeast. Henceforth the Cambodian power center – successively at Lovek, Oudong, and Phnom Penh – would remain in this new location, close to the Mekong and Tonle Sap rivers and thus enjoying greater access to the coast. It seems likely that even before the permanent shift of capital away from Angkor, the kingdom was taking initiatives to profit from the reinvigorated regional trade which came with the foundation of the Ming dynasty in 1368. The combination of a powerful, aggressive neighbor to the west and new trade patterns along the coast made the southeastern region a more attractive center than the agricultural heartland around Angkor.

From the mid-1400s until roughly 1600 Cambodia enjoyed a period of relative prosperity although not one of peace. Moving the capital to the Phnom Penh region did not eliminate the Siamese threat, but Ayutthaya's problems with the Burmese weakened it sufficiently that Cambodia was able at least to hold its own militarily through the sixteenth century. It even seized the initiative in campaigns against its neighbor in the 1570s, although a revived Ayutthaya took its revenge later in the century. Meanwhile, the Cambodian kingdom acquired some of the ethnic diversity and variety of commercial contacts that characterized Siam during this period as well. Refugees from the shrinking Cham territory along with immigrants from different parts of the Malay world and the omnipresent Chinese contributed to economic growth while adding a certain degree of cosmopolitanism to the capital.

As in Siam and elsewhere, heightened contacts with foreigners could be a mixed blessing. A brief but troublesome episode occurred in the late 1590s when the Cambodian ruler made an appeal to the Spanish colonial government in Manila to come to his aid against the latest threat from Ayutthaya. What he received was arms and small-scale Spanish intervention under a pair of European adventurers. Although Cambodia managed to avoid becoming a Spanish colony, this incident, as David Chandler has noted, set several important precedents for the kingdom's future history: a Cambodian ruler's willingness to listen to promises from foreigners, the attractiveness of foreign arms, and the general tendency of the elite to further their political and economic interests through reliance on outsiders.

The threat of European intervention quickly faded and did not re-appear until the mid-nineteenth century, but from roughly 1600 onward Cambodia was caught between two powerful and ambitious neighbors: Siam and Vietnam.

By this point the Nguyen lords in Hue had completed their conquest of the Cham territories along the coast and were now eyeing the Mekong delta. For the next two-and-a-half centuries, the Cambodian ruling class would generally be divided between pro-Siamese and pro-Vietnamese factions, with a king from one side occupying the throne while the other side schemed to remove him. A united kingdom might conceivably have mustered the determination and fire-power to hold onto its independence and its territory, but the long-term court factionalism left the country in a weakened state. In exchange for supporting particular rulers, the Vietnamese bargained for economic and territorial conces-sions which could not be reversed, and the court's cession to the Nguyen of customs rights at Prey Nokor (the future Saigon) in the 1620s began the irre-versible erosion of Cambodian sovereignty over the Mekong delta.

Although historians generally agree that Angkor never 'fell', there is no doubt that much was irretrievably lost when the Angkorean age came to an end. Cambodian culture, with its wealth of *cbap* (moral tales), the strength of its Theravada beliefs, and the omnipresence of the *neak ta* (spirits), possesses a resilience which has preserved its foundations through not only the tribulations of the fifteenth–seventeenth centuries, but later the crisis of colonization and the horrors of civil war and the *Khmer Rouge*. Yet after the abandonment of Angkor as a capital, Cambodia found itself increasingly vulnerable to foreign intervention. It is small wonder that the memory of a strong and powerful king-dom continues to hold sway over the national imagination.

Melaka, c.1400–1511

The western part of the Malay-Indonesian archipelagic zone was well suited for an entrepôt. The Straits of Melaka represented a funnel through which passed much of the trade between China and Japan in the east and India, the Middle East, East Africa and even Europe in the west. The pattern of monsoon winds also suited this area. Ships heading east though the Indian Ocean could sail down the relatively calm waters of the Straits and there rest, resupply, and purchase local goods while waiting for the change of monsoon winds that could take them northeast to China. Traders sailing southwest through the South China Sea could do the same while waiting for the winds to take them into the Indian Ocean and to trading points to the west. When traders met in the western archipelago, they could exchange goods, such as European nails and Indian textiles for Chinese porcelains, Japanese swords, and the much-valued spices of eastern Indonesia. At least from the time of Śrivijaya in the seventh century, local people recognized the opportunities for themselves that lay in this happy geographical, meteorological, and economic conjunction.

International Asian trade was unarmed. Traders carried weapons to defend themselves, but trading ships that were simultaneously men-of-war were a European innovation not yet seen in Asia c.1400. So if one were to create an entrepôt – where traders from all of Asia would meet to exchange goods – what was needed was not a great armed force but a policy that traders would find beneficial, one that would facilitate commerce rather than bleeding it to death through taxes. It was this sort of policy that underlay the success not only of Melaka but of its successor states, down to present-day Singapore.

There is some uncertainty about the origins of Melaka, but the broad outlines seem clear enough. In the late fourteenth century, the Javanese empire of Majapahit under Hayam Wuruk still sought to extend its sway over vassal states outside Java. In 1377 it attacked Palembang in Sumatra and put to flight a local Hindu-Buddhist prince named Parameswara (d. *c.*1414). He crossed the Straits and eventually established himself in Melaka *c.*1400. Of the potential entrepôt sites of the western archipelagic zone, Melaka was one of the best. It had a good harbor accessible in all seasons and was on the narrowest part of the Straits, where shipping was most concentrated. Parameswara first had to get those ships to call at his new port. He turned for help to the so-called 'sea people' (*orang laut*). In the southern Straits of Melaka, the proliferation of small islands made for ideal pirate territory and the *orang laut* were experienced privateers. Parameswara converted them into his seaborne police force, and as he did so he created a bond of loyalty between his dynasty and the *orang laut* that would last for three centuries, until the Melaka line was extinguished by murder in 1699.

Passing ships were compelled to call at Melaka but there, rather than being robbed, maltreated or taxed heavily, they found trade and warehousing facilities and fair administrative systems. So it came to be in the interest of traders to meet there. Thereby Melaka became one of the two great Asian nodes of international commerce (along with Cambay in Gujerat) in the vast trading system that stretched from East Asia and eastern Indonesia at one end to South Asia, East Africa, and the Mediterranean at the other.

The recently established Siamese state of Ayutthaya had its own aspirations to be a major center of world trade and had no interest in a competitor being established in the Straits of Melaka. To counter the Thai threat, Parameswara sent emissaries to the Ming dynasty, then led by one of its greatest emperors, Yongle. He declared his loyalty to the Ming and sought the emperor's protection. This Chinese protection was powerfully displayed in the form of the extraordinary seaborne expeditions of the great Ming admiral Zheng He. His gigantic fleets visited Melaka from 1405 to 1433. The first three kings of Melaka themselves all went on tribute missions to China, guaranteeing Ming protection from Ayutthaya.

The seaborne trade of Asia at this time was largely dominated by Muslims and there was a process of Islamization going on in maritime Southeast Asia, as discussed in the previous chapter. So it is not surprising that the Melaka dynasty, too, converted to Islam. The sequence of events, however, is not clear and has given rise to scholarly debate. Evidently Parameswara converted very late in his reign, taking the name Iskandar Syah. His successors Megat Iskandar Syah (r. 1414–23/4) and Muhammad Syah (r. 1424–44) were Muslims. It seems that there was an attempted Hindu restoration under Parameswara Dewa Syah, who reigned only briefly (1445–46) before being killed in a Muslim coup that placed his half-brother Sultan Muzaffar Syah on the throne (1446–59). Thereafter Melaka remained Islamic, became a center of Islamic scholarship, supported the spread of the religion elsewhere, and was forever after the model of what an Islamic Malay state should be.

The trade network centered on Melaka was extensive. There was much trade in high-value items such as diamonds, gold, benzoin and other wood resins, rosewater, sandalwood, and the spices of Maluku (nutmeg, clove and mace). But there was also very large-scale bulk trade in things such as Indian and Javanese textiles, Chinese silks and porcelains, rice (particularly from Java, the rice-bowl of the archipelago) and slaves (many of them captured in the Philippines and sold in the slave markets of the western archipelago). Ships themselves were bought and sold in Melaka.

The background to Portuguese interest in Melaka is discussed in Chapter 6. After initially attempting to negotiate their way into Melaka's trade, without success, the Portuguese turned to military force. Under the command of Afonso de Albuquerque, they attacked Melaka in 1511 with some 1200 men. The fighting went on for several months and was far from easy for the Portuguese, but in August 1511 Melaka at last fell to them. Now they controlled the great eastern entrepôt of the Asian trade system – or so they thought. In fact they were regularly attacked and almost permanently besieged in Melaka, undermanned, undersupplied, and poorly led. The crucial element in Melaka's success for over a century had been its international community of traders. In their attempt to dominate the trade of Asia, the Portuguese would soon discover that they might conquer the city of Melaka itself, but when they destroyed that community they destroyed the trade.

Java in the sixteenth century

During this time Java went through a fundamental religious-cultural and polit-ical transformation, but our sources are few and of uncertain veracity, so we have only an imperfect picture of how this happened. We have to rely heavily on Javanese chronicles (*babad*) which only survive in copies made well after the events. Nevertheless, some things are reasonably clear.

At the start of the century, the Hindu-Buddhist kingdom of Majapahit was in decline and threatened by north coastal Islamic states. In these circum-stances, it is possible to imagine that internationally connected Muslim commercial interests were in the ascendant on the coast, at the expense of a less commercially inclined, aristocratic Hindu-Buddhist culture centered in the interior of East Java – both of these variants being mystical in religious orienta-tion, as noted above. We should, however, be wary of imposing such simplistic interpretations just because there is little evidence to contradict them. By the end of the sixteenth century, the center of political gravity was in the process of returning to the now-Islamized interior of Central Java.

The first of the coastal Islamic states to rise to prominence was Demak. Its mosque is traditionally believed to be the first to have been built in Java. It is said to have been constructed personally (and, in part, magically) by the legendary nine *walis* – the bringers of Islam to Java. Demak seems to have been founded in the late fifteenth century by a Chinese Muslim. Its greatest ruler was known as Trenggana (r. *c.*1505–18, 1521–46), who is described as 'Sultan' in the chronicles, but this title may be an anachronism. He consolidated Demak's hegemony over other states and led the final Islamic assault on the rump of

Majapahit, then at Kediri, which fell c.1527. It is of interest that, despite the transition from the hegemony of Hindu-Buddhist Majapahit to Islamic Demak, Javanese *babads* emphasize continuity. They wrongly date the fall of Majapahit *Śaka* 1400 (CE 1478–79) and depict the ruler of Demak who conquered Majapahit– whom they call Raden Patah – as a son of the last king of Majapahit by a Chinese princess.

In West Java was located the Hindu-Buddhist port city of Banten. This was prospering as European demand rose for pepper, its main export product. C.1523–24, Demak dispatched an army under one of the *walis*, Sunan Gunungjati, which threw out Banten's lord and established Islamic rule. Banten soon became independent of Demak's authority. It conquered the very fine port of Jayakerta – today Indonesia's capital with the name Jakarta. Gunungjati's successor Hasanuddin (r. c.1552–70) also imposed Banten authority over the pepper-growing area of Lampung in South Sumatra and conquered the last significant Hindu state in Java, Pajajaran in the West Java highlands, c.1579.

The disintegration of Demak's hegemony in the later sixteenth century facilitated the rise of other states. Surabaya was one of these, but it was only in the early seventeenth century that it became a major trading state.

Meanwhile, in the interior of south-central Java, in very rich agricultural zones but rather remote from the north coastal trading routes, new forces were arising. A state called Pajang was founded in the area of present-day Surakarta. Its history is, however, most obscure. If we are to believe the *babads*, it was ruled by a single 'Sultan' who was initially a vassal of Demak, but who became independent of his coastal overlord around the middle of the century and died c.1587.

In the district of Mataram, the area of present-day Yogyakarta, a new state began to emerge c.1570. Evidently the first significant ruler of the line was Panembahan Senapati Ingalaga (r. c.1584–1601). In the mid-seventeenth century, the VOC ambassador Rijklof van Goens was told that it was Senapati who had imposed Islam by force in the district and renounced his previous loyalty to Pajang. He went on to defeat Pajang in battle c.1587–88 and thereby laid the foundations of a new Mataram dynasty, the longest lasting of all Javanese dynasties, which even today is still represented by four princely lines in Surakarta and Yogyakarta.

Indonesian outer island states, c.1400–1600

While Melaka was developing on the Malay peninsula, there were no major competitors on the Sumatran side of the Straits. But towards the end of the fifteenth century, Aceh began to gather strength. Indeed, it is possible that if the Portuguese had not attacked and conquered Melaka in 1511, the Acehnese might have tried to do so themselves.

Aceh was not so well placed for trade as Melaka, but its position at the northern tip of Sumatra was still a strategic one. Thus, it attracted many of the traders who left Melaka after the Portuguese conquest. As the westernmost port of the Malay-Indonesian region, Aceh could be traders' first port of call after an eastward crossing of the Bay of Bengal, or their last stop if sailing west. With the Portuguese in control of Melaka from 1511, a period of triangular warfare involving Melaka's successor Malay state at Johor, Portuguese Melaka, and Aceh ensued in the Straits of Melaka. This made navigation there insecure and thus disrupted trade. As a result, the longer route down the west coast of Sumatra and through the Straits of Sunda seems to have begun to be used more by traders. Thus Johor, Portuguese Melaka, and Aceh might contend for the mantle of Malay Melaka as the sole entrepôt of the western archipelago, but this was an objective that none of them could achieve, for the trading community was disrupted and dispersed.

It is important to note that this triangular warfare was not a conflict in which loyalties were determined by religion. Although there was a long history of Muslim-Christian conflict in Europe and the Middle East that was certainly well known to the Portuguese and probably as well known to the Acehnese and Johorese, this was not primarily a religious conflict in the Straits. Alliances and animosities shifted about from time to time, but the consistent enemies throughout the period were Aceh and Johor, the two Muslim states. For them, the point about the Portuguese was not that they were a Christian power but that they sought hegemony in the local trade system. So did Aceh and Johor, so the competition was about power, trade, and wealth, not about faith. Perhaps the king of Aceh also disliked the Portuguese because they were Christians, but we may be sure that he did not dislike the Johorse any less because they were Muslim.

Aceh's ruler Ali Mughayat Syah (r. 1514–30) launched expeditions that extended Aceh's control further down the eastern coast of Sumatra, where gold and pepper were produced. In 1524 he expelled the Portuguese from Pasai and defeated them in battle at sea. But Johor also claimed dependencies in East Sumatra, so from c.1540 it battled with Aceh for supremacy from Aru southward. In 1537 an Acehnese attack on Melaka was defeated and about this time Ali Mughayat Syah was deposed by his brother.

Sultan Alauddin Riayat Syah al-Kahar (r. 1537/39?–71) was a major military figure. He failed in attempts to conquer Melaka, but sacked Johor in 1564 or 1565 and took its ruler to Aceh. There the Johor ruler was executed. Yet Alauddin's reign demonstrated that it was nearly impossible for Aceh to establish any permanent form of control on the Malay peninsula. After his time, internal dissension within Aceh reduced its role in the Straits until it was revived by the greatest of its Sultans, Iskandar Muda, in the early seventeenth century (see Chapter 7).

In the sixteenth century – and, as will be seen in subsequent chapters, well into the seventeenth – Aceh and Java saw the foremost warrior kings and expanding states in maritime Southeast Asia. This was a turbulent century from Java to the west, its turbulence exacerbated by the disruptive presence of the Portuguese. Elsewhere in the archipelago there were also significant political entities, but the evidence about them is much more limited.

The Portuguese were of course interested in the spices – mace, nutmeg, and clove – from the Maluku islands in east Indonesia, the so-called 'Spice Islands'. From 1512 onwards they attempted to establish a presence there, often finding themselves entangled in local conflicts in which Portuguese firearms made them attractive allies. Here they also bumped into the Spanish, who were establishing themselves in the Philippines and similarly interested in the Spice Islands. Whereas the Spaniards were committed to Christianizing the Philippines, however, the Portuguese were tepid Christianizers at best.

The two small, nearby islands of Ternate and Tidore were the main contenders for regional pre-eminence. The Portuguese were invited to build a fortress on Ternate, which led the Sultan of Tidore to ally with the Spanish. Portuguese relations with locals – allies and enemies alike – were poor. They deposed the ruler of Ternate in 1535 and murdered the successor Sultan in 1570. But in the meantime the deposed ruler had converted to Christianity in Portuguese Goa (in India) and, before dying, presented his Portuguese godfather with a gift of the island of Ambon in 1545. Ambon now became the main center of Portuguese activity. There the Spanish Jesuit Francis Xavier began mission work in 1545–46 that laid the foundations for Christianity in Ambon and surrounding areas.

The murdered king of Ternate was succeeded by his son Sultan Baab Ullah (r. 1570–83), in whose reign genuine religious motivation was evident. He was a devout Muslim who oversaw the expulsion of the Portuguese from his realm in 1575, whereupon the Europeans moved to Tidore. Baab Ullah and his son Sultan Said ad-Din Berkat Syah (r. 1584–1606) spread Islam in surrounding islands and checked the Jesuits' hopes for widespread conversions to Christianity in northern Maluku. By the end of Baab Ullah's reign, Ternate was clearly the dominant power in the Maluku area, fiercely Islamic and wealthy from trade. Similarly, the island of Banda, which produced nutmeg, rejected Portuguese overtures and wanted nothing to do with Christianity. Some Christian communities remained in eastern Indonesia, but they were clearly minorities. Unlike the Philippines, Eastern Indonesia was not to be the westernmost outpost of Christian expansion around the globe, but rather the easternmost outpost of Islam.

One other area – Bali – resisted both Islam and Christianity, but its history in the sixteenth century is hardly known at all. Under its semi-legendary ruler Dalem Baturenggong and his chief Hindu priest Nirartha, the kingdom of Gelgel appears to have dominated Bali itself and its influence seems to have reached to the eastern tip of Java, Lombok, and Sumbawa.

6
Non-Indigenous Actors
Old and New

Introduction

It is clear from preceding pages that Southeast Asia has long been a crossroads where ideas and people met, bringing new influences and styles. Sometimes these novelties were accepted by local Southeast Asians, flourished, and became part of Southeast Asian life.

In looking at the actors who played significant roles in Southeast Asia but who were initially not from the region, we must address the question of what it meant to be 'foreign', to be 'them', in Southeast Asia. In all times and all cultures, human individuals and communities typically distinguish between 'them' and 'us'. But some communities seem more open to the possibility that 'they' might become 'us', or that 'we' might benefit from becoming more like 'them'. There is no satisfactory explanation available as to why communities differ in this way – every reader of this book may have her or his own theory – but that there are such differences is difficult to deny.

Even without a truly satisfactory causative explanation, however, we can say that Southeast Asian societies often absorbed new ideas, as seen in the discussion of new religions in Chapter 4 above. And to a large extent, at least until the high colonial age of the later nineteenth century, they also often absorbed new people. In this book we will see examples of 'foreigners' – 'them' – who before long became part of the 'us' of Southeast Asian societies. There was also conflict, but nevertheless communities and individuals who were 'hybrid', 'creole', 'mestizo', or 'mixed' have been a feature of Southeast Asian history. When we study the languages of Southeast Asia, we find many foreign words that have been imported and thereby became indigenous. If you could do a large-scale genetic analysis of Southeast Asians, you would surely find many genes whose origins are similarly to be traced to people from other parts of the world.

At the same time, however, we must not idealize Southeast Asia as a happily multi-cultural region. There was plenty of conflict and violence along 'us-and-them' lines, plenty of bloodshed and suffering. Being an Indian, European, Chinese, or Arab seafarer shipwrecked on a Southeast Asian coast might mean enslavement or a violent death. Traders in many parts of the region – both indigenous and foreign – had to take great care to protect both their goods and their persons. Being an ambassador from an outside power to a local potentate could mean lavish reception and gifts, or a quick death. When the high colonial period swept across the region in the later nineteenth century – a period after that discussed in this chapter – Southeast Asian history was full of 'us-and-them' violence.

Yet hybridization, creolization, mestizoization, and mixing did occur and constitute one of the characteristic features of the dynamic societies in the period discussed in this part of the book. Before the later colonial period, the engine driving 'us-and-them' interactions was very often trade. So trade looms large in the pages that follow.

Chinese in Southeast Asia

Chinese in Southeast Asia to the eighteenth century

From earliest recorded history, the Chinese have had close contacts with Southeast Asia. Overland contact was facilitated by physical proximity and, quite possibly, the prospects of trade. The southwestern provinces of China lie astride present-day Vietnam, Laos, Thailand, and Burma, and, while little is known about early trade routes, it seems likely that some trading contacts would have been established. As early as the second century BCE, Chinese trade routes apparently appeared between Yunnan and the Irrawaddy and Salween valleys. China's security concerns about the tribal peoples along its porous southwestern frontier provided yet another form of contact: military expeditions to assert China's political and cultural domination southwards. The first Qin emperor, for instance, after his successful conquest and unification of China in the third century BCE, dispatched soldiers against the so-called Yue peoples, who spanned the area that is now southern China and northern Vietnam. It is not clear, however, that his control extended into what is now Vietnamese territory. Following the collapse of the Qin, a new kingdom of Nanyue (Nam-Viet) appeared, whose frontiers eventually extended from Canton in southern China to present-day northern Vietnam. Nanyue's conquest of 'Vietnamese' territory brought the latter into the Chinese sphere of influence, and when Nanyue was defeated by the new Han dynasty early in the second century BCE, the ancestors of the Vietnamese came under long-term Chinese rule.

Seaborne contact between China and Southeast Asia was apparently slower to develop. As foreign trading vessels were prepared to call at Chinese ports, there was little need for Chinese merchants to sail their own ships over dangerous waters to the *Nanyang* – the 'southern ocean' – and beyond. In the absence of Han court encouragement, initial seaborne contact was probably undertaken by the few Chinese merchants, possibly from South China ports, bold enough to venture out on foreign vessels crewed by more adept Southeast Asian sailors. Chinese sepulchral pottery objects of the Han period found in Sumatra, Java, and Borneo – including one bearing an inscription dated 45 BCE – suggest that some form of seaborne trading contact had been established. While some Chinese seafaring merchants might have spent months in these southern territories, selling and buying products before returning to China, there is no record of Chinese from the Han period residing permanently in the *Nanyang*.

With the introduction of Buddhism to China in the third century CE, another form of contact came into being through the passage of Chinese pilgrims who, by the fifth and sixth centuries, were using land and maritime trade routes to India, the sacred land of their faith. The Buddhist monk Faxian, for instance, traveled overland to India but returned via Southeast Asia in 413 on a Malay-crewed ship, stopping at either Java or Malaya, where he apparently found no Chinese settlers, before proceeding to Canton. Another pilgrim, Yijing (I-tsing), reached Langkasuka in the Malay peninsula in 692. The passage of these pilgrims transformed some of the principal Sumatran port cities into centers of Sanskrit learning, where Chinese monks broke their journey for a year or more for language study before proceeding to India. Buddhist pilgrimages also stimulated Southeast Asia-China trade in Buddhist paraphernalia and related products such as aromatic woods for incense.

Following the collapse of the Han dynasty in 220, Chinese envoys from the state of Wu, the southernmost of the three kingdoms into which China split, were sent to the Mekong delta state they called 'Funan', discussed in Chapter 2 above. Such contact served an imperial Chinese purpose, for it facilitated, through demonstrations of ritual superiority, the so-called tributary system that traditionally governed China's relationship with its 'vassal' states. From the third century CE, missions from Southeast Asia bearing 'tribute' arrived at the Chinese court. As the Chinese emperor would often reciprocate with more valuable gifts than those brought by the Southeast Asian envoys, such missions also in fact represented mutually beneficial trading expeditions, and may not have carried the same connotation of 'vassalage' in the consciousness of Southeast Asian rulers.

For Southeast Asian lords, recognition of China's superior status through the ritual of tributary relationships was mutually beneficial, as it was reciprocated by Chinese recognition of their own rule and authority, as well as representing the foundations of a profitable trading relationship. 'Funan' – the first Southeast Asian recipient of Chinese envoys – must have found such a relationship worth cultivating, for it dispatched six such tributary missions to China during the third century and continued to send them up to the sixth century. Other Southeast Asian kingdoms did so as well. The arrival of such tribute-bearing trade missions from the region was recorded in Chinese dynastic records, as were accounts of Chinese missions to Southeast Asian kingdoms, such as in CE 607 when the Sui emperor, Yangdi, dispatched a seaborne mission to an unidentified area in Southeast Asia for the purpose of opening up trade. From the fourth century CE, Chinese ships began to venture out on their own along the coast and seas to trade in the *Nanyang*, with the result that by the beginning of the second millennium, Southeast Asia had become for the Chinese a place not only for trade and imperial diplomacy but also for settlement. The first record of Chinese settlers or permanent residents in the *Nanyang* came from the Yuan envoy Zhou Daguan, who reported in 1296 that there were Chinese residents at the Khmer capital of Angkor, most of them sailors who had settled there, become traders and taken local wives. This may in fact describe a situation already in existence for several centuries. On rare occasions, seaborne contacts were more belligerent: in 1292 the Yuan emperor, Kublai Khan, not satisfied with trade, attempted conquest by sending a huge fleet carrying some 20,000 soldiers to Java – an expedition that was defeated.

Under the Ming, which replaced the Yuan dynasty in 1368, the tributary system was placed on a more formal footing. Bordering tributary states, such as Dai Viet (Vietnam), were required to send tribute every three years while more distant countries, like those in maritime Southeast Asia, were permitted to send tribute infrequently. Only the port of Canton could receive tribute missions from Southeast Asia. An elaborate ceremonial ritual was instituted for the reception of tribute missions as well as for Chinese envoys sent to tributary states. To curtail contacts between Chinese and non-Chinese that might generate friction, only officially sanctioned trade through the tributary system was permitted and private Chinese overseas trade and travel were prohibited. This drastically reduced the volume and value of trade, forcing private Chinese merchants to circumvent restrictions by engaging in smuggling, while Southeast Asian states adapted by sending more tribute missions to increase trade. The Sumatran-based kingdom of Śrivijaya, for instance, dispatched six missions in the course of seven years, while Java and Ayutthaya, in the first and second half of the 1440s respectively, employed ethnic Chinese merchants to lead several official missions. To ensure the security of China's southern borders, aggressive military action was employed under the Ming, whose forces invaded Yunnan in 1381, the Tai principalities along China's southern edge in 1388, and Vietnam in 1406. The Ming sought to establish a ring of tributary kingdoms to keep the peace along China's southern frontier that included Luchuan and Cheli, the Lao principality of Lan Sang, and Lanna in northern Siam, and Ava in Burma.

The Ming desire to establish a Chinese-centered world order, a peaceful southern frontier, and a stable *Nanyang* through which trade could flow inspired the dispatch of seven great seaborne expeditions between 1405 and 1433 led by the grand imperial eunuch, Admiral Zheng He (frequently spelled Cheng Ho), a Muslim from Yunnan. These massive fleets patrolled Southeast Asian waters and sailed across the Indian Ocean as far as the Persian Gulf and the east coast of Africa. The largest of them carried nearly 30,000 men in some 300 armed ships, including the largest ocean-going vessels of that era – four-decked 'treasure ships' some 120 meters in length and 50 meters wide (approx. 400 x 165 feet), with up to nine masts. These great expeditions were perhaps designed as much to overawe foreign rulers and enroll them as tributaries of China, as to police China's long-distance Asian trade at a time when marauding hordes had shut down the overland trade route while domestic Chinese demand for luxuries was increasing.

To ensure the security of shipping through the strategic Straits of Melaka, a Chinese naval base – probably the first by an external power in Southeast Asia – was established at Melaka. This meant that the Ming fleet could be refurbished and wait in port for the change in monsoon winds. Ming sea power was also used to support local allies. As was noted in Chapter 5, Zheng He's fleet protected the fledgling state of Melaka against Ayutthaya. Ming sea power was also used to crush challenges to the existing order in the Straits, such as in 1405, when its armada defeated the naval forces of a Chinese pirate, Chen Zhuiyi, who had usurped power in Palembang in eastern Sumatra.

The records of Zheng He's expeditions reported Chinese residents in many countries, principally in the Malay peninsula, Sumatra, and Java. Muslims among these Chinese seem to have played a significant role in bringing Islam to maritime Southeast Asia. One visible legacy of the Ming expeditions was the erection of numerous temples and mosques dedicated to Zheng He in Southeast Asia, reflecting the degree to which he was revered by the Overseas Chinese communities in the region. After 1433, however, the naval expeditions were abruptly abandoned as the Ming court reoriented itself landwards to face Mongol attacks from the north. The long-standing imperial ban on private Chinese maritime trade remained, but the profitability of maritime commerce was a powerful inducement for the rise of a covert trading system by the late 1400s involving the southern Chinese provinces and Southeast Asian ports. Chinese officials could neither fully stem nor tax this trade. Following the subsequent overturning of the Ming trade ban in 1567, Southeast Asian ports experienced an upsurge in commerce and, with increased commerce, many Chinese began to settle permanently in Southeast Asia, marrying local women and setting up families, and forming Overseas Chinese communities at major trading port-cities in Brunei, the Philippines, Java, Sumatra, and the mainland states of Vietnam (particularly Dang Trong), Cambodia, and Ayutthaya, where Chinese dominated much of the commerce.

China's interest in Southeast Asia waxed and waned over successive centuries. With the upsurge in trade between China and Southeast Asia following the lifting of the ban on private merchant trade, rattan-sailed Chinese junks from southeast China became the preferred long-distance carriers for the Southeast Asian trade routes, until they were gradually eclipsed by European shipping from the late eighteenth century. The decline of Ming naval ambitions in Southeast Asia after 1433 and China's increasing isolationism meant that there was no Asian sea power capable of expelling the Portuguese and Spaniards when they first appeared in Southeast Asian waters in the early sixteenth century, or the Dutch who followed at the end of the century.

The development of colonial port-cities by the European powers, like the Portuguese at Melaka (1511), the Spaniards at Manila (1571), and the Dutch at Batavia (1619), brought new commercial opportunities that the Chinese were quick to seize. Resident Chinese communities soon became recognized features in the ports of Southeast Asia. They were especially relied upon by the European colonialists for their role in trading with China and their value as middlemen, extracting wealth from the indigenous people and servicing the colonial cities as traders, agriculturalists, harbor supervisors, local administrators, city builders, and artisans. In Melaka the Chinese became so numerous by the late sixteenth century that the Portuguese had to deal with them through an appointed local *Kapitan Cina*, usually a wealthy local Chinese merchant who was well respected by the community. Chinese also formed the commercial backbone of the Spanish colonial economy of Manila. By 1600, the Chinese in the Manila area had swelled to a population of 20,000. Substantial Chinese communities also emerged in parts of mainland Southeast Asia. In 1606, a Portuguese account recorded that some 3000 Chinese were living in Phnom Penh, while a French source put the Chinese population in Siam at 3000–4000 by the mid-seventeenth century.

The land-based Manchus from the northeast conquered China and established the Qing dynasty in 1644 and then imposed a maritime trade ban in 1656, as Qing forces battled remnant Ming loyalists in the south for the next 40 years. These Ming partisans were particularly located in the provinces of Fujian and Guangdong and relied extensively on Overseas Chinese communities in the *Nanyang* for help. The circumstances of constant warfare and political turmoil on the one hand, and close affinity between the loyalists and the *Nanyang* Chinese on the other, provided further impetus for Chinese, especially refugees from these two southern provinces, to flee to Southeast Asia. In 1679 and 1680, thousands of defeated Ming soldiers from southern provinces like Guangdong and Guangxi fled to the Mekong delta where they established armed self-governing settlements under the patronage of the Nguyen rulers, who considered their presence a useful counterweight against their Cambodian foes. The Nguyen lords' authority over these immigrants allowed them to bring parts of the delta under the control of their kingdom of Dang Trong.

When the loyalist threat subsided, the Qing reversed the overseas trade ban in 1684. Still-remaining anti-Qing sentiment was institutionalized in the rise of secret societies that subsequently formed an important facet in the social life of the southern Chinese who remained and those who moved overseas. Fearing subversion by renegade anti-Qing Chinese from abroad, the overseas trade ban was reinstituted in 1717 but lifted again in 1727 after coastal officials argued that the ban would undermine the maritime trade on which the prosperity of the southern provinces depended. Nevertheless, the security implications of allowing long-staying Overseas Chinese sojourners to return to their home communities remained controversial until 1754, when the emperor allowed them to do so after an indefinite time abroad. With the lifting of the overseas ban in 1727, a new wave of Chinese immigration descended on the *Nanyang*, with many settling in territories under European administration and contributing to their development. In Dutch Batavia, for instance, the Chinese population, managed by their own *kapitans*, played a vital role in the growth of the town. By 1739, the Chinese population had increased so substantially that there were around 15,000 living in and around Batavia alone. In areas where the political structures were weak or absent, as in western Borneo, enterprising and prospecting Chinese immigrants from the 1760s and 1770s set up self-governing independent regimes and mining confederations.

Along with Chinese expansion and indispensability also came suspicion. Chapter 7 below discusses the bloody history of Chinese massacres in Manila in the seventeenth and eighteenth centuries, in which tens of thousands were killed; the 1740 massacre of Chinese in Batavia; and the Chinese War that followed. But despite expulsions and violence against them, Chinese continued to be drawn to Southeast Asia by commercial opportunities in areas under European administration, where their resourcefulness made them indispensable to these colonial regimes. The gradual rate of immigration during the early colonial period allowed many of these immigrants to adapt to their new environs by absorption into local communities and cultures. In the Philippines, for example, intermarriage and conversion led to the creation of a distinct hybrid 'Mestizo' community, arising from unions between Chinese and Catholic Filipino women. By 1800, these Mestizos numbered around 120,000, or about 5 percent of the total Philippine population, the number of 'pure' Chinese being only about 7000. Similar hybrid 'Peranakan' and 'Baba' communities, sustaining a culture with both Chinese and indigenous Malay features, could be found in Batavia, Melaka, Penang, and Singapore. But unlike the Mestizos in the Philippines, the Peranakans and Babas in Java and Malaya retained more of their Chinese identity as neither their Dutch nor British rulers enforced an official policy of Christian conversion on them. In more tolerant societies like Siam, where assimilation was neither encouraged nor discouraged by economic necessity, and where their economic functions were complementary rather than competitive to the Thais, the Chinese found it easy to embrace widespread biculturalism and bilingualism – behaving as Thai when dealing with the majority population but remaining culturally Chinese. That Chinese ancestry was no barrier to rising to the highest levels of Siamese society could be seen in the example of King Taksin (r. 1767–82) who was born of a Chinese (Teochiu) father and a Thai mother.

Indians in Southeast Asia

The history of Indian communities in pre-colonial Southeast Asia must be disentangled from the cultural process of Indianization. As was discussed in Chapter 2, an earlier generation of scholars believed that the influence of Indian culture in the region was attributable to a fairly substantial presence of settlers from India through a process of colonization and migration. This theory is no longer tenable, and we can now safely assume that inscriptions in Sanskrit or Pali, temples in Indian-influenced architectural styles, and statues of Hindu and Buddhist deities were in most cases the product of Southeast Asian hands. This does not mean, however, that we must totally reject the idea of any sort of Indian presence in early Southeast Asia. There is evidence from various sources of priests and monks from India and Central Asia traveling through the region and on to China in the early centuries of the first millennium. Moreover, given the strength and vigor of trade around and beyond the Indian Ocean, it is logical to assume that Indian merchants criss-crossed at least the coastal parts of the region as well. By the early second millennium, the record becomes clearer, as a few inscriptions written by groups of these merchants have been found. Finally, with the expansion of Islam a few centuries later, the presence of Indian Muslims becomes an important phenomenon in Southeast Asian history.

The earliest Indians to appear in Southeast Asia were probably religious men traveling through the region. Although the ethnicity of Brahmin priests who are mentioned in early inscriptions is still in doubt, it is certainly possible that some came from India and then trained Southeast Asian counterparts. At a much later point in time, Brahmins of Indian origin were found in the Siamese and Cambodian courts as well, performing specific rituals which were outside the sphere of Buddhist culture. It is also known that Buddhist monks traveled as missionaries to China and to northern Vietnam (Giao Chau) when it was under Chinese rule. It seems likely that these individuals would have stayed for some time, as missionaries often do. One source has an interesting reference to a locally born but ethnic Chinese governor in Giao Chau who, whenever he went out in his carriage, was accompanied by *Hu* priests – a term which refers to those of Indian or Central Asian origin. The information on these individuals is scattered and anecdotal but suggests that their presence was significant, if not necessarily large. One place which may have had a more sizable community of Indian religious men is Śrivijaya, which is known to have been a major center for the study and translation of Buddhist texts.

Over the long term, the major links between India and Southeast Asia were of course based on trade. Between the ninth and thirteenth centuries, the powerful Chola dynasty of Tamil-speaking southern India was expanding its political, military, and commercial influence along the eastern edge of the Indian Ocean. During this period, Tamil merchant guilds also expanded their activities to parts of Southeast Asia, and several inscriptions have been found which attest to their presence. Tamil inscriptions have been found in Sumatra, peninsular Thailand (Nakhon Si Thammarat), and in Pagan. There are also references to traders from various parts of India in Javanese epigraphy during the same period. It should be emphasized that 'India' as an entity did not exist at this time. Southeast Asians sources distinguished several different categories of 'Indians', based on their region of origin.

If the arrival of Hinduism and Buddhism in the first millennium represented the first great nexus of trade and religion between India and Southeast Asia, the second such connection was forged beginning in the thirteenth century with the arrival of Islam. The Muslim faith came to Southeast Asia along different paths and through different agents at different times. It seems quite clear that more than one of these paths led from India, particularly the Malabar (south-western) and Coromandel (southeastern) coasts, areas which spoke Malayalam and Tamil respectively. Some scholars have also hypothesized a connection with Bengal, which also has a significant Muslim population, but there is less evidence for this link on any significant scale. Muslim Indian communities were also found in cities like Ayutthaya which were home to foreign traders from many countries; they would have lived and worshipped with Arabs, Persians, and co-religionists from Southeast Asia.

During the pre-colonial period, the Indian communities in Southeast Asia undoubtedly included both short-term residents and settlers who remained permanently. They would have been relatively few in number and would have blended in well in ethnically diverse capitals and cosmopolitan courts. Being Hindu or Muslim in a society which was not could have posed problems, but Muslim Indians in a Muslim kingdom would probably have been very much at home. It is also likely that these early Indian communities were mainly involved with trade and did not compete with local Southeast Asians in other crafts. Under colonial rule, however, patterns of migration would shift, and Indians would immigrate to the region in much larger numbers, significantly changing the demographics of some Southeast Asian societies. They would come to dominate particular occupations and often achieved considerable financial power.

The tensions arising from these developments will be discussed in later chapters. The point to be made here is that in earlier centuries Indian communities were smaller, and their presence in local societies was almost certainly less controversial. Much of their role in pre-colonial Southeast Asian history is, however, 'off the record' and cannot be reconstructed with any certainty.

Arabs in Southeast Asia

Arab traders were interested in Southeast Asia from quite early times, but it is unclear to what extent their information was second-hand via international trading networks. A significant Arab presence in Southeast Asia seems to have begun only in early Islamic times, which corresponded with a period of expanding international trade that enriched the Sumatran kingdom of Śrivijaya. As noted in Chapter 4, already in the seventh century Muslim emissaries from newly Islamic Arabia arrived at the Chinese court. Ninth-century Arab accounts show that Arab ships were reaching China and there was a community in Canton of several thousand Arabs. These ships and people can only have reached China by traveling via Southeast Asia. From the early tenth to the mid-twelfth centuries, the kingdom of Śrivijaya sent emissaries with Arab names to the Chinese court – although we cannot be sure that these were actually Arabs, given the widespread custom of Muslim converts adopting Arabic names. So we can assume that there were Arabs at least traveling through, and perhaps living for a time in, Southeast Asia from the early days of Islam.

Arab involvement in Southeast Asia seems, however, to have fallen away somewhat after the tenth century. This is reflected in Arabic textual references from that period, which contain little new information and tend instead to reproduce information from earlier works. This evidently reflected a decline in trading connections with Southeast Asia.

With the spread of Islam in Southeast Asia from around the thirteenth century, the Arab presence seems again to have grown. It was once assumed that Arabs were the main bringers of Islam to Southeast Asia, but it is generally agreed now that there were Muslims from many areas involved in this process. Nevertheless, Arabs have often been accorded a certain pre-eminence in Islamic societies. So Arab traders, travelers, and preachers begin to appear in the history of Southeast Asia's Islamic regions from the time of Islamization.

One of the foremost Arab travelers to record his experience in Southeast Asia was the Moroccan Ibn Battuta, who visited Samudra on the northern tip of Sumatra in 1345–46. When the Muslim Chinese writer Ma Huan visited the north coast of Java in 1413–15, he noted three kinds of people there: Chinese, many of them Muslims; local people, whom he describes as 'devil-worshippers'; and Muslims, 'from every foreign kingdom in the West who have migrated to this country as merchants'.[1] Among this last group there would certainly have been Arabs.

---

1   Ma Huan, *Ying-yai Sheng-lan: The overall survey of the ocean's shores (1433)*, ed. and trans. J. V. G. Mills (Cambridge: Cambridge University Press, 1970), 93.

Arabs had little political influence in Southeast Asia. In some places, they did become local rulers. There were three Arab rulers of Aceh in the years 1699–1726, but this was a period when the Sultanate was weak. In the eighteenth century, Arab *sayyids* (descendants of the Prophet) from Hadhramaut – whence most Arabs in Southeast Asia have come – were influential in the trade of the western archipelago and particularly in Siak, Palembang, Perlis, and Pontianak. In the mid-eighteenth century the Sultan of Banten had an Arab wife who was influential in disastrous court intrigues there. But it is important to note that in no place in Southeast Asia did a community of Arabs take over power and establish their own kingdom. Nor did they ever exist in sufficient numbers to be a military force in the region. There were Arab traders, Arab travelers, and Arab religious, but no Arab armies and no Arab dynasties in Southeast Asia.

A shared Islamic faith would have made it easy for Arabs to integrate into local Southeast Asian societies if they wished to do so, and we may presume that this often happened. But at the same time, the Arab claim to pre-eminence among Muslims – which may have been particularly strong and useful in the case of communities recently converted to Islam – has not infrequently inclined them to live as exclusive communities. Arabs who claim to be descendants of the Prophet himself, the *sayyids*, frequently married only within their own *sayyid* community. Thus, ironically, while Arabic language and culture and the Islamic faith had widespread influence in Southeast Asia, Arabs themselves sometimes remained rather aloof from local societies.

Europeans in Southeast Asia: the background

In the fourteenth and fifteenth centuries, Christian Europe was, in global terms, a rather backward place. Its technology was in many respects inferior to that of China. The non-Christian Vikings undertook daring voyages into the Atlantic, but in the early fifteenth century China was the greatest seafaring country of the world. Zheng He's fleets were described earlier in this chapter. It was not Christian civilization that was then spreading across the globe, but rather Islam, as we saw in Chapter 4. In 1453 Ottoman Turkey conquered Constantinople, bringing to an end the Eastern Roman Empire (Byzantium). In 1529 the Ottomans besieged Vienna, albeit without success. Again in 1683 they failed to take Vienna, a story that gets rather ahead of the discussion here.

It was in Spain and Portugal that Europeans first regained the initiative. Arab armies conquered the Iberian Peninsula in the eighth century. European Christians thereafter sought to regain control of these lands. So the reconquest – in Spanish and Portuguese 'the *Reconquista*' – began at an early stage of Muslim rule and, from the perspective of Christians, gradually became linked to the medieval Crusades against Islam (1095–1492). There were periods of warfare and periods of peace, and fluctuating borders, but by the thirteenth and fourteenth centuries the *Reconquista* was winning. Major turning points included the reconquest of Cordoba in 1236, of Seville in 1248, and finally of Granada in 1492, ending the rule of the 'Moors' (*Moros* in Spanish and Portuguese) in the Iberian Peninsula. This last year, 1492, was indeed historic, for only a few months after the fall of Granada, Christopher Columbus – an Italian (Genoese) navigator with experience in Portugal who sailed on behalf of the Spanish crown of Castile – discovered the new world of the Americas.

How was it possible for Europeans to sail the oceans for thousands of kilometers, to circumnavigate the globe for the first time in human history and to become – eventually – a force in Southeast Asia and elsewhere? What was it that made them take an interest in Southeast Asia? The answers to these questions, as seen from the twenty-first century, seem remarkably simple, but at the time they were revolutionary.

Three areas were important: ship-building, navigation, and warfare. Medieval European square-rigged sailing ships or rowed galleys, which usually used sails as well, were fine in the Mediterranean, but neither was appropriate for long-distance ocean voyages. So Europeans borrowed from Arabs the lateen sail – a triangular device that is more maneuverable and enables craft to sail closer to the wind. When lateen sails were combined with square-rigging, European ships achieved greater speed and maneuverability. In other respects, too, they were being built to an improved standard.

Navigation was crucial. Medieval shipping mostly navigated by landmarks. But out of sight of land, sailors had to navigate by the positions of the sun, moon, and stars. And that, in turn, depended on the best possible astronomical knowledge. Arab astronomy was in advance of European – which is why so many astronomical and other scientific terms and star names in European languages are of Arabic derivation, words such as algebra, Algol, algorithm, Alioth, Alkaid, Alphard, alchemy, amber, and azimuth. With a cross-staff or mariner's astrolabe in hand, sailors could then determine latitude out of sight of land. The problem of determining longitude, however, was not solved until the later eighteenth century, so ocean navigation was still a crude and dangerous exercise.

Finally, gunnery was important. In warfare, medieval European ships were used as floating platforms for bowmen or ramming devices. Asian trading ships of the time were only lightly armed, or in fact mostly unarmed. It was the northern European Hanseatic League which began to arm merchant ships as a way of protecting them. In the early fourteenth century, gunpowder – which had been known to the Chinese for several centuries – was introduced into Europe. This had a revolutionary effect on warfare, both on land and at sea. European advances in metallurgy made heavier guns possible and Europeans began to place these cannon on their ships which, because of the weight, had to be placed on lower decks. This in turn required the invention of water-tight portholes, so that waves or a ship's angle would not cause flooding of the lower decks. Thus ships became floating artillery platforms and the formidable broadside technique became possible. With better, faster, and more maneuverable ships, heavy guns on board and means of finding their way on long voyages, the Europeans began their search for Asia.

European interest in Asia arose largely out of intellectual and technological backwardness. Through the European winter, large animal herds could not be fed, so many animals were slaughtered and their meat then had to be preserved. Common methods were vinegar and salting. But the best preservatives were the expensive spices that came from Indonesia: pepper, nutmeg, mace and, above all, cloves. These came in on the Asian trade network dominated by Muslims and then into Europe mainly via Venice. There were travelers' accounts of the exotic – and fabulously wealthy – lands of Asia, the most famous being the thirteenth-century travels of Marco Polo. And there were tales of a lost Christian kingdom – that of Prester John – mainly deriving from vague information about the Coptic Christians of Ethiopia or the Saint Thomas Christians of India. So Europeans wanted to get around the Muslim traders – the old enemy of Crusading Europe – and to reach Asia themselves.

Thus, by the late fifteenth century the Spanish and Portuguese had the motivation and the means to seek their own routes to Asia. Among their principal objectives were the 'Spice Islands' of the eastern Indonesian archipelago – although of course they had no idea where those islands might really be. In fact, Europeans believed that nutmeg came from Muscat (Oman), as a consequence of which nutmeg is still today called *muskaatnoot* in Dutch, *Muskatnuss* in German, and *muscade* in French.

The Spanish and Portuguese in Southeast Asia, to the sixteenth century

In the course of the fifteenth century, the Portuguese began to explore outside Europe. The first European colony overseas was established when they took Ceuta, across the Straits of Gibraltar in Morocco, in 1415. Ceuta passed into Spanish hands in the seventeenth century and remains an autonomous city under Spanish rule – one of the very few European colonies overseas still existing in the twenty-first century. Then the Portuguese searched southward along the west coast of Africa, hoping that the route would turn east towards Asia.

'Gold, God and glory' were said to drive the Portuguese: the gold of Africa and, symbolically, the vast wealth of Asia; the Christian God in whose name they sought to outflank and if necessary fight the Muslim enemy; and the glory (and potential wealth) of conquest. This extraordinary adventure, which took Europeans on voyages longer than any yet attempted by humankind, into lands almost entirely unknown to them, was thus in their minds partly a seaborne extension of the *Reconquista*. Needless to say, they also sought the spices of Indonesia, imported into Europe via a near-total Muslim monopoly. Among the patrons of these voyages of discovery down the African coast, the most famous was the Portuguese prince known as Henry 'the Navigator' (d. 1460), who combined Catholic piety and crusading instincts with a measure of curiosity about the lands beyond Europe.

Eventually – after Prince Henry's time – Bartolomeu Dias rounded the Cape of Good Hope in 1488, thus opening a potential route to India. In 1497 Vasco da Gama reached India itself. There the Portuguese found much that surprised and, indeed, disappointed them. Certainly there was wealth to be seen, but Prester John was not there to greet them – although the Portuguese did briefly mistake an image of a Hindu goddess for a slightly odd depiction of the Virgin Mary. Most importantly, it became clear that the Portuguese had limited prospects in the trade of Asia, for European goods could hardly compete with what was available in India's markets. So the Portuguese had to take another approach. Rather than trading their way into Asia, they would try to dominate Asia's trade through military force. Looking back from the present and bearing in mind the tiny size of Portugal and the vast expanse of Asia, this plan is breathtaking. Not surprisingly, it failed, but nevertheless the Portuguese had a significant impact in several places as they tried to implement this audacious strategy.

Afonso de Albuquerque was given the task of implementing the Portuguese strategy. He was probably the most outstanding naval commander of the age. The plan was to capture strategic points on the Asian trade routes and, from them, project Portuguese naval power and thereby dominate the trade. The first stage was the conquest of Socotra (now part of Yemen) in 1507 near the crucial Horn of Africa. Then Goa on the west coast of India fell to Albuquerque in 1510 – and the Portuguese held it as a colony until, 451 years later, an independent Indian government marched in and expelled them.

With strategic posts at the western end of the Asian trade network and in India, the Portuguese now turned to the vital Southeast Asian entrepôt at Melaka. The Portuguese king sent an emissary to make an amicable agreement with Sultan Mahmud Syah (r. 1488–1528), but this ended in hostility, as local Muslims traders persuaded Mahmud not to deal with the Europeans. So Albuquerque decided to attack Melaka.

Albuquerque set sail from Goa in 1511 with some 1200 men and 17 or 18 ships. But fighting Melaka was no easy task. The Portuguese had superior ships with heavy cannon on board, but Melaka was also well defended by cannon. Indeed, artillery was one of the fields of military technology in which innovations – from whatever source – often transferred rapidly around the world. But Melaka was internally divided, for Sultan Mahmud was in conflict with his son, whom he later murdered, and some local merchants supported the Sultan while others sided with the Portuguese. Eventually, after many bloody encounters, Melaka fell to the Europeans.

With the fall of Melaka to the Portuguese, that city's eminence in the trade of the western archipelago came to an end. The Portuguese had imagined that whoever controlled the city could dominate the Asian trade. But Asian trade was a more fragile thing than that. Ship-borne traders could simply decide to gather elsewhere to do their deals and, in the wake of Melaka's fall, many decided to do so. The Portuguese found the trade of Asia slipping through their fingers. But the greatest of all prizes, the 'Spice Islands', now seemed to lay before them: in 1512 the first Portuguese voyage reached Indonesia's Maluku archipelago, and was shipwrecked there.

While the Portuguese were exploring eastwards around the globe to reach Asia, the Spanish were exploring westwards out into the Atlantic. They miscalculated the size of the globe and thought that Asia was not an interminable distance to the west. They were wrong, but when Columbus first discovered the Americas in 1492, he and others were persuaded that they must have reached India. Thus the local people they encountered were dubbed Indians.

With both the Spanish and the Portuguese thinking that they were on the way to Asia, there arose competition between them about which had the right to dominate what they were discovering. Thus arose one of the most astonishingly presumptuous episodes of this early stage of European expansion. The Pope drew a line down the Atlantic Ocean and decreed that what was west of that line would belong to the Spanish and what was east would belong to the Portuguese. No one involved in this had much idea of the actual geography being carved up in this way, but that was a matter of little concern. The Portuguese were unhappy with the Pope's arrangement, so in 1494 Spanish and Portuguese negotiators settled on their own deal, but one still consistent with the idea that these small European states could divide the world in two and take half each. At the Treaty of Tordesillas (subsequently ratified by another Pope), they agreed on a line that left what had been discovered in the Americas to the Spanish and what was being found by the Portuguese down the coast of Africa to them. The line was drawn in such a way that Brazil fell on the Portuguese side of the line, which is why Brazil today is a Portuguese-speaking nation in a Spanish-speaking continent. More problematically, no one knew where this line might fall if it were to be extended all of the way around the globe. This became a serious matter when the Spanish reached the Philippines.

The Spanish were at first fully occupied with the conquest of their new discoveries in the Americas, discoveries which soon proved to be the source of so much silver and gold that Spain became the richest nation in Europe. But they still sought a way to the 'Spice Islands', which meant navigating across the greatest of all the world's oceans, the Pacific. Ferdinand Magellan, a Portuguese who sailed for the Spanish Crown, led the first expedition to achieve this crossing, the very longest stage in the first circumnavigation of the globe in 1519–22. The trip was fraught with great difficulty – attempted mutinies, shipwrecks, illness, shortage of supplies, and much else – and of the original five ships and crew of 270 men only one ship and 19 men lived to see Spain again. Nor did their commander survive the voyage. In 1521 the expedition reached the Philippines, where Magellan (as described in Chapter 4) became involved in a local dispute and was killed. It was some time before the Spanish established a real foothold in the Philippine islands, but from their first contact, the question necessarily arose of whose territory this was – the Spanish or the Portuguese? Both claimed that they were the rightful possessors of the 'Spice Islands', for the Portuguese said they had reached the area by sailing east, and it was thus theirs by virtue of the Treaty of Tordesillas, while the Spanish could now say that they had reached it by sailing west and it was thus theirs by virtue of the same treaty. In 1529 the two sides agreed in the Treaty of Zaragoza on a partition of their territories in Southeast Asia. It was still the case that ideas of longitude were very shaky, but the two agreed that the Philippines could be claimed by Spain and Maluku by Portugal.

Neither the Spanish nor the Portuguese, of course, had consulted local people about what they thought of these Christians who now claimed to be their rulers or of the new faith they brought. Many Spaniards and Portuguese would die discovering that local people in fact thought very little of either.

It is one of the ironies of this global age that, following on the Iberian *Reconquista*, the Spanish sailed westwards around the globe just as Islam was spreading eastwards in Southeast Asia. When the Spanish arrived in the

Philippines, they discovered an archipelago in the process of Islamization. Thus, having gone in opposite directions around the globe, Catholics and Muslims faced each other again at the end of their expansion on the other side. Unsurprisingly, the Spanish called the local Muslims *Moros*, a term still used for Filipino Muslims today.

The Spanish were to have a massive impact on Filipino society (see Chapter 7) but the impact of the Portuguese was far more limited. The Portuguese took Melaka and established various positions in eastern Indonesia, but their social impact was quite restricted. Even Christianization was limited, as already noted in Chapter 5. Their actual control of territory was limited to a few specific posts and they never achieved their aim of dominating the spice trade of Indonesia. In the western archipelago, Portuguese became participants in both the trade of the region and the so-called triangular warfare that plagued the Straits of Melaka, as discussed in the previous chapter. It would be wrong to think the Portuguese insignificant, but it would be equally wrong to see them as a dominant power in Southeast Asia. By the end of the sixteenth century, they were challenged and, ultimately, displaced by northern Europeans.

The northern Europeans

The cold winters of northern Europe made the preservative spices of Indonesia's 'Spice Islands' all the more important as trade items. In the sixteenth century, the Portuguese had nearly a total monopoly of the supply of these spices into Europe. In the north, the Dutch acted as middlemen for Lisbon in the sale of these spices. Needless to say, they and other northern Europeans desired to get their own direct access to those spices and thereby cut out the Portuguese.

But this was not just a commercial matter, for the competition between the northern Europeans and the Iberians was religious as well. It was in some ways not really 'national', for we are discussing an age before nationalism was a dominant sentiment, before the modern concepts of nation and national identity were firmly established, indeed before many of the nations we are used to today – Germany or Italy for example – had been created. When we discuss the activities of the VOC, it is worth noting that many of its officers were men whom we would not now call Dutch at all, but rather Scots, Poles, Swedes, Danes, Norwegians, Prussians, Bavarians, Wurttemburgers, Swiss, Irish, English, and so on. Religion was, however, an important form of identity, for this competition was caught up in the bitter, bloody hatreds generated by the Protestant Reformation.

In the early sixteenth century, the first stages of the Protestant Reformation began, denying the authority of the Pope and, as Protestant preachers saw it, the corrupting influence of the Catholic Church. Instead, they argued, one must return to the Bible and there find the true, unsullied message of Jesus's teachings. In this book, we will see this idea that one embraces the modern world by restoring the texts of an ancient time recurring in other, much later, modernizing movements in Asia as well as in Europe. Ignoring many complexities, we may observe that in the course of the sixteenth century, Europe became generally divided between a Protestant north and a Catholic south, a religious difference that sparked bitter conflict. The bloody wars of religion of the sixteenth and seventeenth centuries cost tens of thousands of lives and left legacies of animosity, the traces of which are sometimes still visible even in twenty-first-century Europe.

The people of the 'Low Countries' – today's Netherlands, Belgium, and Luxembourg – were central both to the commercial and to the religious conflicts of the age. These lands were under the control of Spain in the early sixteenth century, but the 'United Provinces' of the Netherlands launched a war of independence against their Spanish overlords from the 1560s. This was a war of Calvinist Dutchmen against Catholic Spain, which led to movements of population within the Low Countries themselves. Thus the southern provinces (today's Belgium and Luxembourg) became more homogeneously Catholic while the northern (today's Netherlands) became more homogeneously Calvinist. When the Spanish and Portuguese Crowns were united in 1580 (until 1640), the Spanish-Dutch war meant that the supply of Portuguese spices to northern Europe via Dutch middlemen was disrupted, enhancing the incentives for Dutchmen to get into the spice trade directly.

Jan Huygen van Linschoten was one of several Dutchmen who had experience in Portuguese service and who knew something about the route to Asia and the problems the Portuguese were facing there. In 1595–96 van Linschoten published *Reys-gheschrift vande navigatien der Portugaloysers in Orienten* ('Travel Account of Portuguese Navigation in the Orient') and *Itinerario naer Oost ofte Portugaels Indien* ('Itinerary to the East, or Portuguese, Indies'). The Portuguese had tried to keep information about the route to Asia secret, but van Linschoten provided maps and descriptions of what they had discovered in their voyages. This gave Dutch navigators confidence both that they could find the route and that the Portuguese would be no match for them. Indeed, by this time the Dutch had better ships, better armaments, better funding, and better organization than the Portuguese, and were well accustomed to fighting Catholics.

The military aspects of this period deserve emphasis. The wars fought in Europe in the sixteenth and seventeenth centuries were a major engine of technological advance, as has often been true of war, and of progress in the social organization of warfare. In this the Dutch were leaders. Under Prince William of Orange, the Dutch initiated their Eighty Years' War against Spain from the 1560s to 1648. After that they were engaged in the First (1652–54), Second (1665–67), and Third (1672–74) Anglo-Dutch Wars. William of Orange's son Prince Maurits of Nassau is generally regarded as the greatest European soldier of his age. The Dutch also produced great admirals and military engineers. So this small area on the northwest tip of Europe – in due course to become the colonial overlord of the vast Indonesian archipelago – in the sixteenth and seventeenth centuries became one of the great warrior nations of Europe. Improved artillery, small arms, siegecraft, fortifications, drill, tactics, and logistics all came out of these wars, with the northern Europeans generally in advance of the southern.

The first Dutch voyage to Southeast Asia set off from the Netherlands in

1595, and produced mixed results. It was commanded by another Dutchman with experience in Portuguese service, Cornelis de Houtman, but he was not a competent leader and there was much conflict within his own crew. Of his original crew of 249 men, only 89 survived to reach home in 1597. De Houtman got to Banten in 1596, which (as noted in Chapter 5) was by now a Muslim-governed port. There he wanted to buy pepper, but he generated conflict with both the locals and the Portuguese there. So he left and sailed along Java's north coast to Madura and Bali, causing conflicts at several places as he did so. Despite such problems, the expedition returned with enough spices on board to show a profit.

This inspired other Dutch shippers to sail for the east. A period known as the 'wild voyages' (*wilde vaart*) followed, as various companies were formed to get into the spice trade. In 1598, 22 ships belonging to five competing companies sailed from the Netherlands. The expedition led by Jacob van Neck reached the 'Spice Islands' of Maluku and returned with enough spices on board to show a 400 percent profit. This of course inspired others to seek their fortunes in this lucrative trade. In 1601, 14 separate expeditions set sail from the Netherlands.

But it was becoming clear that this unregulated competition would undermine profits. Competition among competing Dutch agents was driving purchase prices up in Asia while increasing supply was driving sales prices down in Europe. So the Dutch parliament – the States-General – pressed competing companies to merge into a joint enterprise in the mutual interest of all. Eventually the companies agreed to this, and in 1602 they came together to form the *Vereenigde Oost-Indische Compagnie* (VOC: United East India Company), which was granted a charter by the States-General. This charter established the VOC as a semi-sovereign power. It could enlist personnel on an oath of allegiance, sign treaties, build fortresses, and wage wars in Asia. It was funded by people buying and trading its shares on the Amsterdam stock market, also created in 1602 for this purpose. This was the first stock market in history and the VOC was one of the earliest examples of a joint-stock company. The distribution of ownership through the sale of shares and the small size of the Dutch population (perhaps some 670,000 in the 1620s) compared to that of the Indonesian archipelago (unknowable, but perhaps somewhere between 8 and 11 million at that time) – not to mention the other places where the VOC became active – together meant that for the Netherlands the VOC was a major, 'national' enterprise that involved much of the population, including even working-class people who purchased shares. The wealth that the VOC brought to the Netherlands led the seventeenth century to be regarded as the nation's 'Golden Age'.

If the VOC was an early joint-stock company, however, it was not the first, for the English had already created such corporate structures to support their colonization of North America and intrusion into the spice trade. English contact with the Maluku 'Spice Islands' began when Sir Francis Drake called there during his circumnavigation of the globe in 1577–80, even before the first Dutch voyages. But the English had less enthusiasm for the spice trade than their neighbors across the North Sea. In 1591 Queen Elizabeth I approved a voyage led by Sir James Lancaster and George Raymond which proved to be a disaster. Many died during the voyage and Raymond was lost at sea along with his ship. Lancaster got to Sumatra and the Malay peninsula but on his way home sailed across to the West Indies and was there marooned. A French privateer brought him home to England in 1594. The English were not encouraged by this experience, but when the news arrived of the great profits won by the first Dutch voyages, minds were changed. In 1600 Elizabeth I granted a royal charter to the English East India Company (EEIC). In 1602 the EEIC built a trading post at Banten, which was to remain its main post in Southeast Asia for 80 years. Two years later a voyage commanded by Sir Henry Middleton got to Maluku. Thus began years of intense rivalry and conflict between the English and the Dutch for control of the spice trade. In 1623 this rivalry peaked – after a failed effort at collaboration between the English and the Dutch – in what was known in England as the 'Amboyna [i.e., Ambon] massacre'. The Dutch tortured and executed ten English trading agents, ten Japanese, and a Portuguese who were said to be part of a conspiracy against the VOC. After some diplomatic outrage in Europe, the English withdrew from direct involvement in Maluku and concentrated on the pepper trade of the western archipelago. The main activity of the EEIC would, in the future, be not in Southeast Asia, but rather in India, where it laid the foundations for the British Empire.

7

Early Modern Southeast Asian States

Introduction

In preceding chapters of this book, we have emphasized the new elements that came into play in Southeast Asia in earlier centuries of its history. After the time of the 'classical' pre-modern states, the new religions, new actors, and new ideas of Chapters 4 and 6 swept across Southeast Asia. These formed part of the background and context of the new states discussed in Chapter 5.

Now we turn to the states we are calling 'early modern' – a classification that would not necessarily be accepted by all Southeast Asian historians, but which will serve our purposes here. This category is meant to distinguish these states both from the foundational states of Chapter 5 on the one hand – states that typically prospered before significant European impact – and from the colonial-era polities of Chapter 8 on the other – places where European and American impact was profound.

In these early modern states we will see consolidation, factionalism, revolution, and much significant involvement by Europeans, but we will not see societies and states fundamentally transformed by Western colonialism. Here the formative, new, globalized influences were principally those of the religions discussed in Chapter 4, which influenced societies and political systems before they were disrupted by European and American colonialism. From the perspective of the twenty-first century, we may come to the view that these globalized religions not only influenced Southeast Asia before there was any deep European impact, but also that their influence was – and remains – more profound and enduring than that of the West.

But we should not see these early modern states as creations solely or even mainly of those globalizing religions. Local idiosyncrasies abounded and local issues, considerations, and actors were the principal shapers of developments. In Southeast Asia's rich cultural forms we will see local genius powerfully molding the way in which foreign ideas became part of indigenous life.

Burma under the Konbaung dynasty, c.1752–1824

The founding of the Konbaung dynasty

In the 1750s, a provincial leader, known later as Alaungpaya (Embryo Buddha), defeated local rivals and crowned himself in Ava as the new Burmese king (r. 1752–60). He moved southward to defeat Pegu and its satellite centers in 1757. Unification of the Irrawaddy river basin ushered in new administrative, cultural, and economic reforms that were adopted and developed to differing degrees under subsequent kings such as Hsinbyushin (r. 1763–76), Bodawpaya (r. 1782–1819), and Bagyidaw (r. 1819–37). By 1759 Alaungpaya had re-conquered the Shan and re-established control in Manipur. In the 1760s and 1770s, his successors not only breached the defenses of Ayutthaya but also repelled four major Chinese invasions.

Pacification of the Shan territories, managing disputes with China over Yunnan, renewing competition with Ayutthaya, and initiating resettlement programs in the delta region were indicative of larger attempts by the court to administer the population, define the boundaries of the kingdom, and strengthen its authority over provincial territories. As early as 1753, Alaungpaya already invited former officials from the old Ava administration to help manage his affairs and attracted key monks to help purify the religious sector. Additionally, the cultural processes connected to forming ideas of 'Burmeseness', a trend that could be traced back to classical Pagan, received innovative contributions from the new 'Konbaung' authorities – a name deriving from the region Alaungpaya had once ruled as its chieftain.

Challenges facing the Konbaung monarchy were similar to those faced by earlier kings. Factionalism in the court, ministerial rivalries, and a relatively powerful – yet divided – religious sector continued to offer alternative patronage opportunities for bondsmen, thus depriving the state of unchallenged access to talent, labor, and expertise. The Konbaung court introduced administrative reforms to address both domestic and foreign policy concerns, many of them directed towards the allocation and organization of resources. Burmese dealings with the western frontier, however, became an unprecedented problem, for the military capabilities and worldviews of the English East India Company – which by then ruled much of India – were unlike anything the Burmese had experienced before.

Konbaung administrative reforms, 1752–1824

Konbaung domestic policy reproduced many earlier approaches towards managing manpower. The central issue was the need to curb provincial leaders and the religious sector from attracting labor and talent away from the crown service corps. Alaungpaya reorganized the military service, re-established authority over headmen, created new subordinate officials, and raised the level of oversight in regional centers. Whereas earlier kings might have assigned relatives to manage secondary territories (*bayins*) beyond the core of the kingdom, Konbaung kings kept these potential claimants to the throne very close to the

capital, opting instead to appoint members of the court with minimal credentials for succession as governors (*myo-wuns*) of these territories. Furthermore,
lower officials were directly appointed by the throne, giving greater access to
local affairs and limiting opportunities for governors to threaten the authority
of the monarchy. New patronage networks through marriage and personal ties
were also forged which tightened control over lowland areas and highland
zones that had previously maintained more autonomous relations with the
distant court. Following the precedent set by King Thalun in 1635, these measures enabled the court to conduct kingdom-wide censuses in 1783 and 1802,
in order to fix new taxes and more effectively manage service contributions
from townships and villages. The dynasty also streamlined its governance by
modifying military organization and quotas, standardizing silver coinage,
expanding the tax system, and extending its legal system to reflect the wide
range of commercial contracts and land sale documents that were now being
used.

Burmese cultural trends, 1752–1824

Seventeenth-century territorial expansion and administrative reforms managed
an increasing population and Konbaung monarchs continued these policies in
the eighteenth century. They extended the reach of the state through village
monasteries, which also served as educational centers. Broader-reaching and
more penetrating policies required greater literacy and systematic instruction.
With the expansion of monastic education, literacy probably became more
widespread and the quality of administration was presumably thereby enhanced.
Factionalism and sectarianism within the Buddhist *Sangha* – highlighted in a
famous 'robe controversy' over whether monks should cover one or both shoulders – drew intervention from King Bodawpaya in the beginning of the nineteenth century, reflecting several Crown attempts to define and standardize
Buddhist 'orthodoxy' throughout the kingdom. Debates over calendar reform,
religious festivals, secular practices, and technical understandings of Buddhist
thought were addressed through committees and councils of senior monks of
the king's choosing. Ideas of what constituted 'Burmese Buddhism' would
continue to be fluid, however, as each new king appointed a different head of
the monastic order (*thathanabaing*) upon coming to the throne.

Attempts to define religious orthodoxy were mirrored by similar court
efforts to influence notions of identity, values, and status through popular
culture. Normative works of fiction, history, architecture, law, poetry, drama,
and dress styles spread to local courts and thence to provincial communities.
These texts emphasized pan-Burman notions of identity and loyalty, synthesiz-
ing local histories into visions of the past focused on the central court. In doing
so, local symbols and notions of sanctity were made to seem less auspicious than
those officially sanctioned by the Crown. Through these processes, local
communities were presented with different and perhaps more attractive options
through which their own worldviews and loyalties could be expressed.

Another indicator of a growing sense of a 'Burmese' community was the
proliferation of popular theatre from as early as the 1730s and 1740s. This

trend was continued under Konbaung kings such as Bagyidaw, who compiled immense records of plays, dance, and music that no doubt reached local audiences as provincial leaders emulated the center. Traveling troupes performed – and thereby promoted – current understandings of Buddhism, notions of social hierarchy, and imperial history to rural audiences.

Communities and boundaries

Konbaung kings maintained complicated foreign relations with their neighbors. The challenge for the state was how to manage fluid borders with neighboring kingdoms and tributary dependencies when those boundaries were often not recognized by communities living there. Much of the conflict that evolved with colonial foreign powers (notably the British) was a result of competing notions of where legal authority began and ended over people, resources, and land. An episode with an Arakanese chief from Chittagong was an example of such tensions. In 1811, a man named Chin Pyan led a violent movement that took control of Arakan, killing nearly the entire Burman population in the capital city of Mro-haung. He then offered to become a vassal to the British. Although this offer was rejected and a British emissary was sent to King Bodawpaya's court to report this position, this event and the failure of the East India Company to neutralize Chin Pyan significantly affected Anglo-Burmese relations and highlighted the instability of the kingdom's borders with Arakan, Assam, and Manipur. Securing the western border and avenging Burmese losses became as important a priority as the kingdom's dealings with Siam in the east. Multiple cross-border raids exacerbated the problem, for dissident communities sought refuge in British territory after engaging in military activities against areas claimed by Burma. The Burmese army occupied Assam in order to secure the region against these raids, but the EEIC interpreted these operations as unduly aggressive, even suggesting that the Burmese intended eventually to occupy Chittagong and Bengal. With different and competing notions of what constituted the relevant boundaries, war was declared by the EEIC in March 1824. By 1826, British forces had pushed the Burmese army out of Assam, Manipur, and Arakan; in the Treaty of Yandabo (discussed below), King Bagyidaw ceded these territories to the Company.

Siam

Ayutthaya, 1688–1767

The Ban Phlu Luang dynasty which ruled Ayutthaya after the coup staged at King Narai's death in 1688 has traditionally been described as having overreacted against the strong influence of foreigners during his reign by moving towards a more isolationist and 'closed-door' policy. Recent scholarship has shown that this is an unfair characterization and that there was a greater degree of continuity with the seventeenth century than earlier accounts acknowledged. Trade with Asian and European partners remained an important priority for the Siamese elite. Unfortunately, this last Ayutthayan dynasty also suffered from the same fundamental weaknesses as its predecessors, which made it equally vulnerable to Burmese aggression.

These weaknesses were twofold: contentious disputes within the ruling class and the perennial problem of manpower. Almost every succession of a Ban Phlu Luang ruler gave rise to a dispute among princes, each backed by his own faction of nobles. The dynasty to some extent consolidated the power of the royal family by multiplying the number of *krom*, bureaucratic offices headed by princes which controlled a specific number of men (*phrai*). In times of intra-familial squabbles, this structure arguably aggravated the political crisis by multiplying the lines of authority. Moreover, the fragmentation of control over manpower combined with the increasing tendency of many *phrai* to escape state control completely meant that the kingdom as a whole remained structurally weak.

Late seventeenth-century Ayutthaya saw a marked decline in the role of Westerners after their strong presence under Narai, whose *Farang* (European) clients had even included a government minister, the Greek adventurer Constantine Phaulkon. The VOC and other Western traders remained in Siam until Ayutthaya's fall, but their role was somewhat more restrained than before. Conversely, several families whose ethnic roots lay elsewhere in Asia (China, India, and Persia) became increasingly powerful through their domination of top government posts, a development which had already begun in the 1600s. These families would remain influential well into the nineteenth century.

Ayutthaya's political vicissitudes notwithstanding, Thai culture in the eighteenth century flourished, especially during the reign of King Borommakot (r. 1733–58), with the construction of new temples and the production of new works of literature. The Siamese *Sangha* had the opportunity to 'repay' Sri Lanka for centuries of Sinhalese influence when it was asked to send a delegation of monks to the island (at that time British Ceylon) to repair the spiritual damage done by successive colonial rulers. Unfortunately, within a few years of Borommakot's death the Burmese would mount an extended campaign against Ayutthaya, culminating in the fall and destruction of the capital in 1767 and bringing an end to its more than four centuries of power and influence.

King Taksin (r. 1767–82)

The heroic ruler who reunited Siam after this shattering defeat was in many ways an unlikely candidate for the task. Half-Chinese, Taksin had been a provincial governor in the final months of Ayutthaya's existence, and during the chaos after the fall of the capital, he established a power base in the southeastern part of the former kingdom. There were several contending power centers at the time, but only Taksin proved strong enough to defeat his rivals and have himself crowned king. Rather than attempting to restore Ayutthaya, he located his capital in Thonburi, now part of metropolitan Bangkok but at that time a separate site on the opposite side of the Chao Phraya river.

Taksin's greatest successes were military. In addition to consolidating his control over what had been the territory of Ayutthaya, he dealt with the

Burmese and drove them out of the northern Lanna kingdom as well. At the same time, he worked to strengthen Siam's long-term security by increasing its influence over the Malay peninsula – both ethnically Thai and Malay areas. Taksin was also able to take advantage of internal weakness in Cambodia and the Lao kingdoms to project Thonburi's power over these neighbors

Taksin's ability to rule his own people, however, was more problematic. His 'outsider' status always jeopardized his legitimacy in the eyes of the powerful families who had served the Ayutthayan rulers. There was no shortage of officials from the *ancien régime* who looked askance on this half-Chinese interloper, military hero though he may have been. Exactly what went on in Taksin's mind is a matter of debate, but it is clear that he aspired to a higher spiritual status than was normally attached to even the most devout Buddhist ruler, and he attempted to force the Siamese monkhood to acknowledge this status. This led to physical abuses of monks and seems to have provided the justification for Taksin's downfall. Whether or not he was actually crazy, as later accounts portrayed him, he had certainly overstepped the bounds of proper behavior for a Theravada monarch and paid the price for it. In 1782 he was overthrown and executed, and one of his generals took the throne as the first ruler of the new Chakri dynasty.

Early Bangkok period

The reigns of the first three Chakri kings are usually known collectively as the Early Bangkok period, and the rulers themselves are most easily referred to in English as Rama I (r. 1782–1809), Rama II (r. 1809–24), and Rama III (r. 1824–51). Together they spanned nearly seven decades and presided over an important time of prosperity and stability after the chaos of the mid-eighteenth century. While this was not a peaceful period, the episodes of warfare were largely offensive rather than defensive, as Siam continued the process of territorial consolidation and expansion begun under Taksin. Foreign trade flourished as well, both with China and, increasingly, with the West.

The chain of events which led to Taksin's deposition and the coronation of Rama I are sometimes portrayed as a coup by those linked to the 'old regime' of Ayutthaya, and to a large extent this was the case. The new dynasty shifted its capital across the river to Bangkok, rather than attempting to revive Ayutthaya as a power center. Nevertheless, there was considerable continuity with the social and political structures of the former kingdom. Moreover, Rama I was linked by various kinship and marital ties to several of the powerful noble families of Ayutthaya.

The Chakri kings, however, were able to avoid a repetition of the structural weaknesses which had plagued Ayutthaya for centuries. The succession of Rama II to his father's throne in 1809 was peaceful despite tensions earlier in the reign. While the choice of Rama III over his half-brother (the future King Mongkut) in 1824 is generally believed to have resulted from court rivalries, there was no violence and the unsuccessful candidate entered the monkhood and remained there throughout the long Third Reign. At the same time, while the nobility continued to play a dominant role in the government, there were a number of powerful princes as well, so that the balance of power between nobles and royalty was relatively stable.

The Early Bangkok period saw the Siamese sphere of influence expand to its greatest historical limits. Although there was renewed conflict with Burma during the First Reign, by the second decade of the nineteenth century that country no longer posed a serious threat, and thereafter Siam became preoccupied with the British menace. Bangkok continued to consolidate its hold over the northern Malay peninsula, Cambodia, and the Lao kingdoms. This expansionist agenda did not go unchallenged: Britain's acquisition of Penang and Singapore, in 1785 and 1819 respectively, injected a new element into the dynamic of Siam's relations with its Malay vassals. While the Anglo-Siamese rivalry in the peninsula did not result in open conflict, it led to decades of tensions which were only resolved in the early 1900s.

To the east, Bangkok was confronted after 1802 with a newly unified Vietnamese empire determined to assert its authority in the areas then dominated by Siam. In the 1820s Hue was briefly able to project its power all the way to the Mekong, but generally speaking the Lao regions remained closely linked to Bangkok. The Vietnamese were more successful in re-establishing their influence in Cambodia, where the long-term pattern of rival pro-Vietnamese and pro-Siamese court factions reappeared, punctuated by episodes of open warfare and an extended Vietnamese occupation.

This period also brought expansion and consolidation of the regions closer to the capital which are now within the borders of Thailand. The former kingdom of Lanna was finally rid of the Burmese but never regained the status and independence it had once enjoyed. Although a ruling family continued to reign in Chiang Mai, the northern *muang* became increasingly subordinated to Bangkok over the course of the nineteenth century. At the same time, Bangkok expanded its direct control throughout the northeastern region on the western side of the Mekong. Finally, it continued to consolidate its authority in the ethnically Thai regions north of the Malay states, notably the important power center of Nakhon Si Thammarat. The areas mentioned in this paragraph would remain under Bangkok's control even after the territorial concessions to Britain and France later in the century and were thus eventually incorporated into the Thai nation-state.

Siam maintained – and, indeed, heightened – the ethnic diversity which had characterized Ayutthaya, particularly in the capital. Chinese immigration was on the rise from the Third Reign onward, while military campaigns across the Mekong resulted in the forced resettlement of large numbers of Lao families within Siamese territory. Bangkok as the capital was particularly cosmopolitan, with a large Chinese population and a sophisticated ruling elite which dabbled in the art and literature of China, India, Persia, and other Asian cultures.

Siam's foreign trade during the early 1800s was dominated by the ruling elite, operating in conjunction with the local Chinese community, and direct trade with China itself played a key role. The increasing Western economic presence in Southeast Asia could not be ignored, particularly after the establishment of Singapore. The rise of this new entrepôt almost immediately translated into pressure on the Siamese to offer more favorable opportunities for Western merchants. In 1826 an Anglo-Siamese treaty was negotiated by Henry Burney which weakened the traditional royal monopoly on trade and adjusted Siam's taxation of foreign ships to make it more equitable for Western traders.

The Burney Treaty, however, was only a small part of a broader pattern of economic change taking place in the early nineteenth century and its impact should not be overstated. Trade was flourishing and in more diverse forms than before. The force of the royal monopoly was giving way in the face of other opportunities for the elite to make money. Siam was exporting more of its own commodities than before, rather than functioning mainly as an entrepôt for those from other countries. Royal family members and nobles alike were able to participate in this trade through the ownership or rental of ships, most of them constructed locally.

The major catalyst for this rise in trade was not Westerners, but Chinese. The immigrants from China were a diverse lot. Some of them remained more 'Chinese' in behavior and identity – maintaining, for example, the pigtail worn by men in Manchu-ruled China. Others, however, were ready and willing to assimilate into the Siamese socio-political system by accepting official positions and noble titles. One of the most important categories of Chinese to emerge was the tax farmer. As elsewhere in Southeast Asia, the tax farm allowed the government to shift responsibility for collecting revenue on a particular item or activity to an individual who bid for the privilege. Tax farming became a major institution during the Early Bangkok period as the ruling class discovered that it was more efficient and more profitable to rely on Chinese to collect such revenue than to do it themselves. The increase in foreign trade generated an increase in the production of items (mostly agricultural) to be traded, and tax farming proved the best way to ensure that the government got its share. Revenue from tax farmers went through several pairs of hands before ending up in royal coffers, and towards the end of the century the government would abolish the system, but in the period under consideration in this chapter, the tax farm flourished.

The increase in Chinese immigration had a significant impact on Siam's social structure as well. The system of relations between *naai* (masters) and *phrai* (clients or subordinates) was still in place during the Early Bangkok period. Its most important function, aside from mobilizing men for war, continued to be the annual periods of labor service (*corvée*) required of all those who held *phrai* status. By the early 1800s, however, the influx of Chinese offered the government an alternative to using *phrai* service: the wage laborer. Chinese were not considered as *phrai* and thus were exempted from *corvée*. They could travel around the country as merchants and traders, or they could be hired to work on government projects such as digging canals. The expansion of the economy meant that more cash was in circulation with the shift from payment 'in kind' (i.e., using rice or some other commodity), and this change also facilitated the rise of Chinese wage labor. The *phrai* system remained important as a means of manpower control, particularly for the nobility, but its actual economic necessity began to decline.

Let us briefly return to the Burney Treaty and its context. The treaty required a certain amount of arm-twisting on the part of the British, but there was no direct military threat, and certainly it did not open Siam to foreign intervention as was the case with similar agreements signed elsewhere in the region. Bangkok was obliged to settle border issues with what had become British Burma, but its influence in several northern Malay states was also formally recognized. For most of the Early Bangkok period, the Western threat was still largely on the horizon and, with the exception of the Malay states, the Siamese had a relatively free hand to expand their territory and otherwise do things their own way. This situation would change abruptly after the Third Reign, however, and Kings Mongkut (r. 1851–68) and Chulalongkorn (r. 1868–1910) would be confronted with a dramatically different geopolitical situation.

Laos

The death of King Soulignavongsa in the 1690s not only brought an end to Lan Sang's golden age, it ushered in the collapse of the kingdom itself as a relatively unified entity. Following a dispute within the ruling family, Lan Sang fragmented into three separate kingdoms: Luang Phabang, Vientiane, and Champassak in the south, bordering on Cambodia. The ethnically Lao Phuan area in Xieng Khouang also went its own way as a distinct polity. This state of affairs left the various smaller kingdoms vulnerable to external pressure and interference from their more powerful neighbors, particularly Siam (beginning in Taksin's reign) and Vietnam (under the Nguyen dynasty). Like the Cambodians, the Lao would henceforth be caught between these two rival powers until their colonization by the French in the late 1800s.

The eighteenth century in Lao history is characterized predominantly by warfare, both among the various kingdoms – particularly Vientiane and Luang Phabang – and with outside powers. During the period when Burma was an active and aggressive player in the Tai world, it represented a possible ally to be used by one ruler against his neighbor, as did Ayutthaya and the Vietnamese, particularly after the establishment of the Nguyen dynasty in 1802. As was the case in Cambodia during this period, the willingness of various Lao rulers to seek external alliances in order to further their own interests resulted in chronic instability and warfare rather than providing any kind of political equilibrium.

The Siamese were in the best position to interfere in the affairs of the Lao kingdoms, both because they were the closest geographically – the Mekong river was no barrier – and because of their ethnic and cultural ties. Once Taksin had eliminated Burmese control over Lanna and blocked further attacks on his kingdom, he had a free hand to extend his authority over his Lao neighbors. Through a combination of diplomacy and threats and a two-pronged military campaign in 1778, Thonburi made vassals of Vientiane, Champassak, and the territory in between along both sides of the Mekong. Luang Phabang, which had aided Siam in its attack on its enemy Vientiane, submitted to Taksin's authority as well. These events marked the end of Lao independence until the mid-twentieth century, a fact driven home by the removal to Siam of the famous Emerald Buddha and Phabang statues. The latter was subsequently returned to the city which bore its name, but the former remains in Bangkok as one of Thailand's most sacred icons.

Siamese overlordship under Taksin and his Chakri successors was very much 'hands-on'. Taksin's forces brought the Vientiane royal family back to the capital, and they remained there for decades, with successive rulers being chosen from among their ranks. Siam chose Champassak's rulers as well, and as suzerain had a hand in selecting Luang Phabang's kings. Bangkok was gradually able to extend its authority over most of the Lao *muang* in what is now northeastern Thailand, since it now controlled the kingdoms on the east bank of the Mekong that had been the overlords of these territories. Siam also began to project its power further east through the area that is now eastern and northeastern Laos, though in these regions it did not have a completely free hand because of Vietnamese influence.

Although the subordination of the former Lan Sang territories to Siamese overlordship was – and is still – deeply resented, the fragmented Lao kingdoms were unable to seriously challenge Bangkok's suzerainty. The only exception was the revolt by Anou (r. 1804–27), the last ruler of Vientiane, who mounted a major revolt against Siamese control in 1827. Despite considerable popular support in some areas and at least lukewarm support from the Vietnamese, to whom Vientiane still paid occasional tribute, he was betrayed by a supposed ally, captured by the Siamese, and left to die of exposure in an open cage in Bangkok. Vientiane was almost completely destroyed, and many of its people were removed and forced to relocate on Siamese territory. Luang Phabang and Champassak maintained an existence as separate kingdoms, but Siamese dominance of the Lao territories was nearly complete – except for Vietnamese activities along the eastern edge of those territories – until the new challenge from the French in the 1880s.

Vietnam

The two kingdoms

The eighteenth century, as elsewhere in Southeast Asia, was tumultuous, culminating in three decades of civil war. Both the Le/Trinh regime in Tonkin (Dang Ngoai) and the Nguyen regime in Cochin China (Dang Trong) underwent crises of governance which engendered dissatisfaction and triggered unrest. In 1771 the Tay Son rebellion broke out and swept both regimes from power. The Nguyen eventually defeated the Tay Son forces, however, and henceforth ruled a united Vietnam as a full-fledged empire rather than a *de facto* autonomous kingdom.

A truce reached between the two Vietnamese kingdoms in 1672 held for just over a century, but a state of peace could not guarantee stability and prosperity. Tonkin in particular faced a prolonged agrarian crisis due to the poor governance of incompetent and often oppressive mandarins combined with the machinations of village elites who were able to appropriate land for themselves which should have been available as a safety valve for their poorer neighbors. The traditional mechanism of periodic redistribution of communal lands – held by the village instead of by private individuals – only functioned effectively when done fairly, and often it was not. At best, those peasants who did not have enough land could expect to find themselves tenants farming for wealthier land-lords; at worst, they would simply abandon their villages and become bandits or rebels.

Rebellions began to occur in the northern countryside in the 1730s and continued sporadically until the outbreak of the Tay Son. In the capital, resources and energy were frequently expended on intra-elite struggles, especially between the Le emperors and the Trinh lords, who were often at odds with each other despite the latter's theoretical subordination to the former. Dang Ngoai society experienced a considerable degree of militarization, and the presence of larger numbers of troops heightened instability rather than relieving it.

The southern kingdom had access to large tracts of land thanks to its conquest of Cham territory and the gradual extension of its control over parts of the Mekong delta, but this expansion did not automatically translate into economic well-being for the population as a whole. Much of the central coast consisted of fairly poor farmland, while the Vietnamese settlement of the sparsely populated delta gave rise to landlordism. High rents and taxes combined to produce widespread indebtedness. The Nguyen government, although not plagued by the chronic political conflicts which characterized the regime in Tonkin, did have its share of corrupt, incompetent officials. By 1744, moreover, the ruling family had formally adopted the title of 'king' (but not 'emperor') and was investing large sums of money in palaces and other trappings of a royal lifestyle.

The Tay Son rebellion

Although the northern kingdom was arguably in a greater and more prolonged state of crisis, none of the rebellions which broke out there proved as serious as the Tay Son movement in Dang Trong, which was to last a full 30 years and came close to establishing itself as a long-term dynasty. The rebellion is named for the home village in the central province of Binh Dinh of the three brothers who instigated it: Nguyen Nhac, Nguyen Lu, and Nguyen Hue. The main target of the rebellion when it was launched was a corrupt minister serving in the government in Hue (then called Phu Xuan), but as it gained momentum, it undermined the government's authority in large stretches of the kingdom. Tay Son supporters drove corrupt local officials from power and burned the land and tax registers which served as the basis for exploitation in the villages. One of the reasons for the movement's success was its ability to appeal not only to a broad rural base, but also to Chinese merchants in the towns and even to some groups of Cham and highlanders who were alienated from the Hue regime.

The chronology of the tumultuous final decades of the eighteenth century is complex, but it can be divided into several phases. During the first phase (1771–76) the reigning Nguyen family in Dang Trong was overthrown. (It should be noted that 'Nguyen' is the most common Vietnamese family name; it is thus only coincidental that the rulers and rebels shared the same surname.) The outbreak of rebellion encouraged the Le/Trinh regime in the north to break the long-standing truce and attack the southern kingdom in 1774, and they drove the Nguyen lord out of his capital. The northern forces began to push southward, but in 1776 a truce was reached with the Tay Son which left the latter free to fight the Nguyen while the northern part of the kingdom was annexed to Tonkin.

The second phase lasted from 1776 until 1786. During this period the Tay Son and Nguyen engaged in nearly constant warfare, concentrated in the Mekong delta region, then known as Gia Dinh. Leadership of the Nguyen lords' cause was now assumed by a prince named Nguyen Phuc Anh. He was driven off the mainland and briefly sought refuge in Bangkok, where he obtained a promise of assistance from the new ruler, Rama I. When the Siamese actually intervened on the side of the Nguyen in 1785, however, they were defeated by the Tay Son. With the Nguyen forces smashed for the time being, the Tay Son brothers turned their attention northward.

During the third phase (1786–92), the Tay Son dominated the conflict, and much of the political and military action shifted to the north. In 1786 they mounted a campaign first to drive the northern forces out of former Nguyen territory and then to overthrow the Trinh family completely. By now the main leadership of the Tay Son forces came from the youngest brother, Nguyen Hue. When his troops reached the northern capital of Thang Long in 1786, he drove out the Trinh but did not attempt to overthrow the Le dynasty, and in fact he took a Le princess as his wife. He left the northern provinces under the emperor's authority while he and his brothers divided up the central and southern regions.

The situation changed dramatically when Nguyen Hue's father-in-law died, and his successor – the last Le emperor – decided to flee to China and ask for help from the Qing dynasty. Chinese forces invaded in late 1788, but Nguyen Hue and his troops rushed northward to attack them, and the Qing were defeated during the Lunar New Year of 1789. Hue now proclaimed a new dynasty with himself as emperor, adopting the reign title Quang Trung. He took serious measures to restore some kind of order and stability in the areas under his control, encouraging peasants to return to their villages and transferring back into their hands some of the lands previously appropriated by local elite. The new emperor demonstrated considerable skill as a ruler, but his untimely death in 1792 put paid to the ambitions of his family.

The final phase (1792–1802) was once more an extended confrontation between the Tay Son forces and Nguyen Phuc Anh, who had succeeded in re-establishing a power base in the Gia Dinh region. Although the Tay Son still had substantial support in some areas, their military leadership never recovered from the loss of Nguyen Hue despite the valiant efforts of their chiefs, such as the famous woman general Bui Thi Xuan. The Nguyen forces gradually fought their way from south to north, liberating their former capital in 1801 and the imperial capital at Thang Long the following year. Nguyen Phuc Anh now established his family as an imperial dynasty ruling from Hue and assumed the title Gia Long (r. 1802–20).

Vietnamese Marxist historians have frequently hailed the Tay Son as the precursor of the revolution for which their Party fought in the mid-twentieth century, but this characterization is in some respects oversimplified. It is certainly true that this was the largest-scale civil conflict in Vietnamese history up to that point in time; neither the war between the Le and Mac in the 1500s nor any of the peasant rebellions that occurred sporadically through the centuries achieved anything like the scale of the Tay Son. Moreover, in terms of the diversity of groups of people involved (beyond just peasants) and the ability to attack government local structures at the local level, the Tay Son did to some extent resemble the August Revolution which broke out in 1945. At the same time, however, when Nguyen Hue set himself up as emperor and began to settle into power, his new dynasty was not so dramatically different from its predecessors.

The most significant long-term impact of the Tay Son rebellion arguably lay in its defeat, since it paved the way for the Nguyen to take power, ruling over a stretch of territory larger than anything their ancestors had controlled. This was both a triumph for a family which had more than two centuries of autonomous government and expansion to its credit and a major challenge, given that roughly half of its new kingdom had never before been under its rule. The northern half of the country had gone from the Le/Trinh to the Tay Son to the Nguyen in a period of less than two decades, and its loyalty to the new dynasty was doubtful.

Nguyen Vietnam, 1802–1858

The Nguyen have frequently been reviled as the dynasty which lost – or 'sold out', depending on one's perspective – Vietnam to the French, but their failure to stand up to the power of a Western imperialist nation at full strength should not color history's view of the half-century before the first European troops landed on Vietnamese soil. Before the final loss of Vietnamese independence in 1884, Vietnam – known for most of this period as Dai Nam ('the great South') – was a relatively strong power by the standards of the time. It was able (up to a point) to expand its influence and its territory at the expense of its weaker neighbors, and it engaged diplomatically and commercially with the West and with European colonies in Southeast Asia.

During the eighty years between the establishment of the dynasty in 1802 and the establishment of the final French protectorate in 1884, Vietnam had only four emperors: Gia Long, Minh Mang (r. 1820–40), Thieu Tri (r. 1840–47) and Tu Duc (r. 1847–83). Apart from a brief succession crisis at the death of Thieu Tri, Nguyen court politics were relatively stable. The rulers were intelligent, cultured men who aspired to be model Confucian rulers and who remained constantly involved with the day-to-day affairs of the empire, served by a large bureaucracy and regulated by a new law code promulgated under Gia Long which was much more heavily influenced by Chinese law – in this case, the Qing – than its fifteenth-century predecessor had been.

Confucian government and a lack of dynastic quarrels did not, however, always translate into political stability. During Gia Long's reign he had to share power with two regional warlords, Nguyen Van Thanh in the north and Le Van Duyet in the south. These men had been his generals during the war with the

Tay Son and could not be pensioned off to a quiet retirement once he came to power. Thanh was eventually executed on rather shaky charges of treason, and Duyet died in Minh Mang's reign; the latter attempted to dishonor the warlord's memory, provoking a serious rebellion by Duyet's adopted son Le Van Khoi in 1833. The Nguyen also faced challenges from elements still loyal to the Le dynasty. In addition, the resurgence of the kinds of rural problems which had occurred in the eighteenth century, combined with natural disasters, engendered frequent small, localized revolts during the early decades of Nguyen rule. None of these seriously endangered their power and no successor to the Tay Son brothers appeared to lead a new movement. Nevertheless, chronic instability hardly served to strengthen the dynasty or its legitimacy.

The various conflicts, overt and latent, which characterized Vietnamese society in the nineteenth century are reflected in the literature of the period. *Kim Van Kieu* by Nguyen Du, the long poem which is the most famous work of Vietnamese literature, subtly tells of the author's dissatisfaction at having to serve what he views as the upstart dynasty of the Nguyen. Ho Xuan Huong, a poetess who made lavish use of ribald puns and scathing satire, mocked many of the pretensions of the patriarchal society of her day. One of the century's more prominent poets, Cao Ba Quat, was a failed scholar who was executed after leading a rebellion against the government. This was not a time of peace and tranquility, even for the educated elite who were sheltered from the problems of the countryside.

As was true of their counterparts elsewhere, the Nguyen's main challenge was dealing with the West. Gia Long had considerable experience with Europeans, particularly the French. He had had Frenchmen among his supporters during his war against the Tay Son, and several of them stayed on to serve him as emperor. One of his most important allies in the earlier conflict had been a missionary named Pierre Pigneau de Béhaine, who had actually negotiated a treaty with France on his behalf in 1787. This treaty, which would have provided the French with economic and territorial concessions in exchange for their military support for the Nguyen cause, remained a dead letter because of the French Revolution, but it shows that Gia Long was ready to cooperate with diverse allies outside the region. He and his successors kept a relatively open mind towards the Western powers. Even after the first Opium War in China (1839–42) drove home the potency of the European threat, Minh Mang insisted that Dai Nam should not shut its doors either diplomatically or commercially.

What ultimately soured Vietnam's ties with Europe was the issue of Nguyen policy towards Christianity. Catholicism had retained a significant, though minority, presence despite two centuries of off-and-on bans and persecution. By Minh Mang's reign, official suspicion of both foreign missionaries (French and Spanish) and Vietnamese Christians was growing, and sporadic episodes of renewed persecution occurred. Unlike the seventeenth and eighteenth centuries, there was more awareness in Europe of developments in countries like Vietnam, and, more importantly, France was now ready and able to use gunboat diplomacy to back up protests over the dynasty's treatment of Christians. French warships appeared in 1845 and 1847, the first actual clash occurring in the latter year. Vietnamese defenses and diplomacy alike would be put to the test, and both were found wanting.

Cambodia

As was mentioned in Chapter 5, from the early 1600s onward Cambodia was increasingly vulnerable to intervention from the Siamese to the west and the Vietnamese to the east. This vulnerability was due both to its geographical location – with no natural barriers on either side – and to the protracted conflicts within its ruling class. While there were occasions during the eighteenth and nineteenth centuries when Cambodia was able to muster up enough strength to resist one or the other of these interventionist neighbors, victory was usually short-lived and, as with the Lao during this period, warfare was all too frequently the norm.

Cambodia's weakness was partly economic. Although it did participate in regional trade, it had relatively few natural resources or commodities of its own to offer, and many of its neighbors were in a more advantageous position to function as entrepôts. Moreover, the gradual extension of Vietnamese control over the Mekong delta meant that Cambodia's main outlet to the sea was now in foreign hands. Trade – such as it was – continued, but the revenue contributed little to the country as a whole. The cession of what would now be called its economic sovereignty together with the effective loss of its political sovereignty at the hands of both the Siamese and the Vietnamese sapped whatever vitality Cambodia had been able to achieve in the late 1500s.

During the eighteenth century, the fragmentation within the court between pro-Siamese and pro-Vietnamese factions was compounded by infighting which was not directly linked to foreign support. When Cambodia enjoyed a respite of two decades or so from outside intervention in mid-century, violence and murder occurred among rivals within the royal family. One would logically expect that the kingdom as a whole would have collapsed, but it did not. Cambodia to some extent lapsed back into a sort of *mandala* state whereby the court (ruling at Oudong) was unable to control large stretches of territory, an overall administrative structure remained in place, and local officials and families seem to have provided some degree of long-term continuity. Because networks of relationships and patronage were as important in Cambodian society as they were in Siam, provincial officials were able to maintain their authority based on these structures even when the administrative system itself was malfunctioning or even breaking down.

The late 1700s, with the rise to power of Taksin and then the Chakri dynasty in Siam combined with the outbreak of the Tay Son rebellion among the Vietnamese, allowed the Siamese temporarily to obtain the upper hand in Cambodian affairs. Cambodian rulers were chosen and crowned in Bangkok before taking the throne in their own kingdom. Like their Lao counterparts, they were forced to subordinate themselves to the Chakri court, and many princes spent long periods of time in residence there. The long-time cultural and religious links between the Siamese and Cambodians made these connections easier and more natural than would have been the case in the Vietnamese court in Hue, and it can be suggested that Siamese overlordship in some respects came more naturally and was less culturally alien. Siam's position was also strengthened in the early years of the Chakri dynasty when a Cambodian official ceded the northwestern areas of Battambang and Mahanokor (the region around Angkor) in exchange for Bangkok's support for his authority – although he functioned more as a governor or minister rather than as a king. Cambodia only had a king in residence from 1794 onward (Eng, r. 1794–97), and his realm was now shorn of a sizable and important piece of territory, which remained under Siamese control until the early twentieth century.

With the end of the Tay Son conflict and the establishment of the Nguyen dynasty in 1802, Vietnam was once more in a position to exercise its authority in Cambodia and, more importantly, to challenge directly Siam's dominant position there. A key factor in the rivalry was the Cambodian king named Chan (r. 1797–1835), who was much more hostile to Bangkok than his father Eng and therefore disposed to reopen the door to Vietnamese involvement. Since neither Bangkok nor Hue was willing at this point in time to allow the other a major role in Cambodian affairs, this meant that conflict between the two rival overlords was inevitable. From 1811, when fighting took place between Siamese and Vietnamese armies on Cambodian territory, until 1847, when Hue finally withdrew its forces, Cambodia experienced episodes of violence and unrest which led historian David Chandler to see this half-century as 'the darkest portion of [its] history before the 1970s'.[1]

The Vietnamese are unquestionably the primary 'villains' of the story during this dark period, and much of the antagonism between Vietnam and Cambodia can be traced to these chaotic decades. Emperor Minh Mang steadily tightened his country's hold over its vassal, both administratively and militarily, and from 1834 until 1847 Cambodia was effectively under Vietnamese occupation. Vietnamese attempts to remodel Cambodia's government and even its culture along more 'civilized' (i.e., Sino-Vietnamese) lines were deeply resented, and numerous episodes of resistance and rebellion took place. By the mid-1840s, it was clear that the attempt to eliminate Siamese overlordship and to replace it completely with that of Vietnam was doomed to failure, and one of Thieu Tri's last acts before his death in 1847 was to bring an end to this experiment. Cambodia could now find some kind of peace under a new king (Duang, r. 1848–60) with joint Siamese and Vietnamese overlordship. Only a decade later, however, France's appearance on the scene would change the power equation.

The Malay states, c.1600–1870s

The triangular contest among Johor, Aceh, and Portuguese Melaka for control of the Straits region continued into the seventeenth century. As the Portuguese had neither the resources nor the will to dominate both sides of the Straits of Melaka, Aceh – emboldened by the influx of new wealth from Muslim merchants using its ports after the fall of Melaka – emerged as a formidable rival

---

[1] David Chandler, *History of Cambodia*, 3rd edn (Boulder, CO: Westview, 2000), 117.

to Johor for hegemony in the Malay world. In 1564, Aceh retook Aru (previously lost to Johor in 1540) and sacked Johor's capital at Johor Lama. The entire royal family was carried off to Aceh, save for the Sultan's son who ruled Johor as a vassal state. In 1570 Acehnese forces sacked Johor Lama again after Johor had attempted to break away. Further punitive Acehnese raids were also carried out against Johor in 1613 and 1623.

It was almost two decades before Johor came out of its dark years of struggle against both Aceh and the Portuguese. Aceh's ambitions led to clashes with the Portuguese at Melaka throughout the sixteenth and seventeenth centuries and drove the latter and Johor together, as in 1582 when the Portuguese assisted Johor to ward off an Acehnese attack. But the alliance broke down in 1587 when Johor attacked the Portuguese, and precipitated, in turn, the retaliatory destruction of Johor Lama. Acehnese attacks on Melaka culminated in a siege in 1627 that lasted two years, before an armada from Goa destroyed Aceh's forces, heralding Aceh's decline, as will be seen below. Portuguese power also started to unravel by the early decades of the seventeenth century, and by 1640 Portuguese Melaka was again under siege – this time from the Dutch VOC. Assisted by their new ally, Johor, VOC forces captured Melaka in January 1641. Thereafter, both of Johor's erstwhile enemies – Aceh and the Portuguese – were no longer serious rivals.

Boosted in part by its alliance with the VOC and a peace treaty with Aceh in 1641, brokered by the Dutch, Johor tried to reclaim its former standing. The VOC focused on establishing its positions in Java and Maluku, and exhibited no strong territorial ambitions in Sumatra or the Malay peninsula except for Melaka. So Johor re-established its suzerainty over many former dependencies, but was not able to dominate both sides of the Straits completely. It imposed control over the east Sumatran kingdoms of Siak (1662) and Indragiri (1669) and brought Pahang back into its fold, but was unable to dominate the northern Malay states. Kedah remained under Siam's tutelage while Terengganu and Perak retained close, but independent, relations with Johor. Johor's revival stuttered temporarily after an emerging east Sumatran rival, Jambi, looted and destroyed Johor Lama in 1673, forcing the relocation of its capital to Riau. This Johor-Jambi war ended in 1679 in the former's favor, and Johor was once more the pre-eminent power in the Straits, but its position was soon undermined by court intrigues and power struggles between the rival *Laksamana* and *Bendahara* families (names deriving from their functional titles in the court). This culminated in the assassination of the last ruler of the Melaka line, Sultan Mahmud, in 1699. As Mahmud left no heirs, this led to the ascension of a new *Bendahara* dynastic line under Sultan Abdul Jalil Riayat Shah IV (r. 1699–1720).

Johor never recovered completely from the regicide of 1699. With a new authority in the court of Johor that lacked the legitimacy of the Melaka dynasty, cracks appeared within the center and periphery. Vassals asserted their independence and new rivals, like the Minangkabaus from Sumatra and the Bugis from Sulawesi, challenged Johor for much of the eighteenth century. The turmoil that ensued brought war and destruction to Selangor, Perak, and Kedah, but also provided opportunities for new sultanates like Terengganu

(1724), Kelantan (1764), and Selangor (1766) to come into existence, while other kingdoms like Negeri Sembilan asserted their independence, as the authority of the Riau-Johor empire waned.

The VOC's presence precluded the rise of a new Malay center on the old Melakan model, even though the Company remained neutral in local disputes, intervening only briefly in 1756–57 to curb the Bugis threat to its maritime trade and again in 1759–61 to crush a revolt by the Malays of Siak. In the late eighteenth century, renewed English rivalry and fears of a Malay alliance with the EEIC compelled the Dutch to enforce more restrictive measures, ending in the seizure of Riau in 1784 and the expulsion of the Bugis from both Riau and Selangor, making the Riau-Johor Empire, in essence, a Dutch vassal state.

Any hope of Malay economic and political revival was further dashed by the EEIC's founding of ports at Penang (1786) and Singapore (1819) and the conclusion of the Anglo-Dutch Treaty of London in 1824. This treaty partitioned the Riau-Johor Empire into British and Dutch 'spheres of influence', with the former inheriting Singapore and the Malay peninsula, including Melaka, while the latter were to be dominant on the other side of the Straits, notably in Sumatra. Further consolidation of the British position followed the formation of the Straits Settlements (Penang, Melaka, and Singapore) in 1826 and their transfer from the EEIC's authority to that of the India Office in 1858, before being finally placed under the Colonial Office in 1867.

With the exclusion of the Riau court from peninsular affairs and the further weakening of Malay central authority, civil war engulfed many Malay states. Feuding elites fought over succession issues, territorial rights, and control of tin production, as demand for tin grew from Straits Settlements traders. By the early 1870s, civil disturbances in the Malay states and the appearance of new European powers in the area obliged the British to reconsider their policy of non-intervention in those states.

Brunei

By the mid-nineteenth century, the Malay sultanate of Brunei had experienced nearly two centuries of decline since its 'golden age' in the first half of the sixteenth century, when the decentralization of Melaka's trade after its fall to the Portuguese in 1511 contributed to Brunei's growth as a commercial entrepôt, strategically located on the maritime trade route between China and the western archipelago. At its height, Brunei claimed suzerainty over northern and western Borneo and its influence spread to the Sulu archipelago and elsewhere in the Philippines. But as the Spanish established control over the Philippines from the later sixteenth century, Brunei's influence correspondingly shrank. In 1578, Brunei itself was temporarily captured by the Spanish. During the next two centuries, the sultanate was plagued by civil strife and royal succession struggles, while Dutch and English commercial activity further weakened the economic and political bases of Brunei power. Brunei lost its territory in northern Borneo to its former vassal, Sulu, in the eighteenth century. Sarawak was ceded to an English adventurer, James Brooke, who became its first 'White Rajah' in 1842, as a reward for his help in quelling a local rebellion. From 1881,

North Borneo was run by the British North Borneo Chartered Company. Between 1853 and 1888, Sarawak and North Borneo extended their territories by stages at the expense of a crumbling Brunei. In 1888, a British protectorate was proclaimed over all three.

Java, c.1600–1808

Around 1600, Mataram in south-central Java and Surabaya at the northeast corner of the island were beginning to emerge in Java as leading powers. For a quarter of a century, competition and conflict continued between these two, until Mataram established itself as the new hegemon of central and east Java. Surabaya had extensive trading networks outside Java and claimed overlordship over other smaller states on the island itself. From 1610 Panembahan Senapati's son and successor as ruler of Mataram, Panembahan Seda ing Krapyak (r. c.1601–13), began annual campaigns against Surabaya, burning the rice crops in the fields that fed it. Krapyak also contacted the newly arrived VOC to see if an alliance against Surabaya might be possible, for the Company could provide naval forces that Mataram lacked, but nothing significant came of this.

In 1613 Krapyak was succeeded by the greatest of all of Java's kings, the man known as Sultan Agung ('the great Sultan', r. 1613–46), even though he actually assumed the Sultan title only in the last years of his reign. This was the greatest warrior the Mataram dynasty ever produced, the most successful king and a major figure in the reconciliation of Islamic and local Javanese cultures and identities. His successors would measure themselves by the standards of Sultan Agung.

Agung's campaigns picked off coastal towns under Surabaya's overlordship one by one and continued Krapyak's pattern of annual campaigns. In 1625 the besieged city was forced to surrender. Now Agung stood alone as the overlord of Central and East Java. The far west of Java – the state of Banten – remained beyond his control, as did the eastern salient of the island, but the Javanese heartland was in his hands. These conquests had done much damage to the land and people of Java, particularly along the north coast. Suffering among the people did not, however, deter Agung from continuing his campaigns. Indeed, in kingdoms such as Java, constant demonstration of the king's invincibility was part of proving his supernaturally sanctioned legitimacy and potency. There were so few institutionalized structures of authority and the geopolitics of the place were so challenging – with populated areas separated from one another by difficult mountainous forests – that such demonstrations were essential to maintaining the loyalty of subordinate lords.

The new challenge for Agung was the VOC. In 1619, Governor-General Jan Pietersz. Coen (1619–23, 1627–29), conquered the west Javanese port of Jayakerta and turned it into the VOC's headquarters, with the name Batavia. This was to remain the capital of the VOC and, after it, of the colonial state in Indonesia for 330 years (Figure 18), until the victory of the Indonesian Revolution in 1949; since then, renamed Jakarta, it has been the national capital. Agung sent his army to besiege Batavia in 1628. There were times when it looked as if the Javanese would be victorious but, crucially, they failed to dam

Figure 18   Batavia c.1750, print by Giuseppe Filosi

the Ciliwung river, upon which Batavia depended for its water supply. The beleaguered VOC held on and the Javanese army withdrew. In 1629 Agung launched a second campaign, but this time the VOC discovered and destroyed stockpiles of rice and boats for the advancing army even before it reached Batavia. This second siege was a complete failure for the Mataram side, which never again attempted to expel the VOC from its capital city.

As has already been seen, Southeast Asian monarchs relied on the belief that they had supernatural forces supporting them, but behind such pretensions there lay the capacity to project military force if necessary. When Agung's army was defeated before the walls of Batavia in 1628–29, his supernatural aura was called into question and rebellions broke out in several places, all of which he put down with force. The most significant rebellion was that of 1630 based at the holy grave of Tembayat, where the Islamic saint Sunan Bayat is buried. This, too, was crushed by Agung, but that was not enough to deal with the threat of religiously legitimated resistance. In 1633 Agung undertook some sort of pilgrimage to Tembayat as a means of harnessing its spiritual authority to his cause. Legend has it that he communed with the spirit of Sunan Bayat, who taught him the secret mystical science of kingship. Agung had a ceremonial gateway erected at the grave site (Figure 19), inscribed with his name and the time of his visit, which still stands. Also in 1633, Agung abandoned the Hindu *Śaka* calendar, which had remained in use for court purposes despite the conversion to Islam, and embraced a hybrid version that employed the Islamic lunar months but continued the enumeration of years from the old system, thus creating a clearly Islamic but nevertheless uniquely Javanese calendar (the *Anno Javanico*, AJ).

At or about the time of his pilgrimage, Agung also invited to the court the surviving scion of the house of Surabaya, Prince Pekik, married one of his own sisters to the prince, and through him introduced into Javanese courtly literature

Figure 19   Sultan Agung's gateway, Tembayat, 1633

three major literary works of Islamic inspiration. These were *Serat Yusup*, an elaborate romance based on the story of Joseph in Egypt (as found in the *Qur'an*); *Kitab Usulbiyah* concerning many figures of early Islamic history with a central episode concerning an encounter between Jesus and Muhammad; and *Carita Sultan Iskandar*, which is based on the Qur'anic account of Alexander the Great. These works were regarded as being spiritually potent. Another poetical work called *Suluk Garwa Kancana* ('The Song of the House of Gold') survives only in an eighteenth-century copy but may represent the lessons in kingship said to have been given to Agung by the spirit of Sunan Bayat; it depicts the Javanese king as an ascetic Sufi monarch. Thus, it seems, did Sultan Agung seek to reconcile Javanese martial aristocratic traditions with Islamic notions and thereby make Islam a pillar of – rather than a threat to – his state. This was a powerful step in the deepening Islamization of the Javanese state and society.

Agung was not alone in fostering the Islamization of his land in this period. As will be seen in the next section of this chapter, in the early seventeenth century Aceh was a major center of Islamic thought and literature. In the west Javanese state of Banten, the ruler Abdul Kadir (r. 1596–1651) was a student of Sufism and, in 1638, became the first ruler in Java definitely known to have adopted the Islamic title of Sultan, upon being authorized to do so by the governor – the Grand *sharif* – of Mecca. In the wake of this, Sultan Agung, too, sent a mission to Mecca that returned with authorization for him to take the Sultan title in 1641. When Agung died in early 1646, he was the most powerful ruler in Java since the time of Majapahit as well as a major reconciler of Islamic and Javanese identities.

We would be wrong, however, to understand this Islamization in more modern or puritanical terms. Much of the rich pre-Islamic legacy of Java survived. Old Javanese literature was evidently still patronized in court circles until around the middle of the eighteenth century. Similarly, the *wayang* shadow-puppet theatre with its tales based on the *Bharatyuddha* (derived from the Indian *Mahabharata*) and *Ramayana* remained a major part of Javanese culture. The dominant form of Islam was mystical Sufism, the doctrines of which not infrequently crossed theoretical boundaries of orthodoxy. In the historical accounts and legends of Agung's reign, the unmistakably non-Islamic Goddess of the Southern Ocean plays a major role as his supernatural wife. So Agung's reconciliation of Islamic and Javanese identities did not mean a thorough-going reconstruction of Javanese culture or society, but it did mean harnessing Islam's supernatural powers and authority to the cause of the monarchy.

Agung's son and successor, Amangkurat I (r. 1646–77) differed from his father in several respects. Whereas Agung was ever after seen as the greatest of Java's kings, Amangkurat I was stigmatized as the quintessential tyrant. He did not take the Sultan title, but instead used the Javanese title *Susuhunan*. Senior courtiers were murdered upon his orders and at the start of his reign, he carried out the largest slaughter of Islamic religious leaders ever to take place in Java. It seems that these religious had supported an attempted rebellion by the king's younger brother, so in 1648 Amangkurat I summoned some 2000 Islamic divines and their families. Upon his signal, they were murdered on the great square in front of the court – according to a VOC ambassador, a total of 5000–6000 men, women, and children. Amangkurat I sought to centralize the state administratively as well as to crush all dissent, but the basic geopolitical realities of Java made this extremely difficult. As a consequence, he managed to concoct a potent combination of forces against himself: (1) outlying and coastal areas whose prosperity was threatened by royal demands and interference; (2) aristocrats who feared for their lives and the welfare of their families; and (3) Islamic leaders who were not killed in 1648 but might reasonably wonder when they would be. Amangkurat I's tyranny thus precipitated the collapse of the Mataram state.

In 1675 a rebellion broke out led by Trunajaya, a prince of Madura whose father had been murdered at the Javanese court in 1656. A Javanese holy man, Raden Kajoran, protected Trunajaya and lent religious authority to his ambitions. Behind the scenes the Mataram crown prince – shortly to become Amangkurat II (r. 1677–1703) – also plotted to support the rebellion, which he naively expected to be in his interest. Trunajaya's forces were joined by marauding Makassarese, who had fled their homeland after the VOC and Arung Palakka's conquest of Gowa in 1669 (described below). Natural disasters – rains out of season, an eruption of Mount Merapi in 1672, and lunar eclipses – seemed to foretell calamity. There was a Javanese tradition that a court would fall at the end of every century (calculated in the AJ calendar): AJ 1600 would begin in March 1677, and in a kingdom as fragile as this, widespread expectation that a court would fall could lead many to believe that resisting the rebellion was futile.

The VOC was uncertain what its role should be, but in 1676 decided upon limited intervention. In early 1677 the Company and Amangkurat I renewed a treaty they had signed in 1646, which had become a dead letter. The Company promised to aid the king against his enemies so long as all its costs in doing so were repaid – a bargain that would prove impossible to implement. The Dutch were also to have commercial concessions such as freedom from tolls. This first military intervention by the VOC in the Javanese heartland – the beginning of over 270 years of direct European intrusion there – forced Trunajaya out of Surabaya, which drove the rebel forces farther inland towards the capital of Mataram.

But the VOC could not initially stop the rebellion. Trunajaya's forces conquered the Mataram capital in May or June 1677, putting Amangkurat I to flight. With him went the crown prince, who had completely lost control of the rebellion. Trunajaya had his own ambitions, which had no room for the dynastic heir. He looted the Mataram treasury and withdrew to Kediri. Amangkurat I died during his flight; his son now became Susuhunan Amangkurat II, but he had no means of regaining his kingdom except to turn to the VOC. The Company demanded more concessions in return for its support – including monopolies in the purchase of rice and sugar and the importation of opium and textiles, and direct control of the port of Semarang. Trunajaya's rebellion was defeated in the end by combined VOC and Javanese forces which attacked Kediri in late 1678. Trunajaya himself was personally stabbed to death by Amangkurat II. Thus the Mataram dynasty was restored to the throne, a victory made possible by the assistance of the VOC.

A pattern of Dutch interference in internal Javanese affairs was thereby established. The Company was never capable of controlling events in Java or winning wars by itself, but in alliance with local forces it could frequently tip the balance of events towards those with whom it was allied. Its presence, however, called into question the legitimacy of monarchs whom it supported, for they clearly needed foreign forces to hang onto their throne. Thus VOC support could generate more dissent and rebellion, and thereby precipitate yet more VOC intervention. Not infrequently, opposition to the Dutch was justified on religious grounds – the opposition of Muslims to the presence of the Christian interlopers. But it is important to note that the Company had no Christianizing agenda. It did not support Calvinist missionizing except in the case of East Indonesian populations previously converted to Catholicism by the Portuguese. Amangkurat II, too, was unhappy about Dutch pretensions. He failed to meet his obligations to the Company and connived in the assassination of a VOC ambassador at the court in 1686, which had the effect of breaking off relations between the Company and the court – by then at a new location, Kartasura, near present-day Surakarta. At this stage, the Company's intervention looked unlikely to bring it much benefit.

The VOC also intervened in the West Javanese state of Banten. The greatest of Banten's rulers, Sultan Ageng (r. 1651–82), oversaw the kingdom's golden age. Banten ships traded widely and many foreign traders were active in its port. Such success of course irritated the VOC in nearby Batavia. Banten was also a leading center of Islam. The Makasarese Sufi teacher Shaikh Yusuf Makasar was active there from 1672. Sultan Ageng was strongly opposed to the VOC and declared war on the Company in 1680, which precipitated an internal dynastic conflict with the crown prince. VOC forces successfully intervened in 1682, put the crown prince on the throne, and expelled other European traders from Banten. Yusuf was captured in 1683 and exiled, eventually to die at the Cape of Good Hope in 1699. Banten was dominated by Batavia thereafter, except for another rebellion in 1750, led by a religious teacher named Kyai Tapa, which inflicted significant losses on VOC forces before they were victorious the following year.

The Company again intervened in Central and East Java only in 1704, when a dissident prince sought its support to take the throne as Susuhunan Pakubuwana I (r. 1704–19). Thus began the First Javanese War of Succession (1704–08). Pakubuwana I and his VOC allies were victorious, but resentment about the restored European presence at court seems to have remained. At the end of his reign, Pakubuwana I's kingdom fell apart in a rebellion based in Surabaya, which soon spread to other areas of East Java. When the king died and was replaced by his ineffectual son, other princes rebelled with the support of the entire religious establishment of the court and the king's formidable widow Ratu Pakubuwana (d. 1732). This rebellion, too, was eventually brought to an end with the aid of the VOC by 1723.

Ratu Pakubuwana remained a powerful figure in the court during the reign of her grandson Pakubuwana II (r. 1726–49). She was a Sufi and a major literary figure. She and her allies decided to make the 16-year-old monarch into the model Sufi king, which might again turn Islam into a pillar of the state rather than a threat to it. Sultan Agung was evidently her inspiration. She revived the supernaturally powerful books first written in his reign, *Serat Yusup*, *Kitab Usulbiyah*, and *Carita Sultan Iskandar*, and had new versions written in 1729–30. The introductions to these versions make clear both the extraordinary religious authority ascribed to Ratu Pakubuwana and the supernatural power claimed for the books. She also produced the only surviving copy of *Suluk Garwa Kancana*, perhaps the lessons in kingship said to have been given to Agung by the spirit of Sunan Bayat in 1633. This was the most powerful effort at Islamizing the state and society by the court since the time of Agung and it seems to have had success. In many ways the malleable young king and his court became more pious, more Islamic (but mystical) in style.

But the Islamizers were in charge of a fragile state and when violence again erupted, their faith had no answers. In 1740 a massacre of Chinese broke out in Batavia, with some 10,000 killed. Along the north coast of Java, other Chinese went to war against the VOC. The Company's unpopularity inspired thousands of Javanese to join the war against it. This 'Chinese War' was the beginning of nearly 17 years of fighting in Java. The vacillating Pakubuwana II first joined the anti-Dutch side and conquered the VOC garrison at his court in 1741. The survivors were ordered to convert to Islam. But the tide of war then began to turn, so the king released these surviving Dutchmen and sought reconciliation with the Company which, needless to say, was deeply distrustful of him. This change of sides turned many other Javanese against him, with the result that the court itself fell to rebels and was sacked in mid-1742. Pakubuwana II fled into the countryside and was prepared to promise the VOC anything it wanted if it would restore him to his throne.

In 1743 the rebellion collapsed and the VOC propped Pakubuwana II back up on his throne. The Company and king signed a treaty that gave the Europeans extensive territorial concessions. But there was still no resolution of the deeply rooted problems of the Javanese kingdom. The king's brother prince Mangkubumi found these concessions unacceptable and rebelled in 1746, thereby initiating the Second Javanese War of Succession (1746–57).

Mangkubumi and the king's nephew Mas Said were the leading figures in a rebellion that fought the VOC to a standstill and nearly conquered the court (rebuilt at Surakarta in 1746 by Pakubuwana III, r. 1749–88). At last the Company had to recognize that it could not keep the Javanese state united under a king whom it could control. In 1755 the Company was obliged to give in to Mangkubumi's demands and, at the Treaty of Giyanti, agreed that he should become ruler of half of the kingdom. Prince Mangkubumi thus became Sultan Hamengkubuwana I (r. 1749–92), the first ruler since Sultan Agung to use the Sultan title and the greatest ruler since that time. In 1755 he established his new court at Yogyakarta. Mas Said fought on for two more years until agreeing in 1757 to become a subsidiary, but senior, prince under the Susuhunan in Surakarta, as Mangkunegara I (r. 1757–95).

The division of the kingdom between Surakarta and Yogyakarta posed problems for legitimation, for how could two kings both be 'shadows of God upon the earth' or mystic spouses of the Goddess of the Southern Ocean? In the interest of at last ending the civil wars that had plagued Java since the previous century, and which had necessitated the destabilizing interventions of the VOC, the monarchs contrived a means of avoiding such difficult questions by ignoring each other's existence. Legal agreements between their courts dealt with matters that might cross their boundaries without the kings needing to become involved, or to go to war. And magical books were written to prove that this was all supernaturally legitimate. As a consequence, the VOC – by now well on its way to bankruptcy, exhausted by the costs of its interventions and by corruption – could concentrate on its coastal interests. Only once, in 1787–90, was there a threat of military conflict, when a group of religious advisors encouraged the new Surakarta monarch Pakubuwana IV (r. 1788–1820) to attempt to overturn the division of the state – mainly by using magical means, it seems. The Sultan of Yogyakarta, Prince Mangkunegara I, and the VOC surrounded Surakarta and the mercurial monarch surrendered his new advisors. Yogyakarta prospered under Sultan Hamengkubuwana I and Java enjoyed the longest period of peace (1757–1825) since at least the early sixteenth century.

As was often the case, however, a great ruler such as Hamengkubuwana I was succeeded by a lesser figure, Hamengkubuwana II (r. 1792–1810, 1811–12, 1826–28). Surakarta was under Pakubuwana IV, a man consistently unable to judge his political surroundings. The intrigues in each court and between them contributed to a decline of both states. Meanwhile, the VOC was taken over by the Netherlands government (1800). In the wake of the French takeover of the Netherlands in 1795, a Napoleonic Governor-General, Marshal H. W. Daendels (g. 1808–11) was sent to Java, initiating a new age in Javanese-European relations, as will be seen in the following chapter.

Indonesia's outer islands, c.1600–1800

Outside of Java, before the nineteenth century we have adequate historical evidence only for certain places and periods, among them Aceh at the height of its power under Sultan Iskandar Muda (r. 1607–36), the contemporary of Java's Sultan Agung. He, too, was a great warrior. He conquered much of Sumatra's east coast and defeated Johor in 1613. He also took Pahang and Kedah in the Malay peninsula, but maintaining control of such conquests was always difficult. His campaigns were brought to a halt in 1629 – the same year as Sultan Agung's failure before Batavia – when he attacked Portuguese Melaka and suffered a massive defeat: the Portuguese reported that Iskandar Muda's entire fleet and 19,000 men were lost. The Portuguese had no means to subdue Aceh itself, but this defeat did give Aceh's rival Johor a chance to rebuild its influence in the Malay peninsula.

Iskandar Muda's reign demonstrates the strengths of such states, but also their limitations. Like Johor, Portuguese Melaka, or VOC Batavia, Aceh was a trading state situated on the coast, with a hinterland hardly under its control. Such states depended on surrounding areas for manpower, food, timber for building ships and houses, and other products. As the non-agricultural population of a state grew, dependence on the hinterland increased. Yet hinterlands were often mountainous or swampy, and inhabited (usually thinly) by people of different ethnicity and/or religion with little interest in being subject to a coastal overlord. So growth bred challenges to the survival of such states. Denys Lombard attributes the decline of Aceh in the later seventeenth century partly to its growth to such a size that it could no longer feed itself. Trading success also bred another challenge: local lords who sought to benefit directly from trade by escaping the demands of the monarch. Iskandar Muda created an elite of war leaders – called *uleëbalang* in Acehnese – who after his death evolved into such local lords. They asserted their influence from the 1640s and reduced the Acehnese throne to a weak symbolic institution until the nineteenth century.

The Sultan was also a patron of Islamic culture. In Iskandar Muda's court flourished a tradition of Sufi Islam associated with the Malay writers Hamzah Pansuri and Syamsuddin of Pasai. In the reign of Iskandar Muda's successor Sultan Iskandar Thani (r. 1636–41), the Gujerati Nuruddin ar-Raniri – the most prolific of these Sufi writers – was the dominant religious figure in the court. He denounced Hamzah and Syamsuddin's writings as heretical, their works were burned and their followers were persecuted. Nuruddin's books included his *Bustan as-Salatin* ('The garden of kings'), one of the greatest works in Malay literature. But he, too, fell from favor in the reign of the next monarch, Iskandar Muda's daughter Queen Taj ul-Alam (r. 1641–75). Now Abdurrauf of Singkil was the dominant religious writer. Works by these Sufis were translated into other Indonesian languages and thereby influenced other parts of the archipelago. Early seventeenth-century Aceh was thus one of the major creative sites for Indonesian Islamic thought, albeit one marked by conflict over the question of orthodoxy.

In South Sulawesi were found two related ethnic communities, the Bugis and the Makassarese, both famous as fierce and professional warriors. They adopted chain mail armor and translated Spanish and Portuguese treatises on gunnery, the only Indonesians to do so. They were also major seafaring traders, selling slaves, gold, spices, foodstuffs, and other locally available products. Before the early seventeenth century, several small states had competed for hegemony in this region. The Portuguese arrived there in the 1540s and made a few attempts at spreading Catholicism before losing interest in the idea and settling down to take part in the trade. The Makassarese state of Gowa became the dominant local power by the end of the sixteenth century, but Islam had not yet made significant inroads there.

In 1605 the ruler of Gowa adopted Islam, becoming Sulawesi's first Sultan, named Alauddin Tumenanga ri Gaukanna (r. 1593–1639). This region had strong pre-Islamic religious traditions, led by transgender priests called *bissu*, so Islamization of the population proceeded slowly. Sultan Alauddin was determined to spread Islam, so he conquered and forcibly imposed the faith on the main Bugis-Makassarese lands by 1611. These so-called 'Islamic wars' remind us that, while no outside, non-Southeast Asian army imposed Islam in the region, at the local level it was sometimes imposed by conquest. In subsequent centuries, the Makassarese and Bugis became renowned as fervent Muslims.

Sultan Alauddin was also a conqueror outside Sulawesi. His influence was felt on the east coast of Kalimantan, in Lombok, and eastwards in the Aru-Kei island group. Gowa's role as the main spice-trading state of eastern Indonesia attracted Asian and European trading communities, among them the Dutch VOC, whose ultimate aim was not to share in Gowa's trade, but rather to destroy it; to expel the English, Danish, French, Spanish, and Portuguese traders there; and then to impose a VOC monopoly. Limited Gowa-VOC warfare began in 1615. Peace treaties were agreed in 1637, 1655, and 1660, but none of them brought Gowa's trading eminence to an end or met the VOC's ultimate objective.

During the seventeenth century, the VOC made progress towards commercial hegemony in eastern Indonesia. In 1605 it expelled the Portuguese from Ambon and thereby acquired the Company's earliest colonial territory in Indonesia. The Dutch converted the local Catholics to Calvinism. Thereafter, except for Gowa, the VOC faced no large-scale military competitors in the area. Since most of the populations lived near the coasts, the Company's naval power could be deployed effectively. There were bloody conflicts and rarely was victory easy, but the VOC managed to dominate Hitu, Hoamoal, Ternate, and Tidore by the later years of the century. Problems arose thereafter from time to time, but generally the VOC established itself as regional hegemon over such small places, even though it never actually won the monopoly over the spice trade that it wanted. Anti-VOC resistance in these campaigns often had the support of Makassarese, so Gowa remained a principal strategic target for the Company.

Some Bugis lands, particularly the state of Bone, were chafing under Gowa's dominance. In 1660 the Bone prince Arung Palakka rebelled unsuccessfully and was forced to flee with a small group of compatriots. In 1663 the VOC enlisted them in its army and allowed them to live in Batavia, thereby acquiring a formidable and reliably anti-Makassarese force. The Company then renewed its war against Gowa, combining its naval superiority with a ground campaign led by Arung Palakka, to whom many Bugis rallied. In 1669 Gowa fell. Arung Palakka thereafter dominated South Sulawesi with the support of the VOC – which frequently found its ally to be troublesome, but never dared resist his wishes. He punished his local adversaries and, by his hard-fisted rule as king of Bone (1672–96), set off an emigration of Bugis and Makassarese from South Sulawesi that led to them intervening in the affairs of many places in the archipelago and Malay peninsula, and even as far abroad as Siam. After Arung Palakka's death in 1696, South Sulawesi again saw a series of conflicts among rival states and leaders, often pitting Makassarese against Bugis. The VOC could do little more than maintain a defensive position in its local headquarters at Ujung Pandang (now Makassar).

In contrast to places like Aceh, Java and eastern Indonesia, Bali had limited contact with Europeans in the seventeenth and eighteenth centuries and no European base was established there. Historians therefore lack the benefit of European records which, however frequently they misunderstood or misrepresented local events, are nevertheless useful sources alongside local evidence. We do know that Bali resisted Islamization and that the kingdom of Gelgel was dominant until c.1650. After this time its hegemony disintegrated and Bali became a battlefield of conflicting kingdoms, which it remained until the Dutch conquest of the nineteenth and early twentieth centuries. The foundation of VOC Batavia in 1619 opened a new market for slaves, and one of the functions of Balinese warfare was to capture people for export as slaves. As a result of Batavia's importation of these slaves, even today the local Indonesian dialect of Jakarta reflects Balinese influence.

In the 1660s Buleleng was established as the dominant kingdom of North Bali. Karangasem (East Bali) expanded its control overseas to Lombok, where it had to fight Sumbawan and Sulawesi forces for control. In the south, Mengwi became the dominant kingdom by c.1700. Buleleng and Mengwi competed with each other to control the eastern salient of Java, where the Balinese elite believed their roots to lie, as aristocratic refugees from the Islamic takeover of Java. But by the later eighteenth century they had lost control of the eastern salient to the VOC and Bali was poised for a century of natural and political disasters that would end in Dutch conquest, as will be seen in the following chapter.

The Philippines

Sources on the Philippines in the seventeenth and eighteenth centuries are scant. Spanish records celebrate conquest and conversion to Catholicism but materials about the Filipino reaction to the *conquistadores* hardly exist. From 1589 onwards the Spaniards imposed yearly tribute upon adult males between the ages of 18 and 60, to be paid in labor, goods, or specie. This annual tax was collected via both Crown and private *encomiendas* (grants) which were awarded as a reward for service to the Crown. For colonizing the Philippines, Miguel Lopez de Legazpi received a number of *encomiendas* which he apportioned among his men. The awardee, an *encomendero*, taxed his Filipino subjects and was expected to protect and prepare them for baptism. *Encomenderos* were often brutal, demanding scarce commodities later resold for profit. Although in 1721 the Crown declared that vacated *encomiendas* would revert to itself, this meant nothing to Filipinos, for until the end of Spanish rule they were required to pay tribute.

The tribute system operated through the chiefly class (*principalia*), themselves exempt from payment. For collaborating with the Spanish, a chieftain retained his role in the *barangay* (community), with the title *cabeza de barangay*, the head of some 40 to 50 families. The *cabeza* maintained peace and order, collected taxes and assigned the males of his constituency to the *polo y servicios* (compulsory labor system). *Polo* allocated Filipinos' labor according to the *conquistadores*' whim. Annually the system required males to labor for 40 days, excluding the *principalia* and those who bought their way out. The exigencies of Spain's 'religious' wars – the Hispano-Dutch War (1609–48) and the Moro Wars (1565–1878) – negated theoretical limits on labor demands. Thousands worked for months as woodcutters, shipbuilders, crewmen, and munitions makers in Cavite and Zamboanga shipyards.

Catholic Spain was unable to check the Protestant Netherlands' expansion in Indonesia. In the 1648 Treaty of Westphalia, Spain was forced to recognize Dutch independence and claims in Southeast Asia. This did not, however, stop further Dutch harassment of the Spaniards. Periodically they attacked southern Mindanao (Maguindanao) or incited the Muslim rulers there to resist the Spanish. Several phases comprised the war between Mindanao Muslims – dubbed 'Moros' as already noted, the term used for Muslims in medieval Spain – and the Spaniards. The first phase (1565–81) saw the Spanish defeat Brunei, whose monarchs were kinfolk to the Sulu rulers. From 1578 to 1597 Mindanao Muslims admitted Jesuit missionaries but refused to become a Spanish colony. In the third phase (1598–1635) Sultan Buisan of Maguindanao (r. 1597–1619) battled the Spaniards and competed with them in demanding tribute from the Visayas. From 1649 to 1668 Muslims raided Christian communities in southern Luzon, the Visayas, and northern Mindanao. By 1662–63 these raids and the threat of an invasion of Luzon by the Ming partisan Koxinga (Zheng Chenggong) from his base on Taiwan forced the Spaniards to retreat from Mindanao and to concentrate their forces in Manila. Fifty years later, the Spanish renewed the southern war but met with further Muslim resistance. These on-and-off Moro conflicts constituted the longest anti-colonial resistance in history, ending only after over 300 years with a peace protocol in 1878.

The Spaniards faced multiple threats even in Luzon and the Visayas. From 1596 to 1764 towns in Ilocos and Cagayan, Pangasinan and Pampanga, Luzon, Bohol, and Leyte sporadically revolted, protesting a combination of oppressive tribute and labor demands, Christianization and suppression of traditional religion, and the burdens of supporting the Spaniards' wars. Although directed against the *encomenderos*, uprisings also attacked friars and churches. The Igorot (1601) and Gaddang (1621) rebellions of northern Luzon and the Tamblot (1621–22), Bankaw (1622) and Tapar (1663) rebellions of the Visayas targeted Catholic symbols. The Spanish put down such resistance with the support of locals from other provinces.

In the eighteenth century, longer and more complex rebellions challenged the regime. In the Visayas, the long-lasting Dagohoy Rebellion (1744–1829) established an independent government in the mountains of Bohol and attracted some 20,000 followers. It outlasted its leader and 20 Spanish Governors-General. In Luzon a two-year Tagalog uprising (1745–46) pitted peasants against the new holders of economic power – the friars. Religious orders took over huge *encomiendas* from lay control – vast tracts called *haciendas* – after private *encomiendas* were transformed into land grants. *Haciendas* cultivated cash crops, undermined local subsistence agriculture, and thrived on the dependence of landless tillers.

In 1762, because the Philippines were ruled by the Spanish Bourbons who were allied with the Bourbon monarchs of France, the islands became embroiled in the Seven Years War between Britain and France. The British sailed with a major force from India and conquered Manila, heartening Filipinos also to take up arms against the Spanish regime. A widespread Ilocano rebellion led by Diego Silang, however, failed. Silang was assassinated and his wife executed by the Spaniards. The Paris Peace Treaty of 1763 ended the war between Britain and France and restored Spain's colonial possessions.

Protests at Spanish rule also came from Chinese migrants. They served as conduits between mainland China and the Spanish Philippines, trading in such items as silk, food items, and metals. The profits to be made persuaded many to stay, becoming farmers, gardeners, and artisans. This influx, however, alarmed the Spanish. The colonial government set a quota of immigrants from China and taxed those who stayed. Chinese had to carry identification papers and to live in a ghetto called the *Parián* outside Manila's city walls, which they could only leave with formal approval.

Inspired by a false belief that the Chinese emperor would support them, in 1603 Manila Chinese rebelled. They raised dragon banners and sounded war-gongs, burned establishments in Quiapo and Tondo, murdered many Filipinos, and then assaulted the walled city of Manila. The authorities suppressed them, killing some 25,000. Subsequent revolts in 1639, 1662, 1686, and 1762 resulted in similar tragedies. These massacres, however, hardly slowed the flood of Chinese immigrants. Therefore the Spanish issued expulsion ordinances against non-Christian Chinese in 1744, 1755, 1769, and 1785, only to be thwarted by their own corrupt officials and zealous missionaries. Chinese escaped repatriation either by bribery or joining in mass baptisms. The regime sighed in relief when Chinese eventually dispersed throughout the colony and integrated in local society. Their yearly influx slowed down after the abolition of the galleon trade with Spanish Mexico (1811) made migration less financially attractive.

For over two centuries the galleon trade served to link China, Spain's Pacific colony, and the Spanish Americas. Yearly some 40 ships brought trade items from China to the Philippines. Much of this merchandise was loaded into the locally constructed Manila galleon. Only government officials, the clergy and their friends, and widowed and retired Spaniards received tickets for cargo compartments, which could be profitably resold to Manila merchants, who expected up to 500 percent profit from the voyage across the Pacific to Mexico. In the Spanish homeland, competing Seville and Cadiz merchants lobbied to restrict the galleon trade, but Manila merchants got around this by bribing officials to look away while they overloaded the ship.

Every July or August the Manila galleon commenced the hazardous, trans-Pacific voyage of some 200 days to Acapulco. Beside tradeware, it carried around 400 passengers and correspondence from the Philippine colonial government to the Viceroyalty of Mexico. Storms, overloading of cargoes, incompetence of navigating officers, and piracy meant that many galleons failed to reach their destination. In Acapulco a galleon drydocked for at least six months before the 90-day journey back to Manila in the following February or March, carrying payment for trade items in Mexican silver, newly assigned Spaniards, and missionaries – except for those who managed to flee from being appointed in the Philippines – the Viceroyalty's subsidy, and correspondence, arriving back in Manila nearly two years after the initial departure. In Manila the galleon's arrival was a festive occasion, signalling continuation of the politico-economic lifeline of the colony.

The fortified city of Manila hosted multiple ethnicities and lifestyles. As the center of colonial and religious governance it was also home to around 1200 Spanish families and 150 religious. Formal education was available. In 1595 the Jesuits established a boys' grammar school that later became the Ateneo de Manila University. The Dominicans founded the University of Santo Tomas in 1611. Spanish girls received practical instruction in boarding schools like Santa Potenciana (1591) and Santa Isabel (1632) or they went to a *beaterio* (combined school and nunnery) for religious education, such as Santa Catalina (1696), San Sebastian (1719), and La Concordia (1869). The Beaterio de la Compañia de Jesus (1725) was exclusively for Filipino girls.

The Spanish Philippines are unusual in Southeast Asian history insofar as the archipelago was under full-fledged colonial rule so much earlier than the rest of the region. There are parallels with Spanish America in the period discussed in this chapter, but fewer with other Southeast Asian areas. The colonial impact was thus earlier here and, arguably, deeper; it will be explored further in the following chapter.

8
Colonial Communities, *c.*1800–1900

Introduction

The nineteenth century witnessed dramatic redirections of life in Southeast Asia, as indeed it did in most parts of the world. Scientific, engineering, medical, and other advances – almost entirely achievements of the West – and the concomitant industrialization of Europe and North America propelled modernization and globalization to a new level. Neither was new in the world, but both now accelerated.

Britain was the first country to begin industrialization from the eighteenth century but was followed in the course of the nineteenth century by other European nations and the United States. New nations also emerged, particularly Germany and Italy, brought together from congeries of smaller political units. Germany became an industrialized major power, creating a new constellation in European and world geopolitics that would eventually lead to World Wars I and II in the twentieth century.

Industrialization brought with it a demand for new raw materials and in increasing quantities. Railways, steamships, tin-plating, the advanced weaponry of the industrial age, photography, electric lighting, the internal combustion engine, the motor car and many other products drew European attention to Southeast Asia (among other parts of the world), just as spices had done in the sixteenth century. For the industrializing West, Southeast Asia had several strategic offerings, including:

- tin, coal, and other minerals needed in industrialization;
- rubber and petroleum, which were developed in Southeast Asia and became vital by the late nineteenth century;
- valuable agricultural products such as rice, sugar, and abaca (which produces the fiber commonly but inaccurately known as 'Manila hemp');
- a narrow waterway – the Straits of Melaka – of crucial significance for world trade; and
- significant populations in some areas that formed pools of labor for estate agriculture and, at least potentially, markets for finished goods.

Western nations looked upon Southeast Asian states and saw both opportunities and threats. Local monarchies often sought to resist colonial rule. The new weaponry of the West – improved artillery, repeating and breech-loading rifles, automatic weapons, high explosives, steam-powered gunships, and the like – altered the military balance. Although some local lords acquired such weapons and effectively resisted European forces, few were able to do so for long. The poet Hilaire Belloc captured the brutal reality of the age in his poem 'The modern traveller':

> Whatever happens, we have got
> The Maxim Gun, and they have not.

The nineteenth century was a time of frequent and brutal armed conflicts both among Western powers and between them and others: the Napoleonic Wars, the War of Greek Liberation, the Anglo-American War of 1812, the Java War, the Anglo-Chinese Opium Wars, the Mexican-American War, the American Civil War, the Crimean War, the Afghan Wars, the German and Italian wars of unification, the Franco-Prussian War, three Anglo-Burman Wars, the Aceh War, the Zulu War, the Boer War, the Spanish-American War among others, along with multiple smaller conflicts fought out on frontiers in America, Africa, and Asia. The great nineteenth-century German military thinker Carl von Clausewitz appropriately observed that war was an extension of state policy and politics by other means. Along with these many wars went strategic competition for influence and position. In this chapter we will see cases where a European power felt obliged to move into some Southeast Asian territory less because there were strategic commodities or geographic locations to be won, than out of fear that some other European power would get there first.

These changes in the West had profound impacts in Southeast Asia, for there they washed up against complex local realities, already discussed in preceding chapters. Southeast Asians were affected by, and responded to, the West's modernities and its aggression in multiple ways in the nineteenth century. These Southeast Asian-Western interactions produced both consolidation and division of communities and cultures, and set the stage for much of the history of the twentieth and twenty-first centuries. We will see below that colonial powers drew new boundaries on the ground in Southeast Asia – boundaries that largely shaped the geographical limits of today's nation-states. But this consolidation of land areas also separated communities to whom these borders were artificial lines on pieces of paper. Indeed, in one respect these boundaries inverted Southeast Asian geopolitical traditions. In Southeast Asia, generally water connected communities and land – often covered with less accessible hills, mountains, and jungles – divided them: Sumatran states had links with Malay states across the Straits of Melaka, south Kalimantan was more connected to north Java across the Java Sea than to Brunei in the north of the island, southern Philippine Muslim states were linked by sea to north Borneo, the states of mainland Southeast Asia and Java were formed along river valleys, and so on. But the Western imperial powers – building on the geopolitical traditions of Europe – viewed water as dividing and land as connecting, no matter how impenetrably jungled or precipitous the Southeast Asian land reality might be. So communities were artificially divided, and in many cases their response was to ignore the presumptions of the Western colonizers. Such communities continued to interact with each other, becoming 'smugglers' in Western eyes for carrying on as they had for centuries. Sometimes, however, this was real smuggling, for Western imperialism also created lucrative new markets – in such areas as drugs, illegal firearms, counterfeit currency, and people trafficking.

Western colonialists were almost never able to govern a place entirely on their own: local allies were needed, which gave rise to multiple consequences that, again, both consolidated and divided Southeast Asian communities. In many places, the Western powers worked to create an indigenous administrative elite. This often made previous social hierarchies more rigid and inflexible, and the social distance between the local elite and the masses of people greater, even hostile. There were also those who resisted colonial encroachments and regarded collaborators with contempt – a social division that not infrequently led to bloody acts of revenge when colonial power was weak or when, in the twentieth century, it came to an end. Ethnic divisions were also often hardened, particularly where 'race' seemed to the colonial rulers a natural way to divide and define their subjects.

Locals who worked with the colonial regimes were not passive actors. Many viewed the intellectual advances of the West with admiration and sought to use Western learning to modernize their own societies – often with the ultimate aim of making foreign rulers redundant. But this Western-style modernity also came with a cultural packaging that was not always welcome. In particular, the nineteenth century was a time of active Christian missionizing in the non-Christian world. This produced converts in some places, but animosity in many others. In general, Christian missions were most successful among peoples who had not yet embraced a world religion. This sometimes led to an association of religion and self-interest between colonial rulers and subject peoples who were once looked down on as backward by dominant societies, a socio-cultural distinction which was thereby hardened by the colonial and Christian intrusion. In general, Christian missions had least success among Muslim and Buddhist societies.

In Muslim societies, there was a sort of competition between alternate forms of globalization – that offered by reformed, universalist Islam and that offered by the West. In Indonesia, administrative elites working with the colonialists found Western-style reforms more attractive than Islam's offerings, while religious elites embraced Islamic reformism and – almost invariably – disliked Western 'Christian' rule, even if that rule was fundamentally secular in nature. Thereby another form of cultural division strengthened. In Malaya, the indigenous elite simply prevented Islamic reformism from gaining a foothold, to both their and British satisfaction. In Thailand – the only Southeast Asian state to escape full-fledged colonial rule – the indigenous royal elite embraced Western technology, education, and governing techniques along with Buddhist reform. This unique combination, along with a favorable geopolitical position – for both the French to the east and British to the west found a buffer state useful – enabled Thailand to escape many of the divisive effects of colonial rule elsewhere.

But one caution is in order. While undoubtedly the new imperialism of the 1800s was of decisive importance, we should remember that in much of Southeast Asia it came rather late in the century. Indeed, many places that formed part of the British, French, Dutch, Spanish, or American colonial states, particularly on their fringes, only came under Western rule early in the twentieth century. As we look at this decisive century in the following pages, it is thus important to bear in mind that, while significant change is a common theme, any suggestion that these changes were the same everywhere would do violence to the complex historical reality of nineteenth-century Southeast Asia.

The conquest of Burma

The First Anglo-Burmese War (1824–1826)

The border disputes that triggered the First Anglo-Burmese War in 1824 had their origins in the eighteenth-century expansionist policies of the Konbaung court, its efforts to integrate western frontier zones into the Burmese state, and the growing territorial influence of the English East India Company (EEIC) in Southeast Asia. The semi-autonomous kingdoms of Arakan, Manipur, and Assam that had once provided a buffer between the EEIC's territories and the Ava kingdom were by the early nineteenth century under more direct Burmese control. This made London and Calcutta officials somewhat nervous about security, resulting in the deployment of forces along British India's borders to thwart any penetration by Burmese forces. Suspicion, ignorance, and over-confidence on both sides of the border compounded matters as diplomatic missions attempted to cool the already heated situation. Communities along and between the borders took advantage of the disputes, sometimes playing one power off against the other in order to maintain autonomy but thereby contributing to the escalation of tensions in the region.

When Bodawpaya came to the Burmese throne in 1782, he turned his attention towards reintegrating Arakan into the imperial fold. Arakan was linguistically Burmese and religiously Buddhist and thus within the cultural orbit of the Burmese court, yet it enjoyed a degree of political autonomy, which provided opportunities for Muslim minorities and other Indian influences to settle there. Within three years the kingdom was annexed, resulting in the deportation of nearly 20,000 people to the Burmese capital, along with the ancient Maha Muni image of the Buddha. By the late eighteenth century, the rise of a reinvigorated Siamese state on the Burmese eastern front prompted the Konbaung court once again to direct its attention towards the kingdoms of Manipur and Assam, just north of Arakan, so as to secure the western front. Manipur had once been nominally connected to the Toungoo court through tributary relations but by the early nineteenth century its king no longer recognized Burmese authority. In 1819 Burmese troops commanded by General Thado Maha Bandula reoccupied the Manipur valley and installed indirect administrative rule. As was true in their earlier contests with Ayutthaya, the Burmese were less concerned with territory than with securing new conscripts for their Crown service corps, resulting in the deportation of skilled artisans, religious bondspersons, and Indian advisors to the Burmese court.

In neighboring Assam succession disputes destabilized what had once been a Burmese tribute state. A Burmese force of 8000 men installed a leader loyal to the Konbaung throne in 1817, but in 1821 Bodawpaya had to send another force of 20,000 under Maha Bandula. By 1823 a permanent base was established and the Assamese throne was abolished.

These developments, along with growing disputes over events in Arakan, sparked EEIC concern, for the Company's Indian territories now had a common border with Burma. Infrastructure projects and the expansion of irrigation works in Upper Burma created a demand for Arakanese labor, which precipitated a massive exodus of refugees into British territory. Resistance followed flight: Arakanese fought Burmese forces from safe havens well within Company territory, knowing that the British would not allow the Burmese to pursue them. The Company's tacit approval of these bases within its territory convinced Burmese officials that the British were not to be trusted.

A similar refugee situation in Manipur provided the final context for open military confrontation. Burma's occupation of Manipur in 1823 sparked a refugee exodus into territories such as Cachar that the British deemed essential to the security of Bengal in particular and India as a whole. Cachar's *raja* asked the Burmese to help stabilize the refugee problem, but the advance of Burmese troops into the region prompted Calcutta to declare it a British protectorate. With the arrival of British forces to secure the territory, the situation worsened.

On 5 March 1824 the EEIC declared war on the Burmese kingdom, commencing the First Anglo-Burmese War (1824–26). While past successes may have emboldened Maha Bandula and his troops at the start, the might of the British expeditionary force and the relative ease with which it moved against Burmese forces soon dampened initial optimism. Expecting a confrontation in Chittagong, Maha Bandula directed his troops across the Naaf river only to receive intelligence that a major force had arrived at Rangoon. He attempted to reach Lower Burma while other forces were directed southward from the capital, but the Burmese were unable to come to Rangoon's aid. The British took the city and then broke through Burmese lines, moving northward towards Prome and central Burma. Maha Bandula was killed in battle in 1825. Superior weapons, a steamship, and better tactics allowed the British to move all the way to Pagan, where finally negotiations were opened with the Burmese court. On 24 February 1826 King Bagyidaw signed a peace treaty at Yandabo, which imposed a large indemnity upon the Burmese and gave the British Assam, Manipur, Arakan, and Tenasserim.

The Second Anglo-Burmese War (1852)

The Treaty of Yandabo required the Burmese government to pay an indemnity of a million pounds sterling and provided for an exchange of diplomatic representatives. The court hoped that the ceded territories might be returned once the payment had been completed, but they soon realized that the terms of the treaty were final and binding in the eyes of the British. The war had a significant effect on the court, as the loss of territories, resources, and labor was soon exploited by claimants to the throne who interpreted these losses as a direct reflection of the king's diminishing merit and inability to rule effectively. British perceptions that the court was being difficult were exacerbated by Burmese port officials in Rangoon who reportedly enforced regulations in an unbending manner, antagonizing members of the powerful foreign business community. When two British ships were fined by the governor of Rangoon for evading customs duties in December 1851, Governor-General Lord Dalhousie ordered two Royal Navy vessels to the port with an ultimatum that the fines be dropped and the governor be replaced. Fully aware of the potential for a new war, the Burmese court accepted the terms but the British continued to blockade the coastline. Consequently, a new ultimatum was issued by Calcutta for a payment of a million rupees. Believing that war was inevitable regardless of the Burmese response, British forces took control of Rangoon, Bassein, and Martaban. The Burmese attempted to defend their territories, but the British nevertheless seized Pegu in 1852 and created a new Province of Burma, comprising nearly all of Lower Burma south of Prome.

A royal attempt at reform

King Mindon Min (r. 1853–78) came to the Burmese throne in the wake of the Second Anglo-Burmese War and the annexation of Lower Burma, with the very existence of his kingdom threatened by the British imperial thrust. He embraced an ambitious program of reforms intended at least in part to forestall claims that his kingdom was a barbaric atavism that must fall to colonial rule. At about the same time, as will be seen below, the Siamese King Mongkut was undertaking reforms which were inspired by his own understanding of the Western threat – not least as it was illustrated in Burma's two successive defeats at British hands. But Siam's geopolitics would prove more favorable than Burma's, for Mongkut could balance the interests of several Western powers and the most dangerous for him – Britain and France – were to find it useful for Siam to be an uncolonized buffer between their territories. For Burma, however, where the British were the unchallenged dominant power, no amount of reform could stave off conquest in the end.

Mindon's reforms were in many ways more ambitious than Mongkut's and more closely resembled the policies of the latter's successor Chulalongkorn. While some of his policies were reminiscent of earlier royal efforts to redefine state-*Sangha* relations, others were of a clearly modernizing variety. With the help and support of his brother (and designated successor) the Kanaung Prince, Mindon introduced new Western technologies, revitalized the arts, modernized the military, and improved access to Western education. Factories began to produce goods with European machinery and in some case involved Western management teams. By the 1870s a standing army was established, telegraph lines had been built, a railway to the Chinese border was planned, and steamships were purchased for security purposes. Administratively, the kingdom improved its governance by bureaucratizing royal agencies, attempting (not entirely successfully) to replace appanages with salaries for officials and princes, revamping the taxation system, centralizing legal authority over the courts, establishing a new fiscal system, and extending the authority of the state over provincial officials through new categories of appointment.

In 1866, however, the Kanaung Prince was murdered in a meeting of the *Hlutdaw* (royal council) by dissident princes. This seems to have shocked Mindon, who thereafter gave more attention to religious affairs and played a less obvious role in modernizing reforms. He did not reappoint a new crown prince immediately because of fear of further violent resistance. Yet the reform process in fact continued and may even have strengthened despite the king's reduced involvement. A new generation of younger officials began to enter the court – many of them European-trained – while some of the more conservative senior ministers who took part in the 1866 rebellion were jailed. These younger figures included the future *Myoza* (governor) of Kyaukmyaung, who was educated at the École Centrale des Arts et Manufactures in Paris, and the *Myoza* of Yaw, who continued the court's interest in importing technology and even developed a Burmese form of the Morse Code, an essential tool in that age of telegraph. Mindon's successor King Thibaw (r. 1878–85), however, was no reformer and the imperial power inexorably closed in on what remained of Burma.

The Third Anglo-Burmese War and final annexation (1885–86)

Strengthening commercial interests domiciled in Burma strongly influenced policy makers in Rangoon, Calcutta, and London. Instability in Mandalay was regarded as bad for Lower Burma's booming rice industry, and this issue intersected with security concerns for India. The British wished to end the inefficiencies and brutality of the state under King Thibaw, knowing also that direct control of Upper Burma would provide foreign companies with access to natural resources and the markets of southwestern China.

Aware of the risk of complete annexation, the Burmese court attempted to secure foreign support by signing a treaty of friendship with the French in early 1885. France had by now emerged as a major power in Southeast Asia after their colonization of Cambodia and Vietnam, and the Burmese hoped to use them as a counterweight against British ambitions. The French were attracted by plans to develop the transportation sector, establish a new bank, and manage the ruby industry. Belligerent voices in the British administration, however, depicted this French interest in Upper Burma as a potential threat to India.

The immediate *casus belli* of 1885 again arose from a commercial dispute. The Burmese government had fined the Bombay Trading Company for allegedly logging in areas beyond their agreed contract. The case went to Mandalay where it was discussed at the highest level in the *Hlutdaw*. While the case was being deliberated, Calcutta issued an ultimatum demanding that the original fine be overturned and that all decisions regarding Burma's foreign relations be ceded to Calcutta's control. In response, the court acquiesced to almost all of the demands, but refused to surrender sovereignty in matters of foreign affairs. As Burmese ambassadors consulted European representatives for advice, the British prepared for war. Conservative figures in British India believed that complete annexation of Burma was necessary, because it was not possible to find an acceptable replacement for Thibaw, who was regarded in official circles and depicted in the press as a tyrant and oppressor of the Burmese people. Others objected that total annexation would be costly, difficult, and administratively challenging due to the weakened nature of the existing infra-structure and the armed resistance that would surely follow.

Major-General Sir Harry Prendergast was ordered to occupy Mandalay as quickly as possible. On the Burmese side, the commander of operations in the northwest (*Hlethin Atwinwun*) was given the task of organizing the Burmese forces and the final defenses of the kingdom. Commanding an armed flotilla and nearly 10,000 troops, Prendergast captured the Minhla fort on 17 November 1885 and a few days later defeated the forces under the *Hlethin Atwinwun*. The court surrendered unconditionally on 27 November 1885.

Upon entering Mandalay, Colonel Edward Sladen informed King Thibaw that he would be exiled to India, where he died in 1916. On 1 January 1886, the British government formally announced the annexation of the kingdom of Burma. By the end of the month, however, civil administration in Upper Burma had collapsed in fierce, armed resistance to British rule and village communities were fighting among themselves for limited supplies of necessities. Within a month, Lord Dufferin (the Viceroy of India) abolished the *Hlutdaw* and announced that Upper Burma would remain under direct British administrative control. On 26 February, the kingdom was formally declared a province of British India.

Establishing borders and pacification (1886–1890)

By June 1886, most of the country was engaged in insurrection, 'dacoity' (an Anglo-Indian word for armed robbery), or other forms of violence. While massive in scale, these rebellions were rarely successful and lacked coordination as no leader was available to link what were essentially local affairs. Counter-insurgency measures were ineffective, at least in part because British Indian troops produced casualties at a far greater rate than King Thibaw's government had ever done. Summary execution of villagers found with arms soon had to be abandoned for fear of escalating an already heated theatre of war. By 1887, nearly 41,000 troops and Indian police were attempting to secure the country-side. As villages began coming over to the British side, however, the situation began gradually to improve. Traders and Buddhist monks provided limited, but important means of contact between British authorities and local communities. Other efforts, such as the construction of the Toungoo-Mandalay railway, also gained the approval of many Burmese who found employment in the three-year project (1886–89).

Peripheral areas required permanent garrisons of troops to deal with ongo-ing resistance by Kachin and Chin tribesmen, but many of these communities were integrated into the province through the appointment of political officers to manage their affairs. The Shan States Act of 1888 established a British super-intendent who was charged with settling disputes, recognizing the status of cooperative *sawbwas* (rulers), and securing the payment of annual tribute. Shan chiefs were given limited legal roles while the British secured rights over all natural resources of the area and maintained authority over local affairs when required. Other administrative zones, such as the large Salween-Kengtung area, the boundary with Siam, and that with Yunnan were established in 1890, 1892, and 1894 respectively.

The new authorities' different understandings of legitimacy and of the obligations of state and society were a barrier to Burmese acceptance of British rule. As dissatisfaction increased from the 1850s onward, the British authorities struggled to devise ways of building public support for the colonial order. Most communities continued to resist. Yet there were minorities such as the Karens, Chinese, and wealthier business interests, who did cooperate with the British, often because their interests seemed to be served by the colonial project. The colonists thus began to build participatory institutions that facilitated the foundations for self-government for such groups.

Administration and education

Administrative reforms began in 1887 under the guidance of Chief Commissioner Sir Charles Crosthwaite, who was tasked with assessing the weaknesses of the local administration. Much of the problem lay in the inability of British officials to recognize the role the monarchy had traditionally played in managing religious affairs, which was at the very heart of ethnic Burmans' identity and conceptual world. The king's duty as a protector-patron of the Buddhist *Sangha* (monastic order) and its *dhamma* (law) were key elements of Burmese life that the secular colonial administration failed to comprehend. Avoiding involvement in religious affairs was a principle of the colonial authorities, but this directly affected how the new government was perceived. By refusing to recognize the authority of the *thathanabaing* (the head of the monastic order, who had previously been appointed by the king), the British lost any hope of winning the hearts and minds of the Burmese at that early stage. To Crosthwaite, the crux of the problem lay at the village level, where local district officials (*myothugyis* and *taikthugyis*) were needed with real authority over financial, judicial, and policing matters. In the wake of the emergency Upper Burma Regulation Act of 1887 and the subsequent 1889 Burma Village Act, the process of appointing a *thugyi* to each of Burma's 17,000–18,000 villages began in earnest. In principle, the new headman would enable the village unit to be the foundation upon which the entire provincial administration would rest, with duties ranging from the collection of taxes to village defense, maintenance of roads, keeping records, maintaining sanitary conditions, and hosting visiting district officers. In practice, the new system faced many challenges, both from detractors within the administration and from locals themselves. The former felt that there were too few local candidates available who could be entrusted with such powers, while villagers distrusted men whose authority derived from appointment by the colonial regime, rather than arising from personal reciprocal relations developed over time.

The transformation from personalized authority to impersonal governance by Rangoon authorities was further enhanced with the introduction of the settlement officer in 1872. This new position was responsible for mapping the geographical, topographical, and cultural landscape of Burma in order to assess the economic potential of the country. Periodic settlement surveys were conducted with the establishment of the Land Records Department in 1900 and they carried considerable bite as tax rates were fixed according to the findings of these reports. Cash payment was expected on a regular basis and collected by headmen, township, and district officers, moving further away from the more flexible system that traditional *myothugyis* had offered their constituents.

Other government agencies expanded the presence of the state in local affairs, notably the Public Works Department (1870s), the Department of Agriculture (1906), the Departments of Public Health and Veterinary Medicine (1906), and municipal corporations. Except for irrigation projects managed by the Public Works Department, many of the initiatives sponsored by these bodies were not appreciated by Burmese as there was little attempt to take local perspectives and concerns into account. Paved streets, lighting, medical services, sanitation, water supply, and other amenities were regarded by some as specifically European priorities and the excessive taxation that went along with these projects led many urban communities to resist being incorporated into the new municipal corporations.

Following the Second Anglo-Burmese War in 1852, colonial legal structures began to be introduced in Lower Burma. An executive officer was responsible for the adjudication of all legal cases, but because his duties were numerous, customary law was still applied where appropriate. This created a considerable disjuncture between common practice and the official courts. Serious matters were still overseen by the Chief Commissioner but appeals rarely reached the colonial government. As the economy expanded and with it a need for greater legal consistency, a judicial commissioner was appointed for Lower Burma in 1872 and the number of appeals multiplied under his more penetrating gaze. In 1890 a subordinate judicial commissioner for Upper Burma was appointed along with the introduction of full-time district level judicial officers. Such central oversight reduced the authority of the lower courts and ended that of the *myothugyis* who handled customary law. In 1900 the Chief Court of Lower Burma was established, followed by the formation of a new judicial branch of the civil service in 1905.

For many local communities, the courts, prisons, and colonial officers that managed them were the most immediate representation of the new colonial authority. Burmese would often find attacks on their personal dignity more alarming than financial transgressions, while marriage, divorce, and inheritance were regarded as matters of traditional custom rather than impersonal state-enforced law. Thus laws gradually became more divorced from the familiar customs and values derived from local traditions. Yet the law also came to be an occupation which generations of Burmese elites would follow, for as the economy expanded, new types of rules, procedures, and relationships needed to be administered and maintained, contributing to the growth of different types of laws and different niches within which a Burmese lawyer could practice. Law would also shape the language in which political debate and nationalism would emerge.

In 1897 British Burma was granted legislative autonomy, with an appointed Legislative Council under the newly designated Lieutenant-Governor. Originally a nine-member body, the council was increased to 17 members in 1909 and 30 by 1915. Several members represented ethnic categories and others the business communities. The council was emasculated from its inception as all legislative matters issued by the body were subject to the vetoes of the Lieutenant-Governor, the Governor-General of India, and the Secretary of State for India. Although by this means the Burmese were legally connected to London, functionally the majority of the population was divorced from the processes associated with the Legislative Council.

A priority of the colonial state was to educate the local population so as to have English-speaking clerks for the civil service and perhaps to support management in the private sectors. Unlike pre-colonial education, which was run by village monasteries and thus connected to local social and ritual life, the colonial school system grew from the needs of the British empire and the priorities of the economy that it sought to foster. Missionary and government-sponsored schools provided elite education but their development was slow; there were only around 900 such schools by the early 1890s. By 1917, however, this number had increased to nearly 5000 and many more students than before attended secondary and tertiary institutions. This increasing education along British lines did not, however, penetrate evenly throughout local society. In fact non-indigenous communities responded to educational incentives to migrate, settle, and compete for lucrative posts within the colonial civil service. While indigenous Burmese retained a bare majority in university enrollment – the essential qualification for commercial and government employment – it was not until the opening of Rangoon University in 1920 and subsequent professional colleges that they came to predominate in higher education.

British Malaya

By the early nineteenth century, the British had gained an important foothold in the Malay peninsula through their settlements at Penang, Melaka, and Singapore. The Anglo-Dutch Treaty of 1824 kept the Dutch at bay and made Malaya a British sphere of influence. The continuing threat since the seventeenth century of Siamese expansion in northern and central Malaya was contained by the Anglo-Siamese Treaty of 1826, whereby Britain recognized Siamese suzerainty over Kedah (and, from 1841, Perlis), Kelantan, and Terengganu, while Siam implicitly acknowledged, in turn, British influence over the remaining Malay states.

Notwithstanding its influence, until the last quarter of the nineteenth century Britain avoided becoming entangled in the affairs of the Malay states, fearing the inherent political and economic costs of such a commitment. It was content to maintain its three Straits Settlements on the fringe of the peninsula to serve as leading entrepôts for imported and regional products, including those from the Malay states, and as entry points for foreign merchants, immigrant Chinese, and later Indian laborers, who hastened the economic development of the peninsula. Nevertheless, where necessary, Britain asserted its prerogatives, as when it intervened in 1831–32 to subdue an uprising in Naning in Negeri Sembilan over British attempts to impose taxes on its people, and again in 1855 when it interfered in the affairs of Johor to fix the line of succession. By and large, however, the British avoided colonial intervention.

From the middle of the century, the relationship between the Straits Settlements and the Malay states began to alter significantly. As new economic forces drew both sides closer together, they also generated intolerable strain. By the 1840s, as the demand for tin from Western industrializing countries expanded, Straits Chinese merchants, often in partnership with rival Malay chiefs, began to invest in tin mines in the western Malay states. Attempts by opposing Malay-Chinese coalitions to gain control of tin-producing districts and their competition for territory and revenue soon gave rise to civil disturbances in Klang (Selangor), Larut (Perak), and Sungai Ujung (Negeri Sembilan). Backed by Straits merchants, the new British Governor, Sir Andrew Clarke, acted immediately upon his arrival in November 1873. Between January and April 1874 he overturned the long-standing policy of non-intervention and brought Perak, Selangor, and Sungai Ujung under British control by inducing each of their rulers to sign a treaty accepting a British Resident, whose advice had to be followed on all matters except those touching Malay religion and custom. Though Clarke had acted on his own initiative instead of waiting on instructions from the Colonial Office, his actions were not repudiated by the latter. Fearing possible German intervention in the Malay states at a time when European powers were expanding their colonial empires, London accepted the Governor's *fait accompli*.

That Malay society did not adapt well to the new British-imposed system of government was evident in the subsequent outbreak of resistance in Perak in November 1875 which resulted in the assassination of its first Resident, J. W. W. Birch. Although the British quashed the resistance by March 1876 and successfully contained smaller outbreaks in Sungai Ujung and an attempted uprising in Selangor, these episodes of opposition gave the British 'forward movement' initial reason to pause, before it resumed again in the 1880s with the extension of the residential system to the remainder of Negeri Sembilan (1887) and to Pahang (1888), where the British yet again encountered sporadic bouts of Malay resistance from 1891 to 1895.

By July 1896 the next stage in the consolidation of British influence in the Malay peninsula was achieved by bringing together Perak, Selangor, Negeri Sembilan, and Pahang as the Federated Malay States (FMS). With the transfer of the northern Malay states from Siamese to British control in 1909 and the appointment of British Advisors to these 'unfederated' states – Kelantan (1910), Terengganu (1919), Kedah (1923), Perlis (1930) – and the acceptance of a 'General Advisor' by Johor in 1914, the extension of British authority to the whole of the deceptively termed 'British Malaya' was, to all appearances, more or less complete. In truth, only the Straits Settlements were formally British colonies; the federated and unfederated states remained legally sovereign and independent Malay kingdoms under the terms of the similar, although not identical, treaties each had concluded with the British. Notwithstanding such legal niceties, it was clear by the early decades of the twentieth century that the

British were *de facto* the dominant power in Malaya, even though the Malay rulers continued to hold *de jure* sovereignty over their kingdoms.

The piecemeal extension of British control had one important consequence: the creation of three separate administrative systems within the boundaries of British Malaya. In the Straits Settlements, which were administered directly as a typical British colony, the Governor in Singapore headed an administration that included an Executive Council of senior officials and a Legislative Council with a majority of nominated members. Day-to-day affairs of the colony were run by a Colonial Secretary. Below them were the Resident Councilors, the local administrative heads of Penang and Melaka. Coordination with the Malay states was achieved by the Governor exercising administrative oversight in his concurrent appointment as the High Commissioner of those states where British rule was more indirect. In the FMS, administrative power was centralized under a Resident-General at Kuala Lumpur with jurisdiction over all the Residents. Selected for their knowledge of, and ability to administer, the Malays, the Residents not only directed a European-style administration in their respective states but also sat in, and dominated, the State Councils, the main legislative bodies, where the Malay rulers and members of the Malay elite and a limited number of Chinese representatives consulted to pass laws. At the lower levels, British District Officers, working closely with village headmen and reporting to the Resident, kept the government in touch with Malay grassroots feelings.

Following the establishment of a Federal Council in 1909, ostensibly to ensure greater uniformity in legislation – though it subsequently assumed the duty of enacting nearly all laws in the FMS – the role of the State Councils and the position of the Malay rulers who presided over them diminished even further. With the High Commissioner, assisted by the Resident-General, now in charge of the Federal Council, the rulers had become in fact only ordinary members without veto powers. The situation was noticeably different in the third component of British Malaya, the Unfederated Malay States (UMS), whose Malay rulers, cognizant of the diminished powers of their counterparts in the FMS, jealously guarded their independence and vehemently opposed any suggestion of incorporating their polities into the FMS. British 'Advisors' appointed to the UMS consequently did not enjoy the same level of influence as their 'Resident' counterparts in the FMS. And with looser British control, the UMS were able to preserve a greater sense of the Malay character of their state governments: Malays continued to occupy many of the positions in the administrative hierarchy, including that of Chief Minister (*Menteri Besar*), State Secretary, and most District Officers.

Although British Malaya was not administratively united, the political stability brought by British rule facilitated enterprise and employment and attracted many Europeans, the great majority British, most of whom settled in the west coast states where the main administrative and commercial centers and planting districts were located. Based on the state censuses of 1891, there were 719 Europeans in the FMS alone. By the time of the 1901 census, their numbers had doubled, and of these some 85.5 percent were British. Employment in the expanding government bureaucracy contributed much of the initial increase but by the second decade of the new century, the number of Europeans engaged in other growth sectors like planting – mainly in rubber – had increased from 12 per cent of all Europeans in the FMS in 1901 to 42 percent by 1911. Those in commerce and finance also registered significant growth and soon outnumbered civil servants. Accompanying the increase in the European population was a corresponding growth in institutions such as churches, hospitals, printing firms, and social clubs, which allowed Europeans to associate with each other. Most of the civil servants and many planters, who formed the largest group of non-officials, shared broadly similar social and educational backgrounds: the great majority were middle class, with officials differentiated from non-officials mainly by the fact that most civil servants had an Oxbridge education. So Europeans formed a generally stable social class, sharing similar outlooks, enjoying a generally high standard of living befitting their status and prestige, and thereby presenting a cohesive social bulwark maintaining British rule in Malaya.

As British rule in the Malay states was indirect, colonial policy encouraged their administrators to associate closely with the people they governed, and especially to secure the allegiance of the ruling Malay elites through whom the all-important Malay base was governed. Because of their focal position within the Malay political and social order, the rulers were provided with a regular stipend and co-opted by the British as local allies and collaborators. Even though they suffered a loss in *de facto* power in relation to the British, their prestige and majesty were carefully preserved and enhanced with British support so that they in fact exercised considerably more influence within the Malay order than their position had previously afforded. Concomitantly, the authority of rival but subordinate Malay chiefs, who had wielded power by controlling revenue and providing the link between the ruler and the villager, was summarily eroded when their roles were usurped by British district officers.

The desire to give their 'partners in rule' and the dispossessed traditional elite a minor share in the apparatus of the colonial government, and thereby to contribute to the overall stability of the Malay order, led colonial administrators to begin educating a small number of young royals and aristocrats in English for government service, with the expectation that they would become future allies. But it was not until the turn of the century, with the opening of the residential Malay College at Kuala Kangsar (Perak) in 1905, that a more concerted and sustained attempt was made to educate the sons of the Malay aristocracy in the fashion of the English public school system, so that they could be the administrative leaders of the country. These administrators were later to form the Malay Administrative Service (MAS), an auxiliary arm of, and subordinate to, the British-dominated Malayan Civil Service (MCS) that was set up in 1920 following an amalgamation of the Straits and FMS Civil Services. With their education in English, many members of the Malay elite were gradually drawn into a European ambience, adopting Western styles of dress, living in Western-style houses, and even taking trips to London in emulation of colonial officials – and widening, in the process, the cultural cleavage between the ruling class and the rest of Malay society.

At the Malay village base, comprising mainly peasants engaged in rice farming and fishing, lifestyles remained relatively unchanged. British policy tended towards minimum interference and entrusted Malay welfare to the chiefs and village headmen. Partly influenced by developments in the neighboring Straits Settlements – where the foundations of a modern system based on English- and Malay-language education were laid in the late 1860s – a rudimentary Malay vernacular education was introduced in the Malay states from the mid-1870s, at first through the personal initiatives of individual British Residents, but more concertedly from 1882, after the dust of the initial British 'forward movement' had settled. Its aim was to offer the Malays a 'practical' education that would make them better farmers and fishermen and thereby advance their welfare. English was not taught to the masses of the Malay *rakyat* (common people) as it would, explained Sir Frank Swettenham – Resident in Selangor and then first Resident-General of the FMS, 1896–1901 – 'unfit them for the duties of life and make them discontented with anything like manual labour'.[1] More worrying perhaps was that it could also create a class of educated and politically conscious Malays who might challenge British rule.

While the British found much about the 'feudal' character of Malay society and the Malays' 'gentlemanly' ways that they admired, they were less enamored by what officials frequently stereotyped as the Malay's lack of industry and commercial ambition – attributes that British officials found in abundance, however, among Chinese immigrants. Described by Swettenham as the 'bone and sinew' of the colonial economy in Malaya, the Chinese became key players in the expanding economies of the Straits Settlements as laborers, traders, entrepreneurs, and professionals, and also in the Malay states, where they had a significant presence in the tin industry. No attempt was therefore made to control Chinese immigration to Malaya until the early decades of the twentieth century. By 1891, the Chinese formed over half the population of Selangor, Perak, and Sungai Ujung, while 79 percent of Kuala Lumpur's population of 43,786 was Chinese. But the British found the Chinese – unlike the Malays – troublesome and difficult to govern, except by their own. Violent power struggles and rioting by rival Chinese secret societies, which commanded the growing communities during the nineteenth century, created anarchic conditions that often threatened the stability of British rule in Malaya. Their policing forces greatly outnumbered, the British had little choice but to turn a blind eye to secret societies' activities, including their trade in opium and women, and to manage them through their community leaders, the *Kapitan Cina* (Chinese Captain). It was not until 1890 that the British banned secret societies in Malaya. Given their numbers and strong social ties to their own communities, it was not surprising that the Chinese retained much of their cultural identity and social organization under British rule. Nevertheless, the availability of English education in the Straits Settlements did engender a class of 'King's Chinese' with strong ties of loyalty to the British Empire.

While the Chinese immigrated through their own communal networking, Indian immigration was assisted by the British for the development of

---

[1]   Quoted in Rex Stevenson, *Cultivators and Administrators: British educational policy towards the Malays, 1875–1906* (Kuala Lumpur: Oxford University Press, 1975), 57.

commercial agriculture. Towards this end, the British provided generous land grants and financial assistance, the initial establishment of transport infrastructure and help with ensuring a regular supply of labor. The plantation economy was initially dominated by the Chinese, but European participation became evident from the 1890s with the cultivation of sugar and coffee. After the fall in coffee prices in the late 1890s, European planters turned to the cultivation of rubber. India was a convenient source of labor as it was already a British colony. Indian immigration initially was on an 'indentured' basis; in 1899 over 5000 indentured migrants arrived in Malaya from Madras. Like the Chinese, Indians also kept very much to themselves: housed mainly on the estates where they worked, they were generally isolated from other ethnic groups.

French Indochina

France's colonization of Vietnam, Cambodia, and Laos – what became known collectively as French Indochina – was a piecemeal process lasting nearly five decades; the final border agreement with Siam was only signed in 1907. This reflected the reality that Indochina was not a natural political or geographical entity, as well as the fact that French ambitions and objectives differed in the various territories in the region. The overarching goal was, of course, to establish a foothold in Southeast Asia for the French colonial empire. While Vietnam was attractive for its ports (particularly Saigon), Cambodia and Laos were of interest mainly because of the Mekong river's perceived potential as a gateway to China. There was also a certain element of what we may call the 'zero-sum game mentality', meaning that France wished to acquire these territories to ensure that they would not fall to imperial rivals, particularly the British. The conquest of Indochina was not merely a matter of Anglo-French rivalry, however, for French expansion directly challenged the suzerainty and influence of both China and Siam, and it had to deal with both of these powers in the process.

Conquest and colonization of Indochina

By the mid-1850s, France was once again a full-fledged empire under Napoleon III (r. 1852–70), grandson of the original Emperor. France was the only major European power without a presence in Southeast Asia, and even its small Indian possessions paled in comparison to the growing British presence there. Siam was a possible target for colonization, but this would have meant a head-on collision with British interests, and Vietnam became a more logical choice. French interest in Vietnam had been piqued by the treaty signed with Prince Nguyen Phuc Anh in the eighteenth century, and although this treaty had remained a dead letter, it did forge a tenuous link between the two countries. Vietnam's share in the thriving regional trade caught the eye of commercial interests in France. More importantly, the Nguyen dynasty's persecution of Western (mainly French) missionaries and Vietnamese Catholics provided a rationale for intervention.

In 1858 France launched an attack on the coastal port known to Europeans as Tourane and to Vietnamese as Da Nang. While the expedition also included some Spanish soldiers from the Philippines (because a Spanish missionary had been martyred), it was predominantly a French undertaking and is generally taken as marking the beginning of France's colonization of Vietnam. The campaign at Tourane was unsuccessful, but the European forces withdrew southward and were able to capture Saigon, which was ultimately a more important prize. Over the next three years, the French expanded the area under their control to include several of the surrounding provinces. There was fierce local resistance, but the court in Hue eventually decided to negotiate rather than fight, and in 1862 a treaty was signed which ceded the conquered provinces to France and promised freedom of religion for Catholics. Five years later the French occupied the rest of the Mekong delta as well.

During this time France was simultaneously establishing a foothold in Cambodia, whose rulers were receptive to the offer of its 'protection' as a counterweight against their two traditional overlords, Siam and Vietnam. A treaty of protectorate was signed with King Norodom (r. 1860–1904) in 1863. Cambodia had little to offer beyond timber and the possibility of finding mineral resources, but any expansion of French authority in the region seemed a step in the right direction to Paris and Saigon. France was not able to push Siam out of the picture, however, and Cambodia's northwestern provinces remained under Siamese control; they would only be ceded to France in 1907, long after Bangkok's suzerainty over the rest of Cambodia had come to an end.

Over the next two decades the French undertook a series of expeditions to explore and map the territory which became their colony of Indochina. Some areas were already under their control, while others remained within the sphere of influence of one or more outside powers, particularly China and Siam. The Mekong remained at the center of French ambitions, not only because it ran through large stretches of territory as yet uncolonized by Europeans, but also because it was viewed as a viable entry point into China. The river's grip on the French imagination was powerful, and it was only weakened when explorers in the late 1860s found that it became unnavigable in parts of Laos, a discovery which shattered the dream of a smooth access route stretching from the South China Sea all the way to China's Yunnan province.

By the 1870s France was looking to the Red river in northern Vietnam as an alternative route into China. In 1873 a trader named Jean Dupuis provoked an incident with Vietnamese authorities when he attempted to force his way up the river from Hanoi to Yunnan. His compatriot Francis Garnier, a naval officer and well-known explorer, came to his aid by force of arms but was defeated and killed in a skirmish with the Vietnamese. The French succeeded in pulling their chestnuts out of the fire by negotiating another treaty with Hue in 1874. In exchange for the removal of French forces from the north, this agreement gave France control over the foreign relations of the Empire of Vietnam and stipulated that Paris would henceforth have a diplomatic representative in Hue. It also opened Hanoi and several ports to French trade and guaranteed free passage for the full length of the Red river.

Like many such agreements, the 1874 treaty created more problems than it solved. The next decade was fraught with tension and confrontation as the

Figure 20 Dung Khiem pavilion, Emperor Tu Duc's tomb, Hue

French were constantly looking for ways to increase their influence over the Vietnamese court while the latter was consistently trying to resist and minimize this influence. By 1882 the French had had enough, and they launched a military campaign targeting Hanoi. When their longtime *bête noire* Emperor Tu Duc (r. 1847–83) died (Figure 20) and the court fell into chaos, the time was ripe for them to take control. After an ultimatum which threatened to destroy the Nguyen dynasty if it refused to accept their 'protection', the 1884 Patenôtre Treaty imposed French control throughout what remained of the Vietnamese empire, and the country's independence came to an end.

The year 1884 also marked a new stage in France's control over Cambodia. Norodom had proved to be a stubborn and frequently uncooperative protégé, and the French were determined to increase both their influence and their revenue, even if it meant deposing him. The arrival of a gunboat was persuasive, and Norodom reluctantly signed a new protectorate treaty which was roughly equivalent to that imposed on his Vietnamese counterpart. Henceforth both the Vietnamese emperors and the Cambodian kings would be 'protected rulers' whose authority over their countries' affairs was largely ceremonial. The traditional royal administrations of both countries were maintained, but were completely subordinated to French officials.

As Vietnam and Cambodia came under complete French control, the remaining prize to be won was the territory lying between lowland Vietnam and the Mekong river. Much of this area was under direct or indirect Siamese control, but the French challenged Siamese claims on the grounds that they had inherited Vietnam's alleged suzerainty over these regions. Vietnamese authority over the Lao areas had in fact never been as strong or as consistent as that exercised by Siam, but France was determined to uphold its claims over as wide a stretch of territory as possible, all the more so given that it (inaccurately) viewed Siam as a proxy for British influence. In 1886 the French successfully pressured Bangkok into allowing them to appoint a Vice-Consul in Luang Phabang. The new official, Auguste Pavie, would devote the next few years to laying the foundations for a 'French Laos'.

By the late 1880s the territories of what is now Laos and northwestern Vietnam were in a state of disorder. Siam was attempting to project its power as far eastward as it could in order to counter French expansion westward, but it met with mixed results. Armed men from China and the ethnically Black and White Thai region around Dien Bien Phu invaded Luang Phabang in 1887, and Pavie strengthened his ties to the local royal family by helping them to escape down the Mekong. The combination of Pavie's assistance and the Siamese failure to deal effectively with this external threat meant that French influence in the area was greatly strengthened, and Siam's correspondingly weakened. France continued to exert diplomatic and military pressure on the Siamese, culminating in the famous Paknam Incident of 1893 when French gunboats blocked the entrance to the Chao Phraya river which runs through Bangkok. The Siamese were forced to sign a treaty ceding all territory east of the Mekong to France; a subsequent agreement in 1904 turned over two more Lao provinces on the western bank of the river.

Mapping Indochina and its borders

More than in almost any other part of Southeast Asia, exploration and mapping played a key role in the expansion of colonial influence. Neither the Vietnamese nor the Siamese had ever produced detailed maps of the areas within their spheres of influence, and an important part of the colonial enterprise for both the British and French was the delineation of boundaries in order to demarcate the territory already under their control, as well as to map out neighboring areas to which they might stake claims. The Siamese government, too, became increasingly aware of the importance of mapping and took its own initiatives in this direction.

As was almost universally true throughout the colonized world, the European presence in Indochina introduced both the concept of territorially-based sovereignty and the policy of establishing and demarcating clearly marked borders. Most powers in the region had traditionally defined their respective spheres of influence in terms of suzerainty (overlordship) rather than sovereignty. Suzerainty was more flexible and in many ways more nominal – or even symbolic – than Western conceptions of sovereignty. More crucially, a particular kingdom could be under multiple suzerains at the same time, as was the case with Cambodia *vis-à-vis* Vietnam and Siam, for example. This system, of course, directly conflicted with the European assumption that territory could only belong to a single ruler. The establishment and consolidation of the French protectorate over Cambodia thus eventually forced the Siamese to renounce all rights of overlordship over their neighbor.

The situation was even more complicated for the Lao territories, where Siamese suzerainty was both recognized and actively exercised, but where the French asserted their own claims based on past Vietnamese overlordship. The French assertions of Vietnamese rights were not invalid, but if it came down to a single country exercising effective authority over the Lao, the Siamese had a stronger case. Moreover, while Vietnam's northern frontier with China was fairly well delineated, the western region was a different story, and the further one traveled away from Hue into the highlands and toward the Mekong, the more difficult it was to demarcate Vietnamese influence.

Exploration missions thus took on considerable geopolitical significance, as the side with better cartographical knowledge was in a better position to stake its claims. Beginning in 1880, Bangkok employed a British specialist, James McCarthy, to undertake mapping along the various edges of the kingdom, and his work considerably increased the court's knowledge of its territory. Where the Lao regions were concerned, however, the best maps in the world could not compete with French gunboats, and Siamese claims to suzerainty ultimately came to naught. In the case of Vietnam, the French were less concerned with mapping the border with China than with convincing the Qing dynasty that this border now represented a dividing line between Chinese sovereignty in the Middle Kingdom and their own in French Indochina. It took the physical destruction of the imperial seal symbolizing Vietnamese vassalage to China and two years of off-and-on conflict between the French and the Qing for the latter to accept that its centuries-old suzerainty had come to an end.

Building a colonial regime in Indochina

Cambodia and Vietnam were brought together administratively as the 'Indochinese Union' in 1887, and Laos was subsequently incorporated into the colony after the 1893 Franco-Siamese treaty. French Indochina was a patchwork of five *pays* ('countries'): Laos, Cambodia, Tonkin, Annam, and Cochin China; the French thus split Vietnam into three parts, each with a slightly different system of government. Although there was an overarching Indochinese government under a Governor-General based in Hanoi, most of the actual administration was done at lower levels, usually through a combination of French and native officials. Cochin China, having been conquered earlier and completely detached from the Empire of Vietnam, was a colony under direct rule. Cambodia remained under its monarchy, as did Tonkin and Annam, although the French drastically reduced the Vietnamese emperor's authority in the northern region. Laos was administratively a single unit, but some provinces were under the authority of the king in Luang Phabang, while others were not.

Throughout Indochina – except for Cochin China – the provinces of the various *pays* were under the authority of a Resident, and each *pays* had a Resident Superior in charge of the whole system. Cochin China's provinces were headed by French officials under a Governor in Saigon. Those provinces which remained under the authority of a native ruler retained the traditional royal administration, which varied according to the monarchy in question, but the French Resident had ultimate authority over his native counterpart and the entire provincial bureaucracy. More importantly, the authority of the emperor in Hue and the kings in Phnom Penh and Luang Phabang was just as firmly subordinated to their respective Residents Superior. While the protectorate structure of indirect rule theoretically placed the French officials in an advisory capacity *vis-à-vis* the 'protected rulers', in reality their control of government affairs was virtually total.

The administrative structure of French Indochina meant that the colony as a whole had multiple power centers. Hanoi was the 'capital' of the entire system, while Saigon became its most important economic center. Hue, Phnom Penh, and Luang Phabang remained the seats of their monarchies, but Hanoi and Vientiane played important roles as administrative and intellectual centers for the Vietnamese and Lao respectively. Hue and Luang Phabang were comparatively less Europeanized, and the French appreciated the more 'traditional' and even exotic atmosphere of these towns which were still so heavily influenced by court culture. Phnom Penh and Vientiane, by contrast, were centers of French power and also home to large populations of Chinese and Vietnamese, which gave them a somewhat more cosmopolitan environment. Saigon, which became France's 'Pearl of the Orient', was probably the most significantly transformed by colonial rule, although the large concentration of Europeans in Hanoi had an impact on its urban culture as well.

Rebellion in the early years of colonial rule in Indochina

After the initial invasion of Vietnam in 1858, it was nearly four decades until the last areas in the mountainous north were pacified. Each stage of the colonization of Vietnam provoked its own wave of resistance; the defeat of imperial troops rarely signaled the end of opposition, and the territorial concessions and treaties forced from the Nguyen tended to heighten resistance rather than putting an end to it. Indeed, a strong case can be made that the Court's decision to negotiate and give in to French demands rather than tapping the strength of popular resistance dealt a fatal blow to the dynasty's legitimacy.

Armed opposition to French control over Cochin China continued well into the 1860s. It was in part the ability of resistance forces to retreat into still uncolonized provinces after 1862 that pushed the French to complete their conquest of the Mekong delta in 1867. Local military commanders like Truong Cong Dinh and Nguyen Tri Phuong led prolonged campaigns against the French, spurred on by the patriotic verses of the famous blind poet Nguyen Dinh Chieu. Eventually the French pacified the region, but the numerous swamps and patches of jungle provided the same haven for rebels that they would during the wars of the mid-twentieth century.

The longest and most concerted resistance movement was the Can Vuong ('loyalty to the king' or 'rescue the king'), which broke out in 1885 after the newly crowned emperor Ham Nghi (r. 1884–85) fled Hue and took refuge in the mountains with a group of royal family members and high-ranking mandarins. Throughout Tonkin and Annam scholar-officials like Phan Dinh Phung – who became the movement's most prominent leader – responded to Ham Nghi's call to arms, mobilizing networks of former students. Ham Nghi was soon captured and sent into exile, but the resistance in his name continued into the mid-1890s. The Can Vuong movement is often seen as the 'last hurrah' of traditional Confucianist loyalty to the monarchy. While two of Ham Nghi's successors – Emperors Thanh Thai (r. 1887–1907) and Duy Tan (r. 1907–16) – also caused trouble for the French, the monarchy as a rallying point for resistance or rebellion became an ever less potent symbol than the nation.

Between the time of the first treaty of protectorate in 1863 and the second in 1884, Cambodia experienced several violent rebellions in various parts of the kingdom. Unrest following the earlier treaty was instigated mainly by Prince Si Votha, a half-brother of King Norodom. As had so often been the case in Cambodia's history, intra-dynastic squabbles and foreign intervention were intertwined. By helping Norodom to suppress the revolts, the French gained greater leverage over his internal affairs. In the years following the 1884 treaty, which eroded royal powers much more than the earlier agreement, the shoe was on the other foot. This time the revolt directly targeted the French; Norodom was in a stronger position and able to gain French goodwill by cooperating in restoring order in the protectorate. Thereafter, there was no major unrest until after World War I.

In Laos, the main source of unrest seems to have been less the colonization of the Lao in the lowland regions than the extension of colonial power to the upland areas. Much of the dissatisfaction was caused by the colonial state's efforts to squeeze revenue and labor out of the highland populations, most of which had generally been beyond the reach of any government throughout their history. Unrest was concentrated in several main areas: the Boloven plateau (sporadically throughout this period), the area along the border with Yunnan (inhabited by the Leu ethnic group, now separated from their kin in China); and the northeastern region along the border with Vietnam, where there were large populations of Hmong. Many of these rebellions were led by 'holy men' of various kinds who claimed special powers and made predictions about cataclysmic change. Ong Kommadam, a highlander in the Salavan region, led attacks on the French for more than three decades beginning in 1905; he was killed only in 1936, and the southern highlands were not really pacified until just before World War II. While some of these movements did attract ethnic Lao followers, the momentum for resistance came mainly from the uplanders.

Expanding European control of Indonesia

In 1800, European power in the Indonesian archipelago was in a rather odd state. The Dutch had been gathering bits of territory for nearly 200 years, but there was no question of them dominating all of the various polities throughout the archipelago. In the later eighteenth century, the VOC's decline into bankruptcy meant that some Company posts were reduced or closed altogether. So in 1800, the Dutch no longer controlled even some places where they had once had a presence. In that year the VOC was dissolved and its territorial claims in Indonesia passed to the Netherlands government.

War in Europe influenced developments in Indonesia. The Dutch king fled to Britain to escape Napoleon's armies in 1795 and there issued what were known as the 'Kew letters', named after his place of residence in exile. These authorized Dutch officials to hand colonial possessions over to the British to prevent them falling into French hands. In some places this happened, but elsewhere the British, who were far more powerful, took Dutch positions by force. The earliest Dutch acquisition in the archipelago was Ambon, taken from the Portuguese in 1605. In 1800 the Dutch didn't even control that island, for the British held Ambon for two periods (1796–1803, 1810–17). The British also took Padang (1781–84, 1795–1819), Banda (1796–1803), and Melaka (1795–1818).

In 1808 the Napoleonic administration of the Netherlands dispatched H. W. Daendels to be Governor-General in Java (g. 1808–11), thereby initiating an intensification of the European presence that would eventually lead to true colonial rule. Prior to this time, the Javanese rulers of Surakarta and Yogyakarta had regarded their relationship with the VOC in Batavia as an alliance. They had even loaned around 2300 soldiers to the Dutch to defend Batavia from an expected English attack (which did not in fact take place) during the Fourth Anglo-Dutch War (1780–04). But now Daendels decreed that these Javanese monarchs were to be treated as vassals of the European colonial power. He was right in principle, for a treaty with the king of Surakarta in 1749 had ceded sovereignty to the VOC, but that treaty had become a dead letter: never before had the Dutch actually tried to exercise such sovereignty. The ruler of Surakarta, Susuhunan Pakubuwana IV (r. 1788–1820) agreed to the new arrangements but the Sultan of Yogyakarta, Hamengkubuwana II (r. 1792–1810, 1811–12, 1826–28), objected. Thus began a period of tension and conflict that would culminate in the devastating Java War (1825–30).

Daendels was an intellectual heir of the French Revolution, with its doctrines of the universal rights of man and opposition to the 'feudal' order, the *ancien régime*. To him, the rulers of Yogyakarta and Surakarta were oppressive feudal monarchs whose power needed to be curbed. Other senior aristocratic Javanese – the *bupatis* – should be cogs in a European-governed bureaucratic regime, rather than feudal lords over their societies. This was a radical assault on the Javanese sense that they were proud, independent rulers of their domains.

This conflict inspired a revolt against the European regime in 1810, led by a senior lord of the Sultan's domains. The revolt was crushed and Daendels marched on Yogyakarta to impose punishment for what he presumed was the Sultan's complicity in the revolt. The Sultan was forced to step down, his son Hamengkubuwana III (r. 1810–11, 1812–14) was put on the throne in his place, substantial money was confiscated, and a treaty of 1811 annexed extensive territories from the Sultanate. European regimes always followed a policy of keeping a balance between the two Javanese states, so Surakarta lands were annexed as well.

Warfare between the European powers now spilled over into Java. Having taken the other Dutch posts mentioned above, by 1811 the British were ready to take Java. Daendels had just been replaced as Governor-General by J. W. Janssens, who had had to surrender the Cape Colony in South Africa to the British in 1806. Now he had to do the same in Java. In August 1811 the British attacked. Batavia's forces resisted for a few weeks, but in the end were no match for the British. In the confusions surrounding the British take-over, several indigenous rulers who had been chafing under Daendels' rule took steps to restore their authority. Hamengkubuwana II retook the throne of Yogyakarta from his son and ordered the murder of the chief administrative officer of the kingdom, who he believed had conspired with Batavia. In Palembang, Sultan Mahmud Badaruddin (r. 1804–12, 1813, 1818–21), slaughtered the 87 men (24 of them Dutch) at the local Dutch garrison.

If rulers like those of Yogyakarta or Palembang expected the British to be more amenable to their pretensions than Daendels, this was a dangerous miscalculation. The man installed as Lieutenant Governor of Java (there was no Governor-General there under the British) was Thomas Stamford Raffles. However much Raffles and his fellows opposed the French, they were as much children of French Revolutionary ideology as Daendels. They, too, wished to bring to an end what they saw as feudal-style *ancien régimes,* of which they perceived prime examples in places like Palembang and Yogyakarta. Because the British were far more powerful militarily than the Dutch or Napoleonic administrations had been, local lords were in even more threatening territory than before.

In 1812 the British acted to chastise both Yogyakarta and Palembang; they attacked and sacked both courts and deposed both rulers. In Palembang, Badaruddin was replaced by his younger brother. Badaruddin fled, submitted in 1813, was briefly allowed back on his throne but was then deposed again on Raffles's orders. In Yogyakarta, this was the only time a European force had ever conquered a Javanese court: a profound humiliation for the Javanese aristocracy. The court was sacked, its library and archive looted, and large sums of money confiscated. Sultan Hamengkubuwana II was deposed and this time was exiled to the British colony of Penang. His son again assumed the throne as Hamengkubuwana III.

Thus commenced a period of rising tension as the British interfered more intensively in Javanese life than the Dutch ever had. Like Daendels before him, Raffles annexed extensive territories from Yogyakarta and then, in the interest of maintaining a balance between the two kingdoms, did the same to Surakarta. In the areas directly controlled by the colonial regime, market taxes and toll gates were auctioned ('farmed'), mostly to Chinese. They then exploited this taxing power in ways which seriously burdened local society and restricted trade. Raffles also introduced 'land rent': a land tax resting on the presumption that, as the sovereign power, the European colonial regime owned all land and was due a tax from those who occupied it. Although the administration of this tax was haphazard, it reflected the colonialists' pretension to more direct control of local society. All of this added up to a radical colonial revolution, the purpose of which in Batavia's eyes was to save Javanese from feudal exploitation by the local aristocracy. In 1814–15 Susuhunan Pakubuwana IV of Surakarta plotted a rebellion, in concert with Indian sepoy soldiers whom the British had brought to Java. But the plot was discovered, the sepoy ringleaders were executed or imprisoned, and Pakubuwana IV was fortunate not to be deposed.

When the British handed Java back to the Dutch in 1816 – over Raffles's objections – the Dutch continued this generally aggressive approach to local society. Europeans and Chinese entrepreneurs were now developing plantations for sugar, coffee, indigo, and pepper in Java. There, local people and their customary social arrangements were often treated with contempt. Increasing opium usage and brigandage were symptoms of deepening social malaise. Watching this colonial revolution, and the increasing decadence of court life and the social dislocations that seemed to go with it, was the Yogyakarta prince Dipanagara, the greatest of Indonesia's nineteenth-century anti-colonial heroes. He was a mystic, a student of local Javanese cultural and historical traditions, and a popular prince with widespread social networks. He was opposed to what he saw as the corrupting interference of the Europeans and to those court circles that benefited from it. Through a series of visions he came to believe that he was a divinely appointed future king, whose task was to bring about a bloody destruction of the colonial age.

In 1825 Dipanagara rebelled and thereby initiated the Java War (1825–30). Initial assaults on Europeans and Chinese took a heavy toll and the colonial regime was undermined in much of Central Java. The religious elite of Java strongly supported Dipanagara, as did many ordinary villagers and a significant proportion of the aristocracy. But the colonial side was able to gain the initiative by 1827. Cholera, malaria, and dysentery exacted a heavy toll on all sides in the conflict. Finally, in 1830 Dipanagara recognized that his cause was lost; he surrendered and was exiled from Java. The war had cost around 15,000 lives on the colonial side and at least 200,000 on the Javanese.

From 1830 the Dutch were at last able to rule Java without any serious opposition. Although there were some localized resistance movements and small-scale rebellions, there was no longer either a European or a local aristocratic power that challenged them. They had, however, learned an important lesson from the events of 1808–30, namely that radical intrusions into local society – and particularly that offending the local aristocracy – were recipes for trouble. So now the Dutch adopted a conservative strategy of associating the local elite with colonial rule, allowing them to enjoy their 'traditional' prerogatives – often, in fact, an exaggerated version of what they had enjoyed before – as lords over their societies, an arrangement which meant cheaper administration – for it required fewer Europeans – and less social disruption.

But how were the Dutch to make any money from Java? For over two centuries no one had found an answer to that question. The VOC had bankrupted itself in large part because of military and administrative costs in Java that were far greater than the profit to be had there. The Netherlands state administration of Java had just spent enormous resources in winning the Java War without significant income from Java to cover those costs. A new Governor-General (g. 1830–33), Johannes van den Bosch, was sent out to Java because he had an idea of how to turn a profit. This was the so-called *Cultuurstelsel* (Cultivation System), which sounded both profitable and humanitarian. As will be seen below, however, while it certainly produced profit for some – particularly for the Dutch – its humanitarian benefits were sharply limited.

While these dramatic events were going on in Java, in theory the Dutch were trying to avoid further involvement in the outer islands of the archipelago. Van den Bosch was of the view that the Dutch should be involved only where there was profit to be made, which meant Java (where his new Cultivation System was expected to produce a profit), Sumatra (for pepper and other products), and Bangka (for tin). The rest of the outer islands were of little or no interest to him. And while the Dutch were dealing with Javanese affairs, and particularly until they won the Java War, there were limited resources available to contemplate establishing a presence in the rest of what is now Indonesia.

Despite this policy of resisting expansion, however, the Dutch found themselves drawn into local conflicts, so that in the end they established their colony of the Netherlands East Indies in spite of their theoretical reluctance to do so. Several factors led to this outcome. One was the presence of competing European interests in the region. The British had long been a factor in Dutch calculations; in the course of the nineteenth century the emergence of new powers such as the United States, Italy, and Germany gave the Dutch further causes to intervene in some places simply in order to prevent anyone else from doing so – the 'zero-sum game' mentality mentioned above. Furthermore, the rise of new products such as coal and oil stimulated Dutch interest in some areas previously of little attraction to them. The technological balance shifted as well. The nineteenth century saw a technological revolution that shifted the balance of power decisively in favor of European powers. Previously, local potentates could acquire or copy European-style flintlock muskets, bayonets, or sailing ships, but steamships, repeating rifles, manufactured ammunition, barbed wire, high explosives and the telegraph required different sorts of societies to produce them.

Returning to Sumatra after the British interregnum, the Dutch had to send military expeditions against Palembang in 1818–19 to restore their dominance. Difficulties did not end there: only after a final anti-Dutch rebellion was suppressed in 1849 was the Dutch position reasonably secure. Further north on the island, the Dutch encountered the first major Islamic reform movement of modern times in Indonesia. This so-called Padri movement – the derivation of the term is debated – was inspired by the rising tide of reformism in the Middle East, spearheaded by the Wahhabis of Arabia. The Padris did not share all of the puritanism of the Wahhabis, but they agreed on the legitimacy of violence as a means to reform society. They commenced a civil war against the ruling aristocracy in Minangkabau in the name of reformed Islam. With the killing of almost the entire Minangkabau royal family in 1815, the Padris had effectively won this war. But then remnants of the defeated aristocracy approached the Dutch – who returned to Padang after the British interregnum in 1819 – and offered them sovereignty over Minangkabau, which was, by any consideration, no longer theirs to give. This precipitated a colonial invasion and what is known as the Padri War (1821–38). Dutch offensives had to be largely suspended in 1825–30 while the Java War demanded so many resources, but thereafter the Dutch resumed this costly attempt to subdue Minangkabau and finally triumphed in 1838.

Increasing Dutch influence in Sumatra was, however, interrupted by British objections in the 1840s. In their 1824 Treaty of London, the Netherlands and Britain had agreed a demarcation of spheres of interest that ran down the Straits of Melaka. Dutch political interest was to prevail on the Sumatran side, but British freedom of commerce was also guaranteed there. Now Straits

Settlements merchants protested that the Dutch were imposing discriminative tariffs in Sumatran ports in violation of that treaty. In response to pressure from the far more powerful British, the Dutch withdrew posts north of Palembang and broke off negotiations for a treaty with Siak. For several years, the Dutch advance in Sumatra was halted, giving Aceh's rulers the fatal impression that the British would act to prevent a Dutch advance. For the time being the Dutch did not threaten Aceh, where the Sultanate was in the process of recovering its influence under the leadership of Tuanku Ibrahim, who dominated Aceh from 1838 to 1857. Increasing world demand for pepper – by the 1820s over half of the world's supply of which came from Aceh – made Aceh both increasingly wealthy and the site of intensifying European competition.

During this period, Dutch imperial expansion was mainly limited to more easterly parts of the archipelago. In most of eastern Indonesia, Dutch influence was non-existent or little more than nominal in 1800. This was even true where their involvement had a long history. In 1817 they had to put down a rebellion in Ambon. They also had to fight significant campaigns in 1825, 1858–60, and even as late as 1905–06 to establish control in South Sulawesi. The Dutch had little interest in the island of Borneo (the Indonesian part of which is called Kalimantan) until the intervention of James Brooke in Sarawak in the 1840s. Suddenly they saw the specter of British influence just across the Java Sea, and were impelled into more active involvement. In the west and southwest of Kalimantan, Chinese gold miners resisted the Dutch but were suppressed in 1850–54. Banjarmasin produced a major dynastic conflict that culminated in the Banjarmasin War (1859–63). This conflict placed a heavy burden on the Dutch colonial forces. Even after their victory of 1863, resistance in the interior of Banjarmasin continued until 1906.

Bali suffered terribly in the nineteenth century, even before the Dutch intervened. The 1815 eruption of Mount Tambora on neighboring Sumbawa left a death toll estimated at 117,000 in Bali, Lombok, and Sumbawa. Mouse plagues and epidemics (mainly cholera and smallpox) raged in Bali several times during the century. Meanwhile, the politics of the island disintegrated into something approaching permanent civil war among the ten or so kingdoms there. The plundering of shipwrecks produced several conflicts with Batavia, leading to the imposition of Dutch control over the northern part of Bali in the 1850s. The southern Balinese kingdoms and the Dutch thereafter played a complex game of subterfuge, bluff, and threat while postponing what, in retrospect, may be thought to be the inevitability of colonial rule.

From the 1890s the pace of events picked up. The Sasak Muslims of Lombok, who were subjects of the Balinese kingdom of Karangasem, rebelled against their Hindu overlords in 1891. The Dutch were thereby handed an excuse for intervention, which followed in 1894. After a bloody campaign the Dutch defeated the Balinese *raja* in what was known as a *puputan* – a 'final battle' in which the defeated Balinese fought to the death sacrificially against the superior colonial forces. Karangasem in eastern Bali thereby became directly ruled Dutch territory. Recognizing the inevitable, the king of Gianyar voluntarily became a Dutch colonial subject.

In 1906–08 Balinese independence came to an end. The Dutch were by now motivated by the 'Ethical policy' discussed in Chapter 9, and wished to bring an end to internecine warfare, opium smuggling, slavery, plundering of ship-wrecks, and aristocratic widow-burnings in Bali. Another ship was plundered in 1904, so in 1906 Dutch colonial forces attacked; the result was *puputans* at Den Pasar and nearby Pamecutan. The *rajas*, their families, and followers ritu-ally prepared themselves for death and marched into the colonial guns, pausing only to kill their own wounded. More than a thousand Balinese probably died in this way. In 1908 the final *puputan* took place in Klungkung and Bali was added to Dutch colonial possessions.

With the eastern part of the archipelago increasingly under Dutch control, Batavia's interest again focused on Sumatra. By the later years of the century, the British and the Dutch realized that their treaty arrangements posed prob-lems for them. By mutually agreeing that Aceh should remain independent – that is, that neither of them would attempt to conquer it – they effectively left Aceh open for some other power to intervene. Meanwhile Aceh's increasing wealth and influence posed a threat to Dutch pre-eminence in Sumatra. Dutch commercial policy became more liberal after 1848, diminishing British concerns about Dutch control. So in 1871 the British and Dutch agreed new arrange-ments which gave the Dutch a free hand throughout Sumatra.

In 1873 the Acehnese contacted the Americans about a possible treaty, which impelled the Dutch to act quickly. In March they attacked the Acehnese capital but were repulsed with the loss of their commander – the only Dutch general to die in action in Indonesia. In Aceh the Dutch now faced the most motivated, wealthiest, and best-prepared enemy they had ever encountered, one utterly committed to maintaining its independence. Batavia sent a second and larger military force later in 1873 and thus commenced the Aceh War, the longest colonial war in history. The Acehnese side abandoned the capital Banda Aceh and the Dutch thereupon proclaimed the annexation of Aceh as a colony in 1874. But prolonged, bitter guerilla warfare continued for decades. Military action and cholera took a heavy toll on both sides. Gradually the Dutch won members of the local administrative elite – the *uleëbalang* – to their side, while the religious elite – the *ulamas* – led ongoing resistance. In this way the Dutch deepened a conflict between these two leadership groups which would prove even bloodier in the future. The war of resistance acquired the nature of a Holy War against unbelievers. It is hard to say exactly when the Aceh War ended. The Dutch proclaimed it so in 1881 but the Acehnese continued to prove this untrue. By about 1903 Aceh was relatively stable. Several major resistance leaders were killed as late as 1910–12. A powerful Acehnese sense of local identity and resistance to outside domination never-theless persisted, to the dismay of both the Dutch colonial regime and the later Indonesian independent state.

By *c.*1900, much of the outline of today's Indonesia was visible in the boundaries of the Netherlands East Indies. There were still conquests going on into the first decade of the twentieth century, as seen in preceding paragraphs, but generally it was clear that the archipelago was under the domination of the Netherlands. There were few cases where a European nation so small governed a colonial territory so large.

The Spanish Philippines

With the exception of the southern Moro areas, the Philippines had long been under Spanish rule, unlike those parts of Southeast Asia which were newly conquered in the course of the nineteenth century. Colonial ways of doing things were thus more firmly established there and we have a better sense of local social structures than in many other parts of Southeast Asia at this time. The liberal reforms brought about in Spain by the Napoleonic Wars quickly failed. In 1814 King Ferdinand VII, backed by the aristocracy and clergy, over-threw the fledgling representative government. The restored tyrants jailed some 50,000 liberals, re-established the Inquisition, abolished the *Cortes* (House of Representatives) and reversed its acts, including those that sought to liberalize the colonies.

In the Philippines, where also liberalism was brought to an end by this restoration of the old order, rebellions erupted. In Ilocos some 1200 men banded together, sacked churches, and destroyed books and documents in the municipal archives. In 1823 the conservative government replaced military offi-cials who were *insulares* (Spaniards born in America or the Philippines) with *peninsulares* (those born in Spain). Discharged officials and 800 former soldiers seized government buildings in the Intramuros section of Manila. Although suppressed, these uprisings illustrated the volatility of the populace and prefig-ured more politicized movements in subsequent years.

The colonial regime had never fully succeeded in transforming scattered settlements into ideal farmsteads, hamlets, and villages. To protest against taxa-tion and compulsory labor, communities abandoned their homes for the moun-tains. Farmers accepted Christianity, but refused to move from their paddy fields or hamlets. Nevertheless, friars hardly wavered in their mission to concen-trate their flock. This impasse brought about the compromise settlement patterns known as *población-barrio-sitio* or *cabecera-visita-ranchería*, which combined traditional *barangay* dispersion and the Spanish ideal of population concentration. The center of this pattern was the Catholic church which, with its adjacent communities, was known as the *cabecera*. As religious centers *cabeceras* provided the stimulus for an agglomeration of population that formed political and economic centers called *poblaciónes*. Those who refused to relocate there formed *barrios* (subsidiary communities), which resident friars of *cabeceras* reached through *visitas* (chapels). Periodically friars conducted serv-ices and Catholic indoctrination in *visitas*. *Rancherías* or *sitios* comprised the smallest concentration – about 10 families. They were dispersed and isolated and did not have *visitas*; their residents acquired the most shallow exposure to Christian and Hispanic tradition.

By the nineteenth century a veneer of Hispanic urbanism prevailed in the islands. Throughout the colony Spanish planners employed the standard grid-iron arrangement, where communities were arranged around a central plaza surrounded by a system of rectangular street blocks. *Poblaciónes* followed this masterplan; the church and priest's residence served as the center, surrounded by public and private buildings. Associated with diversified function this 'plaza complex' contained three primary structures: the church, town hall, and *principalía* (upper-class residents') houses. Across the central square, the town hall where the Spanish civil authorities held office flanked the church. These halls acted as centers for town fiestas, serving as a venue for everyone in the *población-barrio-sitio* system. *Principalía* residences comprised the third element of the plaza complex. Unlike the palm-thatch and bamboo abodes of most townspeople, *principalía* houses were made of stone and brick. Their proximity to the plaza, seat of Spanish authority, signified their owners' social and political prestige.

The transformation of *barangays* and parallel evolution of the local elite or *principalía* (or *principales*) resulted from a preconceived policy of administrative convenience. By favoring a segment of the local populace, Spaniards also established a source of minor civil servants who served as buffers between themselves and the common folk and as agents of Hispanization. Spaniards retained the loyalty of the *principalía* by providing opportunities for increasing their wealth. *Principales* were exempted from tax payment and given control of vast tracts of land. In general, two principles informed Spanish colonial governance of the islands: direct rule, and divide-and-rule. A colonial civil service provided for direct rule. Authority was in the hands of Europeans; members of the indigenous populace could only have minor roles in governance. The crown fostered Iberian interests across the Spanish empire through a policy of administrative decentralization and bureaucratic competition. It encouraged direct ties between colonies and the mother country, but discouraged any inter-colonial cooperation. Each dependency was a separate commercial and administrative unit. The Philippines were divided into territorial units called provinces, which were subdivided into municipalities. Military provinces were governed by *corregidores*; while the pacified regions or *reducciones* were administered by *alcaldes mayores*. A *corregidor* or an *alcalde mayor* was the highest executive, judicial, and military officer in the district; he was the judge, inspector of *encomiendas*, collector of tribute, and captain-general. Furthermore, at his level of government, he fulfilled the role of vice-patron of the Catholic Church, delegated into his hands ultimately from the king of Spain, who was himself the patron of the Church in all his colonies via the *patronato real* (royal patronage) discussed above.

Each municipality was headed by a *gobernadorcillo* (petty governor) who governed from the *población* and supervised the collection of taxes. This office was the highest an elite *Indio* could have in the government. While in office he was addressed as *Capitan* and after retirement, he had the right to carry a swagger stick and use the cherished title of *Don*. The basis of his administrative structure was a matrix of *barrios* under the charge of tribute collectors called *cabezas de barangay* (*barangay* chiefs).

At the apex of the government sat the Governor-General. As representative of the king he wielded supreme civil power, with absolute executive authority. As captain-general he also commanded the insular armed forces. He presided over the *audiencia*, the judicial arm of the government. And since he was also, in his turn, vice-patron of the Catholic Church throughout the Philippines, he could influence ecclesiastical appointments in the islands. The *audiencia* acted as a check on the Governor-General. It counseled him in executive and legislative matters and safeguarded the royal prerogative by prosecuting any abusive colonial official. At the death or prolonged absence of a Governor-General, the *audiencia* took over his legislative, judicial, and executive functions.

Church officials also curbed powerful civil authorities. In accordance with the *patronato real*, the Church and state were united in governing and propagating Christianity. The Church functioned as a separate bureaucracy but remained financially dependent upon the State. Internal administration and the welfare of the islands' inhabitants were concerns of both the Governor-General and the Archbishop of Manila. Intense conflicts at all levels resulted from their theoretical unity of purpose. Beyond Manila and other larger settlements the Church held formidable authority, comparable to or even surpassing that of the civil administration. The friar stood for both the Church and state, the embodiment of Hispanic power in provincial *poblaciónes*. *Gobernadorcillos* deferred to him regarding municipal government. His residence was the symbol of clerical authority throughout the archipelago.

Throughout the islands, the Spaniard reigned supreme, his social prestige resting on military and religious superiority. Legal and taxation policies enhanced his stature and land ownership assured his wealth and economic power. All but the most minor governmental and clerical positions were reserved for Spaniards. Local inhabitants trained as secular priests (parish clergy) were seldom given parishes, for these remained under the Spanish regular clergy (missionary friars). Yet a social rift existed within the Spanish populace. Those born in Spain (*peninsulares*) looked down on those born in the Americas or the Philippines (*insulares/criollos*). To distinguish themselves from their compatriots, *insulares* called themselves 'sons of the country'. They took up governmental and clerical positions and earned economic and political influence. A number participated in the campaign to reform the Church.

Social stratification hardly changed among the local populace. They were called *Indios*: we now use the term 'Filipino' for indigenous peoples of the Philippines, but this usage only emerged late in Spanish times, as will be seen below. The indigenous *maguinoo* (gentry) class retained their headship as the *principalía*. The *timaua* (freemen) and *alipin* (bondsmen), retained their status as *pueblo* (people). Only Spaniards outranked the *principalía* in the social ladder. The prestige of the local elite rested on their role as favored instruments of the colonial government; eventually their vast tracts of land led them to be thought of as the bosses or *caciques* by the peasant populace. At the bottom of the social ladder were the majority of the indigenous *Indios*. Being landless farmers they were economically subservient to the upper classes and tilled the land for the *principalía* as share-croppers.

Between the *principalía* and the landless *Indios* were the *mestizos*, a term that usually referred to those of mixed Sino-Filipino descent. Spanish-Filipino Eurasians were called *Español Filipinos*: in status they were beneath the *peninsulares* or *criollos* (creoles). *Español Filipinos* were appointed to minor governmental positions. They grew wealthy through inheritance from rich Filipino ancestors or through the economic liberalization of the nineteenth century that is discussed below. Sino-Filipino *mestizos* were of particular significance for the future. Spaniards were dubious about immigrant Chinese, whom they called *Sangleys*; they were usually treated like potential criminals and were charged the highest rate of tribute. To attain more favorable tax and legal status, *Sangleys* could convert to Catholicism. They married Catholic *Indios*, producing descendants who eventually shook the colonial order. Through their dominance of wholesale and retail trade, these *mestizos* acquired wealth to enlarge their landholdings, enter professions, and become Hispanized. Here was emerging a new middle class, but they seldom held positions of power. Spanish priests detested *mestizos*, calling them 'beasts laden with gold'. A number of *mestizos* became secular priests, nonetheless. Scorned by the Spanish authorities, *mestizos* persisted in searching for a place in colonial society. Their well-educated offspring became the eventual shapers of the Philippine nation.

Changes in economic policies began to generate greater wealth in the archipelago. A new spirit of economic liberalism penetrated the Spanish mercantilist curtain through the brief British occupation of the colony (1762–64) during the Seven Years War. Liberal Governors-General Simon de Anda y Salazar (g. 1770–76) and Jose de Basco y Vargas (g. 1759–88) introduced administrative and economic reforms that adapted the colony to free trade. Anda thought that the clergy caused provincial stagnation. He proposed to strip the regulars of their lands, enforce clerical reform through episcopal visitation – that is, imposing the authority of secular bishops – and promote Spanish civilian settlement and trade in the provinces. He encouraged the mining industry and deployed officials to survey tar deposits. Naturally the clergy resisted these reforms.

Basco passed a general economic plan in 1779 to develop natural resources and promote agriculture and industries. He established the *Real Sociedad Ecónomica de Filipinas* (Royal Economic Society of the Philippines) which aimed to promote better farming methods and introduce commercial cultivation. It bolstered the latter by financially rewarding agriculturalists who planted sugar, tobacco, indigo, or coffee rather than traditional crops like rice and corn. Confiscation of farm implements and arrests and imprisonment of indigenous farmers were forbidden. In 1782 Basco instituted the government tobacco monopoly – not, of course, an expression of economic liberalism – ordering tobacco cultivation in Cagayan Valley, Ilocos, Nueva Vizcaya, and Marinduque. Each family was to raise a certain quota of tobacco, which was transported to Manila and there turned into cigarettes and cigars. The monopoly lasted until 1882, bringing in some SP 3,000,000 profits. This gave the colony economic independence and the ability even periodically to finance the Crown.

The *Real Compañia de Filipinas* (Royal Company of the Philippines), established in 1785, also promoted the new economic order. It stimulated trade between Spain and Asia and expanded that of the Philippines. Along with the Royal Economic Society, it encouraged the cultivation of indigo, sugar, pepper, and cotton for export and provided liberal loans to agriculturalists and small-scale manufacturers. Unintentionally, the Company encouraged a plethora of foreign merchant houses in the islands. Acting as intermediaries, these houses linked Manila to world trade starting from 1790. They thereby undermined the Royal Company itself. Massive global debts, internal strife, hostilities in the archipelago, and disputes in Spain almost paralyzed it. The Royal Company was abolished in 1834, when Manila was declared to be what it had already been in fact for four decades – an open port.

These economic developments also transformed the socio-economic land-scape. Expulsions of the the deeply distrusted non-Catholic Chinese in 1755 and 1769 offered economic opportunities for *mestizos*. An imperfectly imple-mented ban on Chinese immigration that slowed arrivals remained in effect until 1850. During this time, *mestizos* could dominate retailing and artisanry and take advantage of the growing agriculture industry by buying crops from the provinces and selling them wholesale in Manila. *Mestizos* then established *haciendas* (large estates) by purchasing adjoining plots through loan contracts. In such agreements the peasant borrower conveyed his land to the *mestizo* lender with the stipulation that he could repurchase it later. The peasant rarely in fact redeemed his land, and thus became a perpetual tenant.

Meanwhile, in Spain, political strife and revolutions from 1834 to 1862 produced four constitutions and 28 parliaments. These power struggles between conservatives and liberals resonated in the Philippines. Between 1835 and 1897, 50 different Governors-General took charge. Periodically anti-cleri-cal liberals held power in the Philippines, and their views influenced those of sidelined and disgruntled indigenous, secular priests. For *insulares, principales, mestizos,* and affluent *Indios* the clerical profession as secular priests was a ticket towards acceptance in the colonial order. In 1768, seculars took charge of parishes vacated by the Jesuits, who were expelled from the Spanish Empire in 1767. When a 'desecularization' policy attended the return of the Jesuits in 1859, a number of local priests lost their offices. The Church did not reassign them, however, claiming that they were inappropriate for positions of high esteem. Clearly the dispossessed seculars were sacked because of racism.

Wanting justice, secular priests – both *insulares* and *Indios* – rallied behind the 'secularization movement', or the plea to transfer parishes under Spanish-born European friars to secular priests without parishes, who were over-whelmingly *Indios*. Unlike their hurriedly ordained predecessors, these indigenous secular clergy of the nineteenth century were university-educated and had even served as parish priests in Spain. Creole scholar Father Pedro Pelaez led the movement. In 1862 in front of Queen Isabella II, he advocated equality among the clergy, but this fell on deaf ears. Palaez died in an earth-quake in Manila a year later. His torch was carried on by a Father Jose Burgos, an *Indio* who wrote pamplets that rejected the superiority of the white race and decried racial discrimination. This movement found support among liberal students of the University of Santo Tomas in Manila and the editors, staff members, and sponsors of the Spanish-language newspaper *El Eco Filipino*. In 1869 the liberal Governor-General Carlos Maria de la Torre (g. 1869–71) passed decrees that favored the movement, only for them to be rescinded by his reactionary successor Governor-General Rafael de Izquierdo (g. 1871–73).

In 1872, 200 workers and soldiers in the Cavite arsenal mutinied over wages and working conditions. The Izquierdo government responded by killing most of the mutineers and imprisoning the rest. Paranoid because of their crumbling overseas empire and the destructive Carlist War at home, the authorities magnified the event into a revolt. They hanged mutineers and implicated liberals, particularly dissenting priests and their supporters. The priests Jose Burgos, Jacinto Zamora, and Mariano Gomes, who advocated secularization of the parishes, were garrotted. Other priests were imprisoned, while accused lawyers, businessmen, and other civilians were deported for life to the Mariana Islands. From 1872 to 1892 terror reigned as a means of preventing rebellion, employing the *Guardia Civil*, a paramilitary police organized in 1867. Everyone needed to carry and produce their government-issued identification papers upon demand. Friars contributed to this suppression by indiscriminately denouncing people whom they labelled violators of dogma, thereby sentencing them to the gallows.

Some *nouveaux riches* (whether *insulares*, *mestizos*, *Sangleys*, or *Indios*) voluntarily went into self-exile in Hongkong, Singapore, Paris, London, and Madrid. Others sent their children to Spain to study, away from oppression in the colony. These students were counted among the new intellectual elite – the *Ilustrados*. They formed the core of what was called the '*Propaganda*' movement, which campaigned for political, agricultural, and educational reforms, secularization of parishes, and expulsion of the friars. José Rizal, Marcelo del Pilar, and Graciano Lopez Jaena were their most prominent members. *Ilustrados* referred to themselves as *los Indios bravos* (proud *Indios*) or as *Filipinos*, expanding the previous scope of this term to refer to all those born or living in the Philippines irrespective of ethnicity: thus was born the modern meaning of the term 'Filipino'.

In 1888 Jaena established the reformist newspaper *La Solidaridad* which served as the venue for progressive articles of *Propaganda* supporters and their liberal allies. From the following year until 1895, Del Pilar took over and moved *La Solidaridad* to Madrid. Intrigues among editors and contributors plagued the paper and it subsequently lost its financial backing from colonial exiles. Rizal wrote the famous novels *Noli Me Tangere* ('Touch me not' – a Biblical quote attributed to Jesus reappearing after his crucifixion; published in Berlin, 1887) and *El Filibusterismo* ('The Subversive', published in Ghent, 1891) which exposed the tyrannical social and political regime in the Philippines. He returned to Manila in 1892, but he was arrested and deported to Mindanao; four years later he was publicly executed. His death signified the failure of the reform campaign, but also provided the stimulus that electrified the oppressed into political action. From these roots the Philippine Revolution was born.

Colonial Southeast Asia in international trade and commerce

British Burma

Like elsewhere in colonial Southeast Asia, Burma's traditional economies that were self-sustaining, diverse, and in most cases subsistence-oriented, were transformed under the new colonial administration into an export-oriented economy concentrating on the production of rice and other agricultural goods. The annexation of Burma and its attachment to British India also brought a marriage of the two economies. This brought significant investment into Burma from Indian and British capitalists who were interested in developing its rice fields, transportation networks, timber, oil, rubber, and mining potential. In Burma, colonial managers also saw a potential market for British and Indian finished goods, while its agricultural production could help to feed the Indian population. Investors saw a rich, but underdeveloped land of resources that could be harnessed through the promise of cheap labor and a business-friendly government. The Irrawaddy's historically rich river-basin attracted companies interested in developing and multiplying its rice output while Indian labor began pouring into Lower Burma, altering significantly the hitherto lightly populated areas that had remained relatively uncultivated. Under British management, the Irrawaddy delta region experienced phenomenal growth between the 1850s and the 1930s, increasing cultivated acreage from just under a million acres (400,000 ha) under the Burmese kings to nearly 8.7 million acres (3.5 million ha).

This steady increase in production required better transportation. Although shipping along the Irrawaddy river, mainly through the Irrawaddy Flotilla Company, provided some transport, it was not until the development of roads and railways that the export economy was able really to take off. Railways, in particular, could move agricultural products and minerals quickly while also providing crucial security infrastructure for the movement of troops between Lower and Upper Burma. The growth in the export economy was thus mirrored by the growth in railroads – from 333 miles (536 km) of railways in the late nineteenth century to nearly 1600 miles (2575 km) in 1914.

With the flow of steady investment into transport projects, the increasing amount of Indian coolie labor, and the migration of local cultivators into the Delta region, Burma's rice industry expanded at record pace. Legislation attempted to facilitate and protect these trends in the economic sector. The Land Revenue Act of 1876 increased the possibility of obtaining and cultivating land through credit, making it relatively easy for a farmer to claim a plot of a land after paying dues on it for one year. The payment acted as a security deposit that would entitle the local cultivator to more loans for equipment, seed, and other expenses. The resultant land rush did not come free of cost: groups would often fight violently over desirable tracts of rice fields, and moneylenders – both local and Chinese – took advantage of cultivators who did not have the capital at these early stages. By the time Indian moneylenders entered the scene, much of the land was already owned by landlords and rented to local cultivators who were unable to purchase and maintain land on their own. High rent and fixed revenue demands eventually alienated many indigenous Burmese cultivators from the rice industry and from the ethnic communities who were perceived to be benefiting from it.

The new face of the Burmese economy was reflected in the emerging ethnic diversity within the colony, as immigrants flowed in from British India and China in order to take advantage of the opportunities provided by colonial market interests. With the flow of capital from India and London, Burma's economy became closely linked to the world economy in ways that it had not experienced before. New notions of cost, value, and need were intertwined with the commoditization of raw materials and products in response to demands that were often beyond the experience of the common cultivator or local manufacturer. Many of the new communities taking shape in Burma were immigrants from India, providing an immediate source of manpower for the new roles that the urban economy demanded. Many Burmese and other local minorities remained wedded to the agricultural sector, though some entered the commercial sector which had previously been dominated by both local and newly arrived Chinese.

J. S. Furnivall, an astute British official who wrote extensively on colonial Burma, observed that colonial society appeared diverse in the number of ethnic communities taking part in the economy but that, in fact, these communities were isolated from one another culturally, personally, and – importantly – in politics. Only in the context of the marketplace did Burmese, Chinese, and Indians interact; otherwise they remained uncommitted to each other and uninterested in the future of any larger community as a whole. The colonial economy promoted principles of individuality, profit, and survival of the fittest as the pathway to success. Values that stressed social welfare, community-bonding, and self-sacrifice ran counter to the priorities of the colonial marketplace. This segmented 'plural society', as described by Furnivall, differed significantly from Burma's pre-colonial society. Similar circumstances were seen in other Southeast Asian colonies.

In general, officials in New Delhi and Rangoon, along with investors in London and elsewhere, saw Burma as a good place to do business. Along with the expansion of the timber and rice industries, oil became another success story for investors as a pipeline was built from the upriver oil fields to the refineries in Syriam. Mining and rubber also developed. Between 1914 and 1942, British investment tripled through the development of these industries, expanding both exports to Europe and a return flow of finished goods into the marketplaces of Rangoon, Mandalay, and other cities.

Few locals prospered from this entrance into the global economy as did Europeans, Chinese, and particular groups of immigrant Indians. Burmese mostly lacked capital and experience in the market, and were unfamiliar with their competitors and the administrative structures that surrounded the economy. In 1911, officials noted that many of the more productive parts of Lower Burma's Thaton district were owned and administered by moneylenders and merchants who rented their plots to local Burmese cultivators. According to one official report, indebtedness among these cultivators often left them at the mercy of credit networks within the Indian Chettiar caste of bankers and moneylenders. There were, however, government attempts to address the declining prosperity of local agriculturalists. Measures were instituted to provide alternative sources of credit, but a lack of facilities and funds limited their effectiveness. Legislation to protect farmers' rights in relation to the land was proposed in 1891 and again in 1908, but was blocked by landlords, Chettiars, and the mercantile industry representatives who dominated the Legislative Council.

Thus economic life within the colonial system must be seen as more than an interaction occurring just between local and European communities. The new economic system, procedures, and expectations placed a wide range of immigrant Asians, locals, and Europeans into multiple mutual relationships. The seeds of anti-colonialism in the countryside were often generated from these complex socio-economic experiences, rather than from direct grievances between a Burmese farmer and a British official.

The British Straits Settlements and Malaya

During the early decades of the nineteenth century, economic change in Malaya was largely set in motion by the founding of the British free ports of the Straits Settlements. The English East India Company (EEIC) established settlements at Penang (1786), Singapore (1819), and Melaka (1824) originally as naval bases to check Dutch power in the region and as ports of call for English 'country' (i.e., private) traders plying the lucrative China-India trade since the late eighteenth century. These free ports – located on the strategic waterway of the Straits of Melaka – soon attracted foreign traders and opened Malaya to international trade and commerce. The conception of free ports (i.e., where no customs duties are charged) had no precedent in Asian or Western economic doctrines when it was first introduced; this innovation gave the British ports a head start in attracting ships and trade. The Straits Settlements were soon transformed into leading regional entrepôts and centers of economic activities. With their rise as regional emporiums, the British settlements soon eclipsed older, less competitive Malay entrepôts that now became feeder ports in the new era of trade dominated by the West.

Singapore soon overtook the other two Straits Settlements to become the leading entrepôt in the region. Melaka suffered from progressive silting of its harbor and Penang's location at the northern end of the Straits left it too far from the main sea routes serving the regional trade networks and the long-distance trade route to China. With its deep harbors, sheltered anchorages, and ideal geographical location at the southernmost tip of the Asian mainland, dominating not only the access to the Melaka and Sunda Straits but also the approaches to the South China Sea and the Pacific and Indian Oceans, Singapore was at the meeting point of regional and inter-oceanic vessels traversing between India and China via the Melaka, Sunda, Lombok, and Makassar Straits. It quickly established trading links with surrounding ports under Western colonial rule, particularly in the Netherlands East Indies, although its entrepôt trade with mainland Southeast Asia states did not grow significantly until after Siam and French Indochina became more open to international trade in the latter half of the nineteenth century. After Southeast Asia, Europe – and Britain in particular – was Singapore's next biggest trading partner. Its trade with India and China, on the other hand, became progressively less important as cheap mass-produced cotton products from Britain replaced Indian cotton in Southeast Asian markets by 1840 and as the new British free port of Hong Kong, after the First Opium War (1839–42), supplanted Canton and became Britain's premier economic base in China, reducing Singapore's share of the trade with East Asia. The discovery of rich tin ore deposits in Sungai Ujung and several districts of the west coast states of Selangor and Perak in the 1840s and

1850s contributed to the growth of the trade of Penang and Melaka through which much of the tin was exported, and boosted their capacities as feeder ports to Singapore. The volume of trade between Singapore and the east coast states exceeded that of its traffic with the west coast states. Gold was the main commodity exported from the Malayan east coast to Singapore and accounted for 47 percent of total peninsula exports to Singapore in 1835–36.

With the growth in trade, the Straits ports attracted European mercantile firms that set up agency houses. These firms appointed agents who were paid a commission for selling imported goods like textiles and exporting local products like spices, sugar, coffee, and tea for re-export to international markets. Fourteen agency houses had been set up in Singapore by 1827; all except one were British, and included firms like Guthrie & Co. (1821) and Boustead & Co. (1828). By 1846, the number of agency houses had risen to 43, of which 20 were British. By 1901, the numbers peaked at 114; 66 were British and European, 24 Chinese, 22 Indian, and 2 Japanese. Until international banks established local branches, these agency houses provided banking facilities as well as handling shipping. Given that their resources were limited, agency houses were not deeply involved in the development of the Malayan hinterland until the second half of the nineteenth century.

Apart from entrepôt trade, the British also encouraged the cultivation of cash crops as a source of revenue in the Straits Settlements, using European capital as well as Chinese finance, management and labor in the process. Agency houses like Guthrie & Co., for example, invested directly in agricultural production and cultivated nutmeg in Singapore in the 1830s. In Penang, European planters controlled sugar estates from 1838, but it was the cultivation of spices, chiefly nutmeg, that dominated the island's agricultural development from the 1830s until the nutmeg plantations were devastated by blight (from 1854) and drought (in 1860), ending Penang's aspirations to become a prosperous agricultural settlement. Singapore's agricultural forays were not much better. Early experiments by European planters to cultivate coconut, sugar, coffee, and cotton ended in failure. Nutmeg proved more successful but, as in Penang, it also succumbed to blight. After devastation in 1864 no attempt was made to revive nutmeg cultivation on the island. Only the gambier and pepper industry thrived under Chinese planters after it was discovered that gambier waste could be used to fertilize soil exhausted by the growing of pepper vines. The growing of gambier, which was valued in the West for tanning and dyeing purposes, peaked in the 1840s and 1850s while pepper continued to survive as a commercial crop until the 1860s. In Melaka, agricultural growth was retarded by inadequate land reform, except for the tapioca industry that thrived for a short time in the 1860s. Poor soil conditions, fluctuating international commodity prices, plant disease, and inexperience doomed the experiment to transform the Straits Settlements into a revenue-generating and prosperous agricultural paradise.

As the Straits Settlements had only small areas of cultivable land, gradually agricultural capital moved into surrounding areas on the Malayan peninsula, which led to opening forested areas for further development. The migratory character of pepper cultivation arising from soil exhaustion, for instance, forced the industry in Singapore to fan outwards from the city area until it reached the Straits of Johor in the 1840s before crossing into Johor itself, and opening the state to capitalist development. Similarly, European sugar estates were established in Province Wellesley (on the peninsula opposite Penang) in 1840, two years after planters first gained a foothold in Penang. The expansion of Penang's trade and population also stimulated Kedah's rice-growing industry for export as the settlement provided a growing market for the state's agricultural products. Attracted by the prospect of heightened trade and financial gain, Straits merchants and European agency houses in Penang and Singapore provided capital to Malay rulers who lacked the resources to develop their states. In return, these agency houses managed the ruler's financial affairs. The volatility of commercial agriculture and its cycles of boom-and-bust did not provide a stable basis for the longer-term growth of the Malayan economy. In the latter part of the nineteenth century it was mining – especially tin – that set the pace for Malaya's economic growth.

Earlier Malay tin mining was limited in scope and technology and was usually a part-time activity to supplement agricultural or fishing income. Malay miners employed only simple mining techniques like panning in the beds of lowland streams where tin-bearing soil had been washed down by heavy rains. The pace of development, however, picked up from around the middle of the nineteenth century when the discovery of rich tin deposits in the west coast states of Perak, Selangor, and Negri Sembilan coincided with the expansion in the tin-plate industry in Europe, and particularly in Britain which became Malaya's biggest market for its alluvial tin as Britain's own supplies were depleted. Only a small number of Chinese worked in the mines before the 1830s, but rising tin prices and the prospects of financial gain and employment in the tin industry stimulated a surge in Chinese immigration to Malaya. By 1872 there were an estimated 40,000 Chinese miners in Malaya. This ushered in a period of Sino-Malay partnership in the industry as Straits Chinese merchants advanced capital to the Malay ruling class who used immigrant Chinese laborers to work the mines. In return the merchants received the right to trade in the tin, while the Malay chiefs collected revenue from the mining rights and tin exports. Their ability to control both capital and labor gave the Chinese dominance over this highly labor-intensive industry until the early decades of the twentieth century, when increasing mechanization by European entrepreneurs brought an end to their supremacy.

In the 1860s, as Straits merchants sought more tin concessions, increasing competition for control over tin-bearing districts among rival Malay-Chinese coalitions, backed by Chinese secret society gangs, gave rise to civil disturbances in Klang (in Selangor), Larut (in Perak), and Sungai Ujung (in Negri Sembilan) between 1867 and 1873. As noted above, this led to the British change to a policy of intervention from 1874. As British dominance brought the rule of law, stability, and security, the tin boom began in earnest, and Malaya became the chief tin-producing area in the world, supplying over half of the world's tin output by the 1890s and jump-starting its own development as a modern economy. A tin-smelting industry, originally the preserve of small Chinese-owned smelters located near the mines, was established and attracted

European entrepreneurs who wanted to break the Chinese monopoly. In 1886, a European firm set up a small smelter at Teluk Anson in Perak. The following year it became the Straits Trading Company and transferred its operations to Pulau Brani, an island off Singapore, where cheaper coal imports and fuel storage space were available. As a result, it was able to process nearly all the tin ore from Malaya as well as a large amount from the region and Australia. By 1896, it was able to smelt up to 20 percent of the world's tin output. In 1901, it set up a second smelting works at Butterworth in Penang, where a Chinese-owned smelting enterprise had also been in operation since 1897.

While tin was the initial driver of Malaya's economic development, it was soon followed by another commodity of spectacular impact – rubber. There was rising demand for rubber to be used in footwear, various industrial contexts, and, particularly, bicycle tires in the nineteenth century; in the early twentieth century there was a dramatic explosion of demand from the developing automobile industry. With improved political conditions following the extension of British influence over the Malay states from the 1870s, the development of commercial agriculture proceeded in earnest. Generous low-cost land concessions and loans were provided by the British administration to attract European capital and entrepreneurship into the plantation economy, particularly rubber. First introduced into Malaya as an experimental crop in the Singapore Botanical Gardens in 1877, rubber came to be cultivated on such a scale, using cheap immigrant labor from India, that it was Malaya's top export commodity by the 1890s, surpassing tin.

Pro-business legislation and infrastructure were also put in place to facilitate economic change in Malaya. To attract European investors, the British introduced a Western-style land tenure system that replaced Malay customary land laws which had previously given peasants rights over land they cleared for cultivation. Roads and railways were extended, especially in the west coast states, to support Malaya's economic transformation. Roads linked tin mines and rubber estates to river systems and railways carried commodities to the coastal ports on the west coast. In 1885, the first railway began to carry tin ore from Taiping (Perak) to Port Weld (on the Perak coast), whence daily steamers ferried it to Penang. Other railway lines were also constructed, such as in Selangor, where a line connected Kuala Lumpur to Klang in 1886 and was extended to Port Swettenham in 1899. In Negeri Sembilan, the Sungai Ujung line from Seremban to Port Dickson was completed in 1891. With the expansion of the tin and rubber industries, the main function of the Straits Settlement ports changed from entrepôt trade to serving as staple ports and centers for the bulking and processing of primary products from scattered estates and mines. By the end of the century, Malaya's spectacular transformation into a globally oriented modern economy was nearly complete.

French Indochina

French writings in the nineteenth and twentieth centuries placed great emphasis on France's 'civilizing mission' (*mission civilisatrice*) in its various colonies, but the fundamental purpose of colonization remained economic gain. Indochina, like European possessions elsewhere, was intended to be profitable. The operative concept was what the French called *mise en valeur*, which literally meant that a place would be made to produce value where it had not before. The assumption was that colonial rule would introduce methods of exploitation of natural resources which would profit rulers and ruled alike. At the same time, the French promised to improve infrastructure (roads and railroads) and provide education and health care. These commitments to the physical and material transformation of Indochina were presented as part of France's duty to provide for those under its tutelage, but at the same time, they were used to justify the financial burdens and other demands placed on the local peoples by the colonial system. On balance, few Indochinese outside the elite felt that they came out ahead in this 'trade-off'. The large rural populations in particular were subject to onerous taxes and other forms of exploitation while receiving little in return.

At the time of colonization, Indochina's prospects for becoming a source of revenue for the imperial system did not look encouraging. Aside from a few scattered mines in various parts of Vietnam and Laos, there were few natural resources. One key economic activity was trade, and Saigon was the most important asset in this respect, along with other Vietnamese ports (notably Hai Phong in the north) and Phnom Penh. In much of the colony, though, the only available resource was land, and generally speaking any tract of land considered remotely arable by local people was already under cultivation. The colonial regime thus faced a dual challenge. First, it needed to find ways to squeeze more revenue out of existing agricultural land and its produce. Second, it needed to open up new areas for cultivation – one of the most important aspects of *mise en valeur*.

The most basic and most readily available agricultural commodity in France's Asian colonies was obviously rice, and the rise of the regional rice trade meant that the markets and networks were already in place. In Siam at the time, the export economy had acquired enough momentum of its own that many peasants were motivated to produce a surplus. Indochina, however, was a different case, as land was in much shorter supply, and just achieving subsistence level was already difficult for many families, particularly in the more heavily populated areas of Tonkin and Annam. In Cochin China the Mekong delta was less densely populated, but much of the land was swampy and, in its present condition, not arable.

The colonial regime felt that the first step to promoting agricultural production to develop an export economy was to grant land concessions to those who would be motivated to increase cultivation if large tracts of land were in their possession. Traditionally Vietnamese land had been primarily divided between small-scale private and communal (village) ownership, but now the colonial regime made it possible for favored individuals to become landlords with substantial holdings. Vietnamese collaborators along with French colonists (*colons*) were given concessions of land, some of it taken from village holdings and some from fields abandoned during resistance to the invaders or else confiscated from those joining this resistance. In the Mekong delta substantial dredging operations were undertaken to drain and clear swamps for cultivation, and much of this newly available land went into concessions to private individuals.

All historical sources agree that the patterns of land tenure in the Vietnamese countryside changed dramatically. On the one hand, wealthy and powerful individuals were able to acquire much larger holdings than had been the case in the pre-colonial period. On the other hand, increasingly large numbers of peasants no longer owned their own land, but were reduced to tenancy (paying a fixed rent) or share-cropping (paying a share of the harvest) in someone else's fields. Whereas exploitation had traditionally occurred at the hands of one's neighbors – local officials or notables – now there was more absentee landlordism, with fewer opportunities for peasants to negotiate or reduce their obligations based on kinship or village ties.

Statistics on land holdings under French rule show clearly that many peasants simply did not have enough land to feed their families. This necessitated borrowing rice and/or money to cover their needs, which created a vicious cycle of debt from which it was difficult to escape. Many rural families were functioning barely at subsistence level to begin with, and the expenses involved in an unexpected illness or death in the family could have drastic consequences. Landlords often became creditors, and professional moneylenders were ubiquitous in many parts of Indochina. Moreover, landlords were generally backed directly or indirectly by the colonial state in the sense that they could use the judicial system and their connections with local authorities to enforce compliance by their tenants.

It is important to understand that the French colonial regime was in almost all respects more powerful than pre-colonial states. It could usually penetrate the villages more effectively, whether through routine visits by officials or more forceful action, which meant both that it could acquire more accurate knowledge about the number of inhabitants to be taxed and also that it could enforce taxation and other policies more effectively. This was particularly significant in Vietnamese villages, which traditionally had enjoyed a certain degree of autonomy *vis-à-vis* the imperial government. More importantly, village officials had often been able to 'cook the books' with their population registers by under-reporting the number of male residents and thus reducing their obligation in terms of tax burdens and draftees for the military and for labor service (*corvée*).

As the French took control, they projected their power into the villages, particularly in the Vietnamese regions, where they discovered that some local populations had been under-reported by as much as two-thirds of the real total. The margin for evasion or for negotiation between village leaders and higher authorities now shrank drastically. The colonial regime also changed the structure of the head tax which male residents had to pay. Previously, it was leveled on the village as a whole and thus subject to underpayment based on deflated population figures, but now it was collected from individuals, often in cash rather than quantities of rice. These changes translated into a drastically heavier tax burden on individual peasants, as well as a significantly heightened degree of pressure on officials at various levels of the hierarchy to enforce the collection of revenue. This pressure in turn provided more motives for extortion and corruption. The French also introduced new taxes and monopolies, the most significant being that on rice wine, which had important social and ritual functions among Vietnamese. Villagers were forced to buy the products of government-owned distilleries, sometimes based on officially determined quotas, and individuals who attempted to make their own wine were punished harshly.

Cambodia was less densely populated than Vietnam, and the land tenure situation was traditionally much less tight. Under French rule, while the colony generally did not see large-scale land concessions on the scale of Tonkin, Annam, or Cochin China, a rise in landlordism did take place. This was largely because Cambodian peasants faced the same demands as the Vietnamese in terms of taxation and the same potential vicious cycle of debt and borrowing. Chinese moneylenders were widespread in rural Cambodia; although legally they could not own land (unless they became French citizens or married Cambodian wives), they could hold mortgages on it, collect rent, and foreclose when debts went unpaid. Over the decades of colonial rule large quantities of land gradually changed hands one or two hectares at a time. Even those peasants who were relatively better off than their Vietnamese counterparts still relied heavily on credit and borrowing to get from one harvest to the next.

Laos was underpopulated to begin with and did not constitute an important source of rice for the export market. Like elsewhere in Indochina, the population became subject to heavier and more consistently enforced taxation than had previously been the case. The most important grievance in Laos, however, was the government's use of *corvée* labor, particularly to build roads in a colony that had few of them. Men were forced to work on public projects for weeks on end, sometimes at considerable distances from their home villages, with little or no compensation. Exemption from *corvée* was possible but required a payment in cash which few could afford. This policy was also found in other parts of Indochina, but it seems to have been most deeply resented in Laos, where the demands of the pre-colonial state had generally been relatively light.

Like elsewhere in Southeast Asia, colonial rule significantly transformed the ethnic composition of some parts of Indochina. Of the three principal ethnic groups, the French felt that the Vietnamese were by far the most dynamic and economically productive, although in their opinion it took the catalyst of the colonial system to realize this productivity. The Chinese, however, were even more dynamic and, more importantly, better connected to markets and trading networks elsewhere in the region. There had of course been Chinese communities in Vietnam for centuries, but the French welcomed further immigration as a contribution to the colony's economic growth. The largest concentrations of Chinese were in Hanoi, Hai Phong, and particularly Saigon, where the Chinese community of Cho Lon became virtually a twin city.

Chinese also migrated in significant numbers to Cambodia and Laos, where their presence in pre-colonial times had been relatively small. The more important – and more deeply resented – wave of immigration in these two colonies, however, came from Tonkin, Annam, and Cochin China. The French felt a paternalistic affection for the Cambodians and Lao, but despaired of ever getting them to work hard enough to rise above self-sufficient rice production. (There is of course a clear parallel here with British attitudes toward the Malays.) To the French, the most logical means to pursue the *mise en valeur* of the two countries was to encourage the more dynamic Vietnamese to immigrate, a policy which would also help to relieve demographic pressure in the overpopulated areas of Tonkin and Annam. Although neither Laos nor Cambodia was initially a particularly attractive destination to most Vietnamese, over time they were persuaded to go, and they poured into the cities and towns of their neighbors to the west.

Not only did the Vietnamese immigrants come to dominate the markets and many of the trades in Cambodia and Laos, they also filled many of the administrative posts. Just as the British 'imported' Indians to become civil servants in Burma, the French packed their government offices and schools with Vietnamese officials and teachers. Vietnamese dominance was particularly evident in Laos, where all of the major towns along the Mekong (Vientiane, Tha Khek, Savannakhet, and Pakse) had populations that were more than half Vietnamese. In Cambodia there was a greater balance between the Chinese and Vietnamese minorities, but the Vietnamese presence was strong nevertheless, particularly in Phnom Penh. The irony, of course, was that part of the original rationale for French protectorates over the Cambodians and Lao was ostensibly to prevent the two peoples from being swallowed up or assimilated by either the Thai or the Vietnamese. While the colonial regime was not unmindful of this irony or the potential fallout of large-scale immigration, the benefits of having large Vietnamese minorities among the more 'indolent' (in French eyes) Lao and Cambodians outweighed the risks. As we will see in the next chapter, however, this policy was to have a significant impact on the evolution of Cambodian and Lao nationalism in ways not unlike the impact that the Chinese presence had on Malay nationalism.

Indonesia: The Netherlands East Indies

By 1800, the spices that had brought the Dutch to Indonesia no longer had significant value on the world market. The clove monopoly had collapsed altogether. In 1769–72 two French expeditions captured clove plants in Ambon and then introduced cloves to Mauritius and other French colonies. In the nineteenth century, it was new products that made Indonesia a commercial success for the Netherlands. As noted above, Governor-General Van den Bosch proposed the *Cultuurstelsel* (Cultivation System) on the basis that it would make Java profitable. Instead of the colonial government relying on an inherently unreliable land tax (the 'land rent'), it would require Javanese villagers to grow agricultural products – especially coffee, sugar, and indigo – for sale on the international market through Amsterdam. They were paid a low fixed price for these products, so that the Dutch could market them at a significant profit. Van den Bosch reckoned, however, that the money paid to the peasants would cover their land rent obligations and, if it exceeded those obligations, they would even have extra income from the scheme. Moreover, villagers would need to set aside less land to meet these targets than had previously been required to cover their 'land rent' obligations. So everyone should profit.

In fact, the Cultivation System was hardly a 'system' at all, for arrangements varied dramatically from place to place. The basic input was villagers' labor, carried out compulsorily under the supervision of the indigenous elites. The amount of cultivated land involved was small – around 4–6 percent on average

– but the labor investment was enormous. In some areas virtually the whole village population had to work on government export crops. The profitability of the system was supported by the increasing population of Java, which exploded in the nineteenth century from something of the order of 4–5 million around 1800 (there is no reliable figure for this period) to 9.5 million by 1850 and 24 million by 1890.

With this system of compulsory labor, great profits were wrung from Java for the first time in history. The Dutch colonial budget was balanced and enormous returns were sent to the mother country. Down to 1850 nearly 20 percent of Netherlands state revenue came from the profits of the Cultivation System; over 1851–66 the figure was about 32–34 percent. These returns supported the industrialization of the Netherlands. For most Javanese villagers, these were hard times. Not only was there much work to do, but the Cultivation System meant competition between export crops and domestic food crops for labor, water, and land. Serious famines broke out from the 1840s, the result mainly of general poverty among the peasants and the greed of their superiors. For many of the Javanese elite, however, these were good times – as will be seen in the following section of this chapter.

Domestic opposition to the Cultivation System grew in the Netherlands from mid-century. Dutch middle-class interests – principal beneficiaries of the country's growing wealth – pressed for 'liberal' reform, freeing Java's peasants from compulsory labor, allowing the growth of wage labor, and encouraging private investment. Demands for reform were further supported when, in 1860, an angry colonial official named Eduard Douwes Dekker published *Max Havelaar*, a novel exposing the corruption and exploitation in Java. Douwes Dekker wrote under the pseudonym 'Multatuli', meaning 'I have suffered much', and his novel is still regarded as one of the greatest works of Dutch literature.

With the Agrarian and Sugar Laws of 1870, Java began to be opened to private enterprise. Thus commenced the so-called Liberal period (1870–1900) of Dutch colonial policy. Government monopolies over export crops were progressively abandoned from the 1860s, first the unprofitable ones and then, last of all, sugar (finally coming to an end in 1890) and coffee (the last areas of compulsory coffee cultivation only ending in 1919). This Liberal period after 1870 coincided with the expansion of Dutch control outside Java. The commercial exploitation of the outer islands mainly occurred in the twentieth century (see Chapter 9) but already in the later nineteenth century new outer island products were entering into Dutch commercial calculations.

Aceh was one of the world's greatest sources of pepper in the nineteenth century, but it was the discovery of oil there that would give Aceh its economic prominence in the twentieth century. Oil had been known to exist in northern Sumatra from the 1860s. In 1883 a Dutch entrepreneur, A. J. Zijlker, began to drill for oil in Langkat – an area once subject to the Sultan of Aceh, by then under Dutch influence, but still turbulent because of the ongoing war in Aceh. In 1890 Zijlker set up a company known as 'de Koninklijke' ('the Royal') and he soon began exporting oil. We should remember that in the nineteenth century, this was used mainly as lamp oil, so the development of the electric light bulb from the 1880s seemed to threaten the oil industry. But around that same time the internal combustion engine was developed, the automobile industry began to grow from c.1900, and oil became one of the most crucial products driving modern economies. In 1907 'de Koninklijke' merged with a British company named Shell to form the first of the world's great oil multinationals: Royal Dutch Shell. By this time other companies were getting into the oil industry and drilling was spreading to other parts of Indonesia.

As a result of all of these nineteenth-century developments, Indonesia became more diverse in an ethnic as well as an economic sense. Many Chinese were attracted to opportunities there, from coolies to miners, shop-keepers, tax-farmers, and opium-traders. Some Chinese became very wealthy, but most remained poor. European investment in Java remained heavily Dutch and more Dutch managers and entrepreneurs were seen, but in the outer islands investment was more international, with British investment being particularly evident. In many places, the most crucial cogs in the economic machine were people of mixed European and Indonesian ancestry – Indo-Europeans or *Indos* as they were called. In fact, in the nineteenth century, many of those in Indonesia who called themselves 'Dutch' were locally born, had never been to the Netherlands, and often had Indonesian ancestry somewhere in their genealogy. Those at the very top levels of the colonial administration and of most economic enterprises, however, remained people from Europe who came out to do a job, remained primarily oriented towards their home country, and – if they survived the many threats to health in the nineteenth-century tropics – returned home when their role was finished.

The most remarkable thing about Indonesia, however, was how very few Europeans there were – and how extraordinarily successfully they governed and exploited millions of Indonesians. This was possible mainly because of European technological advantages and because the nineteenth century was a pre-nationalist age. There was not as yet a sense of Indonesian identity or an idea that Indonesians might stand together to resist European rule. Consider that in 1905 the indigenous population of Indonesia was about 37 million. They had been subdued by colonial military forces that totaled a mere 42,000 in that year, of whom over 60 percent were themselves Indonesians. Indeed, as will be seen in the next section of this chapter, for some of the local elite, Dutch rule represented – not a new threat – but the opening of new horizons.

The Philippines

In 1811, after the last galleon sailed from Manila, the Philippines embarked on an age of separation from Mexico, which had subsidized the archipelago's deficient treasury. This signaled the decline of Spanish political and mercantilist dominance in the Philippines in favor of the more capitalist English and Dutch powers. The Spanish Crown lost most of its colonies in the Americas through revolutions: within a decade of Mexico's independence in 1820, only Cuba, Puerto Rico, and the Philippines remained of Spain's once-affluent empire.

For the Philippines, the dissolution of Hispanic authority in the Americas meant the arrival of more Spanish forces, which made the colonial authorities feel more secure and thus less fearful of foreigners. On the other hand, the abolition of the galleon trade made the Philippines less attractive to Chinese and this, along with the (imperfectly implemented) ban on their immigration, slowed Chinese (*Sangley*) arrivals for several decades. For example, only 5440 arrived in 1822, and 5708 in 1828. At the time, Manila housed 93 percent of the islands' Chinese. After the ban on their immigration was lifted in 1850, however, they arrived in steadily larger numbers and begun penetrating the provincial *poblaciónes*. In 1844 governors were restricted from trading, which allowed *Sangleys* to take charge of bulk and retail trading in the provinces, connecting the archipelago's agricultural economy with Western economies. In territories contiguous to Manila, Chinese settlements sprouted; others followed elsewhere, even in the southernmost Sulu islands.

Other foreign traders also trickled in. In 1809 the authorities allowed the establishment of a British firm in Manila. In 1814, after the end of the Napoleonic Wars in Europe, Spain also permitted other Western nations similar privileges. This foreign penetration was not halted even by the animosity of local Spaniards and their subordinates or a massacre of foreigners that followed an 1820 cholera epidemic. In 1834 the government opened Manila to international commerce. By 1842 North Europeans and Americans owned 12 out of 51 shipping and commercial houses in Manila; in 1859 they owned the 15 most properous. By the 1890s – after Zamboanga, Iloilo, and Pangasinan (1855); Cebu (1860); and Legazpi and Tacloban (1873) were opened – foreign houses monopolized the import–export trade.

Foreign trade increased dramatically. In 1837 exports amounted to 49 percent of total trade; by 1852 total trade more than doubled in value and the share of exports increased to 56 percent. The star performers among exports were sugar and raw abaca. Sugar exports increased nearly 16 times in value between 1840 and 1893, while abaca exports increased 45 times in value between 1840 and 1894. Behind the transformation of the Philippines from a subsistence to an export economy were the foreign merchants who provided banking facilities to participating *mestizo*, *Indio*, and *Sangley* entrepreneurs. Here the government hardly assisted – the *Banco-Español Filipino* (today's Bank of the Philippine Islands), established in 1852, only favored Spanish interests.

The dramatic expansion of abaca and sugar exports reflected the economic impact of foreign merchants. In 1820, naval officer John White brought 'Manila hemp' (as it was called, even though abaca is not related to hemp) to Massachusetts. A market for raw abaca then developed in North America. American merchants provided loans to cultivators in Bicol and the eastern Visayas, then established packing houses, collection stores, and warehouses throughout the archipelago, enabling the dramatic expansion of the industry described in the previous paragraph. Foreign houses also transformed the sugar industry. The British loaned capital to Spaniards, Eurasians and Filipino-Chinese *mestizos* who commenced cultivation in the virgin lowlands of Negros. They introduced steam-powered milling equipment and guaranteed the purchase of sugar cane.

Infrastructural innovation facilitated economic expansion. Steamships secured maritime linkages, providing the navy with self-powered vessels for policing the waters. Governmental and private steamers sailed insular seas and rivers. The comunication infrastructure and postal service were expanded. In 1873 the telegraph service was begun and by 1880, after submarine cables linked Bolinao (Pangasinan) with Hong Kong, the colony was connected with the world telegraphic network. In Manila a public water system was established in 1870. By 1881 an extensive horse-drawn tramway system started operation, linking Manila's commercial center in Binondo to the suburbs. Electric lights replaced oil lamps and a telephone service was offered to more affluent citizens. Despite major engineering and financial difficulties, the Manila-Dagupan railroad was opened in 1892.

The population of the Philippines increased from 1,576,865 in 1799 to 3,815,880 in 1850. Ilocos, Pampanga, agricultural areas around Manila, Cebu, Central Pangasinan, and Southeastern Panay showed early signs of density. From 1820 to 1920 unencumbered mobility allowed the populace to occupy the interior, creating new settlements and farmlands. Pampangos and Tagalogs moved northwards; the Pangasinenses, east; the Ilocanos, southwards into the interior portions of Central Luzon, including today's Tarlac and Nueva Ecija. Tagalogs also went to the Tayabas-Batangas area of southern Luzon. Cebuanos migrated to provincial areas removed from the city. Ilongos shifted to Panay, across the Guimaras Strait towards Negros. They established new towns, thereby spreading lowland, Christian culture across the archipelago and transforming the demographic face of the Philippines.

The increase and mobility of the population strained the outdated Spanish system of administering and collecting tribute. In 1849 Governor-General Narciso Clavería y Zaldúa ordered the distribution of surnames to the populace in order more easily to be able to keep track of them. The government compiled an alphabetical list of words that included indigenous names, Spanish surnames and terms from vegetation, minerals, geography, arts, and others. *Alcaldes* received the list, which was then passed down to the *cabezas de barangay* for allocation. Most favored the names of saints; others who already had surnames were allowed to keep them. Names of pre-Hispanic chiefs like Sikatuna, Salamat, Tupas, and others could only be adopted if consanguinity could be proven.

Repercussions accompanied the economic boom. Commercial agriculture turned land into a commodity. Following an 1804 ordinance, non-elite *Indios* only enjoyed usufruct rights to the lands they tilled. Overruling traditional land rights, the elite *principalía*, Church, and *mestizos* owned most lands. The most oppressive landowners were the Dominicans, Augustinians, Recollects, and Jesuits who controlled vast *haciendas*, accrued from the estates of heirless *conquistadores* and the usurpation of community farmlands. In their spiritual jurisdictions (see Chapter 4) they owned some 460,000 acres (185,000 ha) of farmland. They did not farm, but used an *inquilino* – a Chinese overseer – who took charge of the *hacienda* and its tenants. Eventually *inquilinos* also seized lands from smallholders through purchases and foreclosing mortgages.

The clergy participated in commerce. They sold licenses for the galleon trade until the galleons no longer sailed, and monopolized trade and distribution of goods in their *poblaciónes*. Friars controlled charity foundations funded by bequests of churchmen and lay persons. Foundations like the *Hermanidad de la*

Misericordia (Brotherhood of Mercy), established in 1596, functioned as commercial banks and insurance companies. In this context, friars abused their authority. They sold religious paraphernalia and demanded daily food and even sexual favors from the faithful. Insubordinate *Indios* were corporally punished. In *haciendas* friars required payment from tenants who gathered wood, rattan, and bamboo for personal use. They forbade tenants from fishing in waters, gathering wild fruits, and grazing their water buffalo on the hills owned by religious orders. They raised sharecropping rents yearly, even issuing surtaxes on every tree that peasants cultivated.

The development of commercial agriculture had ecological repercussions. Agricultural expansion cleared lowland forests and drained swamps and marginal lands along riverbanks. This caused frequent flooding and lowered moisture in the environment, paving the way for periodic droughts. Clearing increased grassland areas, where pests like locusts thrived. Tarlac province, for instance, suffered locust plagues in 1804, 1805, 1808, 1815, 1839, and 1865. On densely populated farms, diseases struck both the livestock and the peasantry. Rinderpest and foot-and-mouth disease killed up to 90 percent of cattle in the 1890s. Rice crops were infested with armies of worms, while farmers fell victim to cholera epidemics (e.g., in 1820, 1882–83 and 1902). There were also social and political repercussions, as will be seen below.

Indigenous elites

British Burma

As in other Southeast Asian colonial states, a significant development in Burma was the growth of a new middle class. New priorities, sectors, and demands in the economy and administration called for new types of occupations, unlike those previously needed by the Burmese royal state, the *Sangha*, or other pre-colonial sources of employment and status. This brought new forms of social status and identity, indeed new classes and even ethnic categories.

The middle class emerged from a convergence of needs between former elites and the new colonial government. From 1852 posts were given to ex-princes, ministers, and local officials who were able to align themselves with the administrative needs of the British. Receiving appointments from the Rangoon government, many invested or borrowed money to invest in business or land. As the value of land increased or their holdings grew through the foreclosure of mortgages, these families became rich and powerful, allowing them to send their children (usually sons) overseas for an elite education which would result in a lucrative position upon their return. The first ethnic Burman Deputy Commissioner was appointed in 1908 and the first Burman judge was appointed to the High Court in 1917. With the founding of local tertiary institutions there came the option of staying in Burma for higher education, further contributing to the growth and influence of these elite families.

From about the 1880s to the 1930s this class (the *asoyamin*, government officers) produced not only the community of administrators who ran the colony for the British but also the people who developed and fashioned

Burmese political nationalism – a pattern we will see also in other colonial states. Out of the ranks of those upon whom the colonial regime depended came also the very voices of dissent that challenged the political order and those communities who benefited from it. Burmese nationalism's roots lay partly in the middle class's early interest in social reform. Educated Burmese, garnering funds and encouragement from Western benefactors, began to promote Burmese welfare by combining principles of social change with symbols and values that were familiar to the vast majority of the people. Non-clerical Buddhist schools, with curricula modeled on missionary and other English schools, introduced notions relevant to the new economy and administration. One such institution, the Sam Buddha Gosha Anglo-Vernacular High School, was founded in 1897 at Moulmein, in far southeastern Burma, and was soon followed by other schools administered by secular officers and associations. These sought to discuss issues of modernity through Buddhist idioms. It was in this context that in 1906 students founded the Young Men's Buddhist Association – clearly reflecting the model of the Young Men's Christian Association, founded in London in 1844. The YMBA was originally interested in discussing religion, but its interests soon expanded to local cultural and political issues. This is discussed further in the following chapter.

Burmese students educated in the Western style saw the preservation of Burmese cultural forms as a way to forge new identities. Literature, poetry, and theatre in particular took on a semi-autonomous history in this period, seemingly detached from narratives of the colonial economy and state. Much of Burmese literature had its roots in court traditions that were deeply influenced by Buddhist forms, symbols, and themes. Ladies of the court, monks, and laymen with experience in the capitals were often the authors of pre-colonial works, which focused on love stories, tales of past kings, and adaptations of the *Ramayana* and the *Jataka* tales on past lives of the Buddha. Traveling actors performed these stories before the public, adapting what had been meant to be read as court literature to a new form of drama that could be publicly performed (called *pya-zat*, a term that goes back to earlier plays focusing on the *Jataka* tales). By the later nineteenth century, *pya-zat* companies were touring throughout what remained of the independent kingdom and even within the newly annexed territories of British Lower Burma. Puppet shows, musical performances, and other forms of entertainment contributed to the cultural integration that had been on-going for centuries, slowly evolving into a set of ideas that would be associated with being 'Burmese'.

By the 1870s, plays and other dramas were circulated through the printing press. Readers were hungry for these nearly full-length plays that included songs, stage directions, and other features that recreated the staged performances. Many of the plots and stories were drawn from nineteenth-century events, so that these forms of performance and literature are valuable sources for understanding this period of Burmese history. New words and concepts entered traditional plots, resulting in scenes that involve guns, brandy, champagne, sherry, parliament, and technical legal words that were becoming familiar to Burmese.

With the final British annexation of the kingdom in 1886, the production of court literature all but stopped, but Lower Burmese presses continued to publish traditional stories, poems, and legends. In the view of some Burmese authorities, however, literary quality declined because the pre-colonial elite who were patrons of the arts lost their sources of revenue when the kingdom was taken over by the British. New forms did develop, however, as some local writers were exposed to Western literature and began adopting its themes for a Burmese audience. A Burmese version of the novel developed by the turn of the twentieth century, providing writers with a medium to address new issues and topics. While love stories remained popular, the settings often changed to reflect the new circumstances of local society, with plots set in places such as Rangoon College – established in 1878 and the forerunner of the University of Rangoon, opened in 1920 – and addressing the growing British influence in Burmese life.

The British Straits Settlements and Malaya

In the FMS, the British sought to associate the traditional aristocracies with British rule – the essence of what came to be known as 'indirect rule'. By preserving the traditional governing elite, the British were able not only to give the appearance of indigenous consent to their alien regime but also to address the more practical issues of having an adequate administrative corps for Malaya. Most fundamentally, indirect rule was a means of persuading the Malay elite to accept British governance and thus ensure the overall stability of the political system in Malaya.

In the pre-colonial Malay political order, the ruler – described variously or simultaneously by his Malay title *yang di-pertuan* (he who is made lord), the Hindu term *raja* or the Arabic *sultan* – stood at its apex, and was the symbol of its unity. He derived his authority and ruled his state and *rakyat* (subjects) with the support and assistance of chiefs of various ranks from both royal and non-royal aristocratic backgrounds. Together they formed the ruling elite. The ruler was equipped with royal regalia and purportedly invested with *daulat*, the mystical sanctity conferred by kingship, which found outward form in an elaborate and ritualized installation ceremony. He was both the ceremonial head of state, entitled to particular forms of address and symbolic acts of homage from others, and the defender and arbiter of the Islamic faith, for which he was marked as God's viceroy on earth. The ruler's ability to exercise his authority beyond his royal district, however, depended on his capacity to command his chiefs, whose wealth from collecting revenue and controlling tin-bearing districts in the western states often made them the ruler's natural economic – and also political – rivals. Despite the hereditary nature of the elite's status, some mobility existed: the death or downfall of a chief could lead to another rising up the state hierarchy, and court intrigues could even result in a reigning sultan being replaced by a new ruling lineage. Under the Malay feudal political order, the ruling class held political and administrative power over the *rakyat*, who were supposed to serve them loyally.

The preservation of the traditional political and social order was a hallmark of British rule in the Malay states. In reality, however, the balance of power within the structure shifted. The Malay ruler continued to reign with the assistance of his hierarchy of chiefs, but he no longer ruled – a role that British Residents, ostensibly appointed only to advise the ruler, assumed in practice. Like the rulers, the territorial chiefs also suffered a loss of real power as their functions were largely taken over by British District Officers. Partly to placate the Malay aristocracy and to secure their cooperation in the governance of their kingdoms, the British provided the ruling elite with personal allowances based on their rank and standing within the Malay order. By formalizing their status and position within the hierarchy through such allowances and pensions, the British restricted mobility within the elite structure and sealed off the Malay ruling elite from challenges from below. So while the Malay aristocracy lost much *de facto* political and administrative power to the British, their status and positions within society were in fact enhanced under British rule. Through the retention of such traditional structures and the continued accent on the symbols of status, prestige and ceremonial pomp and pageantry, the British not only boosted the majesty of the rulers but also formalized and strengthened the position of the traditional Malay ruling elite. This was all for the purposes of indirect rule, engendering the systemic stability essential for Malaya's growth and development. The ruling elite thus perceived the British as protectors, a role they depended on increasingly as the Malays faced challenges to their privileged position and status from the immigrant communities from the turn of the twentieth century. Here we see parallels particularly with Cambodia.

The British initially could not find a useful role for the ruling elite to play in the modern but alien administrative system they introduced in Malaya, which operated outside the realms where the sultan and his chiefs dominated. The convenient British stereotype of Malays as polite and courteous but also indolent partly contributed to this failure to involve the elite meaningfully in the new administrative set-up. Though the rulers were associated with the new administrative structures of the FMS through the institution of State Councils, for instance, and were required to affix their seals to all documents passed by the latter, they in fact exercised no real power. British Residents, not the Malay rulers, essentially dominated the proceedings. Accepting Malays into the FMS civil bureaucracy was, moreover, problematic because there the language of government was English, not Malay – unlike the UMS, where each state had its own administration headed by its ruler who controlled the largely Malay-led civil service.

After British dominance over the western states was effectively consolidated, British officials were more inclined to the belief that, as protectors, they had moral and treaty obligations to help Malays become more involved in the administration of their own country. Dissatisfaction among members of the FMS ruling elite at not possessing the administrative autonomy enjoyed by their counterparts in the UMS also reached British ears. However grateful FMS Malay leaders were for the enhanced status and personal benefits that British rule brought them, they entertained aspirations consistent with their status as members of a ruling elite. The increasing cost of running a modern bureaucracy was another compelling reason for change, for European manpower was expensive. Consequently, as already noted earlier, the Malay College was opened at

Kuala Kangsar in 1905 to train young aristocrats in a residential college setting in English to be future administrators in what became in 1920 the Malay Administrative Service (MAS).

Ruling the large Chinese community presented another challenge for the British. For most of the nineteenth century, the acknowledged leaders of the Chinese in Malaya were the heads of secret societies. Given the considerable manpower and financial resources at their disposal, the more powerful of these secret society headmen often also assumed more respectable professions that cast them in roles as philanthropic community leaders and wealthy merchants. Their political weight and influence made them sought-after business partners and political allies of local Malay chiefs who appointed them to State Councils and entrusted them with the task of administering the local Chinese population in their states. So pervasive was the hold of secret societies over the Chinese population that the British authorities often found it necessary to tolerate their existence and enlist the support of their leaders to restore order after outbreaks of rioting by rival Chinese gangs.

Confronted by the challenge of ruling the rather heterogeneous Chinese community, differentiated as it was by different dialect and clan groups, territorial origins, and distinctive types of profession or calling, British officials initially relied on the traditional *Kapitan Cina* (Chinese Captain) to keep the peace. But as the British consolidated their power, they decided to take more positive steps to wean the immigrant Chinese from the influence of the secret societies. A new office of Protector of Chinese was introduced in Singapore in 1877, led by a British official with a command of dialects and Chinese social norms and tasked to look after the welfare of newly arrived immigrants, as well as to maintain surveillance on secret society membership and activities through registration, data collection, and personal contacts. After setting up a representative Chinese Advisory Board in 1889 to assist them in administering the Chinese, the British finally outlawed secret societies in 1890.

In the Straits Settlements, however, the British found their main collaborators among English-educated and locally domiciled members of the Chinese community – the largely pro-British and Westernized Straits-born Chinese. As British subjects, they enjoyed a privileged status in the Colony that was superior to that of Chinese in the FMS, who were vaguely categorized as 'British protected persons'. Proud of their 'British' heritage and identification with British culture, the Straits Chinese were thus inclined to be loyal to the British Crown and to support the colonial status quo. On their part, the British consciously nurtured the Straits Chinese as their local collaborators to help underpin British rule in the Colony and rewarded their allegiance with low-ranking administrative positions as well as appointments to various public bodies where they served as representative spokesmen for the Chinese community.

The Indochinese elite

In most of Indochina colonial rule effectively created two sets of elites, both of whom collaborated with the French to varying degrees. The first was the traditional ruling class linked to the monarchies who continued to function much as they did under the pre-colonial governments. Thus the royal courts in Hue, Phnom Penh, and Luang Phabang maintained their ceremonies and much of the culture linked to them, while the various levels of bureaucracy survived more or less intact. In Annam and Tonkin the French continued to hold the centuries-old examinations to recruit mandarins until around the time of World War I. Royal princes, ministers, provincial governors, and lower-ranking officials carried on as their predecessors had in independent kingdoms, even though their authority was checked – and their orders easily countermanded – by their French counterparts. The protectorates enabled this first group of elite – and the socio-political system that was linked to them – to endure until the end of colonial rule in the mid-twentieth century. While many members of this group did learn French and acquire some elements of Western culture, they tended to be more traditional in their thinking, and it was only during the final decades of colonial rule that more Westernized princes emerged.

The second group of collaborators often came from social backgrounds which would have excluded them from the elite in pre-colonial society. As was true elsewhere, foreign rule brought new opportunities for those of relatively humble status, such as interpreters, low-ranking officials, or officers in the colonial military. In this new social system family background and rank within the traditional hierarchy counted for less than loyalty to the French and at least a working knowledge of their language. As time went on, the development of a French-medium school system within Indochina and the opportunities given to some to study in France created a critical mass of Vietnamese, Cambodians, and Lao who had received a Western education, and whose ideas and interests clearly set them apart from their more traditional compatriots.

The impact of the colonial education system varied from place to place. In the Vietnamese regions of Indochina, the main priority for the French was to break the psychological hold of Chinese culture, linked as it was to the long-time suzerainty which threatened their control. The most important step in this direction was to replace the use of Chinese characters and the Chinese-derived *nom* script with the Romanized alphabet known as *quoc ngu* ('national language'). This writing system had been developed centuries earlier for use by Catholic missionaries and converts, but had never been adopted outside the Christian community. Now it gradually became the main vehicle for writing Vietnamese, and thus for vernacular education, although neither written Chinese nor *nom* completely died out. The ability to read and write *quoc ngu* became one qualification which separated the new elite from the old; as late as the 1920s, there were still scholar-officials trained under the old system who were not comfortable writing the Romanized script.

The role of the Vietnamese language in colonial education, however, remained ambivalent. While it was not France's goal to turn their colonial subjects into 'little Frenchmen' who no longer spoke their mother tongue, the school system was necessarily geared to the language of power. Indochina was given an essentially French-style educational system based on primary schools, *collèges* (lower secondary), *lycées* (upper secondary), and a single university in Hanoi. While there was some use of Vietnamese at the primary level, secondary level education was almost exclusively in French, even in classrooms where neither teacher nor students were European, and many Vietnamese who came through this system tended to converse with each other in French rather than their mother tongue. This was a second dividing line between the two groups of elite.

Cambodia and Laos had no tradition of secular education. As was true also in Burma and Thailand, boys acquired their schooling during a stay in the monastery, and girls generally did without. The colonial regime experimented with using the temple schools to teach Western subjects, but this initiative proved to be a spectacular failure, as the worldview of most Buddhist monks was not compatible with the curriculum prescribed by the French. Temple schools survived as centers for providing a traditional religious education, but they were effectively a dead end for any child with aspirations to success, since they did not provide enough grounding in French and other subjects for their pupils to be able to 'mainstream' into the colonial educational system. As in Vietnam, the regime established bilingual schools for younger pupils, but post-primary education was in French. Nor was there much of it: Cambodia had a single *lycée*, and Laos had nothing above the *collège* level.

As a consequence, the number of Cambodians and Lao who constituted a Western-educated elite was proportionally smaller than was the case for the Vietnamese. A handful made their way to Saigon or Hanoi for secondary school, and an even smaller number studied either at the local university or in France. In these two colonies there was more overlap between the older and the newer groups of elite, both because a number of those receiving a Western education were royal and because there were fewer opportunities for careers outside the royal-dominated bureaucracy. The main exceptions were those involved with journalism or other intellectual pursuits, as will be discussed in the next chapter.

Generally speaking, the elites in Indochina were ethnically homogeneous, and marriage with those from other ethnic groups was relatively rare. There was, for example, considerably less intermarriage with Chinese than was the case among the Siamese ruling class, even though for the Vietnamese in particular, the 'cultural distance' between the two groups was not very significant. Several prominent Lao nationalists were, however, of mixed Lao-Vietnamese parentage. Nor did a sizable Eurasian population develop as was the case in other Southeast Asian colonies. Many Frenchmen who came as bachelors, of course, did take local women as wives or concubines, and a number of children of mixed ancestry (known in French as *métis*) were born over the decades of colonial rule. Very few of them ended up among the local elite, however, because in many cases their European fathers were themselves not of high social class and also because many of these *métis* were socialized as 'French' and eventually returned to France.

In each colony a small core of what we might call 'aspirant Frenchmen' could be found – members of the elite who had usually studied in the metropole and acquired French citizenship and/or a French wife. A well-known example was the Vietnamese journalist Nguyen Van Vinh, whom we will meet again in the next chapter when we consider the various strains of Vietnamese nationalism. Vinh saw himself as a cultural broker whose mission in life was to bring Western culture to his less sophisticated countrymen. He translated numerous works of French literature into Vietnamese and wrote impassioned newspaper articles deploring what he saw as the negative aspects of his culture, such as the tendency to smile even when one was angry or upset. Satirical plays and stories appeared about the '*retours de France*' (returnees from France) who could no longer function in their native society or, in some cases, even in their mother tongue.

Men like Vinh were the exception rather than the rule, however, and most members of the Vietnamese, Cambodian, and Lao collaborator elite were to some extent bicultural – except, of course, for those diehards who adhered firmly to their traditional culture and refused to learn French. Such men – and they were mainly men, for relatively few women from Indochina had the chance to study abroad – combined a strong loyalty to France and a deep appreciation of its culture with a strong sense of their own roots. They might speak, write, and even think in French, but they were certainly aware that they were still 'Indochinese' and 'natives'. Their generally second-class status was quite obvious within the colonial power structure. Thus, a Vietnamese who returned with a doctorate from the Sorbonne would almost certainly rank below a much less educated French colleague in terms of both authority and salary.

The clear racist divide between 'French' and 'native' and the impenetrable glass ceiling that blocked off the top of the colonial system persisted throughout the decades of colonial rule. While a local official could be educated and trained for advancement through the government hierarchy, there was generally a clear division of labor between those positions reserved for Frenchmen and those open to their colonized subjects. This was the ultimate paradox of collaboration: colonial rule shaped – and in some respects arguably created – this elite, yet at the same time it also placed clear restrictions on their authority and kept them firmly in their place. This situation was somewhat less problematic for the first generation of collaborators, who were less Westernized and often more willing to accept their subordinate status, having only recently joined the new regime. For the next generation, however, those who came of age during and after World War I, tough questions began to emerge regarding their status and their stake in the system, and these questions shaped their nationalism.

Indonesian elites

As noted earlier, after the Java War the Dutch truly ruled Java in colonial fashion for the first time. The conflicts of the 1808–30 period had, however, taught them that it was dangerous to meddle with indigenous culture and social structures. So the post-1830 colonial regime adopted a conservative approach, ruling in collaboration with local elites as far as possible. This meant that the Dutch identified in Java and then in each of their new outer island territories a cooperative local elite, almost invariably one whose authority rested on local custom and aristocratic descent, rather than the countervailing elites who claimed leadership based upon their Islamic learning and piety. Thus the Dutch identified and often accentuated a dichotomy between so-called 'customary' or 'secular' and Islamic elites.

The top royal and aristocratic elites – the Sultan and Susuhunan in Java, miscellaneous sultans in the outer islands, *rajas* in Bali – were not encouraged to modernize. Indeed, it was their 'traditional' status and influence that were useful to the Dutch. For those who worked well with the colonial government, their positions were often more secure than under previous indigenous states, their sons' succession to their positions was more certain, and their incomes were often higher. Among some members of this group and more particularly among the higher levels of the indigenous administrative structure there developed enthusiasm for the scientific and technological advances of the nineteenth-century West. For such people, colonial rule represented a broadening of horizons and enhancement of their elite status.

The transformation of indigenous literate culture from one based on hand-written manuscripts to one based on print was decisive. The first vernacular-language newspaper in Indonesian history was published in Javanese in Surakarta beginning in 1855 and was shortly followed by Malay-language papers. These papers – mostly weeklies – published news from around the archipelago, farther afield in Asia, Europe, and North America. Europe's wars and colonial conquests, new inventions, the revival of Meiji Japan, the Boxer Rebellion, and much else was reported in these papers, dramatically broadening the horizons of those who read them. Books were also published, including classical works formerly available only in manuscript, some travel accounts, school books, and so on; not until the twentieth century, however, did Indonesia see the emergence of that characteristically modern literary form, the novel.

Literacy was still very limited. The colonial government began to establish indigenous-language schools for the elite from mid-century. Christian mission schools also began to spread, as did local Islamic schools, discussed below. We have no reliable literacy figures for the nineteenth century, but we do know that in the 1930 census – after several decades of effort by Islamic, Christian, government, and other schools – the literacy rate in indigenous languages across Indonesia was only 7.4 percent. The literacy rate in Dutch was only 0.3 percent, for the Dutch had never made it a priority to teach their language to Indonesians. This contrasted dramatically with the Americans in the twentieth-century Philippines, where more than a quarter of the population could speak English by 1939.

In nineteenth-century Indonesia, it was not only European modernity and Western styles that were embraced, for an elite inspired by Islam was also strengthening. In Java, the Cultivation System rested upon compulsory labor, but there were also opportunities for indigenous entrepreneurs in such fields as transport, shipping, fishing, entertainment, smithing, bricklaying, provision of goods such as gunny-sacks, textiles and pottery, and so on. The 'Liberal' period after 1870 encouraged wage labor as a matter of policy. A census taken in Java in 1900 reported that 16 percent of working males worked exclusively in non-agricultural tasks as officials, schoolteachers, professional religious, traders, fishermen, factory workers, craftsmen, carters and shippers, and so on, while another 15 percent were partly so employed. This census did not include women, who have long been prominent among traders in Java. Thus emerged a Javanese commercial middle class, who often had connections with Arab trading communities in the coastal cities. The Arabs included supporters of Middle Eastern Islamic reform movements. Still more importantly, this Javanese middle class could afford the pilgrimage to Mecca and there encountered reformism first-hand. In the outer islands, too, commercial opportunities allowed the growth of an indigenous Islamic middle class.

Pilgrimage traffic from Indonesia to the Middle East grew dramatically from mid-century. It was enhanced by the opening of the Suez Canal in 1869 and the spread of steam-shipping around the same time, making travel to the Arabian Peninsula easier and faster. While colonial statistics are not entirely reliable, it seems that in the 1850s on average 1600 *hajis* (pilgrims) left Indonesia for Mecca every year. In the 1870s this figure had risen to 2600, in the 1880s to 4600, and by the turn of the century to more than 7000. Of course many of these *hajis* came home with their religious obligations fulfilled, but with no more reformist ideas than they had left with. But many did return with reformist ideas and thus sparked a movement for more fastidious observation of Islam's requirements. This reform movement was reflected in the explosion of Islamic schools. Again, colonial figures are not entirely reliable, but reportedly in 1862 there were 94,000 Islamic religious students in Java, whereas there were more than 162,000 a decade after that. In 1893 there were reportedly almost 11,000 religious schools in Javanese-speaking areas with more than 272,000 pupils. While even less reliable data is available for non-Javanese areas, we may be confident that religious schools also spread there. Many of these schools taught little more than reading the *Qur'an* by rote, but others promoted reform and condemned local practices that had long been part of Indonesian Islamic life. More orthodox versions of Islamic mysticism (Sufism) also spread in Indonesia in this time. Some leaders of anti-colonial uprisings were from these Sufi organizations.

Islamic reform did not, however, win over all Indonesians. The administrative elite who worked with the Dutch knew that an overtly pious Islamic life, especially if it included hints of disaffection with *kafir* (infidel) rule, could bring a bureaucratic career to a rapid halt. Thus there was little obvious religious piety among this elite. At the level of their innermost beliefs, there may indeed have been an attenuation of their religiosity. It seems likely that the steamships, telegraph, photography, railways, electric lighting, and so on of Western modernity attracted many of these elite more than the sober pieties of Middle East reform movements.

In Java, many villagers – the majority, it seems – evidently concluded that if the reformed message they were receiving from *hajis*, religious teachers, and Arab traders represented what proper Islam was, then they were less interested in the faith. This group was castigated as the *abangan* by the pious, meaning the red or brown people. This may have referred to the color of their clothing or their betel-nut-stained teeth, but in any case it was a way of differentiating them from the pious 'white ones' (*putihan*, in more recent times commonly called *santri*). These *abangan* evidently began to attenuate their commitment to Islam and their observation of Islamic ritual, so that daily prayer, the observation of the fasting month, and so on became rare among *abangan* nominal Muslims. These *abangan* first begin to appear in historical sources from the

1850s. By the end of the century, Muslim Javanese were thus polarizing along lines of religious identity: nominal *abangan* versus pious *putihan/santri*. In the twentieth century, these divisions would become dangerously politicized, and eventually bloodily so.

For the first time, Christianity also spread among the Javanese. The VOC had not allowed proselytization among Muslims for fear of arousing local animosities. The Netherlands colonial authority only did so from the middle years of the nineteenth century. Among Muslims, however, European missions had very little success, mainly because their version of Protestant Christianity was not unlike the Muslim reformers' version of their faith in rejecting many local cultural practices. Now, however, there arose charismatic Indo-European and Javanese preachers who combined Christianity with Javanese culture and thereby won converts. The converts were few in number, probably totaling only about 20,000 in Central and East Java in 1900 (only 0.1 percent of Javanese), but they represented a further element in the polarization of Javanese along lines of religious identity, one that would grow in the twentieth century.

The Philippines

The economic developments of the nineteenth century boosted traditionally dominant classes and propelled socially upward both *mestizos* and Chinese. The sources of wealth and its distribution were monopolized by aristocratic families, including creole patriarchs and a host of provincial elites. These people became embroiled in politics, thereby taking part in establishing what would become the Philippine nation, and many of the same families remain influential today. Among the affluent, those who most contributed to unravelling the colonial order were the *mestizos* and Chinese. Ironically these *nouveaux riches* actually desired to be accepted; they embraced integration and adopted a more sophisticated form of Hispanization. During the Spanish occupation the proximity of residential houses to the plaza indicated social prestige. From 1820 to 1870 this arrangement became undone as *mestizos* and Chinese replaced their palm thatch-and-bamboo dwellings at the outskirts with two-storey stone and brick houses like those of the colonizers and local elite. Instead of indicating Spanish or local aristocratic pedigree, such edifices now became indices of new wealth. Other buildings in and around the plaza were also refurbished; tobacco monopoly profits paid for the renovation of town halls.

The *nouveaux riches* who lived in the suburbs brought about the flowering of such areas. Binondo, for example, was part of the old *Parián*. It now hosted imposing structures and expensive shops, serving as home to wealthy Catholic Chinese and their *mestizo* offspring. In their houses they proudly displayed luxurious interior fittings like mirrors, pianos, and imported furniture. *Mestizos* also displayed their newly acquired wealth in dress: men sported knee-length 'Chinese shirts', suspended gold chains around their necks, and wore European hats, shoes and stockings, while women paraded in their '*mestiza* dress', which combined Spanish and *Indio* styles of clothing. Like the *principalía, mestizos* only used the best-quality blouses, shirts, and handkerchiefs.

In 1863, the government decreed the establishment of and compulsory attendance at primary schools in all *pueblos*. Public school buildings grew from 640 in 1866 to 1500 in 1898. Nevertheless, this was still an inadequate number. The affluent province of Bulacan only had a handful of schools, whereas it needed over a hundred. Attendance was also not free; except for the poorest children, everyone paid tuition. Contrary to the ambitious decree, then, education remained a privilege of the wealthy and the authorities appeared to be concerned only with that level of society. In 1865 the government established a normal school to train Filipino teachers for primary schools. The government also approved the foundation of the Jesuit *Ateneo Municipal* which offered higher instruction in the classics and sciences. The *Ateneo*, along with the University of Santo Tomas and *San Juan de Letran*, reinforced the place of Manila as the archipelago's center of learning. From 1861 to 1898, some 40,000 rich children, irrespective of ethnicity, flocked to and rubbed shoulders in the city; these constituted the new intellectual elite, the *Ilustrados*.

Having thrived on liberal *laissez-faire* economics, *Ilustrados* tenaciously held liberal political views. They patronized liberal Spanish-language newspapers like *El Eco Filipino*, which supported the secularization campaign and other colonial reforms. The conservative Izquierdo government, and especially the clergy, considered them a threat. As noted above, after the 1872 Cavite mutiny, in addition to priests and soldiers the government convicted members of the elite for complicity. Several prominent lawyers were exiled to the Marianas. These developments forced members of the elite to choose: they must either comply with, or flee from, the Spanish colonial regime.

The opening of the Suez Canal and subsequently of a monthly steamship link between Manila and Barcelona in 1869 gave new opportunities to the rich. *Principalía* and *mestizo* youths who wanted to study European medicine, law, visual arts, engineering, and industries sailed for Madrid and Barcelona or other European cities. Having been raised in an atmosphere of suppression, these students – aged between 17 and 28 – revelled in the free atmosphere of Spain. They led expensive lifestyles, attended parties, and socialized with the powerful in the metropole. They worked to be better Spaniards and to become ideal renaissance men – multilingual and accomplished in multiple disciplines and in the arts.

Their efforts brought about a flowering of Filipino arts and sciences abroad. From 1880 to 1895 they excelled, bringing out essays, pamphlets, and books. In 1880 Pedro Paterno published *Sampaguitas y poesías varias* (*Sampaguitas and Other Poems*), a book of romantic poetry on the Philippines and its inhabitants. A year later Gregorio Sanciano wrote *El progreso de Filipinas* (*The Progress of the Philippines*) which argued for economic reforms to stimulate progress in the colony. In the 1884 World Exposition Juan Luna won the gold medal for his painting *Spoliarium* while Felix Resurrecion Hidalgo received the silver for his *Las virgenes cristianas expuestas al populacion* (*The Christian Virgins Exposed to the Populace*).

That these students were ethnically diverse – Tagalogs, Ilonggos, Cebuanos, Ilocanos, Bicolanos, Pampangos, *mestizos*, *criollos* – hardly mattered. They formed a community of exiles. They shared a love for their native land which, they agreed, remained backwards because of corrupt Spanish officials and self-serving friars. With the more politicized at the helm, these expatriates lobbied for colonial reforms. Accomplished members Rizal, del Pilar, and Jaena envisaged a liberal and fully assimilated colony, privileged with rights that every Spanish province enjoyed. Their campaign failed. As noted above, Rizal returned to the Philippines in 1892, but he was first exiled to the south and then executed in 1896. The foremost martyr of the Philippine Revolution was thereby created. Del Pilar and Jaena died, sick and poverty-stricken, in Barcelona. Members of the community went their separate ways.

The efforts of the *Ilustrados* were not lost at home. Their scholarly successes enhanced their social prestige. Upon return they served as cultural brokers who propagated a '*mestizo* culture' – a hybrid lifestyle that combined urban Hispanization, liberal ideas from northern Europe, and a dose of traditional Filipino values. Journalism took off, novels and poetry flourished, and dramas and comedies became more prevalent. Manila and its environs became dotted with theaters. The elite adopted this new culture and worldview. They led a conservative and complicit existence, aiming to maintain their socio-economic position so as to continue patronizing literature and art.

Some *Ilustrados*, however, remained committed to political activities and writings. They sustained organizations like the *Comité de Propaganda* (Committee of Propaganda, 1888), *La Liga Filipina* (The Philippines League, 1892) and *Cuerpo de Compromisarios* (Corps of the Committed, 1893) that spread nationalist sentiments and campaigned for reforms of colonial institutions and relationships. But they did not support either rebellion or the rapidly growing *Katipunan* (discussed below). Reform-minded *Ilustrados* gathered to discuss liberal ideas and the evils of friar rule as much as they talked about the latest European fashion and the most recent *zarzuela* (local musical drama). Their immediate concern was how to get appointed to positions in the colonial bureaucracy which were reserved for, but not in fact occupied by, Spaniards.

At lower levels of society, peasants whose lives had been dislocated by economic developments retaliated by violating the law. From 1865 to 1885 they comprised 50 to 60 percent of those accused of committing the crimes of flight, vagrancy, smuggling, banditry, and murder. In Cavite and Camarines Sur, discontented farmers retreated to the mountains and formed gangs that attacked affluent households in *poblaciónes*. In *cabecerías*, voices of dissent also prevailed. Lower-class women worked 11- or 12-hour days for the most meager salaries. In the late nineteenth century, cigar makers, peddlers, embroiderers, and seamstresses petitioned for justice and staged sit-down strikes to demand wage increases and better working conditions.

Rural peasants and laborers found allies among the urban middle sector of petty employees and professionals. Exposure to liberal ideas and association with Europeans in the workplace made them slightly more politicized than their provincial compatriots. In and around Manila, issues of justice and equality dominated clandestine meetings associated with Masonic lodges. *Propaganda* materials, especially Rizal's writings, were translated and read in these gatherings. In 1892, Deodato Arellano, Andres Bonifacio, Valentin Diaz, Ladislao Diwa, and Teodoro Plata among others established the *Kataastaasan*

Kagalang-galangang Katipunan nang manga Anak nang Bayan (Greatest Most Revered Union of the Children of the Nation), a Tagalog name usually abbreviated to *Katipunan*. They entered into a blood compact, signing membership papers in their own blood and swearing to recruit more members to secret cells.

Some Masonic practices like initiation rites and symbolic names characterized the *Katipunan*. 'Father of the Revolution' Bonifacio was known as *May pag-asa* (Hopeful) while the 'Brains of the Revolution', Emilio Jacinto, was *Pingkian* (Battle). *Katipunan* aimed to stimulate nationalist sentiments and redeem the Filipino race from the tyranny of Spain and religious despotism. Its teachings concerning liberty, patriotism, and equality were expressed in Tagalog verse and prose. *Katipuneros* believed that a man's nobility did not come from his race or wealth, but from his character and honor. Nor did it did spring from oppressing or helping to oppress others, but from loving his motherland.

The organization's membership only rose when Bonifacio took over recruitment in 1895 and the newsletter *Kalayaan* ('Freedom') came out. Councils were established in towns, then at the provincial level. To forestall wives' suspicions about their men's nocturnal meetings, women were also accepted in the organization. The Katipunan ballooned from 15,000 to 30,000. In July 1896, however, the organization was betrayed to a priest in confession. The authorities thereupon raided a printing shop where they found printing blocks for the *Kalayaan,* other paraphernalia, and a list of members. The *Guardia Civil* then arrested suspects, who were forced to identify other members.

In August 1896, under Bonifacio's leadership, the *Katipuneros* decided to start the Revolution by seizing Manila. To break their ties with Spain they tore up their identification papers and shouted *Mabuhay ang mga anak ng Bayan!* ('Long live the children of the nation!'). The assault failed, and expected reinforcements from Cavite never arrived. Bonifacio and other survivors retreated to the southern mountains, but news of the assault mobilized *Katipuneros* in Nueva Ecija and Bulacan to take up arms. *Katipuneros* of the two bickering councils of Cavite – *Magdalo* and *Magdiwang* – easily captured Cavite province. Landowner Emilio Aguinaldo, the *Magdalo* head, earned renown as a general, but *Magdalo* towns fell to the Spaniards, endangering the *Magdiwang*-held towns to the rear.

The outbreak of the Philippine Revolution made life more difficult for the Filipino elite. To force them to join the revolutionaries, *Katipuneros* implicated some of them. Among the 4000 whom the Spanish arrested and imprisoned were many *Ilustrados*; some were executed and a number were deported. To escape persecution, others demonstrated their loyalty to the colonial government by donating money to the Spaniards and enrolling their sons as officers in local Spanish militias. But many members of the elite, especially in the provinces, concluded that – as in 1872 – weath, status, and education were ineffective weapons against the declining Spanish empire. Quietly they joined and assumed leadership of various councils of the *Katipunan*. Their *mestizo* culture and *Ilustrado* worldview thereby pervaded and changed the orientation of the organization.

In March 1897 Bonifacio called a general convention in Tejeros (Cavite).

Instead of discussing war plans, the *Magdalo* council there insisted on establishing a government. Bonifacio and other *Magdiwang Katipuneros* were sidelined and Aguinaldo was elected President. His election reflected the elite takeover of the Revolutionary leadership. A *Magdalo* questioned Bonifacio's credibility; infuriated, Bonifacio declared the elected government invalid. He and his brother were later hunted down and summarily killed by Aguinaldo's henchmen. Meanwhile Governor-General Primo de Rivera and his forces steadily regained territories held by Filipinos. By June, Aguinaldo and numerous other leaders had to retreat northwards. An accomplished politician, Aguinaldo signed the armistice of Biak-na-Bato in December and agreed to leave for Hong Kong in exchange for amnesty and remuneration. Peace was brief.

In February 1898, in the midst of the Cuban revolution against Spain, the *USS Maine* blew up in Havana harbor. The United States blamed Spain and declared war. In the Philippines, Commodore George Dewey destroyed the Spanish fleet in Manila Bay in May. Aguinaldo now returned home to lead the renewed Revolution. With Spanish defeat looking inevitable, the upper class supported the fledgling Philippine Republic. Aguinaldo responded by appointing only wealthy and eminent professionals to his cabinet. Provincial elites comprised the 138 members of the constitutional assembly, which was presided over by Pedro Paterno.

On 12 June 1898, Aguinaldo declared the islands independent. This was the first colonial state in Southeast Asia to declare its independence – and the last in the Spanish Empire to do so. The republic formally declared at Malolos the following January, however, would soon be destroyed by the new colonial power, the United States. In December 1898 Spain ceded the Philippines to the United States for USD 20,000,000. War ensued between Filipino and American forces. The latter were clearly more powerful; steadily they pushed Filipino fighters deeper into the mountains of northern Luzon. Aguinaldo's elite allies soon surrendered. In March 1901 the Americans captured Aguinaldo himself. Peace was declared, but resistance by Filipino guerillas continued until 1913.

The outbreak of hostilities between Filipinos and Americans divided the *Ilustrados*. Those like the indomitable paraplegic Apolinario Mabini, who believed in the Revolution, defied the Americans. Others who had seized municipal power and feared restored control from Manila also resisted American rule. But most of the elite chose to take their chances with the new regime, which they saw as an opportunity to gain the positions that they had always craved in the government. They were correct. The Americans won the cooperation of the 'better class' by establishing a political system that rested upon elite participation. Education was the most important qualification for taking part in politics; in 1907 the educated elite dominated the American-sponsored Philippine Assembly.

The exceptional case of Thailand

While the rest of Southeast Asia fell under colonial rule, Thailand (or Siam, as it was then known) remained unconquered. Present-day Thai people point proudly to their country's status as the only part of the region which was never colonized. Having said that, however, it cannot be denied that Siam was deeply impacted by the Western powers, both externally and internally. The amount of territory ruled directly or indirectly from Bangkok shrunk drastically thanks to a series of treaties with the British and French. Western economic interests became prominent in the country, and by the latter part of the nineteenth century Western advisors were scattered throughout the government. The country's political, social, and economic structures underwent substantial changes in response to the Western presence.

In Burma, Malaya, Indochina and Indonesia, colonization progressed in stages in the nineteenth century as set out above, as it did in an earlier period in the Philippines. Consequently we can draw chronological boundaries between the 'pre-colonial' and 'colonial' periods of such histories. In Siam's case the issues are more complex. Most students of Thai history have generally taken the 1850s as a watershed because of two key events: the accession to the throne of King Mongkut (Rama IV, r. 1851–68) and the Bowring Treaty signed with Britain in 1855. This decade would thus effectively mark the transition from 'traditional' or 'pre-modern' Siam to the period of 'modern' history which resulted from the direct and indirect consequences of these events.

In this book we adopt such a periodization by discussing the Early Bangkok period together with the pre-colonial Southeast Asian kingdoms, while examining post-1850 developments in this section devoted to the early colonial period. It should not be inferred from this arrangement, however, that the 1850s mark as dramatic a watershed in Thai history as did colonization elsewhere in the region. On the one hand, there were certain fundamental continuities in Siamese society linking the first and second halves of the nineteenth century. On the other hand, the transformations which did occur under Mongkut and Chulalongkorn (Rama V, r. 1868–1910) were not wholly a response or reaction to heightened contact with the West, for to some extent they had roots in earlier reigns.

Mongkut's succession in 1851 brought to power a king with a sophisticated understanding of the West, who interacted comfortably with missionaries and envoys. His familiarity with Western culture set the tone for the ruling elite in his reign and that of his son Chulalongkorn, leading to a 'permanent Westernization' of the Thai ruling class comparable to that which occurred under colonial rule elsewhere in Southeast Asia. The 1855 Bowring Treaty, while not in fact such a powerful catalyst for economic change as has sometimes been claimed, did provide a major incentive for restructuring the economy as well as the social and political systems with which the economy was interwoven. The treaty helped to level the playing field for Western merchants by reducing taxes and duties on them and by drastically limiting the traditionally dominant role of the Siamese state in foreign trade. Siam became integrated into the regional and global economy to the same extent as its colonized neighbors, with a similar mixture of positive and negative results.

Siam and the West: Mongkut, Chulalongkorn, and the elite

The story of a country's elite is not equivalent to the story of its people as a whole; in nineteenth-century Southeast Asia, however, the elite were particularly significant in at least two ways. First, it was they who were most directly confronted by the political and diplomatic challenges of the West. Second, as Western influences penetrated these countries, it generally spread first among the elite. These observations apply to the Siamese ruling class as much as to their counterparts in their colonized neighbors. While a degree of Westernization became the most significant and most visible cultural transformation taking place in Southeast Asian societies in the nineteenth century, in Siam's case it was not the only such change. The Early Bangkok period, despite the social and political continuities with late Ayutthaya, had already seen the flourishing of cultural forms which had been rare or even non-existent in the eighteenth century. As Thai historian Nidhi Eoseewong has shown, there was greater interaction between the (elite) court and (popular) folk cultures, as well as a strong interest in translations of literature from foreign – but non-Western – sources. This cosmopolitanism and cultural diversification arguably made the ruling class, at least, more open to learning from the West than was the case in, say, Mandalay, Hue, or the Balinese court of Klungkung.

Mongkut, as mentioned in the previous chapter, spent more than a quarter-century in the monkhood before taking the throne in 1851. As a high-ranking prince, he maintained his ties to court culture while simultaneously devoting himself to the study of Buddhism. The Western presence in the Third Reign was still relatively small, but Mongkut made the most of it and actively pursued friendships with Catholic and Protestant missionaries of various nationalities. Proficient in English and Latin as well as several Asian languages, he developed a powerful intellectual curiosity towards Western culture and ideas.

Mongkut's image outside Thailand, for better or for worse, has been shaped by Hollywood, particularly the rather eccentric figure portrayed by Yul Brynner in *The King and I*. His English may have been somewhat erratic, but as a person he was not, and the importance of a future – and then reigning – monarch who could meet Westerners largely on their own terms and in their own language should not be underestimated. Spiritually speaking, Western culture held little attraction for Mongkut, and he was rather dismissive of Christian doctrine. The West had many other things to offer, however, and he took a strong interest in science and technology, particularly astronomy. Moreover, the presence of this foreign religion – and particularly missionary Protestantism, which had not existed in Siam before the Early Bangkok period – encouraged him to take a hard look at the state of Siamese Buddhism, and much of what he saw dissatisfied him. During his time in the monkhood he founded a new reformist sect known as Thammayut, which emphasized personal devotion and meditation, the elimination of more 'superstitious' and less 'rational' Buddhist practices, and a generally more intellectual approach to religion.

Mongkut's interest in the West had a strong element of pragmatism. By the time he became king, Burma had lost a war to the British and was about to lose a second. Britain's diplomatic, military, and economic profile in the region was on the rise. Mongkut and a small group of elite men who shared his intellectual outlook now faced the challenge of navigating Siam through the increasingly troubled waters of Southeast Asian geopolitics. The Bowring Treaty was the first hurdle, and it is generally acknowledged that they cleared it successfully.

Mongkut recognized that the need for Siamese who were equipped to deal with the West could only increase, so he took the important step of bringing in a handful of foreign teachers to educate selected royal and noble children. Anna Leonowens, whose reminiscences were the inspiration for *The King and I* and *Anna and the King*, was one of them, though she was almost certainly less influential – and perhaps less charming – than her film avatars Irene Dunne, Deborah Kerr, or Jodie Foster.

Chulalongkorn, Mongkut's son, took the next logical step, which was to send Siamese abroad for education. Many high-ranking princes – including his younger brothers and later his sons – went abroad as boys and spent several years in Europe. The privilege was gradually extended to other members of the elite as well, often through government scholarships. England was the preferred destination; some young men went to Germany, Russia, and Denmark as well. Countries ruled by monarchies were considered more desirable, and only a chosen few studied in republican France or the United States. Most of the princes spent some time in the military in the country where they studied, and a few served in European royal courts.

There were several motives for the decision to make this large-scale investment in educating young Siamese abroad. The most important was to ensure a critical mass of Western-educated elites who would be able to govern the country and to deal effectively with the European powers. Japan and America, although on the rise during his reign, were still of less immediate importance to Siam than the Europeans, particularly the British and French. A second objective of Chulalongkorn's was to train enough of his family members to eventually achieve a government almost completely dominated by princes; more will be said about this below. Finally, Siam was anxious to be accepted by the European royal houses and governments as a peer worthy of respect.

This preoccupation with Siam's image in foreign eyes was arguably the most salient aspect of the elite's relations with the West. The Siamese ruling class had followed closely the expansion of Western diplomatic and military influence in Asia. It had not escaped their attention that their neighbors (including China) were at their most vulnerable when they were internally weak and when they were unable to cope with Western diplomacy on its own terms. The Siamese were determined to ensure as much as possible that the Europeans would not view them as backward or primitive and that their internal governance would give no pretext for intervention, whether as 'protection' or punishment. This preoccupation had begun to form in Mongkut's time but became much stronger in his son's generation, and on several occasions Chulalongkorn explicitly stated that Siam needed to eliminate its more 'backward' aspects in order to forestall outside intervention in its affairs.

The attitude of the Siamese elite in this respect was complex and reflected some of the same contradictions found among colonized Southeast Asians elsewhere. On the one hand, they were proud of their country's long history and rich culture, and few if any Siamese were prepared to completely jettison their heritage to become like *Farang* (the generic term for Westerners). At the same time, however, the West was clearly associated with 'progress' and being 'modern' – two concepts which only really entered the Siamese worldview in the nineteenth century. The frequently articulated ambition of many Siamese was to be seen as 'civilized'; they used the English word (which they pronounced *siwilai*), and they defined it by purely Western criteria. The more Siam was perceived as *siwilai*, the more it would be able to hold its own in its dealings with the West.

Being *siwilai* did not include adopting Christianity. Missionaries generally made little headway among Theravada Buddhists – just as elsewhere in Southeast Asia they made little progress among Muslims – and generations of young Siamese attended mission-run schools without converting. Siamese who studied overseas brought back elements of Western intellectual currents of various kinds, but their spirituality generally remained Buddhist. For many Siamese, *siwilai* was defined most prominently in terms of material culture. Maurizio Peleggi has shown in particular how the royal family and other members of the ruling class sought to represent themselves as cultured and sophisticated through their familiarity with Western cuisine and dress and their acquisition of Western art. Those who returned from Europe were effectively bilingual and bicultural, mixing English or French words in with their Thai and adopting many cultural elements of an upper-class Western lifestyle.

The Bowring Treaty and economic change

As the previous chapter made clear, significant processes of social and economic change were well under way even before the signing of the Bowring Treaty in 1855. In many respects this treaty, and subsequent agreements signed with other Western powers, accelerated the ongoing changes more than they acted as a catalyst for new ones. It was certainly not a case of a 'closed' country suddenly being forced to open its doors to 'free trade', nor was there a sudden transformation from a static economy to a dynamic one. It cannot be argued either that Siam fell prey to Western economic interests, although the latter did come to play a more important role than before, especially in the area of teak-logging in the North.

Perhaps the most significant consequence of the Bowring Treaty was that it acted as a stimulus to the export economy and more particularly to the commodification of rice. During the second half of the nineteenth century, rice shifted from being something grown primarily for the subsistence of the Siamese themselves to become a major commodity for export. Peasants had a motivation to produce more rice and large areas of land in the central region – particularly in the Chao Phraya river valley – were cleared and converted to rice fields. In the process, land itself became more valuable and land ownership gradually became a source of revenue and wealth, all the more so as the importance of possessing manpower faded. The government promoted the digging of extensive networks of canals for both transportation and irrigation. This activity encouraged the cultivation of rice and the movement of goods between markets, but it also directly enriched the elite who were able to become landowners and landlords. Most peasants had adequate land to farm on, but they often had to rent it as tenants rather than owning it themselves.

The expansion of rice cultivation also provided new opportunities for the

Chinese to consolidate their role in the Siamese economy, both as merchants and as the owners and operators of rice mills. They also contributed significantly to the growth of the tin-mining industry in the southern provinces, although in this area – as in colonial Malaya – they faced more significant competition from Western companies. The most powerful Chinese in Siam continued to be those who held noble titles and functioned within the system, but the ongoing economic transformation brought lucrative financial opportunities that went beyond traditional tax farming. Chinese economic power far exceeded that of the Western companies operating in Siam. It was the treaties signed with the West which helped to further economic structural change, but it was the Siamese elite and the Chinese who reaped most of the profits. To achieve this, however, the ruling class in general and the royal family in particular had to ensure that a significant share of the revenue from land and trade would flow into their own hands: the restructuring of the Siamese government under Chulalongkorn was one of the key strategies for realizing this objective.

Chulalongkorn's reform agenda

If Mongkut was responsible for beginning Siam's intellectual and cultural reorientation, his son is credited with transforming its political, administrative, and social structures. In order to understand what Chulalongkorn accomplished, we must first have a sense of the difficulties and challenges – both internal and external – which shaped his agenda. He was an intelligent and in many ways visionary monarch who deserves his reputation as one of Thailand's greatest kings. At the same time, however, he was driven by specific concerns not only for his country's interests, but also for his own and those of his family.

The reforms of Chulalongkorn's reign have traditionally been explained primarily as a response to external pressure from the Western threat. As we have seen, the French were already establishing their influence in Cambodia in Mongkut's time, and their presence there, as well as in Vietnam, meant that Siam now faced an ambitious and aggressive colonial neighbor to its east. The northeastern region was particularly vulnerable as the French began to assert that they had inherited Vietnamese suzerainty over the Lao regions, a claim which could theoretically be extended to the west bank of the Mekong. The north, although less explicitly threatened, nevertheless bordered on British Burma and contained vast teak forests which would be a tempting prize to a foreign conqueror. Finally, in the Malay peninsula, the Anglo-Siamese rivalry continued as British influence expanded. Even before the 1893 Paknam gunboat incident and the consequent cession of territory to the French, Bangkok had good reason to be anxious about the strength of its authority over these geographically peripheral areas. Particularly important was the fact that these regions were mostly inhabited by non-Siamese, which made them potential targets for manipulation and separation if a Western power chose to intervene.

The external threat, then, was very real. At the same time, however, Chulalongkorn was preoccupied with other social and political issues which were very much internal and had little or no connection to outsiders. It is important to appreciate the very significant differences between the early years of his reign and those of Mongkut's. Mongkut, although having been bypassed in favor of his half-brother in 1824, had a quarter-century to consolidate his personal influence and contemplate his future on the throne. His authority as king was not unchallenged; his main rivals came from one of the noble families, the Bunnag, who had become very powerful and held several key positions within the government. He had a brother, Chudamani, who shared his taste for Western ideas and culture but also his aspirations to power, and this 'Second King' (as he was known to foreigners) was also a potential rival. Generally speaking, neither of these forces proved to be a serious challenge for Mongkut as an adult ruler, but when he died of malaria, leaving 15-year-old Chulalongkorn as his most likely successor, the balance of power shifted considerably.

During Chulalongkorn's early years as king, government affairs were dominated by the powerful regent Chuang Bunnag, who supported the boy's succession but used his position to further consolidate the strength of his own family at the expense of the young ruler. Chuang also managed to appoint Prince Wichaichan, the son of Mongkut's 'Second King' (the latter having predeceased his brother), as heir to the throne. Thus Chulalongkorn was faced with an older, ambitious cousin allied with powerful nobles. As he grew to adulthood, he became determined not only to strengthen his own authority *vis-à-vis* that of his 'Second King', but also to reverse the balance of power between royals and nobles within the government. This balance had been more stable during the earlier reigns, but by Chulalongkorn's time the dominance of the nobility in general and the Bunnag in particular was near-complete. Given Ayutthaya's long history of power struggles between the two groups of elite and the reality that it only took a palace coup to replace a king with another prince or even with a noble, the young king was only too conscious of the weakness of his position.

By the early 1870s, Chulalongkorn had assembled a kind of faction of like-minded young princes and nobles who felt the need for change. The system of government which he had inherited from his father was largely that of the Early Bangkok period – and indeed, in many respects, that of Ayutthaya as well. It was structured around a few key ministries whose respective functions and spheres of influence were not clearly defined, and since Mongkut's reign these offices had been the main power base for the Bunnag family. Even upon reaching his majority, Chulalongkorn did not feel ready to tackle directly the existing power structure, but he did experiment with a new 'Privy Council' and 'Council of State' (using the English terms) which he packed with his young supporters as a potential counterweight to the influence of Chuang and the rest of the old guard. He also attempted some initial reforms in the way the government functioned, aiming for greater efficiency and transparency.

Not surprisingly, the series of challenges from the king and his 'upstart' peers provoked serious resentment among the well-entrenched senior princes and nobles. Matters came to a head in 1874–75 when some of the king's faction attempted to dislodge Prince Wichaichan from his position as heir. There was a direct confrontation between soldiers loyal to Chulalongkorn and those under the Second King's authority, and various British and French diplomats inside and outside the country became involved as well. The Front Palace Crisis, as it is usually known (after the name of the Second King's residence), was eventually resolved peacefully in the young ruler's favor, but it was arguably the closest thing to a palace coup since the establishment of the dynasty nearly a century earlier, and it dashed cold water on most of his short-term plans for reform. The new councils faded from sight, and he had to bide his time for the next decade until the old guard had passed from the scene.

By the mid-1880s, Chulalongkorn was able to resume his reformist agenda, this time with little substantive resistance. His main objective was to create a government that worked more efficiently and was dominated by princes rather than nobles. As the senior government ministers died or retired, he replaced them with his own brothers. Although this group of princes had not been educated abroad as their younger siblings would be, Chulalongkorn had put considerable time and effort into preparing them for government work. Within the space of a few years, the ratio of royal ministers to their noble counterparts shifted dramatically in favor of the former. At the same time, the king made the crucial decision to reorganize the administration along the lines of a Western-style cabinet, although with himself as the head of government rather than a prime minister; this change was made in 1888. The Siamese government henceforth structurally resembled that of Western monarchies, and the spheres of authority of the various ministries were much more clearly differentiated than had previously been the case.

Chulalongkorn also undertook a fundamental transformation of the country's social structure by dismantling the traditional system of control over manpower based on *naai* and *phrai* (discussed in the previous chapter) as well as various categories of debt bondage and slavery. On the one hand, these reforms can be seen as part of his broader vision for a more 'modern' country in which these older kinds of relationships had now come to be seen as outmoded. On the other, the abolition of the entire *phrai* system effectively cut the legs out from under the nobles, as much of their personal power and revenue had been derived from the men under their individual control. As we have seen, the changes taking place in Siam which made this reform possible predated his reign, but it was Chulalongkorn's personal determination to end the system once and for all that brought about such an important socio-political transformation. From now on, the nobility would be essentially bureaucratic in that their status and their revenue would be earned primarily through government service.

It should be pointed out that the end of the *phrai* system had the same implications for the princes as it did for the nobility. Historically, of course, there had been no shortage of conflicts between royal family members as well as between royals and nobles, and in any such dispute the ability to mobilize manpower was always a key factor. The Chakri dynasty was generally less prone to these problems, and by Chulalongkorn's time, once the Front Palace Crisis of 1874–75 had passed, the king had no real opponents among his relatives. Indeed, one of the striking things about his decades in power was the high degree of family unity. True, he had perhaps helped to draw other princes to him by ensuring that they, like the nobles, would now rely on him for their livelihood through salaries and a system of stipends. At the same time, however, it is clear that he enjoyed widespread support within the royal family, and it was this solidarity and shared vision which enabled him gradually to put into place a monarchy which was genuinely dominated by royals.

If control of manpower became less important, control of land became more so, both because it represented an increasingly significant source of revenue and because it was now seen as national territory. The nineteenth century in Thai history can be seen as one long process of expansion and consolidation by Bangkok over the various *muang* and vassal kingdoms with which it – and Ayutthaya before it – had long, but sometimes loose relationships. The Chakri rulers were unable to prevent the loss of the Malay, Cambodian, and Lao lands within their sphere of influence, but they succeeded in incorporating the remaining territories under their control and, more importantly, in preserving these territories within the permanent national borders which now came into existence through the signing of treaties with the British and French.

This process of administrative consolidation peaked under Chulalongkorn. He and his brother Prince Damrong, who headed the new Interior Ministry created by the restructuring of the 1880s, oversaw the centralization of Bangkok's authority over the northern, northeastern, and southern *muang*. These entities were all transformed into provinces, and the structures of political and economic control were standardized throughout the kingdom. In the north, local ruling families still reigned in their respective *muang*, but they no longer ruled over them. In the northeast and south, Chulalongkorn co-opted some local ruling families into his new system of provincial government and retired others who were replaced by Bangkok-appointed officials.

While the Bangkok-based ruling class saw this process of restructuring as tightening their grip over territory which was already theirs, the perspective at the grassroots was different. Closer incorporation into Siam meant not only the loss of political authority and financial revenue on the part of the local elite, but also a significant dose of Siamese culture. The northern, northeastern and southern regions each had their own language, script and identity. One of Chulalongkorn's key objectives was to promote the use of Central Thai as a means of integration, particularly in the area of Buddhism. Religious authorities in Bangkok imposed Thai-language texts on monks in other regions and clamped down on local traditions and practices which were seen as heterodox and even potentially subversive. Such moves were deeply resented and triggered resistance, notably a rebellion of 'holy men' which broke out on both sides of the Mekong in 1902. This short-lived but violent episode reflected the general uneasiness of Lao who now found themselves under Siamese rule in some places and French rule in others; at the same time, it articulated the dissatisfaction of local political and religious elites with the extension of Bangkok's influence over their world.

Assessing the late nineteenth century in Thailand

There are at least two significantly different narratives of Siam's history during this period. Most Thai see their country as having been somewhat 'victimized' in terms of its territorial losses, but rescued from the threat of colonization by its enlightened and modernizing monarchs. Mongkut and Chulalongkorn are viewed as having skillfully appropriated Western knowledge and culture in sufficient amounts to strengthen and modernize Siam without sacrificing the fundamental core of Thai identity. By meeting the colonial powers on their own terms and modernizing the kingdom's government and infrastructure, the two rulers thus preserved Siam's independence and oversaw its transformation into a full-fledged nation-state.

The opposing perspective is both more contentious and more cynical. In this view the ruling Chakri dynasty essentially sacrificed Siam's economic sovereignty in order to preserve its own power. The programs of reform and modernization are largely seen as having strengthened Bangkok's control over its remaining territory, large portions of which were forcibly absorbed into Siam as its borders were shaped by colonial-era treaties. The key roles played by foreign advisors and Western economic interests were, in this narrative, little different from the colonial regimes established elsewhere in the region, and some scholars argue that Siam was in fact a 'semi-colony' of the West. Such 'modernization' as the country underwent is viewed as having consolidated the traditional 'feudal' socio-political structure rather than transforming it.

As is usually the case with such contending views of the same set of historical developments, each has its merits, and certainly each contributes to our understanding of this period of Thai history. It cannot be denied that Siam had to make significant territorial and economic concessions to the Western powers, particularly the British and French, whose empires it most directly confronted. Nor can we understand the emergence of Siam as a nation-state in the twentieth century without recognizing the extent to which Bangkok engaged in 'internal colonialism' in the nineteenth century, extending its direct political, economic, and even cultural control over regions which had previously been peripheral *vis-à-vis* the core of the kingdom. It is also quite clear that the monarchy and the rest of the ruling class ultimately benefited in terms of both power and profits from the internal and external changes which took place through their interaction with the West. At the same time, however, when we compare Siam's political, economic, and diplomatic situation in the early 1900s with that of any of its immediate neighbors, we must acknowledge that it entered the twentieth century on a much more solid footing and in possession of more of its sovereignty.

In what ways, then, can we compare and contrast Siam in the late nineteenth century with the neighboring Western colonies? One of the most dramatic consequences of colonization was the heightened ability of a colonial power to control and tax the people under its control, and to some extent this was true of the restructured Siamese state as well. By 1900 Bangkok exercised more direct political, administrative, and financial power over its subjects than had been the case a century earlier. Peasants and villages were increasingly subject to the requirements of an impersonal government rather than those of a *naai* controlling his *phrai*. These exactions were not necessarily harsher than before, but they were different in nature and in some ways more alien. This was particularly true for the areas which had been peripheral *muang*, but were now under provincial governments dominated by ethnic Siamese, what we have here described as 'internal colonialism'.

Looking at the elite, in many ways these Westernized Siamese resembled their counterparts in Southeast Asian colonies who had either studied in Europe or at least received a Western education in their home country. One key difference, however, was the fact that when the Siamese elite returned home, they did not face the humiliation of being subordinated to foreigners who were inferior to them in terms of social status and education. By the late nineteenth century the Bangkok government had numerous Western advisors, but they were hired employees, not colonial rulers, and the real power remained in Siamese hands. Siam did have to submit to the humiliations of extraterritoriality, but it was later able to gradually renegotiate these concessions, partly with the help and advice of its foreign advisors. There was also a healthy balance among the various nationalities, so that no one Western country dominated – although the British did enjoy a particularly strong position by virtue of the fact that so many members of the elite had been educated in England. Moreover, as noted above, Western economic interests in Siam were not comparable in strength and influence to those found in colonies, and the most visible 'foreign' elements were Chinese.

This situation had at least two important implications. First, the Siamese ruling class – particularly Chulalongkorn – generally had a great deal of autonomy in exercising and restructuring their authority within their borders. As long as they stayed within the bounds of their treaty obligations – recognizing extraterritoriality and teak concessions being two of the most important – they had a free hand. This meant, however, that such resistance and opposition as did occur was very much directed at the Bangkok government and its local agents. Feelings in the Lao northeast and Malay south were particularly strong and would pose serious challenges to Bangkok's authority after World War II. Moreover, Chulalongkorn's success in creating a government and an army dominated by a powerful royal family would generate its own resentments, which just over two decades after his death would bring down the absolute monarchy.

A second consequence was that when nationalism developed in Siam, it was less clearly anti-Western because it was not explicitly anti-colonial. There was of course resentment at the loss of territory to the British and French, but the Siamese nationalist agenda was driven much more by internal forces, particularly concern over defining what it meant to be 'Thai' and fears about the loyalties of the Chinese community. The concept of the 'nation' (*chat*) became operative during Chulalongkorn's reign, as he sought to build loyalty among his ethnically diverse population of subjects. The Lao became 'Northeastern Thai', the Malays 'Muslim Thai', and so forth, in an attempt to downplay ethnic differences and promote the idea of a single 'Thai' nation under the monarchy. 'Nation, Religion, and King' as a basis for Thai nationalism would be articulated more clearly and consistently under Chulalongkorn's son and successor Vajiravudh (r. 1910–25), but its genesis occurred in the late nineteenth century.

9
Reform, New Ideas and the 1930s Crisis (*c*.1900–1942)

Introduction

By 1900, the main centers of population in Southeast Asia were under colonial rule, with the exception of Siam. In outlying areas there was still some colonial 'mopping up' to be done, but by the second decade of the century most of that was complete, too. New lines were drawn on maps in The Hague, Washington, Paris, and London – older maps were recognized in Lisbon – to show which colonial power governed which part of the region. Many local inhabitants, particularly in the outer reaches of colonial states, did not recognize these externally imposed boundaries or indeed were completely ignorant of them. So some degree of resistance carried on, as did a good deal of what colonial powers regarded as illegal population movements and smuggling across borders. For the majority of colonialized Southeast Asians, however, a new *pax colonialis* reigned and life was significantly altered by the fact of foreign rule.

The Western context, however, was changing. The increasingly democratic politics of Europe and America gave space for anti-imperialist ideas to be heard, along with demands for a more rational, indeed more humane, politics. This hope for change was not always secular in outlook, for Christian-inspired political forces played a role, as they had also in the abolition of slavery in the nineteenth century. Simple suppression and exploitation of colonial subjects became more difficult to justify in Western domestic politics and in the minds of many colonial officers. Indeed, in the United States, President William McKinley could only mollify American anti-imperialist traditions by asserting that the United States found itself in charge of the Philippines unwillingly, but unavoidably, as a consequence of the Spanish-American War and, as a great nation, must discharge its duty to look after its 'little brown brothers' – a paternalistic term used to describe the Filipinos. The United States' subsequent performance in the Philippines – aside from the brutal wars to suppress remaining Filipino resistance – was so radically progressive that other colonial powers viewed it with considerable unease.

Thus it was that reform voices became influential in Southeast Asian colonies and the welfare of their subjects became one of the objects of colonial governments. No great cynicism is needed to recognize that the interests of the metropoles remained paramount. Nevertheless, this change facilitated the growth of anti-colonial and nationalist politics among Southeast Asians, and thus set the stage for – and generated many of the early leaders of – the independent nations that emerged after World War II.

Many of the more optimistic ideas of the early part of the century, however, collapsed when the Great Depression spread across the world from late 1929. A speculative bubble and poor bank regulation in the United States led to the stock market crash of October 1929 and the consequent failure of banks, a drastic decline in world trade as a consequence of protectionism, and thus a truly global economic crisis. In the United States this crisis was a major element in the 1932 election of Franklin D. Roosevelt as President. In Germany, it was a major reason for the Nazi Party's electoral successes and Adolf Hitler becoming Chancellor in 1933. In Southeast Asia, the Great Depression was a time of challenge and hardship. The 1930s experience helped to persuade many Southeast Asians that the only way forward was to eject their colonial rulers altogether, by force if necessary.

Southeast Asia's interdependent economies

British Burma

The transformation of Burma's economy from a traditional subsistence system into an export-oriented, rice-producing economy required a range of administrative and operational changes that fundamentally changed society and significantly altered Burmese perspectives on their community and their place in the world. As discussed in the previous chapter, the need to develop the delta area required significant amounts of labor. Initially many rural cultivators migrated to Lower Burma where jobs and growth provided significant opportunities to improve their daily lives. Communication and transportation improvements facilitated bringing the rice to the ports, simultaneously creating new jobs and opportunities. Between 1852 and the early years of the twentieth century, Burmese farmers who migrated to the delta region could expect a fair return for their surplus produce, allowing them to purchase the finished goods that were being imported through the colonial economy. There was little competition during this period from the Indians who, for the moment, provided nominal financial and labor support, allowing local farmers to enjoy the fruits of the general prosperity. Few Burmese farmers, however, were able to collect enough surplus to invest directly in landownership, as the living costs or the allure of consumerism diverted much of their profit. When most of the available land was brought under cultivation by the first decade of the twentieth century, this relative security for farmers was shattered as competition intensified for what was now a fixed resource, eventually bringing to an end Burmese dominance in the rice industry. Much of this was caused by cultivator debt, which had always been present and rose significantly during the 1930s but was part of the rice industry from the beginning.

In the early stages of the developing rice economy, new farmers acquired equipment through credit and loans provided through personal networks.

Local moneylenders, relatives, friends, and family would often provide them with the funds they needed to get started. Some professionals, such as doctors, lawyers, traders, and retired headmen were also sources of rural credit. In the 1880s, other operators entered the credit business with the influx of Indian Chettiars and larger landowners who often had more resources at their disposal.

When World War I overtook Europe, the impact of German submarine blockades, new priorities for export to Europe, subsequent unemployment, and the rising cost of living were felt across British Burma. There were, however, differences depending on where one was situated. In Lower Burma, rice prices fell by a third over 1915–17 because there was a shortage of shipping to move the crop. Drops in income made payments for renting land increasingly difficult, especially when landlords began calling in loans, fearful that they, too, would lose money due to the dip in the world economy. A rise in taxes did not help the situation either, forcing village headmen and collectors to conspire to avoid making payments. Government efforts to ease tax burdens often came too late, which forced many cultivators back into subsistence farming and fueled the work of urban activists within the rural settings.

Upper Burma had a different experience during the war. Here, farmers were able to adapt by shifting their labor to more profitable pursuits within the agricultural sector, an option less available to their counterparts near the delta. When rice became unprofitable, they switched to cultivating cotton, onions, peppers, sugar, and tobacco, which fetched high prices and were supported by British investment into their production. With life more attractive in the north, communities were once again on the move, as farmers from Lower Burma moved into cities such as Mandalay, Sagaing, and Pakokku.

As the social and economic changes initiated by the colonial state became more entrenched, Burma saw the emergence of new communities based along class, ethnic, and generational lines. Each such group brought its own – often mutually contradictory – interests, concerns, and priorities, making it difficult for both urban and rural authorities to manage the differences among them. Some groups were of indigenous origin. Others, notably Indians, steadily increased in numbers due to the labor needs of the lower Irrawaddy delta's agricultural development. The British need for educated civil servants also contributed to the growth of the Indian population, as qualified candidates immigrated to work in the colonial administration as well as in other sectors of the economy. Internally, these patterns in immigration were complemented by the growth of an urban Burmese middle class that began to emerge out of new commercial opportunities, the greater availability of modern education, and the needs of an expanded administrative state. Middle-class Burmese came to be found mainly working as landowners, traders, or white-collar professionals, such as lawyers and educators.

It was from these sectors that ideas of a national community – one that in theory superseded ethnic, religious, and class lines – began to emerge. Yet in reality there was little to unite these disparate groups in the 1920s, with their experiences that varied according to occupation, status, and place within colonial society. So long as the colonial economy continued to prosper, there were enough incentives as well as security measures in place to hinder the middle class from uniting with other communities on a single political platform. In the 1930s, however, the impact of the Great Depression demonstrated that the socio-economic structures that contributed to colonial Burma's growth were also the very elements that would lead to its decline. The experience of the Depression provided nationalist reformers and activists with a single issue that could unify Burma's varying communities behind a common grievance.

In the rapidly growing rice economy, as land values and the rice prices again increased, so did the demand for loans to finance entry into the industry. In the competition among moneylenders, Indian Chettiars could undercut the interest rates of their rivals. By the 1930s, very few Burmese moneylenders could compete, leaving the Chettiars and other urban-based loan institutions unchallenged in the delta region. Peasant cultivators now sought loans exclusively from these new sources of credit, whose ties to Indian banks and joint-stock companies connected rural villagers to quick and accessible capital, but also to demands and influences that were often beyond their understanding.

Initially the expansion of the rice industry in the lower Irrawaddy delta facilitated the growth of indigenous landowners and cultivators, but by the late 1920s and 1930s, many of these lands had fallen into the hands of urban landlords, whose interest was in renting the rice fields to cultivators for a profit. Official census figures reveal that in 1921, there were 33,000 landowners who were not themselves involved directly in the cultivation of rice. By 1931 this group increased to 39,000 while the numbers of cultivator-owners fell by over 50 percent. These absentee landlords, consisting of moneylenders and other urban commercial interests, owned over half of the most important agricultural lands in the Burma delta. The wealth of a small number of landlords who were often Indians was obvious; this enhanced already existing discontent among local cultivators. Not owning their own lands had disastrous consequences for farmers during the Depression. When the Depression brought about a drop in rice prices in Burma, local cultivators were left with inadequate money to pay their rent or other monthly installments, ending in them losing their access to the land they had farmed.

Many of the problems of rural society had roots dating from before World War I, but it was not until the drastic drop in rice prices of the 1930s, coupled with the growing presence of Indian competitors for land and the oppressive regularity of the capitation (*thathameda*) and land taxes, that the delta region was turned into a potential hot-spot of communal tension and political unrest. The regularity of the colonial collection of taxes contributed to the difficulties of rural communities and raised further resentment among rural activists. The *thathameda* tax had existed before British rule but, like elsewhere in Southeast Asia, the colonial administration applied it more efficiently and systematically, backed up by armed regiments. The land tax and an indirect tax on rice production also drew criticism. The former was set at 10 percent of the cultivator's gross return while the latter was effectively an export duty on the country's rice. Such taxes could amount to 25 to 50 percent of a farmer's net income and, in hard times, could reduce his surplus to almost nothing. The local colonial officer at the village level could grant a reprieve from these taxes, but this rarely occurred, further antagonizing cultivators and compounding their financial burdens.

The more impersonal colonial style of administration had a direct effect on the way in which rural communities regarded the state. Where pre-colonial headmen had once acted as intermediaries between the village and higher authorities, now Rangoon-appointed headmen and District Commissioners were required to impose the government's requirements on the villages. In the hard days of the Depression, sympathetic members of the Burma Legislative Council lobbied the government for amelioration of taxation policies, to little avail. Younger and bolder activists began forming direct links with villages through associations (*athins*) to resist paying taxes. Thus the socio-economic grievances of rural communities facilitated a growing sense of community encompassing urban nationalists, rural activists, and peasant cultivators.

British Malaya

For much of the latter half of the nineteenth and early twentieth centuries, Malaya's dramatic economic expansion was powered primarily by rising external demand for its primary commodities, particularly tin and rubber. But this reliance on tin and rubber as the two main pillars of the Malayan economy proved a liability when international demand fluctuated strongly during the interwar period. The result was two extended periods of economic downturn, first in 1920–22 and then again in 1929–32.

By the early years of the twentieth century, the local tin industry had undergone a technological shift that enabled Malaya to maintain its position as the largest tin producer in the world. With increased capital investment and mechanization through the use of hydraulic power, gravel pumps, and the introduction of the more costly bucket dredge that reached Malaya in 1912, the domination of the industry gradually shifted from Chinese to European hands as the use of more efficient large-scale, capital-intensive methods – which proved beyond the pocket of most Chinese mine-owners – not only allowed the European miners to overcome the former's advantage in opencast mining using their abundant supply of immigrant labor but also permitted the mining of more deeply buried tin ore as the more readily accessible deposits nearer the surface were exhausted. With increased mechanization, the total tin-mining labor force shrunk by some 37 percent, from 198,000 to 122,000 between 1911 and 1920, with the Chinese-held opencast sector shedding the most manpower. Chinese-run mines, which accounted for 90 percent of the FMS's tin output in 1900, saw their share of output decrease to 64 percent by 1920, before dropping to 39 percent in 1929, reflecting the shift in control of the industry to European companies. The increase in tin supply, however, was not matched by a rise in world demand, which indeed declined further as a result of World War I from 1914 to 1918 and the post-war recession that followed from 1920 to 1922. To shore up prices and ensure that marginal mines could stay financially afloat, the British government, in collaboration with Dutch Indies authorities, soaked up excess tin stocks and sold them at a profit when tin prices improved in the mid-1920s.

The rubber industry shared a similar fate. As the global demand for natural rubber grew, stimulated by its use in the production of footwear and bicycle tires, and later the motor car industries, Malaya experienced a rubber boom in the early years of the twentieth century. As prices rose, rubber acreage and output increased as planters, backed by the infusion of overseas capital from joint-stock companies floated in London, invested in the industry and bought and converted plantation land to rubber cultivation. From 1903 to 1912, for example, 260 such joint-stock companies were floated in London through the mediation of British agency houses. As with tin, the influx of overseas European capital specifically for rubber soon eclipsed more diversified Chinese capital investment. The resultant expansion in the industry was noteworthy. While rubber occupied some 109,000 ha (about 270,000 acres) in 1908, the total area had nearly tripled to 322,000 ha (about 800,000 acres) by 1913. Rubber exports also grew from 6500 UK tons (about 7300 US tons) in 1910 to 181,000 UK tons (about 203,000 US tons) by 1920. But as in the case of tin, rubber's ability to reap pioneer profits could not be sustained.

The increase in overall rubber supply was accompanied by a fall in European demand brought about by the loss of markets as a result of World War I. This decline was, however, more than offset by strong demand in the United States, which consumed around 70 percent of the global output of rubber. During the short-lived post-war boom in 1919, as consumer demand outran supply with the switch from military to peacetime production, Malaya's exports nearly doubled over those of 1918. But by 1920, the boom had evaporated and unemployment in the West reached new heights with an influx of demobilized troops returning to the workforce and as governments decided on deflationary policies to check inflation caused by accumulated wartime debts. With manufacturers in the industrialized countries cutting back on output, demand for primary commodities like rubber also dwindled. Malayan planters, on the other hand, who had been expanding production, could not reduce output in the short term, further dampening the market with their surplus stocks and causing the price of rubber to tumble.

Unwilling to allow the rubber price to slide further, given that commodity's key role as a US-dollar earner, the British government in November 1922 implemented the Stevenson restriction scheme (named after its author) to limit the export of rubber and thus to stabilize prices at a 'pivotal' level and ensure a 'reasonable' margin of profit. For the first three years of its adoption, the rubber restriction scheme stabilized supply and even contributed to a boom in 1924–25 as prices hit new highs arising from a sudden surge in American demand. But from 1926 the scheme's ability to manage supply was not as successful. With their share of the world's output reduced to 53 percent because of the restrictions, Britain's comparative advantage was slipping, while planters like the Dutch in Indonesia, who did not participate in the scheme, were free to expand. The harder the British cut back on production, the faster the Dutch planted. On 1 November 1928, Britain decided to lift the restrictions, prompting another surge in Malayan exports in 1929 just as the Great Depression was about to set the economies of the world tumbling again.

After the stock market crash in the United States in October 1929 precipitated the Great Depression, demand for Malaya's primary commodities like rubber and tin nose-dived. With Western industrialists cutting back on production as consumer demand diminished, Malaya was hit especially hard given its reliance on the American manufacturing economy. As the Great Depression also coincided with the abandonment of the Stevenson restriction scheme, with more supply now flooding the market ahead of weakening demand, prices for Malayan rubber tumbled to new lows. To curb excess capacity and stabilize prices, in 1931 the British government imposed export quotas on tin for the first time. Three international agreements to control tin output and exports among the major tin producers that included Malaya, Indonesia, Siam, Nigeria, and Bolivia were set in motion in 1931–33, 1934–36, and 1937–41, during which each of the signatory countries exported tin based on an agreed output quota. After a five-year pause, export quotas were implemented again on rubber, this time with greater international participation, through an International Rubber Regulation Agreement involving the main rubber producers – British-ruled Ceylon, India, and Burma; Dutch-ruled Indonesia; French-ruled Indochina; and Siam – from June 1934 to December 1938, and renewed for another five years until 1943. Not surprisingly, the fixing of export quotas in both tin and rubber to control pricing was severely criticized by the United States which opposed this 'monopolistic' practice by the producing countries. As a result, even as export quotas were fixed, the interest of American manufacturers could not be ignored completely, and an adequate supply at reasonable prices had to be maintained.

Malaya's heavy reliance on tin and rubber as the two mainstays of its export-oriented economy revealed its vulnerability during the two extended periods of economic downturn. As more cultivators switched to the more lucrative export-oriented agriculture, domestic rice production lagged behind, despite increased consumption by the growing labor force employed in the export sectors. Between 1925 and 1929, imported rice accounted for 70 percent of consumption. With its export earnings severely hit by the slumps, the import of foodstuffs, including rice, was drastically affected, with losses on rice purchases, for instance, taking more than a third of Malaya's surplus balance as the government intervened with subsidies to stabilize prices. During the Great Depression, as fluctuating export earnings once again affected imports, the FMS government formed the Rice Cultivation Committee to stimulate greater interest in food production. The limited increase in cultivation, however, could not wean Malaya away from its dependence on imported rice, which still remained above two-thirds of consumption in the 1930s. With capital locked up in tin and rubber, and the limited size of the local market, there was also little movement towards the development of a more diversified import-substitution domestic manufacturing industry, apart from some secondary processing services related to the expansion of the export industries.

As mines and estates ceased operations and shed their labor force, the social ramifications of the Great Depression finally hit home, with unemployment driving thousands of workers to return to China and India. In Perak alone, for instance, there were some 10,000 unemployed Chinese miners in 1930. The Indian population also dwindled: across the whole of Malaya, Indian arrivals decreased from 69,114 in 1930 to 20,242 in 1933, while departures during the same period were 151,735 and 32,738 respectively. Major towns like Singapore and Kuala Lumpur saw an influx of discharged workers from the surrounding areas hoping to find work, aggravating the unemployment situation there and contributing to a rise in crime. The period between 1928 and 1932, for instance, saw a 55 percent increase in crime figures in the FMS, while Singapore, with its floating population, earned for itself the appellation 'Chicago of the East' as a result of its spiraling crime rate. With the recovery of world trade beginning in 1933, Malaya's export earnings, bolstered by higher prices resulting from the controls, also showed an upward trend and more than tripled between 1933 and 1937. The outbreak of war in Europe in 1939 precipitated another rush to build up strategic stocks, boosting the Malayan economy in the process, but the recovery was short-lived. By 1942, Malaya itself was occupied by invading Japanese forces. Its trade ties with the West now severed, Malaya's export-oriented economy, particularly its rubber industry, was plunged deep into its 'years of disaster'.

Indochina

The overall economic impact of colonial rule in French Indochina has been outlined in the previous chapter. The period between the world wars brought economic 'development' in terms of industrial agriculture – notably rubber and rice for export – and infrastructure, but little benefit for most Indochinese. Heavy tax and/or rent burdens and the unceasing cycle of debt and borrowing meant that most families, especially in rural areas, were completely divorced from the 'boom' of the pre-Depression years, as well as from the benefits of infrastructural investment. The Indochinese experience thus had much in common with other areas of Southeast Asia.

When the Depression hit in 1930–31, the most tangible impact was the sharp drop in rice prices. This made it even more difficult for most peasants to make ends meet, since their income dropped even further, while there was little relief from the tax burden imposed by the colonial state. In some parts of the colony, rural areas were reduced to little more than subsistence farming, with families barely growing enough to feed themselves, let alone having anything to sell on the market. While Lao peasants were less directly impacted by the rice market because the glutinous variety they grew was not exported abroad, they were nevertheless squeezed tightly by a government desperate for more revenue during the financial crisis.

Hungry and impoverished peasants proved to be willing recruits for the Indochinese Communist Party (ICP) after it was founded in 1930. A second important source of Party support was the small but potentially militant proletariat created by the establishment of a few factories and, more importantly, large rubber plantations. The plantations were located in the 'Red Earth' areas of central Annam and in eastern Cambodia along the border with Cochin China. The French companies operating these plantations engaged in widespread recruiting (often under false pretenses), bringing workers from Tonkin to Annam and Vietnamese laborers from various regions to Cambodia. Working and living conditions were poor at best and literally murderous at worst, with death rates of up to one-quarter of the workforce in some places. These migrant workers constituted a critical mass of support for the ICP in the 1930s.

As will be discussed below, in Cambodia and Laos the Communist movement was initially successful only among Vietnamese immigrant workers. This is not to say that the rest of the population in these colonies was complacent. In Cambodia the oppressive nature of French taxation sparked a series of (generally) non-violent demonstrations in 1916, and subsequently the murder of a particularly oppressive French official named Bardez in a rural village in 1925. In Laos the economic impact of colonization continued to be felt most keenly in the highland areas inhabited by non-Lao ethnic groups. The double burden of taxation and *corvée* labor and the virtually complete lack of any tangible benefits from colonial rule provoked chronic unrest in various parts of the colony – notably the Boloven highlands in southern Laos – until the eve of World War II.

Like most other colonial systems, the French regime faced a fundamental challenge: how to squeeze enough revenue out of Indochina to make the colony pay for itself and, ideally, turn a profit. Above and beyond the basic costs of running a colonial state, France had to invest a sizable amount of capital into infrastructure, both to facilitate the extraction of resources and to demonstrate that it was ostensibly looking after the welfare of its Indochinese subjects. The Indochinese economy did indeed become profitable for a time, particularly during the 1920s, but most of the profits went to French and Chinese economic interests rather than to Vietnamese, Cambodians, or Lao. Moreover, a considerable degree of state coercion was required not only to collect taxes and mobilize people for work projects, but to enforce the monopolies (salt, alcohol, opium) which helped keep the colonial budget in the black. This coercion obviously generated deep and bitter resentment on the part of those who were subject to it.

The operative term in evaluating the colonial economy and French policies in Indochina is *exploitation*. In French the term can have positive connotations, particularly when it comes to making use of resources which have previously been left largely untouched. This kind of exploitation was one of the main objectives of colonial rule, and it was closely linked to the overarching philosophy of *mise en valeur*, as mentioned in Chapter 8. Marxists, of course, would argue that the pre-colonial kingdoms had been exploitative as well in their appropriation of their subjects' surplus – whether in rice or other agricultural products or, more rarely, in cash – and it is certainly true that earlier kingdoms and empires did impose exactions on their people. Neither taxes nor *corvée* were inventions of the colonial state. The colonial regime's brand of exploitation was, however, different in at least two ways. First, it was generally less flexible, with less room for 'negotiation' by villages or compromise on the part of the government. Second, and perhaps more crucially, it was backed by an obviously foreign power, whose alien nature was in no way masked by the use of local officials, whether they were monarchs or tax collectors. At the same time, there was often less opportunity for flight to another area to escape the exactions in a particular place. In many respects, then, the exploitation inherent in this and other colonial economies was both harsher and more relentless than had previously been the case.

The colonial system thus provided its opponents with a variety of targets: the French rulers, the local elite who supported the colonial system and helped enforce its rules and policies, and the alien Chinese and Vietnamese who became their creditors and their exploiters. In some cases the last of these three groups was the most hated, since many Indochinese would have much more frequent contact with a Chinese moneylender or (in Cambodia and Laos) a Vietnamese merchant or civil servant than with French officials. Although well aware of the potential tensions inherent in the decision to favor immigration from China and Vietnam, the French felt that this was an acceptable risk given the immigrants' ability to stimulate the colonial economy. Over the long run, though, they may have miscalculated. As various forms of nationalism evolved across Indochina, different groups focused their anger on particular components of the colonial socio-economic structure. The more moderate among them advocated only a weakening of the Chinese and Vietnamese economic clout; the most radical, by contrast, sought to eliminate all of the enemies named above and to build a new society with a new economy.

Netherlands East Indies

In 1900 the Dutch regime in Indonesia ruled two different kinds of areas. On the one hand was Java, which was well down the road of colonial experience, with a long history of European involvement and real dominance since 1830, and already much changed by Dutch rule. Javanese society was also conflicted along lines of religious identity, as seen in the preceding chapter, heavily populated, and only able to feed itself with difficulty. In the first two decades of the twentieth century, Java would see the greatest development of revival and anti-colonial movements, as will be discussed below.

On the other hand, the Dutch were still fighting to gain control of many areas in Indonesia's outer islands. In 1900 the war in Aceh was not yet over, the final conquest of Bali had yet to be achieved, and colonial rule remained far from unchallenged in places like Jambi, Mentawai, Banjarmasin, Flores, South and Central Sulawesi, and Papua. Except for Maluku (where Europeans had been involved since the sixteenth century) and some other areas discussed previously in this book, large areas of the outer islands had relatively recent experience of colonial intrusion. They were also often sparsely populated. Minangkabau had experienced the Padri religious reform movement, but other areas were still untouched by religious reform. Of modern political organization there was hardly any sign.

Another crucial difference distinguished Java from the outer islands. The natural resources which would so shape the history of Indonesia in the twentieth century – products needed by the industrializing world such as oil, rubber, and tin – were mostly found in the outer islands. Java remained one of the world's foremost producers of sugar, but its famous coffee – the origin of the American slang phrase 'a cup of Java' – and tea were of declining importance and were soon overtaken in value by outer islands products. By 1930 about 55 percent of Indonesia's exports (by value) came from the outer islands. The majority of Java's 45 percent share of exports consisted of sugar, which was falling in value.

Dutch conquest of the outer islands was partly driven by awareness of the resources to be had there, although the strategic issue – to prevent another imperial power becoming established there – was often more important. As noted in the previous chapter, oil deposits in north Sumatra were known from the 1860s. Drilling began there in the 1880s, with financing from what was to become the first of the great oil multi-nationals: Royal Dutch Shell, formed by the merger of a Dutch and a British company in 1907. Oil was soon discovered elsewhere in Indonesia, including on the north coast of Java, but Java's output was insignificant compared to that of the outer islands. From 1900 Brazilian rubber trees were introduced and a vast rubber plantation industry quickly developed, particularly in the outer islands, with exports beginning in 1912. By 1930 Indonesia produced almost half of the world's rubber supply. This development was not just a matter of Dutch entrepreneurship, for British and other investment was also involved. Local people also profited as long as the boom lasted. Indonesian small-scale producers played a significant role in producing rubber, tobacco, coffee, tea, coconut, pepper, and kapok (a source of fiber sometimes also called 'Java cotton').

This economic development made for new economic relationships. Whereas in pre-colonial times much of the archipelago's trade was carried out within the archipelago itself – as we saw in the case of Melaka in Chapter 5 – now much of Indonesia's trade was with industrialized nations. In 1914, the ratio of inter-island to foreign trade in Indonesia was only 5.5 percent and in 1910 only 10.0 percent. Trading relationships that had once contributed to drawing the vast Indonesian archipelago together into a connected trading community now pulled it apart and redirected its economic connections outwards to other parts of Asia, Europe, and North America. Thus an archipelago that once had limited political coherence, but was connected by economics, became one held together by Dutch political authority, but with fewer economic links. Thereby the Indonesian economy and millions of Indonesians could profit from – but also became dependent upon – world market conditions.

Increasing colonial activity in the outer islands meant a complication for the 'Ethical Policy' proclaimed in 1901 (discussed below). Java's population had the greatest claim to the welfare policies that were the core of the Ethical Policy, but Java was of declining economic value to the colonial regime. The outer islands attracted more interest and investment, and made more money. Taxing the inhabitants of Java to fund welfare programs in their own benefit may have seemed an odd approach, but the alternatives of taxing the money being made in the outer islands or expecting Dutch taxpayers to cover these costs were politically unpalatable. So Javanese and Sundanese often found themselves told what was in their interest, then told to pay for it. After World War I there were serious problems in the colonial budget, so already heavy tax burdens on Indonesians were raised still higher. The colonial government invested in infrastructure projects as a contribution both to economic development and to indigenous welfare. More railways, tramways, port facilities, and telegraph networks encouraged the growth and export of local produce for large-scale enterprises, but also facilitated local employment and local smallholders' economic activity. The government also invested in irrigation works, for irrigated rice is more productive than non-irrigated.

Population growth remained high and influenced all developments. To deal with this growth, the colonial government had to run very hard in order just to stand still. For example, between 1885 and 1930 the area of irrigated rice land increased about 1.8 times, but population grew by about the same multiple. The immense difficulties that population growth imposed for educational policy in particular will be discussed below. In 1930 the total population of Indonesia was 60.7 million, of whom 59.1 million were indigenous Indonesians. Java and Madura, comprising only about 7 percent of the land area of Indonesia, had 40.9 million indigenous inhabitants, or slightly less than 70 percent of the total; they were thus heavily populated and had already become a deficit food area. By contrast, the outer islands, with 18.2 million indigenous inhabitants on about 93 percent of the colony's total land area, were sparsely populated. Both circumstances posed difficulties for a colonial government seeking to raise welfare and to promote economic development. The remaining population in 1930 reflected the extraordinary demographics of European colonialism. There were 1.2 million Chinese plus other 'foreign Orientals'. There were merely 240,000 Europeans – 208,000 of them Dutch. So the Netherlands claimed sovereignty over a vast archipelago of 60.7 million people where only three-tenths of 1 percent of the population was Dutch. The domestic population of the Netherlands itself was only 7.9 million in 1930.

When the Depression came, Indonesia was heavily exposed to international market circumstances and was hard hit. In 1930, 52 percent of Indonesia's exports went to industrialized Europe and North America. As those economies contracted after the crash of October 1929 and protectionism spread, many of Indonesia's exports faced sharply restricted markets. Indeed, for 20 years the Depression, the Japanese occupation and then the Revolution did dreadful damage to Indonesia. The value of Indonesia's exports dropped precipitously. By 1935, they were worth roughly one-third of their 1929 value. Some export industries, notably oil and rubber, expanded to try to make up by volume what they were losing in value, but this offered little amelioration. With the price of rubber in 1932 a mere 16 percent of the 1929 figure, there was no way that industry could shield itself from disaster. Java exported 3 million tons of cane sugar before the Depression hit, but by 1936 it was exporting just one-third of that. Shut out of some of its most important markets by protectionism, the sugar industry reduced the area planted. From some 200,000 ha (approx. 500,000 acres) in 1934, by 1939 the total area of sugar cultivation had dropped to only 90,000 ha (approx. 220,000 acres). This reduced the sugar industry's payments to Indonesians by 90 percent, with a devastating effect on the many Indonesians who relied upon this income. Indonesian small-holders played significant roles in rubber, sugar, coffee, and tobacco production and suffered badly. Many government and private employees were laid off, but that ironically produced benefits for some Indonesians: since Europeans, Indo-Europeans, and Chinese were paid more than Indonesians, they were often the first to go and sometimes were replaced by cheaper Indonesian workers. The salaries of people who kept their jobs were cut, but because prices were falling this could mean a rise in real wages. The price fall was dramatic: taking 1929 prices as an index figure of 100, in 1939 the price index stood at 44.0.

Export revenues fell, imports were reduced and consequently government revenues that depended on taxing these things fell also. The result was a major financial crisis for the colonial government. Programs were axed, ending the expansion of education (discussed below) and much else. As welfare needs increased in Java, government welfare programs were cut back. Islamic organizations such as *Muhammadiyah* (discussed below) did what they could to fill the gaps.

Since 1905, the government had been moving people from heavily populated Java to the outer islands, particularly east and south Sumatra, where population was sparse. This was seen as a way of both supporting economic development in the outer islands and reducing population pressure in Java. The benefits of this resettlement for individuals and their families may have been significant, but the impact on Java's population problem was not. By 1930 the population of these colonies totaled 36,000. Meanwhile, between 1905 and 1930 the population of Java increased by about 11 million. In 1930 people living in east Sumatra who originated in Java and Madura totaled over 460,000, representing 31.4 percent of the total population there. In Lampung the figure was just short of 91,000, being 25.9 percent of the population. Many of these were estate laborers. When the Depression devastated economic activity in the area, tens of thousands of these migrant workers returned to Java, increasing the already heavy pressure on resources there.

Indicators of indigenous welfare varied in the period 1900–30, but in general there is little evidence of improvement during that period, even before the Depression. There is no doubt that welfare generally declined in the first half of the 1930s, while statistics suggest some recovery in the second half. Per capita income may have reached 1929 levels again by 1937, but the distribution of the benefits of such a recovery are unclear and, in any case, the circumstances in 1929 were hardly satisfactory. What is clear is that the 1930s were a time of particularly great hardship in Indonesia, as in other parts of Southeast Asia and the world more generally.

The American Philippines

In December 1898, after the once-mighty Spanish empire succumbed to American military might, a new world order began. The Treaty of Paris stripped Spain of its colonies in the Americas and the Pacific and annexed the Philippines to the United States. Almost overnight the United States turned into a global power. Presenting himself as a deeply religious man, President William McKinley expressed distress on accepting this new imperial role. He proclaimed the 'benevolent assimilation' of the Philippines, annnouncing that it was America's duty to educate, civilize, and train Filipinos in self-governance.

To gather information about the islands McKinley authorized a consultative body called the 'Philippine Commission'. Prominent men comprised this Commission: the President of Cornell University, Jacob Schurman, acted as head while Rear-Admiral George Dewey (commander of the Asiatic Squadron), General Elwell Otis (Military Governor), Charles Denby (former US Minister to China) and Dean C. Worcester (Professor at the University of Michigan) served as commissioners. In Manila the Commission held hearings, heard envoys from the Filipino resistance led by Emilio Aguinaldo, and insisted that the Americans had only altruistic aims in the archipelago. It justified American occupation by declaring that Filipinos were unprepared for independence. It recommended the establishment of a legislature composed of an elected lower house and a partly appointed upper house. It proposed the demilitarization of pacified territories and concurrent establishment of civil governments among municipalities and provinces. The Commission also recommended that the archipelago's natural resources be reserved for Filipinos. It suggested that free public elementary schools should be started and that Filipinos of high ability and character be awarded with significant government offices.

As the Philippine-American War – which killed some 225,000 Filipinos – raged in the provinces, the Military Governor who was appointed by the American President ran the government in Manila. Generals Wesley Merritt (1898), Elwell Otis (1898–1900) and Arthur MacArthur (1900–01) established order in the pacified territories. There army officers set up provost-marshall courts. The military regime reorganized the judiciary and established a Supreme Court consisting of six Filipino jurists and three American officers. In 1900 it introduced the Court of First Instance and promulgated a Code of Criminal Procedure. The military took charge of the Manila port and tariff collection. And in Manila the American forces held popular elections for local government officials.

In 1900 another exploratory 'Philippine Commission' made up of civilians was sent to the islands. William H. Taft served as President, with Luke E. Wright, Henry C. Ide, Bernard Moses, and Dean C. Worcester as members. Wright studied the militia, police, and criminal codes; Ide, the courts, banking, and currency; Moses, education; Worcester, agriculture, mining, and health; and Taft, the civil service, public lands, and the role of the remaining friars. The Taft Commission wielded legislative and some executive powers. From 1900 to 1902 it passed 440 laws which established the American colonial government. It created a civil service system, started municipal and provincial governments, provided for a code of civil procedure, organized the Philippine Constabulary, introduced national bureaus like the Bureau of Insular Affairs, and provided for a public school system.

More compelling reasons than altruism drove the United States to the Philippines. Late nineteenth-century industrialization generated a demand for larger markets, enticing American industrialists to venture into overseas expansion. A severe economic depression in 1893 left over a million Americans unemployed. Citizens accepted radical economic solutions, including the imperial doctrine that expansionists peddled as the country's 'manifest destiny'. Expansionism, or the need for a base for the lucrative China trade, lay behind Dewey's attack on the Spanish fleet in Manila Bay. Americans could only watch the European partition of the Chinese 'melon'. To partake in this frenzy, Americans campaigned for an 'open door policy' for China. They assumed that an open China could be penetrated from their new base in the Philippines. That this could succeed had already been proven by Manila-based merchants who had long traded in Chinese and Philippine products.

A colonial territory was of value to the powerful American business lobby. The high domestic tariff on imported raw materials put American companies at an international disadvantage against European competitors in marketing finished goods. Having their own colonial territory from which raw materials such as abaca, indigo, tobacco, and sugar could be imported more cheaply would improve their competitiveness. To support the business sector further, the American government required foreign companies to pay a premium to sell their goods in the Philippine domestic market. The American Sugar Refining Company or Sugar Trust which controlled 98 percent of sugar refining in the United States derived most of its profits from this new tariff legislation. Later, however, American sugar interests opposed the retention of the islands because they feared Philippines competition with Cuban sugar, which they controlled.

Dissenting voices against annexation were also heard in a remarkable harmony from left and right. Industrialists like Andrew Carnegie advocated expansion and opening markets abroad, but not outright occupation. The anti-slavery movement, including the Anti-Imperialist League, was against the subjugation of another people. White supremacists feared contamination by another, inferior 'race'. Labor unions dreaded the influx of a cheap workforce and the market competition that cheap agricultural imports would pose for more expensive American farm products.

The contending anti-imperialist concerns on the one hand and the advantages of imperial expansion on the other shaped American economic policies in the islands. Protectionist clauses for American labor and products were included in the Philippine Organic Act of 1902. This law defined Filipinos as 'citizens of the Philippine Islands', barred from immigration to the United States. Franchises and the lease and ownership of land and mining claims were limited, and only American businessmen and a few Filipino landowners and rich merchants could have access to them. But the law also provided for major interest groups like the sugar bloc. Individuals could own only up to 16 ha (40 acres) of public land but corporations could acquire as much as 1024 ha (2530 acres). This limited competition while at the same time allowing for large-scale agricultural cultivation in the colony.

Before commercial exploitation could proceed, transportation, communication, public utilities, ports and harbors, warehousing, and other facilities needed to be developed. The second Philippine Commission and succeeding civil governments repeatedly tried to attract private investment and get around the restrictions placed on them by the American Congress. In 1901 the insular government provided the initial USD 2 million capital for the improvement of Manila's port and harbor. The contract for this project was won by the firm Atlantic, Gulf and Pacific Co., which later became dominant in heavy construction and in iron and steel work. In 1902, the Manila Electric Railway and Light Co. (MERALCO) – associated with General Electric Co. – invested USD 2.5 million for the development of tramways, light, and power in Manila. In 1905 the Manila electric tramway began operation. The Philippine Commission awarded MERALCO with the 50-year franchise of the tramway and the stipulation that it could fix fares for 25 years.

The Philippine Commission and War Department lobbied for investment in railroad construction and issued bonds for water supply, sewage systems, and construction of public buildings in municipalities and provinces. In 1905, to support these campaigns the American Congress passed the Cooper Bill, which exempted Philippine bonds from taxes and guaranteed the payment of 4 percent annual interest to railroad investors. Despite special concessions, railroad construction was a disappointment. By 1914 only 1400 of the planned 2000 km (840 out of 1200 miles) of tracks were built. Two years after the passage of the Cooper Bill the construction frenzy petered out. In the United States, railroad bonds hardly sold, forcing the colonial government to purchase some itself to ensure that some lines were built. A similar fate met the bonds for municipal and provincial improvement. By 1911 private individuals owned USD 16 million worth of bonds. USD 7 million of these, however, financed the purchase of friar lands and so were unrelated to countryside development. Again the fledgeling colonial government had to get involved in order to realize a few developmental projects in pacified municipalities.

In 1909, with the expiry of a ten-year trade restriction under the 1898 Treaty of Paris ending the Spanish-American War, Congress passed the Payne-Aldrich Act which allowed the free and unlimited entry of American goods to the Philippines. The agricultural lobby ensured, however, that a quota was also set on the entry of Philippine sugar, tobacco, and rice to the United States. In 1913 the Underwood-Simmons Act voided all such quotas, establishing free trade relations between the United States and the Philippines until 1934. This new trade relationship expedited the modernization of transport and communication infrastructure. By 1935 20,826 km (12,500 miles) of roads and 8100 bridges were built. Americans established a modern telephone system, an extensive telegraph line, and radio communication. The country boasted 1000 post offices, providing the most efficient postal service in Southeast Asia.

From PHP 94.7 million in 1910–14, Philippine exports increased to PHP 177.3 million in 1914–18, to 244.7 million in 1919–24, and to 279.9 million in 1924–30. American capital became heavily entrenched in the islands. Its share in the import-and-export trade increased from 41 percent in 1910 to 65 percent in 1920, then to 72 percent in 1935. The favorable land law and the sale of friar lands allowed American companies to purchase, lease, or homestead for large-scale agriculture. Modern sugar centrals (factories) rose in Mindoro, San Carlos, Negros Occidental, Laguna, and others. From 1920 to 1934 the area devoted to sugar cultivation doubled, production rose by 200 percent and exports to the United States quadrupled.

The international rise of the soap and margarine industries encouraged the domestic cultivation of copra, making the Philippines the supplier of a quarter of the world's copra by World War I. Simultaneously demand rose for coconut oil, a crucial ingredient for the manufacture of explosives. By 1930 American capitalists owned some 46 percent of the total investment in copra and coconut mills and refineries. Meanwhile, abaca exports rose by over 500 percent. In 1935, 8 million of the 17.5 million lbs (3.6 million of 7.9 million kg) of cordage were exported to the United States. More than 50 percent of all spindle factories for cordage in the Philippines were American-owned, the rest being in Filipino and Chinese hands.

Linking the economy to the United States had a devastating impact on domestic production, as American-made items displaced local products. In 1899 only 9 percent of imports came from the United States; by 1933 it was 64 percent. Filipinos acquired a taste for everything 'stateside' and equated this consumption habit with modernity. Industrialization was discouraged. Manufacturing remained at the level of home industry, providing communities with basic necessities like clothes, shoes, salt, paper, and furniture. Only assembly and processing factories, which were dependent on imported materials and machines, existed. The country remained incapable of producing its own machinery for manufacture. The tariff policy discouraged exchange with other countries, ensuring the country's dependence on the United States. In fact, the American administration of the Philippines combined the most progressive of all colonial political policies (as will be seen below) with the creation of one of the most dependent of all colonial economic relationships. As a result, almost from the beginning, what the United States was creating in the Philippines was not an ordinary colonial relationship, but rather the earliest example in Southeast Asia of a neo-colonial relationship – one in which political independence is constrained by economic dependence.

The Philippine economy was exposed to the fluctuations of external demand. Cigar exports, which peaked at 510 million units from 1915 to 1920, then suffered from the introduction of American machine-manufactured cigarettes and fell to 200 million units annually in the 1920s. Elaborately laced or embroidered clothing also experienced a similar fate. In the 1920s, as more American women joined the work force, demand for lace and embroidery in the United States dropped. Simpler, machine-made clothes saturated the American market, dislocating the labor-intensive Filipino clothing industry.

The Great Depression resonated throughout the islands. Annual average exports decreased from PHP 297.9 million to PHP 213.2 million over 1930–35. The decline in value of commercial crops led to greater indebtedness and landlessness among farmers. As businesses contracted or failed, urban workers suffered paycuts or lost their jobs. Unionism gained ground, helping workers organize and bargain with their employers. At cigar factories in Ilocos, coconut factories in Iloilo, lumber mills in Negros Occidental, and sugar centrals in Negros, Pampanga, and Laguna, strikes and demonstrations ensued. Transit drivers, employees at the Manila Gas Company, laborers in Davao plantations and Nueva Ecija rice mills demanded higher pay, better working conditions and compliance with the eight-hour-workday law. Tenants were unable to reclaim their land through the courts; some resorted to violence. In Bulacan tenants refused to pay irrigation charges, destroyed dikes, and paralyzed the irrigation system. In Caloocan (Manila area) and Pampanga, farmers forcefully seized the harvest. In Bulacan, Pampanga, and Nueva Ecija, 30,000 farmers in rice and sugar haciendas went on strike to demand that landowners pay a fixed sum for land cultivation and that loans from landowners to purchase farming materials and implements should be interest-free. The colonial government, however, remained unmoved by the demands of the labor movement. Dependent on the patronage of the land-owning elite, it passed laws that only benefitted the upper classes. 'Caciquism'

– the oppressive and despotic dominance of the upper classes – still prevailed in these hard times.

From Siam to Thailand, 1910–1941

The trajectory of Thai history during this period is rather different from that of its neighbors, for it was shaped more by internal than by external or foreign forces. Indeed, developments in Siam prior to World War II resemble more closely, and in many ways anticipate, the problems faced by other Southeast Asian countries after the war, when they confronted the twin challenges of nation- and state-building following decolonization. In the case of the former colonies, however, the 'raw material' they had to work with was mainly bequeathed to them by foreigners, whereas in Siam events were most heavily influenced by the legacy of Chulalongkorn's reign. Foreign ideas and interests played their part, to be sure, but the players on the political stage were Siamese.

The Thai historical narrative in the twentieth century is divided into two parts by the coup staged against the absolute monarchy on 24 June 1932, and most studies of the country's political development are split into 'pre-' and 'post-1932' sections. While the Chakri dynasty remained on the throne, the structures of royal domination put in place by Rama V and maintained by his successors were replaced by a putatively Western-style constitutional system. From the beginning, however, different elements of the new regime had different agendas, and the problems and conflicts which plagued the early years of constitutional government in Siam became part of the long-term political landscape.

King Vajiravudh (r. 1910–1925)

It is acknowledged by all but the most diehard royalists that Vajiravudh (Rama VI) was fundamentally unable to fill his father's shoes when he inherited the throne. The first Siamese ruler to be educated overseas (in England), Vajiravudh was an intelligent and articulate man, effectively bilingual and bi-cultural. He spent 15 years as crown prince and designated heir to the throne, so he had ample time to prepare himself for his reign. Yet once in power, he alienated various groups among the elite while squandering much of the political and moral capital which his father had so carefully built up. Although the political crisis of 1932 did not occur until seven years after his death, his reign is generally viewed as a major contributing factor.

In essence, Vajiravudh attempted to maintain the absolutist system created by his father, but without possessing the same assets, particularly Chulalongkorn's personal charisma and ability to exercise influence over competing interests. Especially serious was Vajiravudh's alienation from many royal family members, including some of his brothers and uncles who occupied important positions in the government. The king sidelined or retired a number of prominent princes and replaced them with nobles from his own entourage. The fact that he had his own clique of young male favorites, many of them promoted from rather low ranks in the hierarchy, generated considerable resentment. He spent lavishly on both himself and these favorites. Another consequence of his preference for male company was anxiety over a future heir. It was only in the final years of his reign that he began to have a consort – several of them in succession, in fact – and in the end he fathered only a single child, a daughter born just before his death.

Vajiravudh also fared badly in his ties with the military. Chulalongkorn's decision to build up a standing army structured and trained along Western lines meant that the military now existed as a political force to be reckoned with. Rama VI professed a fondness for military activities, but the army was generally more loyal to his brother Prince Chakrabongse. The king built up his own rival Wild Tiger Corps, a somewhat amateurish paramilitary organization which became popular with those who were either close to the king or hoped to become so. His patronage of this group sparked resentment in the army, culminating in an abortive coup plot in early 1912.

Siamese society was changing and Vajiravudh was often displeased with the changes. The Chinese community was growing larger and more restive, particularly where discriminatory government policies were concerned. The Chinese press also propagated republican ideas which, although directed at the Qing regime rather than the Chakri, made the king nervous about their possible impact on the Siamese elite. He was equally concerned over those who returned from Europe with ideas about political reform along Western lines. A prolific writer for the press under pseudonyms which did not conceal his identity, Vajiravudh lashed out at those who practiced what he called 'imitationism', aping Western fashions and trying to import alien values into Siamese society. He also attacked the Chinese community – whom he referred to as the 'Jews of the East' – for their failure to assimilate and for their perceived lack of loyalty to their adopted country.

Although Siam under Vajiravudh was relatively stable (apart from the failed coup of 1912), it did not really evolve politically. The king was more concerned with raising the country's profile internationally through networking with European royal families and sending a small contingent to join the Allied war effort than he was with carrying out political reform. He was a vigorous promoter of nationalism, but in his view the monarchy should remain firmly at the center of the nation. While the press had considerable latitude in what it could publish, such political debate as there was led only to frustration among would-be reformers. Vajiravudh's acerbic comments against his many critics may have given him personal satisfaction, but they eroded his personal prestige and that of the monarchy as an institution. His sometimes jingoistic nationalism ultimately did little to strengthen the national community and arguably weakened it by pointedly excluding those who did not fit his definition of 'Thai', whether they were Westernized Siamese or unassimilated Chinese.

The Siamese economy was becoming more complex during this period. As mentioned in Chapter 8, land was an increasingly valuable commodity, and members of the royal family and powerful nobles were allocated large tracts of land in the Bangkok region, particularly around the networks of canals which had been dug to facilitate transport and drainage of the areas being cleared for agriculture. Farmers living in these areas were generally tenants of the families who owned most of the land, because so much of the capital and surrounding provinces was in elite hands, and there was frequent conflict between those who farmed the land and those who profited from it. Further away from Bangkok, however, the situation was different. Along this 'rice frontier', cultivation was expanding under farmers who effectively acted as colonists, clearing and settling lands to which they were usually able to obtain title. Freedom from tenancy did not necessarily translate into prosperity, however, as agricultural conditions even in the Chao Phraya valley were often less than ideal, and government taxation replaced rent as the main burden on farmers.

While the ruling class and large landowners were Siamese, the nascent financial elite was almost completely Chinese. Although tax farms were eliminated in the nineteenth century, migrants from China continued to flourish in banking and various forms of business. The transition from a largely subsistence economy to one based on the export of rice offered particular opportunities for the Chinese community, who had a virtual monopoly over every step of the rice marketing process once the crop had been harvested. Connections with Chinese firms in other parts of the region – notably Singapore and Penang – led entrepreneurial individuals to build family-based financial empires.

Vajiravudh was considerably more concerned about the economic role of the Chinese than he was about the hardships facing Siamese farmers. Although his anti-Chinese invective was usually couched more in cultural than in economic terms, the accusation that this alien community made its fortune in Siam but repatriated much of it to China does appear in his writings. While the Chinese role in banking and trade may not have been universally perceived as exploitative, it certainly made them highly visible targets. Conversely, Rama VI was convinced that his 'true Thai' subjects were happy, prosperous, and loyal. Critics' observations about alleged poverty, he felt, were biased and based on misleading foreign assumptions about what constituted a comfortable lifestyle. Discussion of poverty in Siam was automatically interpreted as unfair criticism of government policy. When one official wrote an economics textbook which painted a dismal picture of the exploitation and oppression faced by many of the kingdom's peasants, the King proscribed its publication.

The last years of the absolute monarchy (1925–1932)

When Vajiravudh died without an heir in 1925, the throne went to his brother Prajadhipok (Rama VII, r. 1925–35), who was Chulalongkorn's youngest surviving son. By his own admission he was a 'dark horse' candidate for the throne, as there were originally three other brothers between Vajiravudh and himself, including the popular and influential Chakrabongse. All of them died during the Sixth Reign, however, which left Prajadhipok as the rather unwilling heir. He differed from his brother in many respects, being rather meek and deferential. He also enjoyed a happy and monogamous marriage, although without children. Under other circumstances he could probably have become a popular ruler, but he faced political and economic challenges which proved beyond his ability to handle.

Prajadhipok was all too aware of the widespread dissatisfaction with his brother, and to his credit he worked hard to be the 'anti-Vajiravudh'. He attempted to counteract the effects of his predecessor's financial profligacy by cutting back on royal spending and adopting a relatively more austere lifestyle. Recognizing the problems that had come from Vajiravudh's cronyism, he returned to his father's policy of filling most top government posts with princes, and he created a special Supreme Council of senior royal family members to act in an advisory capacity. This decision, however, shows that the king mistakenly attributed the monarchy's low prestige to the deeds of his brother as an individual rather than to dissatisfaction with the system of absolutism itself.

For dissatisfaction there was, within both the military and the bureaucracy. In part, this was the legacy of Chulalongkorn's success in shifting the balance of power in favor of the royal family, creating a government and an army dominated by princes. A second factor was the government's generosity in sending young men from noble families overseas for their studies along with the young royals. When these men came back to Siam, they were conscious of a 'glass ceiling' in a system top-heavy with officers and officials who were often there by virtue of their blood rather than their skills. The nobility itself was not a monolithic institution; while the highest echelon enjoyed considerable authority, the middle and lower ranks were more resentful of royal domination. When active opposition to the absolute monarchy emerged, it was concentrated in these ranks, which contained many competent and well-educated men.

Siam's economic situation during the Seventh Reign was another important factor behind opposition to the government. Problems early in the reign were blamed – justly or not – on overspending under Vajiravudh. Certainly the national budget was not in good shape at the time of his death. Prajadhipok was able to establish some degree of financial balance, but when the worldwide Depression hit, Siam was too well integrated into the global economy to escape the consequences. Prajadhipok implemented policies of retrenchment in terms of both budget and manpower, which seemed to be the main weapon available against the crisis. Since it was all too evident that commoners rather than princes were being retrenched, however, this policy heightened the sense of favoritism and injustice. Prajadhipok did not clamp down on the press, and the newspapers from his reign printed many criticisms of the absolute monarchy, both veiled and explicit. The key theme that emerged from these articles was that the government was filled with people who did not necessarily deserve to be there and who were at least partially to blame for Siam's problems. There was talk of constitutions, parliaments, and the general need for reform.

Prajadhipok did not lash out at these critics as his brother had done, but neither did he implement any significant reforms. He at least toyed with the idea of drafting a constitution and possibly restructuring Siam's government along more democratic lines, but the proposals were vetoed by the conservative princes on the Supreme Council. Nor is it clear how much Prajadhipok really believed in the need for such reforms. Although in recent years he has acquired a reputation as a frustrated democrat, at the time he demonstrated little sense of urgency in power-sharing or making the monarchy less absolute.

From absolute to constitutional monarchy (1932–1937)

The plot to overthrow the absolute monarchy was hatched by a group of civilians and military officers studying in Paris a few years earlier. Among the first generation of Siamese sent overseas almost none went to France because of Chulalongkorn's fears of republican influences, and his fears proved justified once a critical mass of lower-ranking nobles had the opportunity to study there. Ironically one of the very few princes educated in France was Prajadhipok, who attended military school there after completion of his studies in England. Among the coup group, which later expanded to include officers trained in Germany, were two men who would later play key roles in Thai politics for more than two decades: Pridi Phanomyong and Phibun Songkhram.

The coup plotters took the name 'People's Party' and gradually built up a group of army and navy officers along with a few civilians. They made their move on 24 June 1932, when Prajadhipok was away at his palace in southern Siam. The plotters temporarily detained a number of high-ranking princes and announced that they had taken control of the government, threatening to replace the king unless he cooperated. Cooperate he did. Shortly thereafter he returned to Bangkok and agreed to reign under a constitutional regime. A temporary constitution was promulgated in June and a 'permanent' one in December. This 'permanent' constitution would actually last 14 years, longer than any of its successors. Siam was endowed with a cabinet, a prime minister, and a parliament.

Prajadhipok and those loyal to him never fully resigned themselves to the loss of the absolute monarchy, and his relationship with the People's Party government was frequently tense. Friction between royalists and Pridi – who unsuccessfully proposed a radical economic plan for the kingdom – led to the latter's temporary exile and then to a military coup in June 1933 which marked a long-term shift in power from civilians to the army. The royalists attempted to stage their own coup in October, but it was repressed, and Prajadhipok left for self-imposed exile in England shortly afterward. When he began negotiations with the government to obtain concessions intended to strengthen his own powers, the regime refused, and he abdicated in March 1935, remaining in exile until his death in 1941.

The 1933 coup brought to power a military officer named Phahon Phahonyusena, who spent the next four years as Prime Minister. He was relatively moderate and was able to balance the various factions within the People's Party, which represented a diversity of views on how the country should be governed. Phahon never particularly enjoyed his role as Prime Minister, however, and tried several times to resign. He finally did so in early 1938, after several members of his government had been implicated in a scandal over land deals. He was replaced by Phibun, who had begun building his own power base ever since he helped to suppress the royalists in 1933. Siam's political development moved in a different direction under Phibun, who was much less moderate than Phahon and preferred to eliminate opposing factions rather than work with them.

Prajadhipok's exile and subsequent abdication removed an important impediment to the People's Party's agenda. When he gave up his throne in 1935, the decision was made to replace him with his ten-year-old nephew Ananda, who became King Rama VIII (r. 1935–46). The new king was the son of Prince Mahidol, another son of Chulalongkorn who had been widely respected for his practice of medicine. He died at a young age before the 1932 change of government, and his widow and children moved to Switzerland. Without the coup, Mahidol's son would probably not have been as high on the succession list, but a high-ranking prince who would have been the likely candidate was now in exile, and neither he nor his own son were acceptable to the regime. It was agreed that Ananda and his family would remain in Europe for reasons of health and schooling; having a young ruler so geographically removed from his kingdom obviously sat well with the government's desire to consolidate its power at the expense of the monarchy.

Phibun in power, 1938–1941

Phibun's assumption of the premiership in 1938 effectively froze Siam's evolution as a parliamentary democracy. According to the 1932 constitution, the parliament was divided into elected and appointed members, based on the argument that the Siamese people were not yet ready or politically aware enough to elect an entire parliament. It was stipulated that by the time that a certain percentage of the population had achieved a primary education or, barring that, by a ten-year deadline, the appointed members of parliament would henceforth be elected. When this deadline elapsed, however, Phibun decided that the country was still not ready to elect its whole parliament and the existence of appointed members was prolonged indefinitely. This was the first salvo in a long-term battle in Thai politics between advocates of a fully elected parliament and those who prefer to have an appointed upper house. Under almost all constitutions, the latter group has won out.

More serious at the time, however, was Phibun's crackdown on political opposition. During his early years in power, numerous arrests were made and a series of special courts was set up to try the accused. Several plots against the government were unearthed, and there were at least two actual attempts on Phibun's life. Thai politics being what it is, there has always been suspicion that some of the plots were fictitious and the assassination attempts staged, but they provided an excellent justification for rounding up opponents of the regime. The government published documents which outlined in detail the various plots and the connections among different groups of alleged opponents. Members of the royal family were implicated as well, as the regime claimed that certain elements were plotting to bring back Prajadhipok. Phibun took the extreme step of arresting and imprisoning Prince Rangsit, who was Ananda's uncle and was very close to his branch of the family.

Phibun is viewed by later critics as having been an admirer of Fascism, and certainly he imitated Hitler and Mussolini to some extent by developing a cult of personality centered on himself as 'The Leader' – a term which had obvious Fascist implications at the time. Although some of his enemies argued that he hoped to overthrow the Chakri dynasty and become king, it seems more accurate to say that he wished to downplay the monarchy's role as much as possible without actually getting rid of it, focusing attention on himself and his leadership instead. Certainly he leaned much more towards totalitarianism than democracy and failed to demonstrate any great respect for the constitution, even though by now it had been added as a fourth element to the slogan of 'Nation, Religion, and King'. His admiration for Japan and its militarism was equally evident and led Siam into an ill-fated alliance with Tokyo once the war broke out.

The two most significant aspects of Phibun's thinking were his pan-Tai (or pan-Thai) ideology and his particular version of cultural nationalism. The first was centered on the assertion that Tai-speaking peoples outside Siam's borders should ideally be within a single nation under Bangkok's rule. This ideology was particularly linked to territorial revanchism aimed at recovering Cambodia and Laos, which Phibun and many others felt had been stolen from Siam by the French. In fact, of course, the Cambodians are not related to the Tai, but Phibun generously viewed them as 'brothers' who needed to return to the Siamese fold. To this end he launched a border conflict with French Indochina in 1940, taking advantage of the colony's weakness after France's defeat by the Germans. Tokyo's connections with both Bangkok and Vichy France (through the Axis alliance) enabled the Japanese to mediate the conflict. The result was that Cambodia's northwestern provinces – those formerly under Siamese rule – and portions of Lao territory on the west bank of the Mekong were returned to Siam.

Phibun's nationalism in many ways resembled Vajiravudh's in that he was preoccupied with 'Thainess'. The best-known example of his thinking is the 1939 decision to rename Siam as 'Thailand' in English and other languages. The name *Muang Thai* was already in use in Thai, but 'Siam' now fell out of favor. The choice of 'Thailand' has two possible implications: first, that the country should include all those considered as 'Thai' (i.e., Tai) and second, that it is really only 'the land of the Thai', meaning that those not considered as 'Thai' do not belong there. For this reason the term 'Thailand' is sometimes criticized as being chauvinistic, although it has remained the country's official name despite occasional attempts to dislodge it.

Like his royal predecessors, Phibun was also very concerned that the Thai should appear 'civilized'. Although he was by no means an advocate of Western democracy, he did believe that Western culture in many ways represented 'civilized' and modern behavior, and he issued a number of 'Cultural Mandates' laying down regulations for the Thai people to follow. Many of them were exhortations about 'proper' dress and behavior, but they also included paternalistic advice about health and exercise. These rules had very mixed results and probably inspired at least as much mockery as they did obedience. The broader force of Thai nationalism under Phibun was very strong, however, and the cause of the lost territories in particular struck a responsive chord among much of the population.

A strong component of Phibun's nationalism was economic, and he had a very clear agenda where the Chinese domination of the country's economy was concerned. By this time many Chinese businessmen had essentially made Siam their home and they viewed themselves as part of the 'domestic' economy, as opposed to the Western companies which continued to enjoy special taxation privileges and extraterritoriality. Many Sino-Thai businessmen, as they are sometimes known, supported the 1932 coup because they resented the elite's domination of the economy in collaboration with foreign interests. The People's Party leaders, however, was generally unsympathetic to the businesses operating in the cities and towns, seeing themselves more as advocates for the farmer or peasant who had been oppressed under the old system.

Phibun's own lack of sympathy for these businessmen was reinforced by a strong anti-Chinese sentiment. He cracked down on Chinese immigration, restricted a number of occupations to 'Thais' – excluding the many Chinese who were not citizens – and attempted to promote indigenous entrepreneurship. The government, with Pridi serving as Finance Minister, did succeed in establishing several state-run trading companies and banks. Over the long run, however, it proved simply impossible to exclude the Chinese from the Thai economy in any significant way, and both sides found it more profitable to form partnerships between the ethnic Thai elite and Chinese business interests.

The People's Party was more successful in attacking the privileges still enjoyed by Western companies. When Pridi was Foreign Minister under Phahon, he successfully forced the Western countries to negotiate new treaties which eliminated the hated extraterritoriality and removed most of the unfair tariff regulations. This move subsequently enabled the Phibun government to carry out a limited degree of protectionism using new tariffs. To protect local business with tariffs was one thing, but to have sufficient local businesses to protect was quite another. Ultimately it was the Sino-Thai who benefited from the government measures as the two sides learned how to cooperate.

Competing models of nationhood in colonial Southeast Asia

British Burma

Before the 1920s, British education in Burma provided students with a command of the English language and a more British-oriented perspective. Many students saw themselves as citizens of the British Empire and sought to uplift their own society within the colonial system. They were influenced by values associated with British legal systems, procedures, and institutions; formed book clubs and other organizations; debated recent politics and ideas coming from Europe; but rarely attempted to challenge the authority and legitimacy of the colonial state. Some regarded Burmese culture as inferior to Western civilization and embraced the colonial ideology of 'rescuing' the Burmese from their own traditions. Such aspiring reformers faced challenges in communicating their ideas to the wider population and negotiating with the colonial authorities to find means of improving the social conditions of their fellow Burmese.

As noted in the previous chapter, the Young Men's Buddhist Association (YMBA) was established in 1906. It was the first modern organization to enroll a large following. Many of its founding members were Western-educated civil servants who could articulate reform in the language of the colonial state. It had some success in bringing together local Buddhist organizations that had been forming in various towns. While its interests were originally to do with Burmese culture, education, and the promotion of indigenous products, the YMBA was one of the first to transform these issues into political questions. In 1916 it initiated long-running controversy by objecting to Europeans wearing shoes in Buddhist pagodas and monasteries, which implied disrespect, even contempt, for the majority Burmese faith. By defining common Burmese traits, values, and symbols, these early reformers planted the seeds for more aggressive uses of culture as a means of stimulating a 'national' consciousness. Differences in political strategy, policy, and commitment to the colonial state split the YMBA along generational lines, with a youthful contingent seeking more direct means of achieving reform. Whereas the YMBA was only marginally political, its successor, the General Council of Burmese Associations (GCBA, founded in 1920) was intended for political action.

Few Burmese were directly affected by the hostilities of World War I – most soldiers sent to Europe were Indians from the Burma Military Police – but Burma's educated urban elite responded positively to new ideas flowing from the West. Japan's victory in the Russo-Japanese War of 1904–05 had already stirred the imagination of Burmese, as it did the thinking of many colonized peoples. Now the Allies' support for the concept of self-determination and the generally progressive war aims that they declared certainly galvanized the growing number of middle-class reformers, who wondered about the contrast between these aims and the actual circumstances of Burma. Above all, Indian anti-colonialism during World War I most influenced Burmese, providing the models, arguments, and thinking behind an emerging climate of protest.

The Government of India Act of 1919 created a system of government known as 'dyarchy' for India – dual government that gave certain executive powers to Indians while others were reserved for the colonial authorities – but British Burma was excluded. In fact the Governor of Burma, Sir Reginald Craddock, intended to introduce a completely different system, one that severed the colony's economic obligations to India, concentrated power in the office of the Governor, and slowed the pace of political evolution envisaged for India. Since these proposals were not consistent with the interests of either British India or London, they were rejected, but not before Burmese nationalists used them to rally support in the countryside. In 1921 the British parliament voted for the extension of dyarchy to Burma as well. These developments made it clear to Burmese politicians and activists that the Rangoon authorities were often at odds with New Delhi and London, which opened up negotiating opportunities for them.

The implementation of Burma's dyarchy in 1923 increased the opportunities for Burmese elites to join the political process. As political conditions evolved in India, the same liberties and democratic institutions were demanded by Burma's activists. Although officials may have doubted that Burma was as prepared for self-government as India, many of the initiatives introduced in the latter were nonetheless subsequently applied to Burma as well. The political path was, however, far from smooth. There emerged a bolder, younger, and more spirited group of students who aimed for more immediate political changes. In December 1920, a group of them protested against plans to tighten entry requirements for the new Rangoon University, which they saw as a ploy to limit Burmese access to higher education and thereby slow progress towards self-government. Inspired by Gandhi's boycott tactics in India, Burmese protesters boycotted the university, an action that also spread to neighboring institutions and lasted into 1921. Education thus became a political issue, as it was also in other colonized territories. In years to come, the GCBA would make education and the establishment of non-governmental schools an aim that would attract the support of both urban and rural parents who were concerned about their children's future.

Secular, middle-class activists were important to mobilizing communities in these early expressions of Burmese 'nationalism', but the monkhood (*Sangha*) was also decisive in the years before World War II. Mirroring in some ways the generational differences among the middle class, younger monks began reacting against the manner in which the colonial state marginalized the role of Buddhism in society. No longer were monks the sole source of education, arbitrators in disputes, or the recipients of state donations for temple and monastic upkeep. In 1922 a group of monks formed the General Council of Sangha Sammeggi (GCSS), an organization that might be considered the religious counterpart to the GCBA. Originally the GCSS sought the improvement of Buddhist practice among the laity and discipline among the monkhood, but it soon became involved in anti-colonial politics. There now appeared the radicals whom the British called 'political *pongyis*' (monks). Prominent monks like U Ottama and U Wisara toured the countryside raising awareness of issues that affected Burmese Buddhists. They organized communications between rural and urban centers. The GCSS trained a corps of special political monks called *dhammakatika* whose role was to communicate new political ideas to rural communities and to act as advisors to the new associations (*wunthanu athins*) being formed at the village level.

Burma's various political organizations reflected the highly complex and often contested range of visions of what was called the 'nationalist' movement. Activists came from different generational, occupational, geographic, class, and educational backgrounds which affected not only the way that they perceived British policies, but also how they envisaged reform. Older middle-class elites of the civil service inclined towards cooperation through the Burmese Legislative Council, but activists of a younger generation took a more confrontational approach, employing methods learned from the Indian nationalist movement such as boycotts, strikes, and non-cooperation.

From among Burma's student activists grew a particularly important group that called itself the *Dobama Asiayone* ('We Burmans Society'), formed in 1935 out of a merger of two antecedent student organizations. These activists called themselves *Thakins* ('lords', 'masters') – a term previously reserved for the British rulers – and thus asserted their equality with those who governed them. The *Thakins* were to play a dominant role in Burmese nationalism over the following decades, among them *Thakin* Aung San (the iconic leader of the Burmese independence movement) and *Thakin* Nu (the first Prime Minister of independent Burma).

Some Burmese vented their anger violently on immigrant communities, such as the violence against Indian dockworkers in May 1930 and against Chinese in 1931, which resulted in a further escalation of tensions among the colonized. With the onset of the Depression and its disastrous impact on rural cultivators, more powerful protest arose out of the rice delta in Lower Burma. As a result of the growing connections between urban reformists, Buddhist political associations, and village leaders, rural communities became more aware of wider questions of colonial rule. Many rice cultivators began to come together to voice their concerns to both colonial officials and urban reformers. Through associations like the *wunthanu athins*, village communities became more aggressive in conveying their concerns over taxes, rising rent, prohibition of access to forest resources, and, by 1930, the decline in rice prices, the last allegedly being controlled by a group of rice companies called the Bollinger Pool. Neighboring village associations began to link up, increasing the likelihood of a shared political agenda even though local and often personal priorities still existed. Colonial authorities were wary of these developments and began monitoring the movements of urban-based nationalists as well as the interaction between village headmen and the *dhammakatikas*, resulting in the arrests of these monks and in some cases, the closure of the associations they helped found. But others remained free, able to move around and gather information about villager's complaints. They trained villagers in political mobilization, provided information regarding regional networks, and kept village activists in touch with issues in the Legislative Council, such as the separation of British Burma from India. Saya San, a member of the GCBA, was one of these traveling reformers, and in December 1930 he allegedly began what would become one of the largest peasant insurrections in Burmese history.

Several acts of armed resistance spread throughout the lower delta districts in the early months of 1931, with others occurring in Upper Burma and even in the Shan States. Burmese cultivators, deeply affected by the drop in rice prices, began attacking and destroying symbols of the colonial state. They attacked railways, district officers, government buildings, and headmen who were deemed collaborators with the British. The government claimed that this was a rebellion aimed at restoring the monarchy by ridding the country of all foreigners. Saya San's role is in fact uncertain, but he was accused of having tricked superstitious peasants into believing that he was the returned king of Burma, endowed with supernatural powers which could make them invulnerable. Recent scholarship shows that these claims were probably overstated and intended to downplay the fact that the peasantry itself was now more politicized and active than before. Even when Saya San and several other alleged leaders were arrested and tried, rural cultivators kept fighting for different reasons, following different leaders and often not even aware that the rebellion might have anything to do with the restoration of the monarchy. In the end, counter-insurgency forces, including several thousand troops from India, suppressed the various rebel groups, although sporadic attacks continued to occur well after Saya San was executed in November 1931.

The lack of coherent leadership and ideology in the 1930–32 rebellions revealed the nature of rural politics in the early 1930s. On the one hand, village associations facilitated a growing sense of connection with urban political organizations. Many of these associations were accused of having been the organizational network for the rebellion and were promptly declared illegal. On the other hand, local concerns often took priority over more 'national' ones, as revealed in the way rebel groups often acted independently of one another. The rebellions of 1930–32 show that the rural villagers were capable of action but that they required more than the common experience of the Depression to unite them into coherent and effective action.

The British government was meanwhile progressing with its own plans for Burma's future. The 1929 Simon Commission was empowered by parliament to consider whether further movement towards self-government should be introduced in Burma and whether it should remain a province of India. The commission met with officials from the government, members of the Legislative Council, and other business interest who all favored separation from India for various political, economic, and social reasons. Politically, some felt that separation would provide the opportunity for Burma's politics to develop independently from the influence of India. Business interests wanted to revise taxes and import duties that were designed to protect Indian industry and to reduce the continuing influx of Indian migrants which was affecting socio-economic stability. On the other hand, many nationalist organizations such as the GCBA were against separation, fearing that Burma would be left behind the pace of liberalization in India if local government were separated from New Delhi. This issue was introduced by urban nationalists to their rural counterparts, who through the *wunthanu athins* voiced their opposition to the Simon Commission's recommendations in various ways.

In 1935, the Government of Burma Act instituted a parliamentary system for Burma, as a step towards eventual self-government. It gave local politicians responsibility for much of Burma's internal governance and allowed the creation of political parties. The first indigenous premier under these arrangements was Dr Ba Maw, a strongly anti-British figure whose government lasted until early 1939. In 1940 he openly opposed the idea of supporting Great Britain in World War II and was consequently arrested and jailed for a year, being released by the Japanese when they took Burma.

British Straits Settlements and Malaya

Although the extension of British power in Malaya and Borneo reached its limits in the decade before World War I, Britain had never been able to bring the various autonomous Malay kingdoms together to constitute a united nation or to bring about an administrative amalgamation of its territorial dependencies in Borneo to achieve greater administrative uniformity and efficiency. The British were hampered in part by their lack of formal jurisdiction in these territories, although there can be no doubt that they would have robustly intervened again, as they did in 1874, had there been a pressing need. But no such pressing need existed before World War II. After World War I, Britain was also wary of employing the tactics of 1874. Imperialism was on the defensive and, confronted by anti-British Muslim agitation in the Middle East, the British were nervous about antagonizing the Islamic rulers of Malaya. Unwilling to pay the political price of annexing the Malay kingdoms to create a united Malaya, British officials during the 1920s and 1930s sought an alternative policy of decentralization in the hope that this would lead to voluntary centralization by the Malay states.

In Malaya, British efforts at administrative centralization in the late nineteenth century initially sought to strengthen links between their two existing 'blocs' of territories – the Straits Settlements and the FMS. From the formation of the Federation, however, the Colonial Office noted worrying signs of the FMS and the Colony drifting apart and going their own separate ways. As both the Straits Settlements and the FMS prospered as stakeholders in the emerging export-oriented economy, they also developed into rival centers. The Resident-General at Kuala Lumpur perceived himself as heading a separate FMS administrative unit that was only nominally linked to Singapore, while the Governor-High Commissioner at Singapore found himself duty-bound to exercise his authority over the whole of Malaya, including not just the Straits Settlements but also the FMS and other Malay states. The balance of power shifted in favor of either Kuala Lumpur or Singapore depending on the mettle of the individual High Commissioners and Resident-Generals taking office.

When the 'father of Federation' and old Malayan hand Sir Frank Swettenham was Resident-General from 1896 to 1900, Kuala Lumpur was able to keep the FMS very much out of Singapore's control. The situation was reversed when Sir John Anderson took over as Governor-High Commissioner from 1904 to 1911. Wanting to dispel the notion that the Resident-General was a 'quasi-independent head of a separate administration', Anderson asserted Singapore's authority over the FMS and left no doubt that the Resident-General was nothing more than the High Commissioner's 'principal adviser and mouthpiece' in the FMS. By presiding over the Federal Council that he created in 1909, Anderson removed any pretension that the Resident-General was the head of a separate FMS administration. In 1910, at his instigation, the post of Resident-General was changed to that of Chief Secretary to reflect the latter's subordinate position to the High Commissioner – in the same way the Colonial Secretary occupied a subordinate position to the Governor in the Straits Settlements.

During the interwar years, the conception of a pan-Malayan federation of all the Malay states – now expanded to include the five Unfederated Malay States (UMS) of Kedah, Kelantan, Perlis, Terengganu, and Johor – dominated British constitutional thinking. Although Anderson considered the idea of a closer association between the FMS and UMS after the transfer of the northern Malay states from Siamese to British control in 1909, he was not able to make much headway because of the UMS rulers' fear of administrative over-centralization. As the more autonomous UMS refused to join the FMS, British initiatives in the 1920s and 1930s turned to 'decentralization', which fundamentally sought to loosen the 'knot' of the existing FMS by devolving more power back into Malay hands as an inducement for the UMS to join a new, loose-knit Malayan federation.

First formulated in 1920 by Sir George Maxwell, who became Chief

Secretary of the FMS (1920–26), the decentralization scheme envisaged restoring power not only to the Residents, but also to the rulers and the individual State Councils, thereby reducing the marked difference between the FMS and the UMS. Maxwell suggested that, as a first step, power be transferred from heads of federal departments to the Residents. But whatever momentum that was generated dissipated after the Chief Secretary found himself locked in a bitter power struggle with the assertive Governor-High Commissioner, Sir Laurence Guillemard (g. 1920–27), over who should direct the policy of decentralization in the Malay states. In 1925, Guillemard advanced his own decentralization plans, the core of which was his abortive attempt to abolish the post of Chief Secretary and devolve his immense powers to the Residents and State Councils. Though Guillemard had the support of the rulers, he was unable to win over the business interests, the English press, or FMS officials who feared that administrative inefficiency would ensue and affect Malaya's economic development. That Guillemard's plans, in reality, meant more control by Singapore was also not lost on them: the removal of the Chief Secretary would transfer *de facto* executive power in the FMS to the High Commissioner at Singapore. Denied strong backing, Guillemard conceded defeat and retired in 1927 without fully achieving his decentralization goals.

A more ambitious scheme to bring all the nine Malay states and the Colony of the Straits Settlements together under a single union did not come about until the administration of Sir Cecil Clementi, who was Governor-High Commissioner from 1930 to 1934. In 1931, Clementi revived the policy of decentralization with a vengeance. Going further than his predecessors, he wanted to dissolve the FMS in order to place it on the same footing as the UMS. To that end, he revived Guillemard's call for the abolition of the Chief Secretary post and argued for the replacement of Resident rule with Advisory rule, advisors in theory having less authority *vis-à-vis* the rulers than Residents did. To strengthen the legislative powers of the State Councils, Clementi was prepared to scrap the Federal Council. He also saw the goal of decentralization as not only inducing the UMS to join the FMS but also including the Colony in the federal set-up. Decentralization to Clementi, however, was only a prelude to eventual recentralization. Taking centralization to unprecedented heights, he also sought to create a revolutionary grand union that would bring together the British territories in both Malaya and Borneo.

Not surprisingly, opposition to Clementi's schemes came hard and fast as old fears revived. The state-oriented UMS rulers reiterated their concern about the loss of their autonomy in a union with the Federation, while their FMS counterparts saw union with the Colony as a first step towards losing their own sovereign status. Officials and commercial interests in the FMS feared a decline in administrative efficiency with the proposed dissolution of the Federation and saw the inclusion of the Straits Settlements and centralization in Singapore as a development that would subordinate FMS interests to those of the Colony. And Straits Settlements commercial interests worried about the loss of the Colony's free-port status and entrepôt economy in a union with the tariff-based producing economies of the FMS.

Clementi's hope of creating a Borneo Federation and drawing the Borneo territories into a union with his proposed Malayan Federation also collapsed as the Colonial Office was in no mood for revolutionary and costly centralizing initiatives during a time of deepening economic crises arising from the Great Depression. On a visit to Malaya to investigate the decentralization issues towards the end of 1932, Sir Samuel Wilson, the Permanent Under-Secretary of State for the Colonies, thus assured the Malay rulers that the British government had no intention of compelling them to join any Malayan league or union. While Wilson endorsed Clementi's proposal that the post of Chief Secretary be abolished, he suggested that the vacated position be filled instead by a junior federal head who would coordinate federal affairs from Kuala Lumpur. He recommended that federal services be progressively transferred to the states and financial authority gradually restored to the State Councils, which would be empowered to legislate on purely state and some federal matters.

Thus, successive British attempts to bring about a united Malaya had had little success. Seen as a prelude to further centralization, decentralization had one major flaw: restoring power to the rulers only served to encourage their centrifugal tendencies and there was little inducement for them to federate voluntarily. The expected recentralization never materialized; decentralization, however, morally committed the Colonial Office to continue the policy as its central strategy for the attainment of the objective of a unified Malaya. Clementi's successor Sir Shenton Thomas (g. 1934–42), for instance, paid only lip service to decentralization as he was a firm believer that economic development, which could only be achieved effectively through centralization, was the primary concern of British rule. While he implemented Wilson's proposal and in 1935 appointed a Federal Secretary, junior in rank to the Residents, to head the FMS, he slowed the devolution of power to the states and State Councils, fearing a backlash in administrative inefficiency if decentralization was accelerated.

Whitehall's reluctance to rock the constitutional boat was matched by the absence of a strong indigenous pan-Malayan nationalist movement that could challenge the logic of British rule in Malaya. Divided by sectional loyalties, the Malays were unable to experience the sense of a common nationhood. The majority of the immigrant non-Malays were, on their part, not sufficiently 'Malayan' to be concerned with local constitutional development. On the other hand, while still insensitive to the concept of a united Malayan nationalism, local perceptions were not entirely unresponsive to nascent political developments elsewhere. The national and international movements of Chinese, Indian, and Indonesian nationalism; Pan-Islamism; and Communism were actively claiming the loyalty and support of the mixed communities in Malaya.

During the early decades of the twentieth century, Malay political consciousness was awakened by the Islamic Modernist movement in the Middle East (discussed below). Malay and Sumatran students who had studied either in Mecca or at Al-Azhar in Egypt brought back reformist ideas they had imbibed from their new environment and propagated these new interpretations of Islamic teachings through the newspapers and journals like *Al-Imam* ('the religious leader') which they and Indonesian colleagues founded. These returnees blamed Malay backwardness on ignorance of the true tenets of Islam, which was not opposed to progress and knowledge. They called upon Malays to study

Western education in order to keep abreast of developments around them. This soon led to doctrinal conflict between the *Kaum Tua* (Old Faction) Traditionalists and the *Kaum Muda* (Youth Faction) Modernists which, in turn, produced in the Malays a new understanding of their place in the fast-changing Malayan situation. By the mid-1920s, Islamic Modernism in Malaya was becoming more political than religious in character, as seen in the Pan-Islam movement that included anti-colonialism and such ideas as union between Malaya and Indonesia. But the movement failed to gain popular support as it was largely urban-based and directed and its influence petered out in the 1930s.

Incipient Malay nationalism between the wars was also influenced by the left-wing tendencies of Indonesian nationalism and Communism. Some students of the Sultan Idris Training College for teachers in Tanjung Malim (Perak) for teachers were increasingly attracted by the revolutionary political ideas stimulated by Sukarno's Nationalist Party (PNI) as well as through personal contact with Indonesian Communists like Tan Malaka and Alimin, who took refuge in Malaya after the abortive Indonesian Communist Party (PKI) uprising against the Dutch in 1926–27 (described below). Fired by their ideals of a Greater Malaysia (involving a union of Indonesia and Malaya) these radicals, who included Ibrahim Yaacob, Ishak Haji Muhammad, Ahmad Boestamam and Dr Burhanuddin Al-Helmi, formed the *Kesatuan Melayu Muda* (KMM) or Young Malay Union in 1938. The KMM's anti-British activities finally led to its suppression in October 1941. Like the religious reformists before them, the political radicals achieved little mass support, for the majority of the Malays still preferred more familiar and less demonstrative leadership.

The conservative elements of the Malay elite, comprising the English-educated aristocracy, were also increasingly aware of the social and economic backwardness of the Malays as well as the growing dangers of what they perceived as the non-Malay threat. Malay feelings were stirred when the Great Depression led to competition for scarce jobs with immigrants. At the same time, Straits Chinese began to contest the priority of rights that the British ascribed to Malays. Between 1937 and 1939, Malay state associations mushroomed in Perak, Pahang, Selangor, and Negeri Sembilan. The nationalistic activities of the non-Malays oriented towards China or India convinced the Malays that their political position could only be secured if they started organizing themselves. But although pan-Malayan conferences were held in August 1939 and December 1940, state provincialism was still strong and no united organization emerged before the Japanese invasion.

Until the turn of the twentieth century, the vast majority of Overseas Chinese in Malaya paid only scant attention to political developments in China. It was, after all, the very political turmoil and economic hardship there which drove them to seek greener pastures in Malaya. But China's humiliating defeat by Japan in 1895, the Reform Movement it subsequently inspired in 1898, and the events leading up to the Chinese Revolution in 1911 both stunned and revived interest in their homeland among the Malayan Chinese. Between 1912 and 1937, political developments in China continued to heighten their political consciousness: events like the May Fourth Incident of 1919, the Tsinan

Affair of 1928, and the Mukden Incident of 1931 aroused their nationalist sentiments, this time against Japan. Finally, with the outbreak of the Second Sino-Japanese War from 1937, China-oriented nationalism among the Chinese community in Malaya reached its most intense manifestation.

Malayan Chinese nationalism was dominated by external issues. Chinese national leaders and political activists came to Malaya, some as political exiles seeking refuge, including the reformist leader Kang Youwei (K'ang Yu-wei) and the revolutionary stalwart Sun Zhongshan – usually known in the Cantonese version of his name as Sun Yat-Sen – who both visited Singapore in 1900. Their presence invariably brought China's pressing problems closer to their locally domiciled countrymen. At the same time, direct appeals for financial and moral support on patriotic grounds offered the Overseas Chinese a channel for heightened, if indirect, political participation in the affairs of the homeland. Chinese political life in Malaya increasingly began to reflect political developments in China. In 1912, when Sun's Guomindang (Kuomintang, Nationalist) party was formed, branches were correspondingly established in Malaya. When the Guomindang's united front with the Chinese Communist Party (CCP) .was formalized in 1924, Communist elements were also introduced into its Malayan branches. In 1927, the split in the united front also led to a split in the Malayan Guomindang, with the Communists forming their own Nanyang Communist Party (NCP), later renamed the Malayan Communist Party (MCP), in 1930. The renewed Japanese attack on China in 1937 led to a grudging reconciliation between the Guomindang and CCP which was also mirrored in the limited collaboration between their Malayan counterparts.

While an externally-oriented nationalism – directed against the Manchu dynasty or Japanese imperialism and away from British colonialism – was not entirely inexpedient to British rule in Malaya, the FMS government began to look upon the increasingly Communist-infiltrated local Guomindang as a dangerously subversive movement that had to be proscribed at all cost. In July 1925, the British government accordingly outlawed the Guomindang in Malaya. In 1930, however, following diplomatic representation from China, Guomindang membership was permitted but not the re-establishment of Guomindang branches in Malaya.

Unlike the China-oriented Guomindang, the outlawed and Malaya-oriented MCP was a more formidable opponent, as its avowed goal was nothing less than the establishment of a self-governing Communist Malaya through violent, revolutionary struggle. By fomenting a climate of unrest and disorder, primarily through organizing massive labor strikes between September 1936 and March 1937, and again between October 1939 and September 1940, the MCP threatened the British government with upheaval and revolution. Capitalizing on a resurgent Chinese nationalist spirit after the outbreak of war in July 1937, the MCP further expanded its anti-British activities under the guise of Chinese patriotism, by giving support to the Chinese Anti-Japanese National Salvation Movement, collecting relief funds for the Chinese government and enforcing a boycott of Japanese goods. In the wake of the outbreak of World War II in Europe in September 1939, the MCP seized the opportunity to denounce British imperialism and called for a general uprising against the British. But pre-emptive police arrests and deportation of MCP leaders consistently undermined the effectiveness of the movement. While its overwhelmingly Chinese membership limited its attraction to the other ethnic groups, its emphasis on a violent anti-colonial struggle also diminished its appeal to the largely conservative Chinese community. Nevertheless, the MCP remained a long-term threat to the British.

The Indian community, unlike the Chinese, was more politically quiescent, as there were few issues that inspired them until the mid-1930s when their political consciousness was slowly awakened by the gathering momentum of the nationalist struggle in India, which was spearheaded by the Congress Party led by leaders like Mohandas Gandhi and Jawaharlal Nehru. More conscious of their status and the discriminatory British policy of favoring the Malays in government posts and in education, the Central Indian Association of Malaya (CIAM) was formed in 1936 and registered in 1937 with the object of safeguarding the political interests of Indians in Malaya. Indian political consciousness was further stimulated by visits of prominent Indian nationalists. Nehru, President of the Indian Congress Party, came to Malaya in 1937, following which a more militant phase began in local Indian nationalism. As a result of an appeal by the CIAM, the Indian government banned the migration of assisted laborers from India to Malaya in June 1938. In 1939, the CIAM started to champion the cause of Indian laborers for wage parity with Chinese plantation workers. Finally, a series of strikes in the Klang rubber estates in May 1941, although quickly suppressed by vigorous police action, provided the occasion for a further resurgence of Indian nationalism, as laborers flew Congress flags and started to wear Gandhi caps.

On the eve of the Japanese invasion of Malaya, however, no Malaya-wide nationalist movement transcending ethnic, political, and economic differences had yet emerged to challenge British rule. Nor was there any common understanding of what would constitute a 'Malayan nation'. It would take the occupation by Japan to push latent divisions and tensions to the surface and radically transform the nationalist agenda in its aftermath.

Vietnam: scholar-officials, a new elite and Communism

The colonial regime's decision to preserve the mandarinate along with the monarchy in Tonkin and Annam and to maintain the traditional examination system for several decades meant that these two areas continued to produce cohorts of scholar-officials educated in the classical manner. Many of the mandarins produced by this system remained loyal to both their sovereign and the French, but some began to question the legitimacy of a monarchy 'protected' by a foreign power. The two most prominent examples were Phan Boi Chau and Phan Chu Trinh, contemporaries who shared the conviction that the existing colonial system was not benefiting Vietnam, but had radically different ideas on just what should be done. The two men, both with one foot in the world of traditional scholars – notably a preference for writing in classical Chinese rather than Romanized Vietnamese – and the other in the world of colonial society, have come to symbolize an entire generation of Vietnamese nationalism.

Phan Boi Chau came to oppose the colonial regime and called for its overthrow, but his idea of what should replace it changed dramatically over his lifetime. In the first years of the twentieth century he remained a monarchist, part of a group of Vietnamese who looked to Meiji Japan for inspiration. He had links to Cuong De, a prince descended from Gia Long's oldest son rather than from the line of Minh Mang, the second son (to which all subsequent Nguyen rulers belonged), whom Phan hoped eventually to enthrone in place of the reigning branch of the family. Japan initially welcomed Vietnamese nationalists, but subsequently turned against them when it decided to court the favor of colonial powers. Phan Boi Chau then became a republican and enthused over the revolutionary movement of Sun Yat-Sen in China. When contacts with Sun and his organization proved disappointing, Phan turned to more radical terrorism, killing a prominent Vietnamese collaborator and setting off a bomb in Hanoi which killed two French officers. He fled to China, where he was arrested by the French in 1925 and sent back to Indochina. He was sentenced to life imprisonment, but ended up spending the rest of his life under a kind of loose house arrest in Hue.

Phan Chu Trinh believed that Vietnam's problems were due not so much to French rule as to the corruption of the traditional government itself. He accepted the French presence on the grounds that the colonial regime alone had the ability to sweep away the monarchy, mandarinate, and other remnants of a feudal past. With a group of like-minded intellectuals he established the short-lived Tonkin Free School (*Dong Kinh Nghia Thuc*) in 1907, modeled on the educational institution founded by Fukuzawa Yukichi in Japan, to equip young nationalists with practical knowledge and skills. After an outbreak of protests against taxes the following year, Phan Chu Trinh was arrested and the school closed. He went to France, where he continued to attack the Vietnamese political system while becoming increasingly cynical about French intentions in his country. Finally allowed to return home in 1925, he died of tuberculosis the following year. His funeral was the occasion for an outpouring of nationalist sentiments.

By the late 1920s, the contribution of men like these to ongoing political developments was largely symbolic, and their generation of classically educated scholars had given way to men born under colonial rule and educated in French-language schools. These men were culturally and intellectually more Westernized and a number of them had studied in France. This common Franco-Vietnamese cultural core did not guarantee agreement on political issues, however, and the nationalists during the 1920s and 1930s became increasingly polarized in terms of their ideology.

At one end of the spectrum were the conservatives like Nguyen Van Vinh (mentioned in the previous chapter) and Pham Quynh, who were prime examples of the new elite created by colonial rule. They were Francophile in both their cultural outlook and their political views, sharing a genuine belief that Western rule was needed to bring 'progress' and 'modernity' to Vietnam so that it would eventually be strong enough to stand on its own. One of their arguments, which certainly had some merit, was that if France were made to give up Vietnam prematurely, it would simply be replaced by another colonial power.

Pham Quynh believed that the monarchy and mandarinate could be modernized into an effective government, and he criticized the French for sabotaging the protectorate by failing to give the imperial system its proper role. Vinh, on the other hand, shared Phan Chu Trinh's contempt for the monarchy and believed that the whole royal government should be done away with.

At the other end of the political spectrum were more radical Vietnamese who took a stronger anti-colonialist stance, although without becoming Communist. Nguyen An Ninh, a journalist trained in law in Paris, returned to Saigon and established a newspaper which was highly critical of the colonial system. He published it in French, which meant it was subject to less severe censorship than newspapers in Vietnamese. In the 1930s Ninh developed links to the new Indochinese Communist Party (ICP, discussed below), but did not join it, operating instead through his own organization. He was finally arrested in 1937 and died in prison. In Tonkin, Nguyen Thai Hoc founded the *Viet Nam Quoc Dan Dang* (Vietnamese Nationalist Party, VNQDD) in 1927. Named and modeled after the Guomindang in China, Hoc's VNQDD was the most successful attempt before the ICP to build a movement that went beyond a small group of personalities. The VNQDD organized an abortive mutiny among Vietnamese troops in Yen Bai in 1930; Hoc and most of its leadership were rounded up and executed, while those who could fled to China.

By the early 1930s, it was clear that the colonial regime was there to stay and had no plans to share power within the foreseeable future. Moreover, its near-zero tolerance for dissent or substantive political dialogue – except during the period 1936–38, when leftist parties were in power in France – meant that moderates were obedient even if disillusioned, while radicals were essentially forced outside the system. Ninh and Hoc paid the price for their opposition, as did many of their comrades. It became increasingly obvious that only a concerted revolutionary effort could bring about substantive change, and it was this realization that led to the rise of the ICP after 1930.

During the period between the two world wars, Cochin China saw the birth of two new religious sects which became a permanent presence on the Vietnamese political stage. The Cao Dai, founded in 1926 by a low-ranking civil servant named Ngo Van Chieu, was a syncretic mixture of the world's major religions structured along the model of the Catholic Church, with a 'Holy See' at Tay Ninh near the Cambodian border. The Hoa Hao, founded in 1939 by a young mystic named Huynh Phu So, was an offshoot of Buddhism whose roots went back to millenarian traditions from the previous century. Both of these sects flourished in the fertile ground of the Mekong delta, where Vietnamese, Chinese, and Khmer beliefs and practices coexisted and intermingled. Both sects relied heavily on messages from various deities and spirits, and these messages were often prophetic in nature. Such religious movements had always been suspect in the eyes of the Vietnamese state, precisely because mediums and self-proclaimed prophets could convey potentially subversive messages which resonated deeply with their followers. Although the Cao Dai and Hoa Hao were both fundamentally religious in character and objectives, they began to develop a significant political role during World War II.

By the late 1920s, a number of Vietnamese nationalists had been exposed to

Marxism, mainly in France or China. With its analysis of political economy, its condemnation of capitalism and colonialism, and its vision of world revolution, Marxism appeared to offer both a clear explanation of Vietnam's problems and an eventual solution. One of the earliest 'converts' was a young man who had many different names over his lifetime but is known to us as Ho Chi Minh. In the early 1920s he was living in France under the name Nguyen Ai Quoc ('Nguyen the Patriot'). He was in contact with members of the French Socialist Party; when, in 1920, its more radical followers split off to form a separate Communist Party, he joined them. One of the main issues was precisely the question of socialism's stance on colonies, and the Communist faction, following Lenin, took a harder line which appealed to Ho. He spent most of the 1920s in Moscow and then in China, where he was working for the Comintern, the international Communist movement. His ultimate goal was to bring about a Communist-led revolution in his native land.

In 1925 Ho (then living in Canton or Guangzhou), founded a Vietnamese revolutionary organization usually known for short as *Thanh Nien* (Youth). The new organization began to build up networks inside Indochina, but doctrinal disputes and personality clashes soon split the movement. By 1930 there were several groups using the 'Communist' moniker, but they were not formally recognized by the Comintern. Ho was tasked by the Comintern leadership in Moscow with unifying the various factions to form the first official Vietnamese Communist party. In a February 1930 conference held in Hong Kong, Ho and like-minded countrymen established the Vietnamese Communist Party. Although the name accurately reflected the group's composition, a few months later Moscow ordered that it be changed to the Indochinese Communist Party, since the entire colony was meant to become a battleground for the revolution.

Even as the ICP was building up its initial infrastructure in the various parts of the colony, it was confronted with a wave of rural and urban unrest, involving both peasants and workers at plantations and factories. There were patches of unrest throughout Vietnam, but the main locus of rebellion was in the northern-central provinces of Nghe An and Ha Tinh, and for this reason the main events of 1930–31 are usually known as the 'Nghe-Tinh Soviets', named for the local government councils set up during the revolts. Not surprisingly, many of the key grievances articulated in the protests were economic, particularly taxes and the monopolies on certain essential products. When village and district governments fell into rebel hands, the fiscal structures put in place by the colonial state were the first things to be destroyed. At the same time, however, the local 'Soviets' represented a concerted attempt to implement revolutionary ideas across the board, including attacks on the less desirable aspects of 'feudal' society and culture, such as gambling and the frequenting of temples.

The exact role of the ICP in these events is still being studied by historians. It seems fairly clear that the Party did not actually instigate the rebellion and in fact some leaders were opposed to it on the grounds that conditions were not yet ripe. Once the movement had started, however, the Party jumped on board. This was the most serious and prolonged challenge to French rule since the initial colonization, and it was only with great difficulty that the regime was able eventually to suppress the rebellion.

The events of 1930–31 were a milestone in the evolution of Vietnamese nationalism. On the one hand, for those who already considered themselves to be Communists, the revolt served to confirm that only Marxism and the leadership of the Party could ever hope to liberate the colony from foreign rule. The enthusiastic support for the uprising in many different regions provided a glimpse of what could be achieved through better organization and more thorough mobilization. On the other hand, for less radical nationalists, the Nghe-Tinh Soviets invoked the specter of class struggle and wide-scale violence and, for the time being at least, confirmed them in their moderate views of colonial rule.

The brutal suppression of these events by the colonial regime provided ammunition for those within the embryonic ICP leadership – scattered throughout Indochina and southern China – who had not been in favor of the movement. One of the victims of the political infighting was Ho Chi Minh himself, and his political star dimmed for several years thereafter as rivals within the Party who were more highly favored in Moscow were able to assert control. Ho was arrested in Hong Kong in 1931 and detained there for two years, after which he returned to the USSR. He did not return to China until 1938, when he began the next phase of his revolutionary career, leading to the establishment of the Viet Minh united front which eventually brought down the French.

The 1930s were very much a period of ups and downs for the ICP. After the initial flush of success in 1930–31 and the consequent suppression of the movement and the arrest of many leaders, the Party was relatively quiescent for several years. The Popular Front government in France directly benefited the Party, as leftist elements gained more breathing space and were even able to engage in open propagandizing in Cochin China, where the political environment tended to be more liberal than in the protectorate areas. A number of leaders were released from jail during this time. Party ranks in general swelled through the recruitment of prisoners from various parts of Indochina. The outbreak of the European war in 1939 brought an abrupt crackdown, but by that time the ICP had sufficiently recovered and expanded to be ready for new anti-colonial initiatives.

During this time the ICP did its best to live up to its name and become a genuinely Indochinese party. It established small cells in Cambodia and Laos, particularly among workers on rubber plantations (in the former) and in tin mines (in the latter). At this time, however, these ICP cells were almost 100 percent Vietnamese, since the majority of the workers in Cambodia and Laos were immigrants. The ICP also had a presence among Vietnamese communities in northeastern Siam, where the government kept a wary eye but exercised a certain amount of tolerance as long as Party activities targeted French Indochina rather than Siam itself.

Cambodia and Laos: different strains of nationalism

Cambodia and Laos both produced a group of French-educated intellectuals, but the numbers were much smaller, and the orientation of their nationalism differed in significant respects from that of their Vietnamese counterparts. In both colonies the main center of intellectual activity was the Buddhist Institute, which attracted monks as well as laymen and became a focal point for nationalist ideas. The Cambodian and Lao press was also much less developed than was the case in the Vietnamese parts of Indochina, which meant that the volume of nationalist writings was correspondingly smaller. Moreover, as mentioned in the previous chapter, many of the prominent Cambodian and Lao intellectuals were less strongly opposed to French rule as such than to the large-scale immigration of Vietnamese which it had produced.

A major French preoccupation in both Cambodia and Laos was to disrupt the traditional political and cultural ties which linked the two peoples to Siam, their former overlord. Because these ties were particularly strong where Theravada Buddhism was concerned, the colonial regime committed itself to providing facilities for the education and training of monks within Indochina so that only the most advanced students had a reason to go to Bangkok. To this end the French established Buddhist Institutes in Phnom Penh and then in Vientiane in the early 1930s. Although these institutes were fairly limited in scope, in colonies where there were few secondary schools and no university – the only university being located in Hanoi – their intellectual impact should not be underestimated. Moreover, because of the close link between Buddhism and national identity among ethnic Cambodians and Lao, such institutes were logical forums for sharing nationalist ideas. Many Vietnamese intellectuals, by contrast, had little or no interest in Buddhism.

In Phnom Penh, the Buddhist Institute drew a number of educated Cambodians. In 1936 a group of men associated with the Institute – notably Pach Chhoeun, Sim Var, and Son Ngoc Thanh (an ethnic Khmer from Cochin China) – established a newspaper called *Nagara Vatta* ('Angkor Wat'), which became the main voice of Cambodian nationalism during this period. All three of these men came to play important roles in Cambodian politics, though from differing ideological stances. The new publication spoke out for the interests of ethnic Khmer and criticized the dominant role played by Vietnamese and Chinese immigrants in the administration and the economy.

A comparable newspaper did not appear in Laos until the wartime period. During the 1930s the banner of Lao nationalism was carried almost singlehandedly by Prince Phetsarath, who belonged to a rival branch of the royal family from that of the reigning monarch. Educated in France and England, Phetsarath became the highest-ranking Lao civil servant. Although a collaborator with the colonial regime, he was critical of certain French policies, particularly the decision to encourage Vietnamese immigration into Laos. The civil service, including the corps of schoolteachers, was heavily Vietnamese, and this fact was a major source of frustration to Phetsarath and other members of the elite.

Towards nationhood in Indonesia

As the twentieth century opened, the Dutch proclaimed a new 'Ethical Policy' for Indonesia, one that contributed to the modernization of Indonesian society and, eventually, to its liberation from colonial rule. The foremost figure among the so-called *Ethici* was the lawyer C. Th. van Deventer. In 1899 he published a decisive article arguing that the Netherlands owed a 'debt of honor' to Indonesia in return for all the wealth derived from there. Henceforth, the welfare of Indonesians should be the guiding principle of colonial policy. Meanwhile, Dutch entrepreneurs realized that the millions of Indonesians were potentially a large market for their products, but for this market to develop, their standard of living would have to be raised. Thus, entrepreneurs also supported 'Ethical' measures. From 1901, 'Ethicism' in principle dominated Dutch policy. But of course no Dutch government figure – in the Netherlands or Indonesia – doubted that the Dutch should continue to rule the colony.

The core ideas of the Ethical Policy were said to be irrigation, emigration, and education. The first two have been discussed above. Irrigation probably helped rice production just to keep up with population growth. Emigration – the relocation of people from Java to the outer islands – had no real impact on population growth in Java. But education was indeed important. Because of the scale of population, the Dutch faced a gigantic issue when they thought about improving the education of Indonesians. Two schools of thought contended within colonial circles. One favored education in the Dutch language for elite Indonesians. This would, they thought, strengthen the commitment of that elite to Western culture and produce indigenous leaders who could work with their Dutch overlords in the new Ethical age. The dominant figure here was Professor C. Snouck Hurgronje, the Netherlands' foremost scholar of Islam and the architect of much of Dutch policy towards 'natives'. Another school of thought favored indigenous-language elementary education for the masses as a direct welfare measure. In the end, both approaches were pursued, but with inadequate resources for either. What the educational reforms did produce, however, was a small but very important number of leaders who were determined to be rid of colonial rule.

The first educational reforms were at the higher levels. The three schools for sons of the elite which taught literacy, numeracy, and practical skills such as surveying were converted in 1900 into civil-service colleges, called OSVIA (*Opleidingscholen voor Inlandsche Ambtenaren*, Training Schools for Native Officials). Over 1900–02, the 'Dokter-Jawa' school in Batavia – which had taught vaccination and other basic medical skills – was turned into STOVIA (*School tot Opleiding van Inlandsche Artsen*, School for Training Native Doctors). Both OSVIA and STOVIA taught in Dutch; they brought together some of the brightest Indonesians from across the archipelago, helped them thereby to think in Indonesia-wide terms, and unintentionally produced some of the earliest leaders of anti-colonial movements.

Mass education provided the greatest challenge for the *Ethici*. How were they to educate the millions upon millions of ordinary Indonesians, given the limited size – and hence resources – of this vast archipelago's tiny 'mother country' on the northwest tip of Europe? Typically, the answer was that the Indonesians for whom this welfare measure was intended would have to pay for most of it themselves. Village schools were set up from 1907, with some government subsidies available but most of the cost borne by the villagers themselves; they taught basic literacy and numeracy. By the 1930s there were about 9600 such schools across Indonesia and over 40 percent of Indonesian children aged 6–9 attended, at least in principle. In fact, many peasant families saw little benefit in this education and many children attended sporadically or not at all.

How little impact this government educational effort had is made clear by the 1930 census. At that time a mere 7.4 percent of indigenous adults were literate. What literacy was achieved was often through channels other than the colonial government's schools. Literacy was generally higher in the outer islands than in Java, partly reflecting the impact of Christian mission schools. In Java and elsewhere, many gained their basic literacy and further education from Islamic schools, particularly from the Modernist *Muhammadiyah* schools, discussed below. And, at least in Java, about one-sixth to one-quarter of literates in various regions gained their skills outside of any school whatever. As noted above, when the Depression hit, government educational programs were among those that were cut back.

Low overall literacy concealed catastrophic illiteracy among women. Across the archipelago, 13.2 percent of adult men were literate in 1930, but only 2.3 percent of women. The utterly inadequate level of education among women was the result of both indigenous and colonial attitudes, and goes some way towards explaining why few women were in government employment or private professions, or were involved in the leadership of social organizations and anti-colonial movements. Women's education was championed by a young aristocrat whose memory is still revered in Indonesia, Raden Ajeng Kartini. She was the daughter of a progressive *bupati* on the north coast of Java who sent his daughters to the local European school. Kartini corresponded with a leading Dutch feminist and was a *protégée* of the wife of the then-director of education in the colonial government. But she found little local support in her wish to establish schools for girls and died tragically young in 1904, a few days after giving birth to her first child. The colonial government never made a serious commitment to women's education, but from 1913 a private Kartini Foundation in the Netherlands collected funds to set up girls' schools in Java, which then received a government subsidy.

The colonial government developed university-level education in Indonesia, but the results were small. Tertiary education only became possible with the opening of a technical college in Bandung in 1920. A law college in Batavia followed in 1924 and in 1927 STOVIA was turned into a medical college. In 1930–31, there were a derisory 178 Indonesians in university-level study in the colony. Again and again, the scale of the Indonesian population and its growth rate defeated even the best-intentioned Dutch policies.

Despite the limited impact of Dutch 'Ethical' reforms, they contributed to creating a new elite, destined to be the first generation to rule the modern, independent nation of Indonesia. Early steps were taken by young Javanese *priyayi* (elite) studying at places like OSVIA and STOVIA. Dr Wahidin Soedirohoesodo was a senior figure, a government-trained doctor who had turned to journalism and sought to advance the interests of the Javanese *priyayi*. He viewed Javanese culture as being mainly of Hindu-Buddhist inspiration and sought to reinvigorate that culture through modern education – embracing the modern to revive the ancient. Many of the Javanese elite held this view, sometimes expressed in a telling play on words. The glorious pre-Islamic age of Java, the age of *Buda*, would be restored by embracing the age of *budi*, modern education and intellect. This view implicitly – and sometimes explicitly – regarded the Islamization of Java as a misfortune. When Wahidin visited STOVIA in 1907, the young *priyayi* there were inspired by him to set up the first modern indigenous organization in Indonesia.

In 1908 students from STOVIA, OSVIA, teacher-training schools, agriculture and veterinary schools established *Budi Utomo* (BU). The name itself probably reflected the *Buda-budi* word play described in the previous paragraph, for among BU leaders were several who regarded the conversion of the Javanese to Islam as a civilizational mistake. BU was modern in organizational style. But it was Java-centered and, although it chose to use the Indonesian (then called Malay) language officially rather than Javanese, it never developed an Indonesia-wide vision, rarely adopted political positions, and never agitated for independence. Its aims were to improve the circumstances, notably the educational opportunities, of the Javanese *priyayi* class.

BU was soon followed by other modern organizations. Some were similarly regionally focused. Trade unions also appeared for the first time from 1905. The first union was for Europeans working in the state railways, but Indonesians soon formed a majority of the membership. Other unions followed. Some of the most important new organizations reflected Islamic reform movements in the Middle East, which found supporters in Indonesia. The Middle Eastern thinkers who created Modernist Islam – notably Jamal ad-Din al-Afghani, Muhammad Rashid Rida, and above all Muhammad 'Abduh – believed that the eternal truths of Islam should be recovered from centuries of medieval legalism by denying the authority of the four Traditionalist schools of law and returning to the original sources, the *Qur'an* and *hadith*. To understand that original message and apply it in the modern world, they embraced modern (i.e., Western) education, science, and technology. So Modernism sought both to return to the past and to embrace the future. Its main center was Cairo, with Traditionalist legalism remaining stronger in Mecca.

Minangkabaus from West Sumatra took the lead in introducing Modernist Islam to Indonesia. In 1906 the first Modernist newspaper, *al-Imam* ('the religious leader') began to be published in Singapore, but its main target readership was in Indonesia. Among the creators of *al-Imam* was the Minangkabau Islamic scholar Shaikh Tahir bin Jalaluddin, who had lived 12 years in Mecca, followed by four years in Cairo. Like most Modernists after him, Shaikh Tahir denounced the Sufi orders as a perversion of Islam – even though his father had been a famous Naqshabandiyya *sheikh*. Attacking Sufism meant attacking a dominant aspect of Traditionalist Islam in Indonesia. Shaikh Tahir was shortly followed by other Minangkabau Modernists, notably Shaikh Muhammad Damil Djambek and – the most determined of them all – Haji Rasul. These Modernists established modern schools. Unlike the Traditionalist *Qur'an* schools, they used desks, pupils were promoted from class to class in the modern fashion, and 'secular' subjects such as geography and history were taught. Arabic was a key subject, offering students direct access to the *Qur'an* and *hadith*, but Western languages were also taught, offering access to Western learning. Minangkabau Modernists opened the first school for girls in the area in 1915.

Modernism won supporters also in Java among the pious (*santri*). Locally domiciled Arabs took the first steps, but the most important organization in Modernist Islam in Indonesia was founded by Kyai Haji Ahmad Dahlan of Yogyakarta. In 1912 he established *Muhammadiyah* (the way of Muhammad), which devoted its energies to proselytization, education and welfare. Because its schools adopted the government curriculum for secular subjects, it received a colonial government subsidy. Dahlan also created a women's branch – called Aisyiyah, after one of the Prophet's wives. In 1925 Haji Rasul introduced *Muhammadiyah* into Minangkabau and from that time it spread rapidly throughout the archipelago. By 1935 *Muhammadiyah* had 43,000 members and in 1938 it claimed a following of 250,000 across Indonesia. By then it had 834 mosques and prayer houses, 31 public libraries and 1774 schools, and had 5516 male and 2114 female proselytizers. *Muhammadiyah* continues even today to be one of the greatest religious, educational, and welfare organizations of Indonesia, and indeed of the entire Islamic world. It has generally avoided political involvement, even though its activities often carried political implications and have inspired political action by its followers. By the early twenty-first century, *Muhammadiyah* had won a following of some 25 million Indonesians.

The Traditionalist Sunni religious leaders of Indonesia were condemned as old-fashioned and backward by the Modernists and reacted to defend their interpretation of the faith. Several Traditionalist organizations were formed. The most important was *Nahdlatul Ulama* (NU, meaning 'the rise of the religious scholars'), established in 1926 by Kyai Haji Wahab Chasbullah, with the support of East Java's most respected Traditionalist scholar, Kyai Haji Hasjim Asjari. East Java was always the heartland of NU, but it spread to all other parts of the archipelago. NU interpretations of religion and ritual and its approaches to education differed from those of the Modernists, but over time many of Modernism's social and educational innovations came to be accepted in NU circles. Because NU was – and is – as much a network of Traditionalist scholars (*kyai*) and their schools as it is a modern organization, it has always lacked precise membership figures. Its following is estimated to be of the order of 40 million in the early twenty-first century, making it the largest organization led by religious scholars in the entire Islamic world.

Meanwhile activist political organizations were being formed, the first major one inspired by Islamic sentiments. This was *Sarekat Islam* (SI, Islamic Union), founded in 1912 and led by H. O. S. Tjokroaminoto. He was not a learned Islamic scholar, but his charisma made him the dominant figure of early Indonesian political movements. SI was the first political organization in Indonesia to acquire a large mass base, but it was a poorly organized and unruly one. It seemed to many long-suffering peasants and the nascent urban proletariat to be a means of defending themselves against the Chinese whom they saw as exploiters, the local elite administrators whom they saw as oppressors, their non-SI neighbors whom they did not trust and – probably last of all – their Dutch colonial rulers, who were responsible for it all but were remote from the lives of most villagers. Peasant millenarianism played a role in SI's spread. Its claim of two million members in 1919 was probably inflated, but it may well have had some 500,000 followers at its peak. SI officially proclaimed loyalty to the Dutch regime, but its members were sometimes quite radical. Village SI branches were prominently involved in a wave of anti-Chinese violence in Java in 1913–14.

Even more radical political doctrines entered with Dutch socialists. H. J. F. M. Sneevliet was later to play a prominent role in the founding of the Chinese Communist Party under his Comintern pseudonym of G. Maring, but his first impact was in Indonesia, where he arrived in 1911. Three years later he established the Indies Social-Democratic Association (ISDV), with an almost entirely Dutch membership. But ISDV sought a mass base and began to attract some SI members to join it. It became a 'bloc within' SI branches, especially in Semarang, the most radical branch of SI. After the 1917 Russian Revolution, ISDV became a more obviously Communist party, although it did not adopt that term until 1920. When it tried to organize soviets of soldiers and sailors, the colonial government acted and exiled the party's European leaders. This allowed the leadership to fall into Indonesian hands, and thus gave ISDV the key to building an indigenous following.

The intellectual foundations of nationalism – seeking an independent Indonesian nation rather than regional interests, Islamic revivalism or international Communism – were meanwhile being laid. The Indo-European E. F. E. Douwes Dekker (a distant relative of the writer Multatuli mentioned in Chapter 8) and the Javanese leaders Tjipto Mangunkusumo and Suwardi Surjaningrat (later known as Ki Hadjar Dewantara) established the Indies Party in 1911. They sought an independent state with citizenship for all who regarded it as their home, without ethnic distinctions. The government regarded this as too radical to be tolerated and in 1913 exiled all three to the Netherlands for several years.

The Communists declared themselves the Communist Association of the Indies in 1920 and the *Partai Komunis Indonesia* (PKI, Communist Party of Indonesia) in 1924. Tension between them and more Islamically inspired SI leaders led to mutual denunciations, open conflict within branches, and finally a formal split in 1921. Members had to decide to be either SI or Communists. In many places this led to the creation of hostile 'red' or 'white' SI branches, contributing to deepening polarization between 'red' *abangan* and 'white' *santri*. As conflict spread among Indonesians themselves, a revolutionary 'section B' of SI was discovered in 1919. Now the colonial administration at all levels became more aggressive in its intelligence-gathering and police monitoring of political organizations. Peasants began to feel that political involvement might only get them into trouble and the mass base that SI once claimed thus began to disintegrate. Only the most radical workers and peasants remained politically involved. As a result, it was the radicals of PKI who became the vanguard of a dying mass political movement.

In 1926–27 the PKI attempted a rebellion. It was disastrously disorganized, badly led – PKI's best leaders were by then in exile or prison – and actually broke out only in Batavia, Banten, Priangan, and West Sumatra. The aspiring revolutionaries killed only two Europeans. PKI was utterly crushed by the authorities. Some 13,000 Communists were arrested, 4500 imprisoned and over 1300 sent to a prison camp in remote Papua built especially to house them. With the destruction of PKI, the first stage of Indonesian anti-colonial movements came to a close.

Into this apparent political vacuum stepped Sukarno, who would become Indonesia's first President. His father was a Javanese schoolteacher in the government system, an *abangan* (nominal) Muslim, and his mother a Balinese Hindu. Sukarno was a Muslim, but he remained one of the *abangan* style. He studied engineering in Bandung and there was much influenced by the nationalist thought of Douwes Dekker, Tjipto Mangunkusuma, and Ki Hadjar Dewantara, all by then returned from their exile in the Netherlands. This thinking persuaded Sukarno to reject Pan-Islam, international Communism, class conflict, or religious revivalism as his core ideology: the nationalist struggle for an independent nation, he argued, must take precedence over all else. Sukarno did not, however, embrace the ethnicity-blind nationalism of Douwes Dekker, Tjipto, and Dewantara, instead taking indigenous Indonesians as the proper nationalist constituency, sidelining particularly local Indo-Europeans and Chinese. Sukarno was a great orator and inspirer of others. In 1926, he entered the risky world of anti-colonial politics. He founded the *Partai Nasional Indonesia* (PNI, Indonesian Nationalist Party) the following year. This was the first anti-colonial organization in Indonesia to have one nationalist goal – independence – and one national constituency – all those who were indigenous to the archipelago.

Other young leaders with such nationalist agendas were emerging among Indonesian students in the Netherlands. Among the dominant figures were Mohammad Hatta and Sutan Sjahrir, both destined to play major roles in the independent state. In 1927 the Dutch arrested Hatta and several others for encouraging armed insurrection in Indonesia, but much to the embarrassment of the government they were acquitted. Dutch justice worked more effectively in the Netherlands than in Indonesia, however, where the authorities were moving decisively to the right, determined to crush anti-colonial agitation.

In 1929 Sukarno and other PNI leaders were arrested and the party was thereby beheaded. Nevertheless, nationalism was now widely accepted as the dominant ideology. In 1928 a Youth Congress in Batavia declared three objectives: one fatherland, Indonesia; one nation, Indonesia; and one language, Indonesian. Hatta and Sjahrir returned to Indonesia in 1931–32 and established another nationalist organization, but both were caught up in a wave of arrests in 1932–34.

By 1942 a generation of Indonesian leaders had established their credentials as popular leaders, but there seemed no prospect of Indonesia ever achieving independence. Sukarno, Hatta, Sjahrir, Haji Rasul, and hundreds of others were in prison or internal exile and posed no significant threat to a determined and repressive colonial regime.

The American Philippines from conquest to Commonwealth

American tutelage of the Philippines towards eventual independence began when the Congress passed the 1901 Spooner Amendment that abolished the military regime and established civilian government in the archipelago. William H. Taft remained President of the Philippine Commission and served as the first civilian Governor-General. Numerous problems plagued his office. Military Governor Arthur MacArthur refused to recognize his government, Filipino guerillas continued to resist American rule, and epidemics ravaged the populace. In 1903 several provinces experienced severe drought and locust infestation. The lack of markets for tobacco, sugar, coconut, and abaca and the depreciation of silver reduced the country's purchasing power and aggravated its economy.

Taft, who exercised full executive and legislative powers, sought first to establish American sovereignty and end resistance. In 1901 the Sedition Law outlawed advocating Philippine independence: dissenting journalists, playwrights, and writers were jailed or sentenced to death. The 1902 Brigandage Act classified guerrilla resistance as banditry, thereby criminalizing guerrillas and their supporters. In 1903 the Reconcentration Act allowed the military to cordon off any outlying *barrio* where guerrillas thrived. In 1907 the Flag Law outlawed any displays of the Philippine flag.

Progressive administrators were convinced that the root of conflict in the countryside lay in land. Accordingly, in 1903 the regime declared all untitled lands public domain; validation of land claims could only be achieved through land titling and registration. Having obtained the sanction of Pope Leo XIII, Taft also negotiated the purchase of 164,594 ha (about 407,000 acres) of friar lands for USD 7,543,000. The Philippine Commission then passed the Friar Lands Act, which stipulated that the retrieved estates should be sold to their former tillers, who numbered some 60,000. Being illiterate, however, these peasants failed to acquire titles for their modest farms. Instead, *caciques* obtained the titles and extended their properties by usurping lands through fraudulent surveys.

When Taft spoke of Filipinos as 'little brown brothers', he had in mind *caciques* or *Ilustrados* in particular. He was impressed by such *Americanistas*. To secure their loyalty he awarded them positions in the Philippine Commission. Pedro Paterno, Felipe Buencamino, and other *Ilustrados* formed the *Asociacion de Paz* (later *Partido Federal*) which aimed to federate the Philippines to the United States. Once he felt that control was sufficiently established, Taft promoted a policy of 'The Philippines for Filipinos' and the placement of Filipinos in government. He endorsed the 1902 Philippine Organic Act which provided for two Filipino Resident Commissioners to sit in the American Congress and for an an elected lower house of the Philippine legislature. Taft fulfilled what the elite wanted: representation and positions at home.

In 1907, after a census and two years of sustained peace, national elections for the Philippine Assembly were held. Only males who held office, paid at least USD 15 in annual tax and were literate in English or Spanish could vote; thus only 6 percent of the populace was enfranchised. They elected 78 representatives from 34 provinces and two from Manila. *Partido Nacionalista* (NP), which stood for immediate independence, won the majority (32), besting the well-organized *Partido Progresista* (formerly *Partido Federal*), which sought some form of eventual autonomy and took 16 seats. Legislators represented a spectrum of the

Christian Filipino elite – ethnically diverse but thoroughly Hispanized. All had studied in and around Manila; ten had done so in Spain. Most were lawyers; 45 percent were landowners and/or merchants. The prominent young leaders Sergio Osmeña and Manuel L. Quezon were elected as Speaker of the House and Majority Floor Leader, respectively.

Anticipating the eventual grant of political independence, the 1916 Jones Act provided the elite with further opportunities to govern. The American Governor-General retained his executive powers and had a cabinet composed of Department Secretaries. But the Jones Law also established an elective bicameral Philippines legislature composed of a 24-member Senate which replaced the Philippine Commission and a 93-member House of Representatives superseding the Philippine Assembly. The law required the Governor-General to secure the confirmation of the Senate for all appointments and limited him to a veto power over acts of the legislature. The franchise was extended to all Filipino males who were literate and could meet a lower property requirement.

After serving as Resident Commissioner in the US (1909–16), Quezon returned home to become Senate President and to displace Osmeña – whom he accused of being an autocrat – as the principal *politico*. Thus a split surfaced in the NP. Quezon's 1922 re-election as Senate President was full of intrigue. His opponents in their new *Partido Democrata* offered their support to Osmeña in exchange for the appointment of Claro M. Recto as Speaker of the House. Osmeña declined and backed Quezon's candidate, Manuel Roxas, instead. Quezon returned the favor by endorsing Osmeña as Senate President Protempore, the second most senior Senate position, signalling the reunification of the NP.

This reconciliation was needed to counter the less-accommodating policies of Governor-General Leonard Wood (g. 1921–27). Unlike his predecessor, Francis Harrison (g. 1913–21), Wood curtailed Filipino political activity. He vetoed 124 out of 411 bills passed by the legislature. In 1923 he demanded that Interior Secretary Jose Laurel reinstate an American detective found guilty of corruption. Laurel complied, but then resigned in protest; the Filipino Cabinet members and the Council of State followed. Unmoved, Wood governed with his advisers. Filipino leaders unsuccessfully appealed for his recall. Wood tackled graft and corruption, stabilized the Finance Department, and provided impetus for the improvement of sanitation, health, transport, and communication. Subsequent Governors-General, however, were more accomodative of the local *politicos.*

From 1929 onwards the American Congress, which turned away repeated independence missions of Filipino leaders, locked horns with Americans who advocated independence. These advocates included agriculturalists who disliked the import of Filipino produce, laborers who were against Filipino immigration, isolationists who were apprehensive about the Japanese menace, and anti-imperialists. This bizarre Right-Left coalition of convenience led to the passage of the Hare-Hawes-Cutting Act, which the Osmeña-Roxas independence mission (1931–33) gladly supported. This law authorized the establishment of a transitional Philippines Commonwealth government for ten years, after which independence would be granted on 4 July 1946. Other colonial powers in Southeast

Figure 21   Manuel Quezon, 1935

© Bettmann/CORBIS

Asia, who were in no hurry to grant independence to their territories, looked askance at this arrangement and at the smug sense of superiority that Americans derived from it.

At home, however, Quezon convinced the legislature to reject the independence bill won by Osmeña and Roxas. He then left for the United States to acquire a 'better' law, only to end up with the Tydings-McDuffie Act – in essence a replica of the Hare-Hawes-Cutting Act. Returning to the Philippines claiming himself to be the winner of independence, Quezon (Figure 21) became the President of the Commonwealth (1935–42) and fulfilled his long-held aspiration to be, in effect, the first Filipino Governor-General. The American-sponsored, dependent Philippine state came to fruition under his watch. To arrange the defense of the archipelago he hired Gen. Douglas MacArthur, the retired Chief of Staff of the American Army and son of the Philippines' first American Military Governor. MacArthur launched an expensive, long-term defense plan, ironically compelling the Japanese to take the Philippines quickly when World War II broke out.

The Americanization of Filipino society proceeded apace, best illustrated by the public school system, which offered free primary education from 1901. The first group of teachers, famously known as the Thomasites, were 600 Americans who arrived on the Army transport ship *Thomas*. The first director of the

Bureau of Public Instruction, David Barrows (1903–09), selected textbooks to promote 'character building' in pedagogy. Educators assumed that Filipinos were inherently corrupt and degenerate, and should be taught the 'American' values of democracy, honesty, industry, thrift, sportsmanship, and patriotism. By imposing English as the medium of instruction, they gave the archipelago a common *lingua franca* but marginalized Filipino languages.

Subsequent legislation bolstered this educational drive. In 1907 the Philippines legislature appropriated PHP 1 million for the construction of schools nationwide. In 1908 the legislature provided for the establishment of teachers' colleges and the University of the Philippines was designed on the American model. Nurses' training under the supervision of the Bureau of Health began and vocational schools like the Philippine School of Arts and Trades and the Central Luzon Agricultural School followed. By virtue of a 1903 Act of the Philippine Commission, the government granted hundreds of annual scholarships to study medicine, education, and law in the United States. These recipients returned home to serve as teachers and other key personnel in the American Philippines. They included some of the country's finest sons, aspiring Filipinos who thus regarded Americans not as colonizers but as benefactors.

Private schools began to compete with their public counterparts by offering more comprehensive education, but public instruction remained a symbol of the progress associated with American rule. Americans endorsed secular education by emphasizing democratic traditions and the practical application of principles. English facilitated academic, scientific, and cultural exchange with the United States. The literacy rate rose from 44.2 percent in 1903 to 65 percent in 1935. Schools trained Filipinos for the civil service, churning out graduates who personified modernity and the new middle class.

Cholera, smallpox, dysentery, malaria, and tuberculosis were endemic in the Philippines, and the Bureau of Health considered Filipinos as incorrigibly unhealthy and thus needing to be drilled, disciplined, and bodily reformed. Interventionist programs that eradicated superstitions and promoted modern sanitation and hygiene were instituted. Officers vaccinated children, spread the benefits of using soap, and propagated the use of toilets. To care for the sick and prevent transmission of disease the government founded dispensaries, leprosaries, and hospitals. Asylums for orphans, the insane, and delinquents were also opened. The government waged war against germs and apathy, transforming the islands into a clean, healthy, cooperative and grateful colony.

While the Filipino elite collaborated in transforming the country into an experiment in American democracy, many others resisted. From 1901 to 1913, revolutionaries mounted guerrilla war. Freed from *Ilustrado* influence, revitalized *Katipunan* cells emerged. In 1902 cells in Bulacan and Rizal of Central Luzon merged under the leadership of General Luciano San Miguel. This New *Katipunan* raided towns looking for weaponry and evaded capture by hiding with sympathetic communities before returning to the hills. American forces retaliated by 'reconcentrating' local people – that is, forcing them into controlled communities where they could be watched and cut off from the guerrillas, a technique later used by the British in the Malayan Emergency ('new villages') and the Americans in Vietnam ('strategic hamlets'). In 1903,

American forces obliterated San Miguel's 200-strong army. His successor, Faustino Guillermo, disbanded his force in Rizal and moved to Bulacan, where he was captured and executed in 1904.

Resistance forces in Rizal, Cavite, Laguna and Batangas consolidated under the *Katipunan*. Its leader, Macario Sakay, had fought with Bonifacio and Jacinto during the Revolution and was among the first prisoners during the Filipino-American War. Upon release he and his generals resumed the struggle and established the *Republika ng Katagalugan* (Filipino Republic) with its own flag, constitution, and government. Sakay did not tolerate dissent, sentencing enemies of his cause to hard labor. Towns that denied revolutionaries shelter were burned and informers were put to death. But the years of fighting and enemy infiltration wore down the revolutionaries. In 1905 the Americans tricked Sakay into surrendering by promising him and his men amnesty and the right to carry firearms; he was hanged in 1907.

Resistance sometimes took on religious overtones. Leaders were believed to possess supernatural powers, endowing followers with *anting-anting* (charms) that rendered invulnerability. In 1907 Felipe Salvador or Papa Ipe led *Santa Iglesia* (Holy Church), which extended to Bulacan, Pampanga, Tarlac, and Nueva Ecija. Salvador officiated at religious rites and predicted a second great flood that would destroy nonbelievers and produce rains of gold and jewels. He promised land to his followers after the overthrow of the government. Success spawned a sister organization, the *Guardia de Honor*, concentrated in northern Luzon with a membership of 5000. The Americans caught and executed Salvador in 1910; his death only magnified his popularity and through the 1920s fighters battled in his name.

Parallel movements raged in the Visayas. In 1902 in Negros, Dionisio Magbuelas or Papa Isio led a group called the *Babaylanes* ('priestesses') who demanded equal distribution of lands, destruction of machinery, and abolition of sugar cane cultivation. In 1907, after losing support, Magbuelas was hanged. In Cebu Quintin and Anatalio Tabal led the *Pulajan* (or *Pulahan*, 'those wearing red') movement, reknowned for their red uniforms and fierce fighting. Eventually the Tabal brothers surrendered. In Leyte from 1902 to 1907, the *Dios-Dios* (also called *Pulajanes*) led by Faustino Ablen preoccupied Americans. Ablen promised to lead followers to the mountaintop where they would find seven golden churches, their dead relatives brought back to life, and their lost water buffaloes returned to them. *Dios-Dios* leaders operated as guerrilla cells. Ablen was captured in 1907, but the last leader, Isidro Pompac or Papa Otoy, was not killed until 1911.

In 1904 the Americans abrogated the Bates Treaty of 1899, a deal whereby the Sulu Sultanate recognized American overlordship but retained local autonomy and was given authority in Mindanao. Now Mindanao became a separate Moro province under American control. In response, Muslim forces battled the Americans in bloody guerrilla warfare until 1913. Traditional leaders Datu Ampuanagus of the Maranaos (of the Lanao region), Datu Ali of the Maguindanaos, and Panglima Hassan of the Sulus mounted bloody and legendary attacks, earning their people's adulation and their enemies' respect. Eventually they succumbed to American might. Panglima Hassan's bullet-ridden body was put on display in 1903, Datu Ali and his three sons were slain in 1906, and Datu Ampuanagus surrendered in 1907. Other leaders carried their torch, only to be neutralized in turn by American forces.

In the 1920s the *Colorum* movement preoccupied the Constabulary nationwide. The name derived from the Latin phrase used in the Catholic Church, *per omnia saecula saeculorum* (world without end). Comprised of disparate groups of both peasant and urban poor origins, *Colorums* shared a form of religious fanaticism. In Tarlac *Colorums* worshipped Jose Rizal and Papa Ipe. From Manila members went on pilgrimages to Mt San Cristobal to listen to the voice of 'Amang Dios' from inside a cave. In Surigao *Colorums* – here devotees of the Sacred Heart of Jesus, Jose Rizal, and the Immaculate Heart of Mary – believed that if they were killed, they would rise again in five days. In 1923 they attacked a military detachment and killed a commander and 12 soldiers. The Constabulary retaliated by slaying hundreds, leaving the corpses to rot. In 1924 in Nueva Ecija some 12,000 displaced peasants and tenants joined a rebellious plot led by Pedro Kabola. The plot was discovered and Kabola was put to death.

Tension escalated between labor and peasant groups on one side and the state on the other. *Ilustrados* used the earliest labor organizations as venues for nationalist propaganda. In 1902 Isabelo de los Reyes founded a federation of some 150 unions of printers, lithographers, cigarmakers, shoemakers, and tailors. This federation provided members with sickness and funeral benefits and organized strikes. It was the last that led to De los Reyes's imprisonment. His successor, Dominador Gomez, was implicated in a militant group. Lope K. Santos reorganized this federation as the *Union del Trabajo de Filipinas* (Labor Union of the Philippines) in 1907. Participation in formal party politics, however, split labor into warring camps and transformed them into adjuncts of parties. Isabelo de los Reyes was also a principal mover along with the priest Gregorio Aglipay in the creation of an independent national church, a sort of Catholicism without the Pope rather like the Church of England or the American Episcopal Church, with which it eventually came to be in communion. In 1902 this *Iglesia Filipina Independiente* was founded with Aglipay as its head, for which reason it is called the Aglipayan Church.

In 1913, in an effort at reunification, labor movement leaders organized the *Congreso Obrero de Filipinas* (COF, Workers Union of the Philippines) which demanded an eight-hour working day, a law on child and female labor, and an employer's liability law. In 1917 the peasant *Union ng Magsasaka* (later *Union de Aparceros de Filipinas*, Union of Sharecroppers of the Philippines) was formed in Bulacan. In 1919 to unionize tenants and rural workers, labor leaders established the *Anak-Pawas* (The Wretched [of the earth]) in Pampanga. A 1922 Tenants Congress resolved to lobby for laws to alleviate the sufferings of the peasantry and incorporated groups into a National Confederation of Tenants and Farm Laborers, NCTFL.

Relations with leftist groups abroad radicalized the leadership. In 1919 COF organizer Crisanto Evangelista met with American labor leaders and radical politicians. Five years later he established the *Partido Obrero de Filipinas* (Labor Party of the Philippines), a Marxist-oriented party that railed against politicians as traitors to independence. The 1924 Tenants Congress lobbied for self-government through the American Federation of Labor, and the small Labor Party, Socialist Party, and American Farm and Labor Party. Labor leaders attended conferences of the League Against Colonial Oppression in the Far East at Hankow and the League Against Imperialism at Brussels. In 1927 COF joined the Red International of Labor Unions. Leaders convened at Moscow, then conferred with the Chinese Communist Party leaders. In 1928 NCTFL became *Katipunan Pambansa ng mga Magbubukid ng Pilipinas* (KPMP, National Union of Peasants in the Philippines), an affiliate of the Peasant International.

In 1929 Evangelista and his group split from the COF and formed the *Congreso Obrero de Filipinas (Proletariat)* or the *Katipunan ng mga Anak-Pawis ng Pilipinas* (KAP). Evangelista became its Executive Secretary and Manahan its Vice-President. In November 1930 they founded the Communist Party: *Partido Komunista ng Pilipinas*. The government arrested Evangelista, Manahan, and others three months later; in 1932 the Party was declared illegal. Clandestine organizations continued to proliferate after its banning. In 1930 Dionisio founded the *Tanggulan* (Refuge), a secret peasant society that advocated armed uprising. The government discovered their plan and Dionisio and his lieutenants were arrested. Another Communist, Teodoro Asedillo, and a revolutionary veteran, Nicolas Encallado, organized peasants in Tayabas, attracting the attention of the Constabulary. In 1935 Asedillo was killed and Encallado surrendered soon after.

In the 1930s Benigno Ramos's *Sakdal* (Accuse) movement went from widespread support to suppression. It grew out of the tabloid *Sakdal* which denounced the state authorities and the Catholic Church. In the 1933 election campaigns, Sakdalistas tackled such issues as the colonial style of public education, the establishment of American military bases, and the American stranglehold on the economy. Sakdalistas won seats in the legislature, a governorship, and municipal posts in Central Luzon. They were primed to become the opposition, when Ramos scaled down party goals. The rank-and-file thereupon revolted. On 2 May 1935 in Bulacan 150 peasants took the municipal building, lowered the American flag and raised the Sakdal emblem. The uprising spread: 1000 took the towns of Tanza and Caridad in Cavite; others seized Cabuyao and Santa Rosa in Laguna and 14 towns in Bulacan, Cavite, Rizal, and Laguna. The long knives and home-made guns of 60,000 peasants were, however, ineffective against the modern firepower of the Constabulary. Fifty-seven peasants were killed, hundreds were wounded, and some 500 were jailed.

From 1935 to 1940, workers and farmers staged more strikes and demonstrations. In Central Luzon, Pedro Abad Santos founded the Socialist Party which advocated radicalism within the law. But problems plagued the movement. *Caciques* prevented the passage of a labor law, tenancy regulation, and land reform. Landlords hired militias that broke up strikes and harassed farmers. Pampanga *hacenderos* sponsored ordinances that forbade evening gatherings and authorized local police to crack down on 'gangsterism' among farmers.

The right-wing Spanish Falange movement became popular among wealthy Filipinos. Catholic schools approved of Francisco Franco and demonstrated an affinity for the Fascist regimes of Europe. To counter these, the Left established the Popular Front – a coalition of unions, peasant organizations, Socialists and Communists, the Aglipayan Church, and professional groups – which won national seats in the 1940 elections and resisted Fascism. Thus stood politics in the Philippines on the eve of World War II, when Japan's version of Fascism would briefly reign there.

10

World War II in Southeast Asia (1942–1945)

Introduction: pre-war Japanese-Southeast Asian encounters

As we saw in the preceding chapter, during the 1930s Depression most Southeast Asians became painfully aware of the socio-economic strains of being connected to the global economy. The Depression also stimulated greater indigenous dissatisfaction with, and undermined confidence in, colonial regimes. Naturally many Southeast Asian reformers and nationalists began to look elsewhere than to Europe for models of independence and modernity. Japan was a particularly powerful model.

By the mid-nineteenth century, some Japanese leaders were already advocating adoption of Western technology as a means to strengthen Japan militarily. The country pursued a dramatic reform and modernization process following the Meiji Restoration of 1868. New forms of ship-building, mining, railways, manufacturing – of armaments, textiles, glass, chemicals, and so on – and other modern activities were introduced. Western styles of clothing and architecture were part of a reform and revival process that, by the early twentieth century, made Japan a world power. These transformations also led Japan to have a more assertive interest in its region: Korea, Manchuria, and the rest of China as regions where it might exercise imperial dominance and Southeast Asia as a source of raw materials vital to its continued growth as a modern industrialized and imperial state.

Japanese intellectuals had long divided Asia into two categories: lands under the influence of Chinese culture and 'outer barbarians', which included most of Southeast Asia. Following the Meiji Restoration in 1868, however, Japan shaped its modernization on Western industrialized models, attenuating its traditional admiration for things Chinese. By the time the two nations went to war in 1894–95, the Japanese side saw the conflict as one between the civilized (Japan) and the backward (China). Along with its European-style modernization, Japan often shared Western colonial images of Southeast Asia backwardness. Racist stereotypes of the kind associated with the contemporary Western mentality can thus be found in the ideas of Japanese observers of Southeast Asia at that time. Recognizing that the natural resources of Southeast Asia were important to Japan's industrialized future, as early as 1893 the Overseas

Development Society was established, devoted to the peaceful immigration of Japanese into the region. Thus, just as Southeast Asians were increasingly looking towards Japan, Japan was intensifying its interest in the region.

In the early twentieth century, it was primarily the potential for securing natural resources and establishing consumer markets in Southeast Asia that attracted the attention of Japanese government, military, industrial, and business interests. In the wake of Japan's colonial occupation of Taiwan (1895), crushing defeat of the Russians (1904–05), invasion of China (1931), and creation of a puppet state in Manzhouguo (Manchukuo, 1932), the Japanese military saw Southeast Asia as another potential sphere of Japanese imperial influence. For their part, Southeast Asian nationalists, such as U Ottama of Burma, Raja Hitam of Riau in the Netherlands East Indies, and General Artemio Ricarte of the Philippines, were impressed with Japan's successes and visited there in hope of gaining financial and political backing. The Indonesian nationalists Mohammad H. Thamrin and E. F. E. Douwes Dekker also built contacts with the Japanese, as did the Islamic *Ulamas* of Aceh, led by Mohammed Daud Beureu'eh. Ironically, despite the attraction Japan held for an earlier generation of Vietnamese nationalists like Phan Boi Chau (see Chapter 9), few of their 1930s counterparts seem to have looked to Tokyo until the outbreak of World War II.

Japan's withdrawal from the League of Nations (1933), its unilateral policies in Manchuria, and the establishment of the Greater Asia Society signaled Japan's growing assertiveness. Yet, peaceful economic engagement was the norm as Japanese banks, sugar companies, and storage conglomerates, along with its Borneo Oil Company and Japanese-owned newspapers began to emerge in the region alongside a growing expatriate Japanese community. For the time being, however, Japan's southward advance policy (*Nanshin seisaku*) was shaped by political priorities in China, which dictated that engagement with Southeast Asia would continue to function within the framework of the Western colonial rule.

The Japanese conquest of colonial Southeast Asia: an overview

Seizing the so-called Southern Resource Area, securing a defence perimeter through the Pacific Islands on its eastern border and against India on its west, and containing China were Japan's primary objectives in its invasion of Southeast Asia in 1941. The Japanese were particularly keen on capturing the region's oil, tin, rubber, and rice, for these were needed to sustain both the war in China and the inevitable conflict with the Western powers. A necessary first step was neutralising the United States Pacific Fleet in Hawaii. On 7 December 1941 (8 December in Southeast Asia), Japanese aircraft attacked the naval and military installations of the United States at Pearl Harbor and on Oahu, sinking numerous American battleships and aircraft and killing thousands of military personnel. Designed to immobilize the American military in the Pacific and to demoralize the American home front, this surprise attack won – if only briefly – the Japanese respite on their eastern flank in their drive towards Southeast Asia.

Japanese plans for conquering Southeast Asia were audacious and ambitious, especially since the majority of their naval power had to be committed in the Pacific Theatre in order to hold back American forces. Expecting a protracted struggle against the European and American powers, the Japanese needed to secure Southeast Asia swiftly and then integrate it into an autarchic economy that would enable Japan to endure a long war.

As discussed below, Japan was able to obtain a military presence in French Indochina through diplomatic pressure, but elsewhere in Southeast Asia it used force. The plan was for almost simultaneous attacks by the 25th Army on British Malaya and Singapore, and by the 15th on Burma and Thailand – the latter was in fact a potential ally, but it was targeted for strategic reasons. The Philippines and Indonesia were to be occupied by the 14th and 16th Armies respectively. More than an hour before the air strikes at Pearl Harbor, the Japanese launched their Malaya-Singapore and Thailand campaigns by landing in northern Malaya. Firepower and speed characterized this operation. Seventy days after landing, the Japanese had advanced 1100 km (approximately 680 miles) south, forcing the numerically superior British forces to capitulate. From the start the British were outmaneuvered by the Japanese, who had clear superiority in the air. The arduous battles that were expected on land barely took place. The poor British strategy of retreating to delay the enemy advance and the quick collapse of British military morale were partly to blame. Their surrender of Malaya and Singapore (15 February 1942) facilitated the subsequent swift seizure of Burma from under-resourced British colonial forces there. The Japanese victory in the Philippines was equally swift and complete.

Japan's sudden emergence as the new occupying power in Southeast Asia had varying effects. It dismantled European and American colonial administrations, forcing their official personnel, military, and civilian employees to escape or to spend the war in horrific imprisonment. In some cases, indigenous political activists could now align themselves with Japanese initiatives to produce an 'Asia for the Asians'. Other politicians who had cooperated with European administrators were often imprisoned or were left with little opportunity to participate within this new system. Similarly, Japan's vision of a Greater East-Asia Co-Prosperity Sphere drew support from some Southeast Asians while others saw it as a new form of colonialism. For some urban nationalists, Japan's vision of an East Asian economic community at first seemed consistent with their visions of an independent national community. For many villages, however, such ideas had little impact, for their lives continued to be based on more traditional forms of kinship, work, religion, and ethnicity. In the Philippines, there were both local collaborators with the Japanese and the most extensive armed resistance against them to be found in Southeast Asia. In short, the new political order introduced by the Japanese drew different responses from various communities within the former Western colonies. The diversity of ways in which student activists, seasoned politicians, soldiers, ethnic minorities, businessmen, women, and rural villagers responded to these new policies would set the stage for many of the issues facing these societies when, after the war, the Western powers reappeared.

The Japanese declared themselves liberators of Southeast Asia from the colonial West, but ironically then imposed similar forms of governance through local elite collaborators and institutions. They attempted to win the support of local populations through a deliberate, yet sometimes haphazard, prapaganda machine. As various case studies below will illustrate, European symbols of governance – buildings, street signs, newspapers, books, schools – were dismantled or censored in favor of local languages and indigenous cultural monuments. In many cases, particular communities, such as the Chinese or Indian minorities and Eurasians who had worked within the colonial administrative system, were persecuted or held as prisoners. For other communities, however, the Japanese provided new political and socio-economic opportunities based on alleged common histories, interests, concerns, and values.

It needs to be remembered that, after Japan's stunning initial victories, the tide of war quickly turned against it as the American Southwest Pacific Command regained the initiative in the Pacific. The Japanese advance was halted in the battles of the Coral Sea in May 1942 and Midway in June. After the American victory at Guadalcanal in the Solomon Islands in February 1943, the Japanese were on the defensive in the Pacific until the end of the war. From early 1944 they were also on the defensive on their western (Burmese) front in the face of the counter-offensive from India by the British-led South East Asia Command. As the imperial Japanese forces collapsed on all fronts, American President Truman authorized the use of atomic bombs against Hiroshima and Nagasaki on 6 and 9 August 1945. Tens of thousands perished in the bombings and many more succumbed to radiation poisoning. On 15 August 1945, less than four years after their attack on Pearl Harbor, Japan's plans for conquest of East and Southeast Asia culminated in surrender – not only bringing to an end Japan's own imperial ambitions, but also opening an era that would bring Western colonialism to an end in Southeast Asia, as will be seen in Chapter 11.

The theatres of war

Singapore and British Malaya

On the same day that Pearl Harbor was bombed, Japanese forces, spearheaded by the 25th Army – veterans of combat in China – landed on the east coast of southern Thailand and northeast Malaya. Capitalizing on British hesitation and failure to launch *Operation Matador* – the pre-emptive Allied plan to advance into neighboring Thailand (at that stage still uncommitted in the conflict but sympathetic to Japan) to destroy the invading force at sea and deny it a beachhead – Japanese troops rapidly swept down the west and east coast of the Malay peninsula towards their prize: the capture of the strategic British naval base and army HQ Malaya Command at 'Fortress' Singapore. At the same time, Japanese naval bombers, flying from airbases in southern Indochina, began their strategic bombing of sites in Singapore. Equipped with the superior and highly maneuverable Mitsubishi A6M *Zero* piloted by experienced aircrew, Japanese fighters soon established air superiority over Malaya as they came up against the obsolete *Vildebeeste* torpedo-bombers, the ageing Brewster *Buffalos*, and the handful of *Hurricane* fighters. On 10 December 1941, Japanese bombers found and sank *Force Z*, comprising the battleship *HMS Prince of Wales*, accompanied by the cruiser *HMS Repulse*, sent to interdict the landings on the east coast.

With the sinking of the two main British warships in the South China Sea off Kuantan, the Japanese forces had complete command of the sea in the battle for Malaya and Singapore. Although the British and Commonwealth defenders outnumbered the invaders, they were unable to concentrate their forces or hold their lines, and were constantly outflanked and overwhelmed by the numerically inferior, but battle-hardened and highly mobile Japanese soldiers equipped with light tanks that the Allied defenders did not possess. And while the big naval guns at Singapore could manage full traverse and fire towards Malaya, their flat trajectory and the fact that most of their ammunition was of the armor-piercing variety for firing at ships at sea over long distances made them ineffective for the bombardment of ground forces. Fifty-four days after their invasion, Japanese forces had pushed the defending British and Commonwealth troops to the doorsteps of Singapore, forcing the British to blow up the causeway that linked Malaya and Singapore on 31 January 1942, delaying the Japanese advance by a week.

The main Japanese assault on Singapore finally began at midnight on 8 February with an amphibious landing on the northwest part of the island, following the launch of a diversionary attack on the island of Pulau Ubin in the northeast the night before. From their beachhead in the northwest, Japanese forces pushed towards the south, west, and center of Singapore, reaching the strategic central Bukit Timah area by 11 February. Overrun Allied units were forced to retreat to the southern and eastern parts of the island, while in the southwest, at Pasir Panjang Ridge, the 1st and 2nd Battalions of the Malay Regiment held on stubbornly and blunted the Japanese advance for 48 hours until the regiments were almost wiped out to a man. As the remaining Allied units fought on, civilian casualties mounted as nearly a million people crowded into the city area in the south. With the capture of the main MacRitchie Reservoir on 14 February, water failure was imminent, and with it the threat of an epidemic. The next day, Japanese troops broke through the north of the city. With dwindling fuel, food and water stocks, and mounting civilian tolls, the noose around Singapore tightened, and Lieutenant-General A. E. Percival, the General Officer Commanding HQ Malaya Command, finally agreed to surrender the 'impregnable fortress' of Singapore to his Japanese counterpart, Lieutenant-General Tomoyuki Yamashita, on 15 February 1942. It was a stellar victory for Yamashita; he achieved in 70 days what he had estimated would take at least 100 days – the destruction of British rule in Malaya and the capture of Singapore.

British Burma

The Japanese invasion of British Burma began in January 1942 and soon destroyed the colonial state. The retreat of the European power was surprisingly swift, suddenly returning the countryside to control by local village leaders. In the cities, evacuating civil servants and soldiers opened the jails, released criminally insane patients from hospitals, closed universities, and even shot animals in the Rangoon zoo in what has been called a 'scorched state' policy. Police stations, municipal offices, courts, hospitals, the Port Trust, and even social clubs were deserted in haste. Fearing that the Japanese would arrest anyone associated with the British administration, many Indians – something like 400,000 – and indigenous personnel fled in panic to India with the British, bringing the machinery of the colonial state to a grinding halt. Many died in this disorderly flight. The British military retreat became a rout in the face of Japanese flanking tactics. Thus, the Japanese invasion of British Burma did within months what generations of rebels, reformers, and radicals had not been able to accomplish for the previous 50 years – the complete removal of British authority.

The Japanese occupation brought Burmese nationalism to an important new stage. In the 1930s, a group of radical students – those who called themselves *Thakins*, as noted in the preceding chapter – feared colonial arrest and therefore fled to China, where they met Japanese agents who convinced them to raise a Burma Independence Army (BIA). Calling themselves 'the Thirty Comrades', these young men went to Japan and received training in intelligence work, military strategy, political organization, and guerrilla warfare. Their leader, *Thakin* Aung San, secretly left Burma only in 1940, hoping to gain aid from the Chinese Communists. He was, however, arrested by the Japanese in Amoy (Xiamen) and, with little choice in the matter, found himself working with the Japanese despite his own distaste for their version of Fascism.

By the time of the Japanese invasion, the BIA had already penetrated Burma's countryside, recruiting locals to its ranks. The BIA supported the invasion through sabotage, securing intelligence, translating, and operating beyond enemy lines. During the war, the Thirty Comrades developed personal relationships with followers that would be crucial to their political careers. Discussions that were once limited to the elite circles in the cities about citizenship, notions of national security and conceptions of a new national community now penetrated the countryside through the recruitment efforts of the BIA, creating new bonds of personal and political allegiance that would last well into post-war Burma. As the BIA swelled in size, Japanese authorities became worried about it. In July–August 1942, they disbanded it in favor of a new Burma Defense Army (BDA) with stricter recruitment requirements, smaller numbers, and better Japanese control.

Because there was little actual Japanese presence in much of the countryside, local networks of authority and patronage re-emerged. This gave village headmen and nationalist leaders opportunities to strengthen their roles at the expense of the central government. Many young men from these communities were tied directly or indirectly to the BDA, so that the very idea of a Burmese nation began to be associated with wartime experience and one's military role. In this manner, nationalist ideas occupied the same space as military ones – the idea of the nation and the army developing symbiotically. This bonding experience was not, however, shared by all, for nearly 30 percent of the population lived in areas too remote to have experienced colonial control in the past or Japanese control in the present. These rural communities, although officially part of what had been British Burma, never quite comprehended or associated themselves with the new identities developing through the BDA.

The American Philippines

In April 1941, as war loomed between Japan and the United States, Manuel Quezon, President of the Philippine Commonwealth, established the Civilian Emergency Administration (CEA). Tasked to prepare Filipinos for war, the CEA conducted tests of sirens, blackouts, and evacuations. Two months later, American President Roosevelt incorporated the Philippine Army and Navy into the American Army in the Philippines, creating the 50,000-strong US Army Forces in the Far East (USAFFE) under the command of General Douglas MacArthur. MacArthur's costly ten-year defense plan included the training of a large reserve of citizen-soldiers to supplement a professional army, who would then be dispersed throughout the archipelago. Meanwhile, the American War Department developed a defensive strategy designed to delay anticipated Japanese aggression in the Pacific. Prolonged defense would be made on Bataan, the gateway to Manila's harbor. There were, however, no preparations in the event of Bataan's fall. Less than a year later this omission would prove deadly for the USAFFE.

On 8 December 1941, just hours after the bombing of Pearl Harbor, the Japanese 14th Army under the command of General Masaharu Homma invaded the Philippines. The bombing of key naval and airforce installations, including Camp John Hay, Clark Field, Nichols Field, Cavite, and Batangas, immobilized the USAFFE. Having secured the Lingayen Gulf in Pangasinan, the Japanese Navy set their sights on the central plains of Luzon, the country's ricebowl. As the USAFFE retreated, MacArthur declared Manila an open city. On 2 January 1942, the Japanese army took control of the capital. To seal off the country's southern reaches from an American counter-attack, the Japanese forces headed toward Mindanao, committing atrocities along the way.

This great offensive forced the Commonwealth government led by Quezon, the High Commissioner's Office, and USAFFE officers headed by MacArthur to flee to Corregidor, an island fort in Manila Bay, where they waited for evacuation to Australia. General Jonathan Wainwright's North Luzon Force held off the Japanese advance in order for General Parker's South Luzon Force to withdraw north and west towards the Bataan peninsula. Fatally, forces on Bataan were ill-prepared for a prolonged stand. To prevent Japanese capture of their supplies, USAFFE logistics officers destroyed food, gasoline, and other provisions. The situation was thus made dire for some 80,000 troops and the 26,000 Filipino refugees who followed them.

From January to March 1942, the remainder of the USAFFE on Bataan and the reorganized US Forces in the Philippines under Wainwright engaged the Japanese army in ferocious battles. Exhaustion, dwindling supplies, disease, and the aggressiveness of the Japanese offensive led, however, to the defeat of the Filipino and American forces. In the aftermath of the fall of Bataan and Corregidor, the 70,000 or so defeated soldiers, including the sick and wounded from the army hospitals, were forced onto the infamous 90-km (56-mile)

Bataan Death March. Some 10,000 of them died in a matter of nine days from exhaustion, illness, hunger, beatings, and executions.

Dutch Indonesia

The Japanese invasion of Indonesia began on 10 January 1942. After the surrender of Singapore on 15 February, the Netherlands East Indies became the front line of the Japanese southward advance, but Dutch colonial and allied forces were no match for the Japanese. In the Battle of the Java Sea in late January, a combined Dutch, British, Australian, and American fleet was destroyed. Most Indonesians gave the colonial forces little or no support. In Aceh, the All-Aceh Union of Ulamas (PUSA), led by Daud Beureu'eh, actually rebelled against the Dutch and drove the colonial power out even before the Japanese arrived. On 8 March 1942 the Dutch Governor-General surrendered in Batavia and the Dutch colonial regime came to an end, never to be restored. Some 65,000 Dutch military men were interned along with about 25,000 other Allied troops and about 80,000 civilians. Some 60,000 of the latter were women and children. The conditions in Japanese prison camps were horrific: about 40 percent of the civilian male internees died, 20 percent of the military, 13 percent of the female civilians, and 10 percent of the children.

The Japanese conquest of Indonesia was thus swift and the consequences of its occupation were momentous. But it was not to last long: barely three and a half years, in fact. From the beginning, the Japanese faced formidable problems. They were few in number when compared to the vast size of Indonesia and its population, which was then around 75 million. Their lines of supply were extended and exposed and it was not long before the depredations of Allied submarines rendered maritime connections with Japan tenuous. The Japanese knew that they might need somehow to hold this vast area and population against an Allied counter-attack; this was one of the principal considerations driving Japanese policy towards the local people, as will be seen below.

Indonesia was now potentially a front line for an Allied counter-offensive launched from the Pacific and Australia, but in fact the Allies decided not to counter-attack the main Indonesian islands. Instead, the Allied re-conquest of Southeast Asia threw the British-led South East Asia Command against Japanese forces in Burma while the American Southwest Pacific Command swung northwards to reconquer the Philippines. As a part of their northward sweep, the American forces took Morotai in eastern Indonesia in September 1944.

French Indochina and Thailand

French Indochina and Thailand had very different experiences from the rest of Southeast Asia, since by the time of the Japanese campaign both had governments directly or indirectly allied with Tokyo. Phibun's militaristic orientation, hostility toward the Western colonial powers, and general admiration for Japan made him an ally whose cooperation was all the more desirable given Thailand's strategic location as a jumping-off point for attacks on Burma and Malaya.

While the Thai put up a token show of resistance when Japanese troops landed on their territory on 8 December 1941, within a few hours Phibun stopped the fighting and then signed a treaty with Tokyo three days later. To consolidate Thailand's links to what seemed likely to be the winning side, in January 1942 he declared war on Britain and the United States, although this action had little real effect because Thai diplomats in those countries remained more sympathetic towards their hosts than towards their Prime Minister.

Indochina's situation was even more anomalous because it was among the colonies controlled by the Vichy government in defeated France, whose pro-German stance made it a *de facto* ally of the Japanese. During 1940–41 the colony came under strong pressure to allow Japanese forces access to its territory and facilities. The French were less than enthusiastic about such demands, but were not in a position to refuse or resist. By the end of 1941, there were Japanese troops scattered around Indochina, particularly in the strategic coastal regions. The colonial regime under Admiral Georges Decoux maintained political control in an uneasy coexistence with the Japanese. While some Japanese diplomats and officers forged links to local nationalists (particularly among the Vietnamese), strategic priorities dictated that they not rock the boat by stirring up any significant trouble against their lukewarm French allies.

This coexistence lasted until March 1945, when the fall of Vichy and the subsequent infiltration of pro-de Gaulle elements into Indochina, combined with fears of an Allied landing in the colony, led the Japanese to seize power from the French. The 9 March *coup de force*, as it is usually known, brought the imprisonment of top-ranking French officials and military officers – although some escaped into the jungle – and the granting of nominal independence to the Vietnamese, Cambodian, and Lao monarchies. In the event, Indochina was spared an Allied invasion, but it did suffer bombing of its ports and coastal shipping during the final months of the war. More importantly, perhaps, the five-month period of Japanese control dramatically changed the political and military status quo in the different parts of the colony and provided the opportunity for new actors to take the stage, as will be seen below.

Japan's impact across Southeast Asia

The Japanese occupation of Southeast Asia was important throughout the region. In broad terms, Southeast Asia was transformed by the destruction of the European colonial states and the emergence of political elites who would come to rule the successor independent states. These leaders were often more radical than earlier politicians who had in some places been able to collaborate with the colonial state in order to press for reform. But in no place was this crucial transition straightforward or free of violence.

British Burma

In Burma, younger politicians were able to achieve a greater presence in the political arena by marginalizing rivals who had cooperated with the British. With Japanese financial and political support, urban reformers mobilized new recruits from the countryside, contributing to the growth of nationalist senti-ment that would frustrate the return of British colonial power. Just as the Japanese espoused 'Asia for the Asians', young Burmese nationalists shouted 'Burma for the Burmese', denoting not only a new-found confidence in who they were and what they stood for, but a sense of common ancestry, history, and cultural identity.

Yet in Burma the Japanese period also allowed pre-existing political patterns and ideals to develop and mature. As we saw in the preceding chapter, since the 1930s nationalist organizations like the Young Men's Buddhist Association (YMBA), the General Council for Burmese Associations (GCBA), and the General Council of Sangha Sammeggi (GCSS) had provided new opportunities to communicate among the many political and religious activists. Political elites such as the *Thakins* were already connecting with rural constituents and communities. Ideas about what constituted an independent national commu-nity were already being discussed among students, seasoned politicians, and politically active monks. Most significant among these groups was the *thakin*-led *Dobama Asiayone* ('We Burmans Society'). Through these efforts, ideas about an independent national community were already being adopted, reshaped, and re-interpreted to fit local concerns, priorities, and agendas.

Thus, cultures of nationalism were already present within British Burma at the time of the invasion in 1942. But because many of the political groups were divided along personal, class, and ideological lines, the influence of the Japanese upon these political communities varied. With the removal of British personnel from Rangoon and other locations, Japanese military officers and political agents and Burmese politicians filled the posts left vacant. Japanese officials allowed a few local, urban-based elites the privilege of displaying symbols of power, rank, and administrative office that had been granted to them only in limited degrees by the British. Those who were associated with the colonial order were arrested, persecuted, or forced to leave with the evacuating British. Many of the new leaders were young nationalists who had been trained by the Japanese in the late 1930s or those who had helped organize and recruit for the BIA. To these young nationalists, fighting alongside the Japanese in the BIA signaled their commitment to independence and an expression of their anti-colonialism. For the moment, differences in ideology, class, experiences, or aspi-rations among these various political elites were put aside. These pre-war tensions, however, remained only slightly below the surface.

The Japanese authorities had only limited success in stabilizing the Burmese political landscape, as personal rivalries among Burmese continued to flourish in the rush to obtain positions of influence. In the political vacuum left by the retreating British, there arose opportunities for rival politicians to settle scores, obtain influence, and move up in the political hierarchy. The Japanese concen-trated on administering the major cities while BIA officers and *Thakins* took control of local areas by erecting new governing committees, often in conflict with one another and with older politicians or the Japanese army. The initial so-called *Baho* (central administration) government was chaotic. Neither it nor the succeeding provisional government established in 1942 – as head of which the Japanese installed Dr Ba Maw – nor indeed the supposedly independent

Burmese government set up in August 1943 under Ba Maw, could do much to promote stability beyond Rangoon as local interests and leaders continued to assert their autonomy. In short, pre-war rivalries re-emerged and influenced the political scene, with an effect on both the growth of nationalism and the newly formed Burma National Army (BNA).

Realizing the complexity of Burmese socio-political culture, Japanese policy-makers attempted to reach out to urban elites, in part because they needed their help to administer the state, but also to produce an image of Japan that might win popular support for the regime. The Japanese identified Buddhism as a key element of Burmese identity. While 'Asia for the Asians' was a call along racial lines that sought to differentiate Asia generally from the West, specific programs tailored for the Burmese were introduced along religious lines, in the hope that the Japanese might be regarded as fellow Buddhists, despite Burmese being Theravada Buddhists while the Japanese were followers of Mahayana. In 1942, the Japanese attempted to tap into local religio-nationalist rhetoric by sponsoring a United *Pongyi* (monks) Association, designed to purge Burma of its enemies and to promote the purification of Buddhism, under the guidance of the Japanese. A Greater East Asia Buddhist Conference in Tokyo was to be a way of bolstering Japan's image not only as a great military power, but as a center of religious authority and pilgrimage. Numerous Burmese relics of questionable origin were gathered and enshrined in a temple in Japan, so as to include Burma's sacred geography within the Greater East Asia Co-Prosperity Sphere.

Other measures included Japanese sponsorship of associations for minorities such as the Karens. These and other minorities were particularly concerned about how their interests would be represented in a government dominated by the ethnic majority Burmans. These associations allowed the Karens to voice their concerns while helping the Japanese curb those within such communities who traditionally were pro-British. Demonstrating sensitivity to minority groups while emboldening them with political support allowed the Japanese to ingratiate themselves with such groups, in much the same way as the British had developed their own relationships with minorities.

The Japanese were most successful in winning popular support through their sponsorship of the East Asia Youth League. Essentially a public service corps, the league was run by Burmese and concerned itself with providing safety shelters, sanitation measures, and library and educational activities for the general society. Membership was broad and included Indians and other minority communities that were only marginally represented in more prominent government institutions. While apolitical in theory, this league provided the inspiration for other corps with strong political leanings. These 'national service' legions included the 'Blood', 'Political', 'Sweat' , and 'Leadership' Armies. These were all initiated under the leadership of the Japanese-installed head of state Ba Maw.

There were also attempts to revitalize royal court customs, which had been in decline since the British conquest and abolition of the monarchy in 1885. Ba Maw incorporated traditional royal symbols – court music, clothing, titles, protocols, and Brahmin attendants – into official activities in an attempt to garner support and legitimacy for his Japanese-sponsored government and to articulate leadership and authority through more traditional symbols. Public events connected to secular politics were repackaged using images and language thought to be congenial to the masses. The launching of the *Mahabama* (Great Burma) Party in 1944 was accompanied by the planting of a sacred tree alongside Rangoon's royal lakes from a region of the country that had seen the birth of many of Burma's most famous kings. Although it is difficult to say whether these measures were actively supported by the Japanese, it is important to note that only under Japanese rule did such cultural symbols re-enter the political arena. It is not at all clear, however, that the Burmese masses were favorably impressed.

The Japanese occupation allowed once-marginalized elites greater participation in affairs of the state while limiting the roles of those who had cooperated with the British. The concepts, terms, symbols, and philosophies that would shape independent Burma remained as mixed as they had been under the British. Differences of class, education, ethnicity, and religion continued to influence how citizens of the future Burma imagined their national community. Once Burmese leaders saw that the tide of the war was turning, they prepared to collaborate with the British in the hope of securing an independent Burma, which had always been their primary objective. Few expected the returning British to be keen on re-establishing their own control.

Japanese control was meanwhile falling apart. The writer John Masters – then an officer in the Indian Army – captured the drama of the final South East Asia Command counter-attack down the Irrawaddy valley in 1945:

> The dust thickened under the trees lining the road until the column was motoring into a thunderous yellow tunnel, first tanks, infantry all over them, then trucks filled with men, then more tanks, going fast, nose to tail, guns, more trucks, more guns – British, Sikhs, Gurkhas, Madrassis, Pathans, Americans … . All these men knew their commanders and as the vehicles crashed past most of the soldiers were on their feet, cheering and yelling. The Gurkhas, of course, went by sitting stiffly to attention, whole truck loads bouncing four feet in the air without change of expression … . This was the old Indian Army going down to the attack, for the last time in history.[1]

On 3 May 1945, the British reoccupied Rangoon. As this western front of the Japanese empire collapsed, the stage was set for a confrontation between the former colonial power and the forces of local nationalism, a confrontation that would end in independence for Burma.

Dutch Indonesia

The Japanese divided Indonesia into three zones of occupation. Sumatra was under the 25th Army, while Java and Madura were under the 16th Army. The

---

[1]   John Masters, *The Road Past Mandalay: A personal narrative* (London: Michael Joseph, 1961), 311.

rest of Indonesia was under the Japanese Navy. Each of these commands had different concerns, priorities, and approaches. The 16th Army recognized that nationalist sentiments were relatively widespread in Java, even though national- ist leaders and organizations had been repressed for the previous decade or more by the colonial authorities. So from early on the 16th Army had to formu- late an approach to local nationalist leaders that might serve Japanese objec- tives. The 25th Army did not face such a situation in Sumatra and was less inclined to pay attention to local nationalism until the very end. The Navy considered the east of Indonesia a 'backward' area and adopted generally repressive policies towards local people.

The Japanese wished to extract Indonesia's strategic resources such as oil, rubber, tin, and bauxite to sustain their war effort. This was, after all, one of the main reasons for the entire southward offensive. But utilizing these products proved difficult in wartime conditions, particularly because of Allied destruc- tion of Japanese shipping. As a consequence, production fell precipitously. Inflation went totally out of control; by the end of the occupation the occupa- tion currency that the Japanese printed was worth only about 2.5 percent of its face value.

The Japanese imposed harsh controls, requisitioned food supplies to the detriment of Indonesians, and forcefully recruited labor. By 1944 famines were occurring. The infamous recruitment of 'volunteer laborers' (*romusha*) for work even as far away as Burma and Siam led to the deaths of something like 150,000–400,000 ordinary Indonesian villagers. Several peasant uprisings occurred and were brutally crushed. The occupiers conducted public punish- ments including beheadings and their military police (*Kempeitai*) created a general atmosphere of terror. Even in the dark days of the Depression and polit- ical repression since the late 1920s, Dutch rule had never been as full of suffer- ing or as brutal as the Japanese period, a situation shared across much of occupied Southeast Asia.

Although the Japanese presented themselves as liberators from European colonial oppression, in fact they were obliged by local realities to use many of the same approaches as the Dutch. They mostly relied on the same classes of local administrators to run the country and kept Dutch colonial law in place except where it was inconsistent with Japanese military law. But other aspects of European influence were abolished. The Dutch and English languages were not allowed and Japanese was introduced – a decision which by itself brought higher education almost completely to a standstill. Streets were renamed and European statues were torn down.

In Java, the 16th Army knew that its principal resource was the 50 million or so people who lived there. The two most promising groups of leaders who might assist to mobilize these people were the pre-war nationalist politicians and the Islamic religious leaders (*kyai*) of the countryside. Modernist Islamic activists also sought opportunities under the Japanese, but the latter never quite trusted them and recognized that, in any case, Modernists' influence was largely restricted to urban areas whereas the bulk of the population was rural. It took some experimentation before the Japanese could create political structures that served their purposes. In April 1942 the 16th Army set up a 'Triple-A

Movement', based on the slogan of Japan as the leader of Asia, the protector of Asia, and the light of Asia – bombast characteristic of Fascist regimes, but it seems not to have impressed Indonesians. The Triple-A Movement flopped and the Japanese decided that they had better press pre-war anti-colonial figures to support them. So they turned particularly to Sukarno, Hatta, and Sjahrir, now released from Dutch detention.

There was, however, a significant difference among the three leading nationalists. Hatta and Sjahrir were European-influenced Socialists and, therefore, anti-Fascist in principle. Despite their imprisonment by the Dutch, on the eve of the war they had offered to support the colonialists against the Japanese. This did not, however, interest the Dutch; it would indeed have required an unusually large leap of imagination for them to accept this offer. With the Japanese now in charge, Hatta decided to try to work with them to advance the cause of Indonesian independence. Sjahrir would remain aloof from the regime, try to build a clandestine network of activists, and attempt to establish contact with the Allies (which proved impossible). Sukarno, on the other hand, although one of the most highly educated Indonesians of his generation, had never been outside Indonesia, had never seen more liberal and open aspects of life in Europe and was instinctively rather attracted to the populist appeals of Fascism. In his experience of the Japanese occupation lay some of the roots of his later bombastic, authoritarian style as first President of Indonesia.

The Japanese also turned towards Islam. By late 1942 they were cultivating rural *kyais*, whose religious schools – which emphasized both martial and spiritual disciplines – resonated with Japanese notions of *Bushido*. But with the more educated and puritan leaders of Islamic Modernism they had problems. The leading Modernist Haji Rasul led objections to bowing towards the Emperor in Tokyo, which he saw as offending Muslims' obligation to pray only in the direction of Mecca and to recognize only one God, and to the Japanese abolition of Arabic in schools. The Japanese had to give way on the latter issue. They also had to abandon the demand that their war be declared a Holy War (*jihad*), a nonsensical idea in Islamic thought, for a Holy War could hardly be fought on behalf of non-Muslim *kafir* such as the Japanese. Such issues enhanced the distrust between the Japanese and the urban Modernists. But cooperation went well with the rural *kyais*, over a thousand of whom underwent propaganda-filled training courses in Jakarta by the end of the war.

Semi-military youth movements were formed from early 1943 onwards. Auxiliary forces called *Heiho* were also formed to support the Japanese military. At the end of the war perhaps 2 million youths were in such organizations and some 25,000 in *Heiho*. The most significant of the proto-nationalist movements were set up from late 1943 onwards. In October *Peta* (an acronym for *Pembela Tanah Air,* Protectors of the Fatherland) was created as an auxiliary guerrilla force. This formed an Indonesian army that at the end of the war had 37,000 men in Java, 1600 in Bali and 20,000 in Sumatra, where it was commonly given its Japanese name *Giyugun* (volunteer soldiers). Peta officers were *kyais*, former teachers, former members of the colonial armed forces and government officials. Among them was Soedirman, a former Islamic schoolteacher who would become the leading military figure of the Indonesian Revolution.

A new organization for controlling Islam was set up in October 1943 called *Masyumi* (from *Majlis Syuro Muslimin Indonesia*, Consultative Council of Indonesian Muslims). The urban Modernist politicians were kept away from its leadership, which was instead given to figures from the non-political *Muhammadiyah* educational system and Kyai Haji Hasjim Asjari of the Traditionalist, rural-based organization Nahdlatul Ulama. In January 1944 *Jawa Hokokai* (Java Service Association) was set up under the leadership of Sukarno and Hasjim Asjari for everyone over the age of 14, but of course was closely supervised by the Japanese. They now promoted Sukarno as the leader of a future state of Indonesia. On 7 September 1944, the Japanese Prime Minister explicitly promised that independence would come at some stage. *Barisan Hizbullah* (God's Forces) was set up as a military wing for *Masyumi* in December 1944; at war's end it had some 50,000 members. *Jawa Hokokai* also got its own guerrilla force called *Barisan Pelopor* (Vanguard Column), with 80,000 members by the time of the Japanese surrender.

Java was now ripe for revolution: mobilized and politicized by desperately hard times and anti-European propaganda, with thousands of young men who had at least basic levels of military training and with Japan's Greater East Asia Co-Prosperity Sphere disintegrating in the face of Allied victories. From March 1945, planning began for Indonesian independence under Japanese auspices – a process which the latter carefully supervised. On the Indonesian side, there was debate about whether the philosophical basis of the state should be Islam or some form of secular nationalism. Sukarno and others favored the latter and carried the day: *Pancasila* (the Five Principles) was to be the foundation of the Indonesian state and, as it turned out, a focus of political contention for decades to come.

By July 1945, with their empire on the point of collapse, the Japanese decided that Indonesia should be given independence soon in the hope of frustrating the re-establishment of a European colonial state. But it was too late. Before the Japanese could arrange the final steps and a declaration of independence, the war came to its horrific end. Because the Allied campaigns bypassed all but a tiny part of the eastern archipelago, when Japan surrendered on 15 August, there was a military vacuum in Indonesia. There had been no Allied reconquest and there were no Allied forces present in the main islands. It was to be several weeks before the first Allied representatives reached Batavia – to which the Japanese had already given its older Indonesian name, Jakarta. So military control rested nervously in the hands of demoralized and apprehensive Japanese forces. Now Indonesians themselves could take the initiative, for with Japanese authority in disarray and no Allied forces present to accept their surrender, there was an unprecedented opportunity for independence to be grasped.

British Malaya and Singapore

To Sir Winston Churchill, the British Prime Minister, the fall of Singapore was the 'worst disaster' that had befallen British arms. Defeat by an underrated power – and an Asian one at that – was a devastating blow to British military pride. That some 120,000 Allied prisoners of war were taken by the Japanese in the Malayan campaign – and paraded openly in the streets for the local population to see – further added to Britain's humiliation. The myth of British invincibility was shattered forever. In London, a reappraisal of Britain's colonial record in Malaya was put into motion and, arising from that review, the Colonial Office undertook the planning of a new constitutional policy that would result in its controversial Malayan Union scheme after the war. That scheme envisaged London taking the unprecedented step of creating a united Malaya through what amounted to the annexation of the legally still-sovereign Malay states and their union with the former British Straits Settlements of Penang and Melaka. Even more ground-breaking was the proposal that Singapore, the remaining settlement, was to be detached from the Malayan Union to remain as a separate colony.

But while the shock of defeat was acutely felt in London, the scale of the tragedy reverberated even more resoundingly in the Asian communities in Malaya and Singapore who now faced a cruel occupation. Notwithstanding Japanese professions of 'Asia for Asians', they made it plain that their mission was empire-building, not liberating Asians from other empires. Singapore was quickly renamed *Syonan-to* or 'Island of the Light of the South' to reflect the island's new position as the center of the southern regions of Japan's Greater East Asia Co-Prosperity Sphere. In short, Malaya was now a Japanese colony within the empire – and its new masters would do as they pleased with it. The pre-war Federation of Malaya was dissolved and the peninsula was divided into ten provinces, each administered by a Japanese governor. Tokyo time, two hours ahead of Malayan time, was adopted as the standard for Malaya and Singapore. In October 1943, the four northern Malay states of Kelantan, Terengganu, Kedah, and Perlis were transferred to Thai control, partly to reward Bangkok for its support of Japanese objectives, but mainly to reduce the Japanese area of command and to release troops for the Burma campaign.

To impose law and order and to subdue the local population during the crucial early days of the occupation, Japanese soldiers of the 25th Army terrorized locals at will with slaps, kicks, arbitrary detention, rape, and torture, and meted out summary executions of looters – their decapitated heads impaled publicly on spikes as a warning. The overt use of terror to intimidate the local population abated only after the establishment of civil administration, although the pervasive presence and brutal tactics of the *Kempeitai*, the notorious military police, continued to strike fear in the local populations throughout the occupation years.

In dealing with Malaya's diverse communities, the Japanese adopted a varied approach. Their attitude towards the Chinese community was initially hostile and reflected their extreme distrust of the Malayan Chinese, many of whom had supported China's cause by participating in anti-Japanese activities before the invasion. Many of the soldiers of the 25th Army had a deep-seated dislike for the Chinese in Malaya as a result of their prior involvement in the protracted war against China. Eager to bring the Chinese population quickly to heel and to weed out hostile elements from within its midst so as to consolidate Japan's occupation and free up its army for combat operations elsewhere, a systematic campaign of public 'mass screening' of the adult male Chinese population, conducted with the help of hooded local informers, was undertaken in Singapore shortly after the occupation in February, and extended throughout Malaya in March. The notorious *sook ching* or so-called 'purification through elimination' campaigns targeted all Chinese men aged between 18 and 50 years, and especially those involved in any form of anti-Japanese activity, secret societies and those who had actively supported the British or Chongqing (Chungking) government. The Japanese took away thousands of Chinese men suspected of hostility towards them for summary execution. The victims included many who had no association with anti-Japanese activities. The number of Chinese who perished in the purge cannot be accurately ascertained but it was estimated that between 6000 and 40,000 could have been killed. The brutal Japanese assault on the Chinese community no doubt weakened open resistance to their rule but it also left an undercurrent of distrust and hatred towards the new masters.

After the initial purge of the Chinese, the Japanese regime – recognizing the value of Chinese wealth and enterprise for overcoming wartime shortages and restructuring the Malayan economy – adopted a more conciliatory policy towards them. An Overseas Chinese Association (OCA) with branches throughout Malaya was created for dealing with the Chinese. Chaired by a respected but reluctant Straits Chinese elder, Dr Lim Boon Keng, the OCA was given the task of raising MD 50 million from the Chinese community as a 'voluntary contribution' to the military administration to atone for their pre-war opposition to Japan. Despite strong Japanese pressure, the Chinese community managed to raise only MD 28 million and the OCA had to take a loan of the remaining MD 22 million from the Yokohama Specie Bank, to be repaid within a year at 6 percent interest. Overall, the large Chinese population in Malaya cooperated outwardly because they valued their lives and wanted to gain profits.

More radical elements among the Chinese refused to cooperate and joined the underground anti-Japanese resistance movement that became the Malayan People's Anti-Japanese Army (MPAJA), the armed wing of the Malayan Communist Party (MCP). British agents from Force 136, a unit of the British covert Special Operations Executive Far East, supplied them with arms and training. The MPAJA conducted raids behind enemy lines and, by the time the occupation ended, had units throughout the country and was then able to gain effective control of Malaya within days.

In contrast to the harsh treatment meted out to the Chinese, the Malays enjoyed generally favorable treatment from the Japanese. Prior to their invasion, the Japanese had cultivated ties with radical non-aristocratic Malay activists belonging to the *Kesatuan Melayu Muda* (KMM, Young Malay Union) whose aim was to achieve independence through a political union of the Malay peoples of Malaya and Indonesia. During the invasion of Malaya, KMM collaborators were involved in fifth-column activities as guides and interpreters for the Japanese army, and contributed to the mistaken perception in British Malaya Command that Malays as a community were actively collaborating with the Japanese.

As the Japanese distrusted the pro-British traditional Malay leadership, they favored and relied initially on the KMM activists to help them establish rapport with the Malay community during the immediate aftermath of their conquest. But five months into the occupation, the Japanese had doubts about encouraging the premature development of radical indigenous nationalist objectives and banned the KMM – just as they had disbanded the BIA in Burma. They thus politically marginalized the KMM. Its leader, Ibrahim Yaacob, however, was given the rank of Lieutenant Colonel and put in charge, under Japanese supervision, of a newly created Volunteer Army (*Giyugun*), also known in Malay as *Pembela Tanah Air* (PETA, Defenders of the Fatherland) – the same terms used for such organizations in Indonesia. The large-scale mobilization and militarization of young Malays were also carried out through other volunteer units like the *Heiho* (Auxiliary Servicemen) and *Giyutai* (Volunteer Corps). The use of such largely Malay units to assist the Japanese in supporting anti-MPAJA operations contributed in no small measure to the worsening of inter-ethnic relations between Malays and Chinese.

With the marginalization of the KMM, and given Japanese distrust of the pro-British Malay rulers, the way was open for the pre-war aristocratic elite and civil servants to assume the leadership of Malay communities. Upon the appointment of Japanese governors to run the Malay states, the status of the traditional Malay Sultans who headed the political and social order before the war was reduced from that of legal sovereigns to being subordinate officials. Confined to their palaces and cut off from their subjects, the rulers were not in a position to help or protect them as in pre-war days. The indigenous aristocratic elite and civil servants were now given the opportunity to rise to higher positions than had been possible under the British. By treating them well and promoting them, the Japanese also ensured their compliance and cooperation. The experience gained by these elites during the war years strengthened their political self-confidence and enabled them to have a head start in asserting the leadership of their communities when the British returned.

Like Malays, the Indians also enjoyed generally favorable treatment under Japanese rule. To encourage Indian nationalist activity aimed at overthrowing British rule in India, the Japanese supported organizations like the Indian Independence League (IIL) whose leadership included Indian nationalists like S. C. Goho, K. P. K. Menon, and Mohan Singh. In a series of mass rallies, Indian prisoners-of-war from the British army were invited to join the Indian National Army (INA) and large numbers did so. But friction with the Japanese over Indian nationalist objectives resulted in the replacement of the leadership and the appointment of the pro-Japanese Subhas Chandra Bose, a charismatic former President of the Indian National Congress, as the new leader of the IIL and INA in July 1943. Bose's call for the forceful liberation of India from British rule through cooperation with Japan and his organization of the Free India Army and the Free Indian Provisional Government aroused strong support among the Indian community. But his death in a plane crash at the end of the war deprived the IIL of its leader.

In Malaya, the shock of British defeat at the hands of Japanese forces left an indelible imprint on indigenous minds that the British were vulnerable rulers.

This set the stage for a simmering anti-colonial nationalism among the more radical elements. But this nascent territorial nationalism was still unable to transcend the ethnic divides that had become even deeper as a result of both Japan's uneven handling of the various communities and the increased ethnic competition and insecurity brought by wartime conditions. Heightened ethno-nationalism was played out violently after the Japanese surrender as Chinese and Malays clashed in parts of Malaya. The communal vendetta and bloodletting that ensued sorely tested inter-ethnic peace and threatened Malaya's increasingly fragile social stability.

French Indochina

The Japanese 'semi-occupation' of Indochina and the continuation of French rule until March 1945 produced a peculiar mixture of continuity and change. For much of the war, the colonial power remained in place and there was only slightly more space for nationalist activity than had been the case in the 1930s. The Japanese gave moral support and inspiration to some anti-colonial elements among the Vietnamese, while in Cambodia and Laos the French encouraged mild cultural nationalism. It was only after the Japanese *coup de force* of March 1945 that the situation changed dramatically, enabling new leaders and forces to emerge during the final months of the war. Most significant was the power vacuum following Japan's surrender, which provided an opportunity for the Indochinese Communist Party (ICP) to launch its revolution in Vietnam, just as it offered an opportunity for Indonesian nationalists to declare their Republic.

Japanese ambivalence towards Vietnamese nationalist aspirations has already been mentioned, but some contacts were established. Shortly before the war, a few Vietnamese nationalists had begun to look to Japan for inspiration and possible assistance, as an earlier generation had done several decades before. There was hope for the return of Prince Cuong De, who was still in exile in Tokyo. In particular, the Cao Dai and Hoa Hao sects developed a strong pro-Japanese orientation and began to disseminate alleged prophetic messages about the eventual defeat of the French and the return of Cuong De, 'the true king'. Japan also found allies among disaffected intellectuals, notably the Confucian scholar Tran Trong Kim and the former mandarin Ngo Dinh Diem, and did take some measures to protect them from French harassment.

Cambodia and Laos were of comparatively less significance and wartime developments in those colonies had little to do with Japanese influence until March 1945. The main threat to French rule came from across the Mekong, where Phibun's pan-Thai policies had revived psychological and cultural connections with Laos and, to a lesser extent, Cambodia. The Buddhist Institutes established by the French for the specific purpose of weakening these links now became gathering places for small groups of nationalist elites. Particularly in Cambodia, the small core of intellectuals associated with the Buddhist Institute and *Nagara Vatta* newspaper began to assert themselves more vocally.

In July 1942 there was an outbreak of anti-French sentiment in Cambodia centered on a prominent monk named Hem Chieu, who became involved in a plot against the colonial regime. He was arrested and forced to defrock without the proper religious ceremonies, which was a grave offence in many Cambodians' eyes. Laymen affiliated with *Nagara Vatta* joined with a number of monks to organize a large-scale protest in Phnom Penh, which was quickly suppressed by the authorities. This event became known as the 'Umbrella War' because so many Buddhist monks carry umbrellas to protect themselves from the sun. Hem Chieu and several other nationalist figures were packed off to prison, where the ex-monk died the following year.

The wartime period saw the appearance of two figures who would dominate the Cambodian scene for the next few decades, often as bitter rivals. King Norodom Sihanouk (r. 1941–55, 1993–2004) was the last 'protected monarch' under colonial rule, while Son Ngoc Thanh, the ethnic Khmer from Cochin China, was among the group of intellectuals linked to the Buddhist Institute. He emerged as a vocal nationalist after the outbreak of the war and was involved with the protests in July 1942. Thanh escaped to Thailand and ended up in Tokyo, one of the few Cambodians to have openly established links with Japan. There is some evidence of Japanese support for the protests, but the nature and degree of this support are not clear.

After the Japanese coup of March 1945, Cambodia was granted nominal independence and King Sihanouk assumed a more active and prominent role in his country's affairs. Son Ngoc Thanh returned and briefly served as Prime Minister in Sihanouk's government. But the two men had different agendas and, for Sihanouk, Thanh soon became a threat rather than an ally. When the Japanese surrender brought first British occupation and then the return of the French, Thanh's efforts to organize resistance were overruled by Sihanouk. In October 1945, Thanh was arrested and sent off to exile in France, temporarily removing an obstacle to the King's ambitions.

Although wartime Laos experienced nothing comparable to the Umbrella War, nationalist sentiments were quietly fermenting just the same. The French were generally more successful at promoting a kind of 'loyalist nationalism' among Lao intellectuals than they were in Cambodia. *Lao Nhai* ('Great Laos' or 'Greater Laos'), the counterpart to the *Nagara Vatta* newspaper, lent its name to a movement – carefully directed by the French – which aimed at a cultural renaissance among the elite. While *Lao Nhai* did discuss nationalist themes, it was generally more critical of Vietnamese immigration into Laos than of the colonial regime. Meanwhile, another group of nationalists took refuge across the Mekong and forged links with prominent Thai figures. These exiles were to appear on the scene in March 1945 as the *Lao Issara* (Independent Lao). The most important figure, however, was Phetsarath, the French-educated prince who had become the highest-ranking Lao in the colonial government. He had often expressed criticism of certain policies, particularly regarding the immigration issue, and had both the popularity and the ambition to play an even greater role. The opportunity came in March 1945. Phetsarath, who had held the newly created post of Prime Minister since 1941, cooperated with the Japanese while strengthening his hand against his cousins the king and crown prince, who remained loyal to the now-disempowered French.

The Japanese surrender in August 1945 left a power vacuum with competing factions of Lao jockeying for power. Although some of the elite refused to be associated with an anti-French movement, Phetsarath was able to cobble together a provisional government with returnees from Thailand and his half-brother Souphanouvong, who had a more radical political orientation and close connections to revolutionaries in Vietnam. King Sisavangvong (r. 1904–59) attempted to restore the protectorate in anticipation of a French return, but he was overruled and forced to abdicate. In October 1945 a full-fledged 'Lao Issara' government was proclaimed in Vientiane. Although Phetsarath declined to head the new government, his personal prestige was to a large extent the glue holding it together. The Lao Issara regime was fragile, however, and its control over more remote parts of the country tenuous. More crucially, it lacked the firepower to oppose the French forces which began to infiltrate across the Mekong in late 1945. After several months of resistance, the Vientiane government (including Phetsarath) fled to Thailand and the king ruled once more from Luang Phabang under French authority.

March 1945 also gave birth to an 'independent' government in Vietnam, as the 'Empire of Annam' re-emerged under Emperor Bao Dai, seconded by Tran Trong Kim as Prime Minister. While the Japanese remained the power behind the throne, the imperial government did exercise more authority than it had under the French – although only in Tonkin and Annam, since Japan retained control over Cochin China. Kim and a newly assembled cabinet made valiant attempts to deal with the country's problems, the most serious being a major famine which had broken out in the northern provinces. This crisis, which was due to a combination of Japanese requisition of grain and the disruption of supplies from the south caused by Allied bombings, caused an estimated two million deaths, and it proved to be more than the regime could manage. Equally serious, however, was the threat from the ICP-led revolutionary movement, which had been building up its strength throughout the war.

In February 1941, Nguyen Ai Quoc – now calling himself Ho Chi Minh, the name he would bear until his death – slipped over the border from China into the homeland he had left nearly three decades before. The ICP held a Party conference at Pac Bo in the northern province of Cao Bang in May 1941 and established a Party-led popular front, usually known as the Viet Minh. Ho and his comrades judged correctly that the French-Japanese coexistence would not last forever, so they concentrated on expanding their rural base of support while avoiding clashes with either foreign occupier as much as possible. Toward the end of the war, Ho was able to build ties with American forces operating out of China. Meanwhile, the famine provided an opportunity to strengthen support for the Viet Minh by confiscating and distributing stocks of grain. The imperial government was able to make some headway in the towns and cities, but increasingly large patches of the countryside belonged to the Viet Minh. When the Japanese surrendered, Ho issued a general call to arms and a series of localized seizures of power ensued throughout the three regions of colonial Vietnam. Although this 'August Revolution' was less organized and more fragmented than Party histories have acknowledged, the Viet Minh was able to seize power. On 2 September 1945, Ho proclaimed the Democratic Republic of

Vietnam to cheering crowds in Hanoi. The euphoria was short-lived, however, as the Vietnamese were soon confronted by British and Chinese occupying forces as well as the threat of an imminent French return.

American Philippines

In January 1942, having secured Manila, the Japanese proclaimed the end of American occupation. Tens of thousands of foreign nationals, including Jews who had escaped Nazi persecution in Europe and fled to the Philippines only to be imprisoned by the Japanese, were interned at the University of Santo Tomas. Filipinos were ordered to sever relations with Americans in any capacity, while fulfilling the needs of the Japanese military. But Filipinos dragged their feet. Only a few obeyed the Japanese order to turn in their arms, for they expected the USAFFE to return, at which time their weapons would prove invaluable. Those caught by the military police (*Kempeitei*) were imprisoned, beaten, decapitated, or shot.

To maintain the order that was needed to extract the country's resources, the Japanese relied on national figures. General Masami Maeda authorized the establishment of the Philippine Executive Commission, staffed by Commonwealth leaders who were left behind by the fleeing Quezon. They included Jorge Vargas, Quintin Paredes, Benigno Aquino, Jose Laurel, Antonio de las Alas, and Jose Yulo. Conceived as an advisory commission, over time it obtained limited powers in administrative and executive matters. For purposes of social control and surveillance, the Japanese created neighborhood associations of five to ten families across the archipelago, as they did in other occupied areas. The associations ensured attendance at public events, functioned as small-scale administrative units, and distributed the meagre provisions the Japanese provided for the populace at large. In a remarkably short time, the Japanese administration had seemingly reached the lives of millions of ordinary Filipinos.

Having banned political parties, the Japanese instituted the supposedly apolitical public service organization known as *Kapisanan sa Paglilingod sa Bagong Pilipinas* (KALIBAPI, Association for Service to the New Philippines). Only members of KALIBAPI could work for the administration (or in a related capacity). Headed by Japanophile Benigno S. Ramos, KALIBAPI's mass drive for membership produced mixed results. By July 1943, it tallied only 350,000 members.

Japanese wartime policy was characterized by repression and co-optation. To build a new Philippines, Filipinos were encouraged to celebrate their Asian nature by shedding the 'degenerate' influence of American culture based on individualism, liberalism, and democracy. Strict censorship was also imposed. The *Kempeitai* closed newspapers, and put all other forms of mass media and publication under the eventual control of the Japanese-run agency *Manila Shinbun-sha*. Of particular concern was preventing Filipinos from listening to foreign radio broadcasts; in their stead, the airways were filled with Japanese propaganda.

In their attempts to de-Americanize Filipinos and celebrate their own putatively indigenous culture, the Japanese banned the use of English, making

Japanese and Tagalog official languages. Streets, for instance, were renamed in one of those two languages. The Japanese also reconstituted public education, which included the rewriting of textbooks. With Japanese as the language of instruction, pedagogy emphasized the role of Filipinos in the Greater East Asia Co-Prosperity Sphere, discouraged materialism, and promoted vocational education. Results did not, however, conform to Japanese plans. Teachers creatively distorted official lesson plans, while the number of enrolled students during this difficult time dropped precipitiously.

Leaders in Tokyo ensured the collaboration of the Filipino elite by promising independence before December 1943. In June, KALIBAPI was permitted to form the Preparatory Commission for Philippine Independence. The constitution it drafted stressed the duties and obligations of the country's citizens in the Greater East Asia Co-Prosperity Sphere. The Japanese administration congratulated the commission on its work. Delegates to the National Assembly were thereafter elected. Benigno S. Aquino was chosen as Speaker of the Assembly and Jose P. Laurel as President of the new Republic. On 14 October 1943, the Japanese-sponsored Republic of the Philippines was officially declared. Veteran of the 1896 Revolution General Emilio Aguinaldo and Japanophile Artemio Ricarte hoisted the Philippines flag as the national anthem played, displays of nationalism formerly banned under the Japanese. Only Japan and its occupied territories recognized the new Republic, whose treaty of alliance with Tokyo provided for close collaboration on political, economic, and military matters. The agreement struck fear among Filipinos, as mandatory conscription beckoned. Laurel tried to assuage their fear by announcing that Filipinos would be deployed only within the Philippines.

In an attempt to demonstrate his authority, Laurel successfully lobbied the Japanese to grant amnesty to citizens convicted of political crimes of sedition, illicit association, engaging in guerrilla activity, rumor-mongering, and the like. As a result, according to the Japanese-controlled daily, *The Tribune*, thousands of guerrillas surrendered. Rehabilitation funds were disbursed to dozens of governors. The exercise was farcical. Under pressure, governors randomly gathered people who 'surrendered' multiple times. Locally, this became a badge of honor.

Meanwhile, food shortages devastated society. By November 1943, the shortfall of rice in Manila reached alarming levels; the starving and dying littered the streets. To alleviate pressure upon resources, the Laurel government transferred civil servants to the provinces. Despite rationing, attempts by the National Rice and Corn Corporation (NARIC) to procure rice were unsuccessful. Dealers hoarded supplies and traded only with the Japanese Army and Japanese companies, who controlled the currency, or with black marketeers. The last paid two to three times government prices, which caused the price of rice in the open market to soar.

In January 1944, the Bigasang Bayan (BIBA, People's Rice Granary) replaced the ineffectual NARIC. This new body – less crippled by corruption than the NARIC – for a short time rather successfully acquired rice and other cereals from Central Luzon. This enabled the government to ration rice at 120 grams per day per person in Manila. Later this was lowered to 60 grams, supplemented with an equal amount of sweet potatoes. But as conditions deteriorated, the rations dried up altogether.

To alleviate the crisis, Laurel created special courts to try profiteers and hoarders but only a few cases were filed. He also mandated governors and mayors to meet rice quotas and expand areas planted with food crops. Filipinos aged 16 to 60 were drafted to labor in the fields for one eight-hour day per week. The lack of transportation, robbery, and frequent attacks by Japanese soldiers and Filipino guerrillas hindered the program. In a measure of last resort, Laurel authorized the Constabulary to confiscate rice from hoarders. Dealers bribed the constabulary, however, and the confiscated rice rarely reached its intended destination. The *Kempeitai* took matters into their own hands, forcibly seizing rice from hoarders and producers without informing the Filipino administration. Laurel demanded that the stocks be returned. Rice only trickled in and its price remained high. Abandoning its resolve to be independent of the Japanese, the government replaced BIBA with a joint Filipino-Japanese Rice and Corn Administration. Most of the produce it obtained was consumed by the Japanese Army.

The worsening economic and social conditions further damaged the standing of the Japanese. Stories of the horrific Bataan Death March demonized them in the eyes of Filipinos, who longed for the fulfillment of General MacArthur's promise to return. Filipinos associated the pre-war American presence with prosperity and contentment. Men were angered by the Japanese officers' penchant for publicly slapping them in the face for small infractions, while rape and the forced sexual slavery of Filipino women further alienated the populace at large. Anger began to solidify into resistance.

In simplified terms, Filipino resistance was divided between the *Hukbong Mapagpalaya Laban sa mga Hapon* (Hukbalahap, United Army Against the Japanese), a left-leaning organization based in Central Luzon that championed independence, and an archipelago-wide network of guerrillas loyal to the Americans and the USAFFE. The former, whose members became known as Huks, espoused equal distribution of land for Central Luzon's peasants. The Huks found ample support among other leftist organizations, including the pre-war CCP and the newly established Squadron 48 (*Wa Chi*). The latter was a China-backed organization consisting of Chinese trade unionists, teachers, clerks, and newspapermen from Manila. The Huks regularly ambushed Japanese troops and confiscated their weapons and foodstuffs. They saw themselves as the people's army. To keep their organization corruption-free, they would punish anyone – even decorated soldiers – who abused his authority.

USAFFE guerrilla units provided MacArthur with intelligence on Japanese troop movements and installations. Many units were led by American or Filipino USAFFE officers who had refused to surrender or escaped from imprisonment. Guerrillas distributed underground newspapers and, by keeping some areas free of Japanese control, they brought about a semblance of stability during the occupation. They were also riddled with infighting and abuse of authority. One infamous case in Rizal pitted two groups, known as Hunters and Markings, against each other, a conflict that ended in significant bloodshed. Other bands instilled fear and hatred among communities by sequestering goods, molesting citizens, and raping women. For their unique assistance to the Americans, guerrillas evaded punishment and even enjoyed post-war rewards while others were subjected to accusations and indictments for collaboration with the Japanese.

In September 1944, in response to American bombing of Japanese installations in and around Manila, the newly appointed General Yamashita assigned his best commanders to defend Leyte, where he rightly assumed the Americans would concentrate their attack. But the American naval onslaught overwhelmed Japanese forces, destroying defense facilities and supply dumps. On 20 October 1944, MacArthur returned to the Philippines as he had promised. American forces and Filipino resistance groups relentlessly pursued the Japanese. By February 1945, they had secured Manila. The Japanese-installed puppet government was forced into exile and the Japanese empire collapsed on its southeastern front.

Conclusion

The Japanese occupation of Southeast Asia produced a wide variety of consequences, but there were some striking parallels across the region. With colonial authority destroyed, urban nationalists sought an opportunity to strengthen their ties with rural comunities and to espouse notions of an independent nation – ideas that under European authorities were often considered seditious or criminal. Within limits, the Japanese occupiers allowed student leaders, politicans, and local activists to articulate such ideas. Japanese brutality meanwhile widened the constituency of those who sought to be rid of all foreign overlords. Older generations of politicans who had worked within the colonial system were often marginalized or even imprisoned on suspicion that they remained loyal to the colonial power. With younger, more outspoken local leaders at the helm, it even appeared at first that the Greater East Asia Co-Prosperity Sphere might be achieved alongside local aspirations for independence. But Japanese oppression and then the defeat of Japan closed that door and opened other possibilities and opportunities for activists to grasp.

Crucially, the Japanese developed and nurtured national armies in the former colonial states. Such indigenous military forces contributed to the mobilization of the countryside and the spread of nationalist ideals. They offered local (and often competing) political, economic, and social interests a common cause worth fighting for. Pre-existing rivalries that stemmed from class, ethnic, religious, and patron-client loyalties were often – but not always – de-emphasized as long as a common enemy and interests were maintained. In British Burma and Dutch Indonesia, the nationalist armed forces tended to diminish the influence of Communist groups by incorporating them into their ranks, although in French Indochina the Communists continued to operate independently and were able to dominate anti-colonial action. The intimate association of national armed forces and the struggle for independence in Burma and Indonesia would help to shape the nature of post-independence politics in those two countries, while the absence of a Japanese-sponsored national army in Vietnam facilitated the growth and popularity of the Communist Party.

At the point when the Japanese surrendered in August 1945, key elements shaping the contested post-war period were already identifiable. The Western colonial powers were poised to attempt to return to their former colonies but – with the exception of the Americans – they had little understanding of how profound the changes during the Japanese occupation had been. Many leaders in British Burma and Malaya, French Indochina, and Dutch Indonesia expected some form of political independence in recognition for their role in opposing the Japanese, but few could reach a concensus on what form their new national community might take. Even in the Philippines – where independence was already scheduled – conflicting elites had wildly different expectations of the political future. The Vietnam War(s), the Indonesian Revolution, the Burmese threat of revolution, the conflicting movements of Laos and Cambodia, and the violence that took place in Malaya and the Philippines after the war were due in part to varying visions of what should constitute the new national community, who should lead it, and what sort of country should emerge. In some cases, claims of legitimacy were drawn from the war experience, but in other cases long-standing patron-client rivalries, ethnic tensions and religious differences re-emerged onto the political scene. A difficult, often violent, road to independence lay ahead.

11
Regaining Independence in the Decades After 1945

Introduction

As we have seen in the preceding chapter, World War II had a major impact throughout Southeast Asia, but the precise nature of that impact varied from place to place. There has been some debate among historians about how the war's legacy shaped the decolonization that followed it. Some regard the Japanese occupation period as a momentous historical epoch that fundamentally transformed Southeast Asia by introducing important psychological, political, and social changes. It not only heightened indigenous peoples' sense of nationalism and ushered in the era of mass anti-colonial mobilization in its aftermath, but also facilitated the rise of new elites who displaced pro-colonial traditional leaders and led the ensuing anti-colonial struggle. Japanese discriminatory policy towards different ethnic groups also intensified social conflict and communal strife, leaving a legacy of simmering social tensions for many years to come. More 'revisionist' historians seek to temper this thesis by pointing to the structural continuities that persisted, but they have not demolished the thesis altogether. In the aftermath of the war, enlightened opinion neither within colonial nor within indigenous ranks seriously believed that the pre-war *status quo ante* could be fully restored. That realization propelled the nationalist leaders to press for independence. Such enlightened thought, however, was hardly a majority view on the colonial side. Nevertheless, after 1945, decolonization – previously unthinkable – became very thinkable. Eventually even reluctant colonial powers were compelled to relinquish political control.

Southeast Asian decolonization is a complex subject. In some places, indigenous nationalism began decades before the World War II; in others it began in earnest only in the war's aftermath. Among Western colonial powers, too, there was no unanimity regarding the future of colonial empires, for European powers had not lost the will to rule non-Europeans. While the principle of preparatory 'trusteeship' for eventual self-government guided British colonial policy, there was no discernible timetable for the transfer of power. Instead, the spread of freedom, as the British Colonial Secretary Malcolm MacDonald said in 1938, was to be a slow, evolutionary process that could take generations or even centuries. For French colonial policy, premised as it was on the tradition of the indivisibility of France and its empire, the concept of decolonization was anathema to its doctrines of 'assimilation' or 'association'. The more obscure colonial aims of the Dutch envisaged neither assimilation nor independence for overseas territories. Only American colonial policy had a timetable setting down independence for the Philippines in 1946. What is incontrovertible is that in all of Southeast Asia, the formal ending of empires was a post-1945 phenomenon, emerging from a world turned upside down by the war.

Theoretical explanations for the fall of European empires tend to emphasize one of three main causes. The first is the international. Decolonization took place in the context of the upheaval wrought upon both the European powers and the colonized peoples by World War II and the emergence in its aftermath of a bipolar world dominated by two avowedly anti-imperialist powers, the United States and the USSR. This created novel conditions hostile to the retention of colonial empires. After 1945, it is argued, imperialism was on the defensive and rear-guard attempts by the colonial powers to cling to their empires were not sustainable in a post-war order that cherished the principle of self-determination, proclaimed by Allied wartime propaganda as the *raison d'être* for the war. The second explanation sees imperial retreat as a deliberate, if not entirely voluntary, choice by waning or indifferent metropolitan powers, for whom the burdens of empire had become too great. Thus, an orderly transfer of power was perceived as an expedient exit strategy. When the crunch finally came, deals were struck with local nationalists and withdrawal timed to ensure that power was transferred only to those whom the colonial rulers considered 'moderate' and 'safe', thereby safeguarding the colonialists' interests within a post-colonial order. A third explanation locates the crucial force in ending the Western empires in the emergence of an irresistible indigenous mass nationalism that demanded independence and threatened the colonial authorities with either rebellion or civil resistance if it was not hastened. This view argues that once local nationalist leaders were able to galvanize mass support for independence, the days of colonialism were numbered.

While theories of decolonization provide useful insights, they are insufficient on their own to explain the complex changes that brought about the ending of empires. Mobilizing *en masse* a strong and cohesive indigenous nationalism from among peoples divided by ethnic, cultural, class, and religious cleavages, for instance, was always more difficult that it appears in hindsight. Nor could it be assumed that the act of mounting a risky war of independence or a sustained campaign of civil disobedience against a determined and well-equipped colonial foe would necessarily succeed. Even if the metropolitan powers realized that they had to adjust to changed post-war circumstances, it is far from clear that they intended a reduction of their imperial roles after 1945. Indeed, some regarded their status as great powers to be inextricably tied to the retention of colonial empires. Few also believed that a colonial war was militarily unwinnable. It is also not evident that metropolitan rulers were either in the mood or in a position to strike bargains and buy off local nationalism in order to dictate the timing of withdrawal. And while it may also be true that seismic changes at the international level altered the balance of power and favored change, it is not clear that these changes really signified the passing of the old

European order and the colonial structures that accompanied it. Both the United States and USSR were preoccupied in other theatres of global competition. American opposition to old-school imperialism turned out to be far more flexible than ideologically inspired, leaving the colonial powers with more latitude to restore their empires in Southeast Asia than had sometimes been expected.

It should be obvious that no single cause will be sufficient to account for the break-up of colonial empires in Southeast Asia. Just as it was the confluence of interlocking circumstances at the international, metropolitan, and indigenous levels that had preserved the stability of the old pre-war colonial order, so it seems reasonable to accept that disruptions at any of these levels were likely to have an effect at other levels, ricocheting off each other to produce further consequential changes that would set off further rounds of adjustments and adaptations. In the dissolution of colonial empires in Southeast Asia, the disruption caused by World War II would appear significant in this respect, as seen in the completeness of the imperial withdrawal in the decades after 1945. Before the war there was nothing in the colonial world to predict what took place after 1945. It is thus appropriate to suggest that, while changes at the international, metropolitan, and indigenous levels created the complex of transformations we call decolonization, it may have been developments at the international level – in particular World War II and its aftershocks – that ignited the series of upheavals which finally destroyed colonial rule in Southeast Asia.

The politics of decolonization

The new international context

The world in the late 1940s faced unique circumstances. In August 1945, the old balance-of-power international order was utterly destroyed. The United States stood alone as the hegemon, richer and stronger than at the beginning of the war, and at the time the world's only nuclear-armed nation. There was no other power to counterbalance the United States. Japan, Germany, France, the Netherlands, and much of the rest of Europe were in ruins, the United Kingdom was exhausted, the USSR was devastated and not yet a nuclear power, China was in the midst of civil war between Mao's Communists and Chiang's Nationalists, and the colonial empires in Southeast Asia were destroyed or (in the case of Burma and the Philippines) only precariously reclaimed from Japanese occupation. So if the European colonial powers were to re-establish themselves in Southeast Asia, they could only do so with at least some degree of acquiescence from the United States, which in principle opposed the whole idea in 1945. America believed that it offered a superior model to the old colonial powers of Europe in its governance of the Philippines, its struggle alongside Filipino allies to defeat the Japanese, and its determination voluntarily to grant independence on schedule in 1946. Another new element was the United Nations, which was founded in 1945 and – still untried – inspired hopes that it could be a truly international force for peace in the world. As the later 1940s passed, this state of affairs evolved into the Cold War, as the USSR revived, dominated Eastern Europe, and became the world's second nuclear power. That introduced anti-Communism as a central element into American policy calculation and altered the context in which Southeast Asian decolonization took place. Some benefited from these changes and some lost by them. As will be seen below, for the Indonesian revolutionaries these international evolutions worked to their advantage; for Ho Chi Minh's fighters, they worked to their disadvantage. The colonial powers and nationalist movements of Southeast Asia all had to negotiate the changing dynamics of the international political world, not least because in all cases the colonial overlords lived in that world.

The Philippines

Of the colonial dependencies in Southeast Asia, the Philippines was unique in that a time-table for independence had been fixed prior to World War II. As we saw in Chapter 9, under the terms of the Tydings-McDuffie Act of 1934, a Philippines Commonwealth government was established with a ten-year transition to full independence, scheduled for 4 July 1946. War disrupted the Commonwealth government, but did not delay the schedule for independence.

On 27 February 1945, while American forces suppressed the last pockets of Japanese resistance in the mountains, the Commonwealth government went back to work in Manila. Sergio Osmeña succeeded as President, Quezon having died in the United States six months earlier. Osmeña's government distributed relief commodities, reopened schools and colleges, and began the arduous task of rehabilitating transport, communication, trade, and industry. General Douglas MacArthur overshadowed everything until he moved to head the Allied occupation of Japan. That he represented a reimposition of American sovereignty was ignored, for many equated him with liberation from Japanese oppression and the return of pre-war affluence.

MacArthur treated the archipelago as his fiefdom and sought to restore the *status quo ante*. The Philippine Civil Affairs Unit distributed relief goods and established civil governments in reoccupied territories. The Counter Intelligence Corps (CIC) screened civil officers before appointment, which allowed the Americans to secure the loyalty of provincial and town authorities with little intervention from the Commonwealth government. Members of the leftist Hukbalahap and USAFFE guerrilla organizations were treated differently. Whereas Americans rewarded the latter with money and government positions, they persecuted the former as criminals and Communists. Huks were disarmed and arrested, accused by the CIC of being enemies of the American and Filipino governments. In 1945 the military held Huk leaders Luis Taruc and Casto Alejandrino for seven months without charges. MacArthur was ambiguous on the issue of collaboration with the Japanese. He ignored the directive that collaborators were under the jurisdiction of civil authorities. A sweeping anti-collaborator policy would imprison most of the political elite and undercut his desire to restore prewar stability. Some former officials of the Japanese-sponsored government such as Jose Yulo, Antonio de las Alas, Quintin Paredes and Teofilo Sison were hence 'captured', while their colleague Manuel Roxas – who was MacArthur's friend and a former USAFFE brigadier-general – was 'liberated'.

In June 1945 the pre-war Philippine Legislature convened for the first time and elected Roxas as Senate President. He used this new position to bolster his presidential campaign and convinced Congress to pass a bill that allowed bail to 5000 Filipinos held by the CIC. Predictably, the Congressmen among these former detainees threw their support to Roxas. Later he and his associates left the ruling NP and formed the Liberal Party. Wealthy Nacionalistas, led by Chinese tycoon Alfonso Sycip, supported their election bid. Later, after becoming President of the Republic, Roxas amnestied all who had collaborated with the Japanese, with the exception of those convicted of crimes of violence.

Osmeña's NP was forced to form a loose coalition with the political group Democratic Alliance, which was a united front consisting of the guerrilla groups Hukbalahap, Free Philippines, and Blue Eagle; the peasant organization National Farmers' Union (*Pambansang Kaisahan ng mga Magbubukid*); the labor group Committee on Labor Organization; and the progressive organizations League for National Liberation, Anti-Traitors League, Anti-Japanese League, and Civil Liberties Union. The Democratic Alliance stood for independence, democracy, social security, agrarian reforms, and industrialization, and was against former collaborators.

The NP-Democratic Alliance coalition isolated Osmeña from the economic oligarchy and made him an unsuitable ally for the United States. Filipino and American backers flocked to his rival Roxas. His contributors included MacArthur's close associates Andres Soriano, Jacobo Zobel, and Joseph McMicking, along with businessmen Joaquin Elizalde and Tomas Morato. The newspapers *Daily News* and *Balita* featured Roxas as the more energetic and intelligent candidate who could tackle the task of reconstruction by attracting massive American investment. He won the 1946 election by 203,000 votes. Keeping precisely to schedule, on 4 July 1946, the Philippines was granted its independence.

After the formal grant of independence, Roxas was inaugurated as the President of the Philippine Republic (1946–48). In several ways he bound the Philippines to the United States. He campaigned for the passage of the Bell Act which extended free trade between the two countries until 1954, thereafter slowly increased import tariffs on American goods over 20 years, and granted Americans parity rights to exploit Philippines natural resources, acquire public land and domain, and operate public utilities in the Philippines on the same footing as Filipino citizens. Roxas neutralized possible votes against this bill by preventing seven Democratic Alliance congressmen from taking their seats. He also signed the Military Bases Agreement which allowed the United States to retain jurisdiction over 23 base sites in the Philippines for 99 years. Under the Military Assistance Pact, the United States furnished military supplies to the Philippines, trained its military personnel, and admitted Filipinos to American military academies. The Philippines received from the American government USD 120 million for road and transport reconstruction, USD 100 million worth of military property, and USD 400 million as compensation for property losses and damages.

The government acted violently against its perceived enemies in the Hukbalahap and National Farmers' Union. Military Police and civilian guards raided and terrorized 'Huk' *barrios* and tortured or shot suspected Huks and PKMs. Huk leaders Mateo del Castillo and Luis Taruc evaded assassination by going underground; peasant leader Juan Feleo was not as fortunate. These persecutions fueled a Huk rebellion which raged in Luzon and the Visayas from 1946 until 1954. In 1947 Taruc's demands for a peace settlement included the enforcement of the Bill of Rights, the dismissal of charges against Huks, the replacement of 'Fascist-minded' officials, the restoration of all Democratic Alliance congressmen, and the implementation of land reform. The government agreed to none of these demands.

In 1948 the Hukbalahap and PKM were outlawed. President Elpidio Quirino (g. 1948–53) briefly achieved a peace agreement with their leaders, but government harassment and killings of their members continued. Hence Huk leaders resolved to overthrow the government via armed struggle, and *c*.1950 seemed close to doing so. American forces became involved through the Joint US Military Advisory Group and thus the threat posed by leftist insurrection was suppressed. The Philippines armed forces were transformed into a counter-insurgency force which deployed agents who infiltrated the Huks and turned them against each other. In October 1950 the Huk politburo was arrested and jailed. To end the resistance of the already demoralized Huks, Defense Secretary Ramon Magsaysay offered them land and economic assistance to resettle in Mindanao.

In 1953, with the help of the CIA, the Catholic Church, professional associations and anti-Communist peasant and labor groups – who formed the election watchdog National Movement for Free Elections (NAMFREL) – Magsaysay became President (g. 1953–57). A hands-on leader, he introduced reforms that built the people's trust in the presidency and alleviated the plight of the poor. To assist farmers, he installed a Presidential Assistant for Community Development. Military officers served in such executive offices as the Bureau of Customs and the Mindanao resettlement programs. Magsaysay's network of public and private organizations mobilized neighborhoods independently of landlords and local bosses. A nation so much in need of such leadership and reconciliation had reason to mourn his tragic death in an airplane crash in May 1957.

Burma

Unlike the experience in the Philippines, the passing of the British empire in Burma was hardly an orderly transfer of power. As we have already seen, the 1935 Government of Burma Act left Burma just short of a self-governing dominion. After elections in December 1936, the new constitution was implemented on 1 April 1937. Despite the evident constitutional progressivism, the system was weighed down by indecisive coalition politics, factionalism, and corruption. The British declared that 'Dominion status' was their goal for Burma, but refused to be tied to a specific timetable.

When the Japanese conquered Burma, British officials led by Governor Sir Reginald Dorman-Smith (g. 1941–46) retreated to India and set up a government in exile at Simla. Planners in London, working in consultation with

Dorman-Smith, came up with ideas for post-war Burma that were published as a White Paper in May 1945. In essence, this plan envisaged a period of 'direct rule' after the war, lasting about three years, to enable the authorities to undertake economic rehabilitation. In due course, elections would be held under the existing 1935 Act and the Burmese legislature restored, following which a new constitution would be drafted to give Burma democratic self-government within the British Commonwealth. The minority-populated hill areas would be excluded from this arrangement unless the minority groups themselves expressed a desire for association with the rest of Burma. The White Paper failed, however, to take into account growing Burmese demands for a swift transition to self-government and indeed placed Burma in a worse constitutional position than before the 1935 Act. It represented political regression, not advancement, and was doomed to failure.

As noted in the preceding chapter, by war's end Burmese nationalism was a formidable force with military capability. After Burma was granted sham 'independence' by the Japanese on 1 August 1943 – and as Burmese acquired greater administrative experience and confidence by filling government positions – return to a colonial relationship was unlikely to be accepted. Aung San, who emerged as the foremost nationalist leader, was determined to rid Burma of both its new Japanese and old British masters. While ostensibly collaborating with the Japanese, in August 1944 he gathered Burmese nationalist forces together under a broad united front organization, the Anti-Fascist Organization (AFO), which shortly became a powerful political party as the Anti-Fascist People's Freedom League (AFPFL). Aung San secretly contacted the British through Force 136 agents in Burma and offered assistance to the Supreme Allied Commander South East Asia, Admiral Lord Louis Mountbatten, who formally assumed responsibility for the administration of Burma from 1 January 1944. Mountbatten agreed in February 1945 to arm Aung San's forces and to regard them as a pro-Allied force, even though Dorman-Smith and his superiors in London had reservations about the merits of a liberal policy towards the former Japanese collaborators, fearing future political difficulties. On 27 March 1945, the AFO rebelled against the Japanese. As British troops reoccupied Burma in stages, the AFO and the BNA took advantage of the Japanese retreat to spread their influence. After the liberation of Rangoon by British-Indian forces on 3 May 1945, a detachment of the BNA joined other formations of Mountbatten's command at a victory parade on 16 June. Mountbatten's decision to recognize rather than to suppress the AFO had far-reaching consequences for Burmese independence, for it allowed Aung San and his political vehicle, the AFO (now renamed the AFPFL), to be thrust into the forefront of the Burmese nationalist movement.

Predictably, Burmese nationalist reactions to the publication of the White Paper of May 1945 were wholly negative. The AFPFL demanded that the right of self-determination be applied forthwith to Burma. But with South East Asia Command forces still in Burma, the AFPFL was not prepared to challenge the British with arms. It did, however, resist British endeavors to demobilize its military arm and to absorb eligible fighters into regular battalions under British command. By early September 1945, Aung San and Mountbatten agreed that willing former Burmese fighters could be enlisted into the Burma Army under their own officers, although under overall British command. Aung San himself was offered the rank of Brigadier, but he turned this down to devote himself to the political struggle for independence – backed by his proven potential to mobilize force.

Relations between the AFPFL and the British worsened with the return of Governor Dorman-Smith and the restoration of civil government in October 1945. Out of touch and refusing to believe that the AFPFL had popular support, Dorman-Smith brushed aside its demand that it be given the right to appoint seven of the 11 members in the Governor's Executive Council. He instead filled the latter with his own loyalist nominees. Ill-advised by his aides, the Governor also considered charging Aung San with the 1942 murder of a pro-British village headman. The Governor dropped the matter after London intervened, but by this time he had left the impression that he had blinked after staring Aung San in the face. Excluded from the government, the AFPFL set its sights on mobilizing the country. As President of the AFPFL, Aung San went on up-country tours and campaigned vigorously for independence, showcasing in the process his masterly ability to stage – and control – spectacular mass rallies that captured the popular imagination. He also gathered new recruits and the substantial number of former fighters who had not enlisted in the Burma Army to form the People's Volunteer Organization (PVO), ostensibly a welfare group engaged in reconstruction and law-and-order activities, but potentially a quasi-military arm of the AFPFL; its members wore uniforms and drilled in public. Aung San kept the British guessing: while he indicated that he would prefer to achieve independence peacefully, he shrewdly gave the impression that he would not shrink from violence to gain Burma's freedom. Dorman-Smith's tactic of ignoring the AFPFL and excluding it from sharing power was not working and had contributed instead to creating a volatile political situation. Stricken with dysentery, the Governor went on home leave in June 1946. At the end of August he was replaced by Sir Hubert Rance, the former head of the post-war military administration in Burma and Mountbatten's choice for the job.

Within a week of his arrival, Rance was greeted by a strike by the Rangoon police over pay. The strike soon widened to include police outside Rangoon and then threatened to bring all public services to a halt. With the AFPFL exploiting the strikers' cause and the government on the brink of collapse, Rance concluded that the White Paper was unworkable and that the inclusion of the AFPFL in the government was necessary to defusing the explosive situation. After consulting London, he opened negotiations with Aung San. Dismissing the Executive Council that he inherited from Dorman-Smith, Rance announced on 28 September 1946 the formation of a new Executive Council with an AFPFL majority – six out of 11. In October, the AFPFL expelled its Communist faction, which controlled the All-Burma Trade Union Congress, after it tried to obstruct the settlement of the strike. In November, the AFPFL upped the stakes: the British must announce before 31 January 1947 that Burma would be free within a year and the Executive Council must be recognized as a national government. At British Prime Minister Attlee's invitation, a six-man AFPFL delegation led by Aung San was in London for talks between 13 and 27 January 1947. It was agreed that Burma would become an independent state within the year and decide itself whether or not to remain within the British Commonwealth, that elections would be held in April 1947 and a Constituent Assembly convened in May, that during the interim period the Executive Council would function as the government of Burma, and that frontier areas would decide themselves whether or not to join the new Burmese nation.

Upon his return to Burma, Aung San met and secured the support of the leaders of the minority Shans, Kachins, and Chins on 12 February 1947 at a conference in Panglong in the Shan States by striking a deal that called for autonomous Shan and Kachin states and the inclusion of a Shan counselor and two deputy counselors (Kachin and Chin) to represent minority interests in the Executive Council. The largest minority group, the Karens, however, did not recognize the agreement, and boycotted the general elections that were held on 9 and 10 April 1947. Those elections produced almost total victory for the AFPFL, which won 204 of the 210 elected seats. Its legitimacy boosted by this strong win, the new government went about drafting the new constitution, which sought independence outside the British Commonwealth. Burma was in fact the only former British colonial territory that refused to join that organization.

Aung San's dominance as Burma's man of the hour was cut short on 19 July 1947 when assassins gunned him down together with five Executive Council members. The killers were subsequently linked to U Saw, a former Prime Minister (g. 1940–42), who was charged with the plot, convicted, and hung. Not wanting to slow the constitutional momentum, Rance immediately called upon U (formerly *Thakin*) Nu to form a new AFPFL government. After the adoption of the new constitution by the Constituent Assembly on 24 September, a treaty was signed in London on 17 October 1947 and, with the endorsement of the Burma Independence Bill by the British parliament, Burma achieved independence on 4 January 1948.

Why did London agree to independence for Burma? Because it had no other realistic option in the face of Burmese demands. Backed by significant popular support, the AFPFL was in a commanding position to negotiate. Not only had it demonstrated its willingness to curb the Communists within its ranks and to resolve outstanding issues with Burma's minorities at Panglong, but its legitimacy had also been bolstered by the strong mandate received at the April 1947 elections. If AFPFL demands were refused, its leaders could take their fight to the streets and countryside. British security assessments were that there would then be a strong chance of widespread rebellion breaking out that would require massive reinforcements to contain – the sort of thing that British forces had already found themselves facing in Indonesia, as will be seen below. But only three battalions of British soldiers were immediately available – grossly inadequate for a security situation that would require up to two divisions. Postwar demobilization had already shrunk the pool of available British troops in Asia, and India's embargo on the use of its troops to suppress nationalist movements – never popular with Indian nationalists – further tied British hands.

Given the dire security situation, London saw little benefit in holding on to Burma for a few more years by force when the principle of eventual independence for Burma had already been accepted, as it was for India. With no other choice, the British concluded that 'If the principle of independence was sound for India it was also sound for Burma.'[1]

Malaya

If the passing of the British Empire in Burma was a case of imperial capitulation to pressure for independence, the same may not be said of Malayan decolonization, which was more a transfer of power. Unlike Burma, where an active anti-colonial agenda was already set in motion during the interwar period, Malaya's British rulers during the same period encountered no significant nationalist challenges to their 'trusteeship', apart from largely containable pressure exerted by small, fringe groups like the left-wing Malayan Communist Party and the Malay radicals in the KMM. This lack of widespread internal pressures for political change reflected in part the difficulties of fashioning a broad-based, united, anti-colonial movement out of Malaya's plural society, where ethnic divisions were a major impediment to the development of a 'Malayan' consciousness. Malays were already nervous and suspicious of an 'immigrant' population who not only dominated them economically but had also, by 1931, outnumbered them numerically – and, potentially at least, threatened them politically. Forming only 41 percent of the population by 1941, indigenous Malays had lost their majority position to the Chinese, who constituted 43 percent. Among Malays, state parochialism further hampered a pan-Malayan outlook, as pointed out in Chapter 9. Despite the pan-Malay congresses of 1939 and 1940, little progress was made before 1941 in linking up state-based associations into a national organization for the purpose of safeguarding Malay interests. The political activities of Chinese and Indians in Malaya during the interwar years, and especially from the latter half of the 1930s, further suggested that whatever nationalist orientation and sympathies these communities displayed were focused more towards their respective motherlands than Malaya. By and large, Chinese and Indians had no wish to be subjects of the Malay rulers, nor were the latter anxious to include non-Malays among their subjects. Within Malaya, all of this meant that there was no strong indigenous pressure forcing the British to reconsider their leisurely pace of constitutional change before 1941 – and they did not.

Malaya's more rudimentary political development also reflected the legal oddity of indirect British rule. From a technical legal point of view, the Malay states were independent, sovereign kingdoms, not British colonies, and the question of their 'decolonization' therefore did not arise. Only in the colony of the Straits Settlements – technically British territory – was 'decolonization' a

---

[1] India and Burma Committee of Cabinet, 19 December 1946, in Hugh Tinker (ed.), *Burma: the Struggle for Independence, 1944–1948: Documents from official and private sources*, Vol. 2 (London: HMSO:1983/84), 203–6.

possible future prospect. Despite this, most British officials believed that they would be in charge of Malaya for the foreseeable future. Malaya's wealth – it was the United Kingdom's chief trading partner in Southeast Asia and principal American dollar earner within the Empire – and strategic importance – for the Singapore naval base was the key to the defense of the British empire in the East – seemed too great to allow the idea of terminating British dominance. Bolstered by their success in enlisting local collaborators within the various communities to underpin their rule, the British were further confident that the interplay of communal differences and competition was not entirely unfavorable to their strategy of *divide et impera:* while Malays needed the continued British presence to protect their interests from further encroachment by non-Malays, Chinese and Indian economic interests also required the political stability that British rule afforded. Confident of their ability to rule well and with no significant indigenous challenges to their rule, colonial administrators saw no pressing reasons before 1941 to alter the arrangements that had kept Malaya economically profitable and politically quiescent for over 70 years, even if it lagged behind more progressive states like British-ruled Burma and India on the constitutional front – let alone the American Philippines, with its fixed schedule for independence.

International pressures during the interwar period were also not such as to cause Britain to reassess its role in Malaya. Although during World War I and after the start of World War II in Europe from September 1939, Allied – and, more prominently, American – leaders reaffirmed publicly their commitment to the principle of self-determination, such declarations did not stir British leaders to contemplate a schedule for Malayan independence. If anything, wartime conditions only made the retention of Malaya even more important to the United Kingdom. It took another global crisis, the onset of the Pacific War in December 1941 and the Japanese conquest in February 1942, to set Malaya upon a new course. The humiliating defeat of British forces, and the capture of their supposedly 'impregnable fortress' in Singapore by an underrated Asian power, as already noted, exerted tremendous pressure for a reappraisal of British policy and rule in Malaya. The outbreak of the Pacific War met the first condition for decolonization: the weakening of British colonial authority.

The metropolitan power, however, was slow to consider any likelihood of imperial retreat. When British forces reoccupied Malaya at the end of the war in September 1945, they did not return with the intention of re-establishing the pre-war *status quo ante*. Instead, they came back with the intention of implementing a revolutionary new scheme – the Malayan Union – that Colonial Office planners had drawn up during the war and which was to set Malaya on a new imperial course. The war exposed the weaknesses of the old order and at the same time seemed to offer an opportunity to clear up Malaya's pre-war problems. Rebuilding a new Malaya required in the first instance the creation of a united Malaya, a goal that had eluded British officials in the past. Departing from the old principles that had underpinned Anglo-Malay relations since 1874 – namely, the sovereignty of the Malay rulers, the autonomy of their states, and the notion that Malaya was essentially a Malay country – the Malayan Union plan revealed in a White Paper in January 1946 called for a centralized state to be created from a 'union' of the former Straits Settlements of Penang and Melaka (but not Singapore, which was to remain as a separate colony) and all nine Malay states. This was achieved by means of new treaties that the Malay rulers were induced to sign by Sir Harold MacMichael, the British special envoy sent to Malaya to conduct negotiations between October and December 1945, effectively transferring sovereignty to the British Crown.

An integral part of this new deal was also the creation of common Malayan Union citizenship for all who regarded Malaya as their home, a scheme that essentially benefited non-Malays, and especially the Chinese in the Malay states, by empowering them politically for the first time. While the Malayan Union's origins might have been long simmering in the various centralizing schemes contemplated before the war, it was the shock of defeat by the Japanese that brought into sharper focus British post-war interests and intentions for Malaya. Although presented as a scheme to set Malaya on a self-governing path, the Malayan Union scheme was, in reality, an act of annexation in technical terms. From a legal point of view, it was a new imperialism foisted on the once-sovereign and only indirectly ruled Malay states, purportedly designed to lay the foundations of a multi-racial Malaya for all Malayans. In short, the British returned to Malaya not intending to withdraw, but with plans to turn the Malay states for the first time into a true colonial territory and then to impose a scheme for their future.

After the war there was no broad-based pan-Malayan nationalist movement to check London's latest colonizing agenda. Whatever nascent anti-colonial nationalism emerged from the war was unable to surmount the ethnic suspicions that had further intensified as a consequence of Japan's treatment of the various communities during the occupation, and the heightened ethnic contestation and insecurity that wartime conditions had engendered. After the Japanese surrender, Chinese and Malays clashed bloodily in several areas, further threatening Malaya's fragile social edifice. With the return of civilian rule and the Malayan Union's inauguration on 1 April 1946, after an interim British military administration, inter-ethnic tensions suffered another blow.

Opposition to the Malayan Union immediately led Malays to close ranks behind a newly established political party – the United Malays National Organization (UMNO) – formed in March 1946 but formally inaugurated in May. Led by the Johor aristocrat Dato Onn bin Jaafar, UMNO aimed to spearhead the campaign against the Malayan Union. The inauguration of the new Governor, Sir Edward Gent, was met by a Malay boycott; mass demonstrations and non-cooperation followed. Chinese and Indian nationalists, who had initially shown scant interest in the constitutional proposals, started to muster their communities as well, partly in response to Malay mobilization but also to safeguard their own collective interests. Indians set up the Malayan Indian Congress (MIC) in August 1946. After British and Malay negotiators met behind closed doors from July 1946 to discuss an alternative Federation of Malaya to replace the unpopular Malayan Union, politically conscious Chinese – alarmed that the British might succumb to Malay pressure to scrap the original plan – also started to organize themselves. A belated campaign by an anti-Federation front from December 1946 failed to derail the Anglo-Malay settlement after the British refused to sanction another volte-face.

On 1 February 1948, the Malayan Union was displaced by the Federation of Malaya, with former governor Gent as its High Commissioner. With the Federation's formation, the British goal of a strong centralized state with multiracial citizenship as the basis for creating a new Malayan nation was more or less achieved. Non-Malays were more empowered politically than ever before: the more liberal Malayan Union citizenship provisions were tightened under Federation, but not forsaken. For Malays, victory was not complete: the pre-war pro-Malay agenda was restored, but not fully. The politics of the Malayan Union period, however, kept inter-communal tensions and suspicions very much alive and made the prospects of a successful pan-Malayan nationalist challenge to British rule even more remote.

The 1948 start of the 'Emergency', an MCP-led armed insurgency for national liberation – just four months into the life of the new Federation – further retarded prospects of Malaya's political development. As the majority of the Communist insurgents were Chinese, and the security forces opposing them included Malay policemen, Sino-Malay tensions intensified. Certainly, the insurgency had the ring of an indigenous nationalist rising against colonial rule, given the MCP's pan-Malayan objectives. But the insurgents' inability to muster broad-based popular support apart from Chinese doomed their prospects as a nationalist front. Malays shunned the movement, except for the community's more radical elements, and closed ranks behind the British in defeating the insurgents. At a time when the Chinese-dominated MCP insurgents threatened to turn Malaya into a Communist state, Malays were also in no mood to seek early self-government. The majority of non-Malays, too, balked at the Communists' campaign of violence, murder, intimidation, and revolution, and yearned for a return to normalcy.

From the metropolitan perspective, top priority was given to defeating the Communists and initially constitutional progress had to be put on hold. But while the Emergency taxed British military prowess, particularly in the early years of the jungle war, the realization that it was also a battle for 'hearts and minds' soon shifted the fight to the political front. Encouraging constitutional advance, not withholding it, was the best way to counter Communist subversion and propaganda, or so it was argued. A stock-taking of British colonial trusteeship in Malaya was also in order for another reason: the rising economic and political costs of fighting the insurgency. Increasing military demands were straining the United Kingdom's limited resources and making Malaya too expensive to maintain. Equally compelling was the belief that it was better for the United Kingdom to seize the initiative on the constitutional front and run risks of its own choosing than to be forced by the pressure of events over which it would have little or no control into capitulating to nationalist demands, as was happening elsewhere in the region. With India out of the Empire by 1947 and safely in the Commonwealth, and Ceylon and Burma also granted independence in 1948, any psychological barrier to the transfer of power had also been breached. Of course, the situation in Malaya was different from Burma as there was no mass-based nationalist movement capable of usurping British rule. But with time on its side, the United Kingdom could at least better prepare Malaya for the day when it would become fully self-governing.

With decolonization at last thinkable, a tentative time schedule for Malaya's self-government began to see light. Privately, the British were thinking in December 1948 of a transition period of about 25 years, with self-government at the earliest in 1973. In 1950 the Secretary of State for the Colonies persuaded the cabinet to quicken the pace and think in terms of 15 years instead, that is, self-government by 1965. Even this target was revised again in December 1952, and shortened to eight years, giving 1960 as the earliest possible date for self-government. Thus, in the end the Emergency clarified and strengthened British convictions that political change could not be stopped and that they had to keep pace with the rapidly developing situation on the ground. Urgent steps would have to be taken to bring about a pan-Malayan orientation as a prerequisite for decolonization.

As decolonization entered the official mind, the question was no longer whether – but rather when – Malaya could be self-governing. The answer to that question depended on how soon moderate political forces could work out a formula of inter-racial cooperation to meet London's prerequisite for social stability before transferring power. British initiatives to encourage inter-communal bonding at the elite level yielded some early results in the formation in 1949 of the multi-ethnic Communities Liaison Committee, sponsored by Malcolm MacDonald, the British Commissioner-General for Southeast Asia, with the aim of finding non-communal solutions to political issues. There followed the establishment in 1951 of the Member System, a prototype cabinet scheme to provide experience in power-sharing and self-governance for local leaders drawn from the different communities. Efforts by the latter's originator, Sir Henry Gurney (who succeeded Gent as High Commissioner in October 1948), to attract a non-Communist base of support within the Chinese community also bore fruit with the launch of the Malayan Chinese Association (MCA) in February 1949.

Attempts to institutionalize popular non-communal politics were less successful. Malays rejected Dato Onn's proposal, which MacDonald had backed, to make UMNO a more inclusive national party by admitting non-Malays; they also snubbed the non-communal Independence of Malaya Party (IMP) that Onn founded in 1951 after resigning from UMNO. Initial British misgivings at the institutionalization of communalism in Malayan politics, however, soon gave way to grudging acquiescence after these moderate communal forces convincingly triumphed over their non-communal rivals in a spate of elections introduced by the British to prepare for self-government. After local branches of UMNO and the MCA entered an informal pact to defeat their main rival, the IMP, in February 1952 municipal elections, leaders of both parties formalized their alliance in March 1953, with the MIC joining in 1954. Taking the form of a coalition of three communal parties, the Alliance Party, as it came to be known, contested the national elections in July 1955 and won a resounding mandate – capturing 51 of the 52 seats.

Backed by the strong mandate from this landslide victory, Alliance leader and new UMNO President Tunku Abdul Rahman gave notice to the British that his party expected an acceleration of the pace towards independence. In December 1955, with independence approaching, the Tunku – against strong British reservations – met top Communist leader Chin Peng for talks at Baling, Kedah, in an attempt to end the MCP's 'war of liberation', and demanded an unconditional surrender from him. Even though the talks collapsed, as the insurgents were unwilling to surrender unconditionally, the Tunku's uncompromising handling of the Communists was reassuring to the British. Impressed by the size of the Alliance's mandate and the commitment of its moderate, anti-Communist and pro-British leaders to independence, London accepted the coalition's demand after talks in London in 1956 and 1957 to end its empire in Malaya sooner rather than later, even though its requirement of a non-communal, multi-ethnic Malayan consciousness had not yet been fully met. Alluding to the lessons of the French debacle in Vietnam, the British Colonial Secretary, A. T. Lennox-Boyd, warned the cabinet that London should seize the initiative to grant independence to Malaya with the tide still flowing in its direction and while it still had the power to decide. In short, the moderate Alliance Party appeared to be the United Kingdom's best bet, the only party the British could trust to safeguard their interests. Failure to accept the Tunku's demands would only weaken his position, damage the credibility of the Alliance, and possibly contribute to the rise of a less accommodating alternative. On 31 August 1957, to loud shouts of *Merdeka*, independence was finally handed to Malayan leaders 'on a silver platter'.[2]

Singapore and Borneo

With Malaya independent and safely in the British Commonwealth, Singapore and the Borneo territories (Sarawak, North Borneo, and Brunei) were the only remaining British-ruled areas in Southeast Asia whose political futures were undecided. Singapore's detachment from the former Straits Settlements and its establishment as a separate colony under its own Governor was one consequence of the British experiment to create a new post-war order in Malaya. The island's exclusion from the Malayan Union in 1946 was a tactical necessity to soothe anticipated Malay resistance to the already controversial scheme. Singapore's economic interests, focusing on entrepôt trade, were distinct from those of the more agriculturally oriented Malayan mainland. Aside from the fact that peninsular Malays resented being ruled from Singapore in the past, the inclusion of the colony's predominantly Chinese population would further tip the delicate ethnic balance and make the Malays a minority in their own land. Still, British officials were cautiously hopeful that Singapore's separation would only be temporary and that, at a future date when more settled circumstances returned, the two territories could be united again. The reality, however, was that separation made the prospect of such a reunion even less likely, as both territories revived their pre-war rivalry and drifted further apart as they tackled distinct, but not totally unconnected, challenges within their borders.

---

2   The words of Deputy Under-Secretary of State at the Colonial Office Sir John Martin, quoted in Brian Lapping, *End of Empire* (London: St. Martin's Press, 1985), 177.

That the war had sparked off a mental revolution and radicalized segments of Singapore's multi-ethnic population is evident in the sprouting of left-wing political parties in the immediate aftermath of war, including the multiracial Malayan Democratic Union (MDU) in December 1945 – the first political party to be constituted – and the more communally oriented Singapore branch of the Perak-inaugurated Malay Nationalist Party (MNP, originally founded in Perak) in February 1946. Led by English-educated intellectuals, the MDU wanted a self-governing, democratic, and united Malaya, inclusive of Singapore. Like the MDU, the MNP also sought the creation of a united Malaya but with the aim of its eventual union with Indonesia to form a larger Malay political unit – an *Indonesia Raya* (Greater Indonesia) or *Melayu Raya* (Greater Malaya). Drawing inspiration from Indonesia's PNI, the MNP's more immediate aim was to mobilize support for the nationalist struggle against Dutch colonialism in the Netherlands East Indies.

Of the anti-colonial forces to emerge after the war, the most pervasive in Singapore was the Chinese-dominated MCP. With its pre-war ban lifted in recognition of its role as a wartime ally of the British, the MCP came out from the war with enhanced prestige, popular support, and restored confidence. Permitted to operate openly again, the MCP revived its anti-colonial agitation and started to infiltrate political parties like the MNP and MDU along with labor groups to further the united front aims of the party. With post-war food shortages, rising costs, low wages, and high unemployment further adding to popular grievances against the interim British military administration, and increasing the scope for anti-colonial activism, militant elements of the MCP revived the General Labor Union in October 1945 to spearhead the anti-colonial struggle on the labor front. The spate of strikes that it organized between October 1945 and February 1946 to pressure and embarrass the British military administration culminated in a general strike on 29 January 1946 supported by some 170,000 workers and the staging on 15 February 1946 of a second general strike to commemorate the anniversary of the British capitulation to the Japanese.

But the emerging nationalist forces were never able to coalesce into a wider anti-colonial movement that could seriously challenge British rule in Singapore. Both the MCP and the MDU saw themselves as 'Malayan' rather than exclusively 'Singaporean' parties. Distracted by their involvement in the Malayan Union controversy, they were slow to concern themselves with constitutional affairs in Singapore and offered only subdued criticism of the island's exclusion from the Malayan Union. It was only in December 1946 that the MDU and the MCP belatedly teamed up with others to form the Council of Joint Action (CJA) in Singapore to protest against the Federation proposals. The fact that it had Malaya and not just Singapore in mind was apparent in the decision to rename the CJA as the Pan-Malayan Council of Joint Action (PMCJA) later in the month to give it a more explicitly 'Malayan' focus as it took its anti-Federation campaign across the causeway connecting the island to the Malay peninsula.

Joining the PMCJA in its opposition to the Federation was the MNP-sponsored *Pusat Tenaga Rakyat* (*Putera*, Center of People's Power), an anti-colonial front of left-wing Malay associations formed in February 1947. But the

MNP's radical agenda did not appeal to moderate Malays in Singapore who were conscious of their minority status and political vulnerability in a Chinese-dominated state. Forging a united front of local left-wing parties was also fraught with ideological difficulties. Reconciling the MNP's objective of *Indonesia Raya* with the Chinese-dominated MCP's aim of an independent Communist Malaya inclusive of Singapore was bound to be problematic. Nor would the majority Chinese in Singapore and Malaya relish the prospect of becoming a minority in a larger Indonesian-dominated state. With its emerging nationalist forces preoccupied with Malayan issues and divided ideologically, no strong Singapore-oriented nationalist movement could arise to contest British rule. Timely police countermeasures, including deportation and the outlawing of subversive organizations, easily contained the more disruptive challenges to British authority in the small island colony.

It was not indigenous pressure but rather the United Kingdom's desire to instill confidence in Singapore's political future after its abrupt severance from the mainland that led to early Legislative Council (from 1955 Legislative Assembly) polls – ahead of the Federation of Malaya – beginning in 1948, followed by elections in 1951, 1955, and 1959, during which the size of the franchise and the number of elected seats expanded. Although public interest in the beginning was lackluster, the pace picked up during the 1955 elections after the British greatly expanded the number of elected seats – from six in 1948 and nine in 1951, to 25 in 1955. By then the political landscape had also changed significantly. The MDU, which boycotted the 1948 elections after claiming that they were not democratic enough, had ceased to operate. The onset of the Emergency in Singapore in July 1948, following its declaration in Malaya the month before, had also driven the now-outlawed MCP underground, never to operate openly again but still exercising strategic influence in the shadows. New right-wing, pro-British collaborationist parties like the Singapore Progressive Party, which appeared in 1947, held the political stage for a time, but they were swept away after the expansion of the political process – in the wake of British successes in containing the Communist insurgency by the mid-1950s – saw a popular surge in favor of left-wing and stridently anti-colonial parties like the newly formed Singapore Labor Front (SLF) and the People's Action Party (PAP) in the 1955 elections. Although these elections brought the SLF into power, it was the PAP which eventually triumphed in a landslide win in 1959, capturing 43 of the 51 seats, and was thus in a position to lead Singapore to self-government as a precursor to eventual independence.

The triumph of the Left in Singapore surprised and worried the British, who had expected their preferred indigenous collaborator, the Singapore Progressive Party, to win in 1955. It was, however, the anti-colonial PAP, led by Lee Kuan Yew, that was in the saddle by 1959. While its moderate leaders were non-Communists, a pro-Communist faction within the PAP harbored plans to hijack the party to fulfill the political objectives of the MCP. Given the MCP's still-pervasive ideological hold over influential segments of Singapore's Chinese population – people attracted by the allure of the socialist revolution and the rise since 1949 of a resurgent Communist China – the prospect of full independence appeared bleak at best. Too small and too vulnerable to be granted independence on its own, Singapore's political future, from the United Kingdom's perspective, lay in it being reunited with Malaya. This was also the solution that moderate PAP leaders advocated, for such a merger would both insure Singapore's political future and neutralize the PAP's radical left opponents within a Malaya ruled by the anti-Communist Alliance government. Kuala Lumpur refused to countenance a merger with Singapore alone, fearing the impact of the island's Chinese majority on Malaya's politics and security, but was more willing to consider a merger that also included the three British Borneo territories as part of a package deal to create an enlarged Federation – a Greater Malaysia.

Such a 'Grand Design' (a term coined by the British) was also exactly what London had quietly lobbied for as a solution to the future of both Singapore and the Borneo territories. The low level of political development in the Borneo territories raised doubts about the wisdom of any swift transfer of power, even if this should be demanded of the United Kingdom. Before the war, Borneo's relative isolation from the outside world, the paternal rule of the Brooke Rajahs, and the commercial interests of the British North Borneo Chartered Company (BNBCC) had left both Sarawak and North Borneo relatively untouched by the spread of nationalist ideas sweeping across Southeast Asia. When the British returned to Borneo after the war, they came back with plans for direct rule and territorial consolidation in both Sarawak and North Borneo, as in Malaya. Such a change was readily welcomed by the BNBCC, not only because government by chartered companies was an embarrassing anachronism but also because the company had neither the financial nor administrative wherewithal for the post-war infrastructural and economic reconstruction of a war-ravaged territory. On 10 July 1946, in a deal struck with the British government, and with hardly any dissenting voice, North Borneo, together with the settlement of Labuan, finally became a British crown colony.

In Sarawak, the transition was less smooth. The 72-year-old Rajah Vyner Brooke was agreeable to cession, having neither energy nor resources to undertake the post-war reconstruction of Sarawak, but other members of the family, including Anthony and Bertram Brooke, and some senior Malay officials in the Sarawak administration opposed the acquisition by the Colonial Office. Anthony Brooke, who was the Rajah Muda and headed a provisional government of Sarawak in London during the war, wanted to re-establish Brooke rule after the war. But the Rajah, backed by the Colonial Office, dismissed his nephew in October 1945 and took personal control of Sarawak's affairs after abolishing the provisional government. After dispatching his private secretary to consult leading local opinion – which was reported to be favorable – Vyner Brooke informed London that he had decided to proceed with the cession of Sarawak. Upon his return to Sarawak, the Rajah convened the *Council Negeri* (the equivalent of a legislative council in other territories) in May 1946 to debate the cession bill and carried it narrowly by 19 votes to 16. The constitution of the new crown colony of Sarawak on 1 July 1946, however, did not cause opposition to subside completely, but provoked instead the rise of an indigenous anti-cession movement within Sarawak that culminated in the assassination by a Malay youth of Sarawak's second governor, Duncan Stewart, in

December 1949. Shocked by this, the British took strong punitive action to crush the anti-cession movement. In 1951, Anthony Brooke, who had been banned from entering Sarawak since December 1946, formally relinquished his claims and colonial government came to be accepted peacefully. Brunei's pre-war protectorate status remained unchanged, except that, for administrative purposes, Brunei was placed under the oversight of its formal vassal, Sarawak, and the Governor of Sarawak in May 1948 became the United Kingdom's High Commissioner to Brunei.

In contrast to Malaya, whose constitutional road had started with a bang, political change in Borneo proceeded excruciatingly slowly. It was only in April 1957 that a new constitution was promulgated in Sarawak which expanded the size of the Council Negeri. Local councils were gradually introduced to awaken political consciousness and to provide training for self-government. Elections to district and divisional councils were held only in 1959. In North Borneo, the pace of constitutional reforms was even slower. A small majority of non-officials in the Legislative Council, but not the Executive Council, came into being only in 1960. Although local councils were introduced in 1952, the electoral process was not implemented in North Borneo before 1962. In Brunei, Sultan Omar Ali Saifuddin III (r. 1950–67) was determined to rid Brunei of its subservience to Sarawak and in 1953 declared his intention to draw up a written constitution. After constitutional talks in London in September 1957 and March 1959, a new treaty was concluded with the United Kingdom in September 1959 granting internal self-government to the Sultan, who was invested with supreme executive powers under the new constitution.

With the withdrawal of the British Resident, a new British High Commissioner with no constitutional connection to Sarawak was appointed with the right to advise the Sultan but with no powers over the internal administration of Brunei, now firmly in the hands of its ruler, who remained in essence an absolute monarch. In the absence of indigenous demands to hasten the tempo of change, attempts at constitutional progressivism had to come mainly from the British themselves. British inspiration was also behind abortive plans from 1953 to revive the pre-war scheme of a Borneo Federation, linking the three territories to give them greater collective strength. Sarawak showed interest, but Brunei recoiled at such an eventuality, fearing not only that its oil wealth would be shared with its poorer neighbors but also that closer association would both offend its sovereignty and open the floodgates to non-Malay immigration that would threaten the Malay-dominated state. North Borneo felt that without the support of a substantial majority of people in each of the three territories, such a federation was premature.

By the late 1950s, however, the idea of an enlarged 'Grand Design' Federation involving not just the Borneo territories but also Malaya and Singapore made another comeback – with more success this time. It was the Malayan Premier, Tunku Abdul Rahman, who on two occasions – in December 1958 and June 1960 – broached the subject privately with the British. Certainly, the proposal had attractions for all concerned. Not only would Malaya benefit by leading an enlarged Federation, and possibly thwarting the future territorial ambitions of either the Philippines or Indonesia in British Borneo (where both countries claimed historical rights), but it would also give Kuala Lumpur oversight over Singapore and neutralize the danger of the pro-Communists toppling the PAP government at the upcoming polls and exposing Malaya to possible security risks from at its southern neighbor. For the PAP, the achievement of its goal of 'independence through merger' would ensure its political survival and the defeat of its extreme leftist rivals. It would also offer prospects of a larger common market to sustain Singapore's industrialization efforts and secure the island's economic survival. Britain naturally welcomed merger as it would resolve the future of Singapore and assure a settled future for its Borneo dependencies, even though it was initially wary about prematurely creating a 'super Federation' that might expose the Borneo territories to the danger of Malayan 'colonialism'. But with the moderate PAP leadership losing ground in Singapore, as seen in its loss of a by-election in April 1961, a more decisive push for the 'Grand Design' and a movement towards independence were necessary, without which the PAP could not hope to hold its position in Singapore by 1963, when the next constitutional review was due.

In May 1961, at a luncheon speech in Singapore, the Tunku publicly signaled, to electrifying effect, his willingness to reconsider Singapore's merger with Malaya within the context of a wider association involving the Borneo territories. In Singapore, the Tunku's announcement triggered a political crisis resulting in yet another by-election loss for the PAP in July 1961, and led to dissidents defecting to form the *Barisan Sosialis* (Socialist Front) later that month. The fear of being politically neutralized forced the extreme left wing of the PAP and Communist elements to come out openly to oppose merger. A year-long campaign by the PAP government to seek endorsement for merger culminated in a referendum in September 1962, confirming popular support in Singapore for joining. In mid-January 1962 the United Kingdom dispatched an Anglo-Malayan commission of enquiry, led by Lord Cobbold, to ascertain popular support for merger in Sarawak and North Borneo, but not Brunei, as the latter's sovereign status meant that it could not be included in the commission's remit. The Cobbold Commission reported that a majority in both territories was in favor of this larger entity – to be called Malaysia – although some wanted more safeguards. Tough negotiations over the terms of merger among the different parties threatened to derail the momentum and on at least three occasions during discussions in London – in November 1961, July 1962, and July 1963 – the Tunku nearly decided to pull out. Frustrated by the stalemate in his talks with Singapore and Brunei, he was ready to proceed with the formation of 'little Malaysia' with only Malaya, Sarawak, and North Borneo, had it not been for British mediation. But while Singapore was able to resolve its differences with Kuala Lumpur, Brunei did not. Faced with local opposition, Sultan Omar's initial enthusiasm for Malaysia cooled significantly, and after an abortive revolt in December 1962, he decided to pull Brunei out of joining Malaysia and to remain under British protection.

Progress was disrupted by opposition from Indonesia, where Sukarno denounced Malaysia as a neo-colonialist plot and embarked on a policy of *Konfrontasi* (confrontation) – discussed further in the next chapter. The Philippines was also opposed, pressing claims over North Borneo as a former dependency of Sulu. Malaysia's scheduled inauguration on 31 August 1963 was consequently postponed so that a UN fact-finding mission could satisfy itself that Filipino and Indonesian claims that Malaysia lacked local support were baseless. On 16 September 1963, Malaysia finally came into being. With its formation, Singapore, Sarawak, and North Borneo (now renamed Sabah) achieved their independence as part of the newly created nation of Malaysia.

Brunei staved off pressure to sever its British connection for as long as it could in the belief that British protection would ensure its continued existence. Limited elections were held in 1965. In 1967 Sultan Omar abdicated in favor of his eldest son, Hassanal Bolkiah (r. 1967–), but continued to wield influence. Control over internal security was transferred from the United Kingdom to Brunei in 1971, but defense and foreign relations remained a British responsibility. Pressure to end this embarrassing colonial relationship continued and in January 1979 the United Kingdom and Brunei agreed to full Brunei independence beginning in 1983. At midnight on 31 December 1983, Brunei finally assumed full responsibility for its own affairs and emerged as a sovereign state on 1 January 1984. All of Britain's Southeast Asian territories were now independent.

The political rivalry and ethnic suspicions that had formerly bedeviled relations between Singapore and Kuala Lumpur, however, resurfaced almost immediately after Malaysia was created. Singapore lasted only 23 months in the new Federation. Both sides attempted to intervene in each other's electoral politics. Two race riots occurred in the island state that the PAP government blamed on incitement by UMNO activists, sparking off a series of political countermeasures that brought the two parties close to collision. In August 1965, Singapore left the Federation to forge a new nation on its own.

Indonesia

Among the states of Asia that won independence after World War II, only Vietnam and Indonesia did so by armed revolution. In the Indonesian case, it was the crucial combination of armed resistance to Dutch re-conquest and a favorable international environment that made independence possible. We have already noted above that in the late 1940s the status of the United States as the sole nuclear power and the strongest economy in the world, while Europe was devastated by the war, altered the balance of international politics profoundly. The presence of the UN as a new world-level organization was also novel, untested, and thought potentially to be of real significance in ensuring world peace. The emergence of the USSR as a nuclear power, the advances of the Communist side in Eastern Europe and in China, and Communist insurrections elsewhere gave birth to the Cold War contest between the United States and its allies on one side and the Soviets and their dependencies on the other. American anti-colonialism thus became alloyed with anti-Communism, a combination which – as will be seen below – happened to suit the dynamics of the Indonesian Revolution.

These international circumstances would, however, have been of no effect without the skills, leadership and determination of Indonesians themselves. In

August 1945, Indonesia had already suffered 15 years of hardship since the onset of the Depression, the most devastating period of all having been the three and a half years of Japanese occupation. Whereas the Dutch had aimed to depoliticize Indonesians after the PKI uprising of 1927, the Japanese in Java – and, to lesser extents, in Sumatra and the east of the archipelago – had mobilized them politically. So on the eve of their Revolution, Indonesians had several of the elements essential to success:

- an educated nationalist leadership, hardened by years of Dutch repression, embittered by Japanese rule, determined not to tolerate foreign rulers ever again, and aware of the historic opportunity they faced;
- religious leaders who had responded to Japanese encouragement to take more active political roles;
- politicized youth activists with at least some military training and imbued with anti-Western propaganda; and
- a desperate and politicized general populace ready to accept leaders who could promise hope of a better future.

There was, moreover, a brief political and military vacuum in Indonesia. In August 1945, the Japanese had surrendered and were demoralized and nervous, but had been commanded by the Allies to maintain order in Indonesia. Those Allies were nowhere to be seen, however, the speed of the Japanese surrender having caught them unprepared. So now was the moment for the Indonesian revolutionaries to grasp the initiative.

In Jakarta on 17 August 1945, Sukarno and Hatta declared the independence of the Republic of Indonesia. They became, respectively, the first President (1945–67) and first Vice-President (1945–56) of the Republic. A constitution drafted under Japanese tutelage in the late stages of the war was adopted, with some changes. A 'Jakarta Charter' in the draft said that the state was to be based upon 'belief in God, with the obligation for adherents of Islam to carry out Islamic law'. This seemed to imply that the state would be responsible for implementing this provision and was thus some sort of quasi-Islamic state. There was also a stipulation that the head of state must be a Muslim. Both of these were dropped in response to objections by eastern Indonesian Christians. A government structure was put in place by simply declaring that Indonesian advisers to Japanese administrators now replaced the latter on behalf of the Republic.

Things did not go so well, however, in military matters. The Republican leaders had expected to take over the Japanese-trained *Peta, Heiho, Barisan Pelopor*, and other such forces as the core of the army. But the Japanese feared that these forces might turn against them – as indeed a *Peta* detachment at Blitar had in February 1945 and as Aung San's forces had in Burma in March – so before the Indonesian leadership could assume command, the Japanese disarmed these forces and sent them home. As news of the declaration of independence spread, it was often local youths who grasped the initiative to form armed 'struggle bodies', take charge of public facilities in the name of the Republic, and pressure (and sometimes attack) local Japanese forces to get access to arms and ammunition. The central Republican leadership had little influence over these groups. *Masyumi*'s *Hizbullah* guerrillas grew rapidly in numbers; rural Islamic teachers (*kyai*) formed other guerrilla forces, mostly called *Sabilillah* (Holy War) fighters. The main Islamic organizations of Indonesia, NU and *Masyumi*, declared that the defense of the new fatherland was Holy War, a religious obligation for Muslims.

The Revolution found strong support among intellectuals. Indonesian artists and writers produced newspapers, magazines, novels, posters, songs, and such like in support. Among these artists were some of the most famous in modern Indonesian art and literature. They included the writers Pramoedya Ananta Toer, Mochtar Lubis, and Bahrum Rangkuti; the poet Chairil Anwar; and the painters Affandi and Sudjojono.

The Revolution was brought to a quick halt in east Indonesia, where the Japanese navy had been in charge. Only at the very end of the war had the navy shown any willingness to mobilize the populace, so the Revolution had shallow roots in the eastern archipelago. Because there were also substantial Christian populations there, the Dutch expected a warmer welcome than elsewhere. Australian troops under the British-led South East Asia Command (responsible for reoccupying Southeast Asia below the 16th parallel except for the Philippines) took the Japanese surrender in east Indonesia except for Bali and Lombok and put down any nascent signs of revolution. By mid-October 1945 the Australians and Dutch administrators who came with them (many of whom had spent the war in Australia) had taken over that area.

British-commanded – in fact mostly Indian – troops accepted the Japanese surrender in Java and Sumatra. The head of South East Asia Command, Lord Louis Mountbatten, generally treated the local Republican administrations that he encountered as *de facto* governments. Violence began to break out in October as fighting began between Indonesians on the one hand and released Dutch prisoners of war, former colonial army soldiers, Chinese, Indo-Europeans, and Japanese on the other. With Allies now present, the Japanese were in a difficult position. Rather than maintaining order as the Allies had commanded, in many places the Japanese had allowed arms to fall into Republican hands and had withdrawn from the center of cities. Now in some places they tried to retake control of these centers, which caused clashes with Republican units that left hundreds dead.

In November 1945 the Battle of Surabaya occurred, one of the turning points of the Revolution. British Indian troops came into the city to evacuate former internees; local Republican forces resisted. Bitter street fighting culminated in the killing of the British commander, Brigadier-General A. W. S. Mallaby. On 10 November – now celebrated annually in Indonesia as 'Heroes' Day' – the British launched a deadly punitive sweep through the city, in the face of fanatical Republican resistance. The British retook most of Surabaya in three days but it was three weeks before they were fully in charge, by which time at least 6000 Indonesians had been killed. This costly defeat became a rallying cry for revolutionaries across the country. For their part, the British had to recognize the depth of support for the Republic and decided that it would be wise to get out of Indonesia altogether. They made it plain to the Dutch that if the latter wanted to re-conquer Indonesia, they could not count on the British to do it for them. The Dutch, too, had to face the reality that the Republic had widespread popular support and was not, as they had imagined, a government created by collaborators with the Japanese, whom other Indonesians would be glad to be rescued from.

Most of this violence was driven by local conflicts, with little control being exercised by the central Republican leadership in Jakarta. In the later months of 1945 and into 1946, the Revolution entered the phase known as the 'social revolution', when pro-Republican Indonesians turned against domestic enemies: collaborators with the Japanese, anti-Republican administrators, local royalty, black-marketeers, and so on. All of this was done in the name of 'the people's sovereignty'. In Java, where *santri-abangan* tensions continued to rise, activists from one side often overthrew a village head from the other. In Aceh, pro-Republican *ulamas* attacked and slaughtered *uleëbalangs* tainted by their service to the Dutch and Japanese regimes. In East Sumatra a general slaughter of aristocrats claimed many victims, among them the poet Amir Hamza. In some areas, Republican army units went into action to suppress local 'social revolutions'.

The central Republican leadership thus had to face domestic disorder as well as the threat of Dutch attack. The Netherlands shipped soldiers to Indonesia as fast as possible, initially giving priority to reoccupying eastern parts of the archipelago, where the Revolution was weaker or, indeed, had not broken out at all. The Republican leaders hoped that Indonesia's independence might be sealed by international agreement and the support of the new UN, so the Revolution also had a diplomatic aspect. In that respect the Republican leadership was disadvantaged by the fact that Sukarno, Hatta, and other prominent leaders had in fact collaborated with the Japanese during the war, a handicap if they were to deal with the victorious Allies. So Sutan Sjahrir and Amir Sjarifuddin emerged as leading figures. Neither had collaborated with the Japanese and Amir had, indeed, made an amateurish attempt at resistance against them, been imprisoned, and only narrowly escaped execution.

In October–November 1945 Sjahrir and Amir engineered a coup within the Central Indonesian National Committee – the interim Revolutionary governing organization – that produced a working party selected by them and a new cabinet in which Sjahrir was Prime Minister and Amir Minister for People's Security (i.e., Defense). Sukarno, as President, was sidelined. Political parties – not provided for in the 1945 Constitution but also not disallowed – were now created. All of this represented a *de facto* overturning of the fairly authoritarian 1945 Constitution in favor of something more like a Western-style democracy. In this evolving atmosphere, discussions began between Sjahrir and H. J. van Mook, the new Dutch Lieutenant Governor-General (g. 1942–48; no Governor-General was appointed after the war).

The political parties that rapidly emerged in late 1945 and early 1946 institutionalized the schisms within the Republic's leadership. The Communist Party (PKI) was revived. Amir Sjarifuddin created an Indonesian Socialist Youth (*Pesindo*) Party, which then merged with the Socialist Party created by Sjahrir. The Japanese-created Islamic organization *Masyumi* became a political party, with Modernist *Muhammadiyah* and Traditionalist NU as corporate members within it. PNI was also revived, but without Sukarno as its head, for as President he was supposed to be above party politics. Nevertheless, PNI's appeal rested on its status as the party once created by Sukarno.

In the turbulence of the early Revolution, the military became a major political force. It was internally divided. Generally speaking, on one side were young revolutionaries with little or no pre-Japanese military training, who saw revolutionary spirit, initiative, comradeship, and personal courage as the main requirements for military leadership. On the other were men with Dutch-era military training who gave priority to professionalism and hierarchical command structures. These groups, however, shared a commitment to the Revolution and a distrust of civilian politicians, whose orders they followed reluctantly, if at all.

The Dutch were meanwhile re-establishing their position in Batavia/Jakarta, which the Republican leaders had declared to be their capital. In January 1946, the Republicans thought it prudent to relocate to Yogyakarta, where Sultan Hamengkubuwana IX (r. 1939–88) was a committed supporter of the Revolution. The Dutch also took over from the Australians in eastern Indonesia and also reoccupied Bangka, Belitung, and Riau, and the city of Bandung in late 1945–early 1946. The South East Asia Command handed over control of all of Indonesia except for Sumatra and Java to the Dutch in July 1946. The Republic was thus being progressively surrounded by areas reoccupied by the Dutch. Pro-Republican activists in those areas were being arrested or forced to go underground, or were making their way to the Republic's heartland in Java.

In such discouraging circumstances, Sjahrir was challenged by more radical voices demanding stronger resistance to the Dutch. A 'Struggle Union' was set up in January 1946 under the influence of Tan Malaka, a 1920s PKI leader who had been outside Indonesia until late in the war, and who had now broken with USSR-led Communism and supported 'national Communism' instead. Sjahrir's and Amir's armed followers were initially part of this Struggle Union, but by March 1946 they had come to blows: Amir's *Pesindo* activists and military police arrested the Union's leaders, including Tan Malaka, who was held for two years without trial. Already the Revolution – like many another – was beginning to consume its own leadership. As a non-PKI radical, Tan Malaka exerted great influence over the left of Indonesian politics for many years, even though he spent most of the Revolution in jail and did not survive to see the end of it.

The belief that a leader like Sjahrir, untainted by collaboration with the Japanese, could negotiate more successfully with the Dutch and the victorious Allies was proving to be questionable. So Sukarno started to re-emerge as a dominant figure – collaboration background or no – to whom contending factions could turn for legitimacy and support. Sjahrir secretly agreed with van Mook to negotiate on the basis of *de facto* Republican sovereignty in Java and Sumatra and Dutch sovereignty over the other islands. When this became known in June 1946, radicals objected in the name of '100 percent independence'. They kidnapped Sjahrir in what is known as the 'July 3rd affair'. Sukarno proclaimed martial law and demanded that Sjahrir be released, but the army commander Soedirman supported the radicals and refused to obey the presidential order. This tense stand-off led to arrests of leading opponents of the Republican government, whom the army then demanded be set free. With armed units supporting both sides, the Republic itself was now very close to civil war. But everyone backed down, Sjahrir was released, and the government blamed Tan Malaka – still in prison – for the entire episode. Soedirman decided to be more flexible in dealing with the civilian leadership thereafter.

As the Dutch tightened their control of the archipelago outside Java and Sumatra, they adopted a strategy to submerge the Republic in a sea of Dutch-sponsored and -dominated federal states. Within a future federal Republic of Indonesia, the Dutch would thereby retain predominant influence. Such states began to be set up in 1946. The Dutch were, however, surprised to discover that even the *rajas*, Christians, and smaller ethnic groups, whom they expected to acquiesce in restored colonial control, aspired to greater self-determination. They also found that Republican guerrilla groups in these areas were prepared to resist their return – however futilely. For the Dutch, it was still difficult to accept just how profoundly Indonesia had changed in ways that made European colonial rule an anachronism; they would soon find that the same was true of the international environment.

In November 1946 the Dutch and Republicans reached their first diplomatic accord (the Linggajati Agreement). This recognized the Republic as *de facto* authority in Java, Madura, and Sumatra; the two sides would work together to create a federal Republic of Indonesia by 1 January 1949. Each distrusted the other, however, and both had to face disgruntled domestic constituencies. The Linggajati Agreement thus had a brief life-span. Sjahrir's government fell in July 1947 and Sjahrir himself traveled to New York to argue the Republic's cause in the UN. The Dutch decided to take military action, partly because of the cost of keeping some 100,000 soldiers in Indonesia without access to income from the most lucrative archipelago products, an arrangement the devastated Netherlands home economy could hardly bear. The Dutch believed that they could defeat the Republic in a few weeks. On 20 July 1947 they launched their first 'police action', reflecting miscalculation both of Indonesian dynamics and of international politics. They took Java's deep-water ports, Madura and parts of East Java (the source of sugar) and oil-, coal- and rubber-producing areas in Sumatra.

Now the UN became directly involved. Barely a week after the 'police action' started, India – just days away from its own independence – and Australia raised the Indonesia issue in the Security Council. There the Americans equivocated, and the British, French, and Belgian colonial powers abstained, but a majority including the USSR called upon the Dutch and Indonesians to cease fire and to resolve their conflict by negotiation or arbitration. No one at this stage knew just what 'teeth' a UN Security Council resolution might have. The Dutch could nevertheless recognize that world opinion was turning against them. And even if the American government equivocated, pro-Indonesian opinion in the American Congress was strengthening. In August the Dutch and Republic declared a cease-fire; the latter was now reduced to the interior of Sumatra and Java, where a flood of refugees made conditions extremely difficult, with Dutch forces surrounding them. Another diplomatic agreement followed, signed on the American warship *Renville* in January 1948; this agreement, too, would last only briefly.

Following the Renville Agreement, the Republican Siliwangi Division withdrew from Dutch-occupied West Java and marched into Central Java. The charismatic Javanese mystic S. M. Kartosuwirjo, who led local Islamic guerrillas in West Java, was so incensed at this abandonment of that area by the Republic that in May 1948 he launched the first of Indonesia's several Islamist rebellions, the Darul Islam uprising, resisting the government in Yogyakarta as much as the Dutch occupiers. In the same year, the domestic politics of Indonesia and increasing anti-Dutch international sentiments were harnessed together by a third factor, the politics of anti-Communism. By 1948 the strengthening of the USSR and the advance of the Communists in China were harbingers of what was soon to be dubbed the 'Cold War'. That same year also saw the start of the Berlin blockade by the Soviets, the rebellion of the Red Flag Communists in Burma, the MCP Emergency in Malaya, the ongoing Hukbalahap rebellion in the Philippines, a Communist *coup* in Czechoslovakia, and other events suggesting a general advance of Communism. In March 1946 Winston Churchill had observed ominously that 'From Stettin in the Baltic to Trieste in the Adriatic an iron curtain has descended across the Continent'; now it seemed that curtain might encompass the globe. This greatly alarmed Western – and especially American – leaders. The United States had anti-imperialist traditions that encouraged an anti-Dutch posture, but fear of a Soviet-led Communist threat to the American-led 'free world' was becoming a more powerful determinant of policy.

In August 1948 a veteran of the 1920s PKI named Musso returned to Indonesia from the Soviet Union. He had not been in Indonesia since 1926, except for a clandestine visit in 1935 to establish an underground Communist network, so he was as out of touch with Indonesian realities as the Dutch. Upon his direction, the main leftist parties merged with the PKI. At this stage Amir Sjarifuddin publicly announced that he had been a member of the underground PKI himself since 1935. PKI was increasingly clearly a party of the *abangan* peasantry; it encouraged peasant take-overs of land, which provoked opposition from *santri* peasants and landlords who supported *Masyumi*. By September 1948 there was open warfare in the streets of Surakarta between pro-Communist and pro-government units.

On 18 September 1948, PKI supporters took over Madiun in East Java. Musso, Amir and other Communist leaders rushed to Madiun to try to take control of this uprising. The rebels announced that they had formed a new Republican government. Soedirman was sympathetic to radicals but had no wish to see the country under Communist rule, and feared that the Dutch would take advantage of this crisis to attack the remaining heartland of the Republic in Java. He hoped to arrange some sort of compromise settlement, but Sukarno – in no mood for compromise – responded with a broadcast denouncing the Communists and their Soviet-style government and calling upon all to rally to the Republican government in Yogyakarta. Siliwangi Division troops went into Madiun and, after bloody fighting, put the rebellion down. The rebels murdered pro-*Masyumi santris* and pro-government officials as they retreated. Musso was killed while fleeing. Amir was captured and later shot. Perhaps 8000 people died in the Madiun uprising, and some 35,000 people were arrested.

The Republic's suppression of the PKI uprising was crucial to the success of the Revolution. The left-wing challenge to the Republican leadership was removed for the duration of the conflict. The army was obliged to recognize that Sukarno was irreplaceable as leader and the Yogyakarta government the only legitimate one in the new nation, and acquired a deeply rooted anti-Communist hostility that remained throughout its subsequent history. The army began its own internal purge of leftist officers and units. Most crucially of all – in this year of evident Communist advances around the globe – the Republic of Indonesia had shown itself to be anti-Communist. This was not just a matter of public ideological positions: the Republic had taken up arms and bloodily suppressed a Communist uprising. Any potential conflict between American anti-imperialism and American anti-Communism was now obviated: both sentiments could lead the United States to support Indonesia's struggle for independence.

The Dutch made a desperate last attempt to defeat the Republic. They launched a second 'police action' in December 1948, an initial military success that proved to be a security headache and an irreversible political disaster. They took Yogyakarta, and the Republican leadership – having assessed the international environment more successfully than the Dutch – allowed themselves to be captured. Sukarno and his colleagues reckoned that there would be international outrage at this and they were right. The army broke into guerrilla units and harassed the Dutch everywhere; the Republican military did not share the political calculation made by the civilian leaders and forever after regarded itself as the sole savior of the Revolution in its darkest hour. Among the Dutch-created federal states, several protested and the cabinets of the East Indonesia state and the West Javanese state of Pasundan resigned in protest.

The UN called for a cease-fire, the return of Sukarno and his colleagues to Yogyakarta and the finalization of Indonesian independence by 1 July 1950. The United States suspended aid to the Netherlands that was supporting its efforts in Indonesia and then threatened to cut off all aid to the Dutch. The Netherlands had nowhere left to turn. A ceasefire was agreed, the Republican government was returned to Yogyakarta, negotiations took place in the Netherlands from August to November 1949 and on 27 December the Dutch recognized Indonesia as an independent state encompassing the former Netherlands East Indies, except for Papua (the western half of the island of New Guinea). The latter omission left a legacy in the form of a decades-long political problem. A combination of Indonesian determination and armed resistance, effective diplomacy, and the favorable circumstances (and lucky timing) of the Cold War had created Southeast Asia's largest nation. East Timor – still a sleepy Portuguese colony – was not part of these arrangements for Indonesian independence. It would, however, later become a major issue when the Portuguese empire collapsed in the 1970s.

Indochina

The West has tended to draw a fairly neat chronological boundary between the First Indochina War, which lasted from 1946 until 1954 and centered around opposition to French colonial rule, and the Second Indochina War, which lasted from 1954 until 1975 and involved Communist-led opposition to American-supported and non-Communist governments. This perspective is shared by non-Communist nationalists from Indochinese countries, who see their countries as having gained independence from France in 1953–54 and subsequently having done battle with Communist insurgencies. Conversely, the narrative constructed by Communist parties in the three countries prefers to see the period 1945–75 as a single revolution against, first, the French, and then their successors, the Americans; in fact, this narrative often dates the beginning of the 'revolution' to the founding of the Indochinese Communist Party (ICP) in 1930. Both views have their strengths and weaknesses. The second allows us to understand better the continuities between the two conflicts, while the first recognizes the fact that the French vision for Indochina differed significantly from that of the United States, even if both Western powers were fighting the same enemies to achieve their objectives.

As discussed in the preceding chapter, the final months of World War II produced three very different scenarios in the different parts of Indochina. The Japanese coup of March 1945 provided opportunities for local political forces to gain power, but it was not the same forces. In Vietnam the government of Emperor Bao Dai and his Prime Minister Tran Trong Kim only lasted a few months and was overthrown by the Viet Minh movement established as a united front by the ICP. This August Revolution, which led to the establishment of the Democratic Republic of Vietnam (DRV) under Ho Chi Minh's leadership in September 1945, temporarily placed the Party in a position of political dominance but did not give it a monopoly of political and military power, as rival forces still existed in different parts of Vietnam. In Laos, March 1945 weakened the authority of the monarchy and strengthened the influence of Prince Phetsarath and the group of nationalists known as the *Lao Issara*, who now took center stage in the new government. In Cambodia, Sihanouk (at that time still holding the title of king) remained the pre-eminent political figure, although initially, at least, he had to share the stage with his nationalist rival Son Ngoc Thanh.

Independence for part or all of Indochina was unacceptable to a French government trying to re-establish its power and prestige after the humiliations of the war. Even before the Japanese surrender, French forces were planning for the re-conquest of the colony. At the Yalta Conference in February 1945 the Allies agreed that Indochina would be occupied by Nationalist Chinese and British troops – north and south, respectively, of the 16th parallel – to handle the surrender and disarmament of the Japanese. The British, of course, had no reason to obstruct the French return to Indochina when they were busy reoccupying their own colonies and were entangled in Indonesia, while the Chinese were pragmatic enough to negotiate with either Indochinese nationalists or the French, depending on where their interests lay.

The British effectively gave the French a free hand to reoccupy the areas of Indochina under their control. In Cambodia there was no significant resistance from Norodom Sihanouk and the elite, and the French helpfully strengthened his position by arresting Son Ngoc Thanh after their return; Thanh subsequently left for exile in France. For the time being, Sihanouk was willing to subordinate Cambodia's political interests to the French; in early 1946 a *modus vivendi* was signed which made Cambodia a kingdom within the French Union, an amorphous structure essentially intended to maintain the colonial empire in a somewhat different form. Cambodia was given a constitution and the fundamental institutions of a democratic multi-party system; the first elections were held in September.

Vietnam was a different story, as the Viet Minh and the DRV government had established an administrative presence in all three regions. In Cochin China their authority was weaker, however, as their main power base had long been in Tonkin and northern Annam. Moreover, not only were there divisions within the southern ICP leadership, but they also faced serious competition for power there, particularly from the Cao Dai and Hoa Hao. The French were able to re-establish their rule in the towns and cities below the 16th parallel, although the countryside was another matter. The DRV government was in an extremely difficult situation, for it maintained that France's future relationship with Vietnam had to be negotiated before any kind of official French presence could be sanctioned, whereas France was determined to return first, and then negotiate. Although the Chinese Nationalists were less favorably disposed toward colonialism than the British, they had little sympathy for the Communist-dominated DRV. With civil war looming back home, the Chinese had little to gain from a prolonged occupation, and in February 1946 they allowed the French to return in exchange for France relinquishing economic rights in China.

Ho and his government were not ready to fight at this juncture, so they negotiated an agreement recognizing the DRV as a 'free state' within the French Union. The rest of 1946 was spent on negotiations over Vietnam's status, but generally speaking the two sides' positions were simply too far apart. France's top representative in Indochina, High Commissioner Thierry d'Argenlieu, did his best to undermine the negotiations going on in France by creating an autonomous Republic of Cochin China and otherwise sabotaging Ho's attempts to weaken or eliminate French authority. Even a *modus vivendi* signed by Ho in Paris in September did no more than delay the inevitable conflict, which broke out in December 1946. The DRV government evacuated Hanoi and relocated to the Viet Bac region to the north, which had been the main Viet Minh base area.

The Chinese presence in Laos also facilitated the return of the French beginning in March 1946. Phetsarath's regime did not have the strength to resist, and in May the *Issara* leaders fled across the Mekong to Thailand. King Sisavangvong, whose cooperation with the *Issara* had been reluctant at best, welcomed back the French. In August a *modus vivendi* similar to that signed in Cambodia formalized the kingdom's status. The following year Laos received a constitution and a National Assembly was established with a cabinet government and political parties.

Cambodia and Laos were now functioning constitutional monarchies, but without full sovereignty over their foreign relations or even their armies, which remained under French command. Their political systems were dominated by the elite. Cambodia's parties were led mainly by royal family members, though they did have genuine ideological differences. The Lao elite included both princes and members of powerful families; the divisions among them were based much more on regional and kin ties than on policies or political views. There were two important differences between the two kingdoms. First, Sihanouk as king dominated politics more thoroughly than Sisavangvong. While sharing the stage with other princes and with Son Ngoc Thanh following the latter's return from exile in 1951, Sihanouk became quite adept at manipulating the system to his advantage and at suppressing opposition, particularly from the Left. Sisavangvong never played such a strong role, and political power was more fragmented. Second, the main challenge to the Lao government came from outside the country, namely the *Issara* exiles in Thailand. They would remain there under Phetsarath's leadership until 1949, when many of them – but not Phetsarath himself – decided to return and join the royal government.

In Cambodia and Laos, the French had ready-made governments who were in no great hurry to see them leave, but in Vietnam an alternative had to be found to compete with the DRV for the population's loyalty. The French eventually turned to ex-Emperor Bao Dai, who had briefly served the DRV as an advisor but then left the country in 1947. After several years of protracted negotiations, in 1950 France created a 'State of Vietnam' under Bao Dai's leadership as head of state, but not emperor. This regime was meant to rally anti-Communists of various political stripes, but the 'Bao Dai solution' did little to strengthen either non-Communist nationalism or the French position in Vietnam. Bao Dai himself was not exactly charismatic, and his political capital had been severely depleted by his years of collaboration with the French. His regime was a hodge-podge of politicians of mixed quality and often dubious reputation, held together primarily by their anti-Communism.

To varying degrees, legitimacy was an issue for all three governments. The Cambodian and Lao regimes were at least buttressed by their monarchies, whose prestige had been less damaged by colonial 'protection' than Bao Dai. All three governments, however, were hampered by the fact that sovereignty over internal and external affairs was only transferred by the French in dribs and drabs, making them vulnerable to accusations of being mere tools of colonialism. By 1950 the French had gathered the three governments together as the Associated States of Indochina. The United States and United Kingdom, who were becoming more involved in Indochina, both pressured France to grant more autonomy to these governments in order to heighten their legitimacy, but ultimately French policy was conceived more in terms of preservation than of evolution. As a result, each of the three governments had to contest its power and legitimacy with a Communist-led rival, and by 1950 there were three revolutionary governments. The DRV, of course, existed before Bao Dai's State of Vietnam and enjoyed widespread support. The resistance government continued to expand the area under its control, leaving mainly the cities and towns for the French and Bao Dai. Sihanouk's regime faced opposition from two groups of insurgents, one operating with Thai support and one linked to the ICP. Over time the first group weakened in strength and influence, but the Communist-dominated resistance continued to strengthen under the leadership of Tou Samouth and Son Ngoc Minh, two of the earliest Khmer ICP members. In Laos, as was mentioned above, many of the *Issara* exiles chose to return in 1949–50. Phetsarath, despite remaining in Thailand, did not actively oppose the regime, but a group of more radical nationalists led by Prince Souphanouvong (Phetsarath's half-brother) linked up with the ICP. Souphanouvong had studied in Vietnam and married a Vietnamese wife; he was the first prominent Lao to cast in his lot with the ICP, and even during his participation in the *Issara* government in 1945–46 his pro-Viet Minh orientation was already evident.

From the ICP's perspective, Indochina was effectively a single revolution on a single battlefield, but the leadership realized the need for national parties for Cambodia and Laos. By the early 1950s there were enough non-Vietnamese members to establish Cambodian and Lao parties, and the ICP was formally dissolved in 1951. The Vietnamese component was renamed the Workers (*Lao Dong*) Party, and a Khmer People's Revolutionary Party was established the same year after the founding of a united front structure in 1950. For reasons which are unclear, a full-fledged Lao party was not established until 1955, but a resistance government existed from 1950 onward. Commonly known as the *Pathet Lao* ('Lao country'), it was led by Souphanouvong and a group of men who would be its leaders for the next four decades: Kaysone Phomvihane, Nouhak Phoumsavan, and Phoumi Vongvichit.

The main military challenge to the French and their allied governments always came from the Vietnamese; the DRV's forces, the People's Army of Vietnam (PAVN), put up a tough fight. The early years of the war were the most difficult for the DRV side, with several important defeats, but a French victory was far from assured. A key turning point came in 1949 with the establishment of the People's Republic of China. The DRV now had a friendly regime in its backyard, and substantial Chinese aid was forthcoming – both *matériel* and personnel. Moreover, as would be the case in the South after 1954, the perception that Bao Dai's State of Vietnam was propped up by a foreign power only served to strengthen the base of support for the DRV cause.

In Cambodia and Laos the situation was more complex. As suggested above, the royal governments themselves had a certain degree of inherent legitimacy, but even so they were still linked to the French. The insurgencies, too, had to 'prove themselves' and to demonstrate that they were not merely tools of the Vietnamese – an accusation which carried a lot of weight given the evolution of Cambodian and Lao nationalism. Neither revolutionary government could claim the base of support achieved by the DRV, nor did their insurgencies really threaten the royal governments – with the exception of Laos in 1953, to be discussed below. Collectively, however, the three components of the Indochinese revolution did achieve a critical mass of support which dramatically affected the evolution of nationalism.

By 1953, the prospects of France remaining in Indochina were increasingly dim. French public opinion was tiring of the conflict, and even with large amounts of American aid, the French-led forces were unable to get the upper hand militarily in Vietnam, which was the most crucial area to be won. In Cambodia, Sihanouk had launched a self-proclaimed 'crusade for independence' to pressure France into speeding up the timetable for full independence. In October France agreed to grant Cambodia and Laos almost total independence, although still within the French Union. These commitments did not satisfy the revolutionary movements, which continued to fight for the expulsion of the French and for new regimes under their own leadership. The final act of the First Indochina War was precipitated by a combined thrust of PAVN and *Pathet Lao* forces into Laos in early 1953 which nearly led to the capture of Luang Phabang. The attack was repulsed, but demonstrated the strategic vulnerability of Laos and its significance for Vietnam. In late 1953 the French began to fortify their outpost at Dien Bien Phu in northwestern Vietnam, which became a quagmire sucking in men and supplies. The outpost fell to the PAVN in May 1954, signaling the final French defeat.

Indochina's future was negotiated at the Geneva Conference which opened in July 1954. In addition to the great powers – France, the UK, USA, USSR and PRC – the conference was attended by Communist and non-Communist delegations from each country. The Khmer People's Revolutionary Party and *Pathet Lao*, however, were not given any official status. The Cambodian resistance gained virtually nothing from the negotiations, as Sihanouk's stature ensured that his government was recognized as the legitimate regime. The *Pathet Lao*, although not recognized as a government, were allowed to occupy two provinces as a resettlement zone but were eventually to be integrated under the Royal Lao Government. The most bitterly contested outcome of Geneva was the partition of Vietnam into two halves, separated at the 17th parallel. The DRV, of course, saw itself as the legitimate government for the entire country, but the British and Americans pushed for partition, and neither the Soviets nor the Chinese exerted the pressure which would have been necessary to block this decision. The DRV was now in power in the northern half of the country, and Bao Dai's State of Vietnam in the southern half. French rule was over, although France maintained close ties with its former colonies. Henceforth, the United States would assume the main role as protector, backer, and ally of the non-Communist governments.

The two Vietnamese governments (North and South Vietnam, with their capitals in Hanoi and Saigon respectively) were in very different positions in terms of strength and legitimacy. During the long years of the war, the DRV had consolidated its control in the rural areas and had been able to gradually implement certain key socialist policies, particularly in agriculture. Initially the Viet Minh, functioning as a united front meant to draw in as many 'patriotic' elements as possible, had tended to downplay the class struggle which was the ultimate goal of a Marxist revolution in favor of solidarity against the common enemy. By the early 1950s, however, the Party was in a stronger position and began gradually to shift its emphasis to attacking the 'feudal' system of land tenure through the confiscation and redistribution of land. At the same time, it attempted to impose more stringent 'socialist' criteria on the artistic and literary works being produced in the resistance zones, alienating a number of intellectuals who were anti-French but not Marxist in their ideology. From the beginning, the revolution had incorporated both nationalism and Marxism, and the tensions between the two began to appear when the Party line shifted in favor of the latter. Even so, the years of resistance considerably strengthened the DRV as a regime, and it faced relatively little internal opposition after partition.

Bao Dai's regime was not significantly bolstered by the departure of the French, given that independence had been gained by the efforts of the revolutionary forces now in power in the North. Even though most of the South had never been directly governed by the DRV, the Viet Minh presence in the rural areas was strong, and many Southerners had served the Revolution, not the State of Vietnam. Moreover, movements like the Cao Dai and Hoa Hao had large numbers of followers loyal only to their own leadership. Although the Saigon government was bolstered by the arrival of roughly one million refugees from the North – many of them Catholics – and by the departure of several hundred thousand Party sympathizers, it nevertheless faced major challenges in imposing its authority.

This observation was true of Bao Dai personally as well. He had spent the final months of the war in France, and in fact never again returned to Vietnam. After a series of unsuccessful prime ministers, just before Geneva he had appointed Ngo Dinh Diem, a Catholic with solid anti-Communist credentials and a fairly strong reputation as a nationalist. Equally important were Diem's good relations with the Americans, whose opinions carried increasing weight as the war went on. Diem had little respect for Bao Dai, however, and did not wish to share power; in October 1955, with American support, he engineered a referendum driving Bao Dai from power and establishing the Republic of Vietnam. The United States also backed Diem in a second crucial decision, namely, to prolong indefinitely the partition of Vietnam. The Geneva Accords had called for elections to reunify the country to be held by mid-1956. Neither the State of Vietnam nor the United States, however, had formally signed up to that part of the agreement, and thus did not feel themselves bound to carry it out. The stage was now set for two decades of civil war.

It was widely accepted that were elections in fact held, Ho Chi Minh (Figure 22) would be victorious. The DRV held back as long as possible before supporting armed resistance to the Diem government. During the first few years after partition the Party concentrated on 'building socialism' in the North while pressuring Saigon to agree to elections. Diem, however, was engaged in his own consolidation, attacking opponents of various kinds. The Cao Dai and Hoa Hao were major targets, along with the Binh Xuyen, a sort of Mafia with powerful financial interests and its own armed forces. The United States, fully committed to supporting Diem's government, was providing large amounts of economic, military, and developmental aid, as well as training for the army and police. Diem was successful in suppressing these particular enemies, but much less so in earning trust and loyalty.

Viet Minh followers in the South – only some of whom had gone North at the time of partition – were fiercely anti-colonialist, and in their eyes Diem (Figure 23) with his American backers was little more than another Bao Dai with a different foreign master. Instead of trying to convince them otherwise

Figure 22 Ho Chi Minh, 1969
Three Lions/Hulton Archive/Getty Images

by working toward the creation of a viable Southern-oriented nationalism, Diem tracked them down and arrested them as subversive elements. He also alienated many farmers by reversing land reform policies implemented by the Viet Minh during the war. By the late 1950s, the countryside was becoming a dangerous place for Party sympathizers and government officials alike. Those accused of Communism were being arrested and, increasingly, executed, while local Party elements in villages around the country were assassinating officials, teachers, and others associated with the regime. Until 1959 these actions did not have Hanoi's sanction; by that year, however, pressure from southern Party members could no longer be resisted, and the DRV leadership formally announced its support for the anti-Diem insurgency. Fighters and weapons from the North began to move over the network known as the Ho Chi Minh Trail (eventually extending through both Vietnams, Laos, and Cambodia). In 1960 the Party also took the important step of establishing the National Liberation Front (NLF), a united front to coordinate opposition to Diem.

By that time Diem faced opponents on all sides, as his intolerance for dissent and favoritism for fellow Catholics – particularly his large and powerful family – had eroded his base of support. In 1963 the 'Buddhist Crisis' erupted when his government openly discriminated against the Buddhists over the issue of

Figure 23   Ngo Dinh Diem, 1963
Horst Fass/AP/Press Association Images

flying their own flags on a religious holiday. Demonstrations by monks, nuns, and lay followers met with brutal repression, including raids on temples. A series of public self-immolations by monks drew instant world attention to the crisis and did much to convince the United States that Diem was no longer an effective ally. When a group of military officers began to plot a coup, they received a green light from Americans in Saigon and Washington. In early November 1963, Diem and his widely hated brother Ngo Dinh Nhu were arrested and shot, and a military junta seized power.

The overthrow of Diem's regime represented an important watershed in at least three respects. First, it marked the end of civilian government in South Vietnam; with the exception of an eight-month period in 1964–65, the country would remain under military rule until its fall in 1975. Second, whereas Diem and Nhu had to some extent kept the United States at arm's length and resisted American pressure for political change, their successors were generally more closely allied with the United States. Finally and most importantly, Diem's fall led to an acceleration of the insurgency and to the large-scale involvement of American combat troops.

Between 1963 and 1967 South Vietnam had a series of primarily military governments which corresponded to the rise and fall of various cliques of officers. Some degree of stability was achieved in 1967 with the election of

Generals Nguyen Van Thieu and Nguyen Cao Ky as President and Vice-President respectively. Thieu and Ky promulgated a new constitution and were able to hold onto power until the final days of the Republic. Their regime was deeply flawed in many ways and had little popular support beyond those who feared the Communist alternative, but it was at least able to forestall further coups. Elections were held under American pressure in 1971 which provided a façade of democracy and maintained Thieu and Ky in power.

Diem's successors had even weaker nationalist credentials than his, and his removal from the scene encouraged the Party to accelerate the pace of the NLF-led insurgency. This in turn provoked a dramatic increase in the scale of American involvement. The United States saw South Vietnam as a legitimate nation-state under attack from external aggression, and American policy was predicated on this assumption. The objective was to shore up the foundations of the Saigon regime through massive doses of economic and developmental aid while training – and, increasingly, fighting alongside – the Army of the Republic of Vietnam (ARVN).

Under Diem, the United States had provided large numbers of advisors, some of whom saw combat after the launch of the insurgency. Now the United States began a two-pronged policy of using American combat troops in the South and mounting bombing campaigns against the North, with the hope of persuading Hanoi to stop its support for the insurgency or at least to cripple its ability to provide that support. From the landing of the first Marines in early 1965, the size of the American troop presence quickly expanded, reaching 500,000 by the end of 1967. This presence was larger, more disruptive, and more violent than anything under the French, even during the First Indochina War. In addition to the casualties of actual combat, the war destroyed villages and killed their residents through the use of napalm and triggered a widespread flight of refugees into the towns and cities. The impact of hundreds of thousands of foreign soldiers severely destabilized the South Vietnamese economy and society.

The revolution in South Vietnam was a complex mixture of forces under the leadership of the *Lao Dong* Party. The NLF was the core of the united front; in 1969 it was supplemented by a Provisional Revolutionary Government which would henceforth represent the revolutionary side overseas. The military forces included the People's Liberation Armed Forces (Southern units linked to the NLF) and PAVN troops infiltrated from the North. There were some tensions between the Northern Party cadres and local revolutionaries in the South, but even so the Party built up a solid infrastructure which gradually extended its control over large areas of the country. In early 1968 the Party launched the famous Tet (Lunar New Year) offensive which attacked American and South Vietnamese facilities throughout the country. This campaign did not produce the hoped-for urban uprisings which might have catapulted the revolution into power, and the months of suppression which followed severely depleted the ranks of the insurgency, in particular the Southern forces. Nevertheless, these setbacks did not destroy the revolution itself, and the televised footage of the fighting at the American Embassy and elsewhere contributed significantly to the erosion of American public support for the war.

While the United States and the South Vietnamese government recognized the need for pacification through development and what became known as 'winning hearts and minds', most of their policies to this end had very mixed results. Although many villagers were lukewarm toward the NLF and resented its demands for young men to fight and taxes and rice to supply the insurgency, successive Saigon regimes failed to provide the honest and competent local governance which would have built loyalty at the grassroots. While both sides committed acts of brutality on civilians, the record of ARVN and the American and allied forces was generally worse. Nor were troops from the North ever as 'foreign' in South Vietnamese eyes as the Americans, despite propaganda efforts to portray them as such. The Party generally depicted the 'anti-American resistance' as a continuation of the 'anti-French resistance', and this argument made sense to the many Vietnamese who had fought first one enemy and then the other with only a few years' respite in between.

By the late 1960s, victory remained elusive for the South Vietnamese regime and its American allies, and the United States slowly began to look for an exit door. Richard Nixon's 'Vietnamization' strategy brought the first troop withdrawals in 1969, the idea being that the burden of fighting would be gradually but steadily shifted to ARVN. Meanwhile, the first concrete initiatives were made for negotiations in Paris between the United States and the DRV, along with the Provisional Revolutionary Government. The main segment of the peace talks began in 1970 and dragged on for more than two years, finally culminating in the Paris Peace Agreements of early 1973.

Like the Geneva Agreements in 1954, the 1973 accords served to give a beleaguered foreign power a way out of Indochina without resolving the conflicts which had provoked its intervention. The military status quo was maintained, with the Communist side's armed forces left in place throughout South Vietnam – a situation which the Thieu government in Saigon had only very grudgingly accepted after considerable arm-twisting and promises of continued support from Washington. Without the presence of American combat troops, however, South Vietnam was even more vulnerable, and the next two years saw a steady degradation of the Thieu regime's position. In early 1975 the revolutionary forces began a final push which turned into a rout for ARVN and culminated in the fall of the South Vietnamese government in April. The Provisional Revolutionary Government took power, but a year later North and South were reunified into the Socialist Republic of Vietnam.

Politically speaking, Cambodian history during this period is divided into two distinct periods: the governments of Sihanouk (1955–70) and Lon Nol (1970–75). It can also be split into a period of relative peace, when the internal conflicts were mainly political, and one of civil war, when the country was increasingly fragmented and torn by insurgency and government attempts to suppress it. No other figure dominates the Cambodian stage to the extent that Sihanouk does and until 1970, at least, he remained the most important leader in the country's politics.

In 1955, after the French departure, Sihanouk abdicated the throne and took the position of Head of State (as a prince), while his father Suramarit (r. 1955–60) replaced him as king. Sihanouk continued his practice of maintaining the structures of parliamentary democracy while dominating and controlling them and, when it suited him to do so, ignoring them. He articulated a national ideology called 'Buddhist socialism' which was in many respects more 'Sihanoukism' than anything else, and he created the *Sangkum Reastr Niyum* (People's Socialist Community) which effectively became his personal political party.

Sihanouk faced opponents on both the Left and the Right. Although much of the Khmer People's Revolutionary Party leadership had left for Hanoi after Geneva, some remained in Cambodia, their ranks enlarged by a group of radicals who had recently returned from study in France. These leftists, who included Saloth Sar (the future Pol Pot), operated through a legal party known as *Pracheachon* (The People); there were other more moderate leftists as well. Much of Sihanouk's rightist opposition was based in either Thailand or South Vietnam; the most significant group was the *Khmer Serei* (Free Khmer) under the leadership of his old nemesis Son Ngoc Thanh. Sihanouk worked to keep the leftists in check but generally left them to operate; particularly important were the numerous radicals who became teachers in secondary schools and universities. He felt more directly threatened by the *Khmer Serei*, particularly because they had foreign support, including – at times – that of the CIA.

The most frequent description of Sihanouk is 'mercurial', and this term accurately characterizes his domestic and foreign policies. Politically, he tacked left and right according to the circumstances and to his threat perception at a given point in time. Diplomatically, he attempted to preserve Cambodia's neutrality by accepting aid from the Americans, French, Soviets, Chinese, and anyone else who would give it. In theory this was a wise policy, but Sihanouk sabotaged his own neutrality to some extent by rhetorical excesses and diplomatic gaffes. He also made the dramatic gesture of refusing American military aid in 1963 and subsequently cutting diplomatic ties with the United States as well.

Sihanouk (Figure 24) invested a considerable amount of money in development projects of various kinds, including schools and hospitals. All was not well in the countryside, however, and the corruption and excesses of the Phnom Penh elite did not earn popular support at the grassroots level, despite the prince's personal popularity. In 1967 a change in the government's rice policy provoked a major episode of unrest at Samlaut in the northwest, leading to brutal repression of the revolt. Meanwhile, most prominent leftists had gradually abandoned the capital for the countryside, preparing to launch an insurgency against Sihanouk, who dubbed them the '*Khmers Rouges*' (Red Khmer).

Although Sihanouk made valiant attempts to keep Cambodia from becoming embroiled in the ongoing conflict in Vietnam, this proved impossible, and his strategy for doing so actually dragged the country into the fray. Banking on an eventual revolutionary victory, in 1966 he cut a secret deal with the DRV which allowed Vietnamese forces to take refuge on Cambodian territory and to receive shipments of arms via the port of Sihanoukville. This agreement benefited Cambodia by preventing it from being a target for hostile Vietnamese forces and by ensuring that Hanoi put pressure on the *Khmer Rouge* to refrain from trying to undermine Sihanouk's regime.

Sihanouk's strategy ultimately backfired, however, in two important respects.

Figure 24   Norodom Sihanouk, 1995
© Pierre Perrin/Sygma/Corbis

The Cambodian Communists were increasingly disinclined to follow the advice of their Vietnamese comrades, whom they correctly viewed as willing to sacrifice the interests of the Cambodian revolution in favor of the struggle in South Vietnam. Moreover, the United States and South Vietnamese were not prepared to ignore the presence of the enemy on Cambodian territory, and they began to cross the border in hot pursuit. By early 1970, the *Khmer Rouge* controlled a sizable chunk of the countryside, while another part was occupied by Vietnamese revolutionary troops. Sihanouk's tolerance of this presence caused considerable resentment among the elite, including the military, as did the cut-off of American aid. Although in his final years in power he restored relations with the United States in an attempt to shore up his government, the situation had deteriorated too greatly. In March 1970, while he was overseas, Sihanouk was overthrown by a coup. His Prime Minister Lon Nol became the head of a new Khmer Republic.

Lon Nol, with American support, was determined to take a much tougher line against Vietnamese and Cambodian Communists alike. He began a series of military campaigns against the two enemies but was generally unsuccessful in reversing the insurgency's gains. The United States began massive bombing campaigns in the countryside which caused heavy casualties and generated widespread anger against the government without significantly weakening the *Khmer Rouge*. After his overthrow, Sihanouk headed a government of resistance which was largely a disguise for the Communist Party, his long-time adversaries. It is unclear to what degree Sihanouk's fronting for the *Khmer Rouge* enabled them to win power, but the five years of the Khmer Republic's existence were tragically similar to the final years of the Republic of Vietnam in terms of their human cost, and in April 1975 the revolutionary forces entered Phnom Penh and seized power.

The Party which took power in 1975 was very different from the one founded in 1951. The two key developments had been the rise to power of the returnees from France and the partial vacuum left by the departure of Son Ngoc Minh and many other former leaders in 1954. The top leader remaining in Cambodia, Tou Samouth, was murdered by Sihanouk's police, leaving Saloth Sar (Pol Pot) and his close associates a free hand to run the Party. In 1960 they renamed it the Khmer Workers' Party, and later it became the Communist Party of Kampuchea. Pol Pot, Ieng Sary, and the other core leaders took the Party in an increasingly radicalized direction while gradually 'emancipating' themselves from what they saw as the oppressive grip of their Vietnamese comrades. These tendencies would come to full fruition in 1975.

Laos differed from Cambodia and South Vietnam in at least two important respects. First, there was a much greater balance between political and military conflicts, as the battle between Communist and non-Communist forces was played out in the halls of government as much as it was in the contested rural areas. Second, Laos possessed a critical mass of genuine neutralists, led by Prince Souvanna Phouma (a brother of Phetsarath and half-brother of Souphanouvong), who sought to reconcile the various factions into some kind of national unity. In South Vietnam a viable neutralist movement was never allowed to develop. Sihanouk adopted 'neutralism' as his foreign policy, but the structure of national politics was very different from that of Laos; and his 'neutral' stance was less ideological, more pragmatic, and frequently violated.

Lao political history during the civil war is structured around three formal agreements and the coalition governments they created: those of 1957, 1962, and 1973–74. Each of these governments was the result of negotiations among the *Pathet Lao*, rightists of various stripes, and neutralists in the middle, usually represented by Souvanna Phouma. The first of them was intended to realize the political and military integration prescribed at Geneva, but it collapsed within a few months. The second coalition was meant to put an end to months of renewed conflict provoked by successive rightist and neutralist military coups but it, too, was sabotaged, largely by the rightists. The failure of the 1962 agreement also led to the split of the neutralist faction into two groups, one effectively allied with the *Pathet Lao*, and the other closer to the rightists. The final coalition came at a time when the *Pathet Lao* controlled much of the countryside and represented a final attempt to find a solution which would prevent a total Communist victory. Souvanna Phouma remained the dominant figure in the government throughout this period, but even his personal prestige and tireless efforts to hold the coalition together proved ineffective. In 1975 the revolutionary forces began to take power in the towns through demonstrations and local uprisings, and by December they controlled Vientiane and established the Lao Democratic People's Republic.

Laos had greater political pluralism than its neighbors, and its various parties – including the *Pathet Lao*, which participated in elections and held cabinet posts in the coalition governments – represented a genuine diversity of regional interests and ideological positions. It is not inconceivable that, if left to their own devices, the Lao could have found a more workable solution to their conflict. But they were never masters of their own house, and much of their own agency – not to mention their sovereignty – was eroded by foreign interference. The

United States exercised as much influence as it did in South Vietnam, although it did so largely through aid and support for the Lao government and army rather than through American troops. American policy was far from consistent, especially where Souvanna Phouma was concerned; while from 1962 onwards the Americans supported him, prior to that time they backed the rightists – of whom the most prominent was the military officer Phoumi Nosavan – in efforts to overthrow him. Genuine neutrality in any part of Indochina was never attractive to Washington, and a preference for leaders who took a strong anti-Communist stance usually prevailed. As Souvanna Phouma became less firmly neutralist, he became more acceptable to the Americans.

Although Laos is sometimes portrayed as being of rather marginal importance compared to the main 'set piece' of Vietnam, its proximity to that country and the close ties between the two revolutions ensured that it would never be peripheral to the Vietnamese conflict. The Ho Chi Minh Trail ran through eastern Laos, and the area was heavily bombed over the course of the war in an unsuccessful attempt to interdict traffic moving from North to South Vietnam. The Plain of Jars region in northeastern Laos was also strategically important, as had been demonstrated in 1953. The provinces of Xieng Khouang and Sam Neua (Houaphan) were key battlegrounds for the *Pathet Lao* and North Vietnamese forces; the training of ethnic Hmong fighters in these provinces was one of the most significant aspects of American activity in Laos. The Hmong elite was split between a faction loyal, first, to the French and then to the Americans and the Lao government, and a faction loyal to the revolution.

The counterweight to the United States in the Lao conflict was the DRV. As we have seen, the Lao revolution was effectively launched by the Vietnamese-dominated ICP. After the establishment of a separate Lao party, North Vietnamese support remained a crucial factor in the success of the *Pathet Lao*, and DRV advisors and troops remained on Lao territory for decades. The Vietnamese presence was not always well received and provided fodder for opposition to the *Pathet Lao*, just as the interference by 'American imperialism' was a constant theme of Communist propaganda. Generally speaking, however, the *Pathet Lao* were more successful than the government in building and expanding their own base of support, their links to the Vietnamese notwithstanding.

The ultimate victory of the *Pathet Lao* (or, more properly, of the Lao People's Revolutionary Party) was due as much to the weaknesses of the royal government as to the strength of the revolutionary movement. There were few other figures among the non-Communist elite who could match Souvanna Phouma's prestige. Even the *Pathet Lao* could boast their own royal leader, Souphanouvong. The Royal Lao Government arguably enjoyed a greater degree of legitimacy than its counterpart in Saigon, but even so it was plagued by corruption and by a general failure to bring about genuine development in the rural areas contested between the two sides. By 1975 disillusionment with the government and general fatigue after decades of civil war meant that *Pathet Lao* promises of a democratic, neutral, and prosperous Laos were increasingly attractive, and the Communist victory was political as much as military.

Dissent was rarely tolerated by any of the regimes discussed here. Those under the control of Communist parties were generally subject to severe limitations on freedom of expression. In North Vietnam the most famous episode of dissent was the *Nhan Van Giai Pham* affair of 1956–57 – coinciding with Mao's 'Hundred Flowers' campaign in China – named for two prominent publications ('Humanities' and 'Distinguished Literary Work') which were briefly allowed to disseminate criticism of the government before being shut down. South Vietnam had several prominent dissidents, notably the Buddhist monk Thich Nhat Hanh; many of these figures were neither pro- nor anti-Communist but simply called for an end to the war. Ironically, their independent stance generally earned them the suspicion of the new government after 1975, and several were either imprisoned or went into exile. Laos during the period of civil war had arguably the most space for articulating political views. Cambodia was somewhere in between. Sihanouk was never able to enjoy a monopoly on public political discourse, although his regime grew increasingly repressive over his years in power. After his fall, the Lon Nol regime had little or no taste for opposition. Yet dissenting voices continued to be heard both on the political stage and in the press, despite periodic crackdowns on both.

The conflict in Indochina spanned three countries (while drawing in several more) and three decades. It began as an anti-colonial struggle yet continued through the decolonization period as the fulcrum of the Cold War in Southeast Asia. While the core of the conflict, particularly in its earlier stages, was located in Vietnam, the protracted civil wars in Cambodia and Laos were by no means peripheral, and at times they were equally destructive, especially when American bombing was involved. Although in each of the three countries the fundamental conflict was between Communist-led and anti-Communist forces – each with the backing of particular foreign powers – the relationships between the foreign and local allies were different in each case. While from the perspective of the Communist forces there was a single Indochinese revolution and in the eyes of their opponents a single 'war against Communist aggression', each country's conflict had its own local dynamics and particularities.

Thailand

The Japanese surrender and the end of World War II found Thailand in difficult diplomatic circumstances. Although Phibun, the author of the alliance with Japan, was no longer in power, the fact remained that Thailand had declared war on the Allies and reclaimed territory from British Malaya and Burma and from French Indochina. Siam under the absolute monarchy had tended to be fairly pro-British, both because so many of the Thai elite had studied in the United Kingdom and because France was generally seen as the more aggressive of the two colonial powers in 'stealing' Thai territory. The relationship had soured under Phibun, however, and by 1945 the British showed little sympathy for the government in Bangkok. Conversely, the United States, which had not had a strong presence in pre-war Thailand, now emerged as the country's new 'best friend' and advocate *vis-à-vis* the other Allied powers. The shift to an alliance with the United States would be the single largest factor in Thailand's political and economic development over the next few decades.

Anxious to get into the Allies' good graces and re-establish itself diplomatically, Thailand was forced to make a number of concessions. It returned the portions of the Malay and Shan states which had come under its control during the war and promised to sell large quantities of rice to the British at low prices. The territories taken from Cambodia and Laos in the earlier conflict with Indochina were returned to the French. The government even agreed to nullify an anti-Communist law from the 1930s in order to gain USSR acceptance of Thailand's entrance into the UN. Although these agreements were painful, particularly the territorial retrocession, they did allow the country to enter the post-war period on a somewhat firmer footing, at least in terms of its relations with the great powers.

Politically and economically, however, the outlook was less promising. Between 1944 and 1947 Pridi dominated the political scene, although he actually held the post of Prime Minister only for a few months in 1946. That year saw the promulgation of a new constitution – more democratic in certain respects than the 1932 charter – and the appearance of a multi-party system. Several new parties were established with discernible ideological differences, which gave some promise of a more functional democratic system. King Ananda, now aged 21, returned home in 1945 and quickly made himself popular among his subjects. For a brief period, there was hope that Thailand had left behind the era of single-party or dictatorial rule.

This hope was shattered in June 1946, when Ananda was found shot dead in his bedroom just days before he was to return to Switzerland to complete his university studies. His death, which remains the greatest mystery in modern Thai history, precipitated a political crisis and undid everything which Pridi and his allies had accomplished over the past two years. Although there was little motive for Pridi – or anyone else, for that matter – to want the king dead, he was held responsible by many conservatives, both because he was Prime Minister at the time and because, as the People's Party's main ideologue, he was believed to be anti-royalist and probably a closet republican. A prolonged series of inquests, trials, and appeals eventually led to the execution of three individuals accused of regicide, even though neither their alleged motive nor their connection to Pridi was ever demonstrated convincingly.

The months after the war were also a difficult time for the Thai economy. The sales of cheap rice to the British and related restrictions, although an improvement over the original plans for forced deliveries of rice at no cost, nevertheless caused significant economic disruption. At the same time, opportunities abounded for corruption and profiteering, despite the government's attempts to control the situation. As is so often the case, the economic crisis weakened the regime's legitimacy precisely at the time when it was facing mounting political opposition for its handling of the king's death. Ananda was of course immediately succeeded by his brother Bhumibol (r. 1946–), so there was no real threat to the monarchy as such, but the uncertainties surrounding Ananda's demise and the question of Pridi's responsibility for it made the political climate very tense.

The prolonged crisis of 1946–47 directly benefited two groups of people. First were the conservative politicians opposed to Pridi, of whom there were many. A number of them were royalist in their orientation, and those who were not found it expedient to shift in that direction. The most prominent was Kukrit Pramote, a British-educated intellectual and journalist who founded the Democratic Party, which is still in existence today. A descendant of the royal family, although not actually a prince, Kukrit was convinced that Pridi had committed regicide and remained violently opposed to him for the rest of his life. The second group was the military, many of whom were still loyal to Phibun and bitter over the turn of events after his fall from power.

Over the course of 1947 the conservatives and military formed an alliance which culminated in a military coup in November. Initially the army appointed a civilian Prime Minister, Khuang Aphaiwong (who had already held the office twice since Phibun's resignation), but a few months later they replaced him with Phibun. Although Phibun once again found himself in the seat of power, which he would hold until 1957, he now had to share it. His two most powerful allies – and at the same time rivals – were Sarit Thanarat, a colonel who rose to power in the army, and Phao Siyanon, who headed the police. This triumvirate would dominate Thai politics for nearly a decade. Thus the 1947 coup, like that of 1933, brought an end to civilian-dominated government and inaugurated a period of military rule. This time the soldiers would remain in power for a quarter-century.

12
Building Nations, to *c.*1990

Political and economic dimensions

Introduction: the democratic experiments and authoritarian alternatives

The ending of colonial empires brought to Southeast Asia the challenges of independence. The new states had to establish viable political frameworks to replace the structures imposed by colonial rule. Several opted – at least on the surface – for Western-style democracy, some more completely than others, rather than seeking inspiration from their own pre-colonial and authoritarian pasts. The Philippines, Indonesia, and South Vietnam took on forms of parliamentary democracy based on a presidential form of government. Malaysia, Cambodia, Laos, and Thailand adopted constitutional monarchy with a prime minister. In several of these cases, however, power was really exercised in quite a different manner: in the Thai case there were only short attempts at real democracy during the decades after 1932. Laos and Cambodia maintained parliamentary systems with periodic elections, but their political stages were largely dominated by the elite. Brunei remained an absolute monarchy with the Sultan playing the role of Prime Minister in a ministerial structure after 1984. Burma and Singapore chose to have a prime minister as head of government with a president as formal head of state. Only North Vietnam began its existence as a Communist state. The other states' adoption of a form of Western-style democracy – the system that had actually been represented in their lives mainly by colonial oppression – requires some explanation.

The choice of democracy was not entirely surprising, given that a rudimentary parliamentary system was one of the legacies that some departing colonial powers bequeathed to their nationalist successors. Colonial powers tended to preach democracy more than they practiced it, but – as pointed out in the introduction to Chapter 9 – it had become difficult for Western democracies to deny their colonies some progress towards eventual self-rule. Thus, America and Britain left the Philippines, Burma, and Malaya with constitutional structures based on Western democratic models. France did as well in Cambodia and Laos, although many of the most prominent political figures in both countries were princes of various ideological stances. As we have seen, the American democratic experiment began almost immediately after wresting the Philippines away from Spain in 1898, with Congress passing legislation in 1902 to establish a bicameral legislature in the Philippines, and granting Commonwealth status to the Philippines from 1934 with the promise of full independence on 4 July 1946. Upon independence, the Philippines adopted a structure of government that reflected its American inspiration. Malaya's experience with the democratic experiment was essentially a post-1945 development. Confronted with the changed political contexts after the war, an environment charged with post-war nationalism, and with a Communist insurrection to boot, the British were belatedly compelled to demonstrate to Malayans and to the world the validity of democracy as a model of political development in Malaya. By transferring power willingly Britain was able to win the trust of the nationalist elites and guide the process of parliamentary transplantation, which Malaya's new rulers embraced. In Burma the British won little trust, but nevertheless in the 1935 Government of Burma Act they granted Burma a status close to that of a self-governing dominion, with a constitution that was inaugurated in April 1937.

Democracy also had an intrinsic appeal to nationalist elites, many of whom were Western-educated and therefore exposed to democratic norms and institutions in the metropoles. In Malaya, the sons of Malay royalty, as we have seen, were schooled in the English way and many studied in England. Malaya's first Prime Minister from 1957 to 1970, Tunku Abdul Rahman, was educated at Cambridge, gaining a first degree in law and history, and later in London, where he became a barrister in 1947. Like the Tunku, Singapore's Lee Kuan Yew, Prime Minister from 1959 to 1990, also trained as a lawyer at Cambridge and was equally at home with Western parliamentary norms. During his time in the United Kingdom, Lee befriended political leaders in the British Labour Party and even campaigned on behalf of a Cambridge friend who was a Labour Party candidate. Burma's U Nu, its first Prime Minister from 1947 to 1958 and again from 1960 to 1962, also had a Western education. Like the Tunku he remained committed to the democratic framework. 'Democracy,' he declared, 'is one of the noblest ideas created by man, and there can be no compromise in its application to human society anywhere in the world.'[1] Dutch-educated Indonesian nationalists like Sukarno and Mohammad Hatta also professed their commitment to democracy, but this case is a revealing one. Hatta was the only one of the two to have studied in the Netherlands and thus to have seen what democracy actually was in practice – which may explain the strength of his, and the weakness of Sukarno's, commitment to the idea. Democracy was one of the five principles of Indonesia's *Pancasila* state ideology, but Sukarno understood this more as an extension of the traditional Indonesian methods of *musyawarah* and *mufakat* (deliberation and consensus) rather than the free political contest of Western parliaments.

The new nationalist leaders were also influenced by their experiences during the struggle against foreign rule. Burmese nationalist leaders had not always been impressed by Western democracy and some were attracted to the Fascism of the 1920s and 1930s. In a speech in 1930, U Nu declared: 'I dislike democracy

---

1   Quoted in Richard Butwell, *U Nu of Burma* (Stanford, CA: Stanford University Press, 1963), 75.

where much time is wasted in persuading the majority and in trying to get the consent of the majority. Democracy is good in name only. It cannot be used effectively. It cannot work in this period of dictatorship of Hitler and Mussolini ... . I like dictatorship where things can be done quickly without any interference.'[2] But wartime experiences changed many such views. The Burmese nationalists' experience with Japanese rule – its brutality and sham Japanese-sponsored independence – dampened their enthusiasm for Fascism and totalitarianism. This was reflected in the very name of the Anti-Fascist People's Freedom League. Now U Nu was of the view that a 'one-party dictatorship' would be intolerable, for Burma had just emerged from an 'evil system in which political power [was] derived from the top few'. 'We must take particular care', he said in a speech in 1958, 'not to allow the exploitation, the tyranny and the oppression that are inherent evils in Communism ... to become any part of the ... state we wish to create.'[3] Such sentiments were also expressed by Indonesian nationalist leaders like Hatta who said that 'Experience with the colonial autocratic government in the form of a police state had given rise to the ideal of a democratic constitutional state in the minds of the younger generation of Indonesia.' Such a state, he added, should be 'based on the sovereignty of the people'.[4]

Accepting democratic norms was also an important tactical weapon in the nationalists' battle for independence. By doing so they hoped to attract Western sympathy and diplomatic support for their struggles against undemocratic colonial rule. Indonesian nationalists, who depended heavily on international support to compel the Dutch to decolonize, realized that their chances of maintaining such outside support were better if they emphasized their democratic nature. In the drafting of the 1950 provisional constitution, Indonesia adopted Western constitutional forms. Such international considerations probably informed Ho Chi Minh's declaration of the independence of the *Democratic Republic* of Vietnam (DRV) on 2 September 1945, which began with a quotation from the American Declaration of Independence of 1776. In Vietnam's case, however, the Americans chose not to recognize the DRV or support its struggle for independence led by the Communist Party. In a few cases, holding elections was a supportive step, for a strong electoral mandate strengthened nationalists' hands in dealing with the colonial powers. In Aung San's inaugural address as President of the AFPFL in 1946, he called for elections to be held so as to demonstrate to the British the strength of the AFPFL's support. Malaya's political elite also sought to impress the British with their ability to lead Malaya's diverse population through favorable election outcomes.

Democracy's emphasis on consensus – rather than authoritarian – politics was also valuable to nationalist leaders who needed to mobilize all social groups not only during the anti-colonial struggle but also in the post-independence

---

[2] Quoted in ibid., 19.

[3] Quoted in ibid., 74, 77.

[4] Quoted in Herbert Feith and Lance Castles (eds), *Indonesian Political Thinking, 1945–1965* (Ithaca, NY: Cornell University Press, 1970), 35.

nation-building phase. The AFPFL, for example, accepted liberal democratic norms in order to win the support of the minority ethnic groups, and to assure them that democratic safeguards would be written into the constitution to ensure their representation. In Indonesia, democracy's emphasis on consensus and consultation offered the best hope of persuading Indonesia's varied social and political groups to support the central government.

Finally, World War II boosted the democratic cause. The Allies claimed that the war was fought to defend the democracies of the world against the onslaught of Axis totalitarianism. Nazism and Fascism had been defeated and discredited by 1945. In Southeast Asia the post-war mood was for greater freedom, not a return to authoritarian rule. The ascendancy of American power in the post-war order was another factor that both colonial powers and their opponents needed to take into account. American favor for newly independent regimes that presented a democratic face and were willing to resist Communism was noticed by all. With democracy apparently in vogue, and upheld by American power, it was not surprising that so many of these new states embraced the democratic experiment, for it would have seemed unfashionable and unprogressive to have done otherwise – except, of course, in the case of elites who were persuaded that Communism was even more up-to-date than democracy, even more the wave of the future.

As will be seen below in the context of particular nations, already by the mid-1950s it seemed increasingly that the democratic fashion had run its course. In 1955, South Vietnam established a republic under the authoritarian rule of Ngo Dinh Diem. In 1957–59, Indonesia abandoned its liberal democratic system when Sukarno declared martial law and introduced 'Guided Democracy'. That year also saw a strengthening of military rule in Thailand when a coup by Marshal Sarit, the Army chief, toppled the newly elected government of Phibun. In 1958 Burma's decade-long experiment with parliamentary democracy under U Nu faltered, and brought the army under General Ne Win to power in a two-year caretaker government. Civilian rule returned for another two years before the army stepped in again in 1962, this time seizing power by force; it has continued to rule Burma down to the present. In 1969, Malaysia's democracy was suspended for two years when communal riots led to the establishment of a National Operations Council which ruled under emergency regulations. In 1970 Cambodia's government under Sihanouk, which had been increasingly dominated by him and his followers within the constitutional framework, was toppled by a coup led by his Prime Minister, General Lon Nol. In 1972 President Marcos of the Philippines, citing threats to the security of the state, imposed martial law and suspended democracy. In 1975, Laos – which had never really established a durable political system – became a Communist state. Only in Singapore has democracy carried on essentially unchanged, but there the island-state's leaders took the view that their parliamentary democracy must be modified to suit local conditions, an approach which produced in effect a predominantly one-party democracy with the PAP always in power.

Where the democratic experiment failed, Southeast Asian states turned instead to military regimes or civilian-led authoritarian rule as alternative structures of governance. By the mid-1970s four states in Southeast Asia were governed by military-dominated regimes: Burma, Indonesia, South Vietnam, and Cambodia. South Vietnam, Cambodia, and Laos were taken over by Communist forces in 1975. Thailand's government had been military-dominated for three decades by then, except for a brief, and in the end bloody, experiment with real democracy, as will be seen below.

Burma

We have seen above how the military's dominant role in Burma had roots in the colonial period and World War II. By 1935, the *Dobama Asiayone*, the university student union, religious organizations, and even a few members of the older generation of politicians formed *tats* (armies) to protect their followers in demonstrations, elections, and other public functions. This contributed to the insertion of military ideas, structures, terminology, and symbols into political life. The group of *Thakins* who sought foreign assistance, who were trained by the Japanese – the famous Thirty Comrades – and worked with them, and then turned against the Japanese in 1945, formed the core of what would eventually become the national army or *Tatmadaw*. Out of the war emerged the Anti-Fascist People's Freedom League (AFPFL), but profound differences about the future remained within the organization.

Factionalism in the AFPFL and among Communist politicians, generational rivalries among the educated elite, and distrust among politicized ethnic groups weakened the state before it could even be assembled. Returning British civil servants and army officers were reluctant to forgive members of the former BIA for initially chasing them out of the country, while Burmese were in turn reluctant to believe that the British would simply grant independence. Supporters of the returning British and followers of the BIA prepared for another struggle. Pro-British battalions, originally recruited from minority ethnic groups, worried about where they would fit in a new national army whose officers had a different educational, social, and religious background.

In September 1945, members of the Allied forces, Aung San, Communist leaders, BNA officers, and British Civil Affairs staff convened the Kandy Conference to determine how to reorganize the army in Burma. They agreed on a two-winged army: one wing for the ethnic minorities and another for the former BIA/BNA. Neither wing trusted the other – reflecting the legacy of the British idea of 'two Burmas', one consisting of the majority Burmans and the other of the ethnic minorities. For Aung San and the AFPFL, keeping their military units intact in this way was essential to preserving their power base. The two-winged army also perpetuated the separate interests of ethnic minorities. Much of this 'two-Burmas' vision was reflected in political cleavages, particularly in the loosely unified AFPFL. Aung San's leadership was crucial; his assassination in July 1947 contributed to fragmentation on both military and political fronts.

Communism was one of the political ideologies circulating among nationalist activists in Burma from colonial days onwards. The first Communist Party cell was formed in 1939, followed in 1943 by an underground Party Congress organized by *Thakin* Soe and six others. The Communists were linked to the

Dobama Asiayone and introduced Marxist-Leninist concepts into the leading nationalist groups, but Communism as an ideology found little support. Key leaders such as *Thakin* Soe and *Thakin* Than Tun shaped the way that Communism was understood, traveling to peasant communities and teaching revolution within the context of an anti-colonial agenda. Each leader had his own vision of Communism's place in the future of the country and, like other figures, won a following based in large measure on personal charisma and patronage. Out of shared animosity towards Japanese Fascism and militarism, the Communist Party-Burma cooperated with the British and (later) BIA forces against the Japanese.

Than Tun won leadership of the Communist Party in competition with Soe in 1946, which caused a split in the Party. *Thakin* Soe's minority 'Red Flag' group thereupon went into rebellion. The appeal of the Communists' agrarian reform programs forced the AFPFL and the colonial authorities to enact similar legislation to undercut the Party's support. The 1947 Tenancy Standard Rent Act redirected tax burdens from peasants to landlords, while the 1947 Agriculturalists Debt Relief Act cancelled all pre-war debts. Although Than Tun was Aung San's brother-in-law, he was unable to gain a significant role for the Communists in the new nation. They were squeezed out of the AFPFL by non-Communists and returning British officials who were wary of Communism's following both in the countryside and within the army. Following independence and the realization that they would not have much influence over the future of the country, three 'White Flag' Communist battalions left the army in 1948; thus, under the leadership of *Thakin* Than Tun began one of the longest Communist insurgencies in Southeast Asia. The 'White Flag' Communists never, in fact, had any prospect of taking over the state. Although the Party in rebellion had considerable support from peasants and workers, it was short of funding, organizationally weak, and without significant military support. The government – for all of its inadequacies – was superior in its military capabilities, infrastructure, and economic resources. Communism in Burma thus never had the prospects of power that it had in Indochina or even Indonesia; nor did it have the capacity to launch an insurrection as serious as in Malaya or the Philippines.

Other battalions defected from the Burmese army in 1948 to join the Karen National Defense Organization rebellion, so that within three months of independence the new government army was falling apart. Aung San's successor, U Nu, could not recreate the loyalty and commitment that his predecessor could claim. From 1948 to 1962 the Rangoon government and its armed forces faced insurgency in nearly every major city and township. This period accustomed the army leadership to making independent decisions, since civilian authority was weak and only the army could keep the insurgencies at bay. Indeed, the weakness of the civilian government and its tumultuous politics were almost as much a security liability as the ethnic and Communist enemies. The AFPFL broke into two main factions in 1958, which also created divisions between field commanders and staff officers. At the same time, it strengthened the military's general view that only it could hold the country together. Prime Minister U Nu's policy of making Buddhism the state religion galvanized ethnic insurgents and exacerbated national divisions. His attempt to placate ethnic demands by creating a Mon State and an Arakan State further worried the military leadership, fearing fragmentation of the country. Finally, when U Nu attempted to meddle in army affairs, in September 1958 three staff generals took over government on behalf of General Ne Win, intending to maintain civil order and forestall conflict between factions within the army. Between 1958 and 1960, this 'caretaker government' ran the state, providing the army with both experience and confidence that it was able to run the nation.

In 1945, the economy had been nearly destroyed by the war. Transport routes, communication lines, factories, distribution centers, capital investment, and key personnel had all been disrupted or destroyed. Returning civil servants, angry at Aung San and the BIA for chasing them out of the country, attempted to assert their authority in the countryside by declaring on 1 March 1945 that all currency issued by the Japanese was worthless. This move directly affected farmers and poor villagers because they had sold their crop to the Japanese army and did not have any British or Indian currency to purchase new seed. Former district officers attempted to collect taxes, conscript labor for rebuilding the infrastructure, and impose curfews, just as touring Communist leaders promised to relieve peasants of such obligations. For many rural communities, the situation between 1940 and 1950 was dire. Income levels were worse than during the Depression.

The social and political instability that followed independence in 1948 compounded the challenges of rebuilding the economy. What economic strategies to adopt, how labor should be organized, and how new industries could be developed were among the more pressing questions facing the new government. Establishing a coherent economic policy required a stable, unified leadership – something hardly visible in 1948. Although unified loosely under the AFPFL umbrella, government stakeholders competed with one another in the economic interests of their various constituencies, stymieing economic advancement. Key businesses were slowly nationalized, including those in banking, transport, agriculture, and heavy industry. There were some joint government-private ventures in the oil industry, but their profits were channeled to the state rather than to foreign shareholders. In the 1950s the Defense Services Institute, whose purpose was to provide discounted consumer goods for the armed services, emerged and, during the military 'caretaker government' (1958–62), became the country's largest economic enterprise. Thus did military influence continue to penetrate deeply into the socio-economic foundations of society. The nationalization of businesses and an attempt to develop import-substitution enterprises between 1948 and 1962 were the keystones of a policy intended to create an economy less dependent on foreign capital.

In 1960, after elections were held, Ne Win (Figure 25) returned the government to U Nu, but the restored civilian government was short-lived. In March 1962, Ne Win led another coup that ushered in a new political order. His Revolutionary Council blended military hierarchy with socialist ideology. Within a few days, the Council concentrated judicial, legislative, and executive power in Ne Win's hands, eliminating the institutions established at independence in 1948. Ne Win announced the nationalization of both foreign and

Figure 25   Ne Win, 1962

AP/Press Association Images

domestic trade, steering Burma along a new path called the 'Burmese Way to Socialism', an explicit rejection of U Nu's ideology of 'Buddhist Socialism'. The Revolutionary Council also took greater interest in activities once considered private: gambling, beauty contests, and art competitions were banned while new holidays that celebrated peasants, martyrs, the military, and the Union of Burma were instituted. U Nu's religious polices were reversed, ethnicity was rejected as a constitutional category, and the regime attempted to promote symbols and ideas to articulate a new national identity. In 1965, the Academy for the Development of National Groups opened: its aim was to encourage students from border areas to appreciate symbols of national heritage and to pursue leadership roles in provincial governments upon graduation. Legislation that was ethnically specific was replaced with laws that applied across all ethnicities. The Revolutionary Council began to isolate Burma from the outside world, so as to cultivate a purer form of 'Burmeseness' that would contribute to the integration of the newly reconceived nation.

Army personnel were key figures in linking the state to rural society, merging state administration and participatory structures with the military hierarchy. Mass and class-defined bodies were established for workers, peasants, and youths. The Revolutionary Council provided rural communities with participatory opportunities by allowing direct voting for the *Pyithu Hluttaw* (People's Assembly). A new constitution in 1974 confirmed Burma as a one-party state dominated by the military and its Burma Socialist Program Party (BSPP). Modernization of the army was meant to support the newly established BSPP as it sought to reach down to rural communities. Many senior BSPP members of the Revolutionary Council were influential military men or their close relatives. A military career was now sufficiently promising to attract talented young people. Thus did Ne Win's regime move still farther away from the kind of state envisaged at independence. Ne Win's closeness to Aung San and experience with the BIA during World War II gave him a standing that few could rival. He was one of the Thirty Comrades, held senior military appointments, and helped to restore order during the 'caretaker government' of 1958–60. He now led the Revolutionary Council, and was the President of Burma from 1974 to 1981 and Chairman of the BSPP until July 1988. He was thus one of the most decisive figures in the post-colonial history of Burma and is given a place of honor next to Aung San in the *Tatmadaw's* Defense Services Museum in Rangoon/Yangon.

While the distinction between the military and the BSPP leadership was blurred, the army did have its own distinct priorities. Military delegations visited a wide range of foreign countries to assess what innovations might be applicable in Burma. Yugoslavia, Israel, and Germany were among the nations that provided military tours for Burmese. In some respects these missions acted as diplomatic exercises, while providing officers with international perspectives that might assist in dealing with Burma's internal challenges. While the state's official ideology claimed to be socialist, military influence remained significant. Government documents, state-sponsored events, and official communiqués employed the military's vocabulary, evoked its battle-field experiences, and projected images of it as the apolitical protector of the nation. Even local infrastructural projects were conducted like small military operations. To some extent the military in Burma became something of a political party in uniform. Like a political party, the military had its own agendas, factions, ideologies, slogans, symbols, and lobbies. As a political entity it penetrated deeply into Burmese society, competed for constituents, and attempted to convince the public that its image of Burma represented the people's vision as well. Yet it is also true that the military differed from most political parties in having leaders who were battle-hardened soldiers, conditioned by experience and training to view the world around them as a series of crises and emergencies. At heart, these men were not politicians but 'war-makers' whose view of the world was filtered through the lens of military operations, maintaining security, and defending the nation from internal and external threats.

The military government attempted to detach the economy from world trade. The economy's integration with the global market was calculated at 40 percent of total trade volume in the 1950s, but dropped to 26 percent by the next decade. Within a year of the 1962 coup, banking, manufacturing, and trade were nationalized. In 1963, for the first of several times, the government declared certain currency notes invalid, in an attempt to control inflation, to destroy the profits of black marketeers (who constituted an ever-larger sector of the economy), and/or to deal with the infiltration of counterfeit *kyat* notes into the economy. These policies had immediate consequences. Most of the remaining Indian business interests were forced out and their enterprises were taken over by nationalized trading corporations. Approximately 125,000 to 300,000 Indians and Pakistanis left the country over 1963–65. Economic control became centralized in the hands of the state managers, which reduced the diversity of the business sector on the one hand, while reducing income disparities within society on the other. Scholars have shown that from 1963 to 1974, industry grew at an annual rate of only 2.6 percent due to governmental intervention in the economy and managerial incompetence. Strict economic policies also limited the ability for private wealth to develop, which served the regime by inhibiting the growth of countervailing political forces.

Twenty-six years of BSPP rule brought the economic collapse of the supposedly socialist state. During the 1970s, the average citizen found meeting basic subsistence levels increasingly difficult as the cost of living rose considerably. Here, as in other societies, the poorer the family, the more income had to be spent on food. In 1961, the average family spent 48 percent of its total income on edibles. In 1975, this had risen to 65 percent in urban areas, while in the countryside it ranged from 72 percent to 79 percent. For the majority of the population, standards of living clearly declined under BSPP leadership. As a result of nationalizing the private sector, general mismanagement, and deliberate isolation from the global market, black-market activity became a major – but unrecorded – part of the Burmese economy. Black-market trade across the borders with Thailand and southwest China was particularly significant. As a result, official statistical calculations reflect only a part of actual economic activity. By the late 1980s, import costs had increased (reflecting a severe trade imbalance), foreign debt was at an all-time high, and lending partners (such as Japan) warned that economic reform was a precondition for further assistance. In December 1987, the United Nations placed the country on its 'least developed nation' list, allowing it to receive loans at a more favorable rate. By now, the country was effectively bankrupt.

In March 1988, a brawl between students at the Yangon Institute of Technology (YIT) and other youths resulted in the police arresting an individual who was then released. YIT students protested, believing that the accused was let go because of connections to a government official. The police responded with gunfire, killing one student. As matters escalated, more students took to the streets. Now the army stepped in with force and at least 41 protesters died from suffocation in a police van. Between July and September 1988, public dissatisfaction grew, with more public demonstrations, violence, and civil disobedience. On 23 July 1988, Chairman Ne Win announced that he and several top officials of the government would resign. He raised with the BSPP itself the issue of whether a referendum should be held on reverting to a multi-party system, which the BSPP Congress rejected. Indecision amongst members of the BSPP only fueled public disorder as protesters shifted from local issues to more fundamental economic and political ones. Burma approached anarchic collapse as the army and police used lethal force to quell the violence and arrested numerous persons. It has been claimed that as many as 10,000 died in the unrest. Thousands left Rangoon out of fear of being arrested and many left the country, particularly for Thailand, to join insurgent groups. New contenders for power also emerged in the chaos, among the more successful being the National League for Democracy (NLD) led by two former generals and, most prominently, by Aung San Suu Kyi, the daughter of Aung San. Civilian leaders proved unable to restore public order in the following weeks, while demonstrations and strikes escalated and the threat of fuel and food shortages loomed, whereupon the military again imposed order and dissolved the BSPP in the name of a new State Law and Order Restoration Council (SLORC).

The new SLORC military government soon dominated all state institutions, assigning officers and loyal civil servants to key positions, and purging officials who were still loyal to the now-defunct BSPP. SLORC leadership claimed, improbably, that it would only hold power until order was re-established. As will be seen in the following chapter, in May 1990 a constituent assembly election was held in which the NLD, led by Aung San Suu Kyi, won 59.9 percent of the vote. But the military regime had no intention of actually handing power to a democratically elected government. The results of the election were ignored and Aung San Suu Kyi was put under house arrest. These events merely confirmed to the international community and opposition parties that the generals intended to hold on to power.

Two groups figured prominently among those who opposed Burma's military regimes, just as they had in the 1920s and 1930s: students and monks. Students mounted strikes and set up underground groups, but were often forced to flee to Thailand for safety. A network grew among dissident students, opposition groups across the eastern border in Thailand, and international networks opposing the Burmese regime. Such student groups became particularly prominent in the years after 1988. They also built links with ordained Buddhist monks. Buddhism was favored by U Nu's government, although he sought to keep monks out of the secular spaces of politics. Ne Win's regime, however, faced protests from monks on several occasions, which were put down with force. Monks were prominent along with students in the 1988 anti-government protests and hundreds of monks were among the thousands who were killed by government forces.

Thailand

In Thailand, the 1947 coup inaugurated a period of military rule that lasted for more than four decades, except for a three-year civilian interlude in the 1970s. The Phibun-Phao-Sarit triumvirate survived until 1957, when Sarit (now a Field Marshal) staged a coup and held power until his death in 1963. The first decade of military rule after 1947 saw the preservation of a certain degree of press freedom, along with a brief period of open speech in the mid-1950s modeled after London's Hyde Park. When it came to explicitly leftist ideology, however, the regime tended to crack down fast and hard, and there were periodic arrests of those accused – rightly or wrongly – of being Communists. In the 1950s the CPT had yet to launch its insurgency, but the strength of Marxist

Figure 26   Sarit Thanarat, 1957

AP/Press Association Images

beliefs among some groups of intellectuals posed a serious threat from the government's point of view. After Sarit (Figure 26) took power in 1957, space for political dissent grew progressively smaller until the final months of the military dictatorship in 1973, when the groundswell of opposition was simply too strong to be suppressed.

Sarit was succeeded by his two chief lieutenants, Generals Thanom Kittikachon and Praphat Charusathien, whose military dictatorship survived until 1973, when they were overthrown by a student-led uprising which brought hundreds of thousands of people into the streets of Bangkok. Between October 1973 and October 1976 Thailand experienced a period of unprecedented openness, with multi-party elections, civilian prime ministers, and the growth of union activism among farmers and workers. Marxist classics were openly sold in bookshops, and radical ideology was widespread among students and intellectuals, including many professors who had recently completed graduate studies at American and European campuses. The three-year-old democracy came to a violent end in 1976 with a police massacre of students on the grounds of Thammasat University, in conjunction with a military coup. Several years of factional rivalry within the army were followed by the stability of 'Premocracy' between 1980 and 1988, so called because of the leadership of General Prem Tinsulanond. Elections were held, and the composition of parliament changed, but Prem remained Prime Minister. The clampdown following the October 1976 coup brutally stifled the voices of dissent, but under Prem in the 1980s the restrictions were gradually relaxed as the threat of a Communist takeover faded. Public discussion of Prem's future plans and other political issues was widespread by the time he stepped down in 1988. Over the long term, the two most potent weapons against opposition were the anti-Communist statutes and the *lèse-majesté* law protecting the monarchy from criticism; both of these could easily be wielded against critics of the government and/or the military.

Coups were now established as a salient feature of modern Thai history. Between 1947 and 1957 several coups were staged under the military, and several more were attempted by dissenting factions. The coup became a convenient way to eliminate rivals, to nullify democratic reforms, and simply to put the entire parliamentary system on hold. Sarit, for example, governed with no parliament and with only a 'temporary' charter instead of a constitution. Thanom and Praphat experimented with a return to a parliamentary system in 1969, but overthrew it with an internal coup three years later. The main victim of these developments was constitutionalism itself, since constitutions were rewritten or scrapped completely with each successive coup.

At the root of the problem was the fundamental tension between two groups of elites: those who advocated a parliamentary system modeled along Western lines and those who favored what they considered to be 'Thai democracy', which could survive nicely with a strong man in power and without allegedly dysfunctional trappings such as elections and parliament. This tension had existed since the People Party's seizure of power in 1932, but it became more acute as time went on, and the conflict between the two sets of values grew more violent. Pridi Phanomyong, who was the most radical among the civilian politicians, was driven from power in 1947, after which he remained an influential and inspirational figure in exile, but was unable to effect political change within the country. More moderate royalists such as Kukrit Pramote and his brother Seni were prominent figures on the political scene, although they did not share the same ideological stance; both had a turn at the prime ministership during the democratic interlude of 1973–76.

The most prominent advocates of 'Thai democracy' were in the military. Like their counterparts in Indonesia, Burma, and elsewhere, they came to see themselves as the most faithful guardians of Thailand's core institutions: nation, religion, and monarchy. The Cold War buttressed this role by providing a menace to all three in the form of Communism. Although the Communist Party of Thailand (CPT) did not initiate armed combat until the early 1960s, leftist ideas were present among some intellectuals by the late 1940s, and Communist insurgencies were active in Burma and Indochina as well. Almost immediately, Phibun and the coup group of 1947 allied themselves with the United States and became a key American partner in the region. This relationship proved tremendously lucrative, bringing millions of dollars in military aid and extensive American support in terms of training and development programs, as well as the construction of highways through the strategic northeast.

The military possessed a fundamental contempt for civilian politicians, who were seen as corrupt, incompetent, and ineffective in protecting the country from the Communists. For opponents of Western democracy, the chaotic years between 1973 and 1976 seemed to prove this point. Thailand always had a plethora of political parties, so that governments had to be constructed from fragile coalitions since no single party ever enjoyed a majority. The mid-1970s saw an explosion of activism among students, workers, and farmers, as well as the proliferation of radical ideas, particularly Maoism. The CPT made considerable inroads in the rural areas, particularly in the impoverished northeast and parts of the north. The combination of Leftist political forces and the growing insecurity provoked a backlash from the Right, targeting both activists and the elected government, and civilian paramilitary groups joined the police in attacking the students at Thammasat in October 1976.

The period between the massacre at Thammasat and Prem's assumption of power in 1980 was a time of major crisis for Thailand. The CPT insurgency was at its peak, its ranks having been swelled by hundreds of students and other activists who fled to the jungle in the final months of the democratic period in 1976. Although the government was never directly endangered, there were patches of insurgent-controlled territory throughout the country. It was the decision of two military prime ministers – first Kriangsak Chomanan and then Prem – to offer amnesties to those who abandoned the revolution which began to reverse the situation. The CPT itself was split by internal debates over strategy and the effectiveness of the Maoist model. By the early 1980s, the Communist threat was fading away, and Prem's eight years in power became a relatively peaceful time of transition between military and civilian rule. Prem himself faced two coup attempts by dissident army officers, but his close ties to the royal family ensured his political survival. In 1988, under increasing pressure to re-establish an elected prime minister, he made a graceful exit and turned power over to an elected successor, Chatichai Choonhawan. For the time being, at least, the military remained in their barracks, and Thailand was back on the democratic path.

Throughout these years Thai economic policy, like that of most of its neighbors, focused predominantly on the twin engines of growth and development. The latter concept was particularly emphasized beginning in Sarit's time, when government policy zeroed in on the need for infrastructural development, especially in the rural areas, and five-year government development plans began to appear in the early 1960s. That decade also saw the promotion of industrialization, first for import substitution and then, on a larger scale, to produce goods for export. Agriculture remained a key economic activity, but many people from farming families shifted to factories and the service sector over the course of time. Beginning in the late 1980s, tourism was also promoted as a major source of income.

Neither economic growth nor development has, however, been consistently strong or evenly distributed. Beginning in the 1950s, the United States and other countries provided extensive development aid which achieved an overall improvement in rural infrastructure. Some of the benefits of this aid were diluted by corruption, however, and poverty remained widespread, particularly in the northeast and among the highlanders in the north – precisely the two areas where the CPT insurgency found the widest support. Moreover, at least some of Thailand's growth during the 1960s and 1970s was linked to income from US military bases, which obviously brought significant social costs as well and which ended abruptly with the closure of the bases in 1975.

By the 1980s, political and economic stabilization combined with the government's emphasis on rural development as a counter-insurgency strategy brought more substantial improvements in many people's lives. Development projects sponsored by the monarchy and the activities of NGOs played an important part in attempts to alleviate rural poverty. The northeast in particu-lar remained poor and underdeveloped, however, and it furnished the lion's share of the many migrants who flocked to the cities to find jobs as factory and construction workers, domestic servants, or taxi drivers. The gap between rich and poor remained prominent, as the rising middle class concentrated in the cities benefited more directly from industrialization and foreign investment than the farmers and workers. In many respects Thailand enjoyed a boom, but the chickens would come home to roost in the 1990s with the Asian financial crisis, discussed in the following chapter.

Indonesia

The political structure established in the Dutch-Indonesian agreement of 1949 was a federal nation, within which the Republic of Indonesia was one state, the others having been set up by the Dutch during the Revolution. Within a year, all of those states had collapsed for a variety of reasons and been absorbed within the unitary Republic of Indonesia – the goal that had inspired Indonesian nationalists for a quarter of a century. But what sort of state was this to be? Everyone who mattered said that it would be democratic, but how would Indonesians create a functioning democracy where none had existed before? The vast majority of Indonesians were still illiterate, hard-pressed by the destructive and violent years they had just gone through, still responsive to the influence of local authoritarian figures and entirely without experience in how to run a democracy.

For the successful revolutionaries, the key to the new democratic Indonesia would be political parties. Those that had emerged during the Revolution remained. Masyumi and PNI were presumed to have the largest constituencies, while the Socialist Party carried on. The 'national Communists' inspired by Tan Malaka formed the Murba Party. PKI was brought back to life in the early 1950s by a new, young leadership team led by D. N. Aidit. In a bitter parting of the ways, the Traditionalist Nahdlatul Ulama withdrew from Masyumi in 1953 and became a party in its own right, leaving Masyumi as the political vehi-cle of urban-based Modernists, led by Mohamad Natsir. Catholic and Protestant Indonesians also formed their own parties.

PKI under Aidit faced a hostile political climate. The Communists were regarded as traitors for their 1948 Madiun uprising, were suspected by religious interests of being atheists determined to destroy religion, had to endure the implacable hostility of the military, and faced competition for the support of Leftists from the Murba Party's 'national Communists'. In this environment, Aidit argued that Indonesia remained a 'semi-feudal' and 'semi-colonial' coun-try; the former raised the prospect of social revolution against the established elite, while the latter suggested a means of tapping nationalist sentiment. But Javanese society – where PKI's greatest strength was to be found – was increas-ingly polarized on lines of religious identity and practice between *abangan* and *santri*. So PKI, which in theory had an ideology based on class analysis, had to fit into a society in which vertical distinctions of religious identity mattered more than horizontal distinctions of class. In practice, PKI became a party of the *abangan* (as was PNI), and prospects for class-based revolution were much attenuated. PKI not infrequently was supported by village leaders who brought the whole village with them into the Party.

The Party recognized the hostility of the Republic's political leadership and concluded that its only defense lay in numbers. So it began a vigorous campaign of recruitment, with remarkable results. By the end of 1952 PKI claimed nearly 127,000 members, by 1954 over 165,000, and by 1955 1 million. Its peasants', intellectuals', women's, and youth organizations added many more adherents. The Communist union organization SOBSI grew rapidly. By mid-1965 PKI claimed that the Party and affiliated organizations had 27 million members. Allowing for overlapping memberships, this probably meant something like 20 million persons. This figure was almost certainly greatly inflated. Perhaps PKI believed it, but perhaps it was a political ploy, for the membership number was itself one of the means the Party had to intimidate its opponents. Nevertheless, it was true that PKI had much more grass-roots organization than any other party and was thus playing the democracy game better than parties whose main interest was distributing the spoils of power in Jakarta (to which PKI never gained access). In fact, however, PKI's extraordinary membership numbers did not make it invulnerable to attack. Instead, it made the Party a greater threat to its enemies and thus a more prominent target.

The military – including the army, air force, navy, and police – was dominated by the army. Throughout the 1950s the army grew increasingly coherent ideologically. Its Islamist wing defected or was purged as a consequence of the Darul Islam rebellion, which spread from its West Java heartland to Aceh and South Sulawesi during the 1950s. The army's Leftist officers were purged after Madiun. So the army was a body characterized by two ineradicable convictions: that it alone was the savior of the Republic and the expression of the people's will, and that civilian politicians in general – and especially Communists because of Madiun and Islamists because of Darul Islam – were not to be trusted.

The civilian politicians were committed to holding general elections, but in practice postponed them until 1955 while playing complicated political games in Jakarta. The election campaign exacerbated social tensions and inter-party rivalries at the village level. The outcome of the elections surprised the political elite. The general expectation was that Masyumi, with its Islamic appeal in a society in which the vast majority was Muslim, would emerge as the largest party. PNI was expected to do well because it was seen as the party of President Sukarno. Sjahrir's Socialist Party was also thought to be important. 'Traditionalist' NU, having recently broken away from Masyumi, was not expected to be particularly large. When the votes came in, Masyumi and PNI were nearly tied, the former with 22.3 percent of valid votes, the latter with 20.0 percent, and both with the same number of seats in the parliament. NU surprised many by being in third place with 18.4 percent of the vote. But the greater shock was that PKI was in fourth place with over 6 million votes, representing 16.4 percent of total valid votes and 15.2 percent of parliamentary seats. From these 'big four' parties it was a long drop to the next nearest party, with just over 1 million votes (2.9 percent of total valid votes). The Socialist Party won only 2.0 percent of valid votes and Murba was behind that with only

0.5 percent of votes. When provincial elections were held in 1957, PKI's vote increased still more. So the political landscape of democratic Indonesia had delivered a major role to PKI and looked like it might even deliver power in the end. There was also an ominous geographical distinction: Masyumi was by far the strongest party in the outer islands, whereas PNI, NU, and PKI had their main strength in Java.

After the economic difficulties of 1930–42 and the chaos of 1942–50, the country's new leadership faced formidable difficulties in producing the prosperity that Indonesians expected of independence. Plantations, transport infrastructure, and factories had all been seriously damaged. Foreign enterprises were still strong in the economy – which stimulated much political animosity – but the indigenous middle class was economically and politically weak. Chinese were often better-placed to develop business enterprises, but faced unpopularity and could count on little or no political support. So it was hard to find adequate investment sources for national recovery. To make the challenge even greater, population growth again took off, increasing pressure on domestic resources. From an estimated population in 1950 of 77.5 million, the number of Indonesians grew to 97.0 million by the time of the 1961 census, 119.2 million in 1971, 147.3 in 1980, and 179.2 million in 1990. This generated domestic demand, particularly for oil, thus undermining efforts to restore oil exports. By 1957 oil output had returned to 1940 levels, but during that same time domestic demand for gasoline rose by two-thirds and for kerosene by some 200 percent.

Nor were world prices for Indonesia's products favorable. Of all the governments of the first parliamentary period, the coalition led by Mohammad Natsir (September 1950–March 1951) faced the most favorable economic circumstances. The Korean War created a boom in commodity prices which led to increased export earnings and government export duties until mid-1951. At this time, rubber was Indonesia's leading export, but its price fell by over 70 percent between early 1951 and September 1952. Thereafter, in the absence of any other commodity boom, the country's economic story became increasingly one of inadequate export revenues or growth, accompanied by increasing political interference in the economy, corruption, smuggling, and black marketeering.

As the 1950s passed, democracy itself came under increasing criticism. Corruption was widespread, although utterly insignificant when compared to what was to come later. The army was disgusted with the doings of the civilian politicians and alarmed at PKI's growth. Sukarno as President was increasingly critical of the self-interested politicking of the parties, and sympathetic to the general disillusionment with the democratic system. Outer island regions were dissatisfied with the trend of the Republic: centralizing, increasingly Leftist in rhetoric, and Java-dominated. The rupiah, Indonesia's currency, was overvalued as a means of subsidizing net-importing Java and the politically volatile residents of the nation's main cities – all located on Java. This disadvantaged the net-exporting outer islands and led to the emergence of various smuggling arrangements, linking outer-island exporters to markets in Singapore and Malaya in particular. These smuggling operations often involved local military commanders, whose resources and incomes were inadequate to sustain their own troops. Many were dissatisfied with the Jakarta commanders' centralizing tendencies and happy to succumb to the temptations of ready money.

These discontents led to a series of regionally based rebellions from 1956 onwards. National politics in Indonesia meanwhile drifted leftwards, as a response both to PKI's increasing influence and to Sukarno's insistence that the Indonesian Revolution remained unfinished. The main evidence that this was so was the refusal of the Netherlands to negotiate the transfer of sovereignty over Papua (Netherlands West New Guinea) to Indonesia. This was consistent also with PKI's view of Indonesia as being still semi-colonial, so Sukarno and PKI moved closer together and the Communists stopped denouncing Sukarno for his role in crushing the Madiun uprising. Sukarno began to say that a new political system was needed to replace '50 percent plus one democracy', which he depicted as an alien Western import into communalist, consultative Indonesia. Non-Communist, anti-Sukarnoist, Masyumi, outer island, and factional military dissatisfactions coalesced in the 1958 rebellion of the Sumatra-based PRRI (*Pemerintah Revolusioner Republik Indonesia*, Revolutionary Government of the Indonesian Republic). This rebellion was quickly crushed in the Sumatran cities by combined military operations. It was thereby reduced to guerrilla action in the countryside which carried on, with little effect, until 1961, when the main rebel leaders and their followers surrendered. Masyumi and Socialist Party leaders were prominent in PRRI so these parties were declared illegal. The American Eisenhower administration had been clandestinely supporting these dissident movements in an effort to counter the Sukarno regime's leftward tendencies. So had Taiwan, Singapore, Malaya, the Philippines, and South Korea. But the downing over Ambon of a plane flown by an American pilot and the Indonesian government's rapid repression of the PRRI rebellion persuaded the United States and others that it would be wiser to deal with the Sukarno regime than to attempt to undermine it.

In the midst of this dissidence and impending collapse of the nation, Sukarno announced a new form of politics, which came to be called 'Guided Democracy' (1959–65). This called for the diminution (but not abolition) of the role of political parties and greater involvement of 'functional groups': women, youth, peasants, and such-like and, crucially, the military. Ideological slogans were manufactured so as to make Guided Democracy seem a uniquely Indonesian contribution to world revolution and radicalism, led by its unique 'people's spokesman' Sukarno (Figure 27). In style, Guided Democracy was a curious combination of the Fascist modes of the Japanese occupation, Soviet-style Socialist Realism, and folksy Indonesian symbolism. While Sukarno stood as the central figure, much of the political dynamism of Guided Democracy came from the increasing competition between the two irreconcilable enemies, the army and the PKI. Indeed, Sukarno was pressed into abandoning the old political system in part to avoid the risk of a military coup under the leadership of General Nasution. In the increasing radicalism of the age, Dutch enterprises were nationalized and their administration taken over by the military. Thus Indonesia's military became an independent economic power as well as monopolizing the use of armed force. The PKI also grew, at least in numbers, but

Figure 27   Sukarno, October 1965
Beryl Bernay/Hulton Archive/Getty Images

never managed to create a significant armed force loyal to itself, despite some success in infiltrating the military. If it came to a physical contest, the military was thus best-placed to win.

In a nation as large and diverse as Indonesia, a multiplicity of views and aspirations is the normal state of affairs. During the 1945–49 Revolution there was much diversity and disagreement, much violence, and next-to-no means of managing dissent. Under the democratic system that prevailed from 1950 to 1959, political differences became increasingly bitter, as implacable hatreds coalesced. The outcome of the PRRI and other regional rebellions was the imprisonment of several major figures, including some who had been instrumental in Indonesia's struggle for independence, notably Sjahrir and Natsir. These political hatreds reached a peak in the Guided Democracy period. Sukarno and the PKI adumbrated a political orthodoxy from which opponents dissented at risk to their freedom. The PKI called for the 'retooling' of government and political figures, major intellectuals were intimidated and/or forced from their jobs, and the hounding of political opponents became common. *Santri-abangan* animosities were hardened by political competition. These hatreds would culminate in the violence of the mid-1960s.

Political chaos, with massive demonstrations and revolutionary posturing, became the order of the day. Just when the 1963 settlement of the Papua issue seemed to remove the basis for radical politics, the creation of Malaysia in September 1963 provided new grounds. Indonesia denounced Malaysia as a neo-colonial plot and announced a policy of 'confrontation'. As it became painfully clear, however, that radical slogans could not feed people, disaffection grew. Islamic organizations joined the military in doubting the radical drift, believing particularly that if this radicalism were to deliver power to PKI, they would suffer. Finally the ramshackle edifice of Guided Democracy began to disintegrate. In 1963 PKI launched a unilateral land-reform campaign, to distribute land to landless peasants. This directly threatened the interests of land-owners, who included military men and, particularly in East Java, prominent NU figures. PKI's opponents began to fight back and, as the violence spread, PKI was put on the defensive, which suggests that its claimed numerical strength was chimerical.

Meanwhile the economy was approaching complete collapse, and was being conventionally described by economists as a 'basket case'. The degree to which radical politics undermined real economic planning was suggested by the eight-year development plan of 1960, which was constructed of 17 parts, 8 volumes, and 1945 clauses to symbolize the date of the independence declaration. From 1961 to 1964, inflation remained at around 100 percent per annum. But by 1965 it was at least 500 percent.

On 30 September 1965 a coup attempt took place in Jakarta. The intrigues of the period were so complex and have generated so much disinformation as well as information, that it is unlikely that the full truth about the plotting will ever be known. The coup group of 'progressive' military officers had links with PKI. Both PKI women's and youth organizations were involved. In the course of that night, six generals and one other military man were murdered. Out of this chaos General Soeharto (Figure 28) emerged from relative obscurity and took charge of the military.

Under Soeharto's leadership, the military recognized an opportunity to be rid of its arch-enemy the PKI and to purge those parts of the military that the Communists had influenced or infiltrated. The Party was outlawed. With the support of the major Islamic organizations and student activists, a slaughter of PKI leaders and members began, while the military purged itself of Communists and their sympathizers. It is not known how many were killed

Figure 28 Soeharto, 1980

© Kapoor Baldev/Sygma/Corbis

across the country in 1965–66, but the figure is generally thought to be of the order of 500,000. Thousands more were arrested, tortured, and held without trial for years. Because political party affiliations had followed *abangan-santri* religious identities in Java, so did much of the killing, with *abangan* victims falling at the hands of *santri*. Sukarno tried to mobilize mass support to maintain his leadership, as he had so often in the past, but his threadbare charisma no longer worked. Over a period of months, Soeharto again and again outmaneuvered Sukarno and his supporters. In 1966 he effectively took charge of the country, with Sukarno reduced to being an ineffectually furious figurehead President. In 1967 Soeharto became Acting President and in 1968 President (until 1998). Thus began what is called Soeharto's New Order.

Under Soeharto, the army clamped down on all dissent, restrained only by the limitations of Indonesia's ramshackle bureaucratic structures. The military had no compunction about banning publications and imprisoning, torturing, or murdering opponents. Regime violence was particularly unrestrained in the outlying areas of Aceh, East Timor (discussed below), and Papua (at the time called Irian Jaya), where there were separatist sentiments and guerrilla resistance. The non-Communist alliance of student activists, Islamic leaders, and the military lasted only briefly. The military created a condominium over the country relying on itself and the bureaucracy. Student activists and Islamic leaders were soon alienated by their exclusion from the core of the regime and by its increasingly obvious corruption. Indeed, it was the regime's ever more extravagant corruption that did most to undermine its legitimacy as years went by. Ethnic Chinese entrepreneurs built mutually lucrative alliances with members of the military elite, thereby exacerbating widespread anti-Chinese feelings in the country.

The role of Islamic groups in the bloody killing of 1965–66 seems to have contributed to some alienation from Islam, which goes far to explain the rapid spread of Christianity and the (more limited) revival of Hinduism and Buddhism among previously Islamic communities, particularly former PKI supporters. In 1933, 2.8 percent of Indonesians were Christians. In 1971, however, Christians were 7.5 percent of the population – nearly 9 million people. In 1990, the Christian population totaled 17.2 million, 9.6 percent of Indonesians. Christianization embittered Islamic leaders, who had assumed that with the demise of PKI, Islam would at last claim its rightful place as the arbiter of the nation's affairs. There were episodes of anti-Christian violence, which the regime put to an end by making it clear that it was prepared to shoot perpetrators. As will be seen below, however, in the end the New Order provided circumstances favorable to deeper Islamization.

One measure taken by the regime with far-reaching consequences was the destruction of the previous political parties. Elections were held periodically, but they were carefully managed and were always won at national level by the government organization Golkar – which claimed to be a working organization of 'functional groups' and thus not really a party, rather like the Sangkum movement in Sihanouk's Cambodia. The old political parties that had not previously been outlawed were forced to merge into two unwieldy coalitions in 1973, which had the effect of emasculating all of them. Thereafter there was

Figure 29 Istiqlal mosque, Jakarta, opened 1978

nothing to threaten the regime except its own corruption and human rights abuses, which gradually rotted it from within. The destruction of the old political parties, however, meant that the institutional frameworks that had supported *abangan* interests were destroyed. This in fact facilitated deeper Islamization at grass-roots level, a social change reflected in the rapid increase in the number of mosques and prayer-houses (Figure 29), as well as in an increasingly religious public style, including among the rapidly growing and prospering urban middle class.

The regime's most difficult challenge came in 1975 when Portugal granted independence to East Timor, where the Leftist group Fretilin was dominant. Indonesia had no intention of tolerating a Leftist regime within its own archipelago, so the Indonesian military invaded, with the tacit approval of Western governments. For 23 years Indonesia – whose self-identification as a nation relied heavily on its successful anti-colonial revolution – ruled East Timor as, in effect, a colonial power itself. Its human rights abuses there did much to undermine its international standing, but in the context of the Cold War this was another anti-Communist measure and thus congenial to Western political interests.

Similarly welcome to Western governments was Indonesian domestic policy towards Islam, whereby religious radicals were uniformly suppressed in the early years of the regime. Soeharto's New Order was favored by Western nations in part because it was seen as successful in domesticating Islam, as well as being pro-development and pro-Western. This was even more true in the wake of the Iranian revolution of 1979, which made both the Jakarta elite and its Western analogues nervous. As a part of the increasing Islamization of society, however, radicalism and fundamentalism also grew underground. There were occasional outbreaks of violence in which the government invariably prevailed. But seeds were already being sown for the terrorist violence that would follow from the later years of the century. In 1991 Soeharto and his family went on the pilgrimage to Mecca for the first time, an event that symbolized a pro-Islamic turning that marked the last decade of the New Order.

Soeharto's greatest achievements were in the economy, and therefore he was often dubbed *Bapak Pembangunan*: the 'father of development'. From the chaos of Sukarno's 'old order', the New Order regime constructed a rapidly growing and modernizing economy. Foreign investment first came into the most profitable industries, particularly extractive industries in the outer islands. In order to fight inflation, domestic interest rates were high, which damaged indigenous (often *santri*) entrepreneurs while favoring those with access to cheaper funds overseas – mainly overseas investors and local Chinese business people. From the early 1970s rising oil revenues and general economic development made possible major investments in welfare measures. Levels of education and welfare began to rise, although Indonesia remained a country with very many extremely poor people. Average food consumption rose as rice production increased. Medical facilities increased dramatically, but remained well behind the level of other ASEAN countries. Indonesia's family planning program, however, was among the most successful in the world. The rate of annual population growth fell from 2.3 percent in the 1960s to 1.97 percent in the 1980s. Literacy went up dramatically, finally addressing a problem that had been beyond the capacity of the former colonial or independent regimes. In 1930 the adult literacy rate was 13.2 percent for men and 2.3 percent for women. In 1980 the rate for males over the age of 10 had risen to 80.4 percent and for women to 63.6 percent. In 1990 those figures were 89.6 and 78.7 respectively.

But corruption by the regime from top to bottom poisoned this economic growth. There were various estimates of how much foreign investment or aid funding went into the pockets of corruptors. A common figure was 30 percent, but of course there was no way of really measuring this. Demonstrations against corruption by students – allies of the New Order regime at its inception in 1965–66 – began as early as 1967. In January 1974, when the Japanese Prime Minister Tanaka was visiting, the worst riots Jakarta had seen since the beginning of the New Order broke out, protesting the Japanese role in the economy. Such demonstrations and protests were always, in the end, suppressed, many activists went to jail or disappeared, and critical newspapers were closed down.

Still the economy grew impressively. From 1971 into the 1990s the real GDP annual rate of growth averaged around 7 percent. Oil was the key export. By 1981 Indonesia had also become the world's largest producer of liquefied natural gas. But the regime could not shake off the criticisms of corruption from both domestic and international sources. The national oil company

Pertamina – run virtually as a personal fief by an entrepreneurial ex-military officer – was one of the world's largest corporations in the early 1970s but it rested
on a combination of excessive overseas debt, chaotic management, and corruption. In 1975 it found itself unable to repay overseas debts and had to be
rescued by the government at a cost of at least USD10 billion. By the 1980s
the Soehartos' six children were coming into their own as entrepreneurs. They
made money in almost unimaginable quantities. Legality was somewhere well
beyond the horizon of this sort of development and governance. People began
to speak of a 'kleptocracy' – government by thieves.

New Order economic development led to a change of crucial significance for
the unity of Indonesia. Colonial economic arrangements had diminished the
trade interconnections that, in the pre-colonial era, had helped to bind the
archipelago (along with the Malay Peninsula) into a regional economic entity.
Now, as Indonesian manufacturing developed, particularly in West Java, it
began to draw in raw materials from elsewhere in the archipelago and sell
finished products back to other areas. For the first time in at least a century, a
community of economic self-interest – a national economy – was thereby being
recreated in Indonesia. This accompanied rapid urbanization and a reducing
role for agriculture in the economy. By 1990, 30.9 percent of the population
was classed as urban and in the early 1990s for the first time agriculture
accounted for less than 50 percent of the work force. Signs of modernization –
electric lighting, motorbikes, televisions, paved roads, schools – were spreading
across the country. There remained, however, regional disparities. Java and Bali
(where tourism produced much wealth) were ahead of Sumatra on most measures, while eastern Indonesia trailed all the rest of the country.

The Philippines

Magsaysay's death brought about a frenzy in Philippine politics, epitomized by
the mudslinging and vulgarity of the 1957 elections. After devising elaborate
ruses to secure the support of the Church, candidates learned that the idea of a
'Catholic vote' was a myth. The well-oiled NP propaganda machine propelled
former Vice-President Carlos Garcia to the presidency (1957–61). As an old-
time *politico*, Garcia admired forerunner Manuel Quezon but allied with
nationalist colleagues Jose Laurel and Claro Recto. Garcia opposed the Bell Act
and the Military Bases Agreement and was elected without American endorsement. His presidency was anchored in his 'Filipino First' policy, advocating
economic independence by setting import and currency controls and promoting Filipino businesses. Association with corrupt Nacionalistas, local warlords,
and strongmen, however, damaged Garcia. Protests from middle-class organizations coalesced with those of marginalized foreign and local businessmen;
rumors circulated that military officers who lost their positions in executive
agencies were plotting a coup. In 1959 Liberal Party (LP) senatorial candidates,
led by Ferdinand Marcos, resoundingly defeated their ruling NP counterparts.
Two years later Garcia failed in his re-election bid, trounced by LP rival
Diosdado Macapagal (g. 1961–65). Macapagal pledged to open the economy
to world trade and foreign investment.

In post-independence Philippines, the pursuit of economic development has been consistently dominated by oligarchic control of production and ties with the United States, through both trade and aid. Presidents Roxas, Quirino, Macapagal, Garcia, and Magsaysay attempted to help the peasantry by expanding agricultural productivity through technological inputs, credits, and social welfare plans but stopped short of displacing landlord power through a land redistribution program. The Bell Trade Act gave Americans the same rights in land ownership, natural resources exploitation, and other fields of economic activity as Filipinos. The Americans pegged the release of war rehabilitation funds for the Philippines to the passage of the Military Bases Agreement that allowed long-term American military facilities in the archipelago.

The Roxas administration only gave access to the rehabilitation funds to its allies: affluent families who invested in land and commerce. The so-called 'special' relationship between the Philippines and the United States benefited American businessmen and Filipino exporters. Free trade proved to be a boom for the landed elite who met American market demand for plantation products like sugar, coconut oil, and abaca. It facilitated the continued dominance of landlordism, even though the newly established Republic in principle stood for democratization and modernization. The flood of American goods into the domestic market hampered small-scale industries, fueled pervasive corruption and overpricing, and precipitated a balance-of-payments crisis that led to capital flight, inflation, and massive unemployment.

With the support of Washington, the Philippine government passed policies favoring import-substitution industries. Imports were limited, while local production was allowed to flourish in a protected environment. The Central Bank prevented unathorized imports and controlled access to the country's USD reserves. Under its supervision, a manufacturing sector that met domestic consumption and export demands developed. By 1953 these policies had stabilized the economy, producing about PHP 655 million in tax revenue and the first budget surplus since 1946. The Central Bank remained committed to implementing technocratic reforms, resisting most of the patronage interests that plagued the Quirino, Garcia, Magsaysay, and Macapagal presidential terms.

Graft and corruption thrived nonetheless. The Quirino government witnessed the rise of cronies called 'ten percenters', officials who demanded bribes from importers and businessmen for licenses in the import substitution business. Magsaysay provided the military with the opportunity to be directly engaged in governance. Garcia's presidency was associated with traditional politics that relied on local warlords and strongmen, and with state corporations known for corruption, bribery, fraudulent transactions, and favoritism. Macapagal outrageously spent millions on unnecessary expenditures, contradicting his pledge to be frugal. He was accused of agreeing to compromises with legislators that allowed American agricultural firms to rent lands for pineapple and banana production cheaply.

To realize his vision for the economy, Macapagal employed US-trained technocrats who were favored by the World Bank, IMF, and the American State and Treasury Departments. After securing pledges for external aid, his administration lifted exchange controls and freely floated the peso. These policies allowed unrestricted exports and led to massive repatriation of profits overseas which depleted the country's reserves. To regain liquidity the government turned to international funding agencies which provided 'stabilization loans' with attached conditions that ensured a hospitable investment climate for multinational corporations but hampered local infant industries. Prices of basic commodities soared, depressing the standard of living. The state pursued a land reform code, riddled with more than 200 amendments, without allocating a budget for its implementation. Amidst growing poverty, Macapagal was accused of wallowing in extravagance, being vindictive towards enemies, practicing nepotism, and compromising the policy agenda. By the 1960s, the policy of import-substitution industrialization had proved inadequate. The stress on commercial cultivation had displaced basic food crops, increased the prices of goods, and caused increasing rural unemployment. A wave of unskilled and unorganized labor entered the cities, forming a new urban proletariat.

In 1965 Macapagal tried to convince his fellow LP member Marcos to join his re-election bid, but the latter was determined to run for the presidency himself. Following a common pattern among Filipino politicians, Marcos changed parties and campaigned as the NP candidate. Extravagance, treachery, disinformation, and chicanery featured in the subsequent contest. Supporters whose personal fortunes hung on the election of their candidate deployed various strategies to win votes and contributed to an increase of criminality and violence. Candidates scrambled to involve religious institutions in the race. Catholics were torn between LP candidate Macapagal and Progressive Party nominee Raul Manglapus. Marcos took another path: he obtained the endorsement of the indigenous church *Iglesia ni Kristo* (Church of Christ), consolidated his northern Luzon bailiwick, secured a tactical alliance with the Lopez sugar-media-energy dynasty and strategically utilized his large war chest of campaign funds. With the prominent support of his beauty-queen wife Imelda Marcos, he proclaimed, 'This nation can be great again.' He won the presidency by a landslide.

Marcos began his first term (1965–69) at a disadvantage. The state – saddled with PHP 400 million of domestic debt – was nearly bankrupt and could hardly afford essential services. The delivery of justice could not keep up with the rapid rise of crime – some 80,000 cases were pending in the courts. Liberals, who felt betrayed when Marcos became a Nacionalista, dominated Congress and stood in the way of legislation intended to improve the grim state of the nation. But Marcos knew that Filipinos yearned for stability, not for more speeches and procastination from Congress. He was also aware of the vast resources and powers that the presidential office wielded, including discretionary funds that could be used to persuade legislators to pass laws. Like Quezon before him, Marcos used public sentiment and the powers of the presidency to control Congress. His executive authority prevailed through the deployment of technocrats working for presidential agencies and the army, which was tasked with the implementation of development programs.

Marcos embarked on an ambitious rural development strategy. Using funds from domestic and external loans and developmental aid, he pumped millions into new irrigation systems, technological innovation, road systems, and social development. The development of high-yielding varieties of rice by the International Rice Research Institute at the University of the Philippines at Los Baños boosted hopes of achieving rice self-sufficiency. Farmers were given access to financial and technical assistance. In 1967 Marcos pushed Congress to pass the Investment Incentives Act which encouraged foreign investors to contribute to the country's industrial development through export production. Despite this export-oriented industrialization policy, and over the objections of technocrats, protection of domestic industries such as food processing, tobacco, and retail continued.

Public discontent rose. Marcos was criticized for assisting the United States in its war in Vietnam. Rampant crime continued, as did the criminal complicity of law officers and politicians. In May 1967, public indignation spiked after 32 members of the millenarian group *Lapiang Malaya* (Free Party) who demonstrated at Malacañang Palace were mowed down by the Constabulary. In Central Luzon the Huks surged back to life and acted as an ersatz government by providing protection from robbers, rustlers, and abusive military. The *Partido Komunista ng Pilipinas* found allies among University of the Philippines and Lyceum University students who later established the militant organization *Kabataang Makabayan* (KM, Nationalist Youth) led by Jose Maria Sison (known as Joma). In 1968, the Communists split between an 'old guard' and a more Maoist 'new guard'. After being expelled from the *Partido Komunista*, Sison and his young 'new guard' comrades established a new Communist Party of the Philippines (CPP). The international context was favorable: the Vietnam War's international unpopularity, the 'continuing revolution' by Mao Zedong, and the rise of the youthful New Left in Western Europe and the United States worked to the advantage of the young comrades at the CPP. They made alliances with workers' unions and peasant organizations, 'national democratic' organizations in schools throughout Manila, and the influential University of the Philippines Student Council. The anti-Marcos legislators Benigno Aquino Jr. and Jose Yap acted as go-betweens in a meeting between Sison and the Huk commander Bernabe Buscayno which led to the establishment of the New People's Army (NPA) as the CPP's armed wing, which trained urban recruits for armed combat. For CPP Chairman Sison, the 'semi-colonial' and 'semi-feudal' economy and the 'bourgeois-dominated' state could only be broken by a protracted war in the rural areas. The NPA advanced across the archipelago, mobilized peasants and workers and built up armed units. In northern Luzon, in traditional strongholds of the landed elite, the NPA established base areas for encircling the cities, where the bourgeoisie remained paramount. In these bases, rebels kept peace and order and earned the reputation of being polite, patient, and helpful in agricultural production.

With Marcos's re-election in 1969, the country plunged further into chaos. Clashes between the military and NPA filled the news. In January 1970 workers, peasants, and students were beaten by the police when they staged demonstrations to protest the death of democracy. Known as the First Quarter Storm, these encounters touched off a year of violent street battles which spurred Maoist revolutionary zeal among the youth. Marcos's discarded allies – the Lopez and Laurel families – used their media consortia to depict him as a 'puppet' of imperialism, feudalism, and bureaucratic capitalism. In the convention that reviewed the 1935 Constitution, delegates redesigned executive power to prevent Marcos from seeking another term. In 1971, after the bombing of an LP rally for which Marcos was blamed, even Nacionalistas joined the opposition in Congress. In response, Marcos suspended the writ of *habeas corpus*, paving the way for the arrest and detention of suspected subversive and Communist academics, students, and professionals. With the support of foreign governments still behind him, Marcos was unfazed by the worsening domestic situation. In September 1972 he signed Proclamation No. 1081 which placed the country under martial law. The President thereby carried out a coup against his own elected government.

Overnight the military subjugated thousands of anti-Marcos forces. They jailed politicians and neutralized their patronage machines and private armies. They arrested activists, forcing those who escaped to join the CPP underground. All media outlets and vital public utilities were seized. Soldiers imposed a daily curfew and an overseas travel ban on citizens. Marcos pronounced the advent of his ideal *Bagong Lipunan* (New Society). Being a trained lawyer, he found it important to inject legality into his rule. He called a convention that promulgated the 1973 Constitution and the tame National Assembly later elected him as both President and Prime Minister. Marcos appointed close associates to the Supreme Court and declared that all subsequent executive decrees and orders had the force of law. Throughout his dictatorship he issued 1941 presidential decrees, 1331 letters of instruction, and 896 executive orders. His party *Kilusang Bagong Lipunan* (KBL, New Society Movement) replaced the two-party system and decorated the dictatorship with a façade of electoral politics. Although some opposition politicians won seats in the countryside, the KBL dominated elections in Manila.

In the Martial Law period the CPP's Yenan-style bases proved disastrous. Seeking to capture Bernabe Buscayno (Ka Dante) and his troops, the army attacked mountain bases in Tarlac and Isabela, causing numerous casualties and destroying what the CPP had spent nearly two years to establish. Under the rubric of 'centralized command, decentralized operations' the CPP Central Committee responded by enforcing a policy of creating autonomous regional organizations, which allowed local members to apply strategies appropriate to their areas and to survive the capture of their leaders. Buscayno and Sison were captured in 1977. The Party still found recruits among detained students and labor leaders and among peasants who were tortured and brutalized or whose families were killed for allegedly supporting the NPA. By 1981 the Party had 48 guerrilla fronts in 43 provinces with 5600 full-time NPA fighters and some 23,000 combat support members (activists and part-time militia). In urban areas it mobilized students through the League of Filipino Students and labor unions through the *Kilusang Mayo Uno* (KMU/May First Movement). Cadres cooperated with Nationalist senators Jose Diokno and Lorenzo Tañada who had sufficient moral authority to be able to publicize Marcos's human rights violations. Nevertheless, the CPP was now on the defensive.

The military and civilian technocrats were the key factors that engineered Marcos's state – a parallel with Soeharto's Indonesia is to be seen here. Freed from legislative constraints and media scrutiny, the Philippines military took over regional political and police networks and launched brutal campaigns against the secessionist Moro National Liberation Front (MNLF) in the southern Philippines and the CPP-NPA. Through able technocrats, Marcos addressed structural problems in the countryside and monitored the budget process and economic planning. He subjected all lands to agrarian reform, providing the landless and tenants with access to land. To compete with the private sector, state corporations engaged in oil production, electric power, mass transportation, and fertilizer production. New investment was fostered through financial institutions and the state-run Philippine National Bank and Development Bank of the Philippines, working closely with the Central Bank. American financial aid further solidified Macros's dictatorship. For 12 years the Philippine economy recorded annual growth of some 6 percent.

From 1972 to 1982 Marcos staved off crisis by eliminating the landlord-dominated legislature and employing technocrats who coordinated economic planning and development. The latter administered a land reform program that included the transfer of lands to tenants occupying rice and corn farms. The self-sufficiency program *Masagana 99* (Prosperity 99) allowed farmers to borrow from rural banks, the Philippine National Bank, and the Agricultural Credit Administration to purchase 3-hectare farms and necessary implements. Technocrats also established state corporations that competed with private counterparts in critical areas like oil, mass transportation, power, fertilizer production, and banking. The government stimulated industrial growth by encouraging foreign investments in designated export-processing zones.

Sustained economic progress, however, remained elusive. Marcos had essentially continued his predecessors' formula for development: economic liberalization, promotion of productivity over land reform, and deployment of executive and military agencies. The promotion of other crops failed: sugar, coconut, and forestry products alone – all subject to global market fluctuations – comprised 70 percent of exports. This narrow export base could not balance the rising cost of imports. Taxes remained unchanged, despite structural changes in the economy. Legislators refused to tax the sugar industry and indirect taxes remained the main source of revenue. This distorted tax structure, weak collection apparatus, and leakages due to corruption depleted state resources which then had to be secured through more borrowing. Government corruption and inefficiency caused the decline of American development assistance and foreign investment. The government deficit thereby reached PHP 1.13 billion.

The early success of the dicatatorship ended in decline. Wealth from the economic success remained concentrated in the hands of the Marcoses and their cronies. Their 'crony capitalism' rested upon monopoly powers, special access, and brute force. A crony network that included the Marcoses profited handsomely thereby. Soon after their founding, however, most crony corporations in sugar, automotive, hotels, and entertainment faltered because of mismanagement. From 1981 to 1983 the government bailed out these corporations through 'equity investments', contributing to the decimation of the state's scarce resources. Meanwhile the administration's continued plunder finally emptied the treasury. The country's balance-of-payments worsened; high import costs could not be covered by the declining value of exports. The state resorted to expensive, short-term borrowing to service past debt and went deeper into deficit spending to pay for its ambitious development programs. By 1983 the Philippines was saddled with USD 25 billion in total debt. Real wages dropped, forcing numerous Filipinos to work abroad. Disenchanted by the dictatorship, local and foreign businesses fled as the international lines of credit were cut.

Still Marcos retained political dominance. The military, whose internal conflicts also drained state resources, supported him. Opposition forces remained divided, and Marcos co-opted some through cushy positions. He also courted the Catholic Church and held the radicals at bay. It was principally the Marcoses themselves who undermined the dictatorship – not unlike the way in which Soeharto and his family undermined his rule in Indonesia, as will be seen in the following chapter. On 21 August 1983 opposition leader Benigno Aquino Jr. returned from exile in the United States, despite warnings that his life was at risk. Within minutes of his arrival at Manila airport, he was assassinated. His lifeless body lying on the tarmac of the country's international airport galvanized political opposition across the nation; even some allies turned their backs on Marcos. Technocrats – whose dreams of transforming the Philippines into a market economy had been shattered by rampant cronyism – were among the first to leave. Dissident elements in the military organized a group called the Reform the Armed Forces Movement and readied for their time to strike.

In 1986 the embattled Marcos inexplicably called for snap presidential elections. Anti-Marcos forces consisted of moderate and elite oppositionists, the Church, left-leaning organizations, and thousands of citizens. They enthusiastically threw their support behind the opposition candidate: Benigno Aquino's widow Corazon 'Cory' Aquino (Figure 30). The opposition won despite limited

Figure 30   Corazon Aquino and Diosdado Macapagal, 1989

AP/Press Association Images

resources, intimidation, and cheating by the Marcos side. Marcos demanded that Congress declare him victorious. His position weakened when election observers publicly walked out in protest over irregularities. The military reformers sought to break the impasse by mounting a coup, only to be thwarted by pro-Marcos loyalists. On 22 February 1986 the presidential security command cornered the rebels and forced their leaders, Defense Secretary Juan Ponce Enrile and Armed Forces Chief of Staff Fidel Ramos, to retreat to two military camps along Epifanio de los Santos Avenue – known forever after as EDSA, the focal point of Philippine street politics. Here, during 'EDSA I', Aquino supporters, the Catholic Church, and millions of citizens gathered; the air force and Manila police force defected to their side. American President Ronald Reagan withdrew his support from Marcos, who was persuaded that he had no choice but to flee the country. On 25 February, Cory Aquino and her supporters declared an end to the dictatorship; the bloodless 'People Power' revolution had won.

After toppling the dictatorship, the Aquino government sought to halt the downward slide of the economy it inherited by honoring the country's debts, dismantling import controls and monopolies, and initiating trade reform. From USD 564 million in 1987, foreign investment rose to USD 2.5 billion in 1992, while export value rose to USD 8.8 billion. But the international debt servicing (equivalent to 10 percent of annual GDP) forced the government into heavy domestic borrowing and deficit spending. The government's failure to enforce land reform perpetuated the continued dominance of landlords, causing persistent unrest among the peasantry. The 1991 reduction of remittances from overseas workers due to the Gulf War and the loss of yearly rental from the American military bases that were closed further strained the economy, precipitating a recession which lasted until 1994.

The CPP was now being bypassed by mainstream politics. It failed to unify the upper- and middle-class factions that were politicized by the Aquino assassination. Its boycott of the 1986 elections isolated the Party from the power-sharing deals that Cory Aquino later made with her allies. NPA commanders Conrado Balweg and Buscayno defected from the movement and denounced armed revolt. Members of the Party's legal organizations were targeted for harassment and assassination. Suspecting spies within their ranks, commanders authorized the torture and execution of fellow members. In 1987 the Aquino government declared 'total war' against the CPP. The Party, for its part, launched a nationwide offensive against the state. It sanctioned political assassinations, including foreign advisers connected with the counter-insurgency measures. But the state was indomitable. By 1988 numerous CPP leaders had been arrested. The party was also beset with internal problems, fast losing members who established 'cause-oriented groups' or chose to work through NGOs. The Party came to be seen widely as following an outmoded form of struggle, an inept player in contemporary radical politics.

Malaya/Malaysia

We saw in the previous chapter how a combination of British and local interests led to the independence of Malaya in the hands of conservative elites whom the

British felt they could trust. Essential to this trust was the fact that these elites proved resistant to any Communist alternative, which in Malaya was represented by the MCP uprising known as the Emergency. Communism failed in Malaya for many reasons, but prominent among them was the inability of the MCP to create a genuine united front that bridged ethnic differences. For that reason, its history has remained something apart, outside the 'mainstream' of Malayan and Malaysian history.

Communism was not the only threat perceived by the Malay leadership, so Malaya/Malaysia maintained preventive detention without trial, perhaps the most significant government weapon for managing dissent. Such powers were first legislated by the British in 1948 during the Emergency and, although the laws were repealed in 1960, their detention powers were retained thereafter under the new Internal Security Act (ISA). This was ostensibly for use against remnants of the Communist insurgents but also applied to anyone considered a security threat to the state. From 1960, the pattern of preventive detention was repeated and fine-tuned as part of the state's repressive apparatus. In 1971 the ISA was amended to cover threats to the essential services and economic life of the country. A further amendment in 1975 imposed a mandatory death sentence for arms possession. In 1989 another amendment removed the court's jurisdiction to hear writs of *habeas corpus* from ISA detainees. ISA arrests had the effect of not only depleting and weakening opposition ranks, especially just before elections, and other challenges to the ruling bloc's hegemony but also served as a tacit warning to the population at large. Among those detained were students, academics, trade unionists, journalists, members of opposition parties, and also members of the ruling bloc. Hopes that Malaysia's fourth Prime Minister, Mahathir Mohammad (g. 1981–2003), would abolish the ISA – as he earlier indicated he might – died in 1987 when he used the ISA instead to detain 106 of his political opponents, both from within and outside UMNO, as well as trade unionist, educationists, and social activists, apparently in order to defuse a challenge to his leadership. Total ISA detentions reached 1199 between 1960 and 1969, rising to 1713 from 1970 to 1979, before falling to 559 between 1980 and 1989.

Apart from the ISA, the state's powers to curb dissent were further supplemented by other laws like the Sedition Act (1948, amended 1971) that restricted public debate on 'sensitive issues'; the Printing Presses and Publication Act (1984) giving the Home Minister 'absolute discretion' in granting annually renewable printing permits; and the Official Secrets Act (1972, amended 1986) which provided a mandatory prison sentence for the collection, possession, and dissemination of state secrets. Under Mahathir's premiership, steps were also taken to curb the independence of the judiciary. After Malaysia's courts ruled on a number of cases against the government, and with several other politically sensitive cases still pending before the courts, Mahathir publicly criticized the judiciary and took precipitous action in July 1988 that culminated in the suspension of five Supreme Court judges and the removal of the Lord President.

The economic rehabilitation of Malaya's economy after the war proceeded relatively swiftly; after grappling with some initial food supply problems, the productivity was restored to the pre-war level by 1949. Malaya's economic priorities remained largely unchanged, relying as before on the export of primary products, especially rubber and tin. By 1947 the rubber industry had surpassed its pre-war output. The rush to stockpile raw materials during the Korean War (1950–51) lifted rubber and tin prices for a time and boosted Malaya's growth. After that war ended, however, there followed a slump, which demonstrated that reliance on a limited range of exports could not sustain long-term economic development. Stiff competition from synthetic rubber depressed the demand for natural rubber, while the tin industry also suffered from fluctuating demand.

With an eye towards independence, from the mid-1950s the Malayan government decided to retain the open, private capital-driven free enterprise system that had served the country well, but to supplement this with more government-interventionist five-year development plans, beginning in 1956. The government's attempts to promote alternative cash crops and encourage import-substitution industries yielded only limited success, in the latter case because of the small domestic market. Plantation agriculture and extractive industries continued to dominate the economy. Investments in rubber still led the way, in large part because of the need to replant existing trees which were nearing the end of their economic life. Palm oil, however, was fast emerging as a new commodity, offering faster returns. Rubber trees and oil palms thus became the main plantation crops.

A fundamental rethinking of Malaysia's economic policies took place after the 1969 riots (discussed below in the context of ethnic and religious issues) underlined the dangers of ethnic distinctions coinciding with socio-economic patterns – a coincidence that had been a principle of British colonial rule. Most Malays found employment in the public and low-income primary sectors, while the high-income private and secondary and tertiary sectors were dominated by Chinese. Seventy-five percent of those living below the official poverty line in Malaya were Malays, who in principle were the 'sons of the soil' with a priority of interest in the Malay state. Predictably, Malays were discontented that the economic fruits of independence had eluded them and benefited the Chinese instead. The launching of the New Economic Policy (NEP) was the result. Vigorous government intervention through four five-year plans beginning in 1971 aimed within 20 years to eradicate poverty and raise living standards in general so as to give Malays in particular a fairer share of the economy. The aim was to do this by creating new sources of wealth through sustained economic growth, but not at the expense of the non-Malays. The NEP also aimed to increase Malay ownership of equity capital from 2 to 30 percent within 20 years. That of 'other Malaysians' would be raised from 35 to 40 percent, while foreigners' share would be reduced from 63 to 30 percent over the same period. Primary production continued to be supported, but the main emphasis of the NEP shifted to export-oriented industrialization. Foreign investment was courted with tax concessions and other incentives. It was, however, initially difficult to attract investment in the wake of the 1969 violence, so the state was obliged to furnish much of the funding through government companies run by Malays.

By 1990, the restructuring of the economy had resulted in a substantial fall in foreign wealth ownership from 63.4 percent in 1970 to 25.1 percent in 1990. The share of 'other Malaysians' exceeded its target – from 34.6 percent to 54.6 percent respectively. Malay ownership saw a substantial jump from 2 percent in 1970 to 20.3 percent in 1990, but this fell short of the 30 percent target. More significantly, the percentage of Malays employed in both the secondary and tertiary sectors rose markedly – from 30.8 to 48 percent, and 37.9 to 51 percent respectively, showing that the NEP was having an effect in shifting Malay employment patterns. Overall, by 1990 Malaysia had successfully made the transition from an economy dependent on the export of primary products to one in which manufacturing – relying largely on foreign enterprise and technology – was the major growth sector. The export value of Malaysian rubber and tin meanwhile tumbled from 54.3 percent of exports in 1970 to only 4.9 percent in 1990.

In North Borneo (Sabah) and Sarawak, direct British rule after World War II facilitated more intensive economic exploitation. From 1959 timber became North Borneo's major export. After 1963, both economies were tied more closely to West Malaysia's, and the discovery of oil off the Sabah coast from the mid-1970s boosted growth. The primary sector, however, remained the most important, absorbing some 80 percent of the workforce, against only 4 percent in manufacturing. Progress was steady, if not spectacular, and well behind peninsular Malaysia's.

Singapore

Independence for Singapore in 1965 was as sudden and sobering as it was cathartic. Separation from Malaysia freed Singapore to pursue its own ideals as an independent state, but it also exposed the infant state to the new politics of survival. Singapore had no natural resources. Other than two infantry battalions, manned in fact largely by Malaysians, its armed forces in 1965 were almost non-existent and grossly inadequate to safeguard its political independence. Adding to its security predicament was the shock announcement in 1967 of Britain's military withdrawal from positions east of Suez (to be implemented in 1971), which Lee Kuan Yew estimated would lead to a loss of some 20 percent of Singapore's GDP and 30,000 jobs at British military bases. Faced with daunting prospects of survival, the PAP government led by Lee, and backed by an able and virtually corruption-free civil service, galvanized Singaporeans to support its pragmatic programs. Compulsory national service for males was introduced in 1967, and a credible citizens' defense force was created from scratch with initial Israeli assistance.

Separation from Malaysia in 1965 destroyed the premises upon which Singapore had based its economic strategy after the war. It had intended to switch its emphasis from the declining entrepôt trade to import-substituting manufacturing, relying upon access to a Malaysia-wide common market. Without that access, Singapore's domestic market was too small to sustain such a strategy. The Singapore government shifted its emphasis to export-oriented industrialization and became one of the first countries in Southeast Asia to make major use of multinational corporations as agents of economic development. It also adopted a more interventionist role in the economy through government-related corporations and statutory boards.

By the early 1980s, increasing competition from lower-wage countries and a tight labor market at home drove Singapore to make yet another radical shift from its low-wage, labor-intensive industries to high-wage, capital-intensive industries. By the 1990s, after having reached the limits of its manufacturing capacity, Singapore embarked on developing a 'second wing' by investing abroad. By combining private enterprise with state participation and attracting foreign and local capital, Singapore defied the odds to create an economy that achieved one of the highest GDP per capita figures in the world, but with a relatively uneven distribution of wealth across its society, as measured by its Gini coefficient – a widely used but hardly perfect measure of wealth distribution – of around 47 in 1990, exceeding that of the United States at approximately 43 and of more egalitarian societies like Sweden, Denmark, or Japan at around 25.

With its popular support at the time of independence further bolstered by its strong economic record and extensive public housing program, the PAP romped home to six more electoral victories before Lee Kuan Yew (by then the longest-serving Prime Minister in the world) stepped down in November 1990 in favor of Goh Chok Tong, a long-simmering process of leadership renewal that Lee had initiated to prepare a group of second-generation leaders to take over. Despite the loss of its parliamentary monopoly from 1981 – an indication of some dissent against the PAP's 'soft authoritarianism' – no serious political alternative to the PAP emerged. Instead, the political longevity of the pro-business PAP remained a stabilizing force in Singapore's political and economic systems. By its third decade of independence, Singapore had been spectacularly transformed into one of the most stable, safe, cosmopolitan, and prosperous countries in Asia, a First World 'oasis' in a Third World region. It had proved wrong those skeptics who believed that a small city-state could not survive in the modern world.

Indochina

The successive Communist victories in Cambodia, South Vietnam, and Laos in 1975 brought an end to the civil wars that had torn these countries apart, but delivered neither the hoped-for prosperity nor, in many respects, the unity necessary to build a socialist future. The brutality of *Khmer Rouge* policies and Pol Pot's decision to attack Vietnam quickly destroyed any remaining revolutionary solidarity with Cambodia's Lao and Vietnamese comrades, and in late 1978 Hanoi mounted an invasion which drove his regime from power and plunged the country into another civil war. The Vietnamese and Lao parties were able to begin the transition to a socialist economy in the areas now under their control, but this proved to be a more difficult and less economically beneficial task than they had anticipated. Vietnam in particular became bogged down with its occupation of Cambodia and suffered from the effects of an international embargo – a consequence of the American position of opposing Vietnam, which now led it bizarrely to defend the idea that the *Khmer Rouge* were still the legitimate rulers of Cambodia. By the mid-1980s, both the Vietnamese and Lao regimes began to abandon the more hardcore aspects of socialist policy and to move towards a market economy.

The short-lived Democratic Kampuchea regime, which was in power from April 1975 until December 1978, oversaw the most tragic and violent period in Cambodia's history. Phnom Penh was evacuated, and the inhabitants forced to join a mass exodus to the countryside. The vision of Pol Pot and his fellow leaders was to turn the entire country into one large worksite, with collective agriculture and construction projects on a scale that rivaled Mao's policies under the Great Leap Forward in the 1950s. Large numbers of people died either of hunger or as victims of the regime's paranoia, which saw enemies everywhere and particularly targeted ethnic minorities such as the Vietnamese and Cham. The Party was also weakened by internal purges and disagreements over the wisdom of pursuing an aggressive policy against Vietnam. These problems caused numerous defections across the border by *Khmer Rouge* cadres, thus providing Hanoi with a critical mass of loyal Cambodians when it invaded the country in December 1978. In January 1979 the People's Republic of Kampuchea was established, marking a return to a Cambodian Communist movement closely linked to Vietnam. Although many Cambodians initially welcomed the Vietnamese as liberators, over time old animosities re-reappeared, and there was growing support for the rural insurgency organized by the *Khmer Rouge* and forces loyal to Sihanouk or a former Prime Minister named Son Sann. This conflict would drag on until the early 1990s, when United Nations intervention brought first a transitional government and then the re-establishment of the Kingdom of Cambodia with Sihanouk on the throne.

In Vietnam, the Lao Dong Party (renamed the Communist Party of Vietnam in 1976) faced the challenge of reuniting a country which had not been ruled under a single government since 1859. The Party's main objectives were to consolidate their power in the South and convert its economy to the socialist model which had been followed in the DRV for more than two decades. This was easier said than done. Culturally, politically, and economically South Vietnam had evolved in a very different direction from the North since the time of partition, particularly in the urban areas. There had also been more widespread physical damage in the South, the destructive bombings in the North notwithstanding. The Party cracked down on what it viewed as the contaminating effects of two decades of Western culture, while also attacking the economic system built on a combination of foreign aid, imported consumer goods, corruption, and a powerful role for the ethnic Chinese minority. The victors also relocated large numbers of urban residents to 'New Economic Zones' in the countryside where they were meant to take up farming.

The fundamental problem – which the leadership only came to realize gradually – was that many South Vietnamese had supported the revolution for various reasons, but few of them were ideologically committed to socialism, at least in terms of collectivized agriculture and a planned economy. Land reform under both the NLF and the Saigon government had put more land into the hands of poor farmers, and they were understandably reluctant to give it up for collectivization. Moreover, imports of agricultural equipment, motorbikes, and other consumer goods had created a certain standard of living in parts of the country which was higher than what the socialist system had to offer. The new government's attack on the 'capitalist' infrastructure in the South, particularly the Chinese, destroyed much of the potential for economic development, as did the flight of many business people in April 1975 and after.

All in all, the first decade of the Socialist Republic of Vietnam was difficult and often painful. The invasion of Cambodia together with the regime's treatment of the ethnic Chinese provoked a destructive, but brief punitive incursion by China in early 1979. Vietnam's costly occupation of Cambodia and the resulting international embargo also severely hampered its growth by restricting aid largely to the socialist bloc allied with the USSR. Internally the various gaps between North and South were proving difficult to bridge. It is difficult to assess just how many of the Southern supporters of the Communist side had really believed that South Vietnam would remain a separate entity for any significant length of time after the Communist takeover. What is clear, however, is that the combination of an influx of Northerners into positions of authority in the South and the sidelining of many non-Party members in the new unified government caused considerable resentment, as did the incarceration in 'reform camps' of many thousands of people linked in one way or the other to the former regime.

By the mid-1980s the economic situation in the country was quite desperate. The transition to socialism in the South was largely halted, and even in the North the end of the war had reduced many people's willingness to make sacrifices and submit to the demands of a collectivized economy. A series of bad harvests only made the situation worse and brought widespread hunger. Prominent voices in the Party began to speak out for change, and in 1986 the policy of *doi moi* – usually translated as 'renovation' – was launched at the Sixth Congress of the Communist Party. This policy began the shift to a more market-oriented economy.

The Lao People's Revolutionary Party faced challenges in integrating its 'liberated zones' with the areas under the control of the Royal Lao Government. It was largely a matter of incorporating the cities into a predominantly rural zone of control, rather than an entire region as in the case of South Vietnam, but the Lao Party confronted many of the same problems as their Vietnamese comrades. The cities and towns were more Westernized and constituted culturally and ethnically alien islands within the new Communist-ruled Lao People's Democratic Republic. Many of the Chinese and Vietnamese residents fled to Thailand, along with many Lao – roughly 10 percent of the population in the early years after the takeover. Laos had few resources to begin with, and it now lost much of its economic dynamic.

Despite the relatively smooth takeover in 1975, the Party remained concerned about possible dissent and opposition, and a number of civil servants and military officers were packed off to 'seminar' camps in the remote northeast. They were later joined by the royal family, who had initially been allowed their freedom after the abdication of King Savang Vatthana (r.

1959–75) but came under suspicion for alleged plots to regain power. The king, queen, and crown prince died in the camps sometime in the late 1970s. The new government also faced sporadic resistance from remnants of the Hmong forces trained by the United States; many Hmong had fled the country, but a number remained in the mountains and continued to resist the Communist regime.

While the Pathet Lao had generally been successful in governing their liberated zones, the transition to governing an entire country was not easy. They worked to shift the Lao economy to a more socialist footing, with very mixed results. Attempts to collectivize agriculture were fairly quickly recognized as failures and were abandoned within a few years of the foundation of the regime. While a Marxist ideology usually required socialist agriculture, it did not seem particularly necessary in Laos, where there had always been plenty of land and a relatively small population. By the mid-1980s, the Party was pursuing 'new thinking', their equivalent of Vietnam's *doi moi*, which involved opening up the country to more foreign trade and investment and gradually cutting back on central planning and government subsidies.

The 1980s represented a major time of transition and change for all three countries in Indochina. Cambodia spent the decade trying to recover from the *Khmer Rouge*, yet the ongoing civil war, the political and economic requirements of the Vietnamese occupation, and the continued international embargo against the Vietnamese-sponsored regime left little room for substantive recovery. The country would not begin to experience any real stability or growth until the 1990s, when the resolution of the conflict and the establishment of a non-Communist regime would pave the way for Cambodia to open its doors to trade and investment.

As has been noted, Vietnam and Laos began this process roughly in step with each other. Laos had the double advantage of not being subject to the international embargo and of having well-established economic links with Thailand which had never been completely severed, and could now be revived. Having only partially socialized its economy, Laos was less far down the path than Vietnam and thus was able to shift directions somewhat more easily. Conversely, when it did so, it had considerably less to work with than its neighbor in terms of both natural resources and human capital. *Doi moi* in Vietnam got underway more haltingly, partly because there was less consensus within the leadership on the desirability of such reforms. Once the government began to take down the barriers on private trade and agriculture and on the movement of goods between different areas, however, the die was cast, and the transition to 'socialism with a market orientation' was irreversible.

The social dimension: managing ethnicity and religion

For the new nations of Southeast Asia, achieving social integration was often as great a challenge as devising a stable and viable political and economic framework. Two major social forces made this task particularly challenging: ethnicity and religion. These were the source of much diversity in Southeast Asia – indeed, often the cause of a divisive and threatening form of diversity.

Indonesia

Ethnic issues were at the very heart of Indonesian identities as they evolved during the colonial period. It was generally agreed that the indigenous ethnicities of the archipelago – Acehnese, Minangkabau, Sundanese, Javanese, Dayak, Madurese, Balinese, Timorese, Ambonese, Papuans, and many more – were without exception 'Indonesians'. Dutchmen were not: the colonialists must go home, regardless of whether they had been born in Indonesia. But what about other minority groups, particularly Indo-Europeans, Arabs, and Chinese?

Indo-Europeans had long lived in the interstices between Dutch colonial masters and their Indonesian subjects. They were mostly Christian in religion and in colonial times had tended to seek equality of status with the higher-up Dutch rather than the lower-down Indonesians. But circumstances were different in independent Indonesia. Indo-Europeans who could claim Dutch citizenship sometimes chose to relocate to the Netherlands. But many others chose to identify with Indonesia and stay in the archipelago, a decision generally accepted by Indonesians. Arabs were Muslims and even though they had a reputation as exploiters of Indonesians in trade and money-lending, they also received much respect, especially the *sayyids* who were descendants of the Prophet. Most Indonesian Arabs were of Hadhrami descent (from modern-day Yemen) and some thought of themselves more as Hadhramis than as Indonesians, but many chose to identify themselves with the new Republic. Several indeed played major roles in the new nation.

The major ethnic issue concerned the Chinese. In 1930, Chinese were a mere 1.9 percent of the archipelago's population. By the early twenty-first century, this group had grown to 8 million, about 3 percent of Indonesia's total population. This small minority was particularly visible because of its concentration in urban areas and its prominence in business affairs. In colonial times they often operated as economic middle-men for Dutch interests and were frequently accused of being contemptuous of 'indigenous' (*pribumi*) Indonesians. They consequently attracted considerable animosity. In independent Indonesia, the position of the Chinese was complicated by PRC policy that claimed all Overseas Chinese as its citizens. This left Indonesian Chinese with a poorly defined dual citizenship status. In 1955 Indonesia and the PRC signed a dual-nationality treaty which obliged Indonesian Chinese to choose either Indonesian or PRC citizenship, but under conditions making it more difficult to choose the former. Because of governmental suspicion and popular hostility to Chinese entrepreneurs, many chose to set up businesses with Indonesian front-men. These were the so-called 'Ali-Baba' firms, with the Indonesian 'Ali' as front-man for a company in fact run by the Chinese 'Baba'.

In the Sukarno period down to 1965, the military remained suspicious of the Chinese, regarding them as being mostly supporters of PKI which, indeed, was overtly supported by Beijing. In 1959 the army decreed that from 1960 onwards non-citizens would be banned from rural trade. This was done mainly to weaken Sukarno's growing friendship with the PRC and to undermine PKI, while also pandering to anti-Chinese sentiments in the general populace. In the end the army forcibly repatriated some 119,000 to the PRC. But since rural trade was a sector dominated by Chinese, along with some Arabs and Indians, the result was greater economic dislocations for ordinary Indonesians and increased anxiety amongst Chinese.

There was a considerable turn-around in Chinese-military relations during Soeharto's New Order regime after 1965. Members of the regime elite (particularly Soeharto, his family, and military leaders) worked with Chinese entrepreneurs who could provide business expertise, overseas connections, and capital, and who posed no political threat precisely because they were Chinese and thus without an indigenous constituency. Now it was Chinese front-men camouflaging vast profits going to corrupt regime leaders: so-called 'Baba-Ali' firms. The most famous was Liem Sioe Liong, also known as Sudomo Salim, who became a multi-billionaire and the richest person in Indonesia through his personal links with Soeharto. Only a few of these business empires made the transition to legitimate business activity after the Soeharto regime fell in 1998. Animosity towards Chinese business tycoons with their extravagant wealth and towards Chinese in general – most of whom, in fact, were far from rich – inspired riots from time to time. Such social violence culminated in terrible anti-regime and anti-Chinese riots in 1998, particularly in Jakarta and Surakarta. Some 30,000 Chinese fled Indonesia at that time.

Malaysia, Borneo, and Singapore

Singapore's separation from Malaysia in 1965 was designed to end the escalating political and ethnic tensions between the two governments that threatened to produce communal mayhem. But before Kuala Lumpur could address the urgent task of forging national unity among its remaining members, new cracks appeared. Singapore's departure was nearly followed by Sabah and Sarawak, which resented Tunku Abdul Rahman's failure to consult their leaders before taking precipitous action to 'expel' Singapore. Fears that their respective states' rights would be similarly brushed aside by Kuala Lumpur fueled their antipathy. Federal leaders, however, moved quickly to nip the secessionist tendencies in the bud by removing the incumbent chief ministers of the two states – Sabah's Donald Stephens and Sarawak's Stephen Kalong Ningkan.

Within peninsular Malayan society, as we have already seen above, one of the main reasons for the MCP's defeat was its inability to forge a movement that bridged ethnic distinctions. After the Emergency, contentious ethnic issues were in some ways overshadowed by the political conflict with Singapore – although much of the debate over merger was in fact directly linked to the question of ethnic balance in a 'Greater Malaysia' – but resurfaced after 1965, now with language as a major area of contestation. As the 1967 deadline approached (after ten years of independence) for making *Bahasa Melayu* (the Malay language) the sole national language of Malaysia, Malay hard-liners pressed the government to implement the policy without exceptions. Just as resolute were the counter pressures from non-Malay, and particularly Chinese, activists who defended the use of English, Chinese, and Indian languages for educational and official purposes. On 3 March 1967, the government formally passed the national language bill recognizing Malay – now called *Bahasa*

Malaysia – as the sole national language and mandating its gradual introduction as the main medium of instruction in all schools, starting at the primary level and reaching the universities by 1982. As a concession to non-Malays, the bill also contained indirect provisions for the continued official use of English and other languages. This highly emotional language debate and the compromise that satisfied no side exacerbated tensions between Malays and non-Malays, prompting disillusioned advocates from both sides to switch their support to non-Alliance parties as the 1969 elections approached.

The ethnic tensions came to a head during the federal elections held on 10 May 1969. The Alliance was chastised at the polls with not only a reduced majority but also a fall in its popular vote from 58.4 percent in 1964 to 48.5 percent. Of the 104 parliamentary seats, the Alliance captured only 66, a fall from the 89 it won in 1964, which meant a loss of its two-thirds parliamentary majority that had previously allowed it to make changes to the constitution at will. While UMNO lost Malay votes to the Islamist *Partai Islam SeMalaysia* (PAS, All-Malaysia Islamic Party), which took 12 seats, the MCA gained only 13 of the 33 it contested, losing half its parliamentary seats to non-communal parties like the Gerakan, Democratic Action Party, and the People's Progressive Party. On 12 May, jubilant opposition supporters took to the streets in a celebratory convoy of vehicles, prompting UMNO supporters to organize a counter-rally on 13 May that quickly erupted into communal violence and mayhem for the next four days, tragically killing 196 people and injuring 406 according to official figures, the majority of the victims being Chinese. On 14 May, a state of emergency was declared, the scheduled elections in Sabah and Sarawak (which were to commence two weeks later) were cancelled, and the constitution was suspended. Over the next 18 months, Malaysia was ruled by an all-powerful National Operations Council headed by Deputy Premier Tun Abdul Razak, who subsequently replaced the now politically weakened Tunku as Prime Minister in 1970, governing until his death in 1976. As we discussed above, this period saw a fundamental rethinking of Malaysian economic policies, with the intention of reducing the pattern of ethnic specialization and Malay disadvantage in the economy.

Given its geographical proximity and its own ethnic diversity, Singapore could not escape the spill-over effects of Malaysia's 1969 riots. The wounds of bloody Chinese-Malay riots in July and September 1964 were still raw and the buildup of tensions, fueled in part by widespread rumors of atrocities committed by Malays on Chinese in Malaysia and fomented also by agitators who had entered the island, finally flared up on 31 May. The clashes, which lasted until early June, left four dead and about 80 injured. Vigorous action by Singapore's security forces – including the enforcement of immigration controls – helped to contain the spread of violence and encourage the return of normalcy.

In Singapore, as in Malaysia, preventive detentions were used to control dissent. The initial tool here was known as the Preservation of Public Security Ordinance (PPSO), which had replaced emergency regulations in 1955. A PPSO security sweep in February 1963, codenamed *Cold Store*, rounded up 113 activists, including 24 leaders of the main opposition party, *Barisan Sosialis* (Socialist Front), crippling its electoral apparatus before the September 1963 elections. When Singapore became part of Malaysia in 1963, it inherited the ISA and kept it even after separation in 1965. ISA arrests were made shortly after in 1966 and, more notably, in 1987, with the detention of 22 Roman Catholic social activists and professionals for involvement in an alleged 'Marxist conspiracy'. Like Malaysia, Singapore employed a variety of other legal instruments to manage dissent and obviate social and religious conflict.

Burma

The colonial experience encouraged Burma's ethnic minority groups and the majority Burmans to continue to regard themselves as distinctively different. At the end of World War II, ethnic identity remained a divisive factor as Burma moved towards independence. We noted earlier that the shape of a new national army was contested along ethnic and cultural lines, ending in the creation of what were in effect two armies. Shan leaders were particularly concerned about how best to protect the future of their people. They faced the threat of being left out of an independent Burma on the grounds that they were politically backward, mirroring the earlier British idea of leaving Burma behind India's pace of progress towards independence. In 1947, several Shan leaders convened the conference at Panglong in the hills of eastern Burma, discussed in the previous chapter. Representatives of Kachin and Chin communities also attended, as did Aung San, Thakin Nu (later U Nu), and the pre-war Prime Minister U Saw. Out of this meeting came the Panglong Agreement of February 1947, which declared that 'full autonomy in internal administration for the Frontier Areas is accepted in principle' – thus entrenching an issue that would haunt nation-building in Burma long afterward. The Panglong Agreement ensured that the ethnic minorities – at least those who attended the conference – would agree to join the new nation but made 'race' a legal and constitutional category. This agreement, however, rested in large part on the minorities' trust of Aung San, whose assassination in July 1947 was decisive in this respect as in many others.

The question of the relationship between the central, 'Burman' state and the minority ethnic groups – many of them Christianized during the colonial period – was central to Burma's subsequent history. Prime Minister U Nu's effort to make Buddhism the state religion antagonized many minorities who suspected from the beginning that their interests would not be met in a Burman-led nation. Following independence in 1948, Karens formed the Karen National Union to defend their identity and autonomy against an increasingly 'Burman' cultural orientation. We have already noted that army battalions defected in 1948 to join the Karen National Defense Organization rebellion. The Karen rebellion and many other separatist movements in the Chin, Shan, and Kachin states added up to one of the longest-running civil wars in Southeast Asian history and denied Rangoon control of its national borders for many years. Karen, Karenni, and Mon refugees in Thailand amounted to well over 100,000, with many more displaced persons within Burma's borders.

Muslims in Burma in some areas met cultural hostility towards non-Buddhists. It became clear on the eve of independence that Indian Muslims still in Burma would be refused Burmese citizenship, so some left for India or

Pakistan. Others struggled for years to define their role in the nation. Many were urban merchants, who were hard hit by the nationalization of the economy under Ne Win. The worst episodes occurred among the substantial community of Muslims living in Arakan (after 1989 called Rakhine) – the so-called *Rohingyas*, whom the government refused to recognize as being Burmese citizens at all. There bloody Buddhist-Muslim hostility went back to colonial and Japanese occupation times. In 1947–48 a Muslim rebellion against Rangoon began in Arakan which precipitated bitter fighting and remained a serious threat into the mid-1950s. In subsequent decades, Buddhist-Muslim conflict and brutal army operations continued to produce a major flow of Muslim refugees across the border with Bangladesh. By contrast, Chinese in Burma – as was also the case in Thailand – were able to assimilate through marriage and shared Buddhist religion.

In common with other new nations of Southeast Asia, Burma's ethnic complexity and political variety made for much dissent. In Burma's case, however, this was true in a heightened degree, for here dissent included one of the longest-lasting series of civil wars in the region. The government in Rangoon had two basic means of dealing with dissent. The first was to crush it militarily – rarely with any need for restraint or concern for civilian casualties. This method was particularly applied to ethnic minority rebellions on the geographic fringes of the nation. The second – favored for urban dissent – was to censor publications, place leaders under house arrest or imprison them, close universities, and – if necessary – unleash the state security apparatus to beat and kill people in the streets.

The Philippines

Muslim Filipinos or *Moros*, as they prefer to be called, comprise about 12 percent of the country's populace and consist of 13 identifiable cultural-linguistic groups in Palawan and Mindanao. The proud remnants of the pre-colonial Sultanates are the majority – the Maguindanao of Cotabato, Maranao-Ilanun of Lanao, and Tausug and Samal of Sulu and Tawi-tawi. These and other ethnic distinctions within the overall Moro group were important, and remain divisive. Unlike their Christian countrymen whose frame of reference has links to Europe and the United States, Moros have always trained their eyes on the Islamic Malay world and the Islamic civilization of Arabia and the Middle East. Their art, dress, music, literature, languages, and lifestyles reveal a closer affinity with neighboring Malaysia and Indonesia than with the northern Philippines.

The Spaniards and Americans alike failed to subjugate the Moros completely but they insisted on regarding them as part of the Philippines polity. The 1934 Tydings-McDuffie Independence Act appointed Chistians to the highest political positions nationwide, further estranging Moros from the nascent state. Christian and Muslim Filipinos were also of differing ethnic origins, thus compounding their religious differences, as has so often been the case across Southeast Asia. Adding insult to injury, the Commonwealth government even encouraged Christians to migrate and homestead in traditional Islamic strongholds in Mindanao. In vain the Moros petitioned the American authorities to be considered a different people from the rest of the archipelago and to be granted a separate independence or, indeed, to be retained as an American colony.

Ironically Moros were advantaged by the Japanese occupation. For participating in anti-Japanese resistance they received rewards that later financed Islamic revivalism in Mindanao. In exchange for patronage, Muslim politicians accomodated their Christian counterparts by maintaining peace and order and promoting the integration of Moros into Philippine life through education. Nevertheless Moros still felt threatened by Christian economic and political superiority in their own homeland. Christian occupation of arable lands, the closure of free trade with Borneo, and competition from non-Muslims in regional waters threatened the livelihoods of the growing Moro population.

In 1968 their relations with the state worsened. On Corregidor the army executed some 28 Muslims, known as Jabidah commandos, who were allegedly training for military operations in Sabah, then still the subject of contending claims between Manila and Kuala Lumpur. This event, known as the 'Jabidah Massacre', aroused outrage and sparked Muslim nationalism, particularly among those Moros who were most affected by Christian immigration. In Cotabato, Datu Udtog Matalag formed the secessionist Muslim (later Mindanao) Independence Movement, followed by Datu Rashid Lucman's establishment of the Bangsamoro Liberation Organization in Lanao. From 1970 to 1971 violent clashes erupted between the Muslim and Christian populations in these provinces, forcing national military intervention that sidelined older Muslim politicians and neutralized their private armies. In mid-1971 former Bangsamoro Liberation Organization members Nur Misuari, Salamat Hashim, and others came together to form the Moro National Liberation Front (MNLF), a movement demanding a Moro Republic comprised of Mindanao, Sulu, and Palawan. Libya and local anti-Marcos politicians provided the organization with armaments, while Malaysia condoned training camps for MNLF forces.

From 1972 to 1977 there was open warfare between the MNLF and the state, transforming Mindanao into a battleground that took thousands of lives, displaced over a million people, and destroyed millions in property. This war strained the Marcos dictatorship financially and politically, while alienating Muslim-majority states that were sympathetic to the rebels. The MNLF, however, failed to exploit the regime's weaknesses. It lost numerous battles and its military front split along ethnic lines. In 1976 some Moro leaders even endorsed a controversial peace pact with the Marcos government known as the Tripoli Agreement, in return for positions in the 'Autonomous Region'. Muslim self-rule nevertheless remained a dream. President Fidel Ramos's appointment of former MNLF Chairman Misuari as governor of the Autonomous Region of Muslim Mindanao and Chairman of the Southern Philippines Council for Peace and Development in 1996 made little difference. Peace and development remained elusive.

In the 1990s, a MNLF break-away faction led by Hashim Salamat and calling itself the Moro Islamic Liberation Front (MILF) boasted some 120,000 regular fighters and 300,000 militiamen in Lanao, Maguindanao, and

Cotabato. Their clashes with the military cost hundreds of lives and billions of pesos in property damage. Meanwhile the Abu Sayyaf Group was established by Abdurajak Janjalani in 1991; it fought for an Islamic state through extremist means. It bombed civilian venues like malls and passenger ships. After Janjalani's death the Abu Sayyaf descended into terrorism and criminality, robbing banks and kidnapping civilians, including on one occasion 20 foreign tourists from a Malaysian resort in 2000. The Abu Sayyaf also built links with other extremist Islamic organizations in Southeast Asia, notably the *Jemaah Islamiyah* terrorists whose main arena of operation was in Indonesia.

Thailand

The greatest challenge to Thailand's national integration has consistently come from the area called the 'Muslim South', the southernmost provinces known collectively as 'Pattani'. ('Patani' is spelled with a single 't' in Malay but is usually written with a double 't' when referring to it as a region of Thailand.) Once the Malay kingdom of Patani, this region was long under Thai overlordship and became a permanent part of Siam when the border with British Malaya was fixed in a 1909 treaty. A significant proportion of the population of these provinces remains ethnically Malay and religiously Muslim, a fact which has produced long-term tensions and conflicts. (It should be noted, however, that in other parts of the country there is also a small minority of Thai Muslims who are not ethnically Malay.)

The modern Thai state has always been ambivalent in its policy towards the Muslim south. Like Christianity, Islam is recognized and tolerated as a minority faith, and Buddhism has never been officially imposed as a state religion. Yet when the triad of 'nation, religion, and king' is invoked, it is clear that Buddhism is the religion being referred to. School textbooks tend to articulate morals and ethics in explicitly Buddhist terms, and Muslim children can only learn about Islam in separate religious schools. Families are thus faced with the dilemma of whether or not to educate their children in their own mother tongue and religion in a system that will not facilitate their transition to university or their integration into Thai society.

At a deeper level, the Muslim minority is also faced with the question of whether or not they are really 'Thai'. In King Chulalongkorn's time the term 'Thai Muslim' came into use, and this seemed to validate the possibility of being both 'Thai' and 'Muslim', even though it also downplayed their Malay ethnicity. Under the absolute monarchy there was relatively little attempt to impose Thai culture on the Muslim south, although the government did pursue administrative integration and the expansion of Thai-language schooling. Phibun's cultural nationalism in the late 1930s and 1940s was more aggressive and official efforts to limit the use of Malay dress and the Malay language met with considerable resistance.

The post-war period saw the appearance of widespread frustration within the southern provinces, with demands for a separate regional government and Islamic court system, as well as more local officials and greater use of the Malay language within the state system. There were also voices calling for Pattani to become independent or to secede and join with Malaya. The military government which took power in late 1947 resisted most of these demands and cracked down on opposition in the region. A separatist movement was born which has existed until the present time under various names. In the 1960s the rise of the CPT insurgency, which included important base areas in the South, also strengthened the position of anti-government forces in Pattani, as did the presence of elements from the MCP who sought refuge on Thai territory after the suppression of the Malayan Emergency. The Thai government used a combination of military repression and 'soft power' – notably a heightened presence for the royal family in the South after the construction of a palace in Narathiwat province – and under Prem the situation stabilized somewhat, but the potential for conflict was never eliminated.

Through the 1950s, however, the Thai government's main concern in terms of integration was less the Muslim southerners than the Chinese community, who constituted an ethnically alien community which was both economically powerful and potentially subversive, given the presence of a critical mass of people sympathetic to the Communist regime in China. The anti-Chinese sentiments of King Vajiravudh and Phibun Songkram have been discussed in previous chapters. Under Phibun's post-war military government there was considerable pressure on the Chinese to assimilate by taking Thai citizenship and Thai names. At the same time the proliferation of business ties similar to the 'Ali-Baba' relationship in Indonesia tended to defuse resentment of Chinese economic domination, since various groups of ethnic Thai elites were now getting a share of the pie. As a result of these policies, the Sino-Thai community has come to be considered one of the best-integrated in Southeast Asia. Their integration into the political and commercial elite and the widespread adoption of Thai Buddhist practices has allowed them to become 'Thai' to a greater extent than most other minorities.

Indochina

The post-colonial states of Indochina faced the problem of integrating minorities to varying degrees. Cambodia was the most ethnically homogeneous and Laos the least. The governments in Hanoi, Saigon, and Vientiane all attempted to create a national identity that would somehow include those minorities, who had enjoyed relative autonomy under French rule, but now found themselves subjects of governments dominated by ethnic groups whom they had often thought more directly oppressive than the Europeans. The Viet Minh had been very successful in recruiting highlanders into the revolution during its struggle against the French. Although a few groups had thrown in their lot with the colonial regime rather than the Vietnamese revolutionaries, after 1954 the DRV enjoyed a considerable degree of stability in its highland areas. Following the model used by the PRC government, it created two large 'autonomous' zones in the northern and northwestern areas of the country, inhabited largely by minorities. These zones would, however, be abolished after reunification in 1976.

The minorities in South Vietnam, located mainly in the Central Highlands, posed a more complex challenge. Some had previously joined the Viet Minh during the anti-French struggle, while others were now recruited by the American army and CIA as part of their Special Forces. Many highlanders felt no loyalty to any Vietnamese side, however, and the emergence of the FULRO (United Front for the Liberation of Oppressed Races), a movement calling for autonomy in the Central Highlands, created a thorn in the side of Vietnamese governments for decades to come. In Laos the large minority population, located mainly in the upland areas, was similarly divided between those loyal to the royal government and those supporting the Pathet Lao. The Hmong, in particular, were split down the middle.

The ethnic situation in these countries was complicated by the fact that Christianity had made considerable inroads among the minorities of Laos and South Vietnam – although much less in North Vietnam, where conversion has only begun in more recent times. The Saigon and Vientiane governments allowed Western missionaries considerable freedom of activity among the minorities. Indeed, the Republic of Vietnam's government ministries worked closely with missionary groups to create writing systems and publish school texts for the country's minorities. The presence of critical masses of Catholic and Protestant highlanders became a long-term source of tension in both Vietnam and Laos after 1975.

The cultural dimension

Each of Southeast Asia's new nations sought also to define themselves in cultural terms. They wanted to create national and cultural identities that would build popular loyalty in an environment in which such national-level, essentially homogenizing efforts often faced formidable barriers posed by local cultures, differing ethnic identities, linguistic variety, and religious differences. Having looked at political, economic, ethnic, and religious aspects above, we now turn to the related process – in some ways even more problematic and certainly more difficult to grasp analytically – of creating national cultures.

Thailand

More than almost any other country in Southeast Asia, Thailand for more than a century has remained preoccupied with defining and preserving its national identity – its 'Thainess' – and its national culture. This preoccupation might seem somewhat paradoxical in view of the fact that the Thai never came under colonial rule and were thus never forcibly exposed to foreign culture. Nevertheless, the constant contact with Western culture, particularly among those who returned from overseas, created a mentality whereby the Thai, on the one hand, are anxious to appear 'modern' and 'civilized' in foreign eyes (as discussed in earlier chapters) and, on the other hand, are obsessed with maintaining their cultural distinctiveness.

Ever since the reign of King Vajiravudh in the early twentieth century, Thai identity has been defined in terms of the 'nation, religion, king' triad. These three institutions are considered to be the main focus of loyalty for all 'true'

Thai and to constitute the bedrock of what it means to be Thai. As was discussed above, this definition can be problematic when it comes to ethnic groups who do not follow the Buddhist religion, particularly the Muslims. It has also been difficult to fit the hill tribes of northern Thailand into this pattern, and in some respects they remain the least 'Thai' of any segment of the population; indeed, many of them remain stateless and do not enjoy the status of citizens. The Chinese, by contrast, although viewed by Vajiravudh and – to a lesser extent – by Phibun as culturally alien, have achieved a much greater degree of assimilation without completely losing a sense of 'Chineseness', as was noted above.

The large Northern Thai and Northeastern Thai (Isan) minorities have also come under a certain degree of pressure to integrate, particularly in the period before World War II. The use of the Central Thai language in government offices and schools, together with the building of links to the royal family through visits and the media from the 1950s onward, have enabled the Tai-speaking groups of other regions to share in the common 'Thai' identity while retaining their own mother tongues (the spoken version, at least) and many of their regional cultural styles. During the first half of the twentieth century, a certain degree of enforced assimilation was also achieved through Bangkok's control over the monkhood, which aimed at imposing the use of Central Thai in religious texts and homogenizing local varieties of religious practice.

Indochina

Both Vietnam and Laos have pursued a policy of creating a 'multi-ethnic' nation characterized by a single national identity combined with individual ethnic identities. Generally speaking, the governments led by Communist parties have gone further along this path than their non-Communist predecessors. To some extent this is because the Vietnamese and Lao revolutions enjoyed fairly strong support among many minorities, as described above. One of the 'carrots' used to attract and maintain this support was the promise of participation first in the revolution and then in the state. Although the Republic of Vietnam and the Royal Lao Government made efforts in this direction (particularly the former), they were generally too preoccupied with politics and war to be able to invest much time and effort into forging some kind of cultural identity. The consequence was that cultural integration of minorities was at least as difficult as political integration, although when a government succeeded in getting children in remote areas into a classroom, the chances of success were somewhat stronger.

These policies have met with mixed results. 'Vietnamese culture' and 'Lao culture' are generally defined in terms of the attributes of the majority ethnic group, so that the minority cultures are somewhat marginalized or represented as exotic fare for tourists. Moreover, the ruling parties have tended to encourage at least partial assimilation into the dominant culture in order to minimize the potential for alienation or secessionist sentiments. Laos has been much slower than Hanoi to promote the use of minority languages, especially in written form. Until the advent of *doi moi* in the mid-1980s, the Vietnamese state also clamped down firmly on many of the rituals, ceremonies, and other practices of minority groups, as much because they were viewed as feudal and backward as because they served to reinforce a separate cultural identity. One of the hallmarks of *doi moi* has been a reversal of the policy among ethnic Vietnamese and minorities alike; this has fueled the revival of many cultural practices that were previously suspect or banned. Among the highland minorities, one reason for increased state tolerance of traditional culture is that the latter is seen as a bulwark against Protestant Christianity, which remains strong among those groups in the Central Highlands among whom missionaries were active before 1975. Protestantism has more recently been spreading also among some minorities in the north where there had previously been few or no converts.

Cambodia has always had a smaller minority population and relatively little dissent articulated in ethnic terms. Both Sihanouk and Lon Nol did place strong emphasis on Khmer identity, however, and there was relatively little interest in minority languages or cultures. Anti-Vietnamese violence broke out under Lon Nol, but this was the result of pent-up political and economic tensions and government instigation rather than any genuine 'cultural nationalism'. The *Khmer Rouge* went much further in imposing their own form of Cambodian culture and in forcibly reducing and suppressing ethnic difference among Chinese, Vietnamese, and Cham. Like their Vietnamese and Lao comrades, they had a strong base of support among the highland populations, who had traditionally been viewed as primitive and in some respects out of reach of the lowland state.

Indonesia

Creating an Indonesian culture and sense of identity was a major challenge in the world's largest archipelago with hundreds of languages and local cultural traditions. The experience of the Revolution itself was one of the glues that helped to bring the nation together, but for many years Indonesian leaders had to work hard to provide content for the idea of Indonesian identity. The way the Dutch fought against the Revolution enhanced an Indonesia-wide sense of identity. The nationalists had long sought a unitary Republic under their control. In an archipelago as complex as Indonesia, a case can be made that federalism is a viable – perhaps the most viable – system of government. But because federal states were set up as a Dutch ploy to undermine the Republic, the very concept of federalism was discredited in Indonesian political discourse. Only a single Indonesian state and identity was politically acceptable.

President Sukarno was a great orator and the most prominent promoter of Indonesianness. In his public appearances he continually hammered the theme of national unity and national identity. He called for the promise, heroism, and sacrifices of the Revolutionary struggle to be carried on, for the Revolution was never finished in his eyes. In his Independence Day address of August 1954, he emphasized the urgency of 'remaining true to the ideals of our National Revolution, for which thousands of our youth have given their lives, for which millions of common people have made their sacrifices, for which the Indonesian people have fought for decades'.[5]

In 1959, as he was leading Indonesia into the chaos of Guided Democracy, Sukarno called upon Indonesians to rally to the spirit of the Revolution, recalling his own greatest moment in 1945:

> We are looking for a realization of the deepest possible kind – a realization which penetrates into the bones, into the marrow, into the mind, into the feeling, into the soul, and into the spirit – the realization ... of the fact that the basic characteristics of our Revolution cannot be any other than the principles and objectives which we proclaimed on August 17, 1945. ... People of Indonesia, awaken again now! Rise up again with the spirit of the Proclamation in your hearts![6]

Literature and art promoted a sense of Indonesian national identity, but it was the spread of radio, television, periodicals, and newspapers using the national language and reporting on national events that was most important. Newspaper circulation remained relatively small for such a large nation – not quite 500,000 copies in 1950 and just over 933,000 by 1956, by which time there were over 3.3 million copies of periodicals being printed. These numbers contracted during the economic chaos of the Guided Democracy period, but nevertheless the impact of such publications – each one often read by multiple people – was considerable.

The national election campaigns of the 1950s and the national role of political parties – for there were no regionally based parties – also cemented the idea that Indonesia was a single nation, even if the campaigns themselves exacerbated social and political conflict within that nation. The most remarkable indicators of the success of this national identity project, ironically, were the regionally based resistance movements of the late 1950s. Except for the 1950 secessionist Republic of South Maluku in Ambon, which was suppressed within months, the other regionally based dissident movements had a vision of themselves as encompassing the whole of Indonesia. The Darul Islam rebellion declared a *Negara Islam Indonesia*, that is, the Indonesian Islamic State, not some separatist Islamic enclave. The PRRI rebellion called itself *Pemerintah Revolusioner Republik Indonesia* – the Revolutionary Government of the Indonesian Republic, not a secessionist Sumatran state. So even the movements that sought to overthrow the existing regime in Indonesia in the 1950s did so in the name of the entire nation.

This sense of national identity was probably most at risk during Soeharto's New Order from 1966. Then a strict centralization of the state was implemented, with efforts at imposing ideological uniformity and a Javanese model of state, society, and culture. The national philosophy of *Pancasila* was declared

---

5 Quoted in Herbert Feith and Lance Castles (eds), *Indonesian Political Thinking, 1945–1965* (Ithaca, NY, and London: Cornell University Press, 1970), 80.

6 Quoted in ibid., 101.

the only acceptable philosophical foundation for any organization. Outer island areas were effectively garrisoned on behalf of Jakarta. Elections were held but carefully managed to ensure that Golkar always came out on top. So Indonesianness, *Pancasila*, the national army, national political parties and all the other things that were essential to the emerging national identity in the 1950s became identified in many people's minds with centralization, domination by Jakarta and by Javanese, discrediting of local identities and traditions and, indeed, with a repressive mode of government. When the Soeharto regime fell in 1998, it released a backlash which provoked more questions about national unity than had been raised since the time of the Revolution itself. In a nation that can never think of itself as federal, because of the Dutch association of federalism with colonialism in the days of the Revolution, one of the most decentralized systems of government in the world – federalism without the name – would spring up from the ruins of the New Order.

Yet the Soeharto regime also left a valuable legacy for unity in the form of literacy in the national language, an important element in Indonesian identity. Although we have no reliable figures, there can be no doubt that at the end of the Revolution in 1949, only a small minority of Indonesians could use the national Indonesian language (which is a developed form of Malay). This did not change until the 1970s oil boom enabled substantial government investment in education across the country. Literacy rates rose dramatically beyond those of colonial times, so that soon a majority of Indonesians – and eventually the vast majority – were literate. As part of this increasing literacy, facility in the national Indonesian language also spread, enhancing national unity. The 1971 census reported that still only 40.8 percent of Indonesians were literate in the national language – a quarter-century after the declaration of independence – but in 1980 the figure was 61.4 percent and in 1990 over 80 percent. The national language was at last truly national, powerfully enhancing the sense of Indonesian national identity.

The Philippines

In the Philippines, linguistic and cultural differences among ethnic groups compounded the task of inculcating a national Filipino identity and culture. The colonial experience hardly helped. The Spanish policy of pitting one group against another created stereotypes that fed animosities and distrust. The American colonial officials favored Filipino Christians to the detriment of their non-Christian counterparts. The public school system which provided Filipinos with the opportunity to participate in the celebrated 'Filipinization' of the government ironically taught children more about American nationalism and the heroic roles of the fathers of the American nation: more George Washington than Aguinaldo.

Filipino leaders later overturned these colonial policies by passing legislation that encouraged their constituents to commit to the Philippine Republic. Quezon centralized power in the presidential office and captured the loyalty of the political elite in national elections. To emphasize patriotism more widely, education was Filipinized in outlook, objectives, and teaching materials. The government encouraged the study of Filipino heroes, the celebration of national holidays, and the use of textbooks and supplementary readings written by Filipino authors and published in the Philippines. It sanctioned the revision of curricula to include more discussions about the archipelago in order to stimulate nationalism among the youth. In 1940, a 'National Language' based on Tagalog was declared to be the official language of the Philippines.

In the post-war period, after full independence, leaders continued to try to forge a truly 'Filipino' nation. Instead of wearing a suit like his predecessors, Magsaysay wore the traditional men's wear, the *Baron Tagalong*, on formal occasions. In 1956 – to the consternation of the Church – he sanctioned the passage of a law that required the inclusion of Rizal's *Noli Me Tangere* and *El Filibusterismo* in the national university curriculum. His successor, Quirino, supported the annual Republic Cultural Heritage Awards for outstanding scientists, artists, musicians, fiction writers, and historians. His 'Filipino First' policy encouraged Filipino participation in business. The Macapagal government, for its part, propagated the use of the Filipino language by using it in passports, diplomatic credentials, traffic signs, and stamps. The government also changed the date of 'Independence Day' from 4 July to 12 June in commemoration of General Emilio Aguinaldo's proclamation of independence in 1898 rather than the date when the United States formally transferred sovereignty (which was also the date of American independence).

By launching *Bagong Lipunan*, Marcos's Martial Law regime began a state-building and nation-building program intended to 'regenerate' Filipinos into civic-spirited, patriotic, disciplined, and vigorous citizens. The dictatorship promoted approved moral values through the mass media and undertook measures like the beautification of cities and *barrios*. It banned lewd films, acted against gambling, relocated pits for cock-fighting outside towns, prohibited ostentatious display of wealth, required character education to be taught in schools, and mandated seminars on moral values for public officials. The regime upheld the idea of nationhood by declaring a national flower, animal, dress, food, and the like. It mythologized the country's history and insisted that the pre-colonial past held the key to understanding Filipinoness. Administratively it even abandoned the Spanish term *barrio* for the smallest governmental unit in favor of the Tagalog term *barangay*.

The Marcos regime failed, however, to stimulate the form of nationalism that it sought. Its programs appeared farcical in the light of its bloody campaign to eliminate perceived enemies. In the 1980s a form of popular nationalism based on anti-Marcos sentiments grew within the populace. The governmentally approved form of Tagalog as the national language began to be rejected as something excessively didactic, formalistic, and sentimental. Instead a more colloquial and vibrant Tagalog arose as the language of *komiks*, movies, radio, tabloids, and television. It took on a casual and syncretic style and functioned as the counter-hegemonic language of 'nationalist' culture; it was prominent in the language of strikes, street demonstrations, semi-clandestine meetings, and protest publications.

Authors, artists, and musicians among others sustained the struggle against the oppressive regime, producing countervailing representations of the

Philippines and Filipinos to the versions in state propaganda. Unlike the officially approved, essentialized Filipino – allegedly descended from pre-colonial nobility – the Filipino of alternative art and literature was rebellious, earthy, and funny. It was this Filipino who outlasted the dictatorship and featured in the novels of Lualhati Bautista, the comic strips of Pol Medina, the flowering Tagalog movie industry, pop music, indigenous jewelry, even in T-shirts which proudly declared *Pilipino ako* (I am Filipino). Symbols of nationhood cropped up in the towering malls nationwide. Filipinoness was transformed into something to be consumed. It could even be transported, something important for an increasingly mobile Filipino labor force.

For lack of opportunities for employment at home, millions of Filipino laborers – construction workers, maids, nurses, and others – were forced to leave their families and seek work abroad. Often overworked and underpaid, overseas Filipino workers symbolized the new subaltern class of the Philippines. Through their letters and newspaper, radio, and television reports, Filipinos at home were kept informed of their overseas compatriots' alienation, suffering, and helplessness. Consequently the murder of the 'Japayuki' Maricris Sioson in Tokyo (1991), the execution for murder of the housemaid Flor Contemplacion in Singapore (1995), and the imprisonment of the teenage housemaid Sarah Balabagan in Abu Dhabi (1995) outraged Filipinos, as was reflected in the countless reports, television exposés, and demonstrations in front of embassies in Manila. Shared experiences moved the populace more than any government-legislated and expensive projects. Clearly the state could seek to build a sense of nationhood and shared culture, but it was the Filipino people who would ultimately decide their shape and content.

Diplomatic dimensions and regional conflicts

Burma

Burma's foreign policy after independence was officially neutralist, but 1950s geopolitics did not make neutralism easy. The greatest threat to post-colonial Burma coming from outside the country – as opposed to the internal threats to its very existence discussed earlier – was posed by Guomindang troops, who were on the losing side in the Chinese civil war. In 1949–50, some 2000 Guomindang soldiers migrated into Burma's Shan states, burning villages in the vicinity of Kengtung. In 1950, better-armed units began to arrive with their families and by 1952 some 12,000 troops were within Burmese borders, with American CIA support for incursions into the Communist-governed PRC. These incursions failed, but the Guomindang fighters stayed on in Burma as opium-smugglers and arms-dealers, taking full control of Kengtung by 1953 in the absence of effective Burmese government. With the consolidation of Communist rule in China and the beginning of the Korean War, U Nu's government worried that the presence of these anti-Beijing forces within its territory might provoke the PRC to invade Burma to forestall an American-backed threat from its southwest border region. Thus, China's internal politics and Cold War tensions with the United States directly affected the security of

Burma, which declared martial law in 22 of the 33 Shan subdivisions. But it was not until 1961 that the Burmese army, in concert with the PRC army, was able to expel Guomindang forces from their shared border region.

Burma's main security preoccupation was with internal ethnic minority resistance, as we have seen. Given the geopolitics of the area, however, such resistance groups often found refuge in the mountainous region along the borders of Burma, Thailand, China, and Laos. Here is located what is known as the 'Golden Triangle' – one of the world's main opium-producing regions. Karen resistance forces set up camps within or just beyond the Thai border, creating the potential for clashes if government troops pursued them on foreign soil and threatening the lives of civilians caught between the sides. Refugees fleeing from these war zones, notably Mons and Karens, sought to enter Thailand in the 1970s and 1980s. This stretched the capacity of local communities to care for the refugees and strained relations between Rangoon and Bangkok, which was reluctant to accommodate the human cost of Burma's internal conflicts.

Thailand and Indochina

Throughout the period covered in this chapter Thailand and Indochina were inextricably linked in terms of their foreign relations, which included not only the usual diplomatic ties (and squabbles) but also various patterns of military intervention and conflict as well. Until 1975, Thailand's role as a major American ally in the region and member of the Southeast Asia Treaty Organization (SEATO), as well as its perception of its own security interests, linked it to other non-Communist regimes while placing it in an adversarial position *vis-à-vis* the various Communist parties in and out of power.

Between 1954 and 1975, Bangkok was aligned with Saigon and Vientiane through their common anti-Communist stance and through their shared links to the United States. Thai combat troops fought in South Vietnam, with the bill being paid by the Americans. Thailand was home to a number of American military bases, some of which were used for bombing raids against Laos and North Vietnam. The American military and the CIA also used Thai for various covert and overt operations in Laos, since their ethnic and linguistic ties to the Lao meant that they could function effectively on the other side of the Mekong. The long history of Thai involvement in Lao affairs, combined with the threat of a Communist insurgency in a neighboring country, meant that Bangkok saw its support of American involvement in Laos as a natural extension of its own national defense. The links were particularly close in the late 1950s and early 1960s because of kinship ties between the Lao military strongman Phoumi Nosavan and the Thai leader Sarit Thanarat, but they outlasted both men and persisted to the end of the Indochina conflict in 1975. As has been mentioned, Thailand was also home to Rightist Cambodian forces opposing Sihanouk, which soured relations with Phnom Penh during the 1960s.

The Communist victories in 1975 meant that Thailand now faced three hostile Communist-ruled neighbors to the east, and relations were almost completely frozen for the next few years. For a time Bangkok used the strategy of shutting its border with Laos to punish the new regime, which was also provoking a mass exodus of refugees whom Thailand had to take in. Refugees from the *Khmer Rouge* began to trickle in as well, causing a considerable humanitarian burden for the Thai. Although the American bases were shut down after the end of the war in Vietnam, thus removing a major source of hostility between Bangkok and Hanoi, the return to power of the military in 1976 and the rising strength of the CPT insurgency inside Thailand meant that the likelihood of real détente was slim.

For the first few years after the fall of South Vietnam, Hanoi's main preoccupation was with Cambodia and China rather than Thailand. The Vietnamese leadership had perhaps held onto the hope that once the *Khmer Rouge* were in power, the three countries of Indochina could restore some semblance of the fraternal ties which had existed until 1954, but this was not to be. What came to be called the 'special relationship' between Vietnam and Laos was strong and relatively free of tensions, but the stability in that relationship was outweighed by the looming crisis between Vietnam and Cambodia. At the same time, the steady degradation of Hanoi's relations with Beijing – due both to Vietnam's treatment of its Chinese minority and to its problems with Democratic Kampuchea, which enjoyed a warm relationship with the PRC – meant that the Vietnamese were facing potential conflicts on two different fronts.

When Vietnam decided that the only way to end Cambodian provocations was to invade, the fall of the Democratic Kampuchea government and the establishment of the People's Republic of Kampuchea in January 1979 changed the power equation within the region. Vietnam and its ally in Phnom Penh now found themselves opposed by a coalition which included the United States, the PRC, and ASEAN, most notably Thailand as the 'front-line state'. The latter country became the main base for the forces allied against the Vietnamese and the Vietnamese-installed Cambodian government while also housing large numbers of Cambodian refugees in camps along the border. Hanoi now had its long-desired fraternal regime in Phnom Penh, but the three states of Indochina found themselves severely isolated within the region, their main friends being the USSR and its European allies. Laos, although it never broke diplomatic ties with Beijing, was forced to choose sides in the Sino-Vietnamese conflict and sided with Hanoi. One important ramification of this decision was that the CPT, which remained closely linked to China, was effectively expelled from Lao territory, where it had established bases and places of refuge.

The Cambodia conflict was a major development in the history of ASEAN, as the organization became directly involved through its support for the anti-Vietnamese resistance coalition. Not all members were equally vocal in their stance against Hanoi, and Indonesia in particular tended to be more sympathetic – a fruit of long-standing mutual respect, particularly between the Vietnamese and Indonesian militaries, on the grounds that they alone among Asian nations had won independence through armed revolution. Ultimately Jakarta's push for a resolution of the conflict allowed ASEAN as a group to take initiatives in this direction, notably preliminary talks among the warring Cambodian factions. Nevertheless, Vietnam's perception of the organization during the 1980s was, not surprisingly, quite hostile; it had always tended to view ASEAN as little better than a reworked version of SEATO, and the group's cooperation with the United States and China – Hanoi's two main enemies at the time – seemed merely to confirm this view.

By the late 1980s, however, the civil war in Cambodia was inching towards a solution, and Vietnam was beginning phased withdrawals of its forces. At the same time, the transition in 1988 in Bangkok from a government dominated by the military to one composed of elected civilians under Chatichai also had direct implications for Thailand's relations with Indochina. Shortly after taking office, Chatichai famously declared his intention to 'turn the battlefield into a market-place' by promoting trade and investment with Thailand's Communist neigh-bors. In the final months of General Prem's regime Thailand and Laos had actually fought a brief border war over three disputed villages, and tensions had been high, but by the turn of the decade the tone of relations was changing for the better. Thai investors poured into Laos and Cambodia and began to explore opportunities in Vietnam as well. More importantly, the resolution of the Cambodian conflict would end the polarization of Southeast Asia between ASEAN and Indochina and pave the way for all three countries (along with Burma/Myanmar) to enter the organization over the next few years.

The conflicts which tore mainland Southeast Asia apart during this period are sometimes rather dismissively characterized as 'proxy wars' among the great powers, but such a perspective is both oversimplified and lacking in historical perspective. The prominent role of external forces cannot be denied; the early rivalry before 1975 between the United States on one hand and the USSR and PRC on the other, and the later marriage of convenience between Washington and Beijing against Moscow were clearly played out within the region. The Southeast Asian countries were never, however, mere pawns in a global chess game. The old struggle between Thai and Vietnamese for domination of the lands in between reappeared all too clearly after 1945, and particularly after the departure of the French. The Vietnamese revolutionaries' view of Indochina as a single anti-colonial struggle remained a powerful vision for more than three decades after the end of French rule, and the allegations of an 'Indochinese Federation' comprising Hanoi and two loyal but subordinate governments fuelled the anti-Communist propaganda machine in more than one country.

Thailand, meanwhile, effectively revived its pre-colonial zone of influence in Cambodia and Laos; even though it no longer enjoyed suzerainty there, with American backing it could – to some degree at least – project its power militar-ily into that zone. China, which had been the principal bogeyman of the Thai ruling elite since the establishment of the PRC in 1949, was now shifting to become more an ally than an adversary, while Vietnam became the main enemy. The resurgence of these historical animosities would pose a major challenge to Indochina's efforts to integrate into ASEAN until the resolution of the Cambodian conflict left Hanoi in a less hostile position *vis-à-vis* its non-social-ist neighbors.

Indonesia and Malaysia

From the beginning of its independence, Indonesia adhered to a foreign policy described as 'free and active', but implementations of that principle varied substantially, from non-alignment to radical Leftism to pro-Western anti-Communism – and almost invariably involved its neighbors, particularly Malaya/Malaysia. In January 1952 a secret aid agreement was signed with the United States that committed Indonesia to the defense of the 'free world': when this became known, the government fell. But changing political circumstances soon led to less fastidious interpretations of the 'free and active' principle. In 1955, Indonesia hosted the Bandung Conference of non-aligned states, which catapulted the nation to international prominence. By this time the PRC was abandoning its animosity toward the non-Communist or neutralist states of Asia, no longer regarding them as implicitly hostile. So China agreed to attend Bandung and while there signed the dual-nationality treaty mentioned above, resolving the nationality status of Chinese in Indonesia. Except for the divided Koreas, Israel, South Africa, and Outer Mongolia, all the major independent states of Africa and Asia were represented at Bandung. A who's who of Asian leaders attended, including Zhou Enlai, Nehru, Sihanouk, Pham Van Dong, U Nu, Muhammad Ali Bogra, and Nasser.

Bandung's final communiqué supported Indonesia's claim to Papua, on which the Dutch were disinclined to compromise. Indeed, they were working towards encouraging a separate Papuan independence movement with local support. This challenged Indonesia's claims, however, and inflamed its nationalism. In 1956 the Indonesian government unilaterally abrogated the meaningless Netherlands-Indonesian Union and repudiated 85 percent of the nation's debt accepted in the 1949 independence agreements, claiming that this represented Dutch expenditures while trying to defeat the Revolution. The Indonesian political public was delighted with these nationalist measures. The UN, however, failed to pass a resolution calling on the Dutch to negotiate with Indonesia over Papua late in 1957. This led directly to takeovers of Dutch firms in Indonesia by PKI and PNI unions. The military then took charge of these enterprises, so that the Dutch economic position in Indonesia was severely damaged and the military gained its own source of revenue, increasing its dominance in the country. The Indonesian economy suffered, particularly since the takeover of the critically important Dutch-owned Royal Mail Steam Packet Company (KPM) was handled so badly that many of the ships escaped and Indonesia's inter-island shipping was handicapped for many years.

Such developments increased outer island dissatisfaction with Jakarta and spurred dissident regionally based movements such as the PRRI rebellion, discussed above. We noted there that administrations in the United States, Taiwan, Singapore, Malaya, the Philippines, and South Korea offered support to PRRI, provoking Indonesian anger. So Indonesia's list of enemies – all, it should be noted, in the American or British sphere of influence – was growing. In 1958 the Guomindang was banned in Indonesia and enterprises owned by pro-Taiwan Chinese were taken over by the army.

Indonesia broke off diplomatic relations with the Netherlands in 1960 over the failure to hand over Papua and now began to contemplate a military campaign there. For the military aid it needed, Indonesia turned to the USSR, which was doing what it could to increase its influence in Indonesia to counter both the United States and the PRC. Thus Indonesia became increasingly a site for triangular USA-USSR-PRC competition, each of these having its local friends or allies. The Soviet Premier Nikita Khrushchev visited Jakarta in January 1960, followed by a visit by General Nasution to Moscow a year later. These visits produced Soviet credits and loans for arms purchases. With the Indonesian military increasingly dependent on the USSR, the new American administration of John F. Kennedy attempted to staunch radicalism and counter Soviet influence in Indonesia by pressing the Dutch into surrendering Papua.

With American mediation and pressure, in 1962 the Dutch transferred sovereignty over Papua to the UN, which turned the territory over to Indonesia the following year. There had not been even a gesture towards ascertaining what Papuans might have wanted. This handover produced a low-level but continuing anti-Indonesian resistance movement in Irian Barat or Irian Jaya, as Papua was then known. The Americans thought that they might now have sufficient prestige and influence to divert Indonesia from its increasingly radical politics and to bring about economic stabilization and rationality. But there were too many domestic players whose interests were served by radicalism: Sukarno with the revolutionary rhetoric that cemented his centrality in a radicalized nation; the military with its dominance under martial law, its income from confiscated enterprises, and its military aid budgets; PKI with its capacity to mobilize masses of people; and many others for whom radical nationalism provided opportunities and encouraged pride in their nation.

Developments in Indonesia's immediate neighborhood soon produced a crisis that propelled the nation into new international adventurism and domestic radicalism. The British still retained sovereignty over Singapore, Brunei, and Sarawak and wanted to get out of these colonial commitments. The Federation of Malaya could hardly just absorb Singapore, however logical that might look on a map. The problem was the issue of ethnic balance, as we have seen. Indonesia had never regarded Malaya as truly independent, since it had not fought for and won its independence like Indonesia and allowed the British to retain a prominent role there. Malaya and Singapore had assisted the PRRI rebels as well. Now, in the radical atmosphere of the time, Jakarta also took the view that the proposed state of Malaysia would be a neo-colonial outpost on Indonesia's doorstep. Indonesian intelligence indeed had links to the leader of the brief Brunei revolt against incorporation into Malaysia, Shaikh A. M. Azahari, who had been in Indonesia during the Revolution.

In early 1963 Sukarno's radical Foreign Minister Subandrio defined Indonesia's attitude towards Malaysia as 'confrontation' (*konfrontasi*) and thereby posed a diplomatic challenge for the Americans. The United States was becoming more deeply entangled in the Vietnam War and was locked into a Cold War worldview that perceived a 'free world' (which included allies that were certainly not paragons of freedom) in opposition to a 'Communist bloc' (which, in the midst of the growing Sino-Soviet split, was in fact no longer a 'bloc'). The British were allies and Malaya/Malaysia was clearly non-Communist and seen as a barrier to the threat of southward expansion of Communism in Southeast Asia, so the United States was committed to support the British plans and the Malaysian state. Yet the Americans also hoped to win Indonesia away from its radicalism, its dependence on the USSR and its friendship with the

PRC, particularly by achieving a settlement of the Papua issue. Sukarno and others indeed desired American aid, and seemed willing to contemplate some sort of compromise, but had no intention of dancing to America's tune in world affairs.

The Philippines under Macapagal complicated all this by claiming sovereignty over Sabah on the basis of historic links. In mid-1963 there were Malayan-Philippines-Indonesian meetings that envisaged some sort of loose confederation to be called 'Maphilindo' – a nonsensical solution to irreconcilable positions. A possible compromise was raised when Malaya said that it would hold a test of opinion in Sarawak and Sabah before bringing them into the new Malaysia. Sukarno seemed inclined to accept this compromise. Brunei was no longer an issue, for it had declared in July 1963 that it would remain out of the new state – and enjoy its massive oil revenues on its own.

The PRC opposed Malaysia. With the Sino-Soviet split beyond reconciliation and American involvement in Southeast Asia growing, the PRC saw itself facing the USSR to the north and west and pro-American states on the east (South Korea, Japan, Taiwan) and south (Philippines, South Vietnam, Thailand). When the Americans and Russians signed the nuclear test ban treaty in August 1963, the PRC saw a sign that the United States and USSR – despite their own animosities – might conspire to contain China. So the last thing the Chinese wanted was either another pro-American state in the form of Malaysia or for Indonesia to abandon its leftward swing. Within Indonesia, the PRC's ally, the PKI, was meanwhile at loggerheads with the USSR-supported military. Thus, Indonesia's domestic political triangle of Sukarno, the military, and the PKI temporarily mirrored a dangerous three-cornered diplomatic contest among the United States, USSR, and PRC.

In September 1963 – in the midst of the increasingly radical Indonesian domestic scene described above – Malaysia came into existence. In a sense, all the main Indonesian players were relieved, for this move by Malaysia was taken as an insult and removed alternatives to a radical posture. Sukarno could again mobilize his people in the name of ongoing revolution, the military could look forward to increased budgets and military aid from the USSR, and PKI could attempt to move towards power on the wave of radicalism. The British embassy in Jakarta and several staff houses were immediately burned down, provoking a retaliatory attack on the Indonesian embassy in Kuala Lumpur. Sukarno declared that he would 'gobble Malaysia raw' (*ganyang Malaysia*, commonly but inaccurately translated 'crush Malaysia').

Indonesia now swung unequivocally into an anti-American diplomatic position, just as the nation swung domestically into the radicalism that, as noted above, was exploited effectively by PKI and, in the end, proved the undoing of Sukarno's ramshackle 'Guided Democracy'. The relatively low-level war in the jungles of Borneo/Kalimantan, however, was going poorly for the Indonesians. There they faced Malaysian and British Commonwealth forces, who dominated military encounters. In these circumstances, the Indonesian army began to feel that the greatest threat it faced was not Malaysia or the United States or possibly reduced budgets, but PKI.

The Americans made a last effort to reclaim Indonesia from its radical path, to no avail. In late 1963–early 1964 the Kennedy administration arranged an Indonesia-Malaysia ceasefire and tried to get Malaysian-Indonesian-Philippines negotiations started, but the effort came to nothing. Sukarno announced in March 1964 that the United States could 'go to hell' with its aid. During 1965 Indonesia withdrew from the UN and Western-linked international organizations (IMF, Interpol, World Bank). Soviet support of the Indonesian military continued, which the PRC tried to counter by offering to arm a force of 'workers and peasants' – code for PKI followers. In his annual Independence Day address on 17 August 1965, Sukarno announced an anti-imperialist Jakarta–Phnom Penh–Hanoi–Beijing–Pyongyang axis.

When 'Guided Democracy' collapsed in the bloody domestic events of 1965–66, Sukarno's foreign policy collapsed with it, almost overnight. The emerging Soeharto regime recognized the high costs of radicalism and acknowledged that *de facto* Western dominance outweighed USSR or PRC influence in Southeast Asia, and quickly aligned itself with the stronger and richer side. Confrontation against Malaysia was abandoned and Soeharto made it clear that Indonesia would seek reconciliation with the non-Communist world, albeit within a formally non-aligned stance. Massive Japanese and Western aid soon began to flow; Indonesia rejoined the UN, IMF, and other international organizations; inflation was brought under control; and overseas investment resumed.

In 1967 Soeharto was one of the main motivators of the creation of the Association of Southeast Asian Nations (ASEAN), the main purpose of which at this stage was to rehabilitate Indonesia as a responsible regional actor. Indonesia's welcome amongst non-Communist nations was symbolized by the visit of US President Richard Nixon in 1969. Indonesia's 1975 invasion and conquest of East Timor were tacitly welcomed by Western powers. President Ronald Reagan visited in 1986. In a regional and world environment in which the Communist side prevailed in Vietnam, Cambodia, and Laos in 1975 and the radical Islamist Ayatollah Khomeini won power in Iran in 1979, Indonesia's pro-developmental, anti-Leftist and non-Islamist government readily won Western support. The Soeharto regime's abysmal human rights record occasionally caused diplomatic difficulties. In the period 1977–80, the American President Jimmy Carter's emphasis on human rights issues led to Indonesia releasing many of the 55,000–100,000 political prisoners it had held without trial since 1965–66. But larger geopolitical issues always prevailed and Western aid continued to grow.

Vietnam's invasion of Cambodia at the end of 1978 to overthrow the Pol Pot regime precipitated a major diplomatic initiative by Indonesia. As we have seen, the Indonesians took the lead in the 1980s to negotiate a settlement in Cambodia.

The Philippines

After the grant of its independence, the Republic of the Philippines pursued a foreign policy resting upon a determination to continue a close relationship with the United States; sympathy towards the independent aspirations of colonies, especially those in Asia; and cooperation with the UN. In 1946 Roxas secured the American funding needed for his administration by manipulating the Philippine Congress to pass the Bell Trade Act which provided American businessmen with parity rights, and then signing the Military Bases Agreement that guaranteed a long-term American military presence in the archipelago. In 1947 he signed the Military Assistance Pact which authorized the Americans to supply and advise the Philippines military. Four years later, to demonstrate their united defense against any external attack, the Philippines and the United States signed a Mutual Defense Treaty, cementing their proclaimed 'special relationship'.

The much-touted 'special relationship' was, however, illusory. The Bell Trade Act profited American businessmen and Filipino exporters alone, perpetuating landlordism that defied the intentions of the Philippines state. If an external aggressor attacked the Philippines, the United States would not automatically come to its rescue: only a declaration of war by the American Congress could unleash the American military against an invader, so the archipelago could not depend on the Mutual Defense Treaty. The American military presence caused recurring problems. In 1964 an American sentry shot a Filipino boy at Clark Field; in the following year a soldier killed a Filipino fisherman at the Olongapo Naval Base. American military personnel who harmed or killed Filipinos inside, or indeed outside, the bases remained outside the Philippine justice system, which angered and frustrated Filipinos. Numerous renegotiations of the terms of the Military Bases Agreement ensued, but the issue of jurisdiction was only resolved when the Philippine Senate refused to renew the agreement in 1991.

Although aligned with the United States, the Philippines nonetheless rhetorically supported the colonies struggling for independence, regardless of their political ideologies. It sent delegates to congresses concerned with social and political issues like those held in New Delhi (1949), Baguio (1950), and Bandung (1955). The country signed treaties of friendship with Indonesia, India, and South Vietnam. In 1954 the Magsaysay government was active in setting up the Southeast Asia Treaty Organization (SEATO) which bound the Philippines, Australia, France, New Zealand, Thailand, Pakistan, the United States, and the United Kingdom to stand against Communism in Southeast Asia. But the organization was a failure, unable to secure the cooperation of neighboring countries in the region. Subsequent efforts by Filipino leaders to establish closer regional ties also fizzled out. The 1961 Association of Southeast Asia (ASA) launched by Garcia and leaders of Malaya and Thailand existed only on paper. The 1963 idea of an organization among the 'Malay' countries Malaysia, the Philippines, and Indonesia (Maphilindo), was – as noted above – a nonsense.

By 1963 diplomatic relations among the aforementioned countries failed when – as noted above – Sarawak and Sabah were amalgamated within the British-sponsored Federation of Malaysia. The Philippines suggested that the World Court resolve the issue of Sabah, but Malaysia refused this. Embassies were withdrawn and relations were officially severed. This impasse was only resolved in 1966, after Marcos was assured that Malaysia was not averse to taking the Sabah territorial claim to the World Court or to peaceful arbitration. In the following year, foreign ministers of the Philippines, Indonesia, Malaysia, Singapore, and Thailand revived the idea of a regional organization and established the Association of Southeast Asian Nations (ASEAN) which, mindful of SEATO's mistakes, carefully steered clear of regional military collaboration. Progressively, Philippine relations within the region improved, leading to significant cultural, social, and economic cooperation. For the first time in several centuries, the Philippines were facing westward to neighbors in Southeast Asia more than eastward to the United States and Latin America.

13

Boom and Bust in Southeast Asia *c.*1990–2008

Introduction

As the sections on individual countries below will make clear, for much of the 1990s most Southeast Asian nations prospered more than ever before. As a result of economic growth, many of the people of Southeast Asia were lifted out of poverty, education spread, a middle class emerged, and Southeast Asia became more urbanized. This region, which had always been open to influences from around the world, saw the beginnings of even more intensive globalization in these years. Then came the financial and economic crisis that originated in Southeast Asia in the late 1990s. After a decade of mixed results in recovering from this, Southeast Asia was hit by another financial and economic crisis – this time one originating in the West.

The years of economic boom (1990–1997)

Thailand

In the early 1990s Thailand was one of the most salient Southeast Asian examples of a boom economy. The policies of industrialization and emphasis on production for export reaped large dividends and helped to raise the country's GDP significantly. The Thai economy was growing across the board, including heavy industry and international finance, two sectors which were relative latecomers on the scene but which made up for lost time. Another major growth industry was property, particularly in metropolitan Bangkok. Not only were skyscrapers proliferating within the capital, but also housing developments were mushrooming all around the city as the middle and upper classes peopled the suburbs, many of which had been little more than villages only a decade or so before.

Wealth produces consumerism, of course, and Thailand was no exception. Consumer goods proliferated around the country; televisions and video recorders could be found even in fairly remote villages. The expansion of industry necessitated the expansion of electricity production, which had a 'trickle-down effect' for many rural areas. The Thai had never been isolated, as we have seen in previous chapters, and the country's many linkages to the rest of the world meant that it experienced the full force of globalization, both the positive and the negative aspects. Poverty was by no means eliminated in either urban or rural areas. Nevertheless, the contrast between the two grew greater, with cities filled with malls and Mercedes-Benzes – as well as slums, particularly in Bangkok – but also with rural migrants earning wages which were low, but still better than they could have earned in their home villages.

One of the most important phenomena of this period was the proliferation of NGOs. These groups had their roots in the democratic interlude of 1973–76, when activism among students, farmers, and workers became a powerful political force. The subsequent years of military rule dampened the activities of NGOs without destroying them, and after the return to civilian-led government in 1988 they began to flourish again. They were particularly active in rural areas, where villagers were mobilized to protest against large dam projects, the loss of forest and farmland to commercial agriculture, failed plans for economic development, and other causes. In 1996 the Assembly of the Poor came into existence, linking rural organizations with slum dwellers and other urban-based movements. This flourishing of civil society permanently transformed Thailand and raised serious questions about the socio-economic policies being pursued by the government, as well as the impact of globalization in general.

A different response to globalization came in the form of new religious movements, beginning in the 1970s with the appearance of Santi Asoke and Dhammakaya. The first is a sect which broke off from mainstream Buddhism by rejecting the authority of the *Sangha* (monkhood) leadership, while the second promoted meditation and particular forms of Buddhist devotion. During the 1980s and 1990s both groups attracted large numbers of followers who gave lavish donations. Along with the proliferation of spirit mediums and heightened devotion to the Mahayana Buddhist deity Guanyin (normally worshipped by Chinese but not usually by followers of Theravada), the popularity of these new movements has been widely seen as a response to globalization. On the one hand, prosperity brought both the commodification of religion and closer linkages between donations and blessings. On the other, there was heightened anxiety about cultural change and the possibility that prosperity would not last forever, thus encouraging people to pay more attention to spiritual matters. This tendency would be heightened after the crisis of 1997.

Indonesia

Indonesia's annual growth remained around 5 percent in the early 1990s. Interest rates remained high, however, and inflation was not far behind rates of economic growth. Many firms sought loans overseas where interest rates were lower, thus building overseas debt that would contribute to the economic crisis of 1997–98. Public and private external debt was over USD 84 billion by 1992, but that probably underestimated private debt; the true figure was probably more like USD 100 billion. Indonesia was also facing a more competitive environment as opportunities for foreign investors opened up elsewhere – sometimes in places with lower costs, less corruption, less red tape, and more legal certainty. Nevertheless, annual economic growth reached 8.1 percent in 1995, 7.5 percent in 1996, and nearly 8 percent in 1997, on the eve of economic disaster. The Soeharto family and their cronies became immensely rich. Economists were impressed, one declaring Indonesia to be 'Southeast Asia's emerging giant'.[1]

Although the economy was in fact teetering on the brink of collapse, the fruits of three decades of development were evident. Jakarta – once a city of ramshackle houses, skeleton-like unfinished buildings, and chaotic traffic – became a metropolis of gleaming skyscrapers, high-class hotels (through whose windows economists and international agencies observed the country and declared it good), burgeoning middle-class suburbs, still-chaotic traffic, and slums barely out of sight off the main streets. Its population soared past 8 million, heading for 13 million by 2004.

Across the countryside, there was more electricity, more educational opportunity, more literacy, more health support, more urbanization, and – crucially – fewer babies. Population nevertheless continued to grow. The total national population in the late 1990s is not entirely clear, since the census of 2000 was carried out in the face of many difficulties. That census reported 203.5 million Indonesians, but the true figure was probably more like 230 million.

The emergence of an Indonesian middle class was a crucial fruit of Soeharto-era development. Agreeing on a definition of just who was in this middle class and then counting them proved elusive, but it was beyond question that there was a new and significant social group in Indonesia. They lived in cities (Figure 31) where they owned their own houses, drove cars, had salaried jobs, sent their children to the best schools they could afford, read books and newspapers, and watched television.

The middle class also participated in the increase of Islamic religiosity visible across the Islamic world. Public displays of religiosity, Islamic dress styles (notably increasing use of the headscarf by women), growing numbers going on the pilgrimage to Mecca, book stores specializing in Islamic inspirational publications, and the emergence of popular Islamic televangelists all reflected the deepening Islamization of the middle class.

Malaysia

Malaysia's New Economic Policy, introduced after the 1969 riots, had significant social impacts, among them the urbanization, better education, and economic advancement of Malays. By 1990 the officially registered population of Kuala Lumpur had passed 1 million and by 2005 it was 1.5 million. Shah

---

[1] Hal Hill, *The Indonesian Economy Since 1966: Southeast Asia's emerging giant* (Cambridge and New York: Cambridge University Press, 1996). Hill's second edition (2000) dropped this subtitle.

Figure 31 Modern Surabaya

Alam with the neigboring Putrajaya capital area then had a population of some 4.7 million, Johor Baharu was over 3 million, Kota Kinabalu was nearly 3 million, and several other urban areas had surpassed the 1 million mark. By the early twenty-first century, 70 percent of the population was urban and nearly 90 percent of adults were literate. An important demographic change was the increasing presence of foreigners willing to take on the jobs that the developing economy required, but that neither Chinese nor Malays were interested in taking themselves. Hundreds of thousands of temporary Indian, Pakistani, Indonesian, Filipino, and Thai laborers in building sites, factories, and plantations complicated Malaysia's already-complex ethnic environment. Among these migrants a significant number were illegal and unregistered, and their presence contributed to criminality and other social ills in Malaysia's growing cities.

The growing urban middle class was more heavily Malay and poverty among Malays, formerly a phenomenon particularly noticeable in rural areas, was diminishing. By 1990 those below the official poverty line in peninsular Malaysia had been reduced from nearly half the population in 1971 to just 15 percent. A higher rate of population growth among the Malays meant that they were a growing proportion of the population, reaching nearly 60 percent in the 1990s. Mahathir's government-sponsored projects contributed to industrialization and modernization. Exports – particularly in electronics and semi-conductors – grew dramatically. In the booming 1990s, the annual GDP growth rate remained of the order of 9–10 percent. In 1991 the government announced the policy of 'Vision 2020', aiming to make Malaysia a fully developed economy by 2020.

In this changing social environment, UMNO faced significant political challenges from the Islamist PAS. Mahathir's (Figure 32) response was to attempt to 'out-Islamize' his opponents, harnessing Islamic – which is to say mainly Malay – identity to economic development, modernization, and (of course) UMNO. As was also true in Indonesia, there was a dramatic increase in the number of mosques and prayer houses, Islamic study groups, Islamic (but not other) religious broadcasts, and all forms of public religiosity. Islamic banking and Islamic (i.e., Middle Eastern) architectural styles spread. The government became more prominent internationally in its support of Islamic political causes around the world. Other Islamist groups developed and were carefully watched by the government. Islam-inspired radical and terrorist groups from the Philippines and Indonesia found it possible to seek refuge from their own governments in Malaysian territory. In such an environment, many non-Muslim Malaysians felt that they were, more than ever, second-class citizens. Set against this trend, however, was another that sought a more inclusive *Bangsa Malaysia* (Malaysian – not just Malay – nationality) that would accommodate other ethnic groups and traditions, something implied in Mahathir's 'Vision 2020'. Malaysia's future social, ethnic, and cultural development lurked somewhere in the tension between these visions.

Figure 32   Mahathir Mohamad, 2006
Andy Wong/AP/Press Association Images

Vietnam

Vietnam pushed ahead with the economic reforms launched under *doi moi* ('renovation', i.e., economic reform) in the 1980s. Although disagreements remained within the leadership as to the proper pace and scope for moving toward a market economy, reforms proceeded. Even before the lifting of the last restrictions of the international embargo in 1994, the country had opened its doors to foreign investors, and foreign ventures proliferated. Like China, Vietnam faced challenges in developing both the physical infrastructure and the legal environment for investment projects, and it was a long, slow process. Once embarked along this path, however, it was difficult if not impossible to turn back, and the leadership recognized this fact. Moreover, the benefits were clear: a steady increase in GDP, particularly through tourism and exports, both of commodities like rice and coffee and of products manufactured in foreign-owned factories. While socialist ideology required the preservation of a state economic sector, it was greatly diversified through the so-called equitization of state-owned enterprises, bringing in outside capital without completely transforming them into private companies. At the same time, the legitimacy of a private sector was acknowledged, first tacitly and gradually more explicitly.

Doi moi also brought an influx of foreign culture, not only from the West but also from Japan and South Korea, particularly through music and television programs. Although restrictions on private satellite dishes were in place, these increasingly became a dead letter, and Vietnamese of all ages enjoyed wider access to information and entertainment from around the world. Direct connections to the Internet were, however, very limited during this period and even e-mail service only began in the mid-1990s. Vietnamese also began to travel more widely overseas, and growing numbers of students headed to the West for undergraduate and graduate degrees.

Figure 33 Living on the Perfume river, Hue, Vietnam

Singapore

In the 1990s the city-state of Singapore continued its growth and transformation into one of the world's most modern cities. One indicator tells much: this is the only city in Southeast Asia where you can drink the tap water safely. Singapore boasted the most modern communication facilities, high-quality roads, fancy shopping malls, top-class restaurants and cheap food courts, high-rise office buildings, excellent public transport, good schools and universities, and a high level of public safety. The decision to move the population into high-rise apartment blocks made it possible for Singapore to reserve a remarkable amount of its limited land area for public parks and green spaces. As a consequence, Singapore became not only one of the most modern cities in the world but also one of the greenest. As noted in the previous chapter, the distribution of wealth in Singapore as measured by its Gini coefficient was (and remains) relatively inegalitarian, but government policies existed to ameliorate such differentials, notably the provision of inexpensive housing. There were clear limits placed upon any form of political dissent, which concerned intellectuals and those with experience of lands of greater individual freedom, but the majority of the populace accepted these as reasonable prices to pay for stability and security under PAP government.

Brunei

Brunei continued to float economically and socially on its sea of oil and gas in the booming 1990s. Efforts to diversify its economy met with little success. Its 330-odd thousand people enjoyed a high GDP per capita (at around USD 18,000 in 1995), paid no income tax, and had free education and health care. The adult literacy rate by the mid-1990s was approaching 90 percent. About 70 percent of the population was Malay and Muslim, and Brunei was a self-consciously Islamic state under the absolute authority of its Sultan. About 13 percent of the population was Buddhist, 10 percent Christian, and 10 percent followers of other – including local – beliefs; the religious activities of non-Islamic communities were carefully monitored.

The Philippines

In the 1990s the Philippines appeared to have overcome the difficulties wrought by the Marcos dictatorship and was well on its way towards full economic recovery. Advised by the IMF and World Bank, the Fidel Ramos government embarked on a liberalization program that included trade, foreign exchange and investment, and bound the country to the international, pro-free-trade architecture of APEC, AFTA, and GATT. In 1993 the state reinvigorated the Philippines Central Bank which was burdened with USD 12 billion of accumulated debt. The two rival stock exchanges merged to facilitate accelerated foreign investment and bring about stability in the Philippine bourse. Economic growth of 5–7 percent per annum ensued from these measures from 1994 to 1997. The unemployment rate steadily declined to 8.5 percent.

Through significant capital investments, the government also sought to upgrade the country's deteriorating infrastructure. It successfully put an end to the daily 8 to 12-hour power outages in Manila that were crippling business operations. The telecommunications sector was liberalized, allowing for the entrance of new providers that increased teledensity nationwide from 1.01 landline phones for every hundred persons in 1992 to 3.88 in 1999. Lower-income groups took advantage of the more accessible and affordable mobile phone service. By 2000 mobile phone subscriptions reached 6.5 million, more than double the landline counterpart. The liberalization of telecommunications served as a model for the shipping and airline industries that afforded consumers numerous transportation choices and more control of their expenditures. Financial optimism abounded: the country appeared to have kicked 'the sick man of Asia' label.

Laos

Like its Vietnamese socialist 'older brother', Laos continued with the economic policies begun in the 1980s. Although the country had less to offer in terms of skilled labor or natural resources, it did its best to market itself as a destination for foreign investment. Infrastructural issues were more serious than in Vietnam, and joint ventures remained fewer in number and size. One of the country's main exports was power, generated through hydroelectric projects and transmitted to Thailand – even though large portions of Laos still had no electricity. Overall, the Lao economy remained heavily linked to, and dependent on, Thailand. In particular, virtually all of its consumer goods were imported from across the Mekong.

Cambodia

Cambodia was in full recovery mode after the end of decades of civil war, and it also sought to reconnect to the world through trade and investment. Like Laos, it had poor infrastructure and few resources. Also like Laos, it was most successful in attracting Thai business, along with investors from Japan and South Korea, among others. One key development was the proliferation of textile factories, for which Cambodia provided a ready labor supply. Foreign aid of all kinds remained a crucial source of support, as indeed was the case in Vietnam and Laos as well.

Burma

Burma did not share in the developmental boom seen in much of the rest of Southeast Asia in the 1990s. Its economic lethargy worsened when creditors began to seek payment for outstanding loans in the late 1980s. The government's inability to generate adequate revenue through decades of economic mismanagement and the freezing of further loans by the World Bank, the IMF, and the Asian Development Bank deepened the country's financial crisis. Efforts to jump-start reform and modernization programs were also crippled by economic sanctions imposed by the international community in response to the government's violent repression of the anti-government demonstrations of 1988.

International consumer boycott campaigns continued throughout the early 1990s when it became clear that a political transition from military rule would not follow as a result of the 1990 elections. Heeding Aung San Suu Kyi's call to apply economic pressure through sanctions, the United States and several other countries banned all new investment after 1997. This isolation from the rest of the world meant that the Asian financial crisis of 1997–98 did not affect Burma's economy as directly as those of its neighbors, but access to regional economic support slowed considerably. Some foreign investment did flow into the energy sector but most foreign aid was directed towards humanitarian relief, which had little effect on providing jobs or stimulating growth.

The politics of the boom years

The international context c.1990–1997

For most of the 1990s, Southeast Asia's international context was dominated by (a) positive economic conditions and (b) the end of the Cold War. The collapse of the USSR left the United States as the sole superpower, which encouraged democratization movements in some places. In East Asia, Taiwan and South Korea continued on their democratization path, but not all Southeast Asian states were similarly inspired. In many respects the 1990s down to the crisis of 1997 were good in Southeast Asia, especially for the growing middle classes. Few could imagine how dramatically their world would change before the decade was out.

Burma

The end of the Cold War brought no improvement in Burma's international standing. Western governments shifted their policy priorities from resisting Communism to promoting human rights and democracy, but Burma appeared in an even worse light in that new context.

In May 1990, multi-party elections were held. Despite much of the National League for Democracy (NLD) leadership being under house arrest, the League received 59.9 percent of the vote, winning 80.8 percent of the constituencies contested. Following the elections, the NLD and external supporters announced that the party should now be allowed to form the legitimate government of Burma, based on its impressive election results. The military rejected these claims on the grounds that the elections had been to determine the makeup of the constituent assembly to draft a new constitution, not to arrange a transfer of power, and this had been agreed upon by all participating parties. The military government's insistence on the NLD's pre-election agreement to this arrangement was regarded by many observers as merely a scheme to keep General Ne Win and the military in power. SLORC refused to give up power to the NLD, confounding expectations of international observers who favored Aung San Suu Kyi and her party to lead Burma. Instead, preparations were made to host a national constitutional convention, while differences over definitions of democracy, legitimacy, and authority characterized both domestic and international controversies about what the elections should mean for the future of the country.

The Burmese regime continued to develop its own special vision of what Burma was. In 1989, the government modified the name of the nation to 'Myanmar', a shortened version of the much longer *Pyi-daung-zu-Myanma-naing-ngan-taw* (The Union of Burma). The term was interchangeable with the indigenous term *Bama*, but the name-change became politicized since opposition groups, activists, and some foreign governments refused to recognize the legitimacy of the new regime and therefore of the country's new name. The United Nations and ASEAN accepted the change while the United States, United Kingdom, Canada, and Australia preferred to use Burma. Other colonial-era spellings of Burmese place-names were also modified to represent more accurately their Burmese-language pronunciations, such as Yangon (Rangoon), Bago (Pegu), and Bagan (Pagan).

Throughout the 1990s, the government's vision was also reflected in the attention given to public history through the restoration of ancient sites, the erection of new commemorative monuments, and the construction of new museum exhibits expressing Myanmar's cultural history from the perspective of the regime. In the mid-1990s the military funded a tour of a tooth-relic of the Buddha that visited the main administrative divisions and major cities throughout the country – and thus asserted the legitimacy of the regime's claims to the state, reflecting much older ideas of Buddhist legitimacy associated with Burmese kingship. The later relocation of the nation's capital to Naypyidaw in Upper Burma (near the thirteenth-century regional center of Pyimanna) in 2006 was consistent with other expressions of national identity, since Yangon was regarded as a 'colonial' capital. At Naypyidaw giant statues depict the great pre-colonial kings Aniruddha, Bayinnaung, and Alaungpaya. In such ways the cultivation of a common heritage became a visible part of nation-building in Myanmar.

While democratic change looked impossible in the early 1990s, important developments were quietly occurring in the domestic political scene as separatist groups along the Chinese-Burmese border entered cease-fire agreements with the government, signaling a significant change after nearly 50 years of civil war. Cold War-era financial and ideological interests were no longer as relevant to the younger generations of the borderlands, who sought to forge new relationships with the Rangoon government. In 1991, groups representing the Kachin, the Pa O National Organization, and the Palaung State Liberation Army also brokered agreements. In 1994, the powerful Karen Nationalist Union (KNU) entered talks as well but did not come to an agreement. Between 1989 and 1997, 17 cease-fire agreements were established for the first time since the eruption of civil war in 1948, including with some splinter groups that broke away from the KNU. Promises were given that once a constitutional settlement was reached, these groups would disarm or be converted into police forces and local militias in the service of the government. The last vestiges of the Cold War era were thus slowly disappearing, even in Burma.

Thailand

The return to a functional democratic system with an elected Prime Minister (Chatichai Choonhawan) in 1988 proved short-lived. Chatichai assembled a group of ministers who came to be known as the 'buffet cabinet' for their enthusiastic participation in money politics and their competition for a share in lucrative contracts. The army, feeling that it was missing out on its share of the pie, staged a coup which overthrew the government in 1991. The coup initially met with some degree of popular support, since Chatichai's administration had not proved particularly competent – above and beyond the corruption problem – and the army promised elections and a return to parliamentary government.

Elections were held in early 1992, but the army showed evidence of planning to hold onto power through its ties to certain political parties. This objective became even more obvious when General Suchinda Kraiprayoon, the most visible figure in the coup group, announced that he would step down from his post as Army Commander to become Prime Minister, even though he had not stood for election. This backtracking on the junta's promises provoked widespread protests in May, which accelerated under the leadership of Chamlong Srimuang, a former governor of Bangkok who enjoyed a solid reputation for personal integrity. When the army began to fire on demonstrators in the streets, killing at least several dozen – the exact number is still unknown – King Bhumibol intervened. He appeared on television with Chamlong and Suchinda kneeling in front of him and called for an end to the conflict. The king appointed a temporary Prime Minister, Anand Panyarachon, who had previously served under the junta but had demonstrated more integrity and independence than the army had expected. Elections followed, and the regular Thai pattern of coalition governments returned.

True stability remained elusive, however, as prime ministers and coalitions shifted every two or three years. Each successive administration was brought down by a no-confidence vote in parliament, generally fuelled by accusations of corruption and incompetence and usually facilitated by defections from coalition parties. Politics and business interests were completely intertwined. Many politicians were powerful 'godfathers' in their respective provinces, and the agendas they pursued through their positions in government were often personal and parochial, having little to do with the national interest. The years after 1992 saw a growing call for deep-rooted structural reform of the political system, but the strength and staying power of vested interests posed major obstacles to significant change.

Years of debate finally culminated in a new constitution in 1997, which was meant to address some of the major weaknesses in the Thai system. It put more emphasis on citizens' rights, built up the judicial system as a tool for attacking official corruption and malfeasance, and changed the Senate from an appointed to an elected body, an objective which very few previous charters had achieved. This 'people's constitution' grew out of many public feedback sessions around the country and represented the hopes and expectations of a wide variety of political and social constituencies. In many respects it did set the scene for a sea change in Thai politics – as long as it remained in effect, that is, for it was to survive less than a decade.

Thailand spent these years expanding its diplomatic and commercial relations with its neighbors, including China. The resolution of the Cambodian conflict and the withdrawal of Vietnamese troops made it possible for Bangkok to develop closer ties with both Phnom Penh and Hanoi, along with its increasingly warm relationship with Laos. For the latter country in particular Thailand came to play the role of mentor, offering scholarships and training opportunities for Lao. Because all educated Lao could communicate in Thai while few were fluent in Western languages, Thailand was a logical 'intermediary' between Laos and the rest of the world. Thai corporate and individual investors also flooded into Cambodia and Laos, being more culturally at home and in many respects less risk-averse than their competitors from other countries. Thai businesses also gained a foothold in the PRC, and the disappearance of the old suspicion of Chinese Communism smoothed the way for closer relations between the two countries.

Vietnam

The world of the Vietnamese leadership was seriously shaken by the end of the Cold War, the break-up of the Soviet Union, and the disappearance of the socialist bloc in Eastern Europe. Even though Hanoi was poised to open a new era in foreign relations with its 1989 withdrawal from Cambodia and the consequent end of the international embargo, it had counted on the support of its long-time allies in Eastern Europe. Not only did the end of socialism mean the end of the ideological basis for the 'fraternal relations' between Vietnam and the Soviet bloc, it also did immeasurable damage to the prestige of Marxism, thus potentially threatening the legitimacy of the Communist Party itself. The Party rushed into damage control, portraying the recent events in Eastern Europe as the result of traitors working in conjunction with hostile foreign powers – notably the CIA and the Vatican – while affirming Marxism as the correct path for Vietnam.

The Party was thus reinforced in its determination to follow the 'Chinese model' of economic reform with minimal change to the political system. Even though by the 1990s many of the old guard among the leadership had either died or retired – the last Party General Secretary of that generation, Do Muoi, was succeeded by Le Kha Phieu in 1997 – the younger leaders shared their elders' suspicion of political reform. Dissident voices speaking out in favor of a multi-party system or political pluralism were severely punished. The press began to enjoy somewhat more freedom to engage in investigative journalism against corruption and other abuses, but government policy in this respect was inconsistent, and publications which went too far found themselves in hot water.

Ambivalence about corruption was the most significant dilemma confronting the Vietnamese leadership. On the one hand, they recognized that corruption was arguably the most significant threat to their regime, as most Vietnamese were far angrier about graft, favoritism, and injustice than they were about the lack of political pluralism. On the other hand, the Party still wished to police its own ranks, and was in a constant state of tension between the desirability of allowing the press to investigate and report on corruption cases and the need for a crackdown when these efforts went too far.

The 1990s saw Vietnam achieve a much stronger footing on the international stage. After the end of the embargo, the two most important developments were the normalization of relations with the United States and membership in ASEAN, both in 1995. Ties with China were normalized at the beginning of the decade, after more than ten years of rupture and conflict. Vietnam was able to pursue increasingly solid bilateral relationships with both Washington (despite occasional spats over human rights and trade issues) and Beijing (despite ongoing border disputes). These developments helped to give the country a greater sense of security and stability after its years of relative isolation and over-reliance on the socialist bloc.

Laos

With the deaths of Kaysone Phomvihane, Souphanouvong, and several other 'founding fathers' of the revolutionary movement, Laos also experienced a leadership transition. Like their Vietnamese comrades, the younger generation of leaders was committed to economic change but not to any significant loosening of political control. There were few dissenting voices, but one or two small episodes of protest did occur and were quickly suppressed. Laos joined ASEAN in 1997, which brought the promise of lessening its dependence on Vietnam and Thailand. China also came to play an increasingly important role as the 'second-generation' leaders sought a greater degree of balance between Hanoi and Beijing.

Cambodia

The 1990s brought dramatic change and tumult for Cambodia but also gradual stabilization. Between 1989 and 1991 the various factions worked toward a solution to the civil war, resulting in a peace agreement in October 1991. A UN peacekeeping mission arrived shortly thereafter, followed by the establishment of UNTAC (UN Transitional Authority in Cambodia) in early 1992. UNTAC oversaw elections in 1993, from which the FUNCINPEC Party – a name deriving from a long French title – led by Norodom Sihanouk's son Prince Ranariddh and the Cambodian People's Party (CPP, formerly the pro-Vietnamese Cambodian Communist Party) emerged in the top two positions.

Cambodia was now (1993) re-established as a kingdom under Sihanouk, with Ranariddh and Hun Sen (the leader of the CPP) as co-Prime Ministers (Figure 34). The rivalry between the two parties was hardly a recipe for stability, and the country's problems were heightened by the refusal of the *Khmer Rouge* forces to participate in the elections or to lay down their arms. Under Pol Pot's leadership, the *Khmer Rouge* continued to maintain an armed struggle in parts of the country until their final surrender in 1996. The following year there was an outbreak of violence between FUNCINPEC and CPP

Figure 34   Prince Ranariddh (left) and Hun Sen (right), 2004
David Longstreath/AP/Press Association Images

supporters which led to an internal coup by Hun Sen, who became the sole Prime Minister.

Malaysia

Down to the financial crisis of the late 1990s, Malaysia continued on its course as a socially conservative, economically progressive, ethnically complicated, developing country under the leadership of Mahathir. But the political dominance of UMNO faced significant challenges in this changing society. After the 1969 riots it was clear that within the Alliance, the MCA and MIC were no longer as effective as they had once been in maintaining Chinese and Indian support. In 1970 a broader *Barisan Nasional* (National Front) was therefore formed that brought in other parties, but with continuing dominance by UMNO. The predominantly Chinese Democratic Action Party, however, stayed outside the *Barisan*. PAS joined in 1973 but was expelled in 1977 and thereafter represented the main opposition to UMNO within the Malay constituency. The *Barisan* continued to dominate the nation electorally through the 1990s, winning 71 percent of the seats in the national parliament in 1990, 84 percent in 1995, and 76 percent in 1999. UMNO was always the dominant partner. PAS was, however, a serious challenger at state level. In the 1990 election an opposition alliance including PAS won all of the parliamentary seats (both state and federal) in Kelantan and PAS took control of the state government, where it sought to introduce elements of Islamic law. In 1999 PAS won control of Terengganu.

As already noted above, UMNO sought to stave off the PAS challenge by itself being a major promoter of Islam at the national level. Among the most active Islamic organizations of the time was ABIM (an acronym for *Angkatan Belia Islam Malaysia*, Malaysian Islamic Youth Generation), established in the

Figure 35   Petronas towers, Kuala Lumpur, built late 1990s

early 1970s under the leadership of Anwar Ibrahim, a former student activist. It was strong among professionals, academics, and public servants. Anwar was arrested during student protests in 1974 and held under ISA powers for nearly two years. He continued to serve as ABIM's President until – to the surprise of many observers – he left the organization to join UMNO as a protégé of Mahathir in 1982. As Anwar rose within UMNO, already holding ministerial posts from 1983, questions were asked whether it was Mahathir who had co-opted Anwar or the reverse. In 1993 Anwar became Deputy Prime Minister, but his rise threatened some of the unofficial sinews of UMNO dominance, especially when he began denouncing the air of cronyism and corruption that lingered around it. When the 1997 financial crisis (discussed below) hit Malaysia, Anwar was also Minister of Finance and accepted the IMF approach to recovery, which differed greatly from Mahathir's. In June 1998 it was suddenly claimed that Anwar was guilty of both corruption and sodomy (a criminal offence in Malaysia); he was deposed from his governmental posts, arrested, beaten while under arrest, and then jailed for six years on the corruption charged, followed by a nine-year sentence for sodomy. The latter charge was dismissed in 2004 upon appeal, but in 2008 Anwar was again charged with sodomy.

The Anwar crisis shook UMNO. Mahathir was already quite unpopular with many voters and Anwar had been seen by many as a hope for the future. He was now destroyed – at least for a time – as a political figure and his moral standing was in tatters except among his own supporters who saw him as a victim of government oppression. Mahathir thus had to face the financial crisis and its aftermath without the threat of competition from Anwar, but with much-diminished personal standing.

The Philippines

In 1986, after the People Power Revolution toppled the Marcos dictatorship, Corazon Aquino assumed the presidency (1986–92) and the task of rehabilitating a devastated country. She inherited an economy in recession. Capital flight and withdrawal of short-term loans caused a severe economic contraction that obliterated a decade of growth. Indicators painted a worsening social picture: most families consumed less than the recommended calorie intake and 22 percent of pre-school children were malnourished. Many doubted the capabilities of the state. Military discontent, which exploded in a series of coup attempts, repeatedly disrupted civil order and frightened off much-needed foreign investment. The previous administration's USD 27.2 billion debt weighed heavily on the Aquino government. About USD 10–15 billion of this arose from fraud. Hence most Filipinos advocated debt restructuring or even debt repudiation. Unsurprisingly, the IMF, World Bank, and creditors in the United States opposed such schemes.

Acquiescing to external pressures, Aquino declined radical changes in economic policy and honored the country's debts. She liberalized the economy by ending agricultural monopolies and industrial favoritism, reducing tariffs, and lifting import controls. Technocrats and social reformers worked on removing Marcos's cronies and protectionism from the domestic industrial sector.

In 1987 Aquino's mandate was bolstered by a national referendum that approved a new constitution, restoring the pre-martial law system with a president and vice-president, a bicameral legislature, and an independent Supreme Court. The new constitution reflected the reformist tendencies of its drafters, limiting the president to one six-year term and senators to two six-year terms in office. Congressmen could be elected by legislative districts or through a party-list system representing national, regional, and sectoral parties or organization. These institutional reforms, however, proved insignificant to the impoverished peasantry. Dominated by traditional politicians (known as 'trapos' – literally 'cleaning rags' in Filipino), the 1987 legislature derailed the comprehensive agrarian reform program. Landlordism continued to dominate the countryside.

The growth brought about by the selective liberalization of the economy was unsustainable. From 1987 to 1991 debt servicing consumed some 40–50 percent of the state budget, thereby severely limiting efforts at economic rehabilitation, infrastructure development, and enhanced social welfare. Domestic borrowing stemmed cash outflow, but also trapped the state in a vicious cycle as it increased deficit spending, which raised interest rates and internal debt-service requirements. As a result, deficits rose even higher. Natural disasters like the 1990 earthquake in Baguio, the 1991 eruption of Mount Pinatubo (Luzon), and floods in the Visayas worsened the country's predicament. In

1991 state resources, as stated earlier, were further constrained by the reduction of remittances from Filipino workers due to the first Gulf War and the loss of USD 480 million yearly rent after the Senate declined to renew the Military Bases Agreement with the United States. The economy plunged into a recession. Poverty and income disparity persisted; 40 percent of the country's income remained in the hands of the top 10 percent, while 10 percent went to the poorest 30 percent. Massive tax fraud, especially among the rich, also led to significant revenue losses. Clearly the Aquino government's ability to foster growth was short-lived. The chance to change the government in the 1992 presidential elections was welcome. Aquino endorsed former Marcos ally General Fidel Ramos.

Like its predecessor, the Ramos administration (1992–98) championed democratization, pledging a 'strong state' that would be anchored in 'people empowerment' and a 'policy environment'. It implemented the 1991 Local Government Code which devolved the powers of national agencies to local government units and increased their share of internal revenue. These units experienced marked economic growth and political stability that featured a marriage of convenience between the politically savvy sons and daughters of traditional politicians and developmentalist NGOs and public organizations. Devolution proved a success in the country's second city Cebu – which became known as 'Ceboom'. But state spending remained high. Decentralization transferred thousands of 'national' employees to local governments where mismanagement of funds and assets prevailed. Local government deficit spending rose from PHP 543 million in 1992 to PHP 2.09 billion in 1998, while unliquidated cash advances increased from PHP 358 million to PHP 2.3 billion in the same period. The provinces of the Autonomous Region of Muslim Mindanao were the worst offenders. Most of their share in taxes and allocation from the Department of Environment and Natural Resources merely paid for local politicians' offices and their personal spoils system. Fearful of compromising the newfound peace in Mindanao, the Ramos government tolerated these distortions of expenditure.

To reposition the Philippines regionally and internationally, the Ramos administration sought to transform the country into an 'economic cub' (as opposed to a 'tiger') by 2000. Ramos presented himself as a capable and hands-on President, always in the midst of work. His *Barong Tagalong* sleeves were always rolled up, while a cigar hung from his mouth. As per the neoliberal agenda, he liberalized, deregulated and privatized the economy. The private sector took over profitable state corporations in the oil industry and water supply. Through build-operate-transfer schemes the government attracted private contractors to develop energy and infrastructure projects in exchange for the right to manage and generate income from the finished product. Restrictions on foreign investment were lifted, highlighted by the opening of the country's highly protected retail sector. The country's balance of payments improved, as economic growth from 1994 to 1996 improved to an annual average of 6 percent. The National Capital Region (Metro Manila), which housed 13 percent of the populace, contributed 30 percent of the GDP. Thousands found employment in corporations housed there. Such growth spilled over into the neighboring regions of Cavite, Rizal, Batangas, and Bulacan. The national unemployment rate dropped from 10.5 percent in 1991 to 8.5 percent in 1996. The improvement in purchasing power and quality of life of ordinary Filipinos proved an exception to the devastation that the 1997 Asian financial crisis wrought elsewhere.

Indonesia

In the early 1990s, many among the growing Indonesian middle class wanted greater freedom, more justice, and less corruption, but had too much invested in the existing system – and were too nervous about potential radicalism among the masses – to contemplate abandoning it. The regime saw parallels between the collapsing USSR and Indonesia: both sprawling, multi-ethnic and multi-religious states with regional disparities, repressive but inefficient governments, rickety infrastructure, and less-than-perfect communications. The Soviets had attempted *perestroika* and *glasnost* (reform and openness) and had seen their empire collapse, whereas in 1989 the Chinese had violently repressed a pro-democracy movement at Tiananmen Square and got away with it – the latter example being more attractive to the military types who dominated Indonesia. Meanwhile Islamic revivalism was producing both more liberal interpretations of the faith and conservative, anti-Western, and anti-Christian versions. So rising aspirations for political change confronted a regime inclined to clamp down lest it be threatened by real democracy. Islam supported both more just and democratic hopes and more repressive ideas.

In Aceh, armed resistance to Jakarta resumed in 1988. Aceh was now among Indonesia's most important provinces, producing much of its liquid natural gas. The profits went mostly to Jakarta and the regime elite, little remaining in Aceh. The regime's stakes in maintaining control of Aceh – already strong on nationalist grounds – were thus strengthened by economic considerations. From 1990 to 1998 Jakarta declared Aceh a 'Military Operations Area', a sort of local martial law area where some of the most brutal Indonesian military units were deployed. Resistance was led by GAM – the *Gerakan Aceh Merdeka* (Independent Aceh Movement) – guided by lay people, for most of Aceh's religious elite (*ulama*) had been co-opted by the New Order.

East Timor was also a growing challenge to Jakarta. From 1989 Indonesian abuses and exploitation there became more widely recognized. East Timor became an international issue of growing significance, an irritant in Indonesia's relations with the rest of the world.

Soeharto and his military supporters – concerned about the potential for globalizing, indeed Westernizing international trends to disturb their dominance – shared interests with the more conservative and anti-Western versions of Islam. Although the regime thwarted Islamic political aspirations, it had long recognized the potential for religion to act as a social force for conformity. Now it began to meet some of the demands of Islam, such as allowing girls to wear the headscarf (*jilbab*) at school. Soeharto and his family went on the pilgrimage (*hajj*) in 1991. But Islam had not only conservative, anti-Western, and ritualistic thrusts, for there was also a strong moral element that was at odds with the extravagant corruption of the regime. Opposed also were the more liberal versions of the faith.

Dr Bacharuddin Jusuf Habibie – briefly to become the nation's third President – emerged as a kind of bridge between New Order developmentalism and Islamic piety. From the mid-1970s, he led Indonesia's nascent high-technology industries, a network of government-backed companies that lost vast amounts of money. He was also a pious Muslim. To many among the pious middle class, he seemed a potential leader for the future. In 1990 ICMI (*Ikatan Cendekiawan Muslim se-Indonesia*, All-Indonesia Union of Muslim Intellectuals) was created, with Habibie as its leader. ICMI grew rapidly, was joined by most prominent Islamic intellectuals, enrolled many bureaucrats who saw in it a path to advancement consistent with their religious identity, and rapidly became influential across government.

The problem for the regime was that social change was producing demands for greater openness, less corruption, and more justice, just as the regime itself, with its military core, was inclined to suspect demands for democratic evolution and prepared to unleash violence to defend itself. The regime was thus pulling away from its middle-class constituency, a dangerous situation for any government. Even within the military, a few leaders were beginning to feel that Soeharto and his cronies were a burden that the nation could no longer afford.

From the mid-1990s social and political violence mounted, including notably Muslim-Christian conflict. These sometimes concealed ethnic aspects, for many Chinese Indonesians were Christians. The Indonesian Democracy Party (PDI, *Partai Demokrasi Indonesia*) was led by Megawati Sukarnoputri, Sukarno's daughter who was to become Indonesia's fifth President. The New Order saw her as a threat and in July 1996 launched a violent attack on her Jakarta headquarters which provoked two days of bloody rioting. The election campaign of the following year was the most violent of the whole New Order period. Golkar dominated again, of course, and Soeharto was re-elected by the parliament as President in 1998, with Habibie as Vice-President.

After 32 years, however, the wheels were falling off the New Order regime, as Indonesia's social and political problems were compounded by the Asian financial crisis, discussed below.

Singapore

The 1990s in Singapore witnessed a significant political transition. Lee Kuan Yew had led the PAP and the government of Singapore since 1959 but in November 1990, at the age of 67, he stepped down. Or, perhaps, we should say that he stepped up. Goh Chok Tong became Prime Minister in his stead (until 2004). Lee's son, Lee Hsien Loong – the future Prime Minister – became Deputy Prime Minister, being thought not yet ready to succeed as head of government. This change was, however, not as momentous as it might seem, for Lee Kuan Yew was hardly a person to enter into a quiet retirement. Instead a new post was created for him called 'Senior Minister' and he continued to have access to Cabinet papers and to play a senior, mainly advisory, role in governmental affairs. This transition was characteristic of the PAP policy of grooming younger members and retiring older ones, a policy that enabled it to avoid the sclerotic, often corrupt, politics that frequently attend states dominated by a single party.

ASEAN

The Association of Southeast Asian Nations has always been a rather curious organization – in some ways, indeed, barely an organization at all. Its history has been described in the following terms:

> From 1967 to 1976 ... ASEAN was characterized by a loose and highly decentralized structure with functions ... and programs driven by national governments. ASEAN itself was labeled as merely a 'letter box' during this early phase. In the next phase, from 1976 to 1992, ASEAN was more like a 'traveling circus' with increasing activity ... but with only minimal ... support from the ASEAN secretariat. Only from 1992 onwards ... did ASEAN require greater coordination and institutionalization.[2]

The key development was the 1992 decision to establish an ASEAN Free Trade Area (AFTA). This was consistent with a global trend towards freer trade – in principle if often not in practice – marked by the emergence in 1995 of the World Trade Organization (WTO). APEC (Asia-Pacific Economic Cooperation, beginning in 1989) was another regional discussion forum with similar goals. Trade liberalization was one element in the increasing foreign investment in ASEAN and the rise in value of its currencies – key factors in the financial and economic crisis that hit in 1997, described below. ASEAN did not foresee the impending crisis and, when it hit, had no solutions to offer. The same was true of APEC.

ASEAN also expanded its membership in the 1990s, including ironically the Indochinese states whose fall to Communist governments in 1975 had impelled anti-Communist ASEAN to enhance internal collaboration. Now that was all water under the bridge. Vietnam joined ASEAN in 1995, Laos and Myanmar in 1997, and Cambodia in 1999. The lower level of economic development in these countries produced a 'two-speed' ASEAN. The inclusion of Myanmar, with its dismal economy and brutal military government, complicated both ASEAN's internal affairs and the group's relations with outside powers.

The crisis of 1997–1998

Economic and social development in Southeast Asia's leading economies was impressive in the 1990s, but rested on shaky foundations. Much of the investment

---

2   Simon S. C. Tay and Jesus Estanislao, in Simon S. C. Tay, Jesus Estanislao and Hadi Susastro (eds), *A New ASEAN in a New Millennium* (Jakarta: Centre for Strategic and International Studies; Singapore: Singapore Institute of International Affairs, 2000), 11.

needed for development came from Japan, where the yen rose in value until 1995. This generated plentiful Japanese overseas investment and much of it flowed to Thailand, Malaysia, and Indonesia, with the Philippines lagging somewhat behind. North American and European investment was also significant, but Japanese money was the main engine of Southeast Asia's export-led development. From the mid-1990s, however, the value of the yen began to fall, reducing Japanese investments in the region. China and India also opened up as competitive sites for overseas investors. As the investment stream into Southeast Asia lessened, crisis loomed.

Southeast Asia's economies were, for the most part, ill-equipped to withstand a financial or economic challenge. There had been little technological development. Most banking systems were poorly regulated. Because of the foreign-funded years of growth, these economies had high levels of overseas debt denominated in Japanese yen or other foreign currency. Government institutions were weak. While Indonesia was, by general agreement, probably the most corrupt nation in the world, other Southeast Asian states were also plagued by corruption and cronyism, as powerful players with access to governments reaped the rewards of development for themselves. Liberalization of capital markets made Southeast Asia's growing economies vulnerable to speculative 'hot money', creating volatile short-term debts: a dangerous mix with the poorly regulated and corrupt local business scenes.

Servicing these high levels of overseas debt required both strong domestic currencies and strong earnings. As Japanese investment decreased, growth slowed, earnings declined, debts could not be serviced and currencies – mostly pegged to the USD – came under pressure.

On 2 July 1997 the Thai government unpegged the Thai baht from the US dollar and thereby unleashed a monetary crisis that swept across Southeast Asia. Almost immediately the IMF arrived with a financial rescue plan, one element of which – consistent with standard IMF policies – was to insist that capital movements be unhindered. A panicked flight of capital followed. The Thai baht fell to some 40 percent of its pre-float level against the USD, then stabilized at around 60 percent.

The monetary crisis then engulfed Indonesia, where it was at its most severe and where it precipitated the fall of the Soeharto regime. Soon after the Thai baht was floated, the Indonesian rupiah went into free-fall, with the Bank of Indonesia recognizing that it could do nothing to defend the currency. It bottomed out in January 1998 at 15 percent of its July 1997 exchange rate against the USD. Virtually every modern business enterprise in Indonesia was bankrupt, the savings of the middle class were mostly wiped out and millions of workers lost their jobs.

It was not only in Indonesia where the impact of the crisis on employment was considerable, as can be seen in the following table (Table 13.1) for the three most 'booming' Southeast Asian nations.

Critics believed that IMF policies in both Indonesia and Thailand actually made the crisis worse. There the political impact was also considerable, for local people regarded the IMF role as both a loss of sovereignty and a Western effort to return Southeast Asians to dependency on the West.

Table 13.1   Unemployment rates, 1995–2001

Year	Indonesia	Malaysia	Thailand
1995	7.2	2.8	1.1
1996	4.9	2.5	1.1
1997	4.7	2.6	0.9
1998	5.5	3.2	4.4
1999	6.4	3.4	4.2
2000	6.1	3.1	3.6
2001	8.1	3.7	3.3

Source: K. S. Jomo (ed.), *After the Storm: Crisis, recovery and sustaining development in four Asian economies* (Singapore: Singapore University Press, 2004), 14.

Malaysia – where the feisty Dr Mahathir was no fan of Western-dominated international institutions or investors – took a different tack and rejected IMF intervention. Mahathir imposed capital controls to control outflows. It is doubtful, however, whether these were of any more than symbolic significance, since they were only imposed 14 months into the crisis, by which time the 'hottest' money had already fled. More importantly, Malaysian banks were better regulated and administered than their Thai and Indonesian counterparts and had less overseas debt to deal with – although there was still significant speculative investment in the country. The Malaysian ringgit dipped in early 1998 to about 70 percent of its January 1997 value, but then recovered quite quickly to around 80 percent.

The Philippines was less affected because it had attracted less foreign investment and had developed less. The Philippine peso fell, as did the Manila stock market, but the damage was less than in Indonesia or Thailand. In Singapore, the government allowed the Singapore dollar to depreciate, whereupon it went down about 8 percent. But Singapore's well-managed economy, strong government, efficient modernity, and absence of corruption positioned it well to withstand the crisis.

The poorest Southeast Asian nations of Burma, Cambodia, and Laos had been less attractive to foreign investors and had developed less, so there the scale of damage was less than in more expansionist economies. Its *doi moi* (economic 'renovation') program notwithstanding, Vietnam still had strict currency controls and a much less developed private economy, so also escaped serious damage immediately, although in later years it was thought to be teetering on the brink of its own local version of the collapse of 1997–98. Brunei rode out the crisis aboard its vast oil reserves, its fortunate citizenry paying no income taxes or interest on housing mortgages, and enjoying free health care.

Southeast Asian politics between crises, 1997–2008

The international context

The international context changed with the election of George W. Bush as American President (2001–09). His policies reflected a conservative, free-market, 'faith-based' ideology, and a distrust of international institutions, while their implementation often betrayed a low level of governmental competence. When Osama bin Laden's Al-Qaeda terrorists attacked New York and Washington DC on 11 September 2001, there was a wave of international sympathy for the United States. Many countries supported the American-led invasion of Afghanistan less than a month later that toppled the Taliban regime and sent Osama bin Laden into hiding. But the Bush administration dispelled this sympathy when its 'global war on terror' led to the much-criticized invasion of Iraq in March 2003. In Southeast Asia as elsewhere, many thought that, whatever was said to the contrary, the neo-conservatives of America were launching a Christian crusade against Islam. The Bush years ended with Southeast Asia, and the rest of the world, facing renewed financial and economic crisis generated again by inadequately regulated markets – but this time the source of the crisis was primarily to be found in the economies of the developed countries.

Myanmar/Burma

As noted above, Myanmar was accepted into ASEAN in 1997, although its inclusion was contested by some members who were concerned that including Myanmar would damage ASEAN's international standing. It did, indeed, produce a 'two-speed' ASEAN economically, with Myanmar, Laos, Cambodia, and Vietnam trailing the development of other members. The decision to join ASEAN marked a significant step away from Myanmar's isolationist policies of the 1970s and 1980s, but continuing international condemnation of its domestic policies kept the nation marginalized.

In the mid-1990s the constitutional convention was convened and treated by the government as a key phase in its proclaimed – but widely disbelieved – 'road-map to democracy'. Despite accusations by foreign governments and NGOs that the process did not include opposition parties that had previously boycotted the convention, the military leadership continued the process of drafting a constitution with those ethnic political groups that had agreed to come to the table. In 1997, SLORC renamed itself the State Peace and Defense Council (SPDC), signaling a transition in the military leadership that had been developing over time. All but four of the top members of SLORC were purged. SPDC included younger commanders, while powerful regional commanders were kicked upwards into ministerial positions in Yangon and replaced by junior officers loyal to those in central command, strengthening the control of the army in borderland areas where cease-fire agreements had been brokered.

In 2000 and 2001, Aung San Suu Kyi began to negotiate secretly with members of the regime despite her continuing house arrest. Her release in 2002 through the mediation of the UN Secretary General's Special Envoy allowed her to tour the country, conduct political activities and begin a series of dialogue sessions with the government's senior leadership. In May 2003, however, her convoy was attacked at the village of Dipeyen and she was once again placed under house arrest, reviving criticism from international observers and even other members of ASEAN.

In 2004, the national convention to draft a constitution was reconvened and met for the next three years. Once again the government invited specifically chosen members who had walked out of the 1995 convention to return, but no agreement could be made in regard to the participation of the NLD, which made the release of Aung San Suu Kyi and the reopening of party offices its conditions for joining the convention.

In September 2007, monks and civilians took to the streets in protest following an inexplicable increase in gasoline and natural gas prices that doubled the cost of public transportation. Earlier that month, a series of conflicts in Pakokku, Sittwe, and other localities had erupted over alleged mistreatment of monks by state authorities. Now initial demands for an apology from the government became politicized and escalated into calls for regime change. By mid-September, 10,000–30,000 students, politically active monks, and concerned citizens were on the streets of Yangon (Rangoon). The army and riot police responded by dispersing the crowds forcefully, resulting in injuries and deaths. But the security forces used considerably more caution than in 1988, aware that images from cell phones and other mobile devices were being shared through the Internet. Monks who disobeyed calls from senior monks to return to their monasteries were arrested. Exile opposition groups and activists were quick to characterize the marches as demands for democratic change, but in fact no clear demands were announced by the loose alliance of monks and civilians on the street.

In May 2008, Lower Burma was hit by Cyclone Nargis with torrential rains and winds of 190 km (115 miles) per hour, destroying villages, rice fields, water supplies, and farm animals. A 3.5-meter (12-foot) tidal surge was reported to have killed nearly 150,000 villagers, displaced millions, and wiped out 65 percent of the country's rice crop. Twenty-four nations immediately pledged nearly USD 30 million in aid, but the military government refused to grant access immediately to those nations, to international agencies, or to NGOs. Criticism of the government's humanitarian indifference mounted as French, British, and American naval vessels with relief supplies were left to float in nearby waters while relief planes sat fruitlessly on runways in Thailand. The infuriated French foreign minister raised the prospect of forceful humanitarian intervention even without the agreement of Burma. When restrictions began to be lifted after several days, access to the disaster zone was limited to nations deemed friendly to the regime such as Bangladesh, Japan, China, and Thailand, and to those NGOs already operating within the country. Within a few days, the government went ahead with a rigged national referendum to approve its new constitution, deepening the impression that this was a government that simply didn't care whether its citizens lived or died. Later reports by NGOs on the ground indicated that the government's efforts were greater than originally thought, but in the eyes of the government's critics the urgency of thorough-going regime change had been underlined by this natural tragedy.

Thailand

The dubious honor of launching the Asian economic crisis of the late 1990s fell to Thailand, although as events quickly demonstrated, it was by no means the only country in the region with structural vulnerabilities. The Thai economic boom had come to rely heavily on two things: a currency (the baht) which was kept at an artificial level and the expansion of its international finance sector. The latter in particular would prove to be a Trojan horse because capital can leave as quickly and easily as it comes, and it is much easier to pull it out through electronic transfers than to close down a factory employing hundreds of workers. Moreover, much of the growth of Thailand's financial industry was not being closely monitored or regulated thanks to pressure from political and business interests alike.

When in 1997 the government decided that the baht had to be allowed to float and re-establish itself at an exchange rate which corresponded better to its real value, it depreciated dramatically, provoking waves of currency speculation which eroded its worth even further. Corporate debts (notably for property construction) which were denominated in American dollars, Japanese yen, or other foreign currencies now became much larger, and many companies defaulted on their loans. The financial industry itself was seriously damaged, and the government had to accept strict conditions on its economic policies in order to receive a large bailout from the IMF. Much of the wealth which had been gained during the recent boom years was now lost: one striking sign was the sudden improvement in Bangkok's long-congested traffic due to the repossession of countless luxury cars.

Although Thailand was able gradually to pull itself back together, the financial crisis had severe implications for the country's leadership. Prime Minister Chavalit Yongchaiyudh took the blame for the crisis, even though the causes obviously preceded his administration. Respected former Prime Minister Chuan Leekpai returned to power with his Democratic Party leading yet another coalition, but a new leader was building his power base. Thaksin Shinawatra, the head of a large telecommunications company and member of a Sino-Thai family from Chiang Mai, founded a new *Thai Rak Thai* (Thais love Thais) party in 1998. Elections were held in early 2001, and Thaksin's party achieved a tremendous victory which swept it into power, opening a new era in Thai politics.

Despite solid electoral victories and widespread popular support, Thaksin remained a controversial leader. He earmarked large sums of money for rural villagers, such as microcredit, low-interest loans, and cash for local development plans, and implemented a government-funded universal health care program. Although his policies were derided by many among the elite as 'Thaksinomics', they obviously addressed genuine needs among the population which earlier governments had generally failed to meet. When elections were held in 2005, the *Thai Rak Thai* became the first party in the country's history to win a parliamentary majority without needing a coalition.

Thaksin was, however, criticized for more than his economic policies. He was generally intolerant of criticism, particularly from the media, and exerted pressure on various sources of media opposition. Although sweetheart deals were nothing new in Thai politics, Shinawatra family companies were widely viewed as profiting excessively from various contracts and concessions. Thaksin launched a war on drugs which included extrajudicial killings of traffickers. At the same time, his period in power saw a resurgence of trouble in the Muslim South. Government repression escalated this into a vicious cycle of violence unprecedented in the region. Finally, Thaksin committed the serious error of mishandling his relationship with the king and was widely perceived as disrespectful and even hostile toward the revered monarch.

The accumulated opposition to Thaksin within various segments of the elite found its catalyst in early 2006 when his family sold their holdings in their flagship Shin Corp to a Singaporean holding company without paying taxes on the deal. A mounting protest movement forced Thaksin to hold new elections, which his Party won, but his grip on power was becoming increasingly untenable. In September 2006 the army seized power, and the longest period of civilian rule in Thailand's history came to an end. Although a military caretaker regime gave way to another elected government led by Thaksin's allies, protests continued as his opponents remained determined to sweep his faction out of power completely.

Thai and foreign observers were dismayed, to say the least, to see the old patterns of the country's political history repeating themselves. Once again the army had stepped in to overthrow a democratically elected civilian regime, and, as has often been the case, they did so with the support of other civilians. Once again there was open conflict between those who advocated a fully-elected parliament – the risk of corruption and vote-buying notwithstanding – and those who favored more 'Thai' mechanisms such as a greater role for the king. The path on which Thailand had been launched by the events of 1932 remained a rocky one, and the transition to a smoothly functioning constitutional monarchy remained incomplete.

Laos

Because its economy was so closely linked to that of Thailand, Laos was also affected by the economic crisis. The Thai baht remained widely used in Laos since the opening up of the economy, and its depreciation dragged down the Lao currency as well. There was relatively little foreign capital to flee the country, but investment slowed. China, already playing an increasingly important economic role, emerged as a major investor in various commercial and infrastructural projects in Laos. Meanwhile, the country continued to open its doors to tourism, which provided much-needed foreign exchange and stimulated growth in the service sector.

Vietnam

Vietnam was at least partially shielded from the worst of the crisis by the fact that, although it relied heavily on the US dollar, its currency was non-convertible and thus much less vulnerable to speculation. Moreover, the country's increasing attractiveness to foreign investment was not significantly damaged, and joint ventures continued to multiply. Export processing zones and industrial zones, although they varied significantly in quality and efficiency, constituted an increasingly important axis of economic growth. Vietnam's GDP

Figure 36   Students in Ho Chi Minh City, 1990s

grew an average 6 percent per year from 1990 onward, quite a respectable figure for a country which was in some respects still recovering from decades of warfare.

One of the most important developments in the Vietnamese economy was the establishment of a stock market. The first stock exchange opened in Ho Chi Minh City in 2000, and its Hanoi counterpart began to operate in 2005. The initial years were slow going, as it took time to build up a critical mass of companies listing on the exchange and, more importantly, to persuade people to invest in them. By the time the Hanoi exchange opened, however, the market as a whole had gained momentum and was attracting much wider interest not only from local investors but from foreign funds as well. The land and property market was also active, as many new construction projects created thousands of new housing units which were snapped up by Vietnamese and foreign buyers. A boom in foreign tourism, facilitated by an increasingly efficient service sector, also made a tremendous contribution to the country's economic growth.

Nevertheless, significant obstacles remained. Private entrepreneurship, while officially allowed and even encouraged, was often weakened by red tape, inconsistent and arbitrary tax policies, and corruption. The government attempted to increase its revenue by a more efficient and broad-based tax system, but this was easier said than done, and it was often easier to cheat than to do one's civic duty as a taxpayer, particularly when the collection process was less than transparent. Infrastructural weaknesses remained, particularly in electricity generation, despite an increase in the country's production capacity. Moreover, despite the recognition of the 'rule of law' as a key objective for government and business across the board, the uneven implementation of this objective posed problems for foreign and domestic investors alike.

On the political scene, one important change was the emergence of the National Assembly as a more vocal and influential organ of government. Once functioning largely as a rubber stamp, the Assembly began to take its role more seriously. Some sessions were televised, including the questioning of government ministers over policy issues. This transition to a more active role took place under the leadership of Nong Duc Manh, who subsequently became General Secretary of the Party in 2001 – marking the first time that the Assembly had been a stepping-stone to a top leadership position. This said, however, the Party rather than the state or government remained the key center of decision-making, although one of the long-term goals of *doi moi* is theoretically to decrease the imbalance in power between the two institutions in the government's favor.

This period also saw several important episodes of unrest within the country. In 1997–8 localized but violent protests broke out in the northern province of Thai Binh against abuses and corruption by local officials. Smaller-scale protests also occurred in other parts of the country, mainly over land issues, which – after corruption – constituted the greatest popular grievance against the government. The implementation of a system of 'land usage rights', intended to function like private property but in a more ideologically acceptable form, did provide a greater measure of security to property owners. At the same time, however, as was true of land distribution in pre-colonial villages, this system relied heavily on the honesty and goodwill of local officials, thus opening the door to numerous abuses. Petitions and demonstrations over land became commonplace, but the authorities were generally unwilling to concede to such demands.

Even more serious were the large-scale outbreaks of unrest in the Central Highlands in 2001 and 2004. Several factors were in play, most of them related to the inflow of lowlanders and highlanders from other parts of Vietnam, who competed with the local ethnic minorities for land and other resources. There was also continued repression of Protestant Christianity in the Highlands, where many followers were organized into churches unaffiliated with the officially sanctioned Protestant denomination. Although there was evidence of involvement by remnants of the separatist movement which had flourished in the Highlands in the 1960s and 1970s (FULRO), most of the unrest was due to government policies and to conflicts over land rather than to any desire for independence.

Cambodia

In the late 1990s, Cambodia was more troubled by political crisis than by economic problems, though like Laos it was affected by its heavy reliance on

Thai investment. The events of 1997, when Hun Sen effectively ejected Ranariddh from power, marked a significant watershed in the country's political evolution. Hun Sen and his CPP became the dominant political force. Although Ranariddh and other leaders of the FUNCINPEC party subsequently returned to Cambodia and rejoined the government, they were now clearly a secondary force. Cambodian politics became increasingly chaotic, and elections brought political violence and accusations of dishonesty. Although opposition newspapers continued to flourish, some editors and journalists were murdered, and space for political dissent gradually shrank.

In early 2003 an outbreak of rioting occurred when a prominent Thai actress was reported to have said that Angkor Wat should be returned to Thai control. This violence poisoned Thai-Cambodian relations, which were even more seriously damaged in 2008 by a dispute over land around the Preah Vihear temple along the border. Cambodia in fact had unresolved border issues with all three of its neighbors, and the determination to take back territory that had been 'stolen' – as Cambodia saw it – continued to stoke the fires of nationalism. Hun Sen's government was even subject to criticism on these grounds by Norodom Sihanouk himself, who abdicated on grounds of poor health in 2004 and was succeeded by his son Norodom Sihamoni. Although largely removed from the political process, Norodom Sihanouk continued to speak his mind when he felt the situation required it.

Malaysia

In the wake of the financial crisis, Mahathir's standing was somewhat strengthened by his determination in standing up to the IMF and his denunciation of Western financiers, which won him sympathy among Malaysians. He continued to oppose all his enemies vociferously – whether local politicians or what he regarded as remnants of Western imperialism. British and Australian press criticisms particularly angered him. The 9/11 attacks were useful to him, for they gave him an excuse to denounce 'extremist' versions of Islam. He represented himself both to the West and to the Islamic world as the spokesman of progressive, modern Islam and Malaysia as the model of the progressive, modern Muslim nation. But his messages were undermined by his tendency to denounce Western and Jewish world conspiracies and by the problems Malaysia was facing in dealing with its own ethnic and religious diversity.

Economic growth recovered after the 1997–98 crisis but did not return to the levels of the boom years, achieving instead some 4 to 6 percent per annum. Despite Mahathir's efforts to turn Malaysia from a primary-produce exporter into an exporter of manufactures, the export of raw materials remained important in the economy. In peninsular Malaysia that meant particularly rubber, palm oil, tin, and timber (in addition to electronics and other light manufacturing outputs), and in Sabah and Sarawak mainly timber and oil.

Mahathir was never a retiring type, so many were surprised when he did retire from the prime ministership – after 22 years and at the age of 77 – in 2003. His chosen successor was Abdullah Ahmad Badawi (g. 2003–09), an amiable but relatively ineffectual man who proclaimed *Islam hadari* (civilizational Islam) to be the guiding principle of Malaysia's future, although it was never quite clear what that was. In 2004 the *Barisan Nasional* did very well in the national elections, but under Abdullah's leadership the government and UMNO declined in popularity, prompting the not-in-fact-so-retired Mahathir to criticize Abdullah publicly. UMNO suffered badly in the 2008 national elections. The *Barisan Nasional* got barely 50 percent of the popular vote and won just 140 seats – a dramatic drop from its previous 198 seats and a loss of its two-thirds majority for the first time since 1969. UMNO itself won just under 30 percent of the votes. The opposition coalition took power in Penang, Selangor, Kedah, and Perak; PAS retained control of Kelantan, but in early 2009 lost control there to the *Barisan* due to the defection of three Legislative Assembly members. Under pressure to quit, Abdullah stepped down and handed the leadership of UMNO and the prime ministership to Najib Tun Razak in 2009. Najib began his prime ministership under the cloud of allegations that he or his associates were somehow involved in the murder of a Mongolian model.

Inter-religious, and thus inter-ethnic, relations were growing more tense on two main fronts. The first had to do with conversions to Islam. There were several cases where a deceased person previously known to be of another faith was said by some family member to have converted to Islam without the knowledge of the surviving spouse, whereupon the Shariah Court refused the spouse access to the body and insisted on an Islamic burial. Other cases concerned divorces where one spouse claimed to have converted the children to Islam and thereby gained sole custody of the children via the Shariah Court, despite the estranged spouse (and the children) having no knowledge of this conversion. The second issue concerned Christians, who were told that they were not allowed to use the Arabic word *Allah* for God in their publications, on the grounds that this might 'confuse' Muslims – and this despite the fact that *Allah* was (and is) used throughout the Arabic-speaking world, as also in Indonesia, by Christians as well as Muslims. Both of these issues were subject to legal challenge and both went to the heart of what it meant to be a non-Malay and non-Muslim in Malaysia. Such events inspired the creation of HINDRAF (the Hindu Rights Action Force) by Indians who felt that the MIC was ineffective in defending them against the creeping influence of Shariah law. In 2007, five HINDRAF leaders were imprisoned under ISA powers.

Singapore

The continuity of PAP control in Singapore and the general recovery from the regional crisis of 1997–98 meant that Singapore's course remained fixed as before. In 2004 Goh Chok Tong stepped up to become 'Senior Minister', which required another new post to be invented – that of 'Minister Mentor' – for Lee Kuan Yew. The latter's son Lee Hsien Loong now became Prime Minister. The main innovation under Lee Hsien Loong was a cabinet decision in 2005 to introduce casinos to Singapore – to be known by the euphemism 'integrated resorts'. Gambling has such a large place in Chinese culture that Lee Kuan Yew (Figure 37) had always opposed having them in Singapore for

Figure 37   Lee Kuan Yew, 2008
© How Hwee Young/epa/Corbis

fear of the social cost that could follow; he continued to dislike the idea but did not stand in his son's way. Various safeguards were promised to prevent poorer citizens ruining their family's finances in the 'integrated resorts'. The crisis of 2008 slowed construction of these 'resorts'; their critics were buoyed by the thought that, when they opened, the 'Asian high rollers' whose pockets they were intended to empty would fail to materialize, having already lost their fortunes in the casino of the world's stock markets instead.

Brunei

Brunei is little and, in the decade after the financial crisis, little happened. The most dramatic episode was a 1998 scandal involving the Sultan's brother, the playboy Prince Jefri Bolkiah, who was Minister of Finance and head of the Brunei Investment Agency. Tens of millions of dollars were alleged to have been misappropriated. The mess was cleared up, claims were settled, and a British national was appointed to head a new national development agency.

Prince Jefri himself – the husband of four wives and father of 17 children – denied any wrongdoing and refused to hand over several billions of his assets to the Sultan. When he failed to show up for a court hearing in 2008, *The Times* of London was moved to observe that he was 'said to have swapped his notoriously decadent lifestyle of vulgarly named yachts and gold-plated lavatory brushes for a fugitive existence'.[3]

---

[3]   *The Times,* 12 June 2008.

The Philippines

The Philippines suffered less damage from the 1997 Asian financial crisis than other countries. Growth slowed, as capital outflow, unemployment, and the price of basic commodities inched upward. Nevertheless, the country recorded 5.1 percent GDP growth in 1997. From May to June 1997, following the collapse of the Thai baht, the Philippines Central Bank spent some USD 2 billion or 13.4 percent of its gross international reserves to protect the Philippine peso against speculation. It tripled domestic interest rates and intervened to keep the peso-to-USD exchange rate stable, but in July floated the peso in a wider band. Contrary to prevalent fears, the devaluation of the peso did not cause a dramatic rise in prices. Inflation was reasonable at 9.7 percent in 1998 and reduced to 6.6 percent in 1999. The strong supply of agricultural products, modest domestic demand, and a relatively stable exchange rate helped to offset the adverse effects of devaluation. Such short-term policy responses seemed effective and the social impact of the crisis was relatively contained. Observers attributed this to the country's sound fundamentals brought about by years of economic and structural reforms. Unlike their Thai counterparts, Filipino businessmen and financiers pursued more conservative investment strategies that guarded against the growth of a 'bubble' economy. Domestic experiences with similar economic crises (in the early 1980s, the mid-1980s, and the early 1990s) also apparently prepared the state to deal with the regional crisis. Previously a site of instability, the financial sector dominated by privately owned commercial banks boasted of its professionalism and technological advances, and was staffed by cosmopolitan bankers who returned from overseas to apply their skills at home. High interest rates kept real estate lending minimal and debt-to-equity ratios of property firms remained low.

Nevertheless, investment rates continued to decline until 1999, investors evidently finding the pace of economic and political reforms too slow. The unemployment rate increased to 9.6 percent, with particularly severe impact on urban males aged 15 to 19. The debilitating effects of the El Niño and La Niña phenomena hit the rural economy hard. The hostile credit environment and prohibitive prices of farming implements contributed to depressed production levels, while demand also slumped. Only the service sector, which accounted for some 45 percent of the country's labor force, expanded. Remittances from overseas Filipino workers also proved to be remarkably resilient. From 1989 onwards these comprised approximately 54 percent of the country's earnings.

As the travails of the fiscal sector continued, Ramos required government departments to reduce expenditures by 25 percent to meet the IMF mandate of keeping a fiscal surplus of 1 percent of GNP. Poor revenue collection convinced the IMF, however, to relax this target and allow a budget deficit. This about-face turned out to be prophetic, for by the end of 1998 the budget deficit stood at more than PHP 50 billion. The subsequent Joseph Estrada government (1999–2001) tried to spur growth, but revenue collection slackened. The deficit reached PHP 112 billion, which wreaked havoc on business confidence and derailed full economic recovery. The government imposed a 25 percent reserve requirement on all expenditures by government departments other than personnel and debt servicing, deferred internal revenue allotment for local governments and suspended tax subsidies of all state agencies and corporations. Expenditures on social services fell 10 percent, seriously affecting investments in public health and education. While some of its harder-hit neighbors were overcoming the economic crisis, however, the Philippines seemed stuck, trapped in a boom-and-bust cycle, unable to sustain growth. The modest 3.5 percent growth brought about by a rebound in agriculture and devaluation of the peso in 2000 hardly impressed foreign investors.

Meanwhile corruption allegations and the slow implementation of anti-poverty measures racked the Estrada administration. The President remained popular among the poor but alienated much of the business and political elite. Military failures against the Abu Sayyaf Group and the MILF sapped the political capital Estrada won after taking a strong stand against Muslim secessionists. The war in Mindanao cost the government from one-half to over two million USD daily, diverting precious cash from other programs. As Estrada began losing allies in Congress, his economic reform agenda stalled. The last straw was his purported complicity in drug smuggling and illegal gambling. On 16 January 2001, after Senate deliberations on charges against him reached a stalemate, tens of thousands of anti-Estrada demonstrators gathered at EDSA. This gathering of predominantly urban middle-class people, known as 'EDSA II', led to Estrada's ousting and propelled his Vice-President, Gloria Macapagal Arroyo – a technocrat and daughter of former President Diosdado Macapagal – to the presidency (2004–10). Estrada's dismissal was backed by the Catholic Church, which felt threatened by his close relationship with such booming alternative religious groups as *Iglesia ni Kristo* and Jesus is Lord, evangelical Christian movements popular among Manila's urban poor.

Within three months, Arroyo found herself needing to defend her claim to the presidency as some three million of her predecessor's supporters assembled at the EDSA shrine. This 'EDSA III' was made up of Manila's subaltern classes, reviled by the urban middle class for being irreverent, dirty, and violent. Their mobilization was successfully contained, however, and denounced as an illegitimate means to pursue change of government by the very political elite who had themselves led EDSA II. Nonetheless, the protests uncomfortably reminded the elite in power of the continuing grievances of the poor.

Gloria Arroyo served out the remainder of Estrada's term. In 2004, despite her previous pledge to the contrary, she ran and won a term of office in her own right. Nonetheless, she found political legitimacy elusive. Through compromise and pork barreling she gained fleeting congressional support. Further liberalization of the retail sector and the rebound in foreign remittances contributed to modest economic growth. Indicators for education, health, employment, and underemployment, however, remained weak. Debt servicing continued to absorb a quarter of the state budget. Pervasive corruption uncovered by independent journalists in a number of departments worsened public perceptions of Arroyo's administration. Other problems plagued her presidency, including a failed 2003 military mutiny, corruption charges against her family, charges of her involvement in vote rigging during the 2004 elections, a 2006 mass mobilization against her regime, a disturbing spike in extrajudicial killings of activists and political opponents, concerted attacks on journalists, several impeachment attempts in Congress, bribery scandals, and the 2007 bombing of the House of Representatives that resulted in the death of a Mindanao congressman. Arroyo weathered these storms by steadfastly holding onto power, but thereby undermined the authority and legitimacy of the state's already weakened institutions. With her term ending in 2010, Arroyo's government lasted over nine years, second only to that of the dictator Marcos.

Indonesia

In 1997–98 the regime was discredited and the economy in near-collapse. The IMF and world leaders pressed Soeharto to undertake reforms, but he preferred to preserve his, his family's, and his cronies' interests. In the face of regime intimidation and murder, university students courageously demanded *reformasi* (reform). Rioting in Jakarta and elsewhere in early 1998 caused hundreds of deaths. Finally Soeharto announced on 21 May 1998 that he would step down as President. From then until his death in January 2008, he avoided accountability for the regime's crimes by claiming to be too ill to stand trial.

Soeharto was succeeded by Habibie, whose 17-month presidency (1998–99) surprised many with its reforms. He released political prisoners, scheduled the first truly free elections since the 1950s and began the process of removing the military from politics. But he achieved no real restoration of the economy. Inter-ethnic and inter-religious violence persisted across the country. Christian-Muslim violence in Maluku began in early 1999 and killed thousands.

Most remarkably, Habibie agreed to hold a UN-sponsored referendum in East Timor, against much opposition from the national elite. In August 1999, 78.5 percent of East Timorese voters chose independence. The Indonesian military and their local militia allies thereupon unleashed violence that killed at least 1300 East Timorese – no doubt as both revenge and a lesson to other restless parts of the nation. UN peacekeepers were sent in and the UN took charge of the transition to independence of the Democratic Republic of Timor-Leste. Thus was born Southeast Asia's newest and poorest nation, within a few years widely regarded as a failed state.

In April 1999 Indonesia held its first free elections for over 40 years. Megawati Sukarnoputri's PDIP (*Partai Demokrasi Indonesia Perjuangan,* Indonesian Democratic Party of Struggle) won a plurality with 33.7 percent of the votes, with Golkar – the electoral vehicle of the unlamented New Order – in second place at 22.4 percent. But it was the charismatic Abdurrahman Wahid of the traditionalist NU, whose PKB (*Partai Kebangkitan Bangsa,* National Awakening Party) won only 12.6 percent of the votes, who put together a sufficient coalition to be elected President (1999–2001), with Megawati as his Vice-President.

Abdurrahman Wahid's 21-month presidency (1999–2001) was characterized by visionary statements, administrative chaos, and evidence that the President – who was blind, had multiple other health problems and had suffered strokes – was not well enough to govern. So the promise offered by one of the most liberal, broad-minded leaders of Islam taking charge of the state came to little.

During Abdurrahman's presidency, the first large-scale Islamically inspired militias came to public notice. The most prominent was *Laskar Jihad* (Holy War Militia) established in 2000 to fight Christians in Maluku, with evidence of support from elements of the Indonesia military. It maintained some 3000 fighters in Maluku until it was shut down in 2002 by a Saudi Arabian scholar's legal opinion (*fatwa*) that it had strayed from its proper purposes. Another group was the Islamic Defenders' Front (FPI, *Front Pembela Islam*), which specialized in attacking bars, houses of prostitution, and other sites of 'immorality'. *Laskar Mujahidin* (Holy Warriors' Militia) was the clandestine military wing of the *Majelis Mujahidin Indonesia* (Indonesian Holy Warriors' Council), led by the extremist cleric Abu Bakar Ba'asyir. These organizations were all led by Indonesians of Arab descent. On Christmas Eve 2000, 38 bombs went off at Christian targets in 11 cities, killing 19. This was the first terrorist plot by *Jemaah Islamiyah* (JI), which was not yet identified as the perpetrator at this stage. JI was generally believed also to be guided by Abu Bakar Ba'asyir.

Abdurrahman Wahid was dismissed as President by the parliament and succeeded (2001–04) by Megawati Sukarnoputri, who generally approached the responsibilities of the presidency with aloof indifference and shopping trips to Singapore. By this time Indonesia was embarked on a decentralization policy that turned one of the most centralized states in the world into one of the most decentralized, dramatically reducing the powers of Jakarta over the nation.

The American-led invasion of Afghanistan prompted large-scale protests by Indonesian extremists, among whom several hundred at least were veterans of the *jihad* against the Soviet occupation of Afghanistan (1979–89). The size of these demonstrations startled the government and the largest Islamic organizations, NU and *Muhammadiyah*, who began to recognize the need for a united stand against extremism.

In October 2002, JI bombed two popular Balinese tourist sites, Indonesia's first large-scale act of terrorism to claim foreign victims. A total of 202 people were murdered, including 88 Australians and 38 Indonesians. The three principal plotters were quickly captured, tried, and sentenced to death, finally being executed in 2008.

Indonesia witnessed multiple terrorist actions thereafter, including bombings of the Jakarta Marriott hotel in 2003, the Australian embassy in 2004, and a second Bali bombing in 2005. These bloody acts alienated many Indonesians and inspired greater resistance to extremism. Indonesian police and intelligence work also proved effective – indeed probably more effective than in any other country – in identifying, capturing and killing terrorists, trying and convicting them, and breaking up their networks.

In the 2004 elections, for the first time in Indonesian history, the president and vice-president were directly elected. Former General Susilo Bambang Yudhoyono emerged as Indonesia's sixth President (2004–09). If Megawati's presidency had seen Indonesia become a site for Islamic terrorism, in Susilo Bambang Yudhoyono's time the nation attracted attention for devastating natural disasters. The worst was the December 2004 earthquake off Aceh, which produced the tsunami that claimed nearly a quarter of a million lives around the Indian Ocean. Some 167,000 died in Aceh. Sri Lanka, India, and Thailand were also hard hit, but none lost so many lives as Indonesia. Earthquakes, floods, landslides, and similar disasters struck the nation with depressing regularity in following years.

As the world's attention focused on restoring Aceh, a solution emerged to the long-standing insurgency there. In 2005 GAM accepted Indonesian sovereignty and Jakarta gave Aceh special autonomy. Local elections were then held and a former GAM figure was elected as governor of Aceh.

Widespread corruption – of business, political parties, government, judiciary, police, military, and bureaucracy – remained a major problem, but there was some progress. Some high-profile and many low-profile criminals and corruptors went to jail during Susilo Bambang Yudhoyono's presidency, but there seemed no shortage of crooks to replace them.

14
Southeast Asia Today

Introduction

Southeast Asia's past – as we have described it in the preceding chapters – shapes its present and future. Each country has its own special issues, but some general patterns can be discerned as we look at the region in early 2010, as this book is being completed. We consider some of the major issues below.

Politics

Above all, it needs to be emphasized that the modern nation-states of the region seem destined to remain for the foreseeable future. Over the years there was significant concern that some of them might break up. Ethnic secession loomed even before the date of independence in Burma, the southern Muslim regions of Thailand and of the Philippines challenged state authority in both nations, and Indonesia had difficulty convincing all of its outlying regions that government from Jakarta was in their interest. Indeed, Vietnam was not even unified as a single nation until 1976, after the Vietnam War. As we look at Southeast Asia from the perspective of early 2010, however, only in Indonesia is there much reality to ideas of secession, for there the future of Aceh within the nation still seems open to question at times. Many Papuans are dissatisfied with Jakarta, but their hopes have no real prospect of being met except within the framework of the Indonesian nation-state. East Timor (now the tiny state of Timor-Leste) having already become independent of Indonesia, and Indonesia having introduced decentralization to over 460 autonomous regions across the archipelago, centrifugal forces generally seem under control in that island state – where about 40 percent of all Southeast Asians live.

Occasionally minor territorial disputes still arise between Southeast Asian nations but no significant conflict follows. Although ASEAN is not a conflict-resolution body, it has evolved from its largely symbolic beginnings to become a regional architecture for interaction, which assists in the management of territorial disputes without serious conflict. Moreover – perhaps most crucially – the middle classes of the more prosperous states reasonably conclude that their hopes for the future are best-guaranteed by the continuing existence of present state structures and interstate relationships. A middle class in rebellion against the existence of any state in the region is almost inconceivable, except perhaps in Burma/Myanmar. It is also true that the militaries of the ASEAN states have productive relationships with one another. It is ironic that ASEAN, which from the start specifically rejected the idea of a military alliance structure, nevertheless constitutes an umbrella under which a network of bilateral military cooperation agreements bind the region together.

That is not to say, however, that these states face no serious issues. We may identify at least four major issues in the political realm before turning to economic and environmental issues below. Those four political issues are the fragility of democracy where it exists, corruption, the continuing presence of authoritarian governments, and the role of religion in political life.

Democracies

Thailand, Malaysia, the Philippines, and Indonesia are democracies, but in most of them the democratic system faces real or potential challenges. One of the most striking phenomena is the emergence of organized mobs as an alternative to electoral politics. It is essential for a stable democratic system that citizens, political leaders, and parties accept the outcome of elections. Beginning with the EDSA 'People Power' action that overthrew the Marcos regime in the Philippines in 1986, the idea of bringing people onto the streets to force political change became a feature in Southeast Asian democracies. Thus followed EDSA II that overthrew President Joseph Estrada and EDSA III that tried – but failed – to topple the government of Gloria Macapagal-Arroyo, both in 2001. In Thailand, 'red-shirt' and 'yellow-shirt' activists used massive street demonstrations to press their cause, rejecting the idea that an election outcome must be accepted even if it is not the one they want. In effect, these campaigns pitted supporters of the Bangkok middle class and its leaders (in yellow shirts), who opposed the elected government of Thaksin Shinawatra, against poorer and rural people (in red shirts). In Thailand there is also the further complication of the role of the king, to whom all sides can appeal rather than taking responsibility themselves for a democratic resolution of conflicts. What would become of this role after the death of King Bhumibol, and the presumed succession of Crown Prince Vajiralongkorn, became the subject of wide concern and covert debate in Thai political circles.

Indonesia is now the third-most populous democracy in the world, after India and the United States. Its democracy, however, has certain oddities that raise concern in the minds of some people. Its electoral process is highly complex – in the 2009 legislative election there were 171 million registered voters, of whom about 104 million actually voted at over 500,000 voting stations, choosing among several thousand candidates from nearly 40 political parties. Political parties are, however, very weak in Indonesia and voting patterns are highly individualistic, revealing little or no party loyalty. It is not clear whether Indonesia is confounding political science theory by creating a strong democracy with a very weak party system, or will face problems if its parties are not better consolidated. In the Philippines, too, the party system is weak.

Other Southeast Asian nations have their own versions of democracy. Singapore has free and fair elections in which the dominant PAP always wins almost all seats, with genuine widespread support. Opposition members are very few and regularly contend that the state marginalizes them, penalizes their supporters, and sues them into bankruptcy. Singapore politics take place more within the PAP than between it and other contenders. Cambodia has an electoral democracy that in fact is entirely dominated by Hun Sen's CPP. It is not clear whether Cambodia can evolve beyond that to a true multi-party democracy. King Norodom Sihamoni has none of the influence of his father, or of the Thai king, so at least there is not a royal barrier to further evolution of the Cambodian system.

Malaysia's National Front (*Barisan Nasional*) is based upon a collaboration at the top level of the leaders of ethnically defined political parties, with overall dominance by UMNO and Malay politicians. The 2008 election outcome seriously challenged UMNO, however, and the future of this sort of system is open to question. Anwar Ibrahim's coalition of opposition parties shook the roots of UMNO dominance but itself is hardly less shaky internally. Whether a non-ethnically defined multiparty democracy can evolve is unknown. A historically precedented alternative could be emergency rule doing away with democracy. Religion is a central issue here and will be discussed below.

Corruption

In all of the democracies mentioned above except for Singapore, abuse of power and financial corruption by politicians are major issues. Southeast Asian states are not alone in this, of course, for corruption is a problem in democracies – as in non-democracies – around the world. But some nations are better at discovering and prosecuting corruptors than others. Regime corruption remains a major issue in the minds of 'yellow shirt' anti-Thaksin activists in Bangkok. It pervades the Indonesian system at all levels, although Indonesia has made great progress in prosecuting corruptors – even 'big fish' up to the level of provincial governors and ex-cabinet ministers. Indonesian elections are, however, dominated by 'money politics', with many voters agreeing to support whichever candidate gives them the most cash. Government-funded projects in Malaysia may betray the heady smell of cronyism. And the Philippines is no cleaner: what Americans call 'pork-barrel politics' is the norm there. Singapore remains the exception to these patterns, with a reputation for incorruptibility that Transparency International ranks at number 4 in the world, just below Denmark, Sweden, and New Zealand.

Transparency International rankings for Southeast Asian nations are as follows (see Table 14.1). They show one significant improvement in the sense that Indonesia is no longer thought to be the most corrupt nation in the world.

Corruption not only diverts public resources into private pockets but discredits the political systems that sustain it. Thus Indonesia's, Malaysia's, or the Philippines' democracies may be discredited by corruption in the eyes of their people, but so are the Burmese 'socialist' military regime or the Communist state in Vietnam. Corruption thus represents a threat to the regimes that allow it to continue. When a state's political leaders, its police, military, and judiciary are all corrupted, however, it is difficult to identify any

Table 14.1 Transparency International rankings for Southeast Asian states, 2008

Country	Transparency International world ranking
Singapore	4
Malaysia	47
Thailand	80
Vietnam	121
Indonesia	126
The Philippines	141
Timor-Leste	145
Laos	151
Cambodia	166
Myanmar	178

Source: http://www.transparency.org/news_room/in_focus/2008/cpi2008/cpi_2008_table
(NB: Brunei does not cooperate with Transparency International)

point in the circle of guilt where a beginning can be made at eradication. This has been a central problem for international organizations such as the World Bank and IMF in their campaigns to improve governance, for the people to whom they must turn to solve the problems of governance – that is, the people in power in particular countries – are usually the leading corruptors themselves.

Authoritarian governments and the military

Authoritarianism has deep roots in the history of Southeast Asia – as has been amply demonstrated in the earlier chapters of this book – and is unlikely to disappear in any grand wave of democratization. Burma/Myanmar's military regime seems a true atavism in today's Southeast Asia – an old-fashioned military dictatorship, run by generals determined to hold onto power and aware that their fortunes and their persons would be at risk if there were truly a transition to democracy. Aung San Suu Kyi (Figure 38) is the best-known pro-democracy figure in Myanmar, but others also vie for relevance. Since the 1990s, the regime's 'Roadmap to Democracy' has guided the transition from a military-run government to a power-sharing structure, an orchestrated process that has attracted criticism. The government's 2008 constitution reserves 25 percent of seats in the national legislature for the military, thereby guaranteeing it a central role. Indeed, the military continues to regard itself as the only institution capable of preventing national disintegration. The 'Roadmap' requires legislative elections in 2010. Opposition groups participating in the process argue that the elections must be meaningful, debate encouraged, and press censorship relaxed. Opposition groups that did not participate in the constitutional convention reject the military's version of democracy altogether. The continuing imprisonment of opposition figures further discredits any claims by the military to be implementing reform.

The Vietnamese and Lao regimes are attempting the sort of transition seen in the PRC: moving toward a more market-based economy and involvement in international trade, while maintaining political control by the Communist Party.

Figure 38   Aung San Suu Kyi, 2009
Khin Maung Win/AP/Press Association Images

In neither state is there leadership of the evident quality of the PRC, but all have to deal with the same inherent tensions between greater economic openness on the one hand, and refusal of political openness on the other. Dissidents are crushed, but in Vietnam there is some greater tolerance of public expressions of dissatisfaction, particularly over land issues. Tiny Brunei is an authoritarian, wealthy welfare state under the rule of its Sultan and presumably will remain so.

Even in democratic states, there can be a risk of military intervention. The risk is greatest in Thailand, as its recent history has shown. In Indonesia, retired military figures still loom large in politics and, although the army has been removed from the parliament and genuinely seems willing to accept a non-political role, from time to time disaffected people wonder whether military rule wouldn't be preferable. In the Philippines, too, the failures of the state make military intervention attractive in the eyes of some. Probably only in Singapore, Malaysia and the Indochinese countries is it reasonable to rule out unilateral military intervention in political affairs.

Religion in public life

In common with much of the world, Southeast Asian societies have witnessed an upsurge in religiosity in public as well as in private life. All the religions of the region have been involved. This has sometimes produced tensions between followers of different faiths but has also frequently promoted divisions within religious traditions.

Burmese identity is so closely tied up with Buddhism that its continuing prominence is unsurprising. Buddhist schools play an important role in education, especially for the poor. The regime itself seeks to use Buddhism as a form of legitimacy and it is here that the faith most obviously intrudes into public life. The regime version, however, is not reformed but rather superstitious Buddhism, where astrology matters more than the teachings or Precepts of the Buddha.

Thailand sees a constant stream of new spiritual leaders and movements, mostly within a Buddhist framework. Spirit mediums are important, too, particularly as Thais seek guidance in uncertain times. After the terrible years of the *Khmer Rouge*, Cambodia has been experiencing a revival of Buddhism and other traditional arts and culture. But here we see also the impact of Christian missions – which historically had little success among either Buddhists or Muslims. Since the 1990s, however, there has been more openness to Christianity among ethnic Khmer, perhaps as a reaction against the psychological trauma of the Pol Pot years.

In the Philippines, Catholic Church leaders have long felt qualified to play public political roles. Now, however, the Church is challenged by the long-established *Iglesia ni Kristo* sect and by more recent evangelical Christian groups like El Shaddai, Jesus is Lord, and Couples for Christ. Evangelical Christianity is also growing in Singapore among the majority Chinese population, although Buddhism remains the largest religion there. In 2009 there were indications that politically active 'born-again' Singapore Chinese Christians were seeking control of a multi-ethnic and multi-religious women's civil-society organization to further an anti-gay agenda. They were defeated in this and the impropriety of such religious intrusion into public affairs was reaffirmed by the government and many other voices.

It is Islam that attracts most attention in discussions of Southeast Asian affairs. Islamically defined insurgencies have occurred – and are almost certain to continue with varying degrees of intensity – in western Myanmar, southern Thailand, and the southern Philippines. Here arise questions about national, ethnic, and religious identities of a kind familiar in Southeast Asian states.

Islam is an even more salient aspect of the domestic social, cultural, and political life of Malaysia, Brunei, and Indonesia. Brunei calls itself *Brunei Darussalam*, meaning 'Brunei, the abode of peace'. This is from Arabic *dar al-salam*, a term found in the *Qur'an* to describe heaven and conventionally used for territories firmly within the Islamic world, as opposed to *dar al-harb*, the lands of war, where *jihad* takes place. Islam is Brunei's official religion and is followed by some two-thirds of its 380,000 or so inhabitants (a population about the size of Tulsa, Oklahoma, or Bristol in the United Kingdom).

In Malaysia and Indonesia, where Islam is the religion of about 60 and 86 percent of the population respectively, religion is – and is likely to remain – a publicly contested issue. Malaysia was declared to be an Islamic state by Mahathir in 2001, although there was no constitutional basis for such a claim.

Non-Muslims fear that they are becoming, or have in fact already become, second-class citizens, a fear that threatens to undermine the ethnic compromises that are the foundation of the Malaysian state. How this issue is handled in the future – in particular, whether UMNO will continue trying to 'out-Islamize' the Islamists of PAS – will be a powerful determinant of Malaysia's future stability as a multi-ethnic, multi-religious state.

In Indonesia, there is conflict between Islamic activists and non-Muslims, particularly new Christian churches, but the main issues are within the Muslim community. Fundamentalist and extremist activists have been involved in terrorism, but Indonesia has an impressive record of eliminating terrorists and reigning in their networks. Terrorism will remain a danger, but there is no prospect whatsoever of an extremist, terrorist takeover of this most populous majority-Muslim nation in the world. Non-violent Islamists may, however, have success in infiltrating, influencing, or even taking over civil-society organizations, the major religious organizations Muhammadiyah and NU, state organs like the Ministry of Religious Affairs, and such semi-official bodies as the *Majelis Ulama Indonesia*. Such a development could threaten the multicultural, multi-religious character of Indonesian public life and poison inter-group relations. The main resistance to such a development comes – not from non-Muslims as in Malaysia – but from the majority Muslim population of Indonesia itself, which regularly demonstrates its opposition to rigid versions of the faith.

Economics

In 2010, all of Southeast Asia – in common with all the rest of the world – awaits anxiously the further development of the worst financial crisis since the Great Depression. Throughout the region, unemployment and underemployment loom as major problems. The degree to which nations are affected by this crisis reflects the extent to which they are integrated into the world's economy. For relatively isolated and isolationist Myanmar, with an economy at a very low level of development, the impact will be slight. For Singapore (Figure 39) – with no resources of its own except a brilliant location, the wit of its people, and a smart, incorruptible government – a booming world economy brought tremendous benefits, measurable in a GDP per capita of around USD 52,000, on a par with oil-rich Brunei and Norway, and above the USA, almost all of Europe and all the rest of Asia. This also means, however, that Singapore is most exposed to a contraction in world trade, which profoundly threatens the nation's well-being.

Myanmar benefits from the PRC's global search for energy security. China and Russia are likely to remain prominent investors in Myanmar's oil and gas sectors. The overall future of its economy will, however, remain obscured by the fact that much of it consists of unrecorded, black-market activity. In Thailand, just as there is tension between globalization and 'Thainess' culturally, so also economic thought reflects tension between international economic integration and autarky; this is particularly true of the royally initiated ideology of 'self-sufficiency' which has been promulgated in some circles since the 1997 financial crisis. The world market for Cambodia's exports (mainly manufactured

Figure 39   Modern bank buildings and restored shop-houses in Singapore, 2010

garments) has shrunk in the international crisis and Cambodia will continue to depend very heavily on international aid for survival. Laos is a very poor country, with a GDP per capita estimated at about USD 2000, but its mountainous terrain running up to 2800 meters (9200 feet) gives it a capacity for hydroelectric power. The dams required for this will have the predictable environmental impacts.

In Timor-Leste, aid has been essential to survival, but oil and gas are changing that picture. Off-shore fields have begun to produce significant income for the country. Because there are no production facilities in the country itself, however, everything is piped to Australia and this income therefore produces next to no employment in Timor-Leste. This tiny land of 15,000 square km (not quite 6000 square miles – about the size of the American state of Connecticut or half the size of Belgium) with a population of around 1 million – faces profound political and human development challenges before it can be regarded as a viable nation.

Globalization and international relations

ASEAN has become more effective as an umbrella organization in dealing with the non-Southeast Asian world as well as a neighborly sort of local organization. In dealing with any major crisis, however – including global economic crises – it has no answers. Countries are on their own when major challenges arise. In the case of Myanmar, the country is largely on its own, anyway, and mainly an embarrassment to ASEAN. Its main international supporters are the PRC and Russia, who have resisted attempts in the UN to impose tougher sanctions.

Southeast Asia's role in globalization is perhaps most obvious with regard to people – particularly, but not always, women. Filipino nurses are found in hospitals around the world; Thai construction workers and prostitutes are seen widely in Asia; and Indonesian and Filipino maids raise the children and look after the elderly of Singapore, Hong Kong, and the Persian Gulf states. These jobs also mean money: remittances from such workers are significant elements in the GDP of several Southeast Asian states. The World Bank lists the Philippines, Indonesia, Vietnam, Thailand, Malaysia, Cambodia, and Myanmar, in that order, among the ten top Asian national recipients of remittances.

We have seen in the preceding chapters of this book that globalization is nothing new in Southeast Asia. In its present form, however, it carries a particularly heavy dose of cultural baggage that raises local issues. In Southeast Asia, two kinds of such baggage are particularly salient: the Western and the Islamic. The cultural differences between these two are profound. The former generally emphasizes the idea of freedom as a means of liberating individual and social potential for good. The latter generally emphasizes the need to control freedom to restrict the individual and social potential for evil; it seeks justice rather than freedom. Neither delivers quite what it promises and neither has been completely welcome among the majority of Southeast Asians. Contests between local cultural expressions – literature, dance, visual arts, myths, faiths – and these globalized ideas are common. Mutual enrichment and cultural bridges also exist. What is called 'liberal Islam' and other such movements seek both the freedom of liberalism and the justice promised by faith. In non-Islamic societies these same challenges are found. We may be confident that Southeast Asians will continue to embrace both the global and the local and thereby produce unique and creative cultural forms.

The natural world

Southeast Asia's geography and geology create permanent challenges to human life there, while human conduct has produced further challenges that now loom large. The archipelago that encompasses Indonesia and the Philippines is one of the most geologically unstable areas of the globe, part of the so-called 'ring of fire' where several of the earth's great tectonic plates collide. Volcanic eruptions are common in Indonesia, sometimes with devastating consequences. Throughout the region a high percentage of the population lives near water, either along Southeast Asia's great rivers or near coastlines. Such conditions explain much of the great human cost of events such as the eruptions of Tambora or Pinatubo, the dreadful earthquake and tsunami of December 2004, Cyclone Nargis in 2008, or the earthquakes, storms, droughts, and floods that occur across the region with discouraging regularity.

For most Southeast Asians, life thus has, and will continue to have, a high degree of unpredictability arising from the natural environment. Climate change is likely to exacerbate this. In April 2009, the Asian Development Bank (ADB) attempted to predict the impact of climate change and concluded that 'Southeast Asia is one of the world's most vulnerable regions ... due to its long coastlines, high concentration of population and economic activity in coastal

Table 14.2   Population and population growth rates, 2009

Country	Population 2009 est. (millions)	Population growth rate 2009 est. (% p.a.)	Population doubling time (years)
Thailand	65.9	0.615	114
Myanmar	48.1	0.783	89
Vietnam	87.0	0.977	72
Singapore	4.7	0.998	70
Indonesia	240.3	1.136	62
Malaysia	25.7	1.723	41
Brunei	0.388	1.759	40
Cambodia	14.5	1.765	40
Philippines	98.0	1.957	36
Timor-Leste	1.1	2.027	35
Laos	6.8	2.316	30

Source: https://www.cia.gov/library/publications/the-world-factbook/print/sn.html

areas, and heavy reliance on agriculture, natural resources, and forestry.'[1] According to the ADB report, extreme weather events are likely to occur more frequently and rice production may decline drastically over the coming century. It suggested that by 2100 Indonesia, the Philippines, Thailand, and Vietnam could suffer a decrease of rice production of some 50 percent from 1990 levels, ranging from 34 percent in Indonesia to 76 percent in the Philippines. If the actual outcome is anywhere near such projections, there will be a terrible economic and human cost to bear. Land-use change is one of the main problems in the region, as its forests are cut down for their timber and the land is converted to plantation agriculture, or sometimes just left to degrade. Soil erosion is a serious consequence of such practices. Much of the logging has been illegal, fueled by heavy international demand and local corruption.

The region's future depends to a great extent on how heavy the demand of its population is upon its resources, especially if the ADB report proves to be correct in predicting declining local rice production. As will be seen in Table 14.2, the larger countries of Southeast Asia have introduced quite successful birth control programs to rein in what were once high rates of population growth. The major exception is the Philippines where the Catholic Church opposes programs to promote contraceptives; there, if current rates of growth hold, the population will double to some 200 million by *c.*2045.

Southeast Asia tomorrow

Southeast Asia as a region is tremendously conscious of its own history. Each country has produced its own narrative of its past – in many cases multiple narratives, as official, government-created versions of history are challenged,

---

1   Asian Development Bank, *The Economics of Climate Change in Southeast Asia: A regional overview.* April 2009. Available at http://www.adb.org/documents/ books/economics-climate-change-sea/default.asp.

contested, and rewritten by dissenting voices within the nation. The struggle continues to reach a balanced assessment of the colonial past, to incorporate immigrant communities into a 'national' story, to write an inclusive history that ideally leaves no minority marginalized without a voice or a share in that story. The contentious issues are not limited to the colonial era, however; the memories of a more distant past, however faint they may be in the twenty-first century, are often evoked as the basis for a particular group's right to power or a government's claim to a disputed territory. At a regional level, the evolution of ASEAN and its expansion to include nearly all of Southeast Asia have generated their own narratives of the past, intended to create bonds where there have often been tensions and conflicts and to build a shared identity where one does not naturally exist. Understandings of the most recent history matter, too; they are often powerful elements in Southeast Asians' conceptions of the present.

It is generally recognized that Southeast Asians would benefit from a more comprehensive study and comprehension of their neighbors' history, not just their own. We may hope that this book, written in Southeast Asia by historians who live there, will contribute to such an understanding. At the same time, a region of such creative people, with so many natural resources, and such a rich history, will continue to deserve the attention of the wider world outside Southeast Asia. Its contributions to that wider world, and to itself, will be shaped by the interplay among the issues discussed above. Perhaps one day there will be a second edition of this book, when it may be possible to assess what that interplay has produced.

Recommended Readings

General histories

There are several good general histories of Southeast Asia, most of them country-based, that readers will find useful, along with the more specific readings mentioned for each chapter below.

The earlier history of all of Indianized Southeast Asia is covered in the venerable work by Coedès, *Les états hindouisés*, available in English as *Indianized States of Southeast Asia*. For island Southeast Asia, Coedès relied upon the even more venerable Krom, *Hindoe-Javaansche geschiedenis*. Tarling, *Cambridge History of Southeast Asia*, consists of four volumes with contributions covering from early times to recent history. Tate, *Making of Modern South-East Asia*, is also a useful reference, particularly for its detailed account of the colonization of the region and its many maps. Owen et al., *Emergence of Modern Southeast Asia*, is a work of collective authorship covering roughly the last three centuries of the region's history. Osborne's books *Exploring Southeast Asia* and *Southeast Asia: An introductory history* provide solid and readable accounts.

Concerning more modern Burma/Myanmar, Taylor's *State in Myanmar* is the best political history from the Konbaung dynasty to 2008. Cady's *History of Modern Burma* – although written in the late 1950s with a supplement going to 1959 – is still useful for the period from the eighteenth century to the time of its writing. A general history of Thailand from early times to the 1990s is Wyatt, *Thailand: A short history*. The best general history of Cambodia from early times to the 1990s is Chandler's *History of Cambodia*. Stuart-Fox, *History of Laos*; and Evans, *Short History of Laos*, are valuable, both emphasizing more recent Laotian history.

For Indonesia, Ricklefs's *History of Modern Indonesia* covers the period from the first signs of Islamization *c*.1200 to 2008. Andaya and Andaya, *History of Malaysia*, covers from early times to the late twentieth century. On Singapore, see Turnbull, *History of Singapore*. Chew and Lee (eds), *History of Singapore*, is also valuable. Brunei's history is surveyed in Ranjit Singh, *Brunei*; and Graham, *History of Brunei*.

On the Philippines, Agoncillo and Gerrero's *History of the Filipino People*; and Zaide's two-volume *Pageant of Philippine history*, provide good overviews of the Philippines from the pre-colonial period to the 1970s. Constantino and Constantino's two volumes *The Philippines: A past revisited* and *The Philippines: A continuing past*, cover the pre-colonial period to the 1960s. Corpuz's two-volume tome, *Roots of the Filipino Nation*, covers the country's history from the sixteenth century until the early twentieth century. And Cortez et al.'s *Filipino Saga*, discusses the archipelago's history from its conquest in the 1500s to its continuing quest towards nationhood in the 1990s.

Vietnam has been less well-served by general histories. An official, but valuable, work is Nguyen Khac Vien, *Vietnam, a Long History*. See also the two volumes by Chapuis entitled *A History of Vietnam* and *Last Emperors of Vietnam*.

1   Ethnic groups, early cultures and social structures

On the pre-history of Southeast Asia, a classic collection of articles is Smith and Watson, *Early South East Asia*; a much more recent and comprehensive collection is in Glover and Bellwood, *Southeast Asia from Prehistory to History*. Bellwood, *Prehistory of the Indo-Malayan Archipelago,* is a thorough study of the maritime world; for the mainland, Charles Higham has authored several important works: *Archaeology of Mainland Southeast Asia; Bronze Age of Southeast Asia*; and *Early Cultures of Mainland Southeast Asia*.

Details on most Southeast Asian ethnic groups can be found in Lebar's works *Ethnic Groups of Insular Southeast Asia* and *Ethnic Groups of Mainland Southeast Asia*. Keyes, *Golden Peninsula,* provides a good historical-anthropological overview of the mainland region. Scott, *Art of Not Being Governed*, is a rethinking of upland-lowland relations. Southeast Asian anthropology as a field has left very few ethnic groups unstudied; King and Wilder, *Modern Anthropology of Southeast Asia*, has a detailed overview of major topics and a comprehensive bibliography. See Moore, *Early Landscapes of Myanmar*, for a wonderfully illustrated source on the pre-Indianized communities of the Irrawaddy river zone.

2   Early state formation (c.0–1300)

The most detailed synthesis of early Southeast Asian history – although it leaves out Vietnam and the Philippines – is Coedès, *IndianizedSstates*. Taylor's *Birth of Vietnam* fills in this gap for Vietnam, covering the period before and during Chinese rule. Smith and Watson, *Early South East Asia*, includes a number of chapters addressing the themes and issues covered in this chapter. Glover and Bellwood, *Southeast Asia from Prehistory to History*, has extensive sections on the proto-history of the various parts of the region. Munoz, *Early Kingdoms of the Indonesian Archipelago and the Malay Peninsula* is a recent synthesis of Western-language scholarship on the maritime world, although it includes some rather dated interpretations. Hall, *Maritime Trade and State Development*, discusses political and economic developments. Wolters, *History, Culture and Region*, is a stimulating discussion of interaction among Chinese, Indian, and Southeast Asian cultural elements. Brown, *Dvaravati Wheels of the Law*, provides an interesting analysis of Indianization from the perspective of art history; while Wheatley, *Nagara and Commandery*, looks at the same phenomenon through historical geography. Wolters, *Early Indonesian Commerce*; and Vickery, *Society, Economics, and Politics in Pre-Angkor Cambodia* focus on specific parts of the region. Nguyen Tai Thu, *History of Buddhism in Vietnam*, is a detailed historical study. Hudson, 'Origins of Bagan', is a much-needed study of pre-Pagan urban centers in the 'Pyu' period. See also the special issue of *Asian Perspectives: The Journal of Archaeology for Asia and the Pacific* (Vol. 40, No. 1, 2001), which covers the development of the field of pre-history in Burma/Myanmar. Aung-Thwin, *Mists of Rāmañña*, controversially challenges the idea of a pre-Pagan Mon kingdom from which the classical Buddhist state emerged.

3   'Classical' states at their height

Coedès, *Indianized States*, provides a detailed narrative of the rise of the 'classical states' except for Vietnam. Munoz, *Early Kingdoms of the Indonesian Archipelago and the Malay Peninsula* extends into the classical period; while Lieberman, *Strange Parallels*, has an excellent discussion of the mainland polities. Krom, *Hindoe-Javaansche geschiedenis,* remains the most comprehensive and authoritative account of the Indonesian 'classical' states. The main sources for fourteenth-century Majapahit are available in translation. In the case of the *Deśawarnana/Nagarakertagama,* see Prapañca, *Deśawārnana* (trans. Stuart Robson); an earlier, less fluent translation is in Pigeaud, *Java in the 14th Century,* which also contains much other useful material. The *Pararaton* is in Dutch translation in Brandes, *Pararaton (Ken Arok).* On the later history of Majapahit, see Noorduyn, 'Majapahit in the fifteenth century'. Old Javanese literature and culture are brilliantly analysed in Zoetmulder, *Kalangwan.* Hall, *Maritime Trade and State Development,* has an extensive treatment of economic issues during the 'classical' period. The chapters in Marr and Milner, *Southeast Asia in the 9th to 14th Centuries;* and Hall and Whitmore, *Explorations in Early Southeast Asian History,* cover a wide variety of topics.

On the Angkorean polity, Briggs, *Ancient Khmer Empire,* is dated but still informative, as is Coedès, *Angkor: An introduction;* Higham, *Civilization of Angkor,* is a more recent synthesis. Aung-Thwin, *Pagan,* is the most comprehensive English-language study of that state; and Aung-Thwin's *Myth and History* addresses important issues in the history of Pagan. See Gosling, *Sukhothai,* on that state. Wyatt, *History of Thailand,* has a good overview of both Sukhothai and Lanna. Chapuis, *History of Vietnam,* has a competent discussion of this period of Vietnamese history, although it is largely narrative; a useful overview is to be found in Lê Thanh Khôi, *Histoire du Vietnam.* Several articles on the Tran dynasty can be found in Wolters, *Early Southeast Asia.* Wolters, *Fall of Śrivijaya* – despite the title – is in fact a study of the polity's history.

4 New global religions and ideas from the thirteenth century

Swearer's works *Buddhism and Society in Southeast Asia* and *Buddhist World of Southeast Asia* contain considerable historical material on Theravada Buddhism. A useful collection of essays is in Smith, *Religion and Legitimation of Power.* An overview of the Buddhist conceptual world is in Aung-Thwin's *Pagan.* Other studies of Burmese Buddhism include Mendelson, *Sangha and State;* Spiro, *Buddhism and Society;* and Collins, *Nirvana and Other Buddhist Felicities,* which places Burmese Buddhism within a larger Sanskrit-Pali context. Spiro's *Burmese Supernaturalism* concerns spirit-worship in Burma.

There are several good introductions to Islam; Saeed, *Islamic Thought,* can be recommended. The very extensive literature on the Islamization of maritime Southeast Asia is surveyed in Ricklefs, *History of Modern Indonesia.* On Southeast Asia early in the Islamic era, see Nakahara, 'Muslim merchants in Nan-Hai'. Sultan Sulaiman's gravestone is discussed in Montana, 'Nouvelle donées'. The Islamization of Java down to the early nineteenth century is discussed in Ricklefs, *Mystic Synthesis.* On the role of Sufis, see Johns's articles 'Sufism as a category' and 'Islamization in Southeast Asia'. Cortesão, *Suma Oriental,* contains an edition of Tomé Pires in Portuguese and English translation. Two sixteenth-century Javanese Islamic books have been edited and translated by Drewes: *Javaanse primbon* and *Admonitions of Seh Bari.* See also Drewes, *Early Javanese Code.* Andaya, *Flaming Womb,* is an excellent discussion of Southeast Asian women and their role within Buddhism, Islam, and Christianity.

Concerning Islamic-period literatures of Southeast Asia, the surveys in Teeuw and Emanuels, *Studies on Malay and Bahasa Indonesia;* and Uhlenbeck, *Studies on the Languages of Java and Madura,* remain useful. Surveys of classical Malay literature are found in Braginsky, *Heritage;* and Winstedt, *History of Classical Malay Literature.* On seventeenth-century Aceh and its mystics, much has been written; see Lombard, *Iskandar Muda;* Johns's contributions 'Malay Sufism', 'Islam in Southeast Asia' and

'Quranic exegetes'; Riddell, 'Earliest Quranic exegetical activity'; van Nieuwenhuijze, *Šamsu'l-Din van Pasai*; al-Attas's works *Mysticism of Hamzah Fansuri* and *Raniri and the Wujudiyyah of 17th Century Aceh*; Drewes, 'Nūr al-Dīn al-Ranīrī's charge of heresy'; Drewes and Brakel, *Poems of Hamzah Fansuri*; Kraus, 'Transformations'; Azra, *Origins of Islamic Reformism*; Ito, 'Why did Nuruddin ar-Raniri leave Aceh?'; and Azra, 'Opposition to Sufism'. Braginsky, 'Structure, date and sources', considers possible Mughal prototypes for *Hikayat Aceh*. See also the edition and translation by C. C. Brown of the *Sejarah Melayu*.

The most comprehensive survey of Javanese literature is in Vol. I of Pigeaud, *Literature of Java*. Zoetmulder, *Pantheisme en monisme*, is still the best analysis of mystical Javanese Islam and is available also in English (*Pantheism and Monism*). On the spiritually powerful books of the eighteenth century, see Ricklefs's books *Seen and Unseen Worlds* and *Jogjakarta under Sultan Mangkubumi*. On the survival of Old Javanese literature in Islamized Java, see Ricklefs, *Seen and Unseen Worlds*. For Bugis and Makasarese literature, see especially Noorduyn's works *Kroniek van Wadjo'* and 'Origins of South Celebes historical writing'.

On Protestantism in the particular context of Dutch history, see Israel, *Dutch Republic*; or Schama, *Embarrassment of Riches*.

5   The rise of new states from the fourteenth century

Attempts to capture broad historical trends and patterns in Southeast Asia (and more widely) have produced major – and contesting – works of synthesis that include this period. The two most important are Reid, *Southeast Asia in the Age of Commerce, 1450–1680*; and Lieberman, *Strange Parallels: Southeast Asia in global context 800–1830*.

This period is covered in Ricklefs's *History of Modern Indonesia*. Malay history in the age of Malacca is in discussed in Wang, 'First three rulers of Malacca'; Wake, 'Malacca's early kings'; and Meilink-Roelofsz, *Asian Trade and European Influence*. On the history of Melaka, see also Wheatley and Sandhu, *Melaka*; and Hashim, *Malay Sultanate of Malacca*.

On Java, see de Graaf and Pigeaud, *Eerste Moslimse vorstendommen op Java*; and de Graaf, *Sénapati Ingalaga*. English summaries of these books and an index can be found in Pigeaud and de Graaf, *Islamic States*. See also Ricklefs, *Mystic Synthesis*. On the later years of Majapahit, see Noorduyn, 'Majapahit in the fifteenth century'.

The history of the western archipelago in this period is covered in detail in Meilink-Roelofsz, *Asian Trade and European Influence*. See also Djajadiningrat, 'Geschiedenis van het Soeltanaat van Atjeh'. On eastern Indonesia, see L. Andaya, *World of Maluku*. Bali is discussed in Vickers, *Bali*; and Creese, 'Balinese *babad*'.

Regarding Burma, Lieberman's two books, *Burmese Administrative Cycles* and *Strange Parallels*, are important. See also Aung-Thwin, *Myth and History*; Gommans and Leider, *Maritime Frontiers of Burma*; and Reid, *Southeast Asia in the Early Modern Era*.

Wyatt, *History of Thailand*, provides the best general overview of the Tai world during this period. Van der Cruysse, *Siam and the West*, is a detailed study of Ayutthaya's relations with European countries. Cushman, *Royal Chronicles of Ayutthaya*, translates the main textual sources for Ayutthaya's history. Kasetsiri, *Rise of Ayudhya*, is a detailed study of Ayutthaya's early years. On other states, see Penth, *Brief History of Lan Na*; and Stuart-Fox, *Lao Kingdom of Lan Xang*.

For Vietnam, Whitmore, *Vietnam, Ho Quy Ly, and the Ming* is an excellent study of the late Tran and Ming occupation periods. Unpublished dissertations by Whitmore ('The development of Le government in 15th century Vietnam') and Ungar

('Vietnamese leadership and order') provide the most detailed treatment of the fifteenth century. Li, *Nguyen Cochinchina*, studies the rise of the southern kingdom of Dang Trong. Manguin, *Les Portugais sur les côtes du Viet-Nam et du Campa*, looks at both Dang Trong and Champa for this period.

On Cambodia, the best general overview is in Chandler, *History of Cambodia*. Vickery's dissertation 'Cambodia after Angkor' is a comprehensive study of the Cambodian and Thai sources. Groslier, *Angkor and Cambodia in the 16th Century*, draws on Spanish and Portuguese accounts. Other valuable works are Mak Phoeun, *Histoire du Cambodge*, for the late sixteenth through early eighteenth centuries. Mak Phoeun and Khin Sok have published a three-volume translation of Cambodian chronicles: *Chroniques royales du Cambodge*.

6   Non-indigenous actors old and new

Sandhu and Mani, *Indian Communities in Southeast Asia*, includes sections on the pre-colonial period. Information on early Arab interest and involvement in Southeast Asia may be found in Tibbetts, *Study of the Arabic Texts on Southeast Asia*. Stuart-Fox, *Short History of China and Southeast Asia*, charts the history of 2000 years of relations between China and Southeast Asia. Concerning the Chinese, see also Kuhn, *Chinese Among Others*; Wolters, *Early Indonesian Commerce*; and Ma Huan, *Ying-Yai Sheng-lan*.

Accounts of Portuguese overseas expansion are found in Boxer, *Portuguese Seaborne Empire*; Subrahmanyam, *Portuguese Empire in Asia*; and in Diffie and Winius, *Foundations of the Portuguese Empire* (but the last includes some errors of detail concerning the Malay-Indonesian area). Boxer, *Dutch Seaborne Empire*, covers early Dutch activity. See also Parry, *Europe and a Wider World*, reprinted as *Establishment of the European Hegemony*; and Masselman, *Cradle of Colonialism*. Dijk looks at early European encounters in *Seventeenth-Century Burma and the Dutch East India Company*. See also Lieberman's article 'Europeans, trade, and the unification of Burma'. Meilink-Roelofsz, *Asian Trade and European Influence*, discusses Portuguese and early English and Dutch activities in Indonesia. A Malay depiction of the Portuguese conquest of Malacca is found in C. C. Brown, *Sějarah Mělayu*.

De Ribadeneira's *History of the Philippines* covers the initial forays of the Spanish in the Pacific. Early accounts of Spanish expansion include De Morga, *Historical Events*; and Mallat, *The Philippines*. Molina's *The Philippines*, gives an overview of Spanish rule of the archipelago. For an introduction on Spanish colonialism, see Alzona, *El legado de España a Filipinas*; or Sánchez Gómez, *Un imperio de la vitrina*.

7   Early modern Southeast Asian states

A detailed overview of Burma c.1752–1824 is available in Cady, *History of Burma*. See also Koenig, *Burmese Polity;* and Lieberman's books *Burmese Administrative Cycles* and *Strange Parallels*. Warfare and technology are described in Charney, *Southeast Asian Warfare*. Charney's book *Powerful Learning* looks at state-*Sangha* relations in Burma in the late eighteenth and nineteenth centuries. Sun, 'Military technology transfers from Ming China', concerns overland trade into the northern mainland of Southeast Asia.

Lailert's dissertation, 'Ban Phlu Luang dynasty', remains the best study of Ayutthaya's final decades. Terwiel, *History of Modern Thailand*, has a good discussion of the Thonburi and Early Bangkok periods, as does Wyatt, *History of Thailand*. Rabibhadana, *Organization of Thai Society*, is a classic study of social structure in the late Ayudhya-Early Bangkok period. Wenk, *Restoration of Thailand*; and Vella, *Siam under Rama III*, focus on the First and Third Reigns respectively. Stuart-Fox, *Lao Kingdom of*

Lan Xang, is the best treatment in English of the fragmentation of the Lao polity, while Ngaosyvathn and Ngaosyvathn, *Paths to Conflagration*, has a detailed examination of the Lao-Siamese-Vietnamese triangle.

For Cambodia, Chandler, *History of Cambodia* provides an overview of this period, which his dissertation 'Cambodia before the French' covers in much greater detail. Khin Sok, *Le Cambodge entre le Siam et le Viêtnam*, is a useful study focusing on Cambodia's tangled relations with its two neighbors.

Regarding Vietnam, Dutton, *Tay Son Uprising*, is a thorough examination of the complex final decades of the eighteenth century; Manguin, *Les Nguyen, Macau et le Portugal*, covers the same period from a different perspective. Woodside, *Vietnam and the Chinese Model*, provides a rich overview of the first three Nguyen reigns, while Choi, *Southern Vietnam*, focuses specifically on that of Ming Mang. Langlet, *L'ancienne historiographie d'état au Vietnam*, is a study of the political and intellectual preoccupations of the dynasty viewed through the lens of its historical writing.

For sixteenth- and seventeenth-century Perak, Kedah and Aceh, see Andaya, *Perak: Abode of Grace*; on Sumatra in the seventeenth and eighteenth centuries, see Watson's very fine book *To Live as Brothers*. Other important studies are Andaya, *Kingdom of Johor*, and Bonney, *Kedah*. Brunei is discussed in Brown, *Brunei*. Also useful is Suwannathat-Pian, *Thai-Malay Relations*. Studies focused more on European activities in the area include Tarling, *Anglo-Dutch Rivalry*; Lewis, *Jan Compagnie*; and Vos, *Gentle Janus*.

There is considerable literature on Java *c.*1600–1830. On the seventeenth century, see de Graaf and Pigeaud, *Eerste Moslimse vorstendommen op Java*; de Graaf, *Sénapati Ingalaga*; de Graaf, *Sultan Agung*, and de Graaf, *Mangku-Rat I*. The first of these books lacks an index, which is to be found along with English summaries of the other books listed here and other of de Graaf's writings in Pigeaud and de Graaf, *Islamic States*. See also Ricklefs, *Mystic Synthesis*, which covers the history of Islam in Java before *c.*1830. On the eighteenth century, see Ricklefs's books, *War, Culture and Economy*; *Seen and Unseen Worlds*; *Jogjakarta under Sultan Mangkubumi*; and *Mystic Synthesis*. For a general overview, see Ricklefs's *History of Modern Indonesia*.

Social life and health conditions in Batavia are analyzed in Niemeijer, *Koloniale samenleving*; van der Brug, *Malaria en malaise*; and Jean Taylor, *Social World*. Vermeulen, *Chineezen te Batavia*, concerns the Chinese massacre. Concerning VOC finances, see de Korte, *Financiële verantwoording*. On colonial issues of the British period, see Bastin's books, *Native Policies of Sir Stamford Raffles*, and *Raffles' Ideas on the Land Rent System*.

On Banten and West Java generally, see Ota, *Changes of Regime*; Djajadiningrat, *Sadjarah Bantěn*; Talens, *Feodale samenleving*; and de Haan, *Priangan*. On Shaikh Yusuf, see Azra, *Transmission*; van Bruinessen, *Naqsyabandiyah*; and Hamid, *Syekh Yusuf*. Concerning Java's northeast coast, see Van Niel's authoritative *Java's Northeast Coast*. The most important work on Java in the period 1792–1830 is Carey, *Power of Prophecy*. The standard history of the Java War itself is Louw and de Klerck, *Java-oorlog*.

An overview of the seventeenth and eighteenth century Philippines is found in the general histories mentioned above. See also De la Costa's *Readings*; Veneracion's *Agos ng dugong kayumanggi*; and Zaide's *Philippine Political and Cultural History*. Manila as the fortified, modern capital of the archipelago is discussed in Barrows, *History of the Philippines*; and Benitez, *History of the Philippines*. The colonial structures that the Spanish built on the islands are analysed in Cushner's publications *Landed Estates in the Colonial Philippines* and *Spain in the Philippines;* and in Phelan's *Hispanization of the Philippines*. See also Salazar's *Kasaysayan ng Pilipinas*. The brief British incursion in the Philippines during the Spanish regime is discussed in Fish, *When Britain Ruled the Philippines*.

8 Colonial communities, c.1800–1900

Thant Myint U, *Making of Modern Burma,* is an important overview of nineteenth-century Burma. A study of the Anglo-Burmese wars can be found in Woodman, *Making of Burma*; while Ni Ni Myint, *Burma's Struggle against British Imperialism,* provides a Burmese perspective of 'pacification' after annexation in 1886. Maung Htin Aung, *Epistles,* offers a rare insight into how the encounter with the British was seen from a Burmese perspective. Major studies of colonial rule include Furnivall's *Colonial Policy and Practice*; Cady's *History of Modern Burma*; and Taylor's *State in Myanmar.* Furnivall, *Fashioning of Leviathan,* is a classic on early British policy in Burma. Early colonial ethnography is best seen in Scott (Shway Yoe), *The Burman.* Harvey's books *British Rule in Burma* and his *History of Burma* are written from a colonial administrator's perspective. Adas, *Burma Delta,* impressively analyzes economic changes in Lower Burma from 1852 to 1941.

Hong, *Thailand in the Nineteenth Century,* spans the social and economic changes covered in Chapters 7 and 8. A somewhat dated, but readable treatment of the Fourth Reign is Moffat, *Mongkut.* A much more thorough study is Wilson's three-volume dissertation, 'State and society in the reign of Mongkut'. Reynolds's dissertation on 'The Buddhist monkhood' looks at Mongkut's impact on Buddhism. The most detailed published account of Chulalongkorn's reign is Wyatt, *Politics of Reform.* Also useful are Engel, *Law and Kingship in Thailand*; and Battye's dissertation 'Military, government, and society'. Peleggi, *Lords of Things,* looks at cultural changes among the Thai elite. Winichakul, *Siam Mapped,* is an important study of Siam's evolving perceptions of space and its relations with the colonial powers who became its neighbors. Tuck, *French Wolf and the Siamese Lamb*; and Jeshurun, *Contest for Siam,* explore the diplomatic and military tussles with the British and French.

Cady, *Roots of French Imperialism in Asia,* remains a useful source for the colonization of Indochina despite its age. Tsuboi, *L'empire vietnamien,* focuses on the Vietnamese side of the story. Osborne's books *River Road to China* and *Mekong* are very readable accounts of the connections between exploration and imperialism. Osborne's study, *French Presence in Cochinchina and Cambodia,* looks at the early decades of colonial rule in those two areas, while Nguyen, *Monarchie et fait colonial*; and Lockhart, *End of the Vietnamese Monarchy,* study the evolution of the protectorate in Annam and Tonkin. Marr, *Vietnamese Tradition on Trial,* focuses on intellectual and cultural changes under colonial rule, as does McHale, *Print and Power.* Duiker, *Rise of Vietnamese Nationalism,* looks at the various groups of Vietnamese elite. Jamieson, *Understanding Vietnam,* has a particularly useful focus on literature during the colonial period.

Tully, *France on the Mekong,* is a detailed study of French rule in Cambodia; a perspective more sympathetic to the colonial regime is in Forest, *Cambodge et la colonisation française.* Edwards, *Cambodge: Cultivation of a Nation,* emphasizes the psychological and cultural changes brought on by French policies, while Hansen, *How to Behave,* focuses on changes in Buddhism and expressions of moral values.

Colonial Laos has received less scholarly attention. Ivarsson, *Creating Laos,* is the most detailed study of French attempts to create a separate Lao political and cultural entity. Evans, *Short History of Laos*; and Stuart-Fox, *History of Laos,* provide overviews of the colonial period.

For studies of the economy of French Indochina, see Robequain, *Economic Development* (from a colonial perspective); and Murray, *Development of Capitalism* (from a Marxist perspective). Gran's dissertation 'Vietnam and the capitalist route to modernity' focuses on Cochinchina. Ngo Vinh Long, *Before the Revolution,* emphasizes the sufferings of the Vietnamese peasantry under colonial rule. Gunn, *Rebellion in Laos*, is a critical study of socio-economic developments under colonial rule. Khieu Samphan, *Economy of Cambodia*, provides a Marxist critique of the colonial economy by a future leader of the *Khmer Rouge*.

On Johor and Singapore, see Trocki, *Prince of Pirates*. See also Nordin, *Trade and Society*, on Melaka and Penang; Kobkua, *Thai-Malay Relations*; Tarling, *Anglo-Dutch Rivalry*; and Turnbull, *History of Singapore*. Valuable works on Sarawak and Brunei include Sandin, *Sea Dayaks*; Pringle, *Rajahs and Rebels*; and Tarling's books *Britain, the Brookes and Brunei* and *Burthen, Risk and Glory*. Warren, *The Sulu zone*, is an important study of that region. British involvement in the Malay states is analyzed in Cowan, *Nineteenth-Century Malaya*; and Parkinson, *British Intervention*. See also Gullick, *Rulers and Residents*; Tarling, *British Policy*; and Khoo, *Western Malay States*. Gullick, *Indigenous Political Systems*, is a major work; see also Milner, *Kerajaan*. Emerson, *Malaysia*; and Sadka, *Protected Malay States*, remain valuable sources on British rule. Economic aspects are authoritatively analyzed in Drabble, *Economic History of Malaysia*.

On the Chinese in Malaya, see the classic work by Purcell, *Chinese in Malaya*; and Trocki, *Opium and Empire*. Blythe, *Impact of Chinese Secret Societies*; and Jackson, *Planters and Speculators*, are both important. On the history of the Straits Settlements and Singapore, see Turnbull's works *Straits Settlements 1826–67* and *History of Singapore*; see also Lee, *British as Rulers*. Aspects of Singapore social history are covered in Warren's books *Rickshaw Coolie* and *Ah Ku and Karayuki-San*. See also Yen, *Social History*. Concerning Indians, see Sandhu, *Indians in Malaya*; or Arasaratnam, *Indians in Malaysia and Singapore*. British colonial social history is studied in Butcher, *British in Malaya*.

There is an immense volume of literature on nineteenth-century Indonesia, much of it listed in Ricklefs's *History of Modern Indonesia*. Important studies of the Cultivation System period are Elson, *Village Java*; and Fasseur, *Politics of Colonial Exploitation*. See also Elson, *End of the Peasantry*; and Boomgaard, *Children of the Colonial State*. On Javanese cultural activities, see Pigeaud, *Literature of Java*; Sears, *Shadows of Empire*; and Florida, *Writing the Past*. Adam, *Vernacular Press*, covers the early history of Indonesian newspapers.

Nineteenth-century Javanese Islam and broader social changes are analyzed in Ricklefs, *Polarising Javanese Society*. See also van Bruinessen, 'Origins and development of the Naqshbandi order' and *Naqsyabandiyah*; and Snouck Hurgronje, *Mekka*; On indigenous Christians, see also Guillot, *L'affaire Sadrach*; Sutarman, *Sadrach's Community*; and van Akkeren, *Sri and Christ*. An important social history of Europeans in Indonesia is Bosma and Raben, *Being 'Dutch'*.

On Indonesia's outer islands after *c*.1880, see Cribb, *Late Colonial State*. Concerning the eastern archipelago, see Chauvel, *Nationalists, Soldiers and Separatists*, on Ambon; Fox, *Harvest of the Palm*, on Nusa Tenggara; and Heersink, *Green Gold of Selayar*. On Southeast Kalimantan, see Lindblad, *Between Dayak and Dutch*. A particularly valuable work on Bali is Schulte Nordholt, *Spell of Power*. Regarding the Padris, see Dobbin, *Islamic Revivalism*; other valuable analyses are in Kraus, *Zwischen Reform und Rebellion*; and van Bruinessen, *Naqsyabandiyah*.

On the nineteenth century in the Philippines, in addition to the general histories noted above, see Molina's *The Philippines*; and Veneracion's *Agos ng dugong kayu-manggi*. The spatial transformation of the archipelago, organization of the colonial government, and hierarchical social engineering under the Spanish are assessed in Cushner's *Landed Estates in the Colonial Philippines* and *Spain in the Philippines*; and in Reed's *Hispanic Urbanism*. The role of the Chinese population in the country's history is tackled in Wickberg, *Chinese in Philippine Life*. On the Filipino reform movement in

Spain, see Schumacher, *Propaganda Movement*. Glimpses of nineteenth century economic development are provided in A.Corpuz, *Colonial Iron Horse*; Camagay, *Working Women of Manila*; Legarda, *After the Galleons*; and Warren, *Sulu Zone*. Bankoff's *Crime, Society and the State*, reviews the history of crime and criminality in Spanish Philippines. The rise of the bourgeoisie is tackled in Cullinane's *Ilustrado politics*. The Philippine Revolution and the development of Filipino nationalism are discussed in Agoncillo's studies *Filipino Nationalism* and *Revolt of the Masses*; and in Ileto, *Pasyon and Revolution*; Almario, *Panitikan ng rebolusyon*; Majul, *Mabini and the Philippine Revolution*; Salazar, 'Si Andres Bonifacio at ang kabayanihang Pilipino'; and Salazar, 'Ang "real": ni Bonifacio bilang taktikang militar'.

9 Reform, new ideas and the 1930s crisis (c.1900–1942)

Much of the literature on colonial Burma has focused on three topics: nationalism, the Depression, and resistance movements. Good analyses are in Cady's *History of Modern Burma* and Taylor's *State in Myanmar*. Other studies of nationalism before World War II include Moscotti, *British Policy and the Nationalist Movement*; Khin Yi, *Dobama Movement*; and Maung Maung's books *From Sangha to Laity* and *Burmese Nationalist Movements*. Studies of the colonial economy, the Depression, and the agrarian revolts that followed include Adas, *Burma Delta*; Scott, *Moral Economy of the Peasant*; and Brown, *Colonial Economy in Crisis*. Sarkysianz's *Buddhist Backgrounds of the Burmese Revolution*; and Adas's *Prophets of Rebellion*, explore peasant mentalities and notions of resistance. On the Saya San rebellion, see further Herbert, 'Hsaya San rebellion;' and Aung-Thwin, 'Genealogy of a rebellion'.

There are two detailed studies of the Thai King Vajiravudh's reign: Vella, *Chaiyo!*; and Green, *Absolute Dreams*. Batson, *End of the Absolute Monarchy*, focuses on the Seventh Reign; Copeland, 'Contested nationalism'; and Barmé, *Woman, Man, Bangkok*, examine the political and social changes which were linked to challenges to the absolute monarchy in its final years. Mokarapong, *History of the Thai Revolution*, is the most detailed study in English of the 1932 coup and its consequences. Wright, *Balancing Act*; and Stowe, *Siam becomes Thailand*, are well-researched narratives of Siam's political development after 1932. Suvannathat-Pian, *Thailand's Durable Premier*, focuses on Phibun's time in power. Prasertkul, 'Transformation of the Thai state', is a critical analysis of the country's political economy before and after 1932. Phongpaichit and Baker, *Thailand: Economy and Politics*, provides an excellent narrative of political and economic forces; while Peleggi, *Thailand: Worldly kingdom*, focuses on social and cultural developments.

McLeod, *Vietnamese Response*, looks at anti-French resistance during the early years of colonization in the south. Fourniau, *Annam-Tonkin*, focuses on resistance in the central and northern regions, while the same author's *Vietnam: Domination coloniale et résistance nationale*, covers all of Vietnam.

The classic studies of colonial Vietnamese nationalism in its various forms are Duiker, *Rise of Vietnamese Nationalism*; and Marr, *Vietnamese Anticolonialism*. Huynh Kim Khanh, *Vietnamese Communism*; Quinn-Judge, *Ho Chi Minh: The missing years*; Duiker, *Ho Chi Minh*; and Zinoman, *Colonial Bastille*; cover the evolution of the ICP in the pre-World War II period. Tai, *Radicalism*, emphasizes the diversity of radical elements between the wars. Woodside, *Community and Revolution*, has important insights on political and social developments during these decades. On the Cao Dai and Hoa Hao, see respectively Werner, *Peasant Politics and Sectarianism*; and Tai, *Millenarianism and Peasant Politics*.

For Cambodia, see the sources listed for Chapter 8 above along with the relevant chapters of Chandler, *History of Cambodia*; and Kiernan, *How Pol Pot Came to Power*. Tully, *Cambodia under the Tricolour*, traces developments through the first quarter of the twentieth century. The sources for Laos have been listed in the previous chapter's recommended readings.

Roff's work, *Origins of Malay Nationalism*, is indispensable for this period in Malaya. See also Khasnor Johan, *Emergence of the Modern Malay Administrative Elite*; Milner, *Invention of Politics*; Emerson, *Malaysia*; Mills, *British Rule*; Sidhu, *Administration in the Federated Malay States*; and Smith, *British Relations with the Malay Ruler*. The decentralization issue in Malaya is analyzed in Yeo, *Politics of Decentralization*. British rule in Singapore is covered in Lee, *British as Rulers*. On Sarawak, see Pringle, *Rajahs and Rebels*; and Ooi, *Of Free Trade and Native Interest*. Allen and Donnithorne's *Western Enterprise in Indonesia and Malaya*, is an important work. See also Drabble, *Economic History of Malaysia*; Courtenay, *Geography of Trade and Development*; and Jackson, *Planters and Speculators*.

On Dutch colonial policy in Indonesia and the impact of the Depression, Furnivall, *Netherlands India*, is still valuable. The most important general study of the new Indonesian elite remains Van Niel, *Emergence of the Modern Indonesian Elite*. An authoritative study of PKI and other organizations down to 1927 is McVey, *Rise of Indonesian Communism*. Trade unions are studied in Ingleson, *In Search of Justice*. The most comprehensive general survey of Islamic reform is Noer, *Modernist Muslim Movement in Indonesia*. Elson, *Idea of Indonesia*, analyzes how the very idea came about. Of various biographies of Sukarno, the best is Legge, *Sukarno: A political biography*. Ingleson, *Road to Exile*, is important on the 1927–34 period. The best study of the Depression in Indonesia is the unpublished study by O'Malley, 'Indonesia in the Great Depression'. For important studies on the peasantry, see Elson, *End of the Peasantry* and *Javanese Peasants and the Colonial Sugar Industry*. An overview is in Ricklefs, *History of Modern Indonesia*.

The American colonization of the Philippines is reviewed in Karnow's *In Our Image* and Kramer's *Blood of Government*. See also Miller, *Benevolent Assimilation*; and Wolff, *Little Brown Brother*. Hutchcroft's 'Colonial masters, national politicos, and provincial landlords' discusses the principle behind American colonial governance. Pomeroy's *American Neo-Colonialism* and *The Philippines: Colonialism, collaboration and resistance!* study the country's political economy under American rule. Constantino's *Making of a Filipino* and Cullinane's *Ilustrado politics* discuss the development of Filipino politics. The American public education system and its enforcement in the Philippines are discussed in Gleeck's *American Institutions in the Philippines*. Colonial efforts towards the modernization of health and sanitation are illustrated in Anderson, *Colonial Pathologies*; and De Bevoise, *Agents of Apocalypse*. The Filipino resistance movements against American rule are covered in Constantino and Constantino, *The Philippines: The continuing past*; and Ochosa '*Bandoleros*'.

10   World War II in Southeast Asia (1942–1945)

Burma's World War II experience is considered in U Nu's *Burma under Japanese Rule*. Ba Maw's *Breakthrough in Burma* sheds light on how some Burmese nationalists viewed the Japanese. The effect of the Japanese occupation on the growth and development of various nationalist movements can be found in Bečka, *National Liberation Movement;* Maung Maung, *Burmese Nationalist Movements 1940–1948;* and Taylor, *Marxism and Resistance*. Callahan, *Making Enemies,* explores the emergence of the army as a key institution during the war period. Research on Allied campaigns in Burma is extensive; a broad overview can be found in Allen, *Burma: The longest war*. Japanese administrative perspectives are covered in Trager's compilation *Burma: Japanese military administration*. An anti-war critique can be found inTakeyama, *Harp of Burma*, a fictional account of Japanese soldiers who fall in love with the country's cultural traditions. See also Ma Ma Lay's translated Burmese-language story, *Blood Bond,* which explores the after-effects of the war.

The bibliography on the military campaign leading to the capture of Singapore and the subsequent Japanese occupation of British Malaya is voluminous. Although slightly dated, the bibliographic essay on British defense policy, the military campaign, and the Japanese occupation of Malaya and Singapore in Turnbull, *History of Singapore*, affords a valuable introductory survey on the relevant historiography on the subject. *Did Singapore Have to Fall? Churchill and the impregnable fortress*, by Hack and Blackburn, includes an introduction with a helpful update on the historiographical contributions of some of the more relevant publications that appeared after 1988. On the Japanese occupation of Malaysia and Singapore, see Kratoska's books, *Malaya and Singapore During the Japanese Occupation* and *Japanese Occupation of Malaya*. Other important studies are Cheah, *Red Star over Malaya*; and Ooi, *Rising Sun over Borneo*.

Thailand's role in World War II is covered in detail in Bruce Reynolds's works, *Thailand and Japan's Southern Advance* and *Thailand's Secret War*. The broader political context for developments in wartime Thailand is studied in Kobkua's *Kings, Country and Constitutions* and *Thailand's Durable Premier*; Wright, *Balancing Act;* and Stowe, *Siam becomes Thailand*.

Nationalism in Indochina as a colony during this period is covered by Dommen, *Indochinese Experience*. The most detailed study of wartime Vietnam is Marr, *Vietnam 1945*. Huynh, *Vietnamese Communism;* and Duiker, *Ho Chi Minh*, focus specifically on the rise of the Viet Minh. For the non-Communist side of the story, see Lockhart, *End of the Vietnamese Monarchy*. A good account of developments in Laos is in Gunn, *Political Struggles*. Norodom Sihanouk's early political activities are studied in Chandler, *History of Cambodia*; and Osborne, *Sihanouk*.

World War II in Indonesia is studied in Aziz, *Japan's Colonialism and Indonesia*; Benda, *Crescent and the Rising Sun*; Sato, *War, Nationalism and Peasants*; Anderson, *Java in a Time of Revolution*; and Legge, *Sukarno: A political biography*. Ricklefs's *History of Modern Indonesia* surveys the period. Friend, *Blue-Eyed Enemy*, is a comparative study of Luzon and Java under the Japanese.

An overview of the Pacific War and consequent Japanese occupation of the Philippines is found in Friend, *Between two Empires*. Detailed studies include Agoncillo, *Fateful Years*; Constantino and Constantino, *The Philippines*; Friend, *Blue-Eyed Enemy*; Escoda, *Warsaw of Asia*; and Malay, *Occupied Philippines*. Some examples of personal accounts are Constantino, *Under Japanese Rule*; Ephraim, *Escape to Manila*; and Morris, *Corregidor*. Hartendorp's *Japanese Occupation* discusses the internment of foreign nationals on the University of Santo Tomas. Henson recounts her experience as a sexual slave for the Japanese army in *Comfort Woman*. A compilation of documents is in Salazar et al., *World War II in the Philippines*. Helpful essays on the period include Jose, 'Food production and food distribution'; and McCoy, 'Politics by other means'.

11   Regaining independence in the decades after 1945

The topics covered in this chapter appear both in the works listed below and in many of the works listed as readings for Chapter 12.

The best study of this period in Burma is Taylor, *State in Myanmar*. There are many valuable analyses of the 1948–62 period. Donnison, *Public Administration in Burma*, provides an early (1953) perspective. Yawnghwe compares the role of militaries in post-colonial Burma, Indonesia, and Thailand in his dissertation 'Politics of authoritarianism'. See also Pye, *Politics, Personality, and Nation-Building*; Silverstein, *Independent Burma at Forty Years*; Callahan, *Making Enemies*; and Tinker, *Union of Burma* (which goes to the 1962 military coup). For the period of military rule, in addition to Taylor's *State in Myanmar* and Callahan's *Making Enemies*, valuable works include Silverstein, *Burma: Military rule*; Taylor, *Burma: Political economy*; and Steinberg, *Burma's Road Toward Development*. Sarkisyanz, *Buddhist Backgrounds of the Burmese Revolution*, sets this period within a longer time-frame of Burmese Buddhist history.

On Thailand, Phongpaichit and Baker, *Thailand: Economy and politics*; Wright, *Balancing Act*; Suwannathat-Pian, *Kings, Country and Constitutions*; and Girling, *Thailand: Society and politics*, all have detailed narratives of political developments during this period. Works which focus on specific leaders or sub-periods include Suwannathat-Pian, *Thailand's Durable Premier*; Chaloemtiarana, *Thailand, the Politics of Despotic Paternalism*; Morell and Samudavanija, *Political Conflict in Thailand*; and McCargo, *Chamlong Srimuang*. Two books which examine the life and political role of King Bhumibol from very different perspectives are Stevenson, *Revolutionary King*; and Handley, *King Never Smiles*.

There are of course hundreds of books written on the conflicts in Indochina, and any abbreviated list will necessarily be incomplete. Only a few titles are informative on all three countries. Hammer, *Struggle for Indochina*, though dated, is still a useful and readable account of the war with the French. Karnow, *Vietnam: A history*, although focused on Vietnam, has competent discussions of Cambodia and Laos. Dommen, *Indochinese Experience*, is the most comprehensive study of developments in all three countries from the colonial period through the post-1975 years. On the conflicts after 1975, see Chanda, *Brother Enemy*; Evans and Rowley, *Red Brotherhood at War*; Elliott, *Third Indochina Conflict*; Westad and Quinn-Judge, *Third Indochina War*; and van Ginneken, *Third Indochina War*.

Readable studies of the Vietnam conflict as a whole include Duiker's works *Sacred War* and *Communist Road to Power*; Young, *Vietnam Wars*; Herring, *America's Longest War*; Turley, *Second Indochina War*; Kolko, *Anatomy of a War*; Post, *Revolution, Socialism and Nationalism*; and Moss, *Vietnam: American ordeal*. Langguth, *Our Vietnam*, is a collection of narratives from the various sides of the war. On the roots of American policy and the First Indochina War, see Bradley, *Imagining Vietnam and America*; Lawrence and Loegvall, *First Vietnam War*; Fall, *Street Without Joy*; O'Ballance, *Indo-China War*; and Statler, *Replacing France*. Several important studies of the Diem years are available: Catton, *Diem's Final Failure*; and Jacobs's publications *America's Miracle Man in Vietnam* and *Diem, Cold War Mandarin*. Detailed studies of the revolutionary side include Pike, *Viet Cong*; Elliott, *Vietnamese War*; and Thayer, *War by Other Means*.

Specific studies of Cambodia include Osborne, *Sihanouk: Prince of light, prince of darkness*; Corfield, *Khmers Stand Up!*; and Shawcross, *Sideshow*. Sihanouk has written numerous memoirs, including *My War with the CIA*; *War and Hope*; and *Shadow over Angkor*. Many of the best studies of the conflict in Laos were written before its resolution: Dommen, *Conflict in Laos*; Toye, *Laos: Buffer state or battleground*; Stevenson, *End of Nowhere*; Fall, *Anatomy of a Crisis*; and Thee, *Notes of a Witness*. Deuve, *Royaume du Laos 1949–1965*, provides a detailed narrative for the timeframe indicated in the title. Overviews of the civil war can be found in Stuart-Fox, *History of Laos*; and Evans, *Short History of Laos*. Gunn, *Political Struggles*, covers the anti-French conflict; while Brown and Zasloff, *Apprentice Revolutionaries*, traces the relations of the Pathet Lao with the

Vietnamese. Castle, *At War in the Shadow of Vietnam*; and Warner, *Back Fire*, focus on US policy.

A detailed overview of the Indonesian revolution is in Reid, *Indonesian National Revolution*. An analysis that is both scholarly and eye-witness, concentrating on Java, is in G. Kahin, *Nationalism and Revolution*. See also the analysis in Legge, *Sukarno: A political biography*. The early stages of the Revolution in Java are analyzed in B. Anderson, *Java in a Time of Revolution*. For essays on areas outside Java, see A. Kahin, *Regional Dynamics*. Robinson, *Dark Side of Paradise*, discusses Bali. Reid, *Blood of the People*, studies Aceh and East Sumatra; while Chauvel, *Nationalists, Soldiers and Separatists*, concerns Ambon. On Islamic aspects, see Boland, *Struggle of Islam*; and van Dijk, *Rebellion Under the Banner of Islam*. International issues are assessed in Taylor, *Indonesian Independence and the United Nations*; McMahon, *Colonialism and Cold War*; and Colbert, *Southeast Asia in International Politics*.

The Malayan Union scheme and its aftermath have attracted much attention. See particularly Stockwell, *British Policy and Malay Politics*; Sopiee, *From Malayan Union to Singapore Separation*; and Lau, *Malayan Union Controversy*. Other valuable works on the period include Harper, *End of Empire*; and Tan, *Creating 'Greater Malaysia'*. On the Malayan Emergency, the following works can be recommended: Stenson, *Industrial Conflict*; Clutterbuck's books *Long, Long War* and *Riot and Revolution*; O'Ballance, *Malaya: Communist insurgent war*; and Short, *Communist Insurrection*. Singapore's road to independence is covered in Lee, *Singapore: Unexpected nation*.

12   Building nations to c.1990

The topics discussed in this chapter are also covered in many of the works listed for Chapter 11 above.

The period since 1988 in Burma has inspired much writing, mostly seeing Burma from a critical liberal-democratic perspective. See Fink, *Living Silence*; Skidmore, *Karaoke Fascism*; Houtman, *Mental Culture*; and Lintner, *Outrage*. A Burmese perspective on the 1988 events is available in Maung Maung, *1988 Uprising*. Aung San Suu Kyi's *Freedom from Fear* contains her views on Burmese history, Buddhism, democracy, and Burmese political potential. Insurgencies and civil war are covered in Lintner, *Rise of the Communist Party*; Smith, *Burma: Insurgency and the politics of ethnicity*; and South, *Mon Nationalism*. Government perspectives can be found in Taylor, 'Government responses'; and Maung Aung Myoe's dissertation, 'Counterinsurgency in Myanmar'. Lang, *Fear and Sanctuary*, provides the best analysis of the problems facing border communities and host nations.

For studies of Thailand's Muslim South, see Pitsuwan, *Islam and Malay Nationalism*; Montesano and Jory, *Thai South and Malay North*; McCargo, *Tearing Apart the Land*, and McCargo, *Rethinking Thailand's Southern Violence*.

Works on post-1975 Indochina include Chanda, *Brother Enemy*; Evans and Rowley, *Red Brotherhood at War*; Elliott, *Third Indochina Conflict*; Westad and Quinn-Judge, *Third Indochina War*; and van Ginneken, *Third Indochina War*. Solid studies of early post-war Vietnam can be found in Porter, *Vietnam: Politics of bureaucratic socialism*; Beresford, *Vietnam: Politics, economics, and society*; Nguyen Van Canh, *Vietnam under Communism*; Duiker's *Vietnam: Revolution in transition* and *Vietnam Since the Fall of Saigon*.

For the Democratic Kampuchea (*Khmer Rouge*) period, see Kiernan, *Pol pot Regime*; Chandler, *Brother Number One*; Jackson, *Cambodia, 1975–1978*; and Becker, *When the War Was Over*. The two most important studies of Cambodia under the pro-Hanoi regime are Gottesman, *Cambodia After the Khmer Rouge*; and Slocomb, *People's*

Republic of Kampuchea. Shawcross, *Quality of Mercy,* looks at the international response to Cambodia's problems after the overthrow of the *Khmer Rouge.* On the early years of the Lao Communist regime after its victory in 1975, see Evans, *Lao Peasants Under Socialism;* Stuart-Fox, *Laos: Politics, economics, and society;* and Stuart-Fox, *Contemporary Laos.*

There is much good writing on Indonesia in the period 1949–90. Ricklefs, *History of Modern Indonesia,* lists much of that work. Important detailed studies include Legge, *Sukarno: A political biography,* the best work on its subject from Sukarno's early years to his end. Feith, *Decline of Constitutional Democracy,* is an exhaustive analysis from the late Revolution to the end of the first parliamentary democracy. Other important works are Hindley, *Communist Party of Indonesia;* Mortimer, *Indonesian Communism Under Sukarno;* McVey, 'Post-revolutionary transformation of the Indonesian army'; Boland, *Struggle of Islam.* Booth's books *Indonesian Economy* and *Agricultural Development* are important works for this period. The authoritative study of the Papua issue is Drooglever, *Daad van vrije keuze.* Mackie, *Konfrontasi: The Indonesia–Malaysia dispute,* covers that important issue. On the issue of national identity, see Elson, *Idea of Indonesia.*

Indonesia's regional crises have been analysed in several studies. See Sjamsuddin, *Republican Revolt,* on Aceh. Van Dijk, *Rebellion Under the Banner of Islam,* describes Darul Islam in Java, Sulawesi, Kalimantan and Aceh. American involvement is discussed in A. Kahin and G. Kahin, *Subversion as Foreign Policy.*

Roosa, *Pretext for Mass Murder,* re-examines evidence surrounding the 1965 Indonesian coup attempt in Indonesia. Elson, *Suharto,* is the best political biography of Soeharto. Concerning the Soeharto period, see also Crouch, *Army and Politics;* Weinstein, *Indonesian Foreign Policy;* Anwar, *Indonesia in ASEAN;* and Feillard, *Islam et armée.* The best sources on East Timor are Jolliffe, *East Timor;* Dunn, *Timor: A people betrayed;* and Carey and Bentley, *East Timor at the Crossroads.* An excellent account of Islamic developments from 1967 to 2005 is in Feillard and Madinier, *Fin de l'innocence?* An analysis of the connections between economic and political power during the 'New Order' is in Robison, *Indonesia: The rise of capital;* and Robison and Hadiz, *Reorganising Power.* Dick et al., *Emergence of a National Economy,* is an important study. Economic affairs are also analysed in H. Hill, *Indonesian Economy.* Significant analyses of Islamic aspects of the period are to be found in Feener, *Muslim Legal Thought;* and Saleh, *Modern Trends.*

There are many studies of the politics and economics of Malaysia and Singapore since independence. Readers will find the following informative: Means, *Malaysian Politics;* Milne and Mauzy, *Politics and Government in Malaysia;* Funston, *Malay Politics;* Crouch, *Government and Society;* Bedlington, *Malaysia and Singapore;* Ratnam, *Communalism and the Political Process;* Milne and Ratnam, *Malaysia: New states in a new nation;* Lim, *Economic Growth;* and Snodgrass, *Inequality and Economic Development.* Studies of the various ethnic communities include Ampalavanar, *Indian Minority;* and Heng, *Chinese Politics.* On cultural and ethnic issues in Malaysia, see further Cheah, *Malaysia;* and Wilmott, 'Emergence of nationalism'. Lau, *Moment of Anguish,* looks at the Singapore-Malaysia tensions that led to the former's separation from Malaysia. Lee, *Singapore: Unexpected nation,* covers nation-building in Singapore in general; while Mauzy and Milne, *Singapore Politics,* focuses on the role of the PAP.

The Indonesian-Malaysian Confrontation episode is described in Mackie, *Konfrontasi.*

Yegar, *Between Integration and Secession,* covers the Muslim minorities of western Burma, southern Thailand, and southern Philippines.

13 Boom and bust in Southeast Asia c.1990–2008

There is considerable literature on the economic crisis beginning in 1997; useful overviews across the region (and wider) are in Jomo, *After the Storm;* and Garran, *Tigers Tamed.*

For Burma/Myanmar, Taylor's *State in Myanmar* is the best study of this period, including an analysis of the 2008 constitution. Skidmore, *Burma at the Turn of the 21st Century,* provides anthropological insights into issues of power, political ritual, identity, and resistance. James's book *Security and Sustainable Development* analyses Myanmar government policies; her *Governance and Civil Society* emphasizes education, health, and environmental issues.

Thailand's rapid transition from boom to crisis is the theme of a number of studies, including Phongpaichit and Baker, *Thailand's Boom and Bust,* and *Thailand's Crisis;* Bello et al., *Siamese Tragedy;* Laird, *Money Politics, Globalisation and Crisis.* Mulder, *Inside Thai Society,* and Van Esterik, *Materializing Thailand,* focus on cultural issues. Thaksin and his regime are the subject of Phongpaichit and Baker, *Thaksin;* and McCargo, *Thaksinization of Thailand.* More general studies of Thai politics since the 1990s include McVey, *Money and Power in Provincial Thailand;* Hewison, *Political Change and Participation* and *Politics in Thailand;* McCargo, *Reforming Thai Politics;* McCargo, *Chamlong Srimuang;* and Connors, *Democracy and National Identity.* Studies of the Muslim South which look at the various stages of the crisis in that region have been mentioned under Chapter 12.

Vietnam under *doi moi* has been studied by a number of scholars: Kolko, *Vietnam: Anatomy of a peace;* Kerkvliet et al., *Getting Organized in Vietnam;* Fforde, *Doi moi: Ten years after;* and Abuza, *Renovating Politics.* Social and economic developments are the focus of several edited volumes, notably Turley and Selden, *Reinventing Vietnamese Socialism;* Chan et al., *Transforming Asian Socialism;* and Luong, *Postwar Vietnam.* Several excellent studies on changes in culture are available: Malarney, *Culture, Ritual and Revolution;* Taylor, *Fragments of the Present,* and *Goddess on the Rise;* and Fjelstad and Nguyen, *Possessed by the Spirits.* Vietnam's foreign relations are covered in Thayer and Amer, *Vietnamese Foreign Policy in Transition;* and Morley and Nishihara, *Vietnam Joins the World.*

Most books on Cambodia in the 1990s focus on the UN-sponsored transition to a non-socialist government. A very thorough collection of articles on Cambodia during this period is Sorpong, *Cambodia: Change and continuity;* see also Brown, *Cambodia Confounds the Peacemakers;* Widyono, *Dancing in Shadows;* Lizé, *Peace, Power and Resistance;* Hughes, *Political Economy of Cambodia's Transition;* and Heder and Ledgerwood, *Propaganda, Politics, and Violence.* Cultural and social change are the focus of Ollier and Winter, *Expressions of Cambodia;* and Ebihara et al., *Cambodian Culture Since 1975.*

General studies of the reform period in Laos include: Zasloff and Unger ed., *Laos: Beyond the revolution;* Rigg, *Living with Transition in Laos.* Bourdet, *Economics of Transition in Laos;* Than and Tan ed., *Laos Dilemmas and Options.* On the country's foreign relations, see Pholsena and Banomyong, *Laos: From buffer state to crossroads?* Pholsena, *Post-War Laos,* focuses on issues of identity and memory. Cultural developments are covered in Evans, *Politics of Ritual and Remembrance;* Ireson, *Field, Forest and Family;* and Hours and Selim, *Essai d'anthropologie politique sur le Laos contemporain*

On Indonesia since *c.*1990, see Ricklefs, *History of Modern Indonesia.* Other important works are Elson, *Suharto;* Robison and Hadiz, *Reorganizing Power;* Schwarz, *Nation in Waiting;* Feillard and Madinier, *Fin de l'innocence?;* Hefner, *Civil Islam;* Hill,

Indonesian Economy; King, *Half-Hearted Reform*; Hasan, *Laskar Jihad*; and relevant reports by the International Crisis Group (accessible via its website http://www. crisisgroup.org/home/index.cfm).

For an overview of Philippine politics from the 1990s onwards, see Abinales and Amoroso's *State and Society in the Philippines*. Hutchcroft, 'Neither dynamo nor domino'; and Krinks, *Economy of the Philippines*, elucidate the country's political economy. The brief economic boom in the 1990s is discussed in Dong-Yeob, 'Economic liberalism and the Philippine telecom industry'. Ball's 'Trading labour' gives an overview on the country's labor export.

The impact of the 1997 financial crisis in the Philippines is reviewed in Balisacan and Edillon's 'Socioeconomic dimension of the Asian crisis'; Lim's 'East Asian economic and financial crisis'; Montes's 'The Philippines as an unwitting participant'; and Valenzuela's 'Philippines' economic recovery'. On the state of the nation after the crisis, see Hicken, 'Politics of economic recovery in Thailand and the Philippines'; Hutchcroft, 'Arroyo imbroglio'; and Timberman, 'Philippines' underperformance'.

The political history of this period in Malaysia is analyzed in Crouch, *Government and Society in Malaysia*; Means, *Malaysian Politics: Second generation*; and Milne and Mauzy's *Malaysian Politics Under Mahathir*. Analyses of Malaysian socio-economic history are to be found in Jomo's publications *Question of Class* and *Growth and Structural Change*; and Kahn and Loh, *Fragmented Vision*; Brookfield, *Transformation with Industrialization*; and Rokiah Alavi, *Industrialization*. The link with politics is explored in Gomez and Jomo, *Malaysia's Political Economy*; Jomo's *Malaysia's Economy in the Nineties*; and in Searle, *Riddle of Malaysian Capitalism*. See further Abdul Rahman Embong, *State-Led Modernization*; and Leete, *Malaysia from Kampung to Twin Towers*. On environmental issues, see Kathirithamby-Wells, *Nature and Nation*.

Among several important works on Islam in Malaysia in this period, the following can be recommended: Nagata, *Reflowering of Malaysian Islam*; Muzaffar, *Islamic Resurgence*; and Mutalib, *Islam in Malaysia*. See also Peletz, *Islamic Modern Religious Courts*.

Bibliography

Serial abbreviations used:

BKI   *Bijdragen tot de Taal-, Land- en Volkenkunde*
JMBRAS   *Journal of the Malaysian Branch, Royal Asiatic Society*
JSEAH   *Journal of Southeast Asian History*
JSEAS   *Journal of Southeast Asian Studies*
VBG   *Verhandelingen van het (Koninklijk) Bataviaasch Genootschap van Kunsten en Wetenschappen*
VKI   *Verhandelingen van het Koninklijk Instituut voor Taal-, Land- en Volkenkunde*

Abdul Rahman Embong. *State-Led Modernization and the New Middle Class in Malaysia*. Basingstoke: Palgrave, 2002.

Abinales, Patricio and Donna Amoroso. *State and Society in the Philippines*. Lanham, MD: Rowman & Littlefield, 2005.

Abuza, Zachary. *Renovating Politics in Contemporary Vietnam*. Boulder, CO: Lynne Riener Publishers, 2001.

Adam, Ahmat B. *The Vernacular Press and the Emergence of Modern Indonesian Consciousness (1855–1913)*. Ithaca, NY: Cornell University Southeast Asia Program, 1995.

Adas, Michael. *The Burma Delta: Economic development and social change on an Asian rice frontier, 1852–1941*. Madison: University of Wisconsin Press, 1974.

——. *Prophets of Rebellion: Millenarian protest movements against the European colonial order*. Chapel Hill: University of North Carolina Press, 1979.

Agoncillo, Teodoro. *The Fateful Years: Japan's adventure in the Philippines, 1941–1945*. 2 vols. Quezon City: R. P. Garcia Publishing, 1965.

——. *Filipino Nationalism, 1872–1970*. Quezon City: R. P. Garcia Publishing, 1974

——. *Revolt of the Masses: The story of Bonifacio and the Katipunan*. Quezon City: University of the Philippines, 1956.

—— and Milagros C. Guerrero. *History of the Filipino People*. Quezon City: R. P. Garcia Publishing, 1974.

Akkeren, Philip van. *Sri and Christ: A study of the indigenous church in East Java*. London: Lutterworth, 1970.

Allen, G. C., and A.G. Donnithorne. *Western Enterprise in Indonesia and Malaya: A study in economic development*. New York: Macmillan. 1957.

Allen, Louis. *Burma: The longest war, 1941–1945*. London and Melbourne: J. M. Dent & Sons and Guild Publishing, 1984.

Almario, Virgilio. *Panitikan ng rebolusyong 1896: Isang paglingon at katipunan ng mga akda nina Bonifacio at Jacinto*. Maynila: Sentrong Pangkultura ng Pilipinas, 1993.

Alzona, Encarnación. *El legado de España a Filipinas*. Pasay: 1956.

Ampalavanar, Rajeswary. *The Indian Minority and Political Change in Malaysia, 1945–1957*. Kuala Lumpur: Oxford University Press, 1981.

Andaya, Barbara Watson. *The Flaming Womb: Repositioning women in early modern Southeast Asia*. Honolulu: University of Hawaii Press, 2006.

———. *Perak, the Abode of Grace: A study of an eighteenth century Malay state*. Kuala Lumpur and New York: Oxford University Press, 1979.

———. *To Live as Brothers: Southeast Sumatra in the seventeenth an eighteenth centuries*. Honolulu: University of Hawaii Press, 1993.

Andaya, Leonard Y. *The Kingdom of Johor, 1641–1728*. Kuala Lumpur and New York: Oxford University Press, 1975.

———. *The World of Maluku: Eastern Indonesia in the early modern period*. Honolulu: University of Hawai'i Press, 1993.

Andaya, Barbara Watson, and Leonard Y. Andaya. *A History of Malaysia*. 2nd edn. Basingstoke: Palgrave Macmillan; Honolulu: University of Hawai'i Press, 2001.

Anderson, B. R. O'G. *Java in a Time of Revolution: Occupation and resistance, 1944–46*. Ithaca, NY: Cornell University Press, 1972.

Anderson, Warwick. *Colonial Pathologies: American tropical medicine, race, and hygiene in the Philippines*. Durham, NC, and London: Duke University Press, 2006.

Anwar, Dewi Fortuna. *Indonesia in ASEAN: Foreign policy and regionalism*. Jakarta: PT Pustaka Sinar Harapan; Singapore: Institute of Southeast Asian Studies, 1994.

Arasaratnam, Sinnappah. *Indians in Malaysia and Singapore*. 2nd edn. Kuala Lumpur and New York: Oxford University Press, 1979.

Asian Development Bank, *The Economics of Climate Change in Southeast Asia: A regional overview*. April 2009. Available at: http://www.adb.org/documents/books/economics-climate-change-sea/default.asp.

Attas, Muhammad Naguib al-. *The Mysticism of Hamzah Fansuri*. Kuala Lumpur: University of Malaya Press, 1970.

———. *Rānīrī and the Wujūdiyyah of 17th century Acheh*. Singapore: Monographs of the Malaysian Branch of the Royal Asiatic Society 3, 1966.

Aung San Suu Kyi. *Freedom from Fear and Other Writings*. New York: Penguin Books, 1991.

Aung-Thwin, Maitrii. 'Genealogy of a rebellion narrative: Law, ethnology, and culture in colonial Burma'. *JSEAS* vol. 34, no.3 (2003), pp. 393–419.

Aung-Thwin, Michael A. *The Mists of Rāmañña: The legend that was Lower Burma*. Honolulu: University of Hawai'i Press, 2005.

———. *Myth and History in the Historiography of Early Burma: Paradigms, primary sources, and prejudices*. Athens: Ohio University Press, 1998.

———. *Pagan: The origins of modern Burma*. Honolulu: University of Hawaii Press, 1985.

Aziz, M. A. *Japan's Colonialism and Indonesia*. The Hague: Martinus Nijhof, 1955.

Azra, Azyumardi. 'Opposition to Sufism in the East Indies in the seventeenth and eighteenth centuries'. Pp. 665–86 in Frederik de Jong and Bernd Radtke (eds), *Islamic Mysticism Contested: Thirteen centuries of controversies and polemics*. Leiden: Brill, 1999.

———. *The Origins of Islamic Reformism in Southeast Asia: Networks of Malay-Indonesian and Middle Eastern 'ulamā' in the seventeenth and eighteenth centuries*. Crows Nest NSW and Honolulu: Asian Studies Association of Australia in association with Allen & Unwin and University of Hawai'i Press, 2004.

Balisacan, Arsenio, and Rosemarie Edillon. 'Socioeconomic dimension of the Asian crisis: Impact and household response in the Philippines'. Pp.167–87 in Yun-Peng Chu and Hal Hill (eds), *The Social Impact of the Asian Financial Crisis*. Cheltenham: Edward Elgar, 2001.

Ball, Rochelle. 'Trading labour: Socio-economic and political impacts and dynamics of labour export from the Philippines, 1973–2004'. Pp.115–38 in Amarjit Kaur and Ian

Metcalf (eds), *Mobility, Labour Migration and Border Controls in Asia*. Basingstoke: Palgrave, 2006.

Ba Maw. *Breakthrough in Burma: Memoirs of a revolution, 1939–1946*. New Haven: Yale University Press, 1968.

Bankoff, Greg. *Crime, Society and the State in the Nineteenth-Century Philippines*. Quezon City: Ateneo de Manila University Press, 2000.

Barmé, Scot. *Woman, Man, Bangkok: Love, sex, and popular culture in Thailand*. Lanham: Rowman & Littlefield, 2002.

Barrows, David. *History of the Philippines*. Indianapolis: The Bobbs-Merrill Company, 1907.

Bastin John. *The Native Policies of Sir Stamford Raffles in Java and Sumatra: An economic interpretation*. Oxford: Clarendon, 1957.

——. *Raffles' Ideas on the Land Rent System in Java and the Mackenzie Land Tenure Commission. VKI* vol. 14. 's-Gravenhage: Martinus Nijhoff, 1954.

Batson, Benjamin. *The End of the Absolute Monarchy in Thailand*. Singapore: Oxford University Press, 1984.

Battye, Noel. 'The military, government, and society in Siam, 1868–1910: Politics and military reform during the reign of King Chulalongkorn'. Cornell University PhD dissertation. Ann Arbor, MI: University Microfilms, 1974.

Bečka, Jan. *The National Liberation Movement in Burma during the Japanese Occupation Period, 1941–1945*. Prague: Oriental Institute in Academia, 1983.

Becker, Elizabeth. *When the War Was Over: Cambodia and the Khmer Rouge revolution*. New York: PublicAffairs, 1998.

Bedlington, Stanley S. *Malaysia and Singapore: The building of new states*. Ithaca, NY: Cornell University Press, 1978.

Bello, Walden, Shea Cunningham and Li Kheng Poh. *A Siamese Tragedy: Development and disintegration in modern Thailand*. London and Bangkok: Zed Books and White Lotus, 1998.

Bellwood, Peter. *Prehistory of the Indo-Malaysian Archipelago*. 2nd edn. Honolulu: University of Hawaii, 1997.

Benda, Harry J. *The Crescent and the Rising Sun: Indonesian Islam under the Japanese occupation, 1942–1945*. The Hague and Bandung: W. van Hoeve, 1958.

Benitez, Conrado. *History of the Philippines: Economic, social, political*. Boston, MA: Ginn & Company, 1929.

Beresford, Melanie. *Vietnam: Politics, economics, and society*. London: Pinter, 1988.

Blythe, W. L. *The Impact of Chinese Secret Societies in Malaya*. London: Oxford University Press under the auspices of the Royal Institute of International Affairs, 1969.

Boland, B. J. *The Struggle of Islam in Modern Indonesia. VKI* vol. 59. The Hague: Martinus Nijhoff, 1971.

Bonney, R. *Kedah, 1771–1821: The search for security and independence*. Kuala Lumpur and London: Oxford University Press, 1971.

Boomgaard, Peter. *Children of the Colonial State: Population growth and economic development in Java, 1795–1880*. Amsterdam: Free University Press, 1989.

Booth, Anne. *Agricultural Development in Indonesia*. Sydney: Allen & Unwin, 1988.

——. *The Indonesian Economy in the Nineteenth and Twentieth Centuries: A history of missed opportunities*. Basingstoke: Macmillan (now Palgrave) in association with the Australian National University, Canberra, 1998.

Bosma, Ulbe, and Remco Raben. *Being 'Dutch' in the Indies: A history of creolisation and empire, 1500–1920*. Trans. Wendie Shaffer. Singapore: NUS Press and Athens, OH: Ohio University Press, 2008.

Bourdet, Yves. *The Economics of Transition in Laos: From socialism to ASEAN integration*. Northampton: Edward Elgar, 2000.

Boxer, C. R. *The Dutch Seaborne Empire, 1600–1800*. London: Hutchinson, 1965; Harmondsworth: Penguin, 1973.

——. *The Portuguese Seaborne Empire, 1415–1825*. New York: Alfred A. Knopf, 1969.

Bradley, Mark. *Imagining Vietnam and America: The making of post-colonial Vietnam, 1919–1950*. Chapel Hill: University of North Carolina Press, 2000.

Braginsky, Vladimir. *The Heritage of Traditional Malay Literature: A historical survey of genres, writings and literary views*. Leiden: KITLV Press; Singapore: Institute of Southeast Asian Studies, 2004.

——. 'Structure, date and sources of Hikayat Aceh revisited: The problem of Mughal-Malay literary ties.' *BKI* vol. 162, no. 4 (2006), pp. 441–67.

Brandes, J. L. A. (ed. and trans.). *Pararaton (Ken Arok) of het boek der koningen van Tumapël en van Majapahit*. 2nd edn, ed. N. J. Krom. *VBG* vol. 62 (1920).

Briggs, Lawrence. *The Ancient Khmer Empire*. Bangkok: White Lotus, 1999. Reprint of the original 1951 edition.

Brookfield, Harold, with the assistance of Loene Doube and Barbara Banks (eds). *Transformation with Industrialization in Peninsular Malaysia*. Kuala Lumpur and New York: Oxford University Press, 1994.

Brown, C. C. (trans.). *Sĕjarah Mĕlayu, or Malay annals*. Kuala Lumpur: Oxford University Press, 1970. Originally published in *JMBRAS* vol. 25, pts 2–3 (Oct. 1952).

Brown, D. E. *Brunei: The structure and history of a Bornean Malay sultanate*. Brunei: Monograph of the Brunei Museum Journal, vol. 2 no. 2, 1970.

Brown, Ian. *A Colonial Economy in Crisis: Burma's rice cultivators and the world depression of the 1930s*. London: RoutledgeCurzon, 2005.

Brown, MacAlister, and Joseph Zasloff. *Apprentice Revolutionaries: The Communist movement in Laos, 1930–1985*. Stanford, CA: Hoover Institution Press, 1986.

—— and ——. *Cambodia Confounds the Peacemakers, 1979–1998*. Ithaca, NY: Cornell University Press, 1998.

Brown, Robert. *The Dvaravati Wheels of the Law and the Indianization of Southeast Asia*. Leiden and New York: Brill, 1996.

Brug, P. H. van der. *Malaria en malaise: De VOC in Batavia in de achtiende eeuw*. Amsterdam: De Bataafsche Leeuw, 1994.

Bruinessen, Martin van. 'The origins and development of the Naqshbandi order in Indonesia'. *Der Islam* vol. 67, pt 1 (1990), pp. 150–79.

——. *Tarekat Naqsyabandiyah di Indonesia: Survei historis, geografis dan sosiologis*. Intro. Hamid Algar. Bandung: Penerbit Mizan, 1992.

Butcher, John. *The British in Malaya, 1880–1941: The social history of a European community in colonial Southeast Asia*. Kuala Lumpur and New York: Oxford University Press, 1979.

Cady, John F. *A History of Modern Burma*. Ithaca, NY: Cornell University Press, 1960.

——. *The Roots of French Imperialism in Eastern Asia*. Ithaca, NY: Cornell University Press, 1954.

Callahan, Mary P. *Making Enemies: War and state building in Burma*. Ithaca, NY: Cornell University Press, 2003.

Camagay, Ma. Luisa. *Working Women of Manila in the Nineteenth Century*. Quezon City: University of the Philippines Press, 1995.

Carey, P. B. R. *The Power of Prophecy: Prince Dipanagara and the end of an old order in Java, 1785–1855*. Leiden: KITLV Press, 2007.

—— and G. Carter Bentley (eds). *East Timor at the Crossroads: The forging of a nation*. London: Cassell, SSRC, 1995.

Castle, Timothy N. *At War in the Shadow of Vietnam: U.S. military aid to the Royal Lao government, 1955–1975*. New York: Columbia University Press, 1993.

Catton, Philip. *Diem's Final Failure: Prelude to America's war in Vietnam*. Lawrence: University Press of Kansas, 2002.

Chaloemtiarana, Thak. *Thailand, the Politics of Despotic Paternalism*. 2nd edn. Ithaca, NY: Cornell University Southeast Asia Program, 2007.

Chan, Anita, Benedict Kerkvliet and Jonathan Unger (eds). *Transforming Asian Socialism: China and Vietnam compared*. Lanham, MD: Rowman & Littlefield, 1999.

Chanda, Nayan. *Brother Enemy: The war after the war*. San Diego: Harcourt Brace Jovanovich, 1986.

Chandler, David. *Brother Number One: A political biography of Pol Pot*. Rev. edn. Boulder, CO: Westview Press, 1999.

——. 'Cambodia before the French: Politics in a tributary kingdom, 1794–1848'. University of Michigan PhD dissertation. Ann Arbor, MI: University Microfilms, 1975.

——. *A History of Cambodia*. 4th edn. Boulder, CO: Westview Press, 2008.

——. *The Tragedy of Cambodian History: Politics, war and revolution since 1945*. New Haven, NJ: Yale University Press, 1991.

Chandra Muzaffar. *Islamic Resurgence in Malaysia*. Petaling Jaya: Fajar Bakti, 1987.

Chauvel, Richard. *Nationalists, Soldiers and Separatists: The Ambonese islands from colonialism to revolt, 1880–1950*. VKI vol. 143. Leiden: KITLV, 1990.

Chapuis, Oscar. *A History of Vietnam: From Hong Bang to Tu Duc*. Westport, CT: Greenwood Press, 1995.

——. *The Last Emperors of Vietnam: From Tu Duc to Bao Dai*. Westport, Conn.: Greenwood Press, 2000.

Charney, Michael W. *Powerful Learning: Buddhist literati and the throne in Burma's last dynasty, 1752–1885*. Ann Arbor, MI: Centers for South and Southeast Asian Studies, 2006.

——. *Southeast Asian Warfare, 1300–1900*. Leiden and Boston, MA: Brill, 2004.

Cheah Boon Kheng. *Malaysia: The making of a nation*. Singapore: Institute of Southeast Asian Studies, 2002.

——. *Red Star over Malaya: Resistance and social conflict during and after the Japanese occupation of Malaya, 1941–1946*. 3rd edn. Singapore: Singapore University Press, 2003.

Chew, Ernest C. T., and Edwin Lee (eds). *A History of Singapore*. Singapore: Oxford University Press, 1991.

Choi, Byung Wook. *Southern Vietnam Under the Reign of Minh Mang (1820–1841): Central policies and local response*. Ithaca, NY: Cornell Southeast Asia Program, 2004.

Clutterbuck, Richard. *The Long, Long War: The Emergency in Malaya 1948–1960*. London: Cassell, 1967.

——. *Riot and Revolution in Singapore and Malaya, 1945–1963*. London, Faber, 1973.

Coedès, George. *Angkor: An introduction*. Trans. and ed. Emily Floyd Gardiner. Hong Kong: Oxford University Press, 1963.

Coedès, George. *Les États hindouisés d'Indochine et d'Indonésie*. New edn. Paris: Editions E. de Boccard, 1964.

——. *The Indianized States of Southeast Asia*. Trans. Susan Brown Cowing, ed. Walter F. Vella. Honolulu: East-West Center Press, 1968.

Colbert, Evelyn. *Southeast Asia in International Politics, 1941–1956*. Ithaca, NY, and London: Cornell University Press, 1977.

Collins, Steven. *Nirvana and Other Buddhist Felicities*. Cambridge: Cambridge University Press, 1987.

Constantino, Renato. *The Making of a Filipino: A story of Philippine colonial politics.* Quezon City: Foundation for Nationalist Studies, 1969.

Constantino, Renato (ed.). *Under Japanese Rule: Memories and reflections.* Quezon City: Foundation for Nationalist Studies, n.d. [c. 1992].

Constantino, Renato, and Letizia R. Constantino. *The Philippines: The continuing past.* Quezon City: Foundation for Nationalist Studies, 1978.

—— and ——. *The Philippines: A past revisited.* Quezon City: Tala Pub. Services, 1975.

Copeland, Matthew. 'Contested nationalism and the 1932 overthrow of the absolute monarchy in Siam'. Australian National University PhD dissertation, 1993.

Corfield, Justin. *Khmers Stand Up! A history of the Cambodian government 1970–1975.* Clayton: Monash Centre of Southeast Asian Studies, 1994.

Corpuz, Arturo. *The Colonial Iron Horse: Railroads and regional development in the Philippines, 1875–1935.* Quezon City: University of the Philippines Press, 1999.

Corpuz, O. D. *The Roots of the Filipino Nation.* 2 vols. Diliman, Quezon City: University of the Philippines Press, 2005–06.

Cortes, Rosario Mendoza, Celestina Puyal Boncan and Ricardo Trota Jose. *The Filipino Saga: History as social change.* Quezon City: New Day Publishers, 2000.

Cortesão, Armando (ed. and trans.). *The Suma Oriental of Tomé Pires and the Book of Francisco Rodrigues.* 2 vols. London: Hakluyt Society, 1944.

Costa, Horacio de la. *Readings in Philippine History: Selected historical texts presented with commentary.* Manila: Bookmark, 1965.

Courtenay, P. P. *A Geography of Trade and Development in Malaya.* London: Bell, 1972.

Cowan, C. D. *Nineteenth-Century Malaya: The origins of British political control.* London and New York: Oxford University Press, 1962.

Creese, Helen. 'Balinese babad as historical sources: A reinterpretation of the fall of Gèlgèl.' *BKI* vol. 147 (1991), nos 2–3, pp. 236–60.

Cribb, Robert (ed.). *The Late Colonial State in Indonesia: Political and economic foundations of the Netherlands Indies, 1880–1942.* Leiden: KITLV, 1994.

Crouch, Harold. *The Army and Politics in Indonesia.* Ithaca, NY, and London: Cornell University Press, 1978.

——. *Government and Society in Malaysia.* Ithaca, NY: Cornell University Press, 1996.

Cruysse, Dirk van der. *Siam and the West, 1500–1700.* Trans. Michael Smithies. Chiang Mai: Silkworm Books, 2002.

Cullinane, Michael. *Ilustrado politics. Filipino elite responses to American rule, 1898–1908.* Quezon City: Ateneo de Manila University Press, 2003.

De Bevoise, Ken. *Agents of Apocalypse: Epidemic disease in the colonial Philippines.* New Jersey: Princeton University Press, 1995.

Cushner, Nicholas. *Landed Estates in the Colonial Philippines.* New Haven, NJ: Yale University Southeast Asia Studies, 1976.

——. *Spain in the Philippines: From conquest to revolution.* Quezon City: Institute of Philippine Culture, Ateneo de Manila University, 1971.

Deuve, Jean. *Le royaume du Laos, 1949–1965: Histoire événementielle de l'indépendance à la guerre américaine.* Paris: École Française d'Extrême-Orient, 1984.

Dick, Howard, Vincent J.H. Houben, J. Thomas Lindblad and Thee Kian Wie. *The Emergence of a National Economy: An economic history of Indonesia, 1800–2000.* Crows Nest, NSW, and Honolulu: Asian Studies Association of Australia in association with Allen & Unwin and University of Hawai'i Press, 2002.

Diffie, Bailey W., and George D. Winius. *Foundations of the Portuguese Empire, 1415–1580.* Minneapolis: University of Minnesota Press and Oxford University Press, 1977.

Dijk, C. van. *A Country in Despair: Indonesia between 1997 and 2000.* Leiden: KITLV Press, 2001.

——. *Rebellion under the Banner of Islam: The Darul Islam in Indonesia. VKI* vol. 94. The Hague: Martinus Nijhoff, 1981.

Dijk, Wil O. *Seventeenth-Century Burma and the Dutch East Asia Company, 1634–1680.* Singapore: National University of Singapore Press, 2006.

Djajadiningrat, Hoesein. *Critische beschouwing van de Sadjarah Bantĕn: Bijdrage ter kenschetsing van de Javaansche geschiedschrijving.* Haarlem: Joh. Enschedé en Zonen, 1913.

——. 'Critisch overzicht van de in Maleische werken vervatte gegevens over de geschiedenis van het Soeltanaat van Atjeh'. *BKI* vol. 65 (1911), pp. 135–265.

Dobbin, Christine. *Islamic Revivalism in a Changing Peasant Economy: Central Sumatra, 1784–1847.* London and Malmö: Curzon, 1983.

Dommen, Arthur. *Conflict in Laos: The politics of neutralization.* New York: Praeger, 1964.

——. *The Indochinese Experience of the French and the Americans: Nationalism and Communism in Cambodia, Laos, and Vietnam.* Bloomington: Indiana University Press, 2001.

Dong-Yeob, Kim. 'Economic liberalism and the Philippine telecom industry', *Journal of Contemporary Asia* vol. 33, no. 4 (2003), pp. 493–509.

Donnison, F. S. V. *Public Administration in Burma: A study of development during the British connexion.* London: Royal Institute of International Affairs, 1953.

Drabble, John H. *An Economic History of Malaysia, c.1800–1990.* New York: St. Martin's Press, 2000.

Drewes, G. W. J. (ed. and trans.). *The Admonitions of Seh Bari.* The Hague: Martinus Nijhoff, 1969.

——. (ed. and trans.). *An Early Javanese Code of Muslim Ethics.* The Hague: Martinus Nijhoff, 1978.

——. (ed. and trans.). *Een Javaanse primbon uit de zestiende eeuw.* Leiden: E. J. Brill, 1954.

——. 'Nūr al-Dīn al-Ranīrī's charge of heresy against Hamzah and Shamsuddin from an international point of view'. Pp. 54–9 in Grijns, C. D., and S. O. Robson (eds), *Cultural Contact and Textual Interpretation: Papers from the fourth European colloquium on Malay and Indonesian studies, held in Leiden in 1983. VKI* vol. 115. Dordrecht and Cinnaminson: Foris, 1986.

—— and L. F. Brakel (eds and trans.). *The Poems of Hamzah Fansuri.* Dordrecht and Cinnaminson: Foris, 1986.

Drooglever, P. J. *Een daad van vrije keuze: De Papoea's van westelijk Nieuw-Guinea en de grenzen van het zelfbeschikkingsrecht.* Amsterdam: Boom, 2005.

Duiker, William. *The Communist Road to Power in Vietnam.* Rev. ed,. Boulder, CO: Westview Press, 1996.

——. *Ho Chi Minh.* New York: Hyperion, 2000.

——. *The Rise of Nationalism in Vietnam, 1900–1941.* Ithaca, NY: Cornell University Press, 1976.

——. *Sacred War: Nationalism and revolution in a divided Vietnam.* New York: McGraw-Hill, 1995.

——. *Vietnam: Revolution in transition.* Boulder, CO: Westview, 1995.

——. *Vietnam Since the Fall of Saigon.* 2nd edn. Athens, OH: Ohio University Center for International Studies, 1989.

Dunn, James. *Timor: A people betrayed.* Milton, Qld: Jacaranda, 1983.

Dutton, George. *The Tây Son Uprising: Society and rebellion in eighteenth-century Vietnam.* Honolulu: University of Hawaii Press, 2006.

Ebihara, May, Carol A. Mortland and Judy Ledgerwood (eds). *Cambodian Culture Since 1975: Homeland and exile.* Ithaca, NY: Cornell University Press, 1994.

Edwards, Penny. *Cambodge: The cultivation of a nation, 1860–1945*. Honolulu: University of Hawaii Press, 2007.

Elliott, David. (ed.). *The Third Indochina Conflict*. Boulder, CO: Westview, 1981.

——. *The Vietnamese War: Revolution and social change in the Mekong Delta 1930–1975*. Armonk, NY: M. E. Sharpe, 2003.

Elson, Robert. *The End of the Peasantry in Southeast Asia: A social and economic history of peasant livelihood, 1800–1990s*. Basingstoke: Macmillan (now Palgrave) in association with the Australian National University, Canberra, 1997.

——. *The Idea of Indonesia: A history*. Cambridge: Cambridge University Press, 2007.

——. *Javanese Peasants and the Colonial Sugar Industry: Impact and change in an East Java residency, 1830–1940*. Singapore: Oxford University Press, 1984.

——. *Suharto: A political biography*. Cambridge: Cambridge University Press, 2001.

——. *Village Java Under the Cultivation System 1830–1870*. Sydney: Asian Studies Association of Australia in association with Allen & Unwin, 1994.

Emerson, Rupert. *Malaysia: A study in direct and indirect rule*. New York: The Macmillan Company, 1937.

Engel, David. *Law and Kingship in Thailand During the Reign of Chulalongkorn*. Ann Arbor, MI: Michigan Center for South and Southeast Asian Studies, 1975.

Ephraim, Frank. *Escape to Manila: From Nazi tyranny to Japanese terror*. Urbana and Chicago: University of Illinois Press, 2003.

Escoda, Jose Ma. Bonifacio. *Warsaw of Asia: The rape of Manila*. Quezon City: Giraffe Books, 2000.

Evans, Grant. *Lao Peasants Under Socialism*. New Haven, NJ: Yale University Press, 1990.

——. *The Politics of Ritual and Remembrance: Laos since 1975*. Honolulu: University of Hawaii Press, 1998.

——. *A Short History of Laos: The land in between*. Crows Nest, NSW: Allen & Unwin, 2002.

—— and Kelvin Rowley. *Red Brotherhood at War: Vietnam, Cambodia and Laos since 1975*. London and New York: Verso, 1990.

Fall, Bernard. *Anatomy of a Crisis: The Laotian crisis of 1960–61*. Garden City: Doubleday, 1969. Published posthumously, edited and with prologue by Roger Smith.

——. *Street Without Joy*. Mechanicsburg: Stackpole Books, 1994. Reprint of original 1961 edn.

Farrell, Brian P. *The Defence and Fall of Singapore 1940–1942*. Stroud, Glos.: Tempus, 2005.

Fasseur, C. *The Politics of Colonial Exploitation: Java, the Dutch and the cultivation system*. Trans. R. E. Elson and Ary Kraal. Ithaca, NY: Cornell University Southeast Asia Program, 1992.

Feener, R. Michael. *Muslim Legal Thought in Modern Indonesia*. Cambridge: Cambridge University Press, 2007.

Feillard, Andrée. 'Islam et armée dans l'Indonésie contemporaine: Les pionniers de la tradition'. *Cahier d'Archipel* 28. Paris: Editions l'Harmattan, Association Archipel, 1995.

—— and Rémy Madinier. *La fin de l'innocence? L'Islam indonésien face à la tentation radicale de 1967 à nos jours*. Paris: Les Indes Savants & IRASEC, 2006.

Feith, Herbert. *The Decline of Constitutional Democracy in Indonesia*. Ithaca, NY: Cornell University Press, 1962.

—— and Lance Castles (eds). *Indonesian Political Thinking 1945–1965*. Ithaca, NY, and London: Cornell University Press, 1970.

Fforde, Adam (ed.). *Doi Moi: Ten years after the 1986 Party Congress*. Canberra: Australian National University Dept of Political and Social Change, 1997.

Fink, Christina. *Living Silence: Burma under military rule*. New York: Zed Books, 2001.

Fish, Shirley. *When Britain Ruled the Philippines, 1762–1764: The story of the 18th century British invasion of the Philippines during the Seven Years War*. Bloomington: 1st Books Library, 2003.

Fjelstad, Karen, and Nguyen Thi Hien (eds). *Possessed by the Spirits: Mediumship in contemporary Vietnamese communities*. Ithaca, NY: Cornell University Southeast Asia Program, 2006.

Florida, Nancy. *Writing the Past, Inscribing the Future: History as prophecy in colonial Java*. Durham, NC, and London: Duke University Press, 1995.

Forest, Alain. *Le Cambodge et la colonisation française: Histoire d'une colonisation sans heurts (1897–1920)*. Paris: L'Harmattan, 1980.

Fourniau, Charles. *Annam-Tonkin 1885–1896: Lettrés et paysans viêtnamiens face à la conquête coloniale*. Paris: L'Harmattan, 1989.

——. *Vietnam: Domination coloniale et résistance nationale, 1858–1914*. Paris: Indes Savantes, 2002.

Fox, James J. *Harvest of the Palm: Ecological change in eastern Indonesia*. Cambridge, MA, and London: Harvard University Press, 1977.

Friend, Theodore. *Between Two Empires: The ordeal of the Philippines 1929–1946*. New Haven and London: Yale University Press, 1965.

——. *The Blue-Eyed Enemy: Japan against the West in Java and Luzon, 1942–1945*. Princeton: Princeton University Press, 1988.

Funston, N. J. *Malay Politics in Malaysia: A study of the United Malays National Organisation and Party Islam*. Kuala Lumpur: Heinemann Educational Books (Asia), 1980.

Furnivall, John S. *Colonial Policy and Practice: A comparative study of Burma and Netherlands India*. New York: New York University Press, 1956.

——. *The Fashioning of Leviathan: The beginnings of British rule in Burma*. Ed. Gehan Wijeyewardene. Canberra: Economic History of Southeast Asian Project and the Thai-Yunnan Project, 1991. Originally published Rangoon, 1939.

——. *Netherlands India: A study of plural economy*. Intro. A. C. D. de Graeff. Cambridge: Cambridge University Press, 1939. Reprinted 1967.

Garran, Robert. *Tigers Tamed: The end of the Asian miracle*. St Leonards, NSW: Allen & Unwin, 1998.

Gerretson, F. C. *History of the Royal Dutch*. 4 vols. Leiden: E. J. Brill, 1958.

Ginneken, Jaap van. *The Third Indochina War: The conflicts between China, Vietnam, and Cambodia*. Trans. David Smith. Amsterdam: The author, 1983.

Girling, J. L. S. *Thailand, Society and Politics*. Ithaca, NY: Cornell University Press, 1981.

Gleeck, Lewis. *American Institutions in the Philippines (1898–1941)*. Manila: Historical Conservation Society, 1976.

Glover, Ian, and Peter Bellwood (eds). *Southeast Asia: From prehistory to history*. New York: RoutledgeCurzon, 2004.

Gomez, Edmund Terence, and Jomo K. S. *Malaysia's Political Economy: Politics, patronage and profits*. Cambridge and New York: Cambridge University Press, 1997.

Gommans, J., and J. Leider (eds). *The Maritime Frontiers of Burma: Exploring political, cultural, and commercial interaction in the Indian Ocean world, 1200–1800*. Leiden: Koninklijke Nederlandse Akademie van Wetenschappen, 2002.

Gosling, Betty. *Sukhothai: Its history, culture and art*. Singapore and New York: Oxford University Press, 1991.

Goto, Ken'ichi. *Tensions of Empire: Japan and Southeast Asia in the colonial and postcolonial world.* Athens, OH: Ohio University Press, 2003.

Gottesman, Evan R. *Cambodia After the Khmer Rouge: The politics of nation-building.* New Haven, NJ: Yale University Press, 2003.

Graaf, H.J. de. *De regering van Panembahan Sénapati Ingalaga. VKI* vol. 13. 's-Gravenhage: Martinus Nijhoff, 1954.

——. *De regering van Sultan Agung, vorst van Mataram 1613–1645, en die van zijn voorganger Panembahan Séda-ing-Krapjak 1601–1613. VKI* vol. 23. 's-Gravenhage: Martinus Nijhoff, 1958.

——. *De regering van Sunan Mangku-Rat I Tegal-Wangi, vorst van Mataram 1646–1677.* 2 vols. *VKI* vols. 33, 39. 's-Gravenhage: Martinus Nijhoff, 1961, 1962.

—— and Th. G. Th. Pigeaud. *De eerste Moslimse vorstendommen op Java: Studiën over de staatkundige geschiedenis van de 15de en 16de eeuw. VKI* vol. 69. 's-Gravenhage: Martinus Nijhoff, 1974.

Gran, Guy. 'Vietnam and the capitalist route to modernity: Village Cochinchina 1880–1940'. University of Wisconsin PhD dissertation. Ann Arbor, MI: University Microfilms, 1994.

Gravers, Mikael. *Exploring Ethnic Diversity in Burma.* Copenhagen: NIAS Press, 2007.

Greene, Stephen. *Absolute Dreams: Thai government under Rama VI, 1910–1925.* Bangkok: White Lotus Press, 1999.

Groslier, Bernard. *Angkor and Cambodia in the Sixteenth Century, According to Portuguese and Spanish Sources.* Trans. Michael Smithies. Bangkok: Orchid Press, 2006.

Guillot, C. *L'affaire Sadrach: Un essai de christianisation à Java au XIXe siècle.* Paris: Editions de la Maison des Sciences de l'Homme, 1981.

Gullick, J. M.. *Indigenous Political Systems of Western Malaya.* London: University of London, Athlone Press, 1958.

——. *Rulers and Residents: Influence and power in the Malay States 1870–1920.* Singapore: Oxford University Press, 1992.

Gunn, Geoffrey. *Political Struggles in Laos, 1930–1954.* Bangkok: Editions Duang Kamol, 1988.

——. *Rebellion in Laos: Peasants and politics in a colonial backwater.* Boulder, CO: Westview, 1990.

Guyot, Dorothy. 'The Burmese Independence Army: A political movement in military garb'. Pp. 51–65 in Silverstein (ed.), *Southeast Asia in World War II* (see below).

Haan, F. de. *Priangan: De Preanger-Regentschappen onder het Nederlansch bestuur tot 1811.* 4 vols. [Batavia:] Bataviaasch Genootschap van Kunsten en Wetenschappen, 1910–1912.

Hack, Karl, and Kevin Blackburn. *Did Singapore Have to Fall? Churchill and the impregnable fortress.* London and New York: RoutledgeCurzon, 2004.

Hall, Kenneth R. *Maritime Trade and State Development in Early Southeast Asia.* Honolulu: University of Hawaii Press, 1985.

—— and John Whitmore (eds). *Explorations in Early Southeast Asian History: The origins of Southeast Asian statecraft.* Ann Arbor, MI: Michigan Center for South and Southeast Asian Studies, 1976.

Hamid, Abu. *Syekh Yusuf Makassar: Seorang ulama, Sufi dan pejuang.* Jakarta: Yayasan Obor Indonesia, 1994.

Hammer, Ellen. *The Struggle for Indochina, 1940–1955.* Stanford, CA: Stanford University Press, 1966. Reprint of 1955 edition.

Handley, Paul. *The King Never Smiles: A biography of Thailand's Bhumibol Adulyadej.* New Haven, NJ: Yale University Press, 2006.

Hansen, Anne. *How to Behave: Buddhism and modernity in colonial Cambodia, 1860–1930*. Honolulu: University of Hawaii Press, 2007.

Harper, T. N. *The End of Empire and the Making of Malaya*. New York: Cambridge University Press, 1998.

Hartendorp, A. V. H. *The Japanese Occupation of the Philippines*. Vol. 1. Manila: Bookmark, 1967.

Harvey, G. E. *British Rule in Burma, 1824–1942*. New York: AMS Press, 1974. Originally published London: Faber & Faber, [1946].

———. *History of Burma, from the Earliest Times to 10 March 1824, the Beginning of English Conquest*. London: Cass, 1967.

Hasan, Noorhaidi. *Laskar Jihad: Islam, militancy and the quest for identity in post-New Order Indonesia*. Ithaca, NY: Southeast Asia Program Publications, Southeast Asia Program, Cornell University, 2006.

Hashim, Muhammad Yusoff. *The Malay Sultanate of Malacca: A study of various aspects of Malacca in the 15th and 16th centuries in Malaysian history*. Kuala Lumpur: Dewan Bahasa dan Pustaka, 1992.

Heder, Steven, and Judy Ledgerwood (eds). *Propaganda, Politics and Violence in Cambodia: Democratic transition under United Nations peace-keeping*. Armonk, NY: M. E. Sharpe, 1996.

Heersink, Christiaan Gerard. *The Green Gold of Selayar: A socio-economic history of an Indonesian coconut island c.1600–1950; perspectives from a periphery*. Vrije Universiteit te Amsterdam doctoral dissertation, 1995.

Hefner, Robert W. *Civil Islam: Muslims and democratization in Indonesia*. Princeton and Oxford: Princeton University Press, 2000.

Heng Pek Koon. *Chinese Politics in Malaysia: A history of the Malaysian Chinese Association*. Singapore and New York: Oxford University Press, 1988.

Henson, Maria Rosa. *Comfort Woman: Slave of destiny*. Manila: Philippine Center for Investigative Journalism, 1996.

Herbert, Patricia. 'The Hsaya San rebellion (1930–1932) reappraised'. Clayton, Vic.: Monash University Centre of Southeast Asian Studies Working Papers, No. 27, 1982.

Herring, George C. *America's Longest War: The United States and Vietnam, 1950–1975*. 3rd edn. New York: McGraw-Hill, 1996.

Hewison, Kevin (ed.). *Political Change in Thailand: Democracy and participation*. London and New York: Routledge, 1997.

——— (ed.). *Politics in Thailand: Power, oppositions and democratization*. New York: Routledge, 1997.

Higham, Charles. *The Archaeology of Mainland Southeast Asia: From 10,000 B.C. to the fall of Angkor*. Cambridge and New York: Cambridge University Press, 1989.

———. *The Bronze Age of Southeast Asia*. Cambridge and New York: Cambridge University Press, 1996.

———. *The Civilization of Angkor*. London: Weidenfeld & Nicolson, 2001.

———. *Early Cultures of Mainland Southeast Asia*. Bangkok: River Books, 2002.

Hicken, Allen. 'Politics of economic recovery in Thailand and the Philippines'. Pp. 206–30 in Andrew MacIntyre et al. (eds), *Crisis as Catalyst: Asia's dynamic political economy*. Ithaca, NY: Cornell University Press, 2008.

Hill, Hal. *The Indonesian Economy*. 2nd edn. Cambridge: Cambridge University Press, 2000.

Hindley, Donald. *The Communist Party of Indonesia, 1951–1963*. Berkeley and Los Angeles: University of California Press, 1966.

Hong Lysa. *Thailand in the Nineteenth Century: Evolution of the economy and society*. Singapore: Institute of Southeast Asian Studies, 1984.

Hours, Bernard, and Monique Selim. *Essai d'anthropologie politique sur le Laos contemporain: Marché, socialisme et génies*. Paris: L'Harmattan, 1997.

Houtman, Gustaaf. *Mental Culture in Burmese Crisis Politics: Aung San Suu Kyi and the National League for Democracy*. Tokyo: Tokyo University Institute for the Study of Languages and Cultures of Asia and Africa, 1999.

Hudson, Bob. 'The origins of Bagan: The archaeological landscape of Upper Burma to AD 1300'. University of Sydney PhD Dissertation, 2004.

Hughes, Caroline. *The Political Economy of Cambodia's Transition, 1991–2001*. London and New York: RoutledgeCurzon, 2003.

Hussin Mutalib. *Islam in Malaysia: From revivalism to Islamic state?* Singapore: Singapore University Press, 1993.

Hutchcroft, Paul. 'The Arroyo imbroglio in the Philippines'. *Journal of Democracy* vol. 19, no.1 (2008), pp. 141–54.

——. 'Colonial masters, national politicos, and provincial landlords: Central authority and local autonomy in the American Philippines, 1900–1913'. *The Journal of Asian Studies* vol. 59, no. 2 (2000), pp. 277–306.

——. 'Neither dynamo nor domino: Reforms and crises in the Philippine political economy'. Pp.163–83 in T. J Pempel (ed.), *The Politics of the Asian Economic Crisis*. Ithaca, NY: Cornell University Press, 1999.

Huynh Kim Khanh. *Vietnamese Communism, 1925–1945*. Ithaca, NY: Cornell University Press, 1982.

Ileto, Reynaldo. *Pasyon and Revolution: Popular movements in the Philippines, 1840–1910*. Quezon City: Ateneo de Manila University Press, 1998.

Ingleson, John. *Road to Exile: The Indonesian nationalist movement 1927–1934*. Singapore: Heinemann Educational (Asia), 1979.

——. *In Search of Justice: Workers and unions in colonial Java, 1908–1926*. Singapore: Oxford University Press, 1986.

Ireson, Carol J. *Field, Forest, and Family: Women's work and power in rural Laos*. Boulder, CO: Westview, 1996.

Israel, Jonathan. *The Dutch Republic: Its rise, greatness and fall, 1477–1806*. Oxford: Clarendon Press, 1995.

Ito, Takeshi. 'Why did Nuruddin ar-Raniri leave Aceh in 1054 A.H?'. *BKI* vol. 134, no. 4 (1978), pp. 489–91.

Ivarsson, Søren. *Creating Laos: The making of a Lao space between Indochina and Siam, 1860–1945*. Copenhagen: NIAS, 2007.

Jackson, James C. *Planters and Speculators: Chinese and European enterprise in Malaya, 1786–1921*. Kuala Lumpur: University of Malaya Press, 1968.

Jackson, Karl (ed.). *Cambodia, 1975–1978: Rendezvous with death*. Princeton, NJ: Princeton University Press, 1989.

Jacobs, Seth. *America's Miracle Man in Vietnam: Ngo Dinh Diem, religion, race, and U.S. intervention in Southeast Asia, 1950–1957*. Durham, NC: Duke University Press, 2004.

——. *Cold War Mandarin: Ngo Dinh Diem and the origins of America's war in Vietnam, 1950–1963*. Lanham, MD: Rowman & Littlefield, 2006.

James, Helen. *Governance and Civil Society in Myanmar: Education, health, and environment*. New York: Routledge, 2005.

——. *Security and Sustainable Development in Myanmar*. New York: Routledge, 2009.

Jamieson, Neil L. *Understanding Vietnam*. Berkeley: University of California Press, 1993.

Jeshurun, Chandra. *The Contest for Siam, 1889–1902: A study in diplomatic rivalry*. Kuala Lumpur: Penerbit Universiti Kebangsaan Malaysia, 1977.

Johns, A. H. 'Islam in Southeast Asia: Reflections and new directions'. *Indonesia* no. 19 (Apr. 1975), pp. 33–55.

——. 'Islamization in Southeast Asia: Reflections and reconsiderations with special reference to the role of Sufism'. *Tonan Ajia Kenkyu* (Southeast Asian Studies) vol. 31, no. 1 (June 1993), pp. 43–61.

——. 'Malay Sufism, as illustrated in an anonymous collection of 17th century tracts'. *JMBRAS* vol. 30, pt 2 (no. 178) (Aug. 1957).

——. 'On Qur'anic exegetes and exegesis: A case study in the transmission of Islamic learning'. Pp. 3–49 in Peter G. Riddell and Tony Street (eds), *Islam: Essays on scripture, thought and society: A Festschrift in honour of Anthony H. Johns*. Leiden: Brill, 1997.

——. 'Quranic exegesis in the Malay world: In search of a profile'. Pp. 257–87 in A. Rippin (ed.), *Approaches to the History of the Interpretation of the Qur'an*. Oxford: Oxford University Press, 1988.

——. 'Sufism as a category in Indonesian literature and history'. *JSEAH* vol. 2, no. 2 (July 1961), pp. 10–23.

Jolliffe, Jill. *East Timor: Nationalism and colonialism*. St Lucia: University of Queensland Press, 1978.

Jomo, K.S. *After the Storm: Crisis, recovery and sustaining development in four Asian economies*. Singapore: Singapore University Press, 2004.

——. *Growth and Structural Change in the Malaysian Economy*. Basingstoke: Macmillan, 1990.

—— (ed.). *Malaysia's Economy in the Nineties*. Petaling Jaya: Pelanduk Publications, 1994.

——. (ed.). *A Question of Class: Capital, the state, and uneven development in Malaya*. New York: Monthly Review Press, 1987.

Jose, Ricardo Trota. 'Food Production and Food Distribution Programmes in the Philippines during the Japanese Occupation', in Kratoska, *Food Supplies and the Japanese Occupation of South-East Asia* (see below).

Kahin, Audrey R. (ed.). *Regional Dynamics of the Indonesian Revolution: Unity from diversity*. Honolulu: University of Hawai'i Press, 1985.

—— and George McT. Kahin. *Subversion as Foreign Policy: The secret Eisenhower and Dulles debacle in Indonesia*. New York: New Press, 1995.

Kahin, George McTurnan. *Nationalism and Revolution in Indonesia*. Ithaca, NY: Cornell University Press, 1952.

Kahn, Joel S., and Frances Loh Kok Wah (eds). *Fragmented Vision: Culture and politics in contemporary Malaysia*. Honolulu: University of Hawaii Press, 1992.

Karnow, Stanley. *In Our Image: America's empire in the Philippines*. Manila: National Book Store, 1989.

Kasetsiri, Charnvit. *The Rise of Ayudhya: A history of Siam in the fourteenth and fifteenth centuries*. Kuala Lumpur and New York: Oxford University Press, 1976.

Kathirithamby-Wells, J. *Nature and Nation: Forests and development in peninsular Malaysia*. Honolulu: University of Hawai'i Press, 2005.

Kerkvliet, Benedict J. Tria, Russell H. K. Heng and David W. H. Koh (eds). *Getting Organized in Vietnam: Moving in and around the socialist state*. Singapore: Institute of Southeast Asian Studies, 2003.

Keyes, Charles F. *The Golden Peninsula: Culture and adaptation in mainland Southeast Asia*. New York: Macmillan, 1977.

Khasnor Johan. *The Emergence of the Modern Malay Administrative Elite*. Singapore: Oxford University Press, 1984.

Khieu Samphan. *Cambodia's Economy and Industrial Development*. Trans. Laura Summers. Ithaca, NY: Cornell Southeast Asia Program, 1979.

Khin Maung Kynunt. 'The Japanese period in Myanmar History', in *Selected writings of Dr. Khin Maung Kynunt.* Yangon: Myanmar Historical Commission, 2004.

Khin Yi. *The Dobama Movement in Burma (1930–1938).* Ithaca, NY: Cornell University Southeast Asia Program Monograph Series, 1988

Khoo Kay Kim. *The Western Malay States, 1850–1873.* Kuala Lumpur: Oxford University Press, 1972.

Kiernan, Ben. *How Pol Pot Came to Power.* 2nd edn. New Haven, NJ, and London: Yale University Press, 2004.

——. *The Pol Pot Regime: Race, power, and genocide in Cambodia under the Khmer Rouge, 1975–79.* 2nd edn. New Haven, NJ, and London: Yale Nota Bene, 2002.

King, Dwight Y. *Half-Hearted Reform: Electoral institutions and the struggle for democracy in Indonesia.* Westport, CT: Praeger, 2003.

King, Victor, and William D. Wilder. *The Modern Anthropology of South-East Asia: An introduction.* London and New York: Routledge, 2003.

Kobkua, Suwannathat-Pian. *Kings, Country and Constitutions: Thailand's political development, 1932–2000.* Richmond, UK: RoutledgeCurzon, 2003.

——. *Thai-Malay Relations: Traditional intra-regional relations from the seventeenth to the early twentieth centuries.* Singapore and New York: Oxford University Press, 1988.

——. *Thailand's Durable Premier: Phibun through three decades, 1932–1957.* Kuala Lumpur and New York: Oxford University Press, 1995.

Koenig, W. J. *The Burmese Polity, 1752–1819: Politics, administration, and social organization.* Ann Arbor, MI: University of Michigan Center for South and Southeast Asian Studies, 1990.

Kolko, Gabriel. *Anatomy of a War: Vietnam, the United States, and the modern historical experience.* New York: Pantheon, 1985.

——. *Vietnam: Anatomy of a peace.* London: Routledge, 1997.

Korte, J. P. de. *De jaarlijkse financiële verantwoording in de Verenigde Oostindische Compagnie.* Leiden: Martinus Nijhoff, 1984.

Kramer, Paul. *The Blood of Government: Race, empire, the United States, and the Philippines.* Quezon City: Ateneo de Manila University Press, 2006.

Kratoska, Paul (ed.). *Food Supplies and the Japanese Occupation of South-East Asia.* New York: St. Martin's Press, 1998.

——. *The Japanese Occupation of Malaya: A social and economic history.* Honolulu: University of Hawai'i Press, 1998.

—— (ed.). *Malaya and Singapore During the Japanese Occupation.* Singapore: Singapore University Press, 1995.

—— (ed.). *Southeast Asian Minorities in the Wartime Japanese Empire.* New York: RoutledgeCurzon, 2002.

Kraus, Werner. 'Transformations of a religious community: The Shattariyya Sufi brotherhood in Aceh'. Pp. 169–89 in Sri Kuhnt-Saptodewo, Volker Grabowsky and Martin Grossheim (eds), *Nationalism and Cultural Revival in Southeast Asia: Perspectives from the centre and the region.* Wiesbaden: Harrassowitz Verlag, 1997.

——. *Zwischen Reform und Rebellion: Über die Entwicklung des Islams in Minangkabau (Westsumatra) zwischen den beiden Reformbewegungen der Padri (1837) and der Modernisten (1908): Ein Beitrag zur Geschichte der Islamisierung Indonesiens.* Beiträge zur Südasienforschung, Südasien-Institut Universtät Heidelberg, Band 89. Wiesbaden: Franz Steiner Verlag, 1984.

Krinks, Peter. *The Economy of the Philippines: Elites, inequalities and economic restructuring.* London: Routledge, 2002.

Krom, N. J. *Hindoe-Javaansche geschiedenis.* 2nd edn. 's-Gravenhage: Martinus Nijhoff, 1931.

Kuhn, Philip A. *Chinese Among Others: Emigration in modern times*. Singapore: NUS Press, 2008.

Lailert, Busakorn. 'The Ban Phu Luang dynasty, 1688–1767: A study of the Thai monarchy during the closing years of the Ayuthya period'. University of London PhD dissertation, 1972.

Laird, John. *Money Politics, Globalisation and Crisis: The case of Thailand*. Singapore: Graham Brash, 2000.

Lang, Hazel. *Fear and Sanctuary: Burmese refugees in Thailand*. Ithaca, NY: Cornell University Southeast Asia Program, 2002.

Langlet, Philippe. *L'ancienne historiographie d'état au Vietnam*. Vol. 1. Paris: École Française d'Extrême-Orient, 1985.

Lau, Albert. *The Malayan Union Controversy 1942–1948*. Singapore and New York: Oxford University Press, 1991.

——. *A Moment of Anguish: Singapore in Malaysia and the politics of disengagement*. Singapore: Times Academic Press, 1998.

Lawrence, Mark, and Fredrik Logevall (eds). *The First Vietnam War: Colonial conflict and Cold War crisis*. Cambridge, MA: Harvard University Press, 2007.

Lé Thanh Khôi. *Histoire du Viêt Nam: Des origines à 1858*. Paris: Sudestasie, 1981.

LeBar, Frank (ed.). *Ethnic Groups of Insular Southeast Asia*. New Haven: Human Area Relations Files, 1972–75.

——, Gerald Hickey and John Musgrave. *Ethnic Groups of Mainland Southeast Asia*. New Haven, NJ: Human Area Relations Files, 1964.

Lee, Edwin. *The British as Rulers: Governing multiracial Singapore 1867–1914*. Singapore: Singapore University Press, 1991.

——. *Singapore: The unexpected nation*. Singapore: ISEAS, 2008.

Leete, Richard. *Malaysia from Kampung to Twin Towers: 50 years of economic and social developments*. Shah Alam: Oxford Fajar, 2007.

Legarda, Benito, Jr. *After the Galleons: Foreign trade, economic change and enterpreneur-ship in the nineteenth-century Philippines*. Quezon City: Ateneo de Manila University Press, 2002.

Legge, John D. *Sukarno: A political biography*. 2nd edn. Sydney: Allen & Unwin, 1985.

Lewis, Dianne. *Jan Compagnie in the Straits of Malacca 1641–1795*. Athens, OH: Ohio University Center for International Studies, 1995.

Lieberman, V. B. *Burmese Administrative Cycles: Anarchy and conquest 1580–1760*. Princeton: Princeton University Press, 1984.

——. 'Europeans, trade, and the unification of Burma, c.1540–1620'. *Oriens Extremus* vol. 27 (1980), pp. 203–26.

——. *Strange Parallels: Southeast Asia in global context, c. 800–1830*. 2 vols. Cambridge: Cambridge University Press, 2003–9.

Lim, David. *Economic Growth and Development in West Malaysia, 1947–1970*. Kuala Lumpur and New York: Oxford University Press, 1973.

Lim, Joseph. 'The east Asian economic and financial crisis: The case of the Philippines'. Pp. 251–78 in Magayoshi Tsurumi (ed.), *Financial Big Bang in Asia*. Aldershot: Ashgate, 2001.

Lindblad, J. Thomas. *Between Dayak and Dutch: The economic history of Southeast Kalimantan, 1880–1942*. VKI vol. 134. Dordrecht and Providence: Foris, 1988.

Lintner, Bertil. *Outrage: Burma's struggle for democracy*. London: White Lotus, 1990.

——. *The Rise of the Communist Party in Burma*. Ithaca, NY: Cornell University Southeast Asian Program, 1990.

Lizé, Pierre. *Peace, Power, and Resistance in Cambodia: Global governance and the fail-ure of international conflict resolution*. New York: St. Martin's, 2000.

Lockhart, Bruce. *The End of the Vietnamese Monarchy*. New Haven, NJ: Yale Council on Southeast Asia Studies, 1993.

Lombard, Denys. *Le Sultanat d'Atjéh au temps d'Iskandar Muda, 1607–1636*. Paris: École Française d'Extrême-Orient, 1967.

Louw, P. J. F., and E. S. de Klerck. *De Java-oorlog van 1825–30*. 6 vols. 's Hage: M. Nijhoff, Batavia: Landsdrukkerij, 1894–1909.

Luong, Hy V. (ed.). *Postwar Vietnam: Dynamics of a transforming society*. Lanham, MD: Rowman & Littlefield, 2003.

Ma Huan. *Ying-yai Sheng-lan: 'The overall survey of the ocean's shores' (1433)*. Ed. and trans. J. V. G. Mills. Cambridge: Cambridge University Press, 1970.

Ma Ma Lay. *Blood Bond*. Trans. Than Than Win. Honolulu: Center for Southeast Asian Studies, 2004.

McCargo, Duncan. *Chamlong Srimuang and the New Thai Politics*. New York: St. Martin's, 1997.

—— (ed.). *Reforming Thai Politics*. Copenhagen: NIAS Press, 2002.

—— (ed.). *Rethinking Thailand's Southern Violence*. Singapore: National University of Singapore Press, 2006.

——. *Tearing Apart the Land: Islam and legitimacy in Southern Thailand*. Ithaca, NY: Cornell University Press, 2008.

——. and Ukrist Pathmanand. *The Thaksinization of Thai Politics*. Copenhagen: NIAS Press, 2005.

McCoy, Alfred. 'Politics by other means: World War II in the western Visayas, Philippines'. Pp. 191–245 in McCoy, *Southeast Asia Under Japanese Occupation* (see below).

—— (ed.). *Southeast Asia Under Japanese Occupation*. New Haven, NJ: Yale University Southeast Asia Studies, 1980.

Mackie, J. A. C. *Konfrontasi: The Indonesia–Malaysia dispute, 1963–1966*. Kuala Lumpur, etc.: Oxford University Press, 1974.

McHale, Shawn Frederick. *Print and Power: Confucianism, Communism and Buddhism in the making of modern Vietnam*. Honolulu: University of Hawaii Press, 2004.

McLeod, Mark. *Vietnamese Response to French Intervention, 1862–1874*. New York: Praeger, 1991.

McMahon, Robert J. *Colonialism and Cold War: The United States and the struggle for Indonesian independence, 1945–1949*. Ithaca, NY: Cornell University Press, 1981.

McVey, Ruth T. (ed.). *Money and Power in Provincial Thailand*. Honolulu: University of Hawaii Press, 2000.

——. 'The post-revolutionary transformation of the Indonesian army'. *Indonesia* no. 11 (Apr. 1971), pp. 131–76; no. 13 (Apr. 1972), pp. 147–81.

——. *The Rise of Indonesian Communism*. Ithaca, NY: Cornell University Press, 1965.

Majul, Cesar Adib. *Mabini and the Philippine Revolution*. Quezon City: University of the Philippines Press, 1996.

Mak Phoeun. *Histoire du Cambodge de la fin du XVIᵉ siècle au début du XVIIIᵉ*. Paris: École Française d'Extrême-Orient, 1996.

—— and Khin Sok (trans. and eds). *Chroniques royales du Cambodge*. 3 vols. Paris: École Française d'Extrême-Orient, 1981–88.

Malarney, Shaun Kingsley. *Culture, Ritual and Revolution in Vietnam*. London: RoutledgeCurzon, 2002.

Malay, Armando. *Occupied Philippines: The role of Jorge B. Vargas during the Japanese occupation*. Manila: Filipiniana Book Guild, 1967.

Mallat, Jean. *Les Philippines: Histoire, geographie, moeurs, agriculture, industrie, commerce*. Paris: Arthus Bertrand, 1846. Translated as *The Philippines. History, geography, customs, agriculture, industry and commerce.* Manila: National Historical Institute, 1998.

Manguin, Pierre-Yves. *Les Nguyen, Macau et le Portugal: Aspects politiques et commerciaux d'une relation privilégiée en Mer de Chine, 1773–1802.* Paris: École Française d'Extrême-Orient, 1984.

——. *Les Portugais sur les côtes du Viêt-Nam et du Campa: Étude sur les routes maritimes et les relations commerciales, d'après les sources portugaises (XVIe, XVIIe, XVIIIe siècles).* Paris: École Française d'Extrême-Orient, 1972.

Marr, David. *Vietnamese Anticolonialism, 1885–1925.* Berkeley: University of California Press, 1971.

——. *Vietnamese Tradition on Trial, 1920–1945.* Berkeley: University of California Press, 1981.

——. *Vietnam 1945: The quest for power.* Berkeley: University of California Press, 1995.

——, and Anthony Milner (eds). *Southeast Asia in the 9th to 14th centuries.* Singapore: Institute of Southeast Asian Studies, 1986.

Marston, Daniel (ed.). *The Pacific War Companion: From Pearl Harbor to Hiroshima.* Oxford: Osprey Publishing, 2005.

Masselman, George. *The Cradle of Colonialism.* New Haven, NJ, and London: Yale University Press, 1963.

Maung Aung Myoe. 'The counter-insurgency in Myanmar: The government's response to the Burma Communist Party'. Australian National University PhD Dissertation, 1999.

Maung Htin Aung. *Epistles Written on the Eve of the Anglo-Burmese War.* The Hague: Martinus Nijhoff, 1968.

Maung Maung. *The 1988 Uprising.* New Haven, NJ: Yale University Southeast Asian Studies, 1999.

——. *Burmese Nationalist Movements, 1940–1948.* Hong Kong: Kiscadale Publications, 1989.

——. *From Sangha to Laity: Nationalist movements of Burma, 1920–1940.* New Delhi: Manohar, 1980.

Moscotti, Albert. *British Policy and the Nationalist Movement in Burma, 1917–1937.* Honolulu: University of Hawaii Press, 1974.

Mauzy, Diane K., and R. S. Milne. *Singapore Politics Under the People's Action Party.* London and New York: Routledge, 2002.

Means, G. P. *Malaysian Politics.* 2nd edn. London: Hodder & Stoughton, 1976.

——. *Malaysian Politics: The second generation.* Singapore and New York: Oxford University Press, 1991.

Meilink-Roelofsz, M. A. P. *Asian Trade and European Influence in the Indonesian Archipelago between 1500 and about 1630.* The Hague: Martinus Nijhoff, 1962.

Mendelson, E. M. *Sangha and State in Burma: A study of monastic sectarianism and leadership.* Ed. John P. Ferguson. Ithaca, NY: Cornell University Press, 1975.

Miller, Stuart Creighton. *'Benevolent assimilation': The American conquest of the Philippines, 1899–1903.* New Haven, NJ: Yale University Press, 1982.

Mills, L. A. *British Rule in Eastern Asia: A study of contemporary government and economic development in British Malaya and Hong Kong.* London: Oxford University Press; Minneapolis: University of Minnesota Press, 1942.

Milne, R.S., and Diane K. Mauzy, *Malaysian Politics Under Mahathir.* London and New York: Routledge, 1999.

—— and ——. *Politics and Government in Malaysia.* Rev. edn. Singapore: Times Books International, 1980.

—— and K. J. Ratnam. *Malaysia – New States in a New Nation: Political development of Sarawak and Sabah in Malaysia*. London: Frank Cass, 1974.

Milner, A. C. *The Invention of Politics in Colonial Malaya*. New York: Cambridge University Press, 2001.

——. *Kerajaan: Malay political culture on the eve of colonial rule*. Tucson: Published for the Association for Asian Studies by the University of Arizona Press, 1982.

Moffat, Abbot Low. *Mongkut, the King of Siam*. Ithaca, NY: Cornell University Press, 1961.

Mokarapong, Thawatt. *History of the Thai Revolution: A study in political behaviour*. Bangkok: Chalermnit, 1972.

Molina, Antonio. *The Philippines Through the Centuries*. 2 vols. Manila: University of Sto. Tomas Cooperative, 1960–61.

Montana, Suwedi. 'Nouvelles donées sur les royaumes de Lamuri et Barat'. *Archipel* no. 53 (1997), pp. 85–95.

Montes, Manuel. 'The Philippines as an unwitting participant in the Asian economic crisis'. Pp. 241–68 in Karl Jackson (ed.), *Asian Contagion: The causes and consequences of a financial crisis*. Singapore: Institute of Southeast Asian Studies, 1999.

Montesano, Michael, and Patrick Jory (eds). *Thai South and Malay North: Ethnic interactions on a plural peninsula*. Singapore: National University of Singapore Press, 2008.

Moore, Elizabeth H. *Early Landscapes of Myanmar*. Bangkok: River Books, 2007.

Morell, David, and Chai-anan Samudavanija. *Political Conflict in Thailand: Reform, reaction, revolution*. Cambridge: Oelgeschlager, Gunn, & Hain, 1981.

Morga, Antonio De. *Sucesos de las islas Filipinas. Mejico: 1609. Translated as Historical events of the Philippine islands*. Manila: Jose Rizal National Centennial Commission, 1962.

Morley, James W. and Masashi Nishihara (eds). *Vietnam Joins the World*. Armonk, NY: M. E. Sharpe, 1997.

Morris, Eric. *Corregidor: The nightmare in the Philippines*. London: Hutchison, 1982.

Mortimer, Rex. *Indonesian Communism Under Sukarno: Ideology and politics, 1959–1965*. Ithaca, NY, and London: Cornell University Press, 1974.

Moscotti, Albert D. *British Policy and the Nationalist Movement in Burma, 1917–1937*. Honolulu: University Press of Hawaii, 1974.

Moss, George. *Vietnam, an American Ordeal*. 4th edn. Upper Saddle River: Prentice-Hall, 2002.

Mulder, Niels. *Inside Thai Society: Religion, everyday life, change*. Chiang Mai: Silkworm Books, 2000.

Munoz, Paul Michel. *Early Kingdoms of the Indonesian Archipelago and the Malay Peninsula*. Singapore: Editions Didier Millet, 2006.

Murray, Martin J. *The Development of Capitalism in Colonial Indochina (1970–1940)*. Berkeley: University of California Press, 1980.

Mya Than and Joseph L.H. Tan (eds). *Laos Dilemmas and Options: The challenges of economic transition in the 1990s*. Singapore: Institute of Southeast Asian Studies, 1996.

Nagata, Judith. *The Reflowering of Malaysian Islam*. Vancouver: University of British Columbia Press, 1984.

Nakahara, M. 'Muslim merchants in Nan-Hai'. Pp. 1–10 in Raphael Israeli and Anthony H. Johns (eds), *Islam in Asia*, Vol. II: *Southeast and East Asia*. Jerusalem: Magnes Press, Hebrew University, 1984.

Ngaosyvathn, Mayoury, and Pheuiphanh Ngaosyvathn. *Paths to Conflagration: Fifty years of diplomacy and warfare in Thailand, Laos, and Vietnam, 1778–1828*. Ithaca, NY: Cornell Southeast Asia Program, 1998.

Ngo Vinh Long. *Before the Revolution: The Vietnamese peasants under the French.* Cambridge, MA: MIT Press, 1973.

Nguyen Khac Vien. *Vietnam, a Long History.* Hanoi: Foreign Languages Publishing House, 1987.

Nguyen Tai Thu (ed.). *History of Buddhism in Vietnam.* Hanoi: Social Sciences Publishing House, 1992.

Nguyen The Anh. *Monarchie et fait colonial au Viêt-nam (1875–1925): Le crépuscule d'un ordre traditionnel.* Paris: L'Harmattan, 1992.

Nguyen Van Canh. *Vietnam Under Communism, 1975–1982.* Stanford, CA: Hoover Institution Press, 1983.

Niemeijer, Hendrik E. *Batavia: Een koloniale samenleving in de zeventiende eeuw.* [Amsterdam:] Uitgeverij Balans, 2005.

Nieuwenhuijze, C. A. O. van. *Šamsu'l-Dīn van Pasai: Bijdrage tot de kennis der Sumatraansche mystiek.* Leiden: E. J. Brill, 1945.

Ni Ni Myint. *Burma's Struggle Against British Imperialism, 1885–1895.* Rangoon: Universities Press, 1983.

Noer, Deliar. *The Modernist Muslim Movement in Indonesia, 1900–1942.* Singapore: Oxford University Press, 1973.

Noorduyn, J. *Een achttiende-eeuwse kroniek van Wadjo': Buginese historiografie.* 's-Gravenhage: H. L. Smits, 1955.

——. 'Majapahit in the fifteenth century'. *BKI* vol. 134, nos. 2–3 (1978), pp. 207–74.

——. 'Origins of South Celebes historical writing'. Pp. 137–55 in Soedjatmoko et al. (eds), *An Introduction to Indonesian Historiography.* Ithaca, NY: Cornell University Press, 1965.

Norodom Sihanouk with Wilfred Burchett. *My War with the CIA: The memoirs of Prince Norodom Sihanouk.* New York: Pantheon, 1973.

——. *Shadow over Angkor: Memoirs of His Majesty King Norodom Sihanouk of Cambodia.* Ed. Julio Jeldres. Phnom Penh: Monument Books, 2005.

——. *War and Hope: The case for Cambodia.* Trans. Mary Feeney. New York: Pantheon, 1980.

Nordin, Hussin. *Trade and Society in the Straits of Melaka: Dutch Melaka and English Penang, 1780–1830.* Singapore: Singapore University Press, 2007.

Nu, U. *Burma Under the Japanese: Pictures and portraits.* Ed. and intro. J. S. Furnivall. London: Macmillan, 1954.

O'Ballance, Edgar. *The Indo-China War, 1945–1954: A study in guerrilla warfare.* London: Faber & Faber, 1964.

——. *Malaya: The communist insurgent war, 1948–1960.* London: Faber, 1966.

Ochosa, Orlino. *'Bandoleros': Outlawed guerillas of the Philippine-American War, 1903–1907.* Quezon City: New Day Publishers, 1995.

Ollier, Leakthina Chau-Pech, and Tim Winter (eds). *Expressions of Cambodia: The politics of tradition, identity, and change.* New York: Routledge, 2006.

O'Malley, William J. 'Indonesia in the Great Depression: A study of East Sumatra and Jogjakarta in the 1930's'. Cornell University PhD dissertation, Ann Arbor, MI: University Microfilms, 1977.

Ooi Keat Gin. *Of Free Trade and Native Interests: The Brookes and the economic development of Sarawak, 1841–1941.* Oxford and New York: Oxford University Press, 1997.

——. *Rising Sun Over Borneo: The Japanese period in Sarawak, 1941–45.* New York: St. Martin's Press, 1999.

Osborne, Milton. *Exploring Southeast Asia: A traveller's history of the region.* Crow's Nest, NSW: Allen & Unwin, 2002.

——. *The French Presence in Cochinchina and Cambodia: Rule and response (1859–1905)*. Ithaca, NY: Cornell University Press, 1969.

——. *The Mekong: Turbulent past, uncertain future*. St Leonards, NSW: Allen & Unwin, 2006.

——. *River Road to China: The search for the source of the Mekong, 1866–1873*. 2nd edn. Singapore: Archipelago Press, 1996.

——. *Sihanouk: Prince of light, prince of darkness*. St. Leonards, NSW: Allen & Unwin, 1994.

——. *Southeast Asia: An introductory history*. 10th edn. St. Leonards, NSW: Allen and Unwin, 2010.

Ota Atsushi. *Changes of Regime and Social Dynamics in West Java: Society, state and the outer world of Banten, 1750–1830*. Leiden and Boston: E. J. Brill, 2006.

Owen, Norman, et al. *The Emergence of Modern Southeast Asia: A new history*. Honolulu and Singapore: University of Hawaii Press and NUS Press, 2005.

Parkinson, C. N. *British Intervention in Malaya, 1867–77*. Singapore: University of Malaya Press, 1960.

Parry, J. H. *Europe and a Wider World*. London: Hutchinson, 1949. Reprinted as *The Establishment of the European Hegemony, 1415–1715*. New York and Evanston, IL: Harper & Row, 1961.

Peleggi, Maurizio. *Lords of Things: The fashioning of the Siamese monarchy's modern image*. Honolulu: University of Hawaii Press, 2002.

——. *Thailand: The worldly kingdom*. London: Reaktion Books, 2007.

Peletz, Michael. *Islamic Modern Religious Courts and Cultural Politics in Malaysia*. Princeton: Princeton University Press, 2002.

Penth, Hans. *A Brief History of Lan Na: Civilizations of North Thailand*. Chiang Mai: Silkworm Books, 2000.

Phelan, John. *The Hispanization of the Philippines: Spanish aims and Filipino responses, 1565–1700*. Madison: University of Wisconsin Press, 1959.

Phinith, Saveng. *Contribution à l'histoire du royaume de Luang Prabang*. Paris: École Française d'Extrême-Orient, 1987.

Pholsena, Vatthana. *Post-War Laos: The politics of culture, history, and identity*. Singapore: Institute of Southeast Asian Studies, 2006.

—— and Ruth Banomyong. *Laos: From buffer state to crossroads?* Trans. Michael Smithies. Chiang Mai: Mekong Press, 2006.

Phongpaichit, Pasuk, and Chris Baker. *Thailand's Boom and Bust*. Chiang Mai: Silkworm Books, 1998.

—— and ——. *Thailand's Crisis*. Singapore: Institute of Southeast Asian Studies, 2000.

—— and ——. *Thailand, Economy and Politics*. 2nd edn. Oxford and New York: Oxford University Press, 2000.

—— and ——. *Thaksin: The business of politics in Thailand*. Bangkok: Silkworm Books, 2004.

Pigeaud, Theodore G. Th. *Java in the 14th Century: A study in cultural history*. 5 vols. The Hague: Martinus Nijhoff, 1960–3.

——. *Literature of Java: Catalogue raisonné of Javanese manuscripts in the library of the University of Leiden and other public collections in the Netherlands*. 4 vols. The Hague: Martinus Nijhoff; Leiden: Bibliotheca Universitatis Lugduni Batavorum; Leiden University Press, 1967–80.

—— and H. J. de Graaf. *Islamic States in Java, 1500–1700: Eight Dutch books and articles by Dr H. J. de Graaf, as summarised by Theodore G. Th. Pigeaud, with a comprehensive list of sources and a general index of names composed by H. J. de Graaf*. VKI vol. 70. The Hague: Martinus Nijhoff, 1976.

Pike, Douglas Eugene. *Viet Cong: The organization and techniques of the National Liberation Front of South Vietnam.* Cambridge, MA: MIT Press, 1966.

Pitsuwan, Surin. *Islam and Malay Nationalism: A case study of Malay-Muslims of Southern Thailand.* Bangkok: Thammasat University Thai Khadi Research Institute, 1985.

Pomeroy, William J. *American Neo-Colonialism: Its emergence in the Philippines and Asia.* New York: International Publishers, 1970.

——. *The Philippines: Colonialism, collaboration and resistance!* New York: International Publishers, 1992.

Porter, Gareth. *Vietnam: The politics of bureaucratic socialism.* Ithaca, NY: Cornell University Press, 1993.

Post, Ken. *Revolution, Socialism and Nationalism in Viet Nam.* 5 vols. Aldershot: Dartmouth, 1989–1994.

Prapañca. *Deśawārṇana (Nāgarakṛtāgama).* Trans. Stuart Robson. *VKI* vol. 169. Leiden: KITLV, 1995.

Prasertkul, Seksan. 'The transformation of the Thai state and economic change (1855–1945).' Cornell University PhD dissertation. University Microfilms, 1989.

Pringle, Robert. *Rajahs and Rebels: The Ibans of Sarawak under Brooke rule, 1841–1941.* London: Macmillan, 1970.

Purcell, Victor. *The Chinese in Malaya.* Kuala Lumpur, London: Oxford University Press, 1967.

Pye, Lucian. *Politics, Personality, and Nation-Building: Burma's search for identity.* New Haven, NJ: Yale University Press, 1962.

Quinn-Judge, Sophie. *Ho Chi Minh: The missing years 1919–1941.* London: Hurst, 2003.

Rabibhadana, Akin. *The Organization of Thai Society in the Early Bangkok Period, 1782–1873.* Ithaca, NY: Cornell University Southeast Asia Program, 1969.

Ranjit Singh, D. S. *Brunei, 1839–1983: The Problems of Political Survival.* Singapore: Oxford University Press, 1984.

Ratnam, K. J. *Communalism and the Political Process in Malaya.* Kuala Lumpur: Published for the University of Singapore by the University of Malaya Press, 1965.

Reed, Robert. *Hispanic Urbanism in the Philippines: A study of the impact of church and state.* Manila: University of Manila, 1967.

Reid, Anthony. *The Blood of the People: Revolution and the end of traditional rule in northern Sumatra.* Kuala Lumpur: Oxford University Press, 1979.

——. *The Contest for North Sumatra: Atjeh, the Netherlands and Britain, 1858–1898.* London: Oxford University Press, 1969.

——. *The Indonesian National Revolution, 1945–1950.* Hawthorn, Vic.: Longman, 1974.

——. *Southeast Asia in the Age of Commerce, 1450–1680.* 2 vols. New Haven, NJ: Yale University Press, 1988–1993.

—— (ed.). *Southeast Asia in the Early Modern Era: Trade, power, and belief.* Ithaca, NY: Cornell University Press, 1993.

Reynolds, Craig J. 'The Buddhist monkhood in nineteenth-century Thailand.' Cornell University PhD dissertation. University Microfilms, 1972.

Reynolds, E. Bruce. *Thailand and Japan's Southern Advance, 1940–1945.* New York: St. Martin's Press, 1994.

——. *Thailand's Secret War: OSS, SOE and the Free Thai underground during World War II.* New York: Cambridge University Press, 2005.

Ribadeneira, Marcelo de. *Historia del archipielago y otros reynos.* Barcelona: Imprenta de Gabriel Graell y Giraldo Dotil, 1600. Translated as *History of the Philippines and Other Kingdoms.* 2 vols. Manila: Historical Conservation Society, 1970.

Ricklefs, M. C. *A History of Modern Indonesia Since c.1200.* 4th edn. Basingstoke: Palgrave; Stanford, CA: Stanford University Press, 2008.

——. *Jogjakarta under Sultan Mangkubumi, 1749–1792: A history of the division of Java.* London: Oxford University Press, 1974.

——. *Mystic Synthesis in Java: A history of Islamisation from the fourteenth to the early nineteenth centuries.* Norwalk: EastBridge, 2006.

——. *Polarising Javanese Society: Islamic and other visions c.1830–1930.* Singapore: Singapore University Press; Honolulu: University of Hawai'i Press; Leiden: KITLV Press, 2007.

——. *The Seen and Unseen Worlds in Java, 1726–49: History, literature and Islam in the court of Pakubuwana II.* Honolulu: Asian Studies Association of Australia in association with Allen & Unwin and University of Hawai'i Press, 1998.

——. *War, Culture and Economy in Java, 1677–1726: Asian and European imperialism in the early Kartasura period.* Sydney: Asian Studies Association of Australia in association with Allen & Unwin, 1993.

Riddell, Peter. 'Earliest Quranic exegetical activity in the Malay-speaking states'. *Archipel* no. 38 (1989), pp. 107–24.

Rigg, Jonathan. *Living with Transition in Laos: Market integration in Southeast Asia.* London and New York: RoutledgeCurzon, 2005.

Robequain, Charles. *The Economic Development of French Indo-China.* Trans. Isabel Ward. London: Oxford University Press, 1944.

Robinson, Geoffrey. *The Dark Side of Paradise: Political violence in Bali.* Ithaca, NY, and London: Cornell University Press, 1995.

Robison, Richard. *Indonesia: The rise of capital.* North Sydney: Allen & Unwin, 1986.

—— and Vedi R. Hadiz. *Reorganising Power in Indonesia: The politics of oligarchy in an age of markets.* London and New York: RoutledgeCurzon, 2004.

Roff, W. R. *The Origins of Malay Nationalism.* New Haven, NJ: Yale University Press, 1967.

Rokiah Alavi. *Industrialization in Malaysia: Import substitution and infant industry performance.* London and New York: Routledge, 1996.

Roosa, John. *Pretext for Mass Murder: The September 30th movement and Suharto's coup d'état in Indonesia.* Madison: The University of Wisconsin Press, 2006.

Sadka, Emily. *The Protected Malay States, 1874–1895.* Kuala Lumpur: University of Malaya Press, 1968.

Saeed, Abdullah. *Islamic Thought: An introduction.* London and New York: Routledge, 2006.

Salazar, Generoso, Fernado B. Reyes and Leonardo Nuval (eds). *World War II in the Philippines.* 3 vols. Manila: Veterans Foundation of the Philippines, 1993.

Salazar, Zeus. 'Ang "real" ni Bonifacio bilang taktikang militar sa kasaysayan ng Pilipinas'. *Bagong Kasaysayan*, Vol.1. Maynila: BAKAS, 1997.

——. *Kasaysayan ng Pilipinas: Isang balangkas.* Quezon City: UP Departamento ng Kasaysayan, 1993.

——. 'Si Andres Bonifacio at ang kabayanihang Pilipino'. *Bagong Kasaysayan*, Vol. 2. Maynila: BAKAS, 1997.

Saleh, Fauzan. *Modern Trends in Islamic Theological Discourse in 20th Century Indonesia.* Leiden: Bill, 2001.

Sánchez Gómez, Luis Ángel. *Un imperio de la vitrina: El colonialismo Español en el Pacífico y la exposición de Filipinas de 1887.* Madrid: Consejo Superior de Investigaciones Científicas, Instituto de Historia, Departamento de Historia de América, 2003.

Sandhu, Kernial Singh. *Indians in Malaya: Some aspects of their immigration and settlement (1786–1957).* London: Cambridge University Press, 1969.

—— and A. Mani. *Indian Communities in Southeast Asia*. Singapore: Institute of Southeast Asian Studies and Times Academic Press, 1993.

Sandin, Benedict. *Sea Dayaks of Borneo Before White Rajah Rule*. London and Melbourne: Macmillan, 1967.

Sarkisyanz, Emanuel. *Buddhist Backgrounds of the Burmese Revolution*. The Hague: Martinus Nijhoff, 1965.

Sato, Shigeru. *War, Nationalism and Peasants: Java under Japanese occupation, 1942–1945*. St Leonards, NSW: Asian Studies Association of Australia in association with Allen & Unwin, 1994.

Saunders, Graham. *A History of Brunei*. Kuala Lumpur: Oxford University Press, 1994.

Schama, Simon. *The Embarrassment of Riches: An interpretation of Dutch culture in the Golden Age*. New York: Knopf, 1987.

Schumacher, John. *The Propaganda Movement, 1880–1895*. Quezon City: Ateneo de Manila University Press, 2002.

Schulte Nordholt, H. *The Spell of Power: A history of Balinese politics, 1650–1940*. VKI vol. 170. Leiden: KITLV, 1996.

Schwarz, Adam. *A Nation in Waiting: Indonesia's search for stability*. 2nd edn. St Leonards, NSW: Allen & Unwin, 1999.

Scott, James C. *The Art of Not Being Governed: An anarchist history of upland Southeast Asia*. New Haven, CT: Yale University Press, 2009.

——. *The Moral Economy of the Peasant: Rebellion and subsistence in Southeast Asia*. New Haven, NJ: Yale University Press, 1976.

Scott, James G. (Shway Yoe). *The Burman: His life and notions*. New York: Norton, 1963.

Searle, Peter. *The Riddle of Malaysian Capitalism: Rent seekers or real capitalists?* Honolulu: Asian Studies Association of Australia in association with Allen & Unwin and University of Hawai'i Press, 1999.

Sears, Laurie J. *Shadows of Empire: Colonial discourse and Javanese tales*. Durham, NC, and London: Duke University Press, 1996.

Selth, Andrew. *The Anti-Fascist Resistance in Burma, 1942–1945: The racial dimension*. Queensland: Center for Southeast Asian Studies, James Cook University, 1983.

Shawcross, William. 'The Minami Organ: A bridgehead in Burmese-Japanese relations'. *United Asia*, 1965, pp. 361–66.

——. *Sideshow: Kissinger, Nixon, and the destruction of Cambodia*. 2nd edn. London: Hogarth, 1986.

Short, Anthony. *The Communist Insurrection in Malaya, 1948–1960*. New York: Crane, Russak, 1975.

Sidhu, Jagjit Singh. *Administration in the Federated Malay States*. Kuala Lumpur and New York: Oxford University Press, 1980.

Silverstein, Josef. *Burma: Military rule and the politics of stagnation*. Ithaca, NY: Cornell University Press, 1977.

——. *Independent Burma at Forty Years: Six assessments*. Ithaca, NY: Cornell University Southeast Asia Program, 1989.

—— (ed.). *Southeast Asia in World War II: Four essays*. New Haven: Yale University Southeast Asian Studies, 1967.

Sjamsuddin, Nazaruddin. *The Republican Revolt: A study of the Acehnese rebellion*. [Singapore:] Institute of Southeast Asian Studies, 1985.

Skidmore, Monique. *Burma at the Turn of the 21st Century*. Honolulu: University of Hawaii Press, 2005.

——. *Karaoke Fascism: Burma and the politics of fear*. Philadelphia: University of Pennsylvania Press, 2004.

Slocomb, Margaret. *The People's Republic of Kampuchea, 1979–1989: The revolution after Pol Pot.* Chiang Mai: Silkworm Books, 2003.

Smith, Bardwell L. (ed.). *Religion and Legitimation of Power in Thailand, Laos, and Burma.* Chambersburg: ANIMA Books, 1978.

Smith, Martin. *Burma: Insurgency and the politics of ethnicity.* New York: Zed Books, 1999.

Smith, R. B., and W. Watson (eds). *Early South East Asia: Essays in archaeology, history and historical geography.* New York: Oxford University Press, 1979.

Smith, Simon C. *British Relations with the Malay Rulers from Decentralization to Malayan Independence, 1930–1957.* Kuala Lumpur and New York: Oxford University Press, 1995.

Snodgrass, Donald R. *Inequality and Economic Development in Malaysia.* Kuala Lumpur and New York: Oxford University Press, 1980.

Snouck Hurgronje, C. *Mekka in the Latter Part of the Nineteenth Century: Daily life, customs and learning; the Moslims of the East-Indian-Archipelago.* Trans. J. H. Monahan. Leyden: E. J. Brill; London: Luzac, 1931.

Sopiee, Mohamed Noordin. *From Malayan Union to Singapore Separation: Political unification in the Malaysia region, 1945–65.* 2nd edn. Kuala Lumpur: University Malaya Press, 2005.

Sorpong Peou (ed.). *Cambodia: Change and continuity in contemporary politics.* Aldershot and Burlington: Ashgate, 2001.

South, Ashley. *Mon Nationalism and Civil War in Burma: The golden sheldrake.* New York: RoutledgeCurzon, 2003.

Spiro, Melford E. *Buddhism and Society: A great tradition and its vicissitudes.* New York: Harper & Row, 1970.

——. *Burmese Supernaturalism.* New Jersey: Prentice-Hall, 1967.

Statler, Kathryn C. *Replacing France: The origins of American intervention in Vietnam.* Lexington: University Press of Kentucky, 2007.

Steinberg, David I. *Burma: A Socialist Nation of Southeast Asia.* Boulder, CO: Westview Press, 1982.

——. *Burma: The state of Myanmar.* Washington, DC: Georgetown University Press, 2001.

——. *Burma's Road Toward Development: Growth and ideology under military rule.* Boulder, CO: Westview Press, 1981.

Stenson, M. R. *Industrial Conflict in Malaya: Prelude to the Communist revolt in 1948.* London and New York: Oxford University Press, 1970.

Stevenson, Charles A. *End of Nowhere: American policy towards Laos since 1954.* Boston, MA: Beacon Press, 1972.

Stevenson, Rex. *Cultivators and Administrators: British educational policy towards the Malays, 1875–1906.* Kuala Lumpur: Oxford University Press, 1975.

Stevenson, William. *The Revolutionary King: True-life sequel to The King and I.* London: Constable, 2000.

Stockwell, A. J. *British Policy and Malay Politics During the Malayan Union Experiment, 1942–1948.* Kuala Lumpur: MBRAS Monograph, no. 8, 1979.

Stowe, Judith. *Siam Becomes Thailand: A story of intrigue.* London: Hurst, 1991.

Stuart-Fox, Martin (ed.). *Contemporary Laos: Studies in the politics and society of the Lao People's Democratic Republic.* St Lucia: University of Queensland Press, 1982.

——. *A History of Laos.* Cambridge and New York: Cambridge University Press, 1997.

——. *Lao kingdom of Lan Xang: Rise and decline.* Bangkok: White Lotus Press, 1998.

——. *Laos: Politics, economics, and society.* London: F. Pinter, 1986.

——. *A Short History of China and Southeast Asia.* Crows Nest, NSW: Allen & Unwin, 2003.

Subrahmanyam, Sanjay. *The Portuguese Empire in Asia, 1500–1700: A political and economic history.* London and New York: Longman, 1993.

Sun Laichen. 'Military technology transfers from Ming China and the emergence of northern mainland Southeast Asia, (c.1390–1527)'. *JSEAS* vol. 34, no. 3 (2003), pp. 495–517.

Sutarman Soediman Partonadi. *Sadrach's Community and its Contextual Roots: A nineteenth century Javanese expression of Christianity.* Amsterdam and Atlanta, GA: Rodopi, 1990.

Swearer, Donald K. *The Buddhist World of Southeast Asia.* Albany: State University of New York Press, 1995. An expanded version of his earlier *Buddhism and Society in Southeast Asia.*

Tagliacozzo, Eric. *Secret Trades, Porous Borders: Smuggling and states along a Southeast Asian frontier, 1865–1915.* New Haven, NJ, and London: Yale University Press, 2005.

Tai, Hue-Tam Ho. *Millenarianism and Peasant Politics in Vietnam.* Cambridge: Harvard University Press, 1983.

——. *Radicalism and the Origins of the Vietnamese Revolution.* Cambridge, MA: Harvard University Press, 1992.

Takeyama, Michio. *Harp of Burma.* Trans. Howard Hibbett. Rutland, VT: C. E. Tuttle, 1966.

Talens, Johan. *Een feodale samenleving in koloniaal vaarwater: Staatsvorming, koloniale expansie en economische onderontwikkeling in Banten, West-Java (1600–1750).* Hilversum: Verloren, 1999.

Tambiah, Stanley Jeyaraja. *World Conqueror and World Renouncer: A study of Buddhism and polity in Thailand against a historical background.* Cambridge and New York: Cambridge University Press, 1976.

Tan Tai Yong. *Creating 'Greater Malaysia': Decolonisation and the politics of merger.* Singapore: Institute of Southeast Asian Studies, 2008.

Tarling, Nicholas. *Anglo-Dutch rivalry in the Malay World, 1780–1824.* St Lucia: Queensland University Press; [London]: Cambridge University Press, 1962.

——. *Britain, the Brookes and Brunei.* Kuala Lumpur and London: Oxford University Press, 1971.

——. *British Policy in the Malay Peninsula and Archipelago, 1824–71.* Kuala Lumpur and New York: Oxford University Press, 1969.

——. *'The burthen, the risk and the glory': The life of Sir James Brooke.* Kuala Lumpur and New York: Oxford University Press, 1982.

—— (ed.). *The Cambridge History of Southeast Asia.* 4 vols. Cambridge, UK: Cambridge University Press, 1999.

——. *Piracy and Politics in the Malay World: A study of British imperialism in the 19th century.* Melbourne: Cheshire, 1963.

——. *A Sudden Rampage: The Japanese occupation of Southeast Asia, 1941–1945.* London: Hurst, 2001.

Tate, D. J. M. *The Making of Modern South-East Asia.* 2 vols. Kuala Lumpur: Oxford University Press, 1971–9.

Tay, Simon S. C., Jesus Estanislao and Hadi Susastro (eds). *A New ASEAN in a New Millennium.* Jakarta: Centre for Strategic and International Studies; Singapore: Singapore Institute of International Affairs, 2000.

Taylor, Alastair M. *Indonesian Independence and the United Nations.* Ithaca, NY: Cornell University Press, 1960.

Taylor, Jean Gelman. *The Social World of Batavia: European and Eurasian in Dutch Asia.* Madison: University of Wisconsin Press, 1983.

Taylor, Keith Weller. *The Birth of Vietnam*. Berkeley: University of California Press, 1983.

Taylor, Philip. *Fragments of the Present: Searching for modernity in Vietnam's South*. Honolulu: University of Hawaii Press, 2001.

———. *Goddess on the Rise: Pilgrimage and popular religion in Vietnam*. Honolulu: University of Hawaii Press, 2004.

Taylor, Robert H. (ed.). *Burma: Political Economy Under Military Rule*. New York: Palgrave, 2001.

———. 'Burma in the Anti-Fascist War'. Pp. 159–90 in McCoy (ed.), *Southeast Asia Under Japanese Occupation* (see above), 1980.

———. 'Government responses to armed communist and separatists movements: Burma.' Pp. 103–25 in Chandra Jeshurun (ed.), *Governments and Rebellions in Southeast Asia*. Singapore: Institute of Southeast Asian Studies, 1985.

———. *Marxism and Resistance in Burma, 1942–1945: Thein Pe Myint's wartime traveler*. Athens, OH: Ohio University Press, 1984.

———. *The State in Myanmar*. Singapore: National University of Singapore Press, 2009.

Teeuw, A., with the assistance of H. W. Emanuels. *A Critical Survey of Studies on Malay and Bahasa Indonesia*. 's-Gravenhage: Martinus Nijhoff, 1961.

Thant Myint U. *The Making of Modern Burma*. Cambridge: Cambridge University Press. 2001.

Thayer, Carlyle. *War by Other Means: National liberation and revolution in Viet-Nam, 1940–1960*. Sydney: Allen & Unwin, 1989.

———, and Ramses Amer (eds). *Vietnamese Foreign Policy in Transition*. Singapore: Institute of Southeast Asian Studies, 1999.

Thee, Marek. *Notes of a Witness: Laos and the Second Indochinese War*. New York: Random House, 1973.

Thio, Eunice. 'The Syonan Years, 1942–1945', in Ernest C. T. Chew and Edwin Lee (eds), *A History of Singapore*. Singapore: Oxford University Press, 1991.

Tibbetts, G. R. *A Study of the Arabic Texts Containing Material on South-East Asia*. Leiden and London: E. J. Brill for the Royal Asiatic Society, 1979.

Timberman, David. 'The Philippines' underperformance in comparative perspective: Past divergence, future convergence'. Pp. 113–50 in Anne Marie Murphy and Bridget Welsh (eds), *Legacy of Engagement in Southeast Asia*. Singapore: Institute of Southeast Asian Studies, 2008.

Tinker, Hugh. *The Union of Burma: A study of the first years of independence*. London: Oxford University Press, 1967.

Toye, Hugh. *Laos: Buffer State or Battleground*. London and New York: Oxford University Press, 1968.

Trager, Frank (ed. and intro.). *Burma: Japanese military administration, selected documents, 1941–1945*. Trans. Won Zoon Yoon and Thomas T. Winant. Philadelphia: University of Pennsylvania Press, 1971.

Trocki, Carl. *Opium and Empire: Chinese society in colonial Singapore, 1800–1910*. Ithaca, NY Cornell University Press, 1990.

———. *Prince of Pirates: The Temenggongs and the development of Johor and Singapore, 1784–1885*. Singapore: NUS Press, 2007.

Tsuboi, Yoshiharu. *L'empire viêtnamien: Face à la France et à la Chine, 1847–1885*. Paris: L'Harmattan, 1987.

Tuck, Patrick J. N. *The French Wolf and the Siamese Lamb: The French threat to Siamese independence, 1858–1907*. Bangkok: White Lotus, 1993.

Tully, John A. *France on the Mekong: A history of the protectorate in Cambodia, 1863–1953*. Lanham, MD: University Press of America, 2002.

Turley, William S. *The Second Indochina War: A short political and military history, 1954–1975.* Boulder, CO: Westview Press, 1986.
—— and Mark Selden (eds). *Reinventing Vietnamese Socialism: Doi moi in comparative perspective.* Boulder, CO: Westview Press, 1993.
Turnbull, C. M. *A History of Singapore 1819–1988.* 3rd edn. Singapore: NUS Press, 2009.
——. *The Straits Settlements 1826–67: Indian Presidency to Crown Colony.* London: The Athlone Press, 1972.
Uhlenbeck, E. M. *A Critical Survey of Studies on the Languages of Java and Madura.* 's-Gravenhage: Martinus Nijhoff, 1964.
Ungar, Esta Serne. 'Vietnamese leadership and order: Dai Viet under the Le Dynasty (1428–1459)'. Cornell PhD dissertation, 1983.
Valenzuela, Ma. Rebecca. 'The Philippines' economic recovery: Trends, issues and strategies for balanced growth'. Pp. 75–94 in Tran Van Hoa (ed.), *The Asia recovery: Issues and aspects of development, growth, trade and investment.* Cheltenham: Edward Elgar, 2001.
Van Esterik, Penny. *Materializing Thailand.* Oxford: Berg, 2000.
Van Niel, Robert. *The Emergence of the Modern Indonesian Elite.* The Hague and Bandung: W. van Hoeve, 1960.
——. *Java's Northeast Coast, 1740–1840: A study in colonial encroachment and dominance.* Leiden: CNWS Publications, 2005.
Vella, Walter F. *Chaiyo! King Vajiravudh and the Development of Thai Nationalism.* Honolulu: University of Hawaii, 1978.
——. *Siam Under Rama III, 1824–1851.* Locust Valley: Association for Asian Studies and J. J. Augustin, 1957.
Veneracion, Jaime. *Agos ng dugong Kayumanggi: Isang kasaysayan ng sambayanang Pilipino.* Quezon City: Abiva Publishing House, 1998.
Vermeulen, J. Th. *De Chineezen te Batavia en de troebelen van 1740.* Leiden: N. V. Boeken Steendrukkerij Eduard Ijdo, 1938.
Vickers, Adrian. *Bali: A paradise created.* Ringwood, Vic.: Penguin, 1989.
Vickery, Michael. 'Cambodia after Angkor: The chronicular evidence for the fourteenth to sixteenth centuries'. Yale University PhD dissertation. Ann Arbor, MI: University of Michigan Microfilms, 1978.
——. *Society, Economics, and Politics in pre-Angkor Cambodia: The 7th–8th centuries.* Kyoto: Toyo Bunko, 1998.
Vos, Reinout. *Gentle Janus, Merchant Prince: The VOC and the tightrope of diplomacy in the Malay world, 1740–1800.* Trans. Beverly Jackson. *VKI* vol. 157. Leiden: KITLV, 1993.
Wake, Christopher. 'Malacca's early kings and the reception of Islam'. *JSEAH* vol. 5, no. 2 (Sept. 1964), pp. 104–28.
Wang Gungwu. 'The first three rulers of Malacca'. Pp. 97–107 in Wang Gungwu. *Community and Nation: Essays on Southeast Asia and the Chinese.* Singapore and North Sydney: Heinemann Educational (Asia) and George Allen & Unwin Australia, 1981. Originally published in *JMBRAS* vol. 41, pt 1 (1968), pp. 11–22.
Warner, Roger. *Back Fire: The CIA's secret war in Laos and its link to the war in Vietnam.* New York: Simon & Schuster, 1995.
Warren, James Francis. *Ah Ku and Karayuki-San: Prostitution in Singapore 1870–1940.* Singapore and New York: Oxford University Press, 1993.
——. *Rickshaw Coolie: A people's history of Singapore (1880–1940).* Singapore and New York: Oxford University Press, 1986.
——. *The Sulu Zone, 1768–1898: The dynamics of external trade, slavery and ethnicity in the transformation of a Southeast Asian maritime state.* Singapore: National University of Singapore Press, 2007.

Weinstein, Franklin B. *Indonesian Foreign Policy and the Dilemma of Dependence: From Sukarno to Soeharto.* Ithaca, NY, and London: Cornell University Press, 1976.

Wenk, Klaus. *The Restoration of Thailand Under Rama I, 1782–1809.* Trans. Greeley Stahl. Tucson: Association of Asian Studies and University of Arizona Press, 1968.

Werner, Jayne Susan. *Peasant Politics and Religious Sectarianism: Peasant and priest in the Cao Dai in Viet Nam.* New Haven, NJ: Yale University Southeast Asia Studies, 1981.

Westad, Odd Arne, and Sophie Quinn-Judge (eds). *The Third Indochina War: Conflict between China, Vietnam and Cambodia, 1972–79.* New York: Routledge, 2006.

Wheatley, Paul. *Nagara and Commandery: Origins of the Southeast Asian urban traditions.* Chicago: University of Chicago Press, 1983.

Wheatley, Paul, and Kernial S. Sandhu (eds). *Melaka: The Transformation of a Malay Capital ca. 1400–1800.* 2 vols. Kuala Lumpur and New York: Oxford University Press, 1983.

Wheeler, Charles James. 'Cross-cultural trade and trans-regional networks in the port of Hoi An: Maritime Vietnam in the early modern era'. Cornell University PhD dissertation. Ann Arbor, MI: University Microfilms, 2001.

Whitmore, John Kremers. 'The development of Le government in fifteenth-century Vietnam'. Cornell University PhD dissertation. Ann Arbor, MI: University Microfilms, 1969.

——. *Vietnam, Ho Quy Ly, and the Ming (1371–1421).* New Haven: Yale Center for International and Area Studies, 1985.

Wickberg, Edgar. *The Chinese in Philippine Life, 1850–1898.* Quezon City: Ateneo de Manila University Press, 2000.

Widyono, Benny. *Dancing in Shadows: Sihanouk, the Khmer Rouge, and the United Nations in Cambodia.* Lanham, MD: Rowman & Littlefield, 2008.

Wilmott, W.E. 'The emergence of nationalism.' Pp. 578–600 in Kernial Singh Sandhu and P. Wheatley (eds), *Management of Success: The Moulding of Modern Singapore.* Singapore: Institute of Southeast Asian Studies, 1989.

Wilson, Constance. 'State and society in the reign of Mongkut, 1851–1868: Thailand on the eve of modernization'. Cornell University PhD dissertation. Ann Arbor, MI: University Microfilms, 1974.

Winichakul, Thongchai. *Siam Mapped: A history of the geo-body of a nation.* Honolulu: University of Hawaii Press, 1994.

Winstedt, Richard. *A History of Classical Malay Literature.* Kuala Lumpur: Oxford University Press, 1969. A reprinting of the revised edition originally published in *JMBRAS* vol. 31, pt 3 (1958; but published in 1961).

Wolff, Leon. *Little Brown Brother: How the United States purchased and pacified the Philippines.* Singapore: Oxford University Press, (1960) 1991.

Wolters, O. W. *Early Indonesian Commerce: A study of the origins of Śrīvijaya.* Ithaca, NY: Cornell University Press, 1967.

——. *Early Southeast Asia: Selected essays.* Ed. Craig Reynolds. Ithaca, NY: Cornell University Southeast Asia Program, 2008.

——. *The Fall of Śrīvijaya in Malay History.* Kuala Lumpur: Oxford University Press, 1970.

——. *History, Culture and Region in Southeast Asian Perspectives.* Rev. edn. Ithaca, NY: Cornell University Southeast Asia Program, 1999.

Woodman, Dorothy. *The Making of Burma.* London: Cresset Press, 1962.

Woodside, Alexander B. *Community and Revolution in Modern Vietnam.* Boston, MA: Houghton Mifflin, 1976.

——. *Vietnam and the Chinese Model: A comparative study of Vietnamese and Chinese government in the first half of the nineteenth century.* 2nd edn. Cambridge, MA: Harvard University Press, 1988.

Wright, Joseph. *The Balancing Act: A history of modern Thailand*. Oakland, CA: Pacific Rim Press, 1991.

Wyatt, David K. *The Politics of Reform in Thailand: Education in the reign of King Chulalongkorn*. New Haven, NJ: Yale University Press, 1969.

———. *Thailand: A Short History*. 2nd edn. New Haven, NJ: Yale University Press, 2003.

———, and Aroonrut Wichienkeeo. *The Chiang Mai Chronicle*. Chiang Mai: Silkworm Books, 1995.

Yawnghwe Chao-Tzang. 'The politics of authoritarianism: The state and political soldiers in Burma, Indonesia, and Thailand'. University of British Columbia PhD dissertation: University of Michigan Microfilm, 1997.

Yen Ch'ing-hwang. *A Social History of the Chinese in Singapore and Malaya 1800–1911*. Singapore and New York: Oxford University Press, 1986.

Yegar, Moshe. *Between Integration and Secession: The Muslim communities of the southern Philippines, southern Thailand, and western Burma/Myanmar*. Lanham MD: Lexington Books, 2002.

Yeo, Kim Wah. *The Politics of Decentralization: Colonial controversy in Malaya 1920–1929*. Kuala Lumpur: Oxford University Press, 1982.

Young, Marilyn Blatt. *The Vietnam Wars 1945–1990*. New York: Harper & Row, 1991.

Zaide, Gregorio F. *Philippine Political and Cultural History*. 2nd edn. Manila: Philippine Education Company, 1957.

———. *The Pageant of Philippine History: Political, economic, and socio-cultural*. 2 vols. Manila: Philippine Education Company, 1979.

Zasloff, Joseph J., and Leonard Unger (eds). *Laos: Beyond the revolution*. New York: St. Martin's Press, 1991.

Zinoman, Peter. *The Colonial Bastille: A history of imprisonment in Vietnam, 1862–1940*. Berkeley: University of California Press, 2001.

Zoetmulder, P. J. *Kalangwan: A survey of Old Javanese literature*. The Hague: Martinus Nijhoff, 1974.

———. *Pantheism and Monism in Javanese Suluk Literature: Islamic and Indian mysticism in an Indonesian setting*. Ed. and trans. M. C. Ricklefs. KITLV Translation Series 24. Leiden: KITLV, 1995.

———. *Pantheisme en monisme in de Javaansche soeloek-litteratuur*. Nijmegen: J. J. Berkhout, 1935.

Index and Glossary